Introduction to
JavaScript® Programming
with XML and PHP

Creating Dynamic and Interactive Web Pages

ELIZABETH DRAKE
Santa Fe College

Boston Columbus Indianapolis New York San Francisco Upper Saddle River
Amsterdam Cape Town Dubai London Madrid Milan Munich Paris Montreal Toronto
Delhi Mexico City Sao Paulo Sydney Hong Kong Seoul Singapore Taipei Tokyo

Editorial Director, ECS: Marcia Horton
Executive Editor: Matt Goldstein
Editorial Assistant: Jenah Blitz-Stoehr
Director of Marketing: Christy Lesko
Marketing Manager:Yezan Alayan
Senior Marketing Coordinator: Kathryn Ferranti
Director of Production: Erin Gregg
Senior Managing Editor: Scott Disanno
Senior Production Project Manager: Marilyn Lloyd
Manufacturing Buyer: Lisa McDowell
Art Director: Anthony Gemmellaro

Text Designer: Gillian Hall/The Aardvark Group
Cover Designer: Joyce Cosentino Wells
Manager, Rights and Permissions: Michael Joyce
Text Permission Coordinator: Jackie Bates/GEX, Inc.
Cover Image: © Shutterstock_58372831/
   Andrea Crisante
Media Project Manager: Renata Butera
Full-Service Vendor: Laserwords, Inc.
Project Manager: Haseen Khan
Printer/Binder: Edwards Brothers, Inc.
Cover Printer: Lehigh-Phoenix Color

Library of Congress Cataloging-in-Publication Data

Drake, Elizabeth, 1948-
   Introduction to JavaScript programming with XML and PHP : creating dynamic and interactive web pages / Elizabeth Drake.
      pages cm
   ISBN 0-13-306830-7 (alk. paper)
  1.   JavaScript (Computer program language) 2.   Internet programming. 3.
XML (Document markup language) 4.   PHP (Computer program language) 5.   Web
sites--Design.   I. Title.
   QA76.73.J39D73 2013
   006.7'6--dc23

                                                    2013000407

ISBN 10: 0-13-306830-7
ISBN 13: 978-0-13-306830-6

Preface

Welcome to *Introduction to JavaScript Programming with XML and PHP*. The motivation behind the creation of this book came from the author's need for an appropriate text that covered this material in her own class, Internet Programming 1, in a two-year Internet Services Programming course of study. Students graduating from a two-year program in web development must be familiar with both client-side and server-side scripting languages. While there are many excellent texts that cover static web page development (HTML, XHTML, HTML5, CSS), beyond the basics, the available books are either trivial in coverage or presented at a level far beyond the scope of a two-year program. This text is designed to fill the need for entry-level programmers who can work comfortably with JavaScript and understand the interaction with server-side technologies.

This book is intended for a one-semester JavaScript programming course for students who have knowledge of HTML and CSS. The fundamentals of programming are covered in a manner that is appropriate for students without prior programming exposure and for those with some prior programming experience. Emphasis is on the application of programming concepts to JavaScript and PHP. Each concept is accompanied by short examples to reinforce the concept and followed by longer examples that are oriented in real-world situations.

Two Case Studies are developed throughout the book: a game website and a classroom website. Each chapter has a section that adds content and functionality to these Case Studies, and students add to this content in the Programming Challenges at the end of the chapter. Two additional websites, one for a landscaping business and another for a jewelry business, can be built from scratch and enhanced by students in the Programming Challenges. This allows instructors to tailor the course toward specific college goals.

The text assumes that students have prior knowledge of HTML and CSS and are proficient in creating static web pages. However, no prior programming experience or specific knowledge of mathematics, finance, or other disciplines is required. While SQL commands are used in the final chapter, students do not need experience with SQL or databases to use this material.

Organization of the Text

The text begins with a chapter on computer basics (Chapter 0), followed by Chapter 1 that focuses on the general concepts necessary to begin programming in JavaScript. Chapter 1 introduces the Case Studies that are developed throughout the text. However, each chapter's Case Study is independent of other chapters. Chapter 2 covers variables, operators, and data types. These chapters are extremely important for students who have never taken a programming course and for students who are familiar with programming concepts. Understanding the interaction between a web page and JavaScript code is one of the most fundamental and important features of learning JavaScript.

Chapters 3 through 5 cover the basic control structures that are required to learn JavaScript—sequence, selection, and repetition. Students with no previous programming experience will learn how these constructs work in general as well as specifically with JavaScript. Students with prior programming experience may be able to move through these chapters swiftly.

Chapters 6 and 7 are specific to JavaScript. Forms and functions, including external JavaScript files, are covered. While most students have used forms in static web pages, here forms are discussed as a means to communicate with JavaScript programs.

Chapters 8 and 9 cover arrays and several advanced searching and sorting techniques. This material, as well as that in the next three chapters, is best suited for students with a solid programming foundation.

Chapter 10 discusses the Document Object Model and introduces students to XML. Chapters 11 and 12 introduce students to PHP. When students complete these three chapters they will be prepared to work on websites that use databases to store and use data. A free program, XAMPP, is used to allow students to host an Apache server on their computers with MySQL and PHP software. The text steps students through this process in detail. No prior knowledge of MySQL or databases is required; MySQL commands are given to the students to allow them to create real-life situations that use databases, a server, and PHP and to create a dynamic website.

There are numerous examples in each chapter. Throughout, **Examples**, **Checkpoints**, and **Review Exercises** increase in difficulty from most basic to very challenging. Each chapter contains a **Putting It to Work** section in which the **Case Studies**, Greg's Gambits and Carla's Classroom, are developed. At the end of each chapter, in the **Programming Challenges**, students add to these **Case Studies**. If followed from the beginning, by the end of the text the **Case Studies** have become robust websites. The **Programming Challenges** contain two additional **Case Studies**, Lee's Landscape and Jackie's Jewelry, that students build completely on their own. A great deal of assistance is provided for the Greg's Gambits and Carla's Classroom projects in the **Programming Challenges**. Much less assistance is given for the Lee's Landscape and Jackie's Jewelry projects. Instructors can decide how much independence is given to students.

Review Exercises contain Fill-in-the-Blank questions, True or False questions, Short Answer questions, and Programming Challenges where students can use what they have learned in the chapter to create their own web pages.

Brief Chapter Overviews

Formatting Notes

Code is distinguished from text by the use of a separate font. Variable and array names are bold. Sometimes certain code must be entered on a single line but it is not possible to display the full line within the confines of the textbook margins. The symbol ↵ indicates that the code on the next line should be part of the previous line but the symbol should not be included. The following code sample should be entered on a single line, without the ↵ symbol. Notice that the variable, **dinner**, is bold:

```
var dinner = prompt("What do you want for dinner? Choose ↵
               P for pizza or S for salad:" , " ");
```

Chapter 0: Computer Basics

This chapter provides an introduction to computers, computer programming, and the Internet. It contains an overview of computer architecture, the structural design of the Internet, browsers, the client/server model, and scripting languages.

Chapter 1: JavaScript Programming Basics

This chapter provides an introduction to programming and an introduction to JavaScript. The general problem-solving strategy for programming is discussed along with the basic structure of a program and the three control structures. Program planning using pseudocode and flowcharts is covered and data types are presented. Students are introduced to creating a JavaScript script that is displayed on a web page. Objects, dot notation, and several important JavaScript methods and events are discussed. The Greg's Gambits and Carla's Classroom websites are introduced and JavaScript is used to create interactive pages on these sites.

Chapter 2: Building Blocks: Variables and Operators

This chapter focuses on variables, JavaScript data types, and operators, including arithmetic, relational, and logical operators. The difference between loosely typed languages, such as JavaScript, and strongly typed languages is covered. The use of the concatenation operator is discussed as well as the way JavaScript treats numbers that are input by a user to a website. The conditional operator is discussed, permitting students to create interesting pages without extensive knowledge of selection structures. The order of operations is covered as well as ASCII code. Students create a game similar to Mad Libs for Greg's Gambits and a spelling lesson for Carla's Classroom.

Chapter 3: Making Decisions: The Selection Structure

Decision (selection) structures including single-, dual- and multiple-alternative structures are covered in this chapter. The switch statement is included, validation is introduced, and the Math object is presented. Programs are developed using nested selection structures and compound conditions. The Math.random() method allows students to create interesting programs. Students create a Fortune Telling program for Greg's Gambits and an arithmetic lesson for Carla's Classroom.

Chapter 4: Going Round and Round: The Repetition Structure

This chapter begins the coverage of repetition structures. The focus is on basic loop structures: pre- and post-test loops, sentinel-controlled loops, counter-controlled loops, and loops for data input and data validation. Loop coverage includes while loops, do...while loops, and for loops. Students create a message encoder for Greg's Gambits and add a good deal of functionality and depth to the arithmetic lesson created for Carla's Classroom in Chapter 3.

Chapter 5: Advanced Decisions and Loops

Chapter 5 expands the coverage of repetition structures and selection structures from Chapters 3 and 4. Several methods of the Math object are used, and computing sums and averages is covered. Nesting selection structures inside loops, loops inside loops, and loops inside selections structures are discussed in depth, including emphasis on desk checking. Various ways to exit loops early are covered. Students create a battle game (a variation of the Rock-Paper-Scissors game) for Greg's Gambits and a grammar lesson for Carla's Classroom.

Chapter 6: Forms

Most students who have taken a web authoring course have worked with forms, but this chapter acquaints students with using forms in conjunction with JavaScript. The basic form controls are discussed (radio buttons, checkboxes, textboxes, textarea boxes, selection lists) as well as hidden fields and special controls (password elements, submit and reset buttons). The chapter focuses on returning form data to a JavaScript program which can then use the data and return other information to the web page or return information to a user by email. Students create an inventory page for a Greg's Gambits site user and a progress report that Carla of Carla's Classroom can send to parents.

Chapter 7: Keeping it Neat: Functions and JavaScript Source Files

Here functions, objects, and JavaScript source files are covered. Built-in and user-defined functions are discussed. The scope of a variable, the use of arguments and parameters, value and reference parameters, and passing by reference versus passing by value are covered. New objects—the Boolean object and the Date object—are introduced and further information about the Math object is provided. Creating and using external JavaScript source files is covered in depth. Students create the game of Hangman for Greg's Gambits and a reading comprehension lesson for Carla's Classroom.

Chapter 8: Arrays

Chapter 8 is the first of two chapters that focus on arrays. The concept of an array as a JavaScript object is discussed. One-dimensional arrays, two-dimensional arrays, and parallel arrays are covered. Various methods of loading arrays are discussed along with several JavaScript array methods that make it easy to add and delete elements in arrays. Students create a game of 15 for Greg's Gambits and a slide show for Carla's Classroom.

Chapter 9: Searching and Sorting

This chapter builds on what was learned in Chapter 8 so that the programmer can quickly sort or search through an array. The JavaScript sort() and reverse() methods are discussed. To maintain the integrity of parallel arrays, alternate methods of searching and sorting are developed. Two sort algorithms—the bubble sort and the selection sort—are covered. Two search algorithms—the serial search and the binary search—are discussed as are some JavaScript methods that facilitate searching. Students create the game of Boggle for Greg's Gambits and a lesson in factoring numbers for Carla's Classroom.

Chapter 10: The Document Object Model and XML

Chapter 10 moves from JavaScript to related topics. The chapter is about the Document Object Model (DOM) and XML. The concepts of DOM nodes and trees and the parent-child model of web pages are discussed. Creating, inserting, removing, and replacing elements with DOM are covered. DOM methods are used to create timers. The chapter introduces XML, XSL, namespaces, and schemas. XML is utilized as an alternate method of displaying data by combining it with JavaScript to create a page for Greg's Gambits. XML is also used with JavaScript to create a spelling lesson for Carla's Classroom.

Chapter 11: PHP: An Overview

This is the first of two chapters about PHP. To use PHP students must have access to a server. This chapter walks students through the installation and use of XAMPP, a free program that includes an Apache server, PHP, and MySQL and can be installed on virtually any personal computer or laptop. The chapter discusses PHP basics including PHP file names, how to access files from the Apache server, PHP data types, PHP operators, and PHP keywords. The basic programming constructs—sequence, selection, and repetition—are covered as they are used with PHP as well as PHP arrays and strings. Emphasis is on creating an appropriate folder organization for a website on a server. Students create welcome pages for Greg's Gambits using PHP to allow users to send data to and return data from the server with the ajax_post() function. Students use PHP to create a page for Carla's Classroom that allows users to type part of a name and then has the program display all entries in a large array or list that begin with those characters (i.e., this program offers the user available options and can eventually be used to autocomplete user entries).

Chapter 12: Using PHP with Cookies and MySQL

This chapter builds on the introduction to PHP in Chapter 11 to demonstrate how to accomplish two specific but significant tasks. Creating and reading cookies is covered. Students are walked through the creation of a database using the phpMyAdmin console which is part of the XAMPP installation. Then, using PHP methods, the database is populated. Since the scope of the text does not include learning MySQL and students are not expected to have knowledge of database management and MySQL, all MySQL commands and statements needed to develop the programs in the chapter are given, with explanations of their purposes. In this way students are able to create and validate an account for a player who wishes to become a member of the Greg's Gambits game site. Students also create a database for Carla's Classroom and learn to pull information from the database to send an email report to a student's parents.

Appendixes

Appendix A: The ASCII Character Set

- A table including both printable and nonprintable ASCII characters with corresponding values in decimal and hexadecimal representation

Appendix B: Arithmetic, Relational, and Logical Operators and Operator Precedence

- Tables of arithmetic operators, relational operators, and logical operators (as used in this text) and charts of operator precedence

Appendix C: HTML Entities

- Tables of most common HTML entities including entities for HTML reserved characters

Appendix D: JavaScript Objects and Methods

- Properties and methods of the following objects: Array, Boolean, Date, Math, Number, String, and RegExp
- Lists of JavaScript global properties and functions

Appendix E: jQuery

- An explanation of jQuery, how to include it with a web page, where to get it and how to store it, and a short sample of jQuery functions

Appendix F: HTML DOM Properties, Methods, and Events

- A list of the most common DOM properties, methods, and events as well as the three important node properties

Appendix G: PHP Reserved Words and Predefined Constants

- Lists of PHP reserved words and keywords and PHP predefined constants

Appendix H: MySQL Functions

- A list of common PHP functions including those used in the book

Appendix I: Checkpoint Answers

- Answers to Checkpoint Exercises from the book

Features of the Text

Examples

There are more than 235 numbered worked **Examples** in the text. All program code lines are numbered, and in the examples, code is explained in detail, referencing line numbers. All code shown has been tested and will, if copied and run by the student, work. Screenshots show results where applicable.

Checkpoints

At the end of each section between five and ten **Checkpoint Exercises** reinforce the most important concepts and coding skills. Answers to the **Checkpoints** are in Appendix I.

Putting It to Work

The **Putting It to Work** section is the last section of each chapter. In this section two websites are developed and expanded. Greg's Gambits is a website about games. In each chapter students are walked through creating a new game or feature for this site. Carla's Classroom is a website for an elementary school teacher. In each chapter students are walked through creating a lesson for students or a feature that a teacher would use in a classroom. The complete code is developed, within the context of each of these sites. The content of these sites is expanded in the **Review Exercises**. The **Programming Challenges** section of the **Review Exercises** contains instructions for students to create either a new game for Greg's Gambits or a new lesson for Carla's Classroom. These may build on what was done in the corresponding site in **Putting It to Work** or may be something new. Concepts used in the Greg's Gambits section of **Putting It to Work** are utilized in a new project in the Carla's Classroom section of the **Programming Challenges.** A new project for Greg's Gambits in the **Programming Challenges** utilizes concepts and skills from the Carla's Classroom section of **Putting It to Work**. Therefore, an instructor who follows one of the sites from the beginning to the end of the book will help students to create real-life projects that encompass virtually all of the important concepts and skills covered, and result in a robust and realistic website.

The **Putting It to Work** section is structured in such a way that students can walk through the projects, using the code provided, and extend that knowledge by creating similar but expanded code on their own in the **Programming Challenges**.

All files necessary for these projects, including images, text files, and the like, are included in the Student Data Files.

Exercises

Each chapter contains more than 40 Review Exercises which vary from easy to complex. The text contains the following diverse selection:

- **Checkpoints** at the end of each section which include several items that test students' understanding of the material covered

- **Review Questions** at the end of each chapter:
  - ☐ Fill in the Blank
  - ☐ True or False
  - ☐ Short Answer
- **Programming Challenges**:
  - ☐ Create short web pages using chapter concepts
  - ☐ Expand pages created in **Putting It to Work** or add new content to Greg's Gambits and Carla's Classroom
  - ☐ Build one of two business sites, Lee's Landscape or Jackie's Jewelry, from scratch, adding to the content with each chapter

Answers to **Checkpoints** are in Appendix I and on the website at www.pearson highered.com/irc. Answers to odd-numbered **Review Exercises** are provided in the Student Data Files resource, including selected answers to the **Programming Challenges**. Where necessary, the entire code is provided. All files, including images, JavaScript source files, and text files, required to complete any project are included in Student Data Files.

VideoNotes

VideoNote

- A series of online videos developed specifically for this book is available at the book's website. Icons in the text alert students to videos that correspond with specific topics.

Supplements

Student Support Web Site

A variety of resources are available with this book. Students may download them at the book's companion website: www.pearsonhighered.com/drake. The following items are available:

- PowerPoint presentations for all chapters
- Solutions to all **Checkpoints**
- Answers to all odd-numbered **Review Exercises**
- **VideoNotes**
- Images, text files, and other external files required for all **Examples, Putting It to Work** websites, and **Review Exercises**

Instructor's Supplements

A variety of supplemental materials are available to qualified instructors from the Pearson Instructor Resource Center, including the following:

- PowerPoint presentations for all chapters
- Solutions to all **Checkpoints**
- Solutions to all **Review Exercises**, odds and evens

- Solutions to selected **Programming Challenges**
- HTML, JavaScript, XML, and PHP programs corresponding to all chapter **Examples**, **Review Exercises**, and **Checkpoints**
- **VideoNotes**
- Images, text files, and other external files required for all **Examples**, **Putting It to Work** websites, and **Review Exercises**
- Testbank with questions for all chapters

To access these materials, visit www.pearsonhighered.com/irc or contact your campus Pearson Education sales representative.

Acknowledgments

Just as there is no one right way to teach programming, there is no one right way to write a book about programming. In creating this text I am fortunate that the following experienced instructors offered varied points of view and numerous helpful suggestions:

> Brenda Terry, Fullerton College
> Leong Lee, Austin Peay State University
> Dave Wilson, Parkland College
> Tony Pittarese, East Tennessee State University
> Dave Sciuto, University of Massachusetts at Lowell
> Janos T. Fustos, Metropolitan State University of Denver
> Sam Sultan, New York University
> Nancy McCurdy, Santa Fe College

Special thanks to Anton Drake, a professional software/web developer who provided invaluable assistance in developing Greg's Gambits and Carla's Classroom for Chapters 10 through 12. Anton contributed as a consultant for the XML, PHP, and MySQL content and assisted in writing code for these chapters.

I am extremely fortunate to work with such a lovely and supportive team at Pearson. Matt Goldstein gave this project a chance and for that I am forever grateful. Kathy Cantwell turned my tendency for wordiness into clean prose. Marilyn Lloyd and Scott Disanno supported me through my first-edition jitters. Greg Dulles and Kayla Smith-Tarbox helped find images to make the websites come alive. Jenah Blitz-Stoehr was on hand to answer all my general questions. Everyone at Pearson is consistently kind, helpful, and encouraging. No author could ask for more.

I would also like to thank Anton and my nonhuman roommates for their patience while I spent many long hours clicking away at the computer and my whole family for their love and encouragement while I spend so much of my free time doing what I love to do—writing.

—Elizabeth Drake

ontents

Chapter 1 JavaScript Programming Basics 29

Chapter 8: Arrays 511

Chapter 9: Searching and Sorting 571

 **ocation of VideoNotes in the Text**

VideoNote

Computer Basics

Chapter Objectives

Why should you learn JavaScript? That's what this chapter is about. Here you will gain perspective on computers, the Internet, and the JavaScript scripting language. A brief history of how computers and the Internet have become such an integral part of everyone's everyday lives is included as well as a short discussion of computer basics, computer programming, browsers and Internet protocols, scripting, and, of course, JavaScript.

After reading this chapter, you will be able to do the following:

- Understand the evolution of computing devices from ancient Babylonia to the twenty-first century

- Understand the rise of computers in the work-place and the history behind the Internet

- Understand how web pages are transmitted over the Internet

- Understand how a URL is constructed

- Understand the components that comprise a typical computer system: the central processing unit, internal memory, mass storage, and input and output devices

- Understand the differences between application software and system software

- Understand the differences between types of programming languages

- Understand how JavaScript evolved

- Understand the basics of how browsers work including similarities and differences among several major browsers.

- Understand the relationship between web pages, HTML, and XHTML

- Understand the difference between server-side and client-side technologies

- Gain a basic understanding of what PHP, DOM, and XML do

0.1 A Brief History of Computers

The calculator, used to increase the speed and accuracy of numerical computations, has been around for a long time. The abacus, an early calculator, uses rows of sliding beads to perform arithmetic operations and has roots that date back more than 5,000 years to ancient Babylonia. More modern mechanical calculators, using gears and rods, have been used for almost 400 years. In fact, by the late nineteenth century, calculators of one sort or another were relatively common. However, these machines were by no means computers as we use the word today.

What Is a Computer?

A **computer** is a mechanical or electronic device that can efficiently store, retrieve, and manipulate large amounts of information at high speed and with great accuracy. Moreover, it can execute tasks and act upon intermediate results without human intervention. It does this by carrying out a list of instructions called a program.

Although we tend to think of the computer as a recent development, Charles Babbage, an Englishman, designed and partially built a true computer in the mid-1800s. Babbage's machine, which he called an Analytical Engine, contained hundreds of axles and gears and could store and process 40-digit numbers. Babbage was assisted in his work by Ada Augusta Byron, the daughter of the poet Lord Byron, who grasped the importance of his invention and helped to publicize the project. A major programming language (Ada) was named after her. Unfortunately, Babbage never finished his Analytical Engine. His ideas were too advanced for the existing technology, and he could not obtain sufficient financial backing to complete the project.

Serious attempts to build a computer were not renewed until nearly 70 years after Babbage's death. Around 1940, Howard Aiken at Harvard University, and John Atanasoff and Clifford Berry at Iowa State University built machines that were close to being true computers. However, Aiken's Mark I could not act independently on its intermediate results, and the Atanasoff-Berry computer required frequent intervention by an operator during its computations.

A few years later in 1945, a team at the University of Pennsylvania, led by John Mauchly and J. Presper Eckert, completed work on the world's first fully operable electronic computer. They named it ENIAC, an acronym for Electronic Numerical Integrator and Computer. ENIAC was a huge machine. It was 80 feet long, 8 feet high, weighed 33 tons, contained more than 17,000 vacuum tubes in its electronic circuits, and consumed 175,000 watts of electricity. For its time, ENIAC was a truly amazing machine because it could accurately perform up to 5,000 additions per second.

For the next decade or so, all electronic computers used vacuum tubes to do the internal switching necessary to perform computations. These machines, which we now refer to as first-generation computers, were large by modern standards, although not as large as ENIAC. They required a climate-controlled room and lots of tender loving care to keep them operating. By 1955, about 300 computers—built mostly by IBM and Remington Rand—were being used, primarily by large businesses, universities, and government agencies.

By the late 1950s, computers had become much faster and more reliable. The most significant change at this time was that the large, heat producing **vacuum tubes** were replaced by relatively small transistors. The **transistor** is one of the most important inventions of the twentieth century. It was developed at Bell Labs in the late 1940s by William Shockley, John Bardeen, and Walter Brattain, who later shared a Nobel Prize for their achievement. Transistors are small and require very little energy, especially compared to vacuum tubes. Therefore, many transistors can be packed together in a compact enclosure. In the early 1960s, Digital Equipment Corporation (DEC) took advantage of small, efficient packages of transistors called integrated circuits to create the minicomputer, a machine roughly the size of a four-drawer filing cabinet. These computers were smaller and less expensive than their predecessors, and they were an immediate success. Nevertheless, sales of the larger computers, now called mainframes, also rapidly increased. The computer age had clearly arrived and the industry leader was IBM's innovative System 360.

Personal Computers

Despite the increasing popularity of computers, it was not until the late 1970s that the computer became a household appliance. This development was made possible by the invention of the microchip in the 1960s. A **microchip** is a piece of silicon about the size of a postage stamp, packed with thousands of electronic components. The microchip and its more advanced cousin, the **microprocessor**, led to the creation of the world's first personal computer (PC) in 1974. The PC was relatively inexpensive compared to its predecessors, and was small enough to fit on a desktop.

Today's Computers

Today, the computer market comprises a vast array of machines. Personal computers, laptops, and tablets are everywhere and range in price from a few hundred to a few thousand dollars. Most computer manufacturers are billion-dollar companies such as IBM, Dell, HP, and Apple. Although PCs are small and inexpensive, they produce a remarkable amount of computing power. Today's tablet PCs, which weigh as little as two pounds or less and fit into a handbag, are far more powerful than the most advanced mainframes of the mid-1970s. And a tiny smart phone that weighs less than five ounces and fits into your jeans pocket can perform virtually all the functions of a desktop computer that the average user wants or needs.

However, content developers of apps, web pages, and online businesses that many of us use every day still depend on the power of a desktop computer. And, in this book, we learn to develop some of that content. So rest assured, your laptop is not outdated yet!

CHECKPOINT FOR SECTION 0.1 ✓

0.1 Which of the following is not true?
  a) A computer is a mechanical or electronic device.
  b) A computer can efficiently store, retrieve, and manipulate large amounts of information.
  c) A computer must be able to communicate over the Internet.
  d) A computer must work at high speed with great accuracy.

0.2 What was the computer designed by Charles Babbage called?

0.3 What significant change occurred in computers in the 1950s?

0.4 What invention led to the creation of the world's first personal computer?

A Brief History of the Internet

Despite the recent advances in computer technology, the most significant development in the last 20 years has been the phenomenal rise in popularity of the **Internet**—a worldwide collection of networks. A **network** consists of two or more linked computers that can share resources and data via cable or phone lines. The Internet dates back to a relatively small U.S. Defense Department project called DARPA (Defense Advanced Research Projects Agency) in the late 1960s. Over the last 40 years, the Internet has grown from a small collection of mainframe computers used solely by universities and the military to more than 1 billion computers used widely by preschoolers to billion-dollar global corporations.

The first recorded description of the social interactions that could be enabled through networking was a series of memos written by J.C.R. Licklider of MIT in August 1962. Licklider envisioned an interconnected set of computers through which data and programs could be accessed from any site. Licklider was the first head of the computer research program at DARPA.

Packet Switching

As might be expected, since the concept of the Internet was developed by the U.S. Defense Department, security was a top priority. The concept of **packet switching** as a means to transmit information is integral to the way the Internet works. The following is a general description of how packet switching works:

When a web page is sent to a computer, the whole page is not sent in one piece. Rather, the page is divided into **packets**. Each packet is sent to a different remote server. For the purposes of this example, and to help you envision the process, we might assume that a web page, housed on a server in Los Angeles, CA, is requested by a student sitting at his computer in Jacksonville, FL. The student's computer sends the request to his **Internet Service Provider (ISP)** and the request is relayed to the server in Los Angeles. When the request is received, the page is divided into four packets which are sent to various servers, based on certain requirements. One packet may be sent to a server in Atlanta, GA, one to Miami, FL, one to Chicago, IL, and one to Baltimore, MD. Then each packet is routed to the next best location, and the next, until it reaches the student's ISP server in Jacksonville. At that location, the packets are reassembled and the ISP sends the web page to the student's computer.

This may seem like a great deal of work. However, this system ensures that, no matter what happens to one server anywhere in the world, communication can continue between the other locations. If, for example, the location in Chicago is compromised, the packet that is sent to Chicago will not be forwarded to Jacksonville. The server in Jacksonville realizes, when the other three packets arrive, that because the page cannot be reassembled correctly, there is problem. A second request is then sent to the initial location in Los Angeles. Then the page is resent, this time perhaps substituting St. Louis, MO for Chicago. And the user in Jacksonville sees the web page without realizing there was a transmission problem.

Transmission Control Protocol / Internet Protocol (TCP/IP)

Together, **Transmission Control Protocol (TCP)** and **Internet Protocol (IP)** are known as **TCP/IP**. This is the official protocol used for Internet communication. TCP breaks the web page file into packets and decides on the best route to use to send those packets. Internet Protocol (IP) routes the packets to the correct address.

Each device connected to the Internet has a unique numeric address, called an **IP address**. Each IP address consists of four groups of numbers and each group is a number between 0 and 255. You can check the IP address of your own computer. Normally, each time you connect to the Internet, your ISP assigns your computer an IP address from a pool of IP addresses available on the network. Because this address changes each time you connect, it is called a **dynamic IP address**. Businesses and other sites may want their IP addresses to remain consistent. They use **static IP addresses**. If you know the IP address of a web page, you can type it into your browser and you'll get to the same place as you would by using the URL! At the time this was written, the IP address of Facebook was `69.171.229.11`. If you type this number into your browser address bar, it will take you to `facebook.com`.

Try It Yourself

If you are using a computer with a Windows operating system (Windows 7 or 8, Vista, or XP), you can check your IP address by following these steps:

- Click `Start`
- Select `All Programs`
- Click `Accessories`
- Click `Command Prompt`
- Enter `ipconfig`

You will get a screen with a lot of information, including one line that provides your IP address. At the time of this writing, two versions of the Internet Protocol (IP) are in use: IP Version 4 (IPv4) and IP Version 6 (IPv6). Each version defines an IP address differently. Because of its prevalence, the generic term *IP address* typically refers to the addresses defined by IPv4. Your `Command Prompt` results will show both IPv4 and IPv6.

What Is a URL?

There is a distinction between the Internet and the World Wide Web. Every resource on the World Wide Web is also part of the Internet but not everything on the Internet is part of the World Wide Web. For example, instant messaging (IM) programs are on the Internet but not on the World Wide Web. IM programs use different protocols for communication. The **World Wide Web (web)** is a system of interlinked hypertext documents accessed via the Internet.

A **Uniform Resource Locator (URL)** is the unique address of every resource on the World Wide Web. Resources include web pages, images, videos, music files, and more. As mentioned, the actual address is the IP address but, for humans, it is much easier to deal with words than with four groups of numbers. A URL consists of four parts: the protocol, the web server, the domain, and the path. We will use the following sample URL as an example to identify and explain each part:

```
http://www.pearsonhighered.com/educator/discipline/Computer/javascrpt.htm
```

The Protocol

In this case, the **protocol** is `http`, which stands for **Hypertext Transfer Protocol**. Most URLs use HTTP; however, there are other protocols such as FTP (File Transfer Protocol) and SMTP (Simple Mail Transfer Protocol). The protocol defines the communication protocol that is used to request a page or source and the response to the request.

The Web Server

In this case, the **web server** is `www`. This is the most common web server but many sites have independent servers.

The Domain

In our sample URL, the domain is `pearsonhighered.com`. The **domain name** locates a specific organization or, as in this case, part of an organization. The format of a domain name is:

```
name-dot-TLD.
```

TLD stands for **Top Level Domain**. It identifies the type of organization or company in that domain. In this example, the `.com` indicates that this is a commercial site. A TLD of `.edu` indicates an educational institution and a TLD of `.org` indicates a nonprofit organization. There are many others, such as .gov, .net, .biz, and so on.

The Path

The last part of every URL is the **path** that takes the user to the exact page or resource requested. The path includes the folder or folders where the page is located and, normally, the exact name of the file requested. In this case, the path is:

```
/educator/discipline/Computer/javascrpt.htm.
```

The page requested is a file named `javascrpt.htm`. It is located on Pearson's server, is inside a folder named `Computer`, which is inside a folder named `discipline`, which is inside a folder named `educator`.

Is It All Necessary?

To go to Google, all we need to do is type `google.com`. So why do we need all those parts of the URL? First, if we simply type `google` into the address bar of a browser, we will get a page that offers many options. The first option will probably be `google.com` but there will be others. The browser doesn't have enough information to know that you want to go to Google's main page.

If we type in `google.com`, we will get to Google's main page but, looking at the browser's address bar, we will see that the address has changed to `http://www.google.com`. The browser has been programmed to fill in the missing (and assumed) protocol and web server.

Browsers are programmed to be user-friendly. However, web programmers are not everyday users. As programmers, when we create a link on our web page to another page, resource, or file outside of our server we must include the entire URL. This type of link is an **absolute reference** because it includes the entire URL to a resource. If we want to create a link to a web page or resource on a page within our own site, we must include the entire correct path to that resource but we do not have to include the protocol, server, or domain. This type of link is a **relative reference** because the resource's path is given, relative to the page that calls it.

CHECKPOINT FOR SECTION 0.2

    0.5 The official protocol used for Internet communication is _____.

    0.6 Describe how packet switching works.

    0.7 Given the following URL, identify the parts listed:

        `http://www.widgets.com/gallery/fidgety_widget.html`

      a) the protocol
      b) the server
      c) the domain
      d) the TLD
      e) the path
      f) the name of the file to be displayed

0.3 Computer Basics

Previously we defined a computer as a mechanical or electronic device that can efficiently store, retrieve, and manipulate large amounts of information quickly and accurately. As the definition implies, a computer must have the ability to input, store, manipulate, and output data. These functions are achieved by five main components of a computer system:

1. Central processing unit (CPU)
2. Internal memory (consisting of RAM and ROM)
3. Mass storage devices (magnetic, optical, and solid-state)
4. Input devices (primarily the keyboard and mouse)
5. Output devices (primarily the monitor and printer)

In a desktop PC, the CPU, internal memory, and most mass storage devices are located in the **system unit**. The input and output devices are housed in their own enclosures and are connected to the system unit by cables or wireless transmitters. Components that are used by a computer but located outside the system unit, are sometimes referred to as **peripherals**. Portable computers house the CPU, internal memory, mass storage devices, keyboard, and monitor in one relatively small package. The physical equipment that makes up the computer system is known as hardware. A simple model of a computer is shown in Figure 0.1.

Input

The computer uses **input** devices to receive data from the outside world. Every computer includes a keyboard and a pointing device such as a mouse to allow users to enter information into a program. Today, there are many input options available including voice activation, touch screens, pens, and so on.

Processing

The **central processing unit** (also called the **processor** or **CPU**) is the brain of the computer. It, along with the **arithmetic logic unit** (**ALU**) receives the program instructions, performs the arithmetic and logical operations necessary to execute

Basic Computer Input–Processing–Output Model

INPUT	PROCESSING	OUTPUT
mouse	CPU	screen
keyboard	(central	printer
touch screen	processing unit)	speakers
light pen	ALU	internet
etc.	(arithmetic	etc.
	logic unit)	

STORAGE
ROM (read–only memory)
RAM (random access memory)
hard drive
DVD
flash drive
etc.

Figure 0.1 The basic Input-Processing-Output model of a computer

them, and controls the other computer components. The processor consists of millions of transistors that reside on a single microchip about the size of a postage stamp and plug into the computer's main circuit board, the motherboard.

Storage

A computer would be virtually useless if there was no way to retain its information and processes. There are two main types of **storage**: volatile and non-volatile. **Volatile storage** is, as the name implies, not permanent. **Non-volatile storage** retains information even after the computer is turned off. A computer uses its internal memory to store the instructions and data to be processed by the CPU.

Internal Memory

There are two types of internal memory: **read-only memory (ROM)** and **random access memory (RAM)**. ROM contains an unalterable set of instructions that the computer uses during its start-up process and for other basic operations. On the other hand, RAM can be read from and written to. It's used by the computer to hold program instructions and data. You can think of ROM as a reference sheet, and RAM as a scratchpad, albeit a very large scratchpad. ROM is an integrated circuit programmed with specific data when it is manufactured. This information cannot be altered by the user; therefore, ROM is a permanent (non-volatile) form of memory storage. RAM is memory used by the computer to hold the data you are working on at a given time. For example, if you are typing an English essay on your computer, as you write the essay you see it on your monitor, and it is also being held in RAM. When you close the word processing program or turn off your computer, the information stored in RAM is lost. Since RAM is a volatile form of memory, it is important to save your work to a permanent storage medium—as most of us, to our dismay, have learned too late at one time or another!

Mass Storage Devices

In addition to ROM and RAM, a computer needs **mass storage**, another form of memory, which stores programs and data semipermanently. The data you store on a mass storage device remains on the device until you erase or delete it. However, to use the information stored on a mass storage device, the computer must first load (copy) that information into RAM. In other words, when you type your English essay, first the computer loads a word processing program such as Microsoft Word or Open Office into RAM. Then, as you continue, your essay is also stored in RAM. When you finish writing your essay or take a break, you save your work to a storage device and close the word processing program. Both the essay and the word processing program disappear from RAM. But the word processing program still exists on your hard drive and the essay is saved on whatever storage device you used.

There are many different types of mass storage and all of them fall into one of the following three categories:

1. Magnetic storage such as hard disks
2. Optical storage such as CDs and DVDs
3. Solid-state storage such as flash drives

Output

Input devices allow us to communicate with the computer; **output** devices make it possible for the computer to communicate with us. The most common output devices are screens, printers, and speakers. However, output is often sent to other devices such as when you use email or a chat room.

CHECKPOINT FOR SECTION 0.3

0.8 Which of the following is not part of the basic computer model?
  a) input
  b) storage
  c) online access
  d) processing
  e) output

0.9 What are the two types of internal memory and how are they different?

0.10 List two or three input and output devices for a laptop computer.

0.11 List two or three input and output devices for a smart phone.

0.4 What Is Programming?

The only way a computer knows what to do with the input it receives is to follow the program instructions. Most people assume that computer programmers write all computer programs. Actually, every time you do anything on a computer you are, in effect, writing a **computer program**. When you change a font to a different size or color, you are creating instructions for the computer about how to display that font. You don't see these programs; nevertheless, they are created for the computer to use. You don't see them because a computer programmer has written the program instructions that translate the mouse click on the *Bold* icon or the red color square into actual program code.

Computer **hardware** consists, basically, of anything a person can touch. All the input, output, and processing devices discussed in the previous section are computer hardware. But even the most powerful hardware cannot accomplish anything independently; it needs software to bring it to life. **Software** consists of programs that allow users to send email, edit photos, play games, run businesses, and perform countless other tasks.

The History of Programming

Before programming languages like C++, Python, Java, or any of today's myriad languages existed, computers were programmed one instruction at a time using binary code. This was an enormously tedious job because code looked like multiple rows of 0s and 1s. Not only were programs difficult to read, but also they were tough to modify and correct. Creating software was not a popular occupation, which resulted in a shortage of programmers. Expensive computers sat idle for long periods while software was being developed. Often, it cost much more to develop software than it did to buy the computer. Assembly language was developed to facilitate writing code. But there were things assembly languages could not do, on top of the fact that this code was still difficult to read. High-level languages were developed to allow programmers to write and edit code much more efficiently and to create programs that supported advanced features.

A Brief Timeline

Like many historic "firsts," the first modern programming language is hard to identify. Some people think that "first modern programming language" status depends on how much power and human-readability is required.

In the 1950s, the first three modern programming languages were designed. In one form or another, they are still in use today: **FORTRAN** (1955), short for FORmula TRANslator and invented by John Backus *et al.*; **LISP** [1958], short for LISt Processor and invented by John McCarthy *et al.*; and **COBOL**, (1959), an acronym for COmmon Business Oriented Language and created by the Short Range Committee, chaired by Joseph Wegstein of the U.S. National Bureau of Standards.

From the late 1960s to the late 1970s there were major developments in programming languages. Many of the main language paradigms, such as object-oriented programming, now in use were created during this time.

While the 1980s were devoted to consolidating and elaborating on previously developed languages, the 1990s brought, along with the increasing popularity of the Internet, the development of a new breed of languages. The new concept centered around introducing languages or modifying languages based on productivity needs. Many RAD ("rapid application development") languages emerged. Often, they were developed from older languages and were all object oriented. The most significant of these was Java.

The 1990s also saw the emergence of scripting languages, such as JavaScript, ASP, and PHP. These languages were developed with productivity in mind. Scripting language code is embedded into an HTML document and interpreted by the browser or server.

Programming and scripting languages continue to develop and evolve with changing technologies. Presently, there is more emphasis on finding a language suited to a specific task rather than fitting a task to a certain programming or scripting language. Importance is on distribution and mobility. Programmers must be able to integrate their programs with databases using XML (Extensible Markup Language). XML is a set of rules for encoding documents in a form that can be read by a computer. XML-based formats have become the default for most popular office productivity software, including Microsoft Office, Open Office, and Apple's iWork.

The distinction between software that is used on a computer and software that is available on and through the Internet has become blurred in recent years. Cloud computing allows for shared resources, software, and information over the Internet, via a browser. Therefore, it is important that programmers understand what a browser is and how it works.

Types of Software

Software is divided into two general categories: **application software** and **system software**.

Application Software

Applications are programs you use to enhance productivity, solve problems, supply information, or provide recreation—reasons one uses a computer. Software applications are often designed to perform multiple tasks. For example, a spreadsheet program may be able to accomplish statistical tasks as well as database tasks and much more. The ubiquitous **app** is simply a small piece of software designed for a specific purpose. The following are some of the more popular kinds of applications:

- *Word processors* help you create, modify, and print documents such as letters, reports, and memos.
- *Database managers* allow you to enter, organize, and access large quantities of data. You might use a database program to create a personal phone directory. A business can use this kind of application to maintain customer lists and employee records.
- *Spreadsheet programs* simplify the manipulation and calculation of large amounts of tabular data (spreadsheets). These programs are used by businesses to predict the effect of different strategies on their bottom line.
- *Photo editors* allow you to download photographs to your computer from a digital camera, modify, and print them.
- *Web browsers* and *email programs* allow you to use the Internet to view an incredible variety of electronic resources and to communicate with others around the world.

Applications are developed and published by many different companies and sold in retail stores, by mail order firms, and over the Internet.

System Software

System software consists of the programs used by the computer to control and maintain its hardware and to communicate with the user. The most important piece of system software is the **operating system (OS)**, which is the computer's master control program. A computer must use an operating system written especially for that computer, although the computer user may be able to choose from among several available operating systems. Without an operating system, the computer would be useless. The operating system has two essential functions:

1. It helps applications communicate with the computer hardware. Applications are written to run under a specific operating system; they need to access the computer's disk drives, memory, and so forth.
2. It provides an interface between the computer and the user so that the user can install and use applications, manipulate files, and perform many other tasks.

Programming and Scripting Languages

Just as a book must be written in a particular language such as English, Spanish, or French, programs must be written in a particular programming language. A programming language is a set of symbols and the rules governing their use that are used in constructing programs.

There are three fundamental types of programming languages:

1. Machine languages
2. Assembly languages
3. High-level languages

Machine Language

A **machine language** program consists of a sequence of bits that are 0s and 1s. Each combination of zeros and ones is an instruction to the computer. Machine language is the only language the computer can understand directly. However, as you might imagine, it is very difficult for humans to read and write machine language programs. Therefore, programmers normally use either assembly or high-level languages.

Assembly Language

Assembly language is a symbolic representation of machine language. There is usually a one-to-one correspondence between the two; each assembly language instruction translates into one machine language instruction. However, assembly language uses easily recognizable codes, which make it easier for people to understand. Before a computer can carry out an assembly language program, the computer must translate it into machine language. This is done by a special program called an assembler, as shown in Example 0.1.

EXAMPLE 0.1 Comparing Machine Language and Assembly Language

The following instruction adds two numbers on a certain computer:

Machine Language Instruction:

```
0110110111110111 0000000100000000 0000000100000000
```

Assembly Language Equivalent:

```
ADD A, B
```

Of course, the computer is not adding the letter A and the letter B. This instruction is actually telling the computer to add the values that are stored in the spaces in the computer's memory, designated by A and B.

High-Level Languages

High-level languages usually contain English words and phrases. Their symbols and structure are very different from those of machine language. High-level languages have several advantages over machine or assembly languages. For example, they are easier to learn and use, and the resulting programs are easier to read and modify. A single instruction in a high-level language usually translates into many instructions in machine language. Moreover, a given high-level language does not differ much from one type of computer to another; a program written on one type of machine usually can be modified for use on another. High-level languages, like assembly languages, must be translated into machine language before they can be understood by the computer.

FORTRAN (FORmula TRANslator), the first high-level language, was developed in the mid-1950s, primarily for engineering and scientific applications. Since then, there has been a flood of high-level languages. The following list includes a few:

- **Ada** is used mostly for programs written under U.S. Department of Defense contracts. It was named for Ada Augusta Byron, a pioneer in the invention of the computer.
- **C++** is used for efficient programming of many different types of applications. Currently, it is one of the most popular languages.
- **Java** is a very popular modern language, especially for web applications.
- **JavaScript** is a scripting language developed by Netscape to enable web authors to design interactive sites. JavaScript can interact with HTML source code, which enables web authors to spice up their sites with dynamic content.
- **Visual Basic** is a new version of BASIC, an older, popular language. Visual Basic is well suited for software that runs on graphical user interfaces (GUIs), such as those on Windows and Macintosh computers.

High-level languages are continually changing. For example, C++ evolved from a language called C. C++ is an important high-level language, but there are two other versions of this C-based language as well: the dot-Net version and C# (C-sharp). Learning about many programming languages may seem overwhelming. If each programming language was as different as English is from Chinese then this would be true. However, basic programming logic applies to all programming languages. Once you have mastered one language, it is relatively easy to learn the rules and structures that govern another.

Writing Programs

To write a program in most high-level languages, first you must have access to the appropriate software. This software usually consists of several programs that work together on your computer to help you create the finished product, including a **text editor** in which you type and edit (modify) the program statements (instructions); a **debugger** that helps you find errors in your program; and a **compiler** or **interpreter** that translates your program into machine language. This software is readily available for many programming languages. Often it is available as a free download.

Scripting Languages versus Programming Languages

It is difficult to characterize definitively the differences between scripting languages, like JavaScript, and programming languages, like C++ and Java. In the past, companies hired C++ programmers or Visual Basic programmers and regardless of the task, the programmer wrote code in his or her preferred language. Today, more often programmers choose a language that fits the job rather than force a given language to do that job. Scripting languages can work efficiently in many cases where a more powerful programming language might make the task tedious and overwhelming.

An important difference between programming and scripting languages has to do with what happens when the program is run. A programming language may more accurately be termed a compiled language. When the code is run, it is translated into machine-readable code. This process is called compilation. The code is compiled, using a compiler, before the program is executed. A scripting language is not compiled. The computer, of course, still needs to have the code translated to the bits and bytes it needs to understand. But, rather than completing this process before the program is run, scripting language code is interpreted "on the fly"—that is, as each line of code is executed, it is translated by an interpreter to the computer.

CHECKPOINT FOR SECTION 0.4 ✓

0.12 List three things that would be classified as computer hardware.

0.13 Briefly describe three types of software applications.

0.14 What are the functions of an operating system?

0.15 What is the main difference between a compiled programming language and an interpreted scripting language?

0.5 Browsers

Normally, as soon as you get on the Internet, whether from your laptop, your smart phone, or your tablet, you're in a browser. Which do you use? Firefox? Internet Explorer? Safari? Chrome? Something else? There are many browsers and most ordinary users hardly think about them. The important thing, for most people, is to get to Facebook, find out what the weather will be, or shop. In fact, the most important thing, when you create web pages, is to consider the browser. Without a browser, none of your pages will be available to anyone but you.

What Is a Browser?

A **browser** is a software application that is used to retrieve, display, and surf for information resources on the World Wide Web. The significant part of that sentence is that the browser is a computer software application. We have discussed software applications so you know that they are programs that reside on *your* computer. The browser program interprets HTML tags, JavaScript code, and most everything the web developer puts in a web page. The browser contacts the web server and requests information. The server sends the information back to the browser, which displays the results on the computer or other Internet-enabled device.

Overview of Major Browsers

The first web browser, WorldWideWeb, was introduced by Tim Berners-Lee in 1991. In 1993, the first graphical web browser, Mosaic, led to an explosion of web use. Marc Andreessen, the leader of the Mosaic team, started his own company, Netscape, and released Netscape Navigator in 1994. It quickly became the world's most popular browser and, at its peak, accounted for 90% of all web use.

Never one to be outdone, in 1995, Microsoft responded with Internet Explorer (IE). By bundling Internet Explorer with Windows, IE gained dominance in the web browser market. Users found it far easier to use what they had when they bought the computer than to download and install a different browser.

Opera debuted in 1996. It never achieved widespread use on computers, but it's used extensively on other devices. Opera is preinstalled on more than 40 million phones and is available on several other embedded systems, including Nintendo's Wii video game console.

In 1998, Netscape launched what was to become the Mozilla Foundation. That browser would eventually evolve into Firefox, which has become a serious IE competitor.

Apple's Safari had its first beta release in January 2003 and, as of 2013, it remains a popular Apple-based web browser.

The most recent major entrant to the browser market is Google Chrome, which was first released in 2008. Chrome has been steadily increasing in popularity, largely at the expense of Internet Explorer.

How Does A Browser Work?

A browser works in a **client/server model**. The **client** is you—or whatever computer the browser resides on. The **server** is where the web page that the client wants to see resides. The browser has two major functions. When a user types a URL (or clicks a link that tells the browser the requested URL), it is the browser that sends a request to the web server, asking for that information. This function goes from client to server and back to client. The server either locates the requested page and sends that information back to the client or, if the page doesn't exist, it returns a message to that effect. If there is more than one file in the page requested, the server sends all of them back to the browser. Once they are on the client-side computer, the browser must display them. You must use a browser to request information over the web because the browser has the ability to transmit information over the web using a set of rules called the HyperText Transfer Protocol (HTTP).

The browser's second main function is to display the information. A web page is created using HTML tags which identify the format of the information. The browser interprets these tags and displays the page as instructed, by the HTML tags. Unless the web page designer specifies otherwise, the browser uses certain defaults for each tag. For example, the <p></p> tag pair may default to displaying text in Times New Roman font, 12 point size, black color, and so on. Unless the designer changes those attributes, all `<p></p>` text will be Times New Roman 12 point black. Styles can be applied with CSS to change the default values, but CSS styles are also interpreted by the browser. The browser has instructions for many other default attributes. However, not all browsers—or versions of the same browser—have the same default values. This is why a page may look different in different browsers.

As the Internet gained popularity and as more "regular" people started publishing web pages, browser developers began to include code that forgave many errors. For example, a person unfamiliar with web programming might not realize the important distinction between uppercase and lowercase letters. One browser may be programmed to ignore case use while another is not. In the first scenario, a web page named **MyPage.htm** would display properly, regardless of whether the user typed **MyPage.htm**, **mypage.htm**, **MYPAGE.HTM**, or any other combination of uppercase and lowercase characters. In the second scenario, a browser might return a **Page Not Found** message for everything except **MyPage.htm**.

Today, browsers have many options that define or restrict what a user will see when requesting a web page. For example, often, the user can change the default fonts or turn off JavaScript. It is essential that professional web developers are aware of these options. Presently, there is no way to control what browser an individual is using or what options he or she has enabled or disabled. There are continuous efforts to create additional standards both in HTML script and in how browsers interpret that script. The process is difficult because the fast growth of the Internet over the past few decades means that web browser developers have endeavored to code ways to excuse and override user errors—not to encourage adherence to strict rules.

HTML5 is a response to the observation that the HTML and XHTML commonly used on the World Wide Web is a combination of features introduced by various specifications and unique conditions introduced by web browsers. It is also a response to the many syntax errors in existing web documents and it attempts to define a single HTML or XHTML markup language.

Is the World Wide Web the Same As the Internet?

The short answer is "no." The World Wide Web and the Internet are not the same but they are firmly intertwined. The Internet (with an uppercase I) is an enormous network of networks. When written with an uppercase I, the Internet refers to the biggest collection of networks on the planet. Any group of networks that are connected is an **internet** (with a lowercase i). The World Wide Web is part of the Internet. The World Wide Web is often referred to as simply the web; it's a way to access information over the medium of the Internet—an information-sharing model built on top of the Internet. The web uses the HTTP protocol to transmit data but HTTP is only one of the languages spoken over the Internet. The Internet, not the web, is used for features such as e-mail, Usenet news groups, instant messaging, FTP, and more. Other protocols used to transmit data include SMTP (Simple Mail Transfer Protocol), FTP (File Transfer Protocol), LDAP (Lightweight Directory Access Protocol), IMAP (Internet Message Access Protocol), Telnet (remote terminal access protocol), and RTP (Real-time Transport Protocol). These are just some of the many protocols used to transmit data over the Internet. The web is a very large portion of the Internet, but it is not the same as the Internet.

This distinction is important to you, as a web programmer because this book is about programming for the web—not programming for the Internet. Often, this may be a distinction without a big difference, but sometimes the distinction is significant.

What Does This Mean to You?

So far, we have discussed how your computer handles data—where the data is input, stored, manipulated, and output. We've talked a bit about programming in general. As you work through this text, you will learn to create programs that will run in web pages. You will create those pages and programs on your computer.

You will need to upload those pages to the web and to view them you will need a browser. There are many available browsers and they have one thing in common: All of them allow users to request data from servers and to display that data on a user's computer. But how that data is displayed may differ slightly or even dramatically, depending on both the browser and the user.

You may create a page that looks fantastic on your monitor. But your monitor has specific resolution settings that may differ from another computer. The screen resolution can turn a beautiful page into a nightmare. Similarly, the user may have altered the default settings on the browser or may be using a browser version with different default settings. These are important considerations when creating web pages.

Additionally, browsers allow users to turn off JavaScript and other scripts. It is good practice to keep this in mind when writing a script. We will discuss how to deal with this issue later in the text.

CHECKPOINT FOR SECTION 0.5

0.16 What is a browser and where does the browser "live"?

0.17 What does the browser do when a user types a URL in the browser's address bar?

0.18 What is HTML5 and why was it developed?

0.19 What is the difference between the Internet and an internet?

0.20 What is the difference between the Internet and the World Wide Web?

0.21 Why is it important for a web developer to understand the differences among browsers?

0.6 JavaScript and the Acronyms: XHTML, DOM, PHP, XML

JavaScript® is one of the most popular scripting languages on the Internet. Called the language of the web, it works in all the major browsers. Browsers have been increasing JavaScript execution speeds with newer versions, allowing sites to make more extensive use of JavaScript. By using JavaScript, a site can send HTTP requests behind the scenes and customize or update certain sections of the site, tailored to a particular user's needs. This makes the user interface much more powerful and user friendly and gives the web developer more ways to exploit JavaScript's capabilities. JavaScript delivers a great deal more interaction with the user.

A Brief History of JavaScript

In the 1990s, when the World Wide Web first became popular, all web pages were static. This meant that a person could view the page but no interaction with that page was possible. The only option was to click a link to go to another page. Web pages were created with HTML, which we know formats what the page looks like. To create a page that allowed the user to interact on any level—to have something on the page respond to a user's actions—meant that some form of programming instructions had to be added. And, for that response to be immediate, the instructions had to run on the same computer as the one the user was operating. This is not as easy as it sounds, because people buy different brands of computers, use different operating systems, load different software, and customize their computers in a myriad of ways. A language was needed that would run on any computer, regardless of the user's choices and configurations. This is almost an impossible task, but JavaScript comes close to doing all these things.

In the 1990s, there were two popular browsers: Netscape Navigator and Internet Explorer. Netscape was the first to introduce a programming language that allowed web pages to become interactive. They called it **LiveScript** and it was integrated into the browser. This meant that anyone who was using Netscape could interact with pages that used LiveScript.

Another programming language called Java also allowed the user to interact with web pages but Java required a separate plugin to run. With this in mind, Netscape decided to rename their language JavaScript. However, although some Java and JavaScript code appears similar, the languages are entirely different and have completely diverse purposes.

Internet Explorer jumped quickly on the bandwagon and implemented two languages into their browser: **VBSscript**, which was based on the BASIC programming language and **JScript**, which was similar to JavaScript. At the time, the Netscape Navigator browser was much more popular than Internet Explorer so IE began to use versions of JScript that were developed to becomes more like JavaScript. By the time that Internet Explorer became the dominant browser, JavaScript had become the accepted standard for writing interactive processing that runs in a web browser.

In 1996, further development of JavaScript was given to an international standards body called ECMA. The language was officially renamed **ECMAScript**, or ECMA-262, but most people still refer to it as JavaScript.

Web Pages and XHTML

A web browser reads HTML documents and creates web pages from them. **Hyper-Text Markup Language (HTML)** is the main markup language for web pages. HTML elements are the basic building blocks of web pages. The browser does not display the HTML tags, but it uses the tags to interpret the content of the page. This text assumes that you already know how to create web pages using HTML or XHTML markup as well as Cascading Style Sheets. Therefore, this overview will be short and should be considered a review.

HTML is written in the form of **elements** consisting of **tags** enclosed in < and > brackets, within the web page content. Many HTML tags are in pairs, such as <p> and </p>, while some, known as **empty elements**, are single tags, such as <img />. The first tag in a pair is the opening tag and the second tag is the closing tag. Between the tags are text, other tags, links, and other content. **XHTML** is a stricter and cleaner version of HTML. The following are XHTML standard requirements:

- XHTML elements must be properly nested.
- XHTML elements must always be closed.
- XHTML elements must be in lowercase.
- XHTML documents must have one root element.

Examples 2 through 5 demonstrate what these requirements mean.

EXAMPLE 0.2

XHTML Elements Must Be Properly Nested

When a set of tags is nested inside another set, the closing tags must work from the inside out. In other words, if text is bold (i.e., <strong></strong>) and italic (i.e., <em></em>) in that order, the closing tags must close the italics first and then the bold.

Incorrect:

```
<strong><em>This is the wrong way to nest tags. </strong></em>
```

Correct:

```
<strong><em>This is the right way to nest tags. </em></strong>
```

EXAMPLE 0.3

XHTML Elements Must Be Closed

All elements, even empty elements that have only one tag, must be closed. Closing an empty element is achieved by inserting a space, then a slash (/) after the name of the element before the closing bracket.

Incorrect:

```
<p>This is the wrong way to write two lines of text.
<p>The first line is missing a closing tag!</p>
A horizontal rule, the wrong way: <hr>
A line break, the wrong way: <br>
An image tag, the wrong way: <img src="kitty_photo.gif" alt="kitty">
```

Correct:

```
<p>This is the right way to write two lines of text.</p>
<p>Both sets of tags are closed.</p>
A horizontal rule, the right way: <hr />
A line break, the right way: <br />
An image tag, the right way: <img src="kitty_photo.gif" alt="kitty" />
```

EXAMPLE 0.4

XHTML Elements Must Be Lowercase

All tag names must be lowercase.

Incorrect:

```
<BODY>
<H1>These tags are not well formed!</H1>
<P>They are uppercase.</P>
</BODY>
```

Correct:

```
<body>
<h1>These tags are well formed!</h1>
<p>They are all lowercase.</p>
</body>
```

EXAMPLE 0.5

XHTML Elements Must Have One Root Element

The `<html></html>` tags are the root element. Everything else must be nested inside these tags.

Incorrect:

```
<p>This is outside the root.</p>
<html>
<head>
<title>Example 0.5</title>
</head>
<body>
<p> other stuff </p>
</body>
</html>
```

Correct:

```
<html>
<head>
<title>Example 0.5</title>
</head>
<body>
<p>This is inside the root. </p>
</body>
</html>
```

You might find that, even if you do not follow the XHTML requirements, your web pages will display as you want. However, you can't be sure what other people might see! In particular, today's market consists of many different browser technologies. Some browsers run on computers, and some browsers run on mobile phones or other small devices. While many browser versions compensate for users who post web pages that do not adhere to standards, smaller devices often lack the resources to compensate for "bad" markup language.

Server-Side and Client-Side Technologies

If web page content can be customized or interactive with users, this interaction is either client-side or server-side. In these terms, the client is the computer that the end-user is using. The server is the computer that generates the web page. For example, if you are using Firefox on your laptop, Firefox is the client. You can think of yourself, your laptop, and your browser as the client.

The machine where the website resides is called the server. In server-side scripting, a user's request is sent to a script that runs on the web server. This is one way to generate dynamic web pages. Normally, server-side technology is used to provide interaction on web sites that interface with databases or other data storage areas. For example, the first time you visit a web site, you might be prompted to enter certain personal information. The next time you log in to the site, you may be greeted by name and reminded that, on your previous visit, you had expressed interest in specific items. The information you provided on your previous visit was most likely stored in the server's database. A server-side program accesses that data and customizes the page it sends to your browser on your following visit.

Server-side scripts are never visible to the browser because these scripts are executed on the server. Some server-side languages are Active Server Pages (ASP), PHP, C/C++, ISAPI, and Java Server Pages (JSP). While this text focuses on the client-side language, JavaScript, we will also learn some PHP.

JavaScript Overview

JavaScript is a scripting language that uses the ECMAScript language standard. **Ecma International** is a nonprofit organization that creates standards for information and communication systems. The organization was founded in 1961 to standardize computer systems in Europe and presently is located in Geneva, Switzerland. ECMAScript is the scripting language standardized by Ecma International and JavaScript can be considered a dialect of ECMAScript. Other dialects include JScript and ActionScript. While JavaScript is compatible with ECMAScript, it also provides additional features that are not in the Ecma specifications.

JavaScript is a dynamic language that contains first-class functions. It is a multiparadigm language, supporting various programming styles. Each of these terms will be defined.

A Dynamic Language

A **dynamic programming language** executes at runtime (while the program is running) as compared to a language that executes after being compiled. This means that some changes can be made, such as adding new code, extending definitions, or modifying a variable's data type, while the program is executing.

First-Class Functions

JavaScript contains **first-class functions**. Thus, it supports passing functions as arguments to other functions, returning them as the values from other functions, and assigning them to variables or storing them in data structures. These concepts will be explained in detail later in this text.

A Multiparadigm Language

A **programming paradigm** is a fundamental computer programming style. Paradigms differ in the way elements of a program (such as objects, functions, and variables) may be represented as well as the steps used to compose assignments, evaluation, and more. A multiparadigm language can use more than one programming paradigm. This allows for extended flexibility in both creating and writing code. JavaScript supports object-oriented, procedural, and functional programming styles.

How JavaScript Is Used

JavaScript is mainly used in web pages to create more interaction between the page and the user. However, it may be used elsewhere, such as in PDF documents or desktop widgets. In this book, we focus exclusively on using JavaScript in web pages. JavaScript uses syntax influenced by the **C** programming language and also uses names and naming conventions from Java.

JavaScript has many uses when creating a web page. Frequently, non-programmers use free JavaScript programs or code snippets to make their web pages more interactive and interesting. Many online websites offer free JavaScript code along with instructions about how to use the code in a web page.

But JavaScript has significant other uses as well. In this text, we will create two websites over the course of the chapters. One site will offer various games, all written in JavaScript, and the other will offer elementary school class programs that enrich learning. We will write programming code for these sites that can be enhanced and customized as desired. You will have the opportunity to do so in the Case Studies at the end of each chapter. By the end of the book, if you complete the Putting it to Work examples and the corresponding exercises in the Case Studies of the Programming Challenges, you will have built two relatively robust websites: one for gamers and one for students. In the Case Studies, you will also be able to build pages for a landscaping business or an online jewelry business, or both.

JavaScript also has significant uses in business sites. Each chapter provides an opportunity for you to create a page using JavaScript for a business site. JavaScript can be used for form validation, to assist a user in purchasing through a shopping cart, to create cookies, and much more.

Cookies are small amounts of data that is stored on the user's computer by the browser. This allows information to be carried from one web page to the next and to be saved between visits to a website. A business site can retrieve information from a cookie on a user's computer and use that information. Not only does this allow the business to customize what the user sees on the website, but also it frees up the user from having to reenter certain information each time he or she returns to that site.

These are just a few examples of how we can use JavaScript. Once you start writing your own code, you will think of other ways to use JavaScript to enhance your web pages and sites.

Overview of DOM, PHP, and XML

In this chapter, we have made passing reference to DOM, PHP, and XML. You may be wondering what these acronyms stand for and what they mean. This section provides a general overview; these subjects will be treated in more depth in Chapters 10, 11, and 12.

The Document Object Model (DOM)

The **Document Object Model (DOM)** is a convention used to represent and interact with objects in HTML, XHTML, and XML documents. When an HTML page is rendered in a browser, the browser parses the markup. This means it looks at the tags and knows how to display the content. For example, assuming no styles have been applied to any tags, the browser knows that the <h1> tag is a header tag and has a higher status than a <p> tag. This hierarchical structure of how tags are rendered is known as a tree structure, called the **DOM tree**. The topmost node in the DOM tree is the Document **object**. Each node has zero or more children. An example of a DOM tree follows:

Hypertext Preprocessor (PHP) or Personal Home Page Tools

When PHP was first created in 1994, its programmer, Rasmus Lerdorf, created a set of scripts in the Perl programming language that he called Personal Home Page Tools. Lerdorf used these tools to maintain his web page and the scripts performed tasks such as displaying his résumé and recording visitors to the page. Lerdorf announced the release of PHP in a Usenet discussion group in 1995 but since then the program has grown to be much more than personal home page tools! Thus, the present **PHP** acronym stands for **PHP Hypertext Preprocessor**. (This, by the way, is a recursive acronym because the expression it stands for refers to itself.)

PHP is now a general-purpose server-side scripting language. It is one of the early server-side scripting languages that is embedded in an HTML source document. However, the code is interpreted by a web server with a PHP processor module. The server generates the web page that results from the PHP processor. PHP can be implemented on most servers. PHP is a competitor of Microsoft's **Active Server Pages (ASP)** server-side script engine. Both scripting languages have particular uses and both are extremely popular. Once you have learned the basic concepts of PHP, it is not difficult to learn ASP and most web developers have knowledge of both.

```
⇨ Document object
   ⇨ Element (<html>)
     ⇨ Element (<body>)
       ⇨ Element (<div>)
         ⇨ text node
         ⇨ Anchor
           ⇨ text node
       ⇨ Element <div>
         ⇨ image node
         ⇨ text node
             ⇨ etc. ...
```

Figure 0.2   The document object model

Extensible Markup Language (XML)

Extensible Markup Language (XML) is a markup language somewhat like HTML but it is specifically designed to transport and store data. Thus, it differs from HTML, which was designed only to display data. XML tags are not predefined; the developer must define his or her own tags.

XML is not a replacement for HTML but it extends the capabilities of web developers. It does not *do* anything, in the way that JavaScript can run a program from the user's computer and PHP can run a program from a web server. XML, on the other hand, was created to set up a structure for information and to store and transport that data.

For example, you might define tags in XML that create, instead of level 1, 2, and 3 headers, a name tag, a message tag, and a greeting tag. The tags would be used inside a root tag for a customer. That information would be sent to a server, stored in fields, and used later. Example 0.6 shows what XML markup might look like after the web developer created the tags mentioned.

XML is extremely important and is the most common tool for data transmissions between all sorts of applications. We will learn more about XML later in the textbook.

EXAMPLE 0.6

XML Tags

The following tags might be created by a web developer who wants to send messages to customers on their return visits to the website. In this example, there are two customers and the greeting and message will be different for each. One customer is delinquent on his account and the other is not.

```
<customer>
    <name>Sally Smith</name>
    <greeting>Final Notice!</greeting>
    <message>Please remit your balance immediately</message>
</customer>

<customer>
    <name>Sammy Smitts</name>
    <greeting>Welcome Back!</greeting>
    <message>We are happy to see you again</message>
</customer>
```

CHECKPOINT FOR SECTION 0.6

0.22 Who first developed JavaScript and what was it originally called?

0.23 What is the difference between HTML and XHTML?

0.24 What is the difference between client-side and server-side technologies?

0.25 List three uses for JavaScript.

0.26 What is PHP?

0.27 What do XML tags do?

Chapter Review and Exercises

Key Terms

absolute reference	interpreter
Active Server Pages (ASP)	IP address
Ada language	Java
application software	JavaScript
applications	JScript
app	LISP
arithmetic logic unit (ALU)	LiveScript
assembly language	machine language
browser	mass storage
C	microchip
C++	microprocessor
central processing unit (CPU)	network
client	non-volatile storage
client/server model	operating system (OS)
COBOL	output
compiler	packet switching
computer	packets
computer program	path
cookies	peripherals
debugger	PHP Hypertext Preprocessor (PHP)
Document object	processor
Document Object Model (DOM)	programming language
DOM tree	programming paradigm
Domain name	protocol
dynamic programming language	random access memory (RAM)
dynamic IP address	read-only memory (ROM)
Ecma International	relative reference
ECMAScript	server
element	software
empty element	static IP address
Extensible Markup Language (XML)	storage
first-class function	system software
FORTRAN	system unit
hardware	tag
high-level language	TCP/IP
HyperText Markup Language (HTML)	text editor
Hypertext Transfer Protocol (http)	Top Level Domain (TLD)
input	transistor
internet	Transmission Control Protocol (TCP)
Internet	Uniform Resource Locator (URL)
Internet Protocol (IP)	vacuum tubes
Internet Service Provider (ISP)	VbScript

Visual Basic
volatile storage
web server

World Wide Web (web)
XHTML

Review Exercises

Fill in the Blank

1. Two or more linked computers that share resources create a _____.

2. When a web page is sent from the server where it resides to the server that requested it, the page is broken into _____.

3. The _____ of any device connected to the Internet consists of four groups of numbers.

4. All computers use the basic _____ - _____ - output model.

5. Computer _____ consists of, basically, anything a user can touch, such as a printer, a monitor, and so on.

6. _____ software is used to control and maintain the computer's hardware and to communicate with the user.

7. A compiler or interpreter translates a computer program into _____ language.

8. The first graphical browser was named _____.

9. A browser works on a _____/_____ model.

10. HTML _____ are the basic building blocks of web pages.

True or False

11. T/F When a request is sent for a web page, the server where that page resides sends the page to the requesting server as a complete file.

12. T/F An IP address that does not change each time that computer is connected to the Internet is a static IP address.

13. T/F A URL is a web page's IP address.

14. T/F When a computer is shut off, all information in its read-only memory is erased.

15. T/F A new game that you buy and install on your computer is a type of application software.

16. T/F All programs written in any high-level language must be either compiled or interpreted.

17. T/F A browser is software.

18. T/F All elements in an HTML document must be closed.

19. T/F PHP is a client-side scripting language.

20. T/F XML is designed to transport and store data.

Short Answer

For Short Answer Exercises 21–24, use the following imaginary URL:

```
http://www.leesland.com/landscaping/services/lawns.html
```

21. What part of this URL designates the protocol?

22. What part of this URL designates the server?

23. What part of this URL designates the domain?

24. What part of this URL designates the path?

25. Why is packet switching considered a secure system?

26. Which of the following is not a high-level computer programming language?
    a) Ada
    b) C++
    c) assembly
    d) JavaScript
    e) Visual Basic

27. a) Describe the client/server model
    b) Assume you want to shop at the Jackie's Jewelry website and you type the following URL. Identify the client and server in this scenario:

    ```
    http://www.jackiesjewelry.com/jackie/
    ```

28. What is wrong with the following XHTML code?

    ```
    <html>
    <head>
       <title> Exercise 28</title>
    </head>
    <body>
       <p>Look at my puppy:
       <img src = "puppy.jpg" alt = "my puppy"> </p>
    </body>
    </html>
    ```

29. What is wrong with the following XHTML code?

    ```
    <HTML>
    <HEAD>
       <TITLE> Exercise 29</TITLE>
    </HEAD>
    <BODY>
       <P>Look at my new car:</P>
       <img src = "lamborghini.jpg" alt = "my new car">
    </BODY>
    </HTML >
    ```

30. JavaScript is considered a dynamic programming language. Describe what this means and explain how JavaScript differs from a compiled programming language like C++.

JavaScript Programming Basics

Chapter Objectives

In this chapter, we'll jump right in and start programming in JavaScript. Of course, you won't be able to create elaborate games or interactive lessons quite yet, but you will learn about the three basic control structures from which all programs are built as well the general problem-solving strategy that must be used to solve programming problems and the program development cycle. You will also learn about data types and how JavaScript operates on various types of data. The chapter introduces objects and how dot notation is used to access various objects on a web page. Several important and basic JavaScript methods are discussed in the chapter as well how and where to put JavaScript code. You'll be introduced to JavaScript events and functions and use these to obtain input from a user on a web page.

After reading this chapter, you will be able to do the following:

- Describe the general strategy used to solve a programming problem

- Describe the basic program development cycle and use pseudocode and flowcharts to plan a program

- Understand the input-processing-output model

- Describe the three control structures: sequence, selection, and repetition

- Understand the differences between numerical and string data

- Understand variables and how to name them

- Understand how to use dot notation to access the document object on a web page

- Use the following methods: `write()`, `getElementById()`, `open()`, and `close()`

- Understand the difference between using JavaScript in a web page `<body>` and using the `<script></script>` tags to put JavaScript in the head section of a web page

- Understand user-defined and predefined functions and how to include parameters

- Understand JavaScript events and use the `onclick` and `onload` events

- Obtain user input on a web page with a prompt

- Display information on a web page with the `innerHTML` attribute

1.1   What Is Programming?

As we go about our daily lives, we encounter problems that are best tackled using a systematic plan of action. Often this plan involves a step-by-step process for resolving the problem. For example, suppose you've invited an out-of-town friend to your new house. To help make the trip go smoothly, you provide detailed directions to your house. In effect, you create a program to be carried out by your friend. Such a program might look like the following:

> Take Route 44 East and exit at Newtown Road.
> At the end of the off-ramp, turn left onto Newtown Road.
> Go three miles on Newtown Road and make a right onto Cedar Lane.
> Follow Cedar Lane for four blocks and turn left onto Duck Pond Terrace.
> Follow Duck Pond Terrace for a quarter mile.
> My house, 68 Duck Pond Terrace, is the gray house on the left.

A General Problem-Solving Strategy

To create a suitable plan of action to solve a particular problem such as providing directions or creating a computer program, it is often useful to apply the following general **problem-solving strategy:**

1. Try to understand the problem completely. If you don't fully understand the problem, it will be difficult, or even impossible, to create a viable plan to solve it.

2. Devise a plan of action to solve the problem and provide precise step-by-step instructions for doing so.

3. Carry out the plan.

4. Review the results. Does the plan work? Does it solve the given problem?

Of course, at any stage of this process, you may notice a flaw in what you've done and have to return to a previous step to reevaluate or modify things.

Now let's apply this problem-solving strategy to a relatively simple programming problem. Suppose your friend has asked you to create a simple program to pick numbers for her to play the lottery. While we aren't ready to actually create that program in JavaScript, we can discuss how to initiate it, using the general problem-solving strategy just described:

1. **Understand the problem.**   First, you need to know a few things: How many numbers must be chosen? What is the range of numbers? You ask your friend these questions and, for the sake of this example, we will assume that the lottery in question requires six numbers, ranging from 1 to 40. You also understand that all the numbers must be whole numbers.

2. **Devise a plan of action.**   Your program needs to select six numbers and each must be no less than 1 and no greater than 40. At this point, your instructions to a computer (i.e., your program) would include the following:
   - Pick a whole number between 1 and 40
   - Repeat five more times

3. **Carry out your plan.**   In this example, we will assume you write the code to represent the plan from Step 2. Six numbers between 1 and 40 are selected.

4. **Review the results.**   However, when you review your results you see that the program has produced the following numbers: 21, 36, 9, 9, 9, 8. Clearly you need to revise Step 2 to ensure that no numbers are repeated. The new Step 2 might look like this:

5. **Devise a plan of action (revised).**
   - Pick a whole number between 1 and 40
   - Pick another whole number between 1 and 40
   - Check to be sure that the new number is not the same as the previous number
     - □ If the two numbers match, select another number
   - Repeat until six distinct whole numbers have been chosen

Now you must repeat Steps 3 and 4. In the course of devising a plan of action, you may discover that you don't have enough information—you don't fully understand the problem. Or in carrying out the plan or reviewing the results, you may find that you have to change your plan. These modifications to previous steps are almost inevitable when applying our problem-solving strategy. We say that problem-solving is a **cyclic process** because we often return to the beginning or redo previous work before arriving at a satisfactory solution.

The Program Development Cycle

The general process for creating a computer program mimics the general problem-solving strategy that we have just outlined: understand the problem, devise a plan, carry out the plan, and review the results. When you solve a problem with a computer program, this strategy takes the following form:

1. **Analyze the problem.**   Determine what information you are given, what results you need to get, what information you may need to get those results, and in general terms, how to proceed from the known data to the desired results.

2. **Design a program to solve the problem.**   This is the heart of the program development process. Depending on how hard or complex the problem is, it might take one person a few hours or it might take a large team of programmers many months to carry out this step.

3. **Code the program.**   Write statements (*program code*) in a particular computer language that implement the design created in Step 2. The result of this step is the program.

4. **Test the program.**   Run the program to see if it actually solves the problem.

This process of analysis, design, coding, and testing forms the core of what is known as the **program development cycle.** It's called a cycle because as with the general problem-solving process, we often have to return to previous steps as we discover flaws in subsequent ones.

Emphasis on Step 4: Test the Program Extensively!

Students are often surprised and upset to receive feedback from a teacher saying that a program did not run correctly. The program may have run fine for the student. Frequently, this surprise is the result of inadequate testing. When you write a program that requires input from a user or uses data that is generated elsewhere in the program, you should imagine all of the possible types of input that the program may encounter. The lottery example, requiring a program to output six random numbers to use as lottery numbers, could have run correctly the first time. It might have generated six different numbers. However, because the original solution did not consider what would happen if duplicates were generated, the program truly would not work.

For example, if you wrote a program that finds the average of numbers a user enters, you would want to test to see what happens if the user enters no numbers. If you wrote a program that asks a user to enter his name, you must test for what would happen if the user enters a name that includes numbers, or a name that contains special characters (such as a hyphen or punctuation), or an unusually long name such as `Throckmortonsteinbrunner`. It is tempting, after spending many hours writing, debugging, and rewriting a program, to shout with joy when the program works. But to avoid embarrassing situations or—worse—loss of assignment points, it's important to spend extra time on the testing phase of the program development cycle.

CHECKPOINT FOR SECTION 1.1

1.1 List the steps in the general problem-solving strategy described in this section.

1.2 Provide a precise list of instructions for traveling from your school to your home.

1.3 List the steps in the program development cycle.

1.4 Assume you have created a program that asks the user to create a password that consists of four to eight characters. The password can include numbers, upper-case, and lowercase characters but no punctuation or spaces. List four things that you, as the programmer, should test for after you write the program.

1.2 The Structure of a Program

Input-Processing-Output

Every computer works on a very simple **input-processing-output model** and every computer program uses the same model. Your computer requires input. Then it processes the input. The computer doesn't need to go any further. But, without seeing the results of that processing, the user remains in the dark. So, the computer must produce some sort of output.

Input

Input comes in many forms. You may use a mouse or keyboard to enter information. Input may come into a computer through a modem, a Wi-Fi connection, or various peripherals that are connected by USB ports (such as a camera, a smart phone, or a calculator). A program may receive input from other parts of the program, from a file that the programmer has instructed the program to use, or from other web pages.

Often, a program receives input from the user through **prompts.** In JavaScript, a pop-up box called the **prompt box** displays information about what the user should enter (see Example 1.1). Then, whatever the user enters is stored in a variable. Variables are covered in depth in Chapter 2, but for now we can say that the variable holds the value of the user input when a prompt box is used.

EXAMPLE 1.1

Using an Input Prompt

The following JavaScript code demonstrates how to create a prompt:

```
1.  <html>
2.  <head>
3.  <title>Example 1.1</title>
4.  <script type="text/javascript">
5.       var name = prompt("Please enter your name"," ");
6.  </script>
7.  </<head>>
8.  <body>
9.  </body>
10. </html>
```

Line 5 is the one JavaScript statement in this example. A variable, name, is declared on the left-hand side. The right-hand side generates a prompt box with the text "Please enter your name". A comma separates the value that will be shown in the prompt box and any default value the programmer wishes to display. In this case, we leave the area in which the user types blank so we set that value to an empty space (" "). Whatever the user types will now become the value of the variable, name. Note that there is a semicolon after the closing parentheses of the prompt box. All JavaScript statements, like statements in most programming languages, must end with a semicolon.

The initial output of this program will be a prompt box that looks like this after the user has typed her name, which in this case is Fiona:

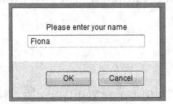

The name Fiona is now stored in a variable called **name**. It can be used later in the program during processing or output.

The appearance of a prompt box may differ slightly depending on the browser and browser version used, but the function of the prompt box is the same.

Input from the user through a prompt box is very common, but data may be input into a program by other means too. In some programs, the user inputs information by clicking or moving the mouse. Another common form of input doesn't involve the user at all—data can be transmitted to a program from a data file, from other web pages, or from other parts of the program.

Processing

In Example 1.1, the prompt allowed the user to input his or her name. But so what? A program must do something with the information it has. This is the **processing** stage. A program can manipulate input received from any source through the instructions coded by the programmer. A program might perform a mathematical operation on data or use data together with other information to create something new or do any of the myriad things computers can do. In Example 1.2, we will show how a program can take the input of a name, received from a prompt box, and join it with other text to create a greeting.

EXAMPLE 1.2

Processing the Input

The following JavaScript code demonstrates how to create a greeting from a name entered at a prompt:

```
1.   <html>
2.   <head>
3.   <title>Example 1.1</title>
4.   <script type="text/javascript">
5.       var name = prompt("Please enter your name"," ");
6.       var greeting = "Hello there, " + name + "!";
7.   </script>
8.   </<head>>
9.   <body>
10.  </body>
11.  </html>
```

At this point, nothing new will be displayed on the screen. However, a new variable, **greeting**, has been created on line 6. If the user has typed Fiona at the prompt, **greeting** now holds the following:

```
Hello there, Fiona!
```

If, instead, the user has typed Horatio at the prompt, **greeting** now holds:

```
Hello there, Horatio!
```

Output

Often, a program will process internally. However, eventually the user wants to see some results. A program's **output** is data sent by the program to the screen, printer, or other destination such as a file, an email link, or another website. The output normally consists, at least in part, of the results of the program's processing component.

In our short example, the output should be a screen display of the greeting that was created. Example 1.3 demonstrates how this is done.

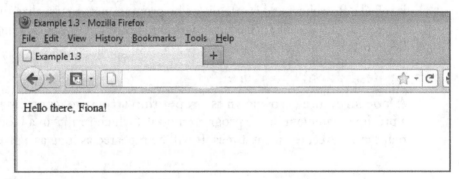

EXAMPLE 1.3

Creating the Output

The following JavaScript code demonstrates how to display a greeting from a name entered at a prompt:

```
1.  <html>
2.  <head>
3.  <title>Example 1.1</title>
4.  <script type="text/javascript">
5.      var name = prompt("Please enter your name"," ");
6.      var greeting = "Hello there, " + name + "!";
7.      document.write(greeting);
8.  </script>
9.  </<head>>
10. <body>
11. </body>
12. </html>
```

Line 7 is an instruction to take the value of the variable, **greeting**, and display it on the user's screen. If the user has typed Fiona at the prompt, the following will be displayed on the screen:

Display on screen in Firefox

The Control Structures

All programs are created using a series of properly organized groups of statements known as **control structures.** In fact, in the 1960s, computer scientists proved that there are only three basic control structures (or constructs) needed to create any program or algorithm. Pretty amazing, right? The three basic types of control structures are as follows:

1. The sequential (or sequence) structure

2. The decision (or selection) structure

3. The loop (or repetition) structure

The Sequential Structure

A **sequential structure** consists of a series of consecutive statements, executed in the order in which they appear. In other words, none of the statements in this kind of structure causes a *branch*—a jump in the flow of execution—to another part of the program module. The following is the general form of a sequential structure:

```
Statement
Statement
  .
  .
  .
Statement
```

Examples 1.1, 1.2, and 1.3 are examples of the sequential structure. Each line is executed in the order in which it appears in the code.

The Decision (or Selection) Structure

Unlike sequential structures, the other types of structures contain *branch points* or statements that cause a branch to occur. In a **decision structure** (also known as a **selection structure**), there is a branch *forward* at some point, causing a portion of the program to be skipped. Thus, depending on a given condition at the branch point, a certain block of statements will be executed while another is skipped. An illustration of how a selection structure works is shown in Figure 1.1. This representation is called a **flowchart** and is often used by programmers to visualize the progression of a program. We will discuss flowcharts and flowchart symbols in more depth in Section 1.4.

The Loop (or Repetition) Structure

A **loop structure** (also known as a **repetition structure**) contains a branch *back* to a previous statement in the program module, which results in a block of statements that can be executed many times. It will be repeated as long as a given condition

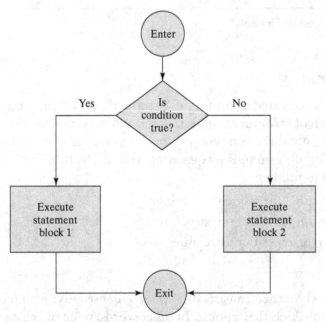

Figure 1.1   Flowchart for a typical decision structure

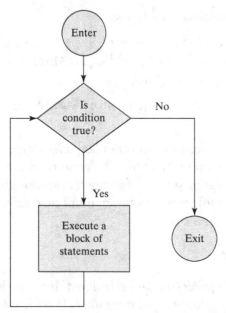

Figure 1.2 Flowchart for a typical loop structure

within the loop structure (for example, "Is the result of a calculation still bigger than 0?") causes the branch to be taken. A flowchart of a typical loop structure is shown in Figure 1.2. Notice that the diamond-shaped decision symbol is used to indicate a branch point. If the condition within the diamond is true, follow the *Yes* arrow; if not, follow the *No* arrow.

CHECKPOINT FOR SECTION 1.2 ✓

1.5 List three ways a computer program may receive input.

1.6 List three ways a computer program can generate output.

1.7 What are the three control structures?

1.8 Describe the difference between the selection structure and the repetition structure.

1.3 Data Types and Operations on Data

When data is entered into any program, it must be stored in the computer's memory. However, when it comes to storage not all data is created equal. How much space will be used to store data and what things a program will be allowed to do to that data depends on the data type. For example, you can take the square root of a number but you cannot take the square root of a person's name. The computer knows what can and cannot be done with some data at a specific storage location by its **data type.**

JavaScript makes use of three primary data types:

- Numbers that include integers (whole numbers) like 13, -456, or 0 and floating point numbers (numbers with a decimal part) like 3.14159, -7.89, or 12.00
- Logical (Boolean) values that are either true or false
- Strings that consist of one or more characters like "Lizzie" or "y" or "Pleased to meet you!"

One thing that distinguishes JavaScript from other languages such as C++ or Java is that JavaScript does not have separate data types for various types of numbers and it does not have separate data types for strings of characters and single characters. In this section, we will discuss the differences between numeric data and string data. We will discuss the other data types later.

Numerical Data

Numbers are values that can be processed and calculated. In many languages, the distinction between integers and floating point numbers is critical from the moment the data is entered through all the processing done with that number. However, in JavaScript when a number is stored in a variable, it is treated initially as a floating point number. All numbers in JavaScript are initially stored as the **numerical data type.** Also, when a number is entered into a prompt box, it is initially stored as a text value, which means it cannot be used in a calculation. The value must be turned into a numeric value, as we will see in later examples.

String Data

Strings are a series of letters, numbers, and other keyboard characters enclosed in quotation marks. JavaScript uses a string literally; it doesn't process it.

A string can consist of words, phrases, sentences, and even whole paragraphs. A string can also be a single character such as a letter, number, or punctuation mark. However, when a number is stored as a string, it cannot be used in a numerical calculation or process.

Boolean Data

When data is stored as a **Boolean** or logical value, it can only have one of two possible values: true or false. We will see many uses for the Boolean type as we progress in this text.

Variables and Named Constants

We have already used variables (see Examples 1.1, 1.2, and 1.3) because **variables** are such an integral part of all computer programs, it's impossible to describe a sample program without referring to them. Therefore, you know something about variables already! Now we will talk about variables in more depth: what they are, how to use them, and how to name them. There will be more information about variables in Chapter 2.

Example 1.4 shows a valid JavaScript program that works fine and does not use variables:

EXAMPLE 1.4

The Cost of Two Sweaters

The following JavaScript code will calculate the cost of two sweaters at an online store. One sweater costs $43.00 and the other costs $58.00. The sales tax rate is 6.5%:

```
1.   <html>
2.   <head>
3.       <title>Example 1.4</title>
4.       <script type="text/javascript">
5.       document.write("<p> The first sweater costs $ 43.00. </p>");
6.       document.write("<p> The second sweater costs $ 58.00. </p>");
7.       document.write("<p> The sales tax is 6.5%. </p>");
8.       document.write("<p> The total cost is: ");
9.       document.write((43.00 + 58.00) * 1.065 + ".</p>");
10.  </script>
11.  </<head>>
12.  <body>
13.  </body>
14.  </html>
```

The output from this program would look like this:

```
The first sweater costs $ 43.00.
The second sweater costs $ 58.00.
The sales tax is 6.5%.
The total cost is: 107.565.
```

The program in Example 1.4 calculated the cost of the two sweaters accurately but, unless you are writing a program for a website that has only two sweaters to sell and their costs remain at $43.00 and $58.00, the program is essentially useless. A computer can do this calculation for us—in fact, we use calculators all the time. We enter the numbers as given on line 9 of this program into a calculator and we get the result. But that's not what programming is all about. A computer program should be written so that the user doesn't have to repeat steps for each result. We will write a program that determines the cost of buying any items, at any price, and considers fluctuating tax rates. We will achieve this by using variables instead of actual values.

Most of the time when we write a program, we don't know the actual numbers or other data that the user will enter while running the program. Therefore, we assign the input data to a program variable. A variable is called a variable because it can vary. It is a quantity that can change value during the execution of a program. Any time we need to refer to that data in a subsequent program statement, we simply refer to its **variable name.** At this point the *value* of the variable—the number or other data value it represents—will be used in that statement.

Let's rewrite this program but now allow the user to enter the cost of any two items and find the total cost based on the sum of the two items and the addition of the sales tax. Later, you will learn to add more features to the program to allow a user to enter any number of items and factor in other options such as shipping costs, coupon codes, sales discounts, and the like. Here, we will use variables for two items, which we will name **item1** and **item2**. These will be the input variables because their values will be input by the user.

We will have a third variable, which we will name **TAX** since it will hold the value of the sales tax. In any single transaction, the sales tax rate will not change. We call this type of variable a **named constant.** While it will not change during execution of the program, later the sales tax rate may change. The programmer can quickly update this program by simply changing the original value of **TAX** once and it will be updated everywhere that variable is used. By convention, named constants are given names in all uppercase characters with underscores separating words, such as **SALES_TAX** or **PERCENT_INCREASE**.

A fourth variable named **total** holds the value of the sum of the costs of the two items. The updated program is shown in Example 1.5.

EXAMPLE 1.5

The Cost of Two Items

The following JavaScript code will calculate the cost of two items at an online store. Costs are input by the user. The sales tax rate is 6.5%:

```
1.   <html>
2.   <head>
3.       <title>Example 1.5</title>
4.       <script type="text/javascript">
5.       var item1 = parseFloat(prompt("Enter the cost of 1 item:"));
6.       var item2 = parseFloat(prompt("Enter the cost of 1 item:"));
7.       var TAX = 0.065;
8.       var total = item1 + item2;
9.       document.write("<p> The total cost, including tax, is: $ ");
10.      document.write(total + (total) * TAX);
11.   </script>
12.   </<head>>
13.   <body>
14.   </body>
15.   </html>
```

If the user input 43.00 at the first prompt and 58.00 at the second prompt, the output from this program would look like this:

```
The total cost, including tax, is: $ 107.565
```

There are some things in this program that might look confusing. The var keyword will be discussed at greater length below but for now, we will simply say that it is an instruction to the computer to set aside some storage space to hold the value of the variable. We will discuss the parseFloat() function in Chapter 2. It is used here to ensure that whatever value the user types at the prompt will be stored as a number. Without parseFloat(), the input given at a prompt is stored as a string and cannot be used in a calculation.

Assignment Statements

We have said that a variable is a name for a storage location in the computer's memory. For example, if we have a variable named **price**, the storage location identified by the computer as **price** will hold the value of the price of an item. There are several ways to inform the computer what that value is. Three of these ways are illustrated in Example 1.5.

One way is for the programmer to assign the value to the variable at the same time it declares the variable. The keyword var tells the computer that a new variable will be created. The format of an assignment statement, which is done at the same time as a variable is declared, is as follows:

```
var variableName = variableValue;
```

Line 7 in Example 1.5 declares a variable named **TAX** and sets its value to 0.065.

However, a variable does not need to be assigned a value when it is declared. You can simply use the keyword var and name a variable as follows:

```
var variableName;
```

At this time the variable is undefined. This is often misinterpreted to mean that the variable has no value. It actually means that the variable has no assigned value. However, the programmer has no control over what may or may not be in that memory location. Therefore, it is important to remember that, until you assign a value to a variable, it should not be used in your program for any calculation or other processing.

Variables can also be assigned values that are input by the user through prompts or values that arise because of other calculations or processing within the program. Lines 5 and 6 in Example 1.5 demonstrate how a value is assigned to a variable from an input prompt. Line 8 from the same example demonstrates how a value is assigned to a variable as a result of adding the values of two other variables.

Naming, assigning values to, and other operations with variables are covered in depth in Chapter 2.

Operations on Data

Programming requires that the data in the program be manipulated in some way to produce some output. The input can be processed arithmetically or combined with other input. Several types of operations are briefly mentioned here and will be discussed in greater depth in the following chapters.

The * symbol used to denote multiplication is an example of an arithmetic operator. JavaScript uses five arithmetic operators: addition, subtraction, multiplication, division, and modulus. Other arithmetic processing, such as taking the square root of a number or raising a number to a power, are done through functions that will be demonstrated throughout the text.

Assigning the value of one or more variables, expressions, input, or any combination of these to another variable is also an important component of programming. JavaScript has six assignment operators.

It is also important to be able to join strings of text with other strings or with user input. Putting these things together requires the use of a string operator.

Arithmetic Operators

Arithmetic operators are used to perform arithmetic operations between variables and/or values (see Example 1.6). The left side of the expression must be a variable. The right side may consist of a single variable with a numeric constant, a combination of variables or other expressions. The JavaScript arithmetic operators are shown in Table 1.1.

EXAMPLE 1.6

Using Arithmetic Operators

Given the following variables:

```
gameCost = 49.95, songCost = 2.00, TAX = .05
```

a) What is the **cost**, before tax of one game and one song?

→ `cost = gameCost + songCost;`

The values of the two variables are added and stored in the new variable, **cost** so `cost = 51.95;`

b) What is the **totalCost**, including tax of one game and one song?

→ `totalCost = cost + (cost * TAX);`

The value of **cost** * **tax** is (51.95 * .05) or 2.5975. This amount is added to 51.95 and the result is `totalCost = 54.5475;`

c) What is the **totalCost** if the consumer applies a $20 coupon to the result of part (b)?

→ `totalCost = totalCost - 20;`

The user now only has to pay the result which is **totalCost** = 34.5475; Later in the text, we will learn to truncate the values so that dollar amounts contain two decimal places only.

TABLE 1.1	**The Arithmetic Operators Using y = 3 As an Example**			
Operator	**Description**	**Example**	**Result, if y = 3**	
+	Addition	x = y + 2	x = 5	
-	Subtraction	x = y - 2	x = 1	
*	Multiplication	x = y * 2	x = 6	
/	Division	x = y / 2	x = 1.5	
%	Modulus	x = y % 2	x = 1	

Assignment Operators

Assignment operators are used to assign values to variables (see Example 1.7). The left side of the expression must be a variable. The right side may consist of a single variable with a numeric constant, a combination of variables or other expressions. The JavaScript assignment operators are shown in Table 1.2.

EXAMPLE 1.7

Using Assignment Operators

Given the following variables:

    gameCost = 49.95, **songCost** = 2.00, **TAX** = .05, **raise** = 5

a) What is the new cost of a game if the seller raises his price by $5.00?

→ **gameCost** += **raise**;

This statement is the same as writing the longer statement:

gameCost = **gameCost** + **raise**; and the result in either case is
gameCost = 54.95;

b) What is the **cost**, before tax of four songs?

→ **songCost** *= 4;

This statement is the same as writing the longer statement:

songCost = **songCost** * 4; and the result in either case is
songCost = 8.00;

c) What is the **totalCost**, including tax of one game at the new price from part (a) and four songs from part (b)?

→ **totalCost** = (**gameCost** + **songCost**)* (1 + **TAX**);

By multiplying the sum of the values of **gameCost** and **songCost** by the sum of 1 plus the tax percent (**TAX**), we can skip one step in the calculation that we did in Example 1.6, part (b). The value of **gameCost** + **songCost** is (54.95 + 8.00) or 62.95. Multiplying this amount by 1.05 gives the result:

totalCost = 66.0975;

d) What is the **totalCost** from part (c) if the consumer now applies a credit of $7.50?

→ **totalCost** -= 7.50;

This statement is the same as writing the longer statement:

totalCost = **totalCost** - 7.50; and the result in either case is
totalCost = 58.5975;

TABLE 1.2	The Assignment Operators Using x = 20 and y = 5 As an Example		
Operator	**Example**	**Equivalent To**	**Result**
=	x = y		x = 5
+=	x += y	x = x + y	x = 25
-=	x -= y	x = x - y	x = 15
*=	x *= y	x = x * y	x = 100
/=	x /= y	x = x/y	x = 4
%=	x %= y	x = x % y	x = 0

The Concatenation Operator (+) Used on Strings

As shown in Example 1.8, the **concatenation operator** is denoted with a + sign but, when used to add string variables or text values together, it does not do addition like the arithmetic operator. For example, if the variable **greeting** holds the value **"Hello, "** and the variable **yourName** holds the value "Jane" the following statement joins together the two strings into a third variable named **welcome**:

```
welcome = greeting + yourName;
```

After the execution of this statement, the variable **welcome** contains "Hello, Jane".

EXAMPLE 1.8

Using the Concatenation Operator

Given the following variables:

```
username = "Kim", cost = 127.87, welcome = "Welcome back,"
```

a) What is the **greeting** that will be displayed?

→ `greeting = welcome + username;`

The variable **greeting** now holds the following:

```
Welcome back,Kim
```

b) How can you add a space between the comma and the name in part (a)? Or add an exclamation point after the name? You can concatenate the string variables with text:

→ `greeting = welcome + " " + username + "!";`

The variable **greeting** now holds the following:

```
Welcome back, Kim!
```

c) How can you tell Kim what she owes for her order on this website? The full text message will be stored in a variable named **result**:

→ `result = username + ", your total cost is $ " + cost;`

The variable **result** now holds the following:

```
Kim, your total cost is $127.87
```

CHECKPOINT FOR SECTION 1.3

1.9 True or False:

a) Boolean variables can only hold one of two values.

b) A string variable can hold a number but no calculations can be done on the number.

1.10 Create an assignment statement that assigns the value of three more than a number to a variable named **calculation**. The value of the number is stored in a variable named **myNumber**.

1.11 Given the following variables, write statements that will do what is requested and store the result in a variable named **result**. Use assignment operators.

> x = 15, y = 7, z = 2, result = 34,

a) Multiply **result** by **z**

b) Add **x** to **result**

c) Divide **result** by 14 using **y** and **z** in your statement

1.12 Given the following variables, write statements that will do what is requested and store the result in a variable named **greeting**. Use the concatenation operator and be sure to include extra punctuation or white space as needed.

> price = 135, shipping = 7,
> name = "Mortimer", hello = "Hi there"

a) Display a welcome message that says "Hi there, Mortimer! Glad you're here."

b) Display a message that tells Mortimer how much the shipping cost will be.

c) Display a message that shows the total cost of the purchase including the **price** and **shipping**. You will have to create a new variable to store the result of adding the two numbers (for example, **total = price + shipping;**).

1.4 Problem Solving: The Importance of Logical Thinking

It really does take a lot of work to create a program that does exactly what it should do, that will work under all circumstances—not just ideal circumstances—and that is written clearly, logically, and efficiently. In fact, if you reread Section 1.1, you will see that writing the actual program code in Step 3 is a four-step process:

1. Analyze the problem.

2. Design a program to solve the problem.

3. Code the program.

4. Test the program.

The analysis and design phases should always take precedence over the coding phase. Once a program has been carefully designed, coding is a relatively easy task. Unfortunately, many eager newbies want to write code before spending enough time on the analysis and design. Similarly, after a program has been written and actually runs, often students are so excited that they skip the final testing phase or they don't test the program thoroughly. In this section, however, we are concerned with analyzing and designing a program. There are two basic tools programmers use to help them create complex programs: pseudocode and flowcharts.

Some programmers swear by one of these tools and eschew the other. But good programmers realize that both pseudocode and flowcharts are valuable assets and one may work better than the other for certain situations. Planning a program often requires the use of both pseudocode and flowcharts. We will discuss both in this section.

Pseudocode

A good way to begin the job of designing a program to solve a particular problem is to identify the major tasks that the program must accomplish. In designing the program, each of these tasks becomes a **program module.** Then if needed, we can break each of these fundamental "high-level" tasks into subtasks. The latter are called **submodules** of the original, or *parent*, module. Some of these submodules might be divided into submodules of their own, and this division process can be continued as long as necessary to identify the tasks needed to solve the given problem. This process of breaking down a problem into simpler and simpler subproblems is called top-down design. Identifying the tasks and various subtasks involved in the program design is called **modular programming.**

Once we have identified the various tasks our program needs to accomplish, we must fill in the details of the program design. For each module, we must provide specific instructions to perform that task. We supply this detail using **pseudocode.**

Pseudocode, as shown in Example 1.9, uses short, English-like phrases to describe the outline of a program. It's not actual code from any specific programming language, but sometimes it strongly resembles actual code. In the spirit of top-down program design, we often start with a rough pseudocode outline for each module and then refine the pseudocode to provide more and more detail. Depending on the complexity of a program module, little or no refinement of its initial pseudocode may be necessary, or we may go through several versions, adding detail each time until it becomes clear how the corresponding code should look.

EXAMPLE 1.9

Using Pseudocode to Design a Program

Imagine you have been asked to write a program to calculate the cost of customer's purchase when a business is offering a 20% discount on all merchandise, must charge 6.5% sales tax, and has a policy of charging $5.00 shipping for all purchases under $100.00 and free shipping for purchases over $100.00

The program appears to require several modules. One of them gets the cost of the total purchase so that the 20% discount can be applied. Next, if the total so far is less than $100.00, the $5.00 shipping cost will be added. Otherwise, there is no cost for shipping. Another module should calculate the tax and add this to the previous amount. Finally, the result should be output.

We will learn to create this program—or others like it—in later chapters. However, we can design the program right now, using pseudocode. It would look something like this:

```
Input module
    Request customer's purchase cost
    Save that amount in a variable named purchase
Discount module
            discountPrice = purchase - purchase * .2
Shipping cost module
    if discountPrice is less than or equal to 100:
        shipping = 5.00
    if discountPrice is greater than 100:
        shipping = 0.00
Tax module
    tax = discountPrice * 0.065
Total cost module
    totalCost = discountPrice + tax + shipping
Output results module
    Display a message that says "Your total cost for this
    merchandise, including a 20% discount, sales tax and
    shipping is: $ " + totalCost
```

Of course, your pseudocode may differ from this pseudocode but regardless of exactly how you write it, the program logic and the necessary calculations should be the same.

Flowcharts

Another common program design tool is the flowchart, which is a diagram that uses special symbols to display the flow of execution within a program or program module. While we will use flowcharts to help develop computer programs, flowcharts are also used in many other fields. Businesses use flowcharts to illustrate manufacturing processes and other industry operations. They are commonly used by industry to help people visualize content or find flaws in a process. A flowchart provides an easy, clear way to see which pieces of your code follow the various programming structures. Flowcharts help you visualize how a program will actually flow.

You can purchase inexpensive plastic templates in an office supply store to help you draw, by hand, the proper shapes for each type of process. Or you can simply draw the shapes by hand. There are also many software applications that will assist you to create flowcharts on your computer. In fact, Microsoft's Word has a flowchart template built into its word processor.

Flowcharts are created from a specific number of standard symbols. This ensures that anyone who knows programming can read and follow any flowchart. A typical flowchart will include some or all of the symbols shown in Figure 1.3:

Flowchart Symbols

■ Start and End symbols are represented as ovals or rounded rectangles, usually containing the word Start or End or another phrase to indicate the start or end of a program segment.

Symbol	Name	Description
	Terminator	Represents the star or end of a program or module
	Process	Represents any kind of processing function; for example, a computation
	Input/output	Represents an input or output operation
	Decision	Represents a program branch point
	Connector	Indicates an entry to, or exit from, a program segment

Figure 1.3   Basic flowchart symbols

- Arrows show the flow of control. An arrow coming from one symbol and ending at another symbol represents that control passes to the symbol the arrow points to.

- Processing steps are represented as rectangles. For example, doing a calculation such as computing the sale price of an item, the sales tax of an item, the shipping cost, or the total new price (as in Example 1.9) are examples of processing steps.

- Input/Output steps are represented as parallelograms. Displaying the results of the computations, such as including the item's name, its sale price, the tax, shipping cost, and the new price from Example 1.9, are examples of output steps.

- Conditional (or decision or selection) segments are represented as diamond shapes. These typically contain a Yes/No question or a True/False test. This symbol has two arrows coming out of it. One arrow corresponds to what happens in the program if the answer to the question is Yes or True, and the other arrow corresponds to what happens next if the answer to the question is No or False. The arrows should always be labeled. In Example 1.9, a True/False question is asked when figuring out shipping costs. If the customer's purchase is less than $100.00, shipping costs will be one amount; otherwise shipping will be free.

- Connectors are represented as circles. These are used to connect one program segment to another.

Other symbols are used less frequently but, for all basic programming, the symbols listed above are sufficient. You have already seen two examples of how flowcharts are used. Figures 1.1 and 1.2 show the general flow of information in the decision and repetition structures. Example 1.10 shows how to design a program using a flowchart.

EXAMPLE 1.10

Designing a Program with a Flowchart

The flowchart shown below creates the same program as given in Example 1.9. It is valuable because the programmer can see the flow of the program.

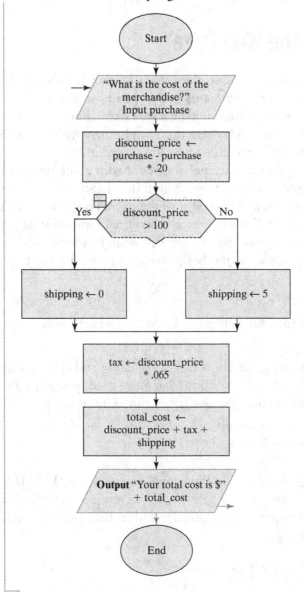

CHECKPOINT FOR SECTION 1.4 ✓

1.13 What is modular programming?

1.14 What is pseudocode and why is it used when designing a program?

1.15 Which flowchart symbol is used when a program must make a decision between two options?

1.16 Use both pseudocode and flowcharts to design the following program: The program will get the values of a student's scores on three exams. Then it will output the exam average for that student.

1.5 JavaScript in the Web Page

Web pages have two main sections: the <head> section and the <body> section. You probably already know that statements in the <head> section are instructions to the browser and do not appear when viewing a web page. The content of the page is normally contained in the <body> section. You also may have formatted your pages with CSS (Cascading Style Sheets). Styles are placed in any of three places: external styles which are created in an external document with a link provided in the <head> section; embedded styles which are written in the <head> section itself; and inline styles which are written into the <body> of the page. JavaScript code can be dealt with in the same manner. You can create an external JavaScript page which is linked to from the web page <head> section; you can write JavaScript code in the <head> section; or you can place some JavaScript code inline within the web page <body>.

The <script></script> Tag Pair

The <script></script> **tag** pair is used to define a client-side script, such as a JavaScript.

Scripting statements are placed between the opening and closing tags. However, since JavaScript is not the only scripting language used, you must also specify the type of script—which, in our case—is JavaScript. The syntax is as follows:

```
<script type="text/javascript">
    JavaScript statements go here;
</script>
```

Normally, these tags are placed in the <head> section. Also, HTML5 will assume the type is JavaScript and may be left out. However, it is strongly recommended that we follow good programming practice and include the script type within the <script></script> tags.

The <noscript></noscript> Tag Pair

The <noscript></noscript> **tag** pair is used to provide an alternate content for users that have disabled scripts in their browsers or for those who have a browser that doesn't support client-side scripting. The <noscript> element can contain all the elements that you can find inside the <body> element of a normal HTML page. The content inside the <noscript> element will only be displayed if scripts are not supported, or are disabled in the user's browser. The syntax is as follows:

```
<script type="text/javascript">
    JavaScript statements go here;
</script>
```

```
<noscript>
     Sorry, your browser doesn't support JavaScript.
</noscript>
```

If a browser has had scripting disabled, instead of executing whatever code is within the <script> </script> tags, the browser will simply display the text:

```
Sorry, your browser doesn't support JavaScript.
```

JavaScript in a Web Page <body>

You may already have used JavaScript in the <body> of a web page without even realizing it. If you've created a button, you've probably used inline JavaScript. First, we'll look at how to use JavaScript with a button, as shown in Example 1.11.

Using Inline JavaScript with a Button

The code to add a button to a web page is as follows:

```
<input type="button" id="myButton" value="Hi there!" />
```

This creates a button that looks like this:

If you click it, however, nothing will happen. The code has simply set up a button (its type is button) with an identifier (myButton) and the text to display on the button (Hi there!). We need to use JavaScript to tell the browser what to do when the button is clicked. We can add various instructions but, for this example, we will add an onclick event which will be explained in more detail later in the chapter. The code for that is as follows:

```
<input type="button" id="myButton" value="Hi there!" ⏎
        onclick="alert('Well, hello my friend.');" />
```

If you add the new code to your button, when the user clicks the button, an alert box will pop up with the message: Well, hello my friend.

Some JavaScript functions can be used within a web page but, in general, it is best to avoid inline JavaScript for several reasons. For one, the HTML code is a lot larger when inline JavaScript is used. Also, the HTML code will never be cached which means HTML code must be loaded for every page each time the user visits that page. This is not the case when JavaScript files are used instead of inline JavaScript. And it makes the code harder to maintain. This may not seem important when a student is working alone and creating small scripts, as we will do in the beginning. But it is important to realize that what you learn now will be applied when you are working on large websites in the future. Web developers and programmers agree that having code in one centralized location is preferable to having code snippets spread all over the files in a single website.

JavaScript in the document <head> section

Most of the JavaScript we will write in the early chapters of this book will be placed in the <head> section of the web page. We do this by enclosing the JavaScript in <script> </script> tags. Some of the other things you may include in the <head> section are the page title, a link to an external CSS file or embedded styles, meta tags, and so on. It doesn't matter where you put the JavaScript in the <head> section; it can be first, last, or anywhere in between.

Often, a web page will load with some content and JavaScript will be executed when the user interacts with elements on that page. It is also possible to have some JavaScript run immediately, before any HTML content is displayed. Example 1.12 shows how a page is loaded first and a JavaScript function which is in the <head> section is called when the user clicks a button.

EXAMPLE 1.12

Calling JavaScript in the <head> Section

```
1.    <html>
2.    <head>
3.        <title>Example 1.12</title>
4.        <script>
5.        function welcome()
6.        {
7.              alert("Hi there, friend!");
8.        }
9.        </script>
10.   </<head>>
11.   <body>
12.   <h1>A New Web Page</h1>
13.   <h3>Click the button! </h3>
14.   <p><input type="button" id="myButton" value="Hi there!" ⌐
                    onclick="welcome();" /></p>
15.   </body>
16.   </html>
```

The page looks like this when loaded:

When the user clicks the button, the JavaScript function named welcome() is called. The function is on lines 5–8 in the page's <head> section. This function is extremely simple and does one thing; it pops up an alert box with the message Hi there, friend! The page looks like this after the button is clicked:

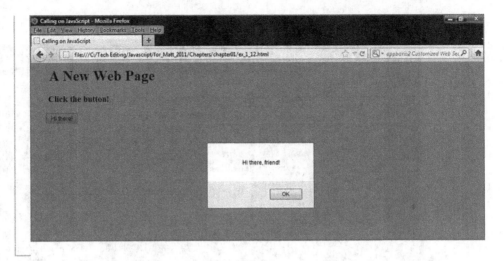

The <body> onload Event

Sometimes you will want JavaScript code to do something before the user even begins to view the page. For this, you can use the onload event. The onload event does what it sounds like it does: It executes some JavaScript as soon as the page or image has loaded. You might use this event if, for example, you wanted an alert to convey some information to the user before he or she even has a chance to look at your page. Example 1.13 will do just that. An alert will appear to warn the user that this site may be more fun than one would expect.

EXAMPLE
1.13

Using the onload Event

```
1.    <html>
2.    <head>
3.    <title>Example 1.13</title>
4.    <script>
5.    function welcome()
6.    {
7.            alert("Warning: This site is a lot of fun!");
8.    }
9.     </script>
10.   </<head>>
11.   <body onload="welcome()">
12.   <h1>More fun than you ever dreamed of...</h1>
13.   <h3>This site is nothing but...</h3>
14.   <h3>    fun...</h3>
15.   <h3>      fun...</h3>
16.   <h3>       fun...</h3>
17.   </body>
18.   </html>
```

The page looks like this when loaded:

Line 11 is the <body> tag, which opens the web page. But, by adding the onload event, the browser immediately, after loading the page content, goes to the <head> section where it acts upon the statements defined in the function that is called. In this example, the function is called welcome() and it does one thing only—it creates the alert. Later, when you become proficient at writing JavaScript code, you will create much more elaborate and interesting functions.

This is what the page looks like after the user clicks the OK button on the alert:

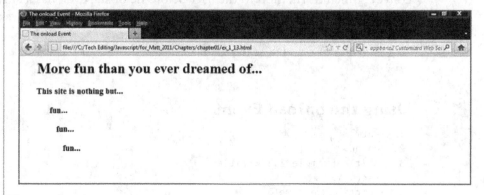

CHECKPOINT FOR SECTION 1.5

1.17 What information must be included in the <script> tag?

1.18 Why would you use the <noscript></noscript> tag pair?

1.19 What will happen if a user clicks a button that has been coded as follows?
```
<input type = "button" value = "Click me" />
```

1.20 What will happen if a user clicks a button that has been coded as follows?
```
<input type = "button" value = "Click me" onclick = "alert('Boo!');" />
```

1.21   What will happen after the user clicks the button, given the following code:

```html
<html>
<head>
<title>A New Page</title>
<script>
    function ouch()
    {
            alert("Ouch! Be gentle, friend!");
    }
</script>
</<head>>
<body>
<p><input type="button" value="Punch me!" onclick="ouch();" /></p>
</body>
</html>
```

1.22   When would you use the onload event?

1.6   Introduction to Objects

Programming languages, up through the mid-1980s, were **procedural.** This means that each step of a program was performed sequentially, after the previous step. Of course, by using branches, some steps could be skipped or repeated, but, basically, the program focused on the actions that would be performed. This method was often known as the top-down modular approach. Today, a new approach, **object-oriented programming,** is used. The focus of a program in an object-oriented language is on the objects in the program, not just on the actions to be performed.

This approach is ideal for the enormous tasks asked of programs today. It uses objects that often can be used and reused for a multitude of tasks. It is ideal for the graphical user interface (GUI) we all now take for granted.

Imagine you were asked to design a game that requires your player to battle with 10 different monsters. In a procedural program, you would write code that described one type of monster—say an ogre who uses a club for a weapon and fights on the ground using his legs to attack—and then you would write code for the battle. Next, you might write code to describe a second monster—say a raptor who uses his beak for a weapon and fights from the sky using his ability to fly to attack—and then you would write code for this battle. You would have to do this for each new monster. But if you wrote code for a general monster that has some weapon (to be defined later) and some method of attack (to be defined later), you could reuse this code for 2, 10, or any number of monsters. This is the basic idea of object-oriented programming: objects are created with certain attributes that can be changed with different instances of the object and certain methods (things the object can do or things that can be done to them) that can be changed with different instances of the object.

What is an Object?

You can think of an object as a noun—a "thing." A chair is an object. Anything that has properties and a function (or functions) is an **object.** Properties are qualities, traits, or attributes common to a specific thing—or object. A function, in this context, is a process or operation executed by or to the object. Objects are all around us—your chair, this book, and your washing machine are objects.

Consider the washing machine. It certainly has properties—it's made of metal; has a tub, motor, and gearbox; and has specific dimensions. After writing a long list of its properties, we may know what a washing machine looks like (which is fine), but we still don't have enough information to define it. We also have to talk about its functions—the processes it carries out: The machine turns on, fills with water, agitates, empties, rinses, spins, and turns off. Finally, we need to know what our object works on. In this case, our object normally works on items such as clothes, towels, and blankets. Combine all these pieces—properties, functions, and something to work on—and we can completely describe a useful object.

The following are important attributes of a washing machine, or for that matter, any useful object:

■ You don't have to know how it works internally to use it.
■ If someone has built a suitable one and it's available for purchase (or better yet, free), you don't have to build it yourself.

In programming, objects containing properties (data) and functions (processes) provide packaged solutions to help us solve problems.

When you write a document in a word processing program, like Microsoft Word, the first time you save your document, after clicking the Save As option, a window opens. The top bar normally says something like "Save As" and the window shows your folders on the left side and the right side shows files and folders. There is a text box on the bottom of the window where you can enter the name of your file as well as other things. When you open Word again and want to open a new document, you click Open and a very similar window pops up. The top bar now says "Open" but the folder list is still on the left, the files and folders in each folder are still listed on the right, and there is a text box where the name of the file you want to open will be entered. This pop-up box has been coded, by the Microsoft programmers, as an object. By changing various properties (such as the text on the top bar) and functions (such as either saving a given file or opening a selected file), the same object can be reused for different tasks.

As you learn to code JavaScript, you will learn that various parts of the web page are considered objects. You can also define your own objects and use them to create more complex programs. However, in this text we will focus mainly on using objects rather than creating our own.

Properties and Methods

You probably have a lot of icons on your computer desktop or dock. Some of these are part of the operating system such as the Recycle Bin icon on a PC or the trash can on a Mac. Many other icons are shortcuts to programs you have installed such as a browser like Google Chrome or a word processor like Microsoft Word. If you right-click on an icon, you will see a popup window that gives you a menu. One option you can select is Properties. The properties are usually descriptions of the program like its size, the date it was created, the type of application it is, and so on. Other options may include the ability to Open the application, Send it to another place on your computer, delete it, and so on. The **properties** describe the object. The other options are the functions it can do or that you can do to it. These are its **methods.** Anything you can click on is an object and all objects have properties and methods.

Attributes and Functions

Sometimes properties are called **attributes** and sometimes methods are called **functions.** There are no differences between properties and attributes or between methods and functions (in this context) except the word used. We will use these words interchangeably throughout the text, often for no reason except to make a sentence more readable.

Since all objects have both things that describe them (attributes or properties, take your pick) and things that can be done to or by them (methods or functions), we need a way to access these things. JavaScript uses something called dot notation for this task and it is described later in this section.

The Document Object

An HTML document is an object. It uses the **Document Object Model (DOM)** which is the browser's view of an HTML page. The browser views a web page as an object hierarchy, starting with the browser window itself and moving deeper into the page, including all of the elements on the page and their attributes. Figure 1.4 is a simplified version of a web page as an HTML Document Object Model.

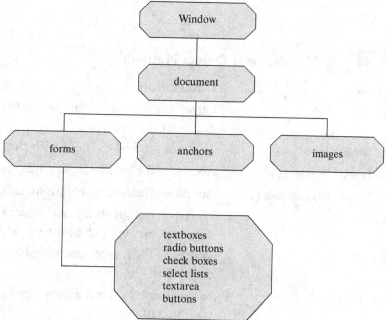

Figure 1.4   The HTML Document Object Model

TABLE 1.3	The document Object Properties
Property	**Description**
cookie	Returns all name/value pairs of cookies in the document
documentMode	Returns the mode used by the browser to display the document
domain	Returns the domain name of the server that loaded the document
lastModified	Returns the date and time the document was last modified
readyState	Returns the loading status of the document
referrer	Returns the URL of the document that loaded the current document
title	Sets or returns the title of the document
URL	Returns the full URL of the document

The top-level object is the window. The document object is a **child** of the window object. Each object except the window object is a child of another object and each object can have child objects of its own. For example, a form is a child object of the document object but a textbox is a child of the form object, as shown in Figure 1.4. We can also say that the document object is the **parent** of the form object and the form object is a parent of the textbox object.

Each HTML document loaded into a browser window becomes a document object. The document object provides access to all HTML elements in a web page, from within a script. Tables 1.3 and 1.4 show lists of the properties and methods of the

TABLE 1.4	The document Object Methods
Method	**Description**
close()	Closes the output stream previously opened with document.open()
getElementById()	Accesses the first element with the specified id
getElementsByName()	Accesses all elements with a specified name
getElementsByTagName()	Accesses all elements with a specified tagname
open()	Opens an output stream to collect the output from document.write() or document.writeln()
write()	Writes HTML expressions or JavaScript code to a document
writeln()	Same as write(), but adds a newline character after each statement

document object. Many of these may not mean a lot to you right now but, as you progress in learning JavaScript, you may use some or all of them.

Dot Notation

You may not care where content appears on your web page. However, it is much more likely that you have a specific place on the page where you want the content to appear. You instruct the browser where to place content by using **dot notation.** The object is accessed, then a dot, and then any further instructions (methods or attributes) are appended. The upcoming examples show how to display HTML text using a JavaScript statement and dot notation.

The write() Method

While there is much more to using JavaScript than simply displaying text or images, you will often need to display text through JavaScript. The **write()** method allows you to display text on an HTML page. Later you will see how to combine text with information you gather from your programs and make your web pages interactive.

For now, however, we will learn to display plain text. First, as mentioned above, the write() method is accessed using dot notation. To place text on a web document, you specifiy the document object, then put in a dot, and then the write() method. The text to display goes inside the parentheses.

However, you cannot simply enter the text. The write() method tells the browser to include text but the browser needs to know how to display that text. Therefore, you must also specify the HTML code that describes how the text is to be formatted. If you don't specify any formatting, the browser will use its default. Example 1.14 shows how to simply display a line of text on a web page document. Notice that the text to display must be enclosed in quotes within the parentheses.

EXAMPLE 1.14

Welcome to the Page, Using JavaScript

This example shows how you would display unformatted text on a web page, using JavaScript and dot notation.

```
1.   <html>
2.   <head>
3.   <title>Example 1.14</title>
4.   <script type="text/javascript">
5.       document.write("Welcome to my first JavaScript page!");
6.   </script>
7.   </<head>>
8.   <body>
9.   </body>
10.  </html>
```

Notice that the document object is accessed with a dot and then the `write()` method. The text to be displayed is in quotes. The output looks like this:

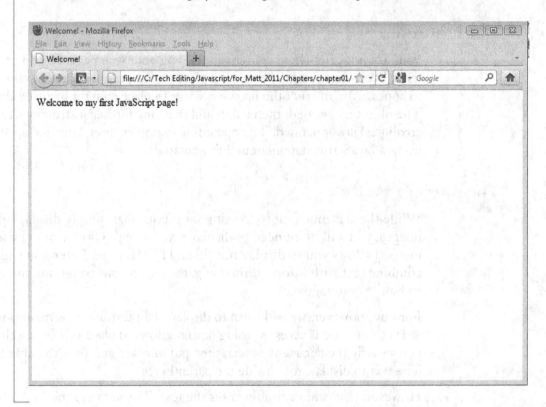

However, if you want your text to be a header, such as <h1> or <h3>, you need to include the header tags within the parentheses, as shown in Example 1.15.

Welcome to the Page, Using Formatted HTML

This example shows how you would display text as a level one header on a web page, using JavaScript and dot notation.

```
1.   <html>
2.   <head>
3.   <title>Example 1.15</title>
4.   <script type="text/javascript">
5.        document.write("<h1>Welcome to my first JavaScript page!</h1>");
6.   </script>
7.   </<head>>
8.   <body>
9.   </body>
10.  </html>
```

Notice that the header tags, <h1></h1> are placed inside the quotes. The browser interprets everything inside the quotes as it would if it were an HTML document. The output looks like this:

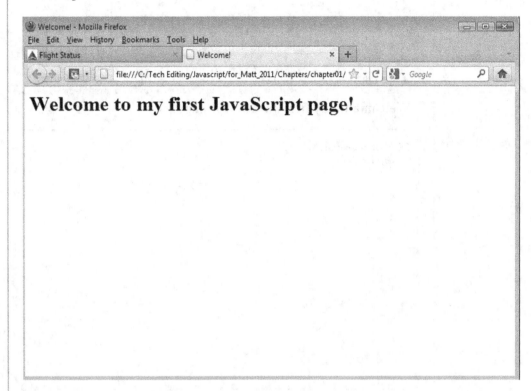

You can put as much HTML as you want within the write() method. Example 1.16 shows how the write() method is used to display several lines of text, each formatted differently.

<table>
<tr><td>EXAMPLE
1.16</td><td></td></tr>
</table>

Using the write() Method Extensively

This example shows how you would display text with various formatting including a header, a horizontal rule, some paragraph text, and a line break.

```
1.   <html>
2.   <head>
3.   <title>Example 1.16</title>
4.   <script type="text/javascript">
5.           document.write("<h2>Welcome to my first JavaScript page!</h2> <hr /> ↵
             <p>This is a short demonstration. <br />Goodbye now...</p>");
6.   </script>
7.   </<head>>
8.   <body>
9.   </body>
10.  </html>
```

Notice that all the HTML tags are placed inside the quotes. The browser interprets everything inside the quotes as it would if it were an HTML document. The output looks like this:

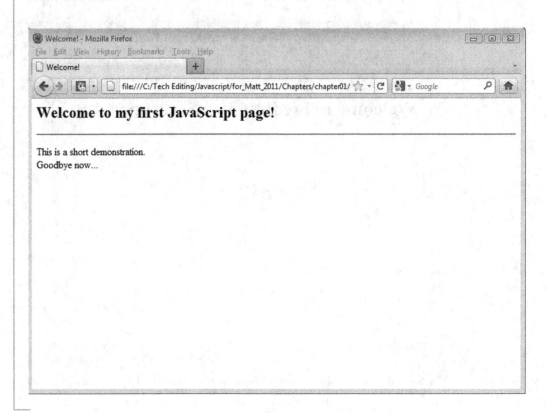

The getElementById() Method and the innerHTML Property

When you create a web page, normally you separate the page into various parts. You may, for example, use <div></div> tags to form a container where you want certain content and other <div></div> tags to place other content. Now, when you create a JavaScript program, you may want your output placed in one of those containers. Or you may want to use content that is in a container in your program. For example, you may have written a program that calculates the total of a user's purchase at an online store and want to display that total in a specific area. To get the contents of an HTML container, you use the getElementById() method.

getElementById()

Each part of a web page is called an **element.** The main way to access specific elements of a web page is to use the **getElementById()** method. This method allows us to access a particular container within a document but that container must already exist when we try to access it.

Therefore, each container must be marked with an identifier. We do this by adding an **id attribute** to the HTML tag. In your web page, be sure to give each container an id, or a name by which it can be identified. The syntax is as follows:

```
<div id = "myContainer"> (or whatever name you want)
```

Notice that the name of the container is in quotes.

Let's assume that you have a container with id = "puppy" and it contains the name of a breed of dog. You can access the content of that container and use it later in your program. You do this by setting a variable (more on variables in Chapter 2) to the value of the content of that container with the getElementById() method. The syntax is as follows:

```
var dog = document.getElementById("puppy");
```

This statement basically says to the browser, "Find the container named puppy in the document and store its contents in a variable named **dog**." Now you can use the variable **dog** in many ways. First, however, you must access the HTML contents stored in **dog**. To do that, you append a new property to the variable. This is the innerHTML property.

innerHTML

In the syntax shown above, the variable **dog** is set to the content of the container named puppy. The **innerHTML** property sets or returns the inner HTML of an element. To display the HTML contents of the container which we have stored in **dog**, we must use the innerHTML property to access just that content. This is done using dot notation, appending the innerHTML property to the variable **dog**. The syntax to display the HTML value of **dog** is as follows:

```
document.write(dog.innerHTML);
```

In Example 1.17 we will use the getElementById() method to retrieve the contents of a container and then display that content using the write() method.

EXAMPLE 1.17

Using getElementById(), write(), and innerHTML

This example shows how you would access content on a web page and use it to display a new message.

```
1.  <html>
2.  <head>
3.  <title>Example 1.17</title>
4.  <script type="text/javascript">
5.  function getValue()
6.  {
7.      var dog=document.getElementById("puppy");
8.      document.write("Your dog is not a terrier <br />");
9.      document.write("It is a ");
10.     document.write(dog.innerHTML);
11. }
12. </script>
13. </head>
```

```
14.   <body>
15.   <h1 id="puppy" onclick="getValue()">Poodle</h1>
16.   </body>
17.   </html>
```

The page originally looks like this:

However, when the user clicks the word Poodle, the JavaScript function named getValue() is called (see line 15). Control then goes to line 5. The instruction on line 7 tells the browser to look on the web page for the container with the identifier (id) "puppy" and store the contents of that container in a variable named **dog**. Lines 8 and 9 use the write() method to display new text on the screen. Line 10, however, does more. It uses the write() method to display new content on the screen but this content is what is stored in **dog.** It uses the innerHTML property to access the HTML part of the content in the "puppy" container which, in this case, is simply the word Poodle.

After clicking on the word Poodle, the screen now looks like this:

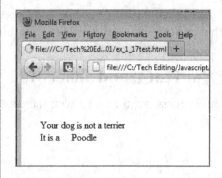

In this example, for simplicity's sake, we did not include an instruction to the user to click the word Poodle but in a real program, you would add this and, probably much more. Also, we will learn more about how to write, call, and use functions and other properties. In the beginning, however, it is often valuable to simply copy code and try it yourself, even if every line is not yet crystal clear.

The open() and close() Methods

Websites almost always contain links to other pages within the site. However, sometimes you may not want the user to leave the current page but you also want the user to see content on a new page. You can use JavaScript to have a new window open when a link is clicked so a user can toggle back and forth between the new page and the original page. Similarly, you can use JavaScript to close that window. The syntax to open a window may look a bit complicated but we will explain each segment and, often, you will not even use all the options:

To open a new window: `window.open(URL,name,specs,replace)`
To close an existing open window: `window.close()`

Let's discuss the **open()** method. The first parameter, URL, specifies the URL of the page to open. If no URL is specified, the browser opens a blank page.

The name parameter is optional. It specifies the target attribute or the name of the window. Any of the following values are supported:

- _blank → The URL is loaded into a new window. This is the default.
- _parent → The URL is loaded into the parent frame.
- _self → The URL replaces the current page.
- _top → The URL replaces any framesets that may be loaded.
- name → This is the name of the window, if desired.

The specs parameter offers you many options. You can use these options to define the size or placement of your new window. For example, you can specify that the new window be a small window, have a scrollbar, or many other options. A list of many of the options supported by most browsers is given in Table 1.5.

TABLE 1.5	window.open() Optional Specifications (separate items with commas)
height = pixels	The height of the window (the minimum value is 100)
left = pixels	The left position of the window
location = yes or no	Whether or not to display the address field; the default is yes
menubar = yes or no	Whether or not to display the menu bar; the default is yes
resizable = yes or no	Whether or not the window is resizable; the default is yes
scrollbars = yes or no	Whether or not to display scroll bars; the default is yes
status = yes or no	Whether or not to add a status bar; the default is yes
titlebar = yes or no	Whether or not to display the title bar; the default is yes
toolbar = yes or no	Whether or not to display the browser toolbar; the default is yes
width = pixels	The width of the window (the minimum value is 100)

Finally, the `replace` parameter is optional. It specifies whether the URL should create a new entry or replace the current entry in the history list. If it is set to `true`, the URL will replace the current document in the history list and if set to `false`, the URL will create a new entry. The `close()` **method** is used to close a window. You might use this in conjunction with a button that allows your user to close a window that was opened for a single purpose. We will combine using the `window.open()` and `window.close()` methods in Example 1.18.

EXAMPLE 1.18

Using `window.open()`, and `window.close()`

This example uses the `window.open()` method to open a small window which displays some text. Buttons are used to allow the user to open or close this new window.

```
1.   <html>
2.   <head>
3.   <title>Example 1.18</title>
4.   <script type="text/javascript">
5.   function openWin()
6.   {
7.         smallWindow = window.open("","", "width=300, height=200");
8.         smallWindow.document.write("<p>Hi again, old friend!<br /> ↵
                    Glad to see you today</p>");
9.   }
10.  function closeWin()
11.  {
12.        smallWindow.close();
13.  }
14.  </script>
15.  </head>
16.  <body>
17.  <input type="button" value="Open a small window" onclick="openWin()" />
18.  <input type="button" value="Close the small window" onclick="closeWin()" />
19.  </body>
20.  </html>
```

When first loaded, the page looks like this:

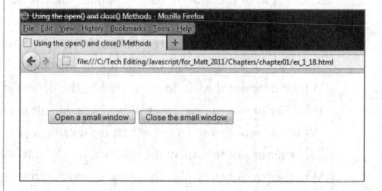

When the user clicks the `Open a small window` button, the instruction on line 17 calls the `openWin()` function in the <head> section, starting on line 5. A variable named **smallWindow** is now created. Its value is a new window, defined by the specifications in the window.open() method. The first specification, the URL is not defined. The set of empty quotes ("") means there is no URL. If a URL had been placed within the quotes, the new window would go to that URL. The second parameter, name, is also empty (another set of empty quotes) which simply means this new window has no identifying name. The third parameter lists the specifications for the new window. This code creates a small window, 300 pixels wide and 200 pixels high. These are the only specs chosen from the list given in Table 1.5. Finally, the last possible parameter, replace, is not given because this window does not need to replace anything in the browser history.

Line 8 defines the content of the new window. Notice that dot notation is used to identify where to place that content. **smallWindow**.document.write() describes where to write the new content—in the document of the new window (**smallWindow**). The content itself is placed within the write() method parentheses and is enclosed in quotes. Notice that any HTML formatting must also be included. In this case, the content is contained within <p></p> tags and even includes a line break (<br />). After clicking the Open a small window button, the screen looks like this:

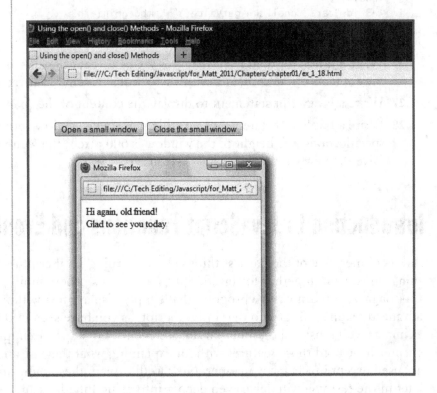

When the user clicks the second button, Close the small window, line 18 calls the closeWin() function on line 10 which simply closes **smallWindow** by using the close()method.

CHECKPOINT FOR SECTION 1.6 ✓

1.23 Fill in the blanks: All objects have _____ and _____.

1.24 Which JavaScript method allows you to display text on a web page?

1.25 Write a JavaScript statement that will, when called, display a welcome message formatted as a level two header. The message should say, "Welcome to my world!"

Use the following code for Checkpoints 1.26 and 1.27

```html
<html>
<head>
<title>Checkpoints 1.26 and 1.27</title>
<script type="text/javascript">
function getValue()
{
        fill in the blank for Checkpoint 1.26
        document.write("Your car is a <br />");
        fill in the blank for Checkpoint 1.27
}
</script>
</head>
<body>
<h3 id="cars" onclick="getValue()">Lamborghini</h3>
</body>
</html>
```

1.26 Write a JavaScript statement that uses the getElementById() method to access the contents of the container with id = "cars". Name your variable **auto**.

1.27 Write a JavaScript statement to display the content of the "cars" container.

1.28 Write a JavaScript statement that will open a new window with the following specifications: the height of the window is 600 pixels, the width is 400 pixels. Give the new window the name "extraInfo".

1.7 Introduction to JavaScript Functions and Events

As a beginner, one of the hardest things about learning JavaScript is that so many things must work together for JavaScript to work. In a programming language like C++ or Java, you can write a program that simply displays text without using any advanced features. But to do that in JavaScript, as you have seen in the previous examples, you must call on functions or use events. So far, the examples in this chapter have used those features without explaining what they are and why they are used except in a cursory manner. Now we'll explain these things further and later in the text you will delve even deeper into using functions and events.

Introduction to JavaScript Functions

A function is used to isolate a group of instructional statements so that other parts of the program can use that code. "Functions" is normally another word for "methods" and the two can usually be used interchangeably. There are some differences between them but, for our purposes, they are insignificant. There are two main categories of functions you will be using in JavaScript: those that have already been created for you and those you create in your code.

To create your own function, type the function **keyword** followed by a name for the function with opening and closing parentheses. The statements in the function are contained within curly brackets ({ }). Here is the syntax for creating your own function:

```
function name()
{
    JavaScript statements...;
}
```

To use a predefined JavaScript function, you merely need to use that function's name with the opening and closing parentheses. For example, we have used the write() method, the getElementById() method, and the open() and close() methods previously in this chapter. These are all examples of JavaScript functions.

Example 1.18 used both user-defined and predefined functions. For convenience, we will repeat the code in Example 1.19 and discuss the various aspects of each type of function.

EXAMPLE 1.19

Two types of Functions

```
1.   <html>
2.   <head>
3.   <title>Example 1.19</title>
4.   <script type="text/javascript">
5.   function openWin()
6.   {
7.           smallWindow = window.open("" , "" , "width=300, height=200");
8.           smallWindow.document.write("<p>Hi again, old friend!<br /> ↵
                    Glad to see you today</p>");
9.   }
10.  function closeWin()
11.  {
12.          smallWindow.close();
13.  }
14.  </script>
15.  </head>
16.  <body>
17.  <input type="button" value="Open a small window" onclick="openWin()" />
18.  <input type="button" value="Close the small window" onclick="closeWin()" />
19.  </body>
20.  </html>
```

Let's discuss this example from the point of view of its functions (or methods). Line 17 calls on the first function from the code onclick="openWin()" which is a user-defined function named openWin(). Control now jumps to line 5 where the openWin() function is defined. Two statements are executed when openWin() is called. They are on lines 7 and 8 between the curly brackets on lines 6 and 9. The first statement on line 7 calls the predefined JavaScript function, open(). The content within the parentheses defines the parameters that will be passed to the open() function. (Parameters will be discussed in more detail later in this section.) The information that is gleaned from the open() function is stored in a variable named **smallWindow** and now can be used elsewhere in the program. The second statement, on line 8, calls the predefined JavaScript function write(). Again, there is some content within the parentheses. The write() function (or method) contains instructions which the programmer does not need to see. The instructions tell the computer to display whatever content is within the parentheses. This information becomes the content of the new window that has been created by the open() function.

After these two statements have been executed, the openWin() function has completed its task. Control now returns to where it left off when the openWin() function was called—i.e., line 17. Since this was the end of line 17, control now goes to line 18.

When the second button is clicked, line 18 is executed. Now the user-defined function, closeWin() is called. Control goes to line 10 where the closeWin() function is defined. This function has only one statement. It calls the close() function to simply close the small window.

There are too many JavaScript predefined functions to list here. We will use many more as we continue through the text. But you will also learn to create your own functions. This is the main difference between a web designer who can use predefined JavaScript functions and a web programmer who actually writes the code!

Parameters

If you have never done any programming, you are probably wondering about all the parentheses that must be included with function names. What do the parentheses do? What should go inside them? Why do some functions have stuff inside the parentheses and others don't? The "stuff" that goes inside the parentheses are called **parameters.** For now, the answers to these questions will be general. Later, when you write your own more elaborate functions, we will discuss parameters in depth.

In general, parameters are values that are passed into a function. A function does something. It may do one simple thing, such as the one statement that closes a window in Example 1.19 or it may do many things. We could, for example, write a function that calculates the sales tax on a user's shopping cart purchases. In this case, the function would probably multiply the total of the purchase amount by whatever state sales tax is required for the user's location. The function would do the same thing for a user who purchased $25.67 worth of merchandise and lived in a state where sales tax was 4.25% as it would for a user who purchased $1,348.97 worth of merchandise and lived in a state where sales tax was 7.5%. The final results would, of course, be very different but the code to get the results is the same for both users. The differences are in the amount purchased and the applicable sales tax. In pseudocode, such a function might look like this:

```
function calculateTotal(amountPurchased, salesTaxRate)
{
    tax = amountPurchased * salesTaxRate;
    total = amountPurchased + tax;
    document.write(total);
}
```

Note that this code is pared down to the basics and, in a real program, we would format the output as dollars and cents and, of course, display an explanation. But the point is that, so long as the function knows the value of the amount purchased and the value of the sales tax rate, it can find the correct result. When this function is called in a program it would have two parameters. These would represent the amount the user purchased and the value of that state's sales tax rate. In the statement that calls the function, the programmer would have to be sure that two values are included within the parentheses.

Not only must the values be included when the function is called, but also they must be included in the correct order. In this pseudocode example, the first value must be the cost of the items to be purchased and the second value must be the tax rate. If the values are passed in the wrong order, the function will still work but the results will be incorrect, as we will see in Example 1.20.

EXAMPLE 1.20

Functions with Parameters

```
1.   <html>
2.   <head>
3.   <title>Example 1.20</title>
4.   <script type="text/javascript">
5.   function calculateTotal(purchaseAmt, taxRate)
6.   {
7.          tax = purchaseAmt * taxRate;
8.          total = purchaseAmt + tax;
9.          document.write("Your total is $ " + total);
10.  }
14.  </script>
15.  </head>
16.  <body>
17.  <p>Amount purchased is $100.00, Tax rate is 0.065</p>
18.  <p>Click Button 1 to calculate the total, passing in 100.00, 0.065</p>
19.  <input type="button" value="Button 1" onclick="calculateTotal(100, .065)" />
20.  <p>Click Button 2 to calculate the total, passing in 0.065, 100.00<p>
21.  <input type="button" value="Button 2" onclick="calculateTotal(0.065, 100)" />
22.  </body>
23.  </html>
```

When this program is run, the output looks like this:

Amount purchased is $100.00, Tax rate is 0.065

Click Button 1 to calculate the total, passing in 100.00, 0.065

[Button 1]

Click Button 2 to calculate the total, passing in 0.065, 100.00

[Button 2]

The actual total for this user's purchase should be $100.00 * 1.065 which is $106.50. When Button 1 is pressed, the values passed to the function are 100 first and 0.065 second. The 100 is stored in the function's variable, **purchaseAmt** and the 0.065 is stored in the function's variable, **taxRate**. Line 7 calculates the tax by multiplying 100 (**purchaseAmt**) by 0.065 (**taxRate**) so **tax** = 6.5. Line 8 calculates the total by adding 6.5 (**tax**) to 100 (**purchaseAmt**) so **total** = 106.5. The result is

> Your total is $ 106.5

However, when Button 2 is pressed, the values passed to the function are 0.065 first and 100 second. The 0.065 is stored in the function's variable, **purchaseAmt** and the 100 is stored in the function's variable, **taxRate**. Line 7 calculates the tax by multiplying 0.065 (**purchaseAmt**) by 100 (**taxRate**) so **tax** = 6.5. But . . . line 8 calculates the total by adding 6.5 (**tax**) to 0.065 (**purchaseAmt**) so **total** = 6.565. The result is

> Your total is $ 6.565

The example demonstrates both the use of parameters which make functions so versatile as well as the importance of passing the information to the function's parameters in the correct order. Example 1.20 also shows us that using a function in this manner is not efficient. It can only calculate the total cost of a purchase of $100.00 with a tax rate of 6.5% We want the function to find the total cost of any purchase with any tax rate. One way to do that is to use a valuable predefined JavaScript funtion: the prompt() function.

The prompt() Function

The prompt() **method** (or function) allows us to prompt the user to input values which can then be used any way the programmer desires. It displays a dialog box that prompts the visitor for input. This method returns a **string** value. That means that if the user enters a number, the number is first stored as text. In Chapter 2, we will learn how to ensure that a user can enter numbers that can be used in calculations. For now, we will use the prompt() function to get text input from a user. The syntax for the prompt() function is as follows:

```
prompt(message,default text if desired)
```

The message parameter is whatever information the programmer wants displayed on the dialog box and the default text is optional. This will go in the area where the user will type his or her response. For example, you may want to ask your user for his name so the message might say, "Please enter your name" and you might leave the default text area blank or you might enter "John Doe" as a default. Example 1.21 uses the prompt() function to receive some information from a user.

Using the prompt() Method

Here we will combine the prompt() method with what we have learned previously to allow a user to enter a favorite food and use that information to display a new message on the web page.

```
1.   <html>
2.   <head><title>Example 1.21</title>
3.   <script type="text/javascript">
4.   function showPrompt()
5.   {
6.           var food = prompt("What's your favorite food?", "carrots and celery");
7.           document.write("It's your lucky day! " + food + " is on today's ↵
                       lunch menu!");
8.   }
9.   </script>
10.  </head>
11.  <body>
12.  <input type="button" onclick="showPrompt()"value="push me" />
13.  </body>
14.  </html>
```

We use a user-defined function named showPrompt() which is called when the user pushes the button (line 12). Control then goes to line 4 where the showPrompt() function begins. The prompt() function is called on line 6. The message on the prompt box is What's your favorite food? and the prompt dialog box will contain the default answer, carrots and celery. However, when the user types in a new favorite food, this is what is stored in the variable, **food**. Line 7 uses the write() method to display a new message on the web page by using the document object with a dot before the write() method. The content of this new message is a combination of text and the value of a variable. The initial page looks like this:

and after the button is pushed, the prompt appears as follows:

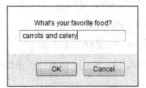

If the user enters pizza at the prompt, the page will display

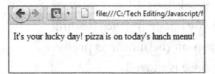

But if the user enters cake, the page will display

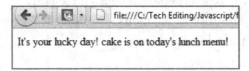

Introduction to JavaScript Events

We have said that each web page is comprised of objects and elements. Some common elements are buttons, links, checkboxes, radio buttons, and other parts of a form. Every element has certain events that can trigger JavaScript. An **event** is an action that can be detected by JavaScript. We've already used two events in previous examples: the onclick **event** and the onload **event.**

Event Driven Programming

Since events occur in a web page, we define what will happen on the web page. We say, in effect, "When this event occurs, do this." Sometimes what happens is simple and sometimes the event can trigger some elaborate programming. Usually events are used in combination with functions; when an event occurs, a function is called. The function will never be executed before the event happens. This is called **event-driven programming.**

Events are considered to be attributes of elements. They are inserted into the element to define what happens when that element is accessed. The following are common events:

- a mouse click
- a web page or image loading
- rolling a mouse over a link, an image, or another hot spot on a web page
- selecting an element or a field on a form

Table 1.6 lists some common events and their triggers.

TABLE 1.6	**Common Events and Their Triggers**
Event Attribute	**When the event occurs**
onblur	an element loses the focus
onchange	the content of a field changes
onclick	the mouse clicks something
ondblclick	the mouse double-clicks something
onerror	there's an error loading an image or a document
onfocus	an element gets the focus
onkeypress	a key is pressed or held down
onkeyup	a key is released
onload	a page or image finishes loading
onmousedown	a button on the mouse is pressed
onmousemove	the mouse is moved
onmouseout	the mouse is moved off an element
onmouseover	the mouse is moved over an element
onmouseup	a button on the mouse is released
onresize	a window is resized
onselect	some text is selected
onunload	the page is exited

The syntax, in general, for using an event is as follows:

```
<element eventName = "some JavaScript code">
```

Example 1.22 demonstrates the use of a trigger (the user clicking a button) to cause the event which, in this case, is a prompt for information.

Using a Prompt and an Event to Greet the User

The following code will prompt the user for a name and then change the greeting text on the web page to include that user's name.

```
1.   <html>
2.   <head>
3.   <title>Example 1.22</title>
4.   <script type="text/javascript">
5.   function greet()
6.   {
7.          var name = prompt("Please enter your name"," ");
8.          document.write("<h2>Hello " + name + "! <br />How are you today?</h2>");
9.   }
10.  </script>
11.  </head>
12.  <body>
13.  <h2 id ="hello">Who are you?</h2>
14.  <button type="button" onclick="greet()">Enter your ⏎
                      name</button>
15.  </body>
16.  </html>
```

Initially, this page has a single line and a button and looks like this:

When the button is clicked, line 14 calls the greet() function that begins on line 5. This function creates a variable named **name** and assigns to it the contents of a prompt box (line 7). Then line 8 uses the write() method to display a new message on the web page. Notice that dot notation is used to place the message on the web page document. Later we will learn to place content in other areas on a web page but for now, we will use the most generic area—the document object. Note that both text and the value of the variable are displayed. The first piece of text, Hello, is placed within quotes. Any HTML formatting we want is also placed within quotes. For this example, we wanted the text to be a level two header so the opening <h2> tag is included. The plus sign (+) means that the text should be followed by the value of the variable, **name**. Then the rest of the text, "! How are you today?" is added by using another plus sign and encasing the text in another set of quotes. We have also placed a line break inside the quotes (<br />) because this is more HTML formatting. And, since an opening <h2> tag requires a closing tag, the closing </h2> tag is placed at the end of the second piece of text, still within the quotes.

If the user clicks the button, types `Helmut Lindstrom` at the prompt, and clicks OK, the page will look like this:

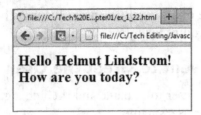

CHECKPOINT FOR SECTION 1.7

1.29 What is a function?

1.30 Create a function that displays the following line of text as a level 3 header to the document object of a web page. Name your function `warning()`.

```
Don't go there! You have been warned.
```

1.31 What are parameters?

1.32 Identify the parameters in the following code:

```html
<head>
<script type="text/javascript">
function showInfo(first, last)
{
    username = first + last;
    document.write("Your username is " + username);
}
</script>
</head>
<body>
<p>pick a username:</p>
<input type="button" value="duck" onclick = 'showInfo("Big", "Quacker")' />
<input type="button" value="dog" onclick = 'showInfo("Big", "Barker")' />
<input type="button" value="cat" onclick = 'showInfo("Little", "Meow")' />
</body>
```

1.33 Rewrite the code of Example 1.22 but add a new event. If the user double-clicks the button, the following message should be generated:

```
Don't be so pushy!
One click is enough.
```

1.8 Putting It to Work

Each chapter of this book includes a section called Putting It to Work. By the end of the book, if you complete the work in this section and continue to work on the problems described in the Review Exercises, you will have developed two large websites—a gaming site (**Greg's Gambits**) and a classroom site for elementary-school age children (**Carla's Classroom**). The Review Exercises also contain projects which add more content to these two sites and will also allow you to create two business sites—one for a landscaping business (**Lee's Landscape**) and one for a jewelry business (**Jackie's Jewelry**).

In this chapter, we will develop information pages for **Greg's Gambits** and **Carla's Classroom**. The code, images, and other material that you need are included with the Student Data Files. Follow along to apply what you've learned so far to create some real-life interactive web pages.

Greg's Gambits: Creating an About You Page

If you open the file in the Student Data Files, entitled index.html, you will see the home page for Greg's Gambits. It will look like this:

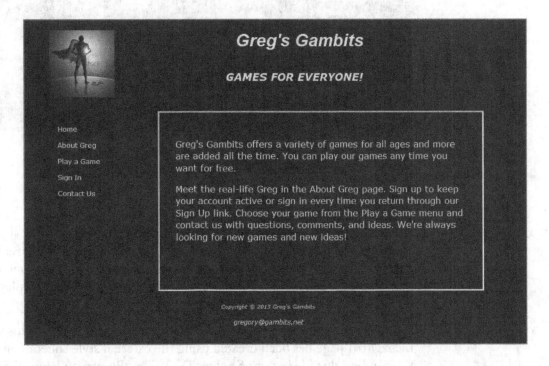

You can edit this page now to change the default email address at the bottom to your own email address or a fake email address. Find the email address at the bottom of the index.html page and change the address. You should also add a link in the navigation bar on the left side to the page we will now create. The page will prompt a user to enter some personal information so we will use Tell Greg About You as the text for the link. The new page will have the filename aboutyou.html and will be stored in the same folder as the index.html page so you should make the link a relative link. The code for this link is as follows:

```
<a href = "aboutyou.html">Tell Greg About You</a>
```

Your page should look like this, with your email at the bottom instead of Greg's:

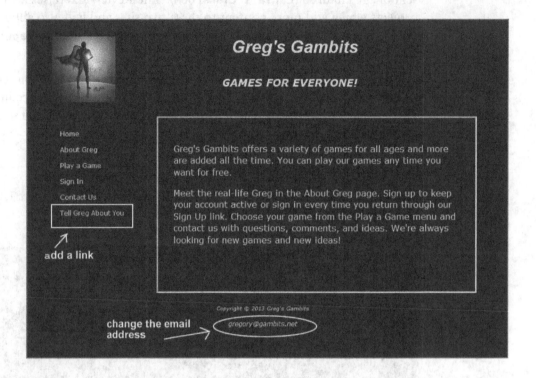

Now we will create the Tell Greg About You page.

Developing the About You Page

We will only ask the user to enter three pieces of information but, if you want, you can use the skills you have learned to add more. For now, we will use functions, methods, and events to get the following information from everyone who plays games at Greg's Gambits: the player's name, a username that the player can select, and an avatar that the player chooses.

First, we need to be sure to use the same styles for every page in this site. The index.html page has been created using the external style sheet named greg.css. You can find this file in your Student Data Files. Be sure to keep all files for this site in one folder on your computer or flash drive. Create this folder and name it greg. It is good practice to keep all images that are used for any web page in a folder named images so create that folder inside the greg folder now. You should also copy the image that is used on the index.html page into your images folder.

You can use the index.html page as a template. The content of the new page will go inside the <div> container with id = "content" so you can delete all the content between these <div></div> tags. You should also change the subheading from GAMES FOR EVERYONE! to TELL GREG ABOUT YOU. Add Greg's Gambits | About You as the page title. Your new page now looks like this:

Writing the Code

This page will prompt the user for a real name and a username and will offer five avatar options for the player to select from. There are five avatar images provided for you but you can find and use others, if you want. We will use the open() method to open a new window that will display the five avatars for the player's selection.

Prompting for the Player's Name

To get the player's name, we will add a button in the content section of the page. The button, when clicked, will call a JavaScript function that will declare a variable called **name** and assign the value of this variable to the result of a prompt box that prompts the player for his name. Then the function will display that value to the page. The relevant code is shown here with a detailed explanation following:

```
1.   ...doctype and other information goes here
2.   <head>
3.   <title>Greg's Gambits | About You</title>
4.   <link href="greg.css" rel="stylesheet" type="text/css" />
5.   <script>
6.   function getName()
7.   {
8.         var name = prompt("Please enter your name"," ");
9.         document.getElementById('myname').innerHTML = name;
10.  }
11.  </script>
12.  </head>
13.   <body>
14.  <div id="container">
15.        ... other code goes here
16.        <div id="content">
17.              <p><button type="button" onclick="getName()">Enter your name ↵
                  </button>
```

```
18.              Hi there, <span  id = "myname" >Greg</span> </p>
19.              <p> </p>
20.         </div>
21.         ... footer code goes here
22.  </div>
23.  </body>
```

Line 9 deserves a little attention. Here we are using the innerHTML property of the getElementById() method to retrieve information from a web page. This line says to go into the element with id = "myname" (i.e., its innerHTML) and fill it with the value of the variable **name**.

On line 17 we add a button that says Enter your name. We use the onclick event to call the getName() function which begins on line 6. We also add some HTML script on line 18. The <span></span> area is given the id = "myname". This will allow us to position the result of the getName() function (the player's name) when we display it on the web page.

The getName() function does three things. On line 8 we use a prompt() to ask the user for his or her name. That same line also declares a variable named **name** and assigns its value to the result of the prompt(). Now **name** contains the player's name. Then, on line 9, that name is displayed on the web page. To do this we must use the innerHTML property. Line 9 is written as follows:

```
document.getElementById('myname').innerHTML = name;
```

This means that we take the value of **name** and use it as the value to replace whatever is in the "myname" container. We use the getElementById() method to retrieve the present contents of myname and the innerHTML property to replace those contents with the value of **name**.

If you add this code to the page you are creating, your page will initially look like this:

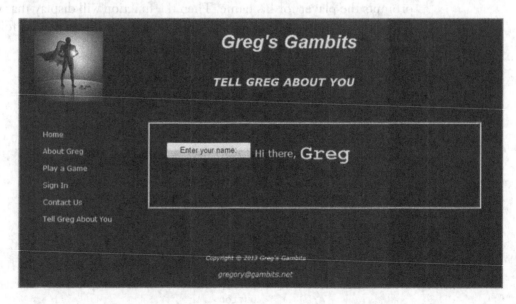

After clicking the button and entering the name Montrose at the prompt, the page will look like this:

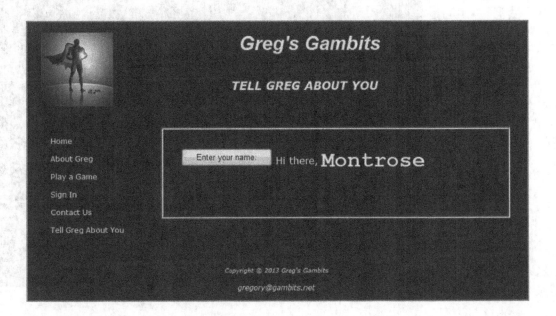

Prompting for the Player's Username

In order to get the player's username, we can use virtually the same code again. We will simply add a second button and a second function. The code for the second button should go directly under the line for the first button and the code for the second function will be placed under the getName() function. We'll call this new function getUsername().

The code for the second button is

```
<p><button type="button" onclick="getUsername()">Enter a username </button>
Username: <span  id = "myusername">KingGreg</span> </p>
```

Notice that we changed the onclick event to call the new function, getUsername(), we changed the text to display, and we changed the <span> id to "myusername".

The new function is almost the same as the first function and the code is

```
function getUsername()
{
    var username = prompt("What do you want for your username?"," ");
    document.getElementById('myusername').innerHTML=username;
}
```

After adding this code, if the user enters `Montrose` for the name and `Troll King` for a username, the page will look like this:

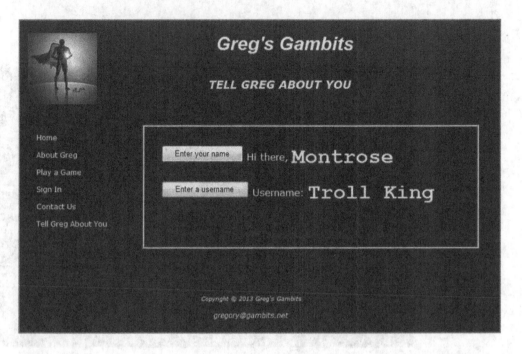

Selecting an Avatar

The third part of this page is more involved. We will create a button, as before, that the player will click to select an avatar. For now, since we don't have too many JavaScript tools to work with yet, we will make the selection of an avatar rather simple. When the player clicks the button to select an avatar, the button will call on a function, `getAvatar()`, which will do things. First, it will open a new window with a new web page. This page will contain the avatar options we are offering. In the future you will be able to design a page that can allow your player to create his or her avatar from many more options and, working in a team with graphic artists, you can allow the player to create a new image. But for now, we will start small. After the player views the options we provide, a button will allow the player to enter the chosen avatar and will display that selection.

Before we add code to the main page, let's create a new page that displays the avatar options for the player. There are five small image files in your Student Data Files that you can use or you can find your own images. The files we will use here are `bunny.jpg`, `elf.jpg`, `ghost.jpg`, `princess.jpg`, and `wizard.jpg`. The page will have the filename `avatars.html` and the page title `Greg's Gambits | Avatars`. The page will contain only brief instructions and the images. The code for this page is as follows:

```
<html>
<head>
    <title>Greg's Gambits | Avatars</title>
</head>
```

```
<body>
<hr />
<h2> Here are your avatar options: </h2>
<h3><hr />
      <img src="images/bunny.jpg" />Bunny
      <img src="images/elf.jpg" />Elf
      <img src="images/ghost.jpg" />Ghost
      <img src="images/princess.jpg" />Princess
      <img src="images/wizard.jpg" />Wizard
<hr /></h3>
<h3>You will enter your selection on the previous page.</h3>
</body>
</html>
```

If you use the images provided for you in the Student Data Files and create this page, it will look like this:

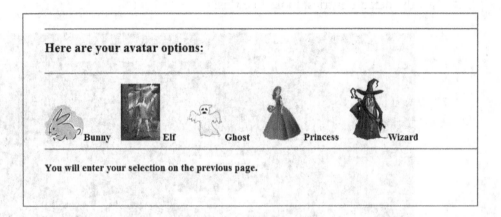

Now we will create the button that the player will click to begin the avatar selection process using code that is similar to the previous two buttons. Place this code underneath the code for the username button:

```
<p><button type="button" onclick="getAvatar()">See the avatar choices</button>
```

This button, when clicked, calls a function named getAvatar(). That function will do one thing—it will open the avatars.html file in a new window. The code for the function should go under the get_username() function. It looks like this:

```
function getAvatar()
{
    window.open('avatars.html');
}
```

The final button will allow the user to enter the avatar he or she has selected. The code is just like the code for the username and name functions and looks like this:

```
<p><button type="button" onclick="pickAvatar()">Select your avatar ↵
        </button><br />
The avatar you selected is: <span  id = "myavatar"> kitty</span> </p>
```

Finally, we will create the `pickAvatar()` function which is called when this button is clicked. It will replace the default contents of the myavatar element with the player's selection. Place the following code for this function under the getAvatar() function:

```
function pickAvatar()
{
    var avatar = prompt("Enter the avatar you want","Bunny");
    document.getElementById('myavatar').innerHTML = avatar;
}
```

This function prompts the player for his avatar selection and displays it on the page. If you published this page on a real website, you would include instructions about how the user should enter the avatar choice or perhaps provide a drop-down menu to facilitate the choice. But, as a beginner, we will assume the player will enter the correctly spelled text name of the selection. The finished aboutyou.html page, with the default entries, looks like this:

Finishing the Code

Now we can put it all together. The final code for this page is given below with line numbers displayed for your convenience. Of course, the line numbers should not be included when you create your own pages.

```
1.  <!DOCTYPE html PUBLIC "-//W3C//DTD XHTML 1.0 Transitional//EN" ⏎
    "http://www.w3.org/TR/xhtml1/DTD/xhtml1-transitional.dtd">
2.  <html xmlns="http://www.w3.org/1999/xhtml" lang="en" xml:lang="en">
3.  <head>
```

```
 4.    <title>Greg's Gambits | About You</title>
 5.    <link href="greg.css" rel="stylesheet" type="text/css" />
 6.    <meta http-equiv="Content-Type" content="text/html;
        charset=utf-8" />
 7.    <script>
 8.    function getName()
 9.    {
10.          var name=prompt("Please enter your name"," ");
11.          document.getElementById('myname').innerHTML = name;
12.    }
13.    function getUsername()
14.    {
15.          var username = prompt("What do you want for your username?"," ");
16.          document.getElementById('myusername').innerHTML = username;
17.    }
18.    function getAvatar()
19.    {
20.          window.open('avatars.html');
21.    }
22.    function pickAvatar()
23.    {
24.          var avatar = prompt("Enter the avatar you want","Bunny");
25.          document.getElementById('myavatar').innerHTML = avatar;
26.    }
27.    </script>
28.    </head>
29.    <body>
30.    <div id="container">
31.          <img src="images/superhero.jpg" width="120" height="120" ↵
                  class="floatleft" />
32.          <h1 id="logo"><em>Greg's Gambits </em></h1>
33.          <h2 align="center"><em> TELL GREG ABOUT YOU</em></h2>
34.          <p> </p>
35.          div id="nav">
36.              <p><a href="index.html">Home</a>
37.              <a href="greg.html">About Greg</a>
38.              <a href="play_games.html">Play a Game</a>
39.              <a href="sign.html">Sign In</a>
40.              <a href="contact.html">Contact Us</a>
41.              <a href="aboutyou.html">Tell Greg About You</a></p>
42.          </div>
43.          <div id="content">
44.              <p><button type="button" onclick="getName()"> ↵
                        Enter your name </button>
45.              Hi there, <span  id = "myname" >Greg</span> </p>
46.              <p><button type="button" onclick="getUsername()"> ↵
                        Enter a username </button>
47.              Username: <span  id = "myusername">KingGreg</span>
48.              </p>
49.              <p><button type="button" onclick="getAvatar()"> ↵
                        See the avatar choices</button>
50.              <p><button type="button" onclick="pickAvatar()"> ↵
                        Select your avatar</button><br />
```

```
51.                 The avatar you selected is: <span  id = "myavatar"> ↵
                        kitty</span> </p>
52.             <p> </p>
53.         </div>
54.     <p> </p>
55.     <div id="footer">
56.         <div align="center">Copyright &copy; 2013 Greg's Gambits<br />
57.             <a href="mailto:gregory@gambits.net"> gregory@gambits.net</a>
58.         </div>
59.     </div>
60. </div>
61. </body>
62. </html>
```

Here is a sample output, given the inputs shown:

inputs:

name = **"Francis"**, username = **"bigbug"**, avatar = **"Wizard"**

output:

Carla's Classroom: Creating an About You Page

Carla, an elementary school teacher, has commissioned you to create exercises for her class. At this point, even though your JavaScript programming skills are limited, you can develop some very good exercises for young children. If you open the file in your Student Data Files entitled `index.html`, you will see the home page for `Carla's Classroom`. It should look like this:

Carla's Classroom

Home   Meet Carla   Reading   Writing   Arithmetic

  Carla is an old teacher with a new attitude. She has been teaching children for three decades (and that means 30 years since a decade is 10 years!*), but Carla has never been old-fashioned. Carla's new classroom is completely online. Lessons change all the time so check back often for new material.

Carla teaches the 3 Rs**. Pick a topic, click on the link, and get started!

**Carla asks: Can you figure out why Reading, Writing, and Arithmetic are called the 3 Rs?

*Carla's Motto: Never miss a chance to teach -- and to learn!

**Answer: Even though Writing and Arithmetic don't start with the letter R, if you say them aloud: Reading, Writing, and 'Rithmetic, they all sound like words that begin with R.

You can edit this page now to add a link to the new page we are creating. Since this page will allow the child to enter personal information, we will name the file `aboutme.html`. Locate the navigation links on the top of the page. The text of your link will be `About Me!`. You can use one of the images included with the Student Data Files or find your own image. Be sure to store the new page, as you create it, in the same folder as the `index.html` page and put your images in an `images` folder. The code for this link is as follows:

```
<a href = "aboutme.html"><img src="images/carla_kids.jpg" />About Me!</a>
```

Your page should now look like this:

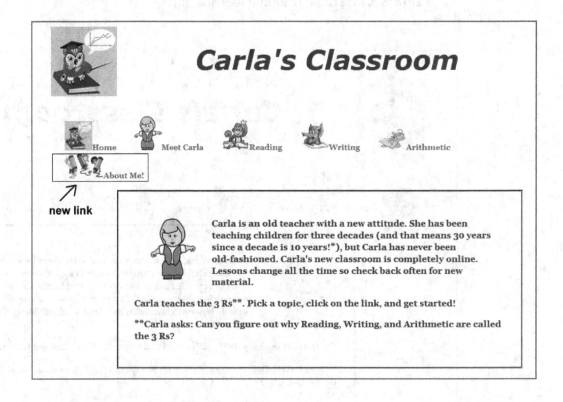

Now we will create the About Me! page.

Developing the About Me! Page

On this page the student will enter four pieces of information but, if you want, you can use the skills you have learned to add more. We'll ask the student to enter his or her name, age, favorite subject, and favorite teacher. To make the page a little more fun, we'll add code so that, regardless of what the child enters for his or her favorite teacher, it will always default to Carla.

We need to be sure to use the same styles for every page in this site. The index. html page has been created using the external style sheet named carla.css that you will find in the Student Data Files. Be sure to keep all files for this site in one folder on your computer or flash drive. Create this folder and name it carla. It is also good practice to keep all images that are used for any web page in a folder named images so create that folder inside the carla folder now. You should also copy all the images that are used on the index.html page into your images folder.

You can use the index.html page as a template. Give this new page the filename aboutme.html. The content of the new page will go inside the <div> container with id = "content" so you can delete all the content between these <div></div> tags, including the image of Carla. Add Carla's Classroom | About Me! as the page title. You can add the girl.jpg and boy.jpg images from your Student Data Files, find images on your own, or leave the content area blank for now. Your new page now looks like this:

Writing the Code

This page will prompt the child for a name, an age, a favorite subject and a favorite teacher. The first three items are coded using the same techniques we used for the Greg's Gambits site. When we finish those three things, we'll focus on the prompt for the favorite teacher and add a little extra code.

Prompting for the Child's Name, Age, and Favorite Subject

To get some information from the child, we will add three buttons in the content section of the page. Each button, when clicked, will call a JavaScript function that will declare a variable and assign the value of this variable to the result of a prompt box. Each prompt box will request different information. Then the function will display that value to the page. The relevant code is shown here with a detailed explanation following:

```
1.    ...doctype and other information goes here
2.    <head>
3.    <title>Carla's Classroom | About Me!</title>
4.    <link href="carla.css" rel="stylesheet" type="text/css" />
5.    <script>
6.    function getName()
7.    {
8.        var name = prompt("What's your name?"," ");
9.        document.getElementById('myname').innerHTML = name;
10.   }
```

```
11.   function getAge()
12.   {
13.         var age = prompt("How old are you?"," ");
14.         document.getElementById('myage').innerHTML = age;
15.   }
16.   function getSubject()
17.   {
18.         var subject = prompt("What do you like best in school?"," ");
19.         document.getElementById('mysubject').innerHTML = subject;}
20.   </script>
21.   </head>
22.   <body>
23.   <div id="container">
24.         ... other code goes here
25.         <div id="content">
26.           <p><img src="images/girl.jpg" class="floatleft" /></p>
27.           <p><button type="button" onclick="getName()">Enter your name ↵
                   </button>
28.         Hi there, <span  id="myname" >Little Fella</span></p>
29.           <p><button type="button" onclick="getAge()">Enter your age ↵
                   </button>
30.         You're <span  id = "myage" > ??? </span>  years old? Wow!</p>
31.           <p><button type="button" onclick="getSubject()">Enter your favorite ↵
                   subject </button>
32.         You like <span  id = "mysubject" > ??? </span>  best. ↵
                   We'll do a lot of that here.</p>
33.           <p><img src="images/boy.jpg" class="floatright" /></p>
34.         </div>
35.         ... footer code goes here
36.         </div>
37.   </body>
38.   </html>
```

The code in this page is similar to the code used for the aboutyou.html page in Greg's
Gambits. On lines 27, 29, and 31 we add three buttons which say Enter your name,
Enter your age, and Enter your favorite subject. We use the onclick event to call
three functions—the getName() function, the getAge() function, and the getSubject()
function. These are in the <head> section. We also add some HTML script on lines 28,
30, and 32. The <span></span> areas are given ids. "myname" identifies the area where
the result of the getName() function will be placed, "myage" identifies the area where
the result of the getAge() function will be placed, and "mysubject" identifies the area
where the result of the getSubject() function will be placed.

The getName() function begins on line 6. After the opening curly bracket on line
7, line 8 uses a prompt() to ask the child for his or her name. That same line also
declares a variable named **name** and assigns its value to the result of the prompt().
Now **name** contains the child's name. Then, on line 9, that name is displayed on the
web page. To do this we must use the innerHTML property. Line 9 is written as follows:

```
document.getElementById('myname').innerHTML = name;
```

This line is an instruction to take the value of **name** and use it as the value to replace
whatever is in the myname container. We use the getElementById() method to
retrieve the present contents of "myname" and the innerHTML property to replace
those contents with the value of **name**.

The same code, replacing all references to a child's name with references to the child's age and favorite subject is repeated in the getAge() function on lines 11–15 and the getSubject() function on lines 16–19.

If you add this code to the page you are creating, your page will initially look like this:

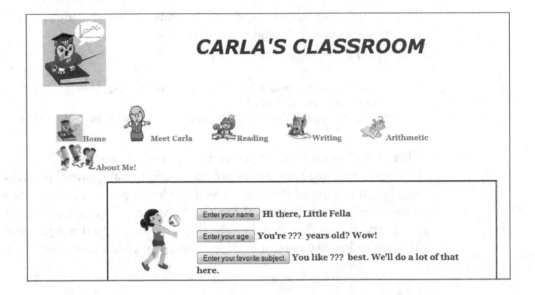

If you enter Lulu for the name, 7 for the age, and music for the subject, the page will look like this:

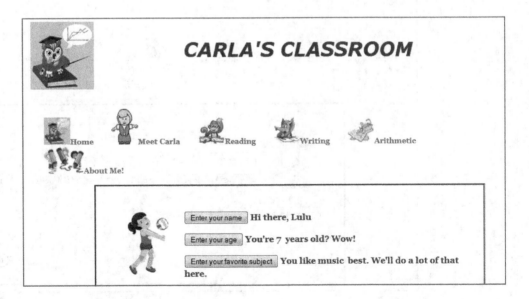

Prompting for the Child's Favorite Teacher

To allow the child to enter his or her favorite teacher, we use the same code as for the previous three buttons and functions. However, this time, as a little joke, we will add a line of code which will force the output to say that Carla is the favorite teacher, regardless of what the child enters.

The code to create the button that the child will click and the `<span>` container to hold the result is as follows:

```
<p><button type="button" onclick="getTeacher()">Who's your favorite teacher? ⏎
        </button>
<span  id = "myteacher" > ??? </span>   is the best!</p>
```

The function, getTeacher(), should be added below the getSubject() function in the `<head>` section. It includes one extra line.

```
function getTeacher()
{
    var teacher=prompt("Who's your favorite teacher?"," ");
    var favorite = "CARLA";
    document.getElementById('myteacher').innerHTML = favorite;
}
```

This code allows the child to enter anything when prompted. That entry is stored in a variable named **teacher**. However, a new variable, **favorite**, is declared on the next line and assigned the value "CARLA". The output sent to the myteacher container is the value of **favorite**, not the value of **teacher**. Thus, regardless of who is the child's favorite teacher, it will always display CARLA. And this is just how Carla wants it! The finished aboutme.html page, before any child has used it, looks like this:

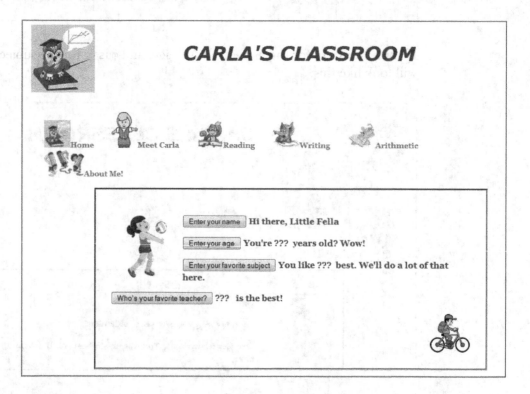

Finishing the Code

Now we can put it all together. The final code for this page is given below with line numbers for your convenience. Of course, the line numbers should not be included when you create your own pages.

```
1.    <!DOCTYPE html PUBLIC "-//W3C//DTD XHTML 1.0 Transitional//EN" ↵
         "http://www.w3.org/TR/xhtml1/DTD/xhtml1-transitional.dtd">
2.    <html xmlns="http://www.w3.org/1999/xhtml" lang="en" xml:lang="en">
3.    <meta http-equiv="Content-Type" content="text/html;charset=utf-8" />
4.    <head>
5.    <title>Carla's Classroom | About Me!</title>
6.    <link href="carla.css" rel="stylesheet" type="text/css" />
7.    <script>
8.    function getName()
9.    {
10.          var name = prompt("What's your name?"," ");
11.          document.getElementById('myname').innerHTML = name;
12.   }
13.   function getAge()
14.   {
15.          var age = prompt("How old are you?"," ");
16.          document.getElementById('myage').innerHTML = age;
17.   }
18.   function getSubject()
19.   {
20.          var subject = prompt("What do you like best in school?"," ");
21.          document.getElementById('mysubject').innerHTML = subject;
22.   }
23.   function getTeacher()
24.   {
25.          var teacher=prompt("Who's your favorite teacher?"," ");
26.          var favorite = "CARLA";
27.          document.getElementById('myteacher').innerHTML = favorite;
28.   }
29.   </script>
30.   </head>
31.   <body>
32.   <div id="container">
33.   <img src="images/owl_reading.jpg" class="floatleft" />
34.   <h2 id="logo"><em>Carla's Classroom</em></h2>
35.          <div align="left">
36.          <blockquote>
37.          <p>
38.              <a href="index.html"><img src = "images/owl_button.jpg" /> ↵
                  Home</a>
39.              <a href="carla.html"><img src = "images/carla_button.jpg" /> ↵
                  Meet Carla</a>
40.              <a href="reading.html"><img src = "images/read_button.jpg" /> ↵
                  Reading</a>
41.              <a href="writing.html"><img src = "images/write_button.jpg" /> ↵
                  Writing</a>
42.              <a href="math.html"><img src = "images/arith_button.jpg" />↵
                  Arithmetic</a>
43.              <a href = "aboutme.html"><img src = "images/carla_kids_3.jpg" /> ↵
                  About Me!</a>
44.              <br />
45.              </p>
46.          </blockquote>
47.          </div>
48.          <div id="content">
49.              <p>
50.              <img src="images/girl.jpg" class="floatleft" /></p>
```

```
51.                <p><button type="button" onclick="getName()">Enter your name ↵
                      </button>
52.                Hi there,<span  id="myname">Little Fella</span></p>
53.                <p><button type="button" onclick="getAge()">Enter your age ↵
                      </button>
54.                You're <span  id = "myage" > ??? </span>   years old? Wow!</p>
55.                <p><button type="button" onclick="getSubject()"> Enter your ↵
                      favorite subject </button>
56.                You like <span  id = "mysubject" > ??? </span>   best. ↵
                      We'll do a lot of that here.</p>
57.                <p><button type="button" onclick="getTeacher()"> Who's your ↵
                      favorite teacher? </button>
58.                <span  id = "myteacher" > ??? </span>   is the best!</p> ↵
59.                <p>
60.                <img src="images/boy.jpg" class="floatright" /></p>
61.          </div>
62.          <div id="footer">
63.          <h3>*Carla's Motto: Never miss a chance to teach -- and to learn!</h3>
64.  <span class="specialh4">**Answer: Even though Writing and Arithmetic don't ↵
              start with the letter R, if you say them aloud: Reading, Writing, ↵
              and 'Rithmetic, they all sound like words that begin with R. </span>
65.          </div>
66.  </div>
67.  </body>
68.  </html>
```

Here is a sample output, given the inputs shown:

inputs:

    name = "Harvey", **age** = "8", **subject** = "gym class", **teacher** = "Mr. Smith"

output:

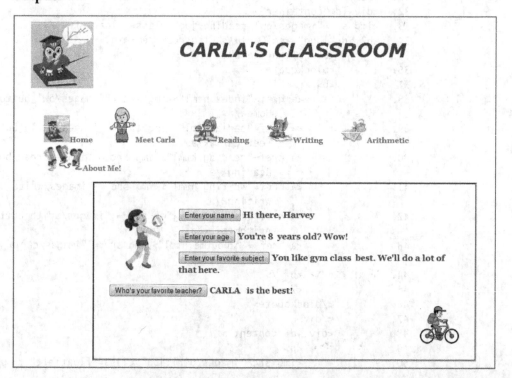

Chapter Review and Exercises

Key Terms

<noscript></noscript> tags
<script></script> tags
arithmetic operators
assignment operators
attributes
Boolean data type
child object
close() method
concatenation operator
control structures
cyclic process
data type
decision structure
Document Object Model (DOM)
dot notation
element
event
event-driven programming
flowchart
function keyword
functions
getElementById()
id attribute
innerHTML
input
input-processing-output model
logical data type
loop structure
methods
modular programming

named constant
numerical data type
object
object-oriented programming
onclick event
onload event
open() method
output
parameters
parent object
problem-solving strategy
procedural programming
processing
program development cycle
program module
prompt box
prompt() method
prompts
properties
pseudocode
repetition structure
selection structure
sequential structure
string data type
submodules
var keyword
variable
variable name
write() method

Review Exercises

Fill in the Blank

1. The steps required to solve a programming problem are known as the _Program Development Cycle_.

2. Computers need _input_ to begin to work on a problem or process.

3. Computer scientists have shown that there are only three basic _Control Structures_ needed to create a program or algorithm.

4. Data stored as a _boolean_ data type can have only one of two possible values.

5. A _variable_ is a name for a storage location in the computer's memory.

True or False

Decision structure 6. T/**F** The sequence control structure consists of a place where, depending on what happens in the program, a portion of the program is skipped.

7. **T**/F If you consider a car to be an object, its color would be one of its attributes.

8. T/**F** If you consider a car to be an object, its make and model (i.e., a Ford two-door sedan, for example) would be two of its methods.

9. T/**F** A program's input must be entered by the user.

10. T/**F** A program's output must be displayed to the screen.

11. **T**/F The repetition structure allows a block of statements to be executed repeatedly.

12. **T**/F If data is stored as string data, it cannot be used in numerical calculations.

13. T/**F** Data entered with the numerical data type must be enclosed in quotes.

14. T/F The process of breaking down a problem into simpler subprograms is called top-down design.

15. T/**F** Pseudocode is rarely used by programmers because it is false code.

Short Answer

16. Assume you have created a program that has the user enter an email address of the form:

    `username@domain.extension`

    An extension for the email should be three letters (no numbers or other characters). List four types of input errors your program should test for.

17. Create a line of JavaScript that will prompt the user for a phone number and will store the entry in a variable named **phone**.

18. Create a line of JavaScript that will display the phone number from Exercise 17. If, for example, the phone number entered is 123-555-6789, the display should be:

    `Your phone number is 123-555-6789.`

19. Which control structure is used in the following pseudocode?

    ```
    If it snows, wear your boots.
    Otherwise, wear your running shoes.
    ```

20. Which part of the input-processing-output model is involved in this JavaScript statement?

    ```
    totalApples = myApples + yourApples;
    ```

21. If you were writing a program, which of the following would you consider to be named constants? Choose all that apply.
    a) the price of a gallon of gas
    b) the number of miles driven
    c) the value of pi ✓
    d) the age of the user
    e) the number of days in a week ✓
    f) the name of the user

22. If **firstName** represents a user's first name and **lastName** represents the user's last name, write an assignment statement that will store the user's whole name in a variable called **fullName** and includes a space between the first and last names.

23. If **firstName** represents a user's first name and **lastName** represents the user's last name, write an assignment statement that will create a user's email address in a variable called **email** and has the following form:

    first.last@goodmail.com

24. In the following statement, identify the assignment operator and the arithmetic operators:

    netPay = **grossPay** * 0.80 - **medIns**;

    Use the following information for Exercises 25–28. Use the concatenation operator when necessary and be sure to include extra punctuation and spaces, if needed. Use variables in your answer wherever possible, given the following variables and values:

    pet = "dog"   **color** = "brown"   **name** = "Spike"
          age = 2   **years** = 4

25. Display a message that says: Spike is a great dog!

26. Create a variable named **newAge** that adds the values of **age** and **years**.

27. Display a message that says: In 4 years Spike will be 6 years old.

28. Create a prompt to allow the user to enter a new pet name. Save the information in a variable named newPet. Then display the following message:

    Your dog, Spike, is brown. Your new pet will also be brown.

    Use the following symbols to answer Exercises 29–32:

29. Which symbol represents a decision?

30. Which symbol represents a process?

31. Which symbol represents input?

32. Which symbol represents output?

33. Given that a pencil is an object, list three properties associated with the pencil object and three methods associated with the pencil object.

34. What is the top-level object of a web page?

35. Use the `write()` method to display the following statement in an HTML document. Format the text as a level three header with a horizontal rule underneath:

    ```
    Lions, and tigers, and bears... oh my!
    ```

36. Given the following HTML, fill in the missing lines in the JavaScript function to replace `Siamese` with `Beagle`:

    HTML: `<h2 id = "cat" onclick="getDog()" > Siamese </h2>`

    JavaScript function:
    ```
    function getDog()
    {
            fill in the code here
            fill in the code here
    }
    ```

37. Fill in the missing line in the `openWindow()` function below to open a new blank window which is 200 pixels high and 200 pixels wide.

    ```
    function openWindow()
    {
        fill in the code here
    }
    ```

38. Edit the answer to Exercise 37 so that the small new window opens and now contains the following message, formatted as a level three header:

    ```
    Welcome, friends, to my small window!
    ```

    (Note: this will probably require two lines of code.)

    Use the following code for Exercises 39–40:

    ```
    function finalExam(time, place)
    {
        document.write("<p>The exam is at " + time + " o'clock.</p>");
        document.write("<p>It is in room " + place + ".</p>");
    }
    ```

39. Create a button which, when clicked, will cause the following to display:

    ```
    The exam is at 9 o'clock.
    It is in room 3.
    ```

40. Create a button which, when clicked, will cause the following to display:

    ```
    The exam is at 3 o'clock.
    It is in room 9.
    ```

Programming Challenges

On Your Own

1. Create pseudocode that could be used as a blueprint for a program that would do the following:

   An employer wants you to create a program that will allow her to enter each employee's name, hourly rate of pay, number of hours worked in one week, overtime pay rate, payroll deductions (such as medical insurance, savings, etc.), and tax rate. The program should output the employee's gross pay (before taxes and deductions) and net pay (after taxes and deductions) for each employee for one week.

VideoNote
Using ids to Replace Web
Page Content
On_Your_Own_2_
Transportation

2. Create a web page that displays the default information shown below about a user's vehicle, then prompts the user to enter his or her own information, and uses that to replace the defaults. The initial page should look like the one shown here. Use ids for each element.

> ## Your Transportation
>
> **Vehicle Type: Sedan**
>
> **Color: orange**
>
> **Years owned: 43**
>
> **Mileage: 376,589**

3. Create a web page that will run a JavaScript script as soon as the page loads, using the onload event. The script should display the following:

   JavaScript rules!

4. Create two web pages. The first page should ask the user if he or she wants to see some pictures. When the user responds positively, a new window should open displaying several images. You can use any images in your Student Data Files or find your own.

5. Create a web page that contains two buttons. When the first is clicked, the user will be prompted to enter a first name, then a last name. These names will be concatenated to form a username with a dot between the first and last names. The second button will prompt the user for a nickname. The buttons and output will be as shown:

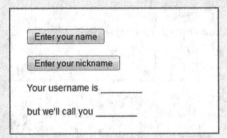

Case Studies

Greg's Gambits

Now you will add to the About You page you created earlier in this chapter. Open the aboutyou.html page and add the following:

- Create a new page with images of possible dwelling places for the avatars. You can use the images provided in your Student Data Files or find your own. Save the file as homes.html.

- Add a button to the `aboutyou.html` page's `content` area. The button should allow the player to see the landscapes and homes offered for the avatars. When the button is clicked, the `homes.html` page should open.

- Add a button to allow the player to select one of the images as the home for his or her avatar and display this information on the `aboutyou.html` page.

Save your page as `greg_aboutyou.html`. Test all the buttons and options in a browser. Submit your work as instructed by your teacher.

Carla's Classroom

Now you will add to the `About Me` page created earlier in the chapter. Open the `aboutme.html` page and add the following:

- Create a new page with images of various activities. You can use the images provided in your Student Data Files or find your own. Save the file as `activities.html`.

- Add a button to the `aboutme.html` page's `content` area to allow the child to see the various activities. When the button is clicked, the `activities.html` page should open.

- Add two buttons to allow the child to select his first and second favorite activities and display this information on the `aboutme.html` page.

Save your page as `aboutme.html`. Test all the buttons and options in a browser. Submit your work as instructed by your teacher.

Lee's Landscape

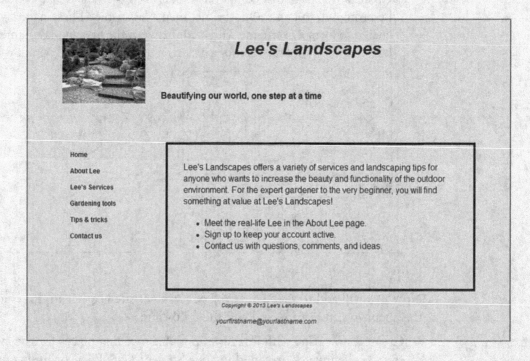

You can develop `Lee's Landscape` site from start to finish if you continue to work on it in the Case Studies in each chapter. A simple `index.html` page is included for this site in the `lee` folder in your Student Data Files along with a `lee.css` file and a `lee_landscape.jpg` file. You can use these files as they are or be as creative as you want. For now, open the `index.html` file and become familiar with the structure of the HTML. Then, create a new page, using the `index.html` page as a template. This page will allow the user to enter some personal information. Give the new page the filename `lee_aboutuser.html` and the page title should be `Lee's Landscapes | About You`. The following information should be requested from the user, using buttons, prompts, and the properties and events you have learned in this chapter to display the information:

- Add buttons which, when clicked, will prompt the user to enter his or her name, level of gardening expertise (novice, intermediate, expert) and specific interest: lawn maintenance, landscaping, growing vegetables, or planting flowers.
- The responses to the prompts should be displayed on the page with a message to the user that says, when complete, the website will provide information on all landscaping subjects.
- Add a link to the `Lee's Landscape` home page to this new page.

Save your page as `lee_aboutuser.html`. Test all the buttons and options in a browser. Submit your work as instructed by your teacher.

Jackie's Jewelry

Jackie's Jewelry

Home

About Jackie

Jackie's Services

Shop

Jewelry Making

Contact Jackie

Jackie makes beautiful jewelry and is eager to share her talents. Custom designs are Jackie's specialty. Browse the site to learn more about Jackie, see finished products, design your own, and learn to make your own jewelry.

- Meet the real-life Jackie in the About Jackie page.
- Sign up to keep your account active.
- Contact us with questions, comments, and ideas.
- And of course, shop, shop, shop!

Copyright © 2013 Lee's Landscapes

yourfirstname@yourlastname.com

You can develop `Jackie's Jewelry` site from start to finish if you continue to work on it in the Case Studies in each chapter. A simple `index.html` page is included for this site in the `jackie` folder in your Student Data Files along with a `jackie.css`. You can use these files as they are or be as creative as you want. For now, open the `index.html` file and become familiar with the structure of the HTML. Then, create a new page, using the `index.html` page as a template. This page will allow the user to enter some personal information. Give the new page the filename `jackie_aboutuser.html` and the page title should be `Jackie's Jewelry | About You`. The following information should be requested from the user, using buttons, prompts, and the properties and events you have learned in this chapter to display the information:

- Add buttons which, when clicked, will prompt the user to enter his or her name, age, and specific interests: buying Jackie's jewelry, designing jewelry for Jackie to create, or learning to make jewelry. There should be three buttons for the interests and the user should enter `yes` or `no` to each question.

- The responses to the prompts should be displayed on the page. If the user enters `yes` to one of the three interests, a message should be displayed thanking the user for his or her interest. If the user enters `no` to an interest, nothing should be displayed. Later, when you learn more JavaScript, you can create more types of responses and also deal with users who enter `no` for all interests. For now, we will assume the user will enter `yes` at least once.

- Add a link to the `Jackie's Jewelry` home page to this new page.

Save your page as `Jackie_aboutuser.html`. Test all the buttons and options in a browser. Submit your work as instructed by your teacher.

Building Blocks: Variables and Operators

Chapter Objectives

This chapter presents variables and operators—the building blocks of all program code. Without variables, computer programs would be limited to a single use. Often, programs must compare and manipulate information, and that information is stored in variables. Several types of operators (arithmetic, relational, and logical) are used to compare and manipulate data. By storing information in variables and using that information in a program, we can write programs that can be reused, each time with different results for different values.

What is a variable? The short answer is that it is a name for a place in your computer's memory. What are operators? The short answer is that they are the tools programmers use to change and compare values. Long answers to these questions is the basis for this chapter.

After reading this chapter, you will be able to do the following:

- Describe a variable and explain why variables are the essential building blocks of program code

- Understand how and where variable values are stored in memory

- Create appropriate variable names

- Know the characteristics of data types: integers, floating point numbers, characters, strings, and named constants

- Understand how a computer uses the hierarchy of operations in mathematical and logical algorithms

- Use the parseInt() and parseFloat() functions to store user input as numerical values, as needed

- Distinguish between the concatenation and addition operators in JavaScript

- Use relational operators for numerical, character, and string comparisons

- Use logical operators

- Use the conditional operator

- Combine the types of operators to create compound conditions

- Use the charAt() function

2.1 | What Is a Variable?

A **variable** is the name of a location in your computer's memory where a value is stored. Whenever you use a variable in a program, the computer knows to look in that memory location for the value stored there. Then it uses that value for whatever instruction is in the program. It sounds simple and, once you understand how variables work, it is. However, before you can use variables appropriately, you must understand what is happening within the computer and within the program code when variables are created and assigned values.

Memory Locations

Technically, a program variable is the name of a storage location in the computer's internal memory, and the value of a variable is the contents of that location. Think of the storage locations as mailboxes. Each variable can be considered as the name printed on a mailbox, and the value of a variable as its contents. These "mailboxes" differ in size and location, depending on many things. Some types of variables can be stored in small mailboxes and others need large mailboxes. The operating system of a computer affects the size of these mailboxes.

When you declare (create) a variable in a program, a memory location is allocated to store the value of that variable. Therefore, you must know how to create a variable.

Variable Names

As the programmer, you choose the names of your variables. This doesn't mean you can pick any names. There are rules you must follow and some conventions you may want to follow. You must understand what types of names are acceptable and what types are unacceptable. If you violate the naming rules, your program will not work. The rules for naming JavaScript variables are as follows:

- A variable name cannot start with a numeral. For example, **6game** or **4thofjuly** are illegal variable names. You can, however, have numbers within a JavaScript variable name. For example, **game_6** or **july4th** are valid variable names.

- You cannot use a mathematical, relational, or logical operator in a variable name. Later in this chapter, we will discuss mathematical, relational, and logical operators. For example, **game*4** is illegal because the asterisk, *****, is the mathematical symbol for multiplication. Similarly, **july/4** is illegal because the slash, **/**, is the mathematical symbol for division.

- You cannot use punctuation in a variable name. The exception is the underscore. For example, **game:4** is illegal (the colon is punctuation) but **game_4** is fine. Similarly, **july,4** is illegal (the comma is punctuation) but **july_4** is fine. The underscore can be used in the beginning, middle, or end of a JavaScript variable name. The following variable names are legal: **_4thofjuly**, **game_6**, and **happy_**.

- JavaScript variable names must *never* contain spaces.

■ You cannot use JavaScript keywords for variable names. **Keywords** are reserved by a programming language for special use. Examples of JavaScript keywords are window, open, and this. There are many keywords in a programming language. If you are unsure whether the variable name you want to use is a keyword, pick something else or alter the word to make it different from a keyword. For example, if you want to use window as your variable name, change it to something such as **my_window** or **wndow**.

■ JavaScript variable names are case-sensitive. An uppercase letter can create a completely new variable if a variable with the same spelling has been previously declared with all lowercase characters. This means that the following names represent four different JavaScript variables: **bluebird**, **Bluebird**, **BlueBird**, and **blueBird**. Remember this as you write programs. A simple error of typing a lowercase letter when an uppercase one is needed can cause hours of frustration.

■ Different programmers use different conventions when naming variables. Some prefer to begin each name with an abbreviated description of the variable's data type. For example, **intAge** indicates an integer and **strName** indicates a string variable. Some programmers use underscores to separate words, such as **my_age** or **first_name**. Others use **CamelBack notation** (or CamelCase) notation. This is the practice of capitalizing the first letter of the second word of a variable name. For example, **myAge** and **firstName** are examples of variables that use CamelBack notation. As a convention, we will use this type of notation for variables in this book, but it is not a problem if you choose to do otherwise.

Example 2.1 lists some variable names with errors and their appropriately corrected names.

EXAMPLE 2.1

What's in a Name?

Variable Name	Error	Corrected Name
5thstudent	Begins with a number	Student_5
last+name	Includes a mathematical operator	lastName
first.name	Contains punctuation	firstName
my dog	Contains a space	myDog
floatAge	Contains the keyword "float"	fltAge

Naming Tips

When naming variables remember the following tips:

■ Variable names can be long; in fact, JavaScript variable names can be 500 characters or more. But remember, you will have to type the variable name throughout your program. If you create a lengthy or complicated name, you are introducing the chance for more errors. It's a lot easier to remember **player6** than to remember **the_name_of_the_sixth_player_in_this_game**.

■ Many programmers use uppercase letters to distinguish one word from another within a single name. For example, `MilesTraveled` works as well as `Miles_Traveled` and may be easier to type.

■ Variable names should be meaningful. If you name your variables perfectly acceptable names such as `variableNumber_1`, `variableNumber_2`, `variableNumber_3`, and so forth, you may find that you are spending time trying to remember the meaning of each variable instead of fine-tuning your program.

It's best to name variables with the shortest possible names that provide some meaningful representation and do not conflict with the rules stated here. Example 2.2 lists some variable names with errors and their appropriately corrected names.

EXAMPLE 2.2

Variable by Any Other Name Can Be As Sweet

Variable Name	Error	Corrected Name
`customers_order_before_tax`	No error but too long	`preTax`
`sale1item`	No error but hard to understand	`sale_1_item`
`usersscore`	No error but hard to understand	`usersScore`
`variable1`	No error but meaningless	`num1`

Declaring Variables

Now that you know how to name variables, you need to know how to create them in JavaScript. This is called **declaring variables.** The rules for declaring variables in JavaScript are somewhat looser than for other object-oriented programming languages. In many languages you must not only create and name a variable, but also you must define its data type immediately. Data types are covered in the next section of this chapter. Luckily, in JavaScript you do not need to identify the data type when you declare a variable. You simply use the keyword **var.**

Example 2.3 shows how to create several variables in JavaScript. Note that you must end each variable declaration statement with a semicolon. If you have more than one variable of the same type, you can declare all of them in one statement, separating the variable names by commas and using the semicolon at the end of the declaration.

EXAMPLE 2.3

Declaring Variables

a) The following statement creates a variable which is named **car**:

```
var car;
```

b) The following statements create two variables, named **cat** and **dog**, with two statements:

```
var cat;
var dog;
```

c) The following statement creates three variables named **burger**, **chips**, and **soda** on a single line. The variable names are separated by commas and, when the list of variables is complete, a semicolon is added to show that the statement is ended. Multiple variable declarations like this are possible only when all the variables in the list are of the same type (see Section 2.2).

```
var burger, chips, soda;
```

CHECKPOINT FOR SECTION 2.1

2.1 Where is the value of a variable stored?

2.2 Who chooses the name of the variables in a program?

2.3 List five rules you must follow when creating variable names.

2.4 What (if anything) is wrong with each of the following variable names?
   a) **Shipping Cost**
   b) **1_number**
   c) **JackAndJillWentUpTheHillForWater**
   d) **oneName**
   e) **thisName**
   f) **Bob,Joe,and Mike**

2.2 Data Types

In Section 2.1, you learned that the value assigned to a variable is stored in the computer's memory. The name of the variable is similar to the name on your mailbox; it tells the computer (or mail carrier) where to store the value of the variable (or mail) and where to retrieve that value (or pick up your mail) when a variable is accessed in a program. But there are many different types of values you can store in a variable. For example, you can store a zip code. A zip code is a whole number with five digits from 00000 through 99999. For a computer, the number 99, 999 is a small number. Computers can deal with numbers that are many times larger than this and many times smaller than 0. You can also, doubtless, think of many situations that involve numbers that are not restricted to **integers** (whole numbers). For example, when you purchase something, your total is in dollars and cents. Numbers that have decimal parts are called **floating point numbers** and are, in a computer program, significantly different from integers.

Often, computer programs store single characters in variables; for example, when asking yes/no questions, you may be asked to enter 'y' for yes or 'n' for no. Variables also store words and phrases. Single **characters** are, in terms of computer storage, significantly different from long **strings** of characters.

You can imagine that a computer would use a smaller memory location to store a single character than it would need to store a whole sentence. Similarly, the computer needs a smaller space to store an integer than it needs to store a floating point number. For this reason, the programmer has to tell the computer not only what the variable will be named but also what type of data will be stored in that variable. The **data type** tells the computer what type of memory location is needed for that variable and also tells the computer a lot about what types of things (**operations**) can be performed on that data. We can multiply two numbers but we cannot multiply two characters.

JavaScript is not as strict about defining data types as some other languages but identifying the data type of a variable is still very important when using variables in programs.

A Loosely Typed Language

Many programming languages, such as C++ and Java, require the programmer to declare the **type** of a variable when a variable is created. This means that, once a variable has been declared as one type, it retains all the properties of that type and cannot be changed through the program except by specific notation. This type of language is called a **strongly typed language.** Here, the word "typing" does not refer to pressing keys on the keyboard. It refers to assigning or checking the data type of a variable. These languages use what is called **static typing,** which means that type checking occurs when the program is compiled. Thus, if a variable has been declared to be of a certain type, it must retain the properties of that type throughout the program because the compiler checks the whole program for consistency before the program is run.

Other languages—JavaScript is one—are **loosely typed languages.** PHP, Python, and Lisp are examples of loosely typed languages. In these languages, type checking is done during runtime; that is, the variable's type is checked as the program runs. These languages use what we call **dynamic typing.** Data types can change after a variable has been declared.

Programmers experienced in strongly typed languages sometimes hold this feature of JavaScript in low regard. But for us, it may make our coding jobs simpler.

Numbers

While many programming languages have two or more completely distinct data types to represent integers and floating point numbers, all numbers in JavaScript are represented as floating point values. JavaScript represents numbers using the 64-bit floating point format defined by the IEEE 754 standard. JavaScript can represent numbers as large as $\pm 1.7976931348623157 \times 10^{308}$ and as small as $\pm 5 \times 10^{-324}$. These are very big and very small numbers and it is doubtful you'll need to go beyond that range! Integers can be represented between $-9,007,199,254,740,992$ and $9,007,199,254,740,992$, inclusive.

JavaScript's dynamic typing means that initially you can give a variable an integer value and later use it as a floating point number. While this gives you more freedom in some respects, it may cause unforeseen consequences in other situations. At this point, you simply need to know that number variables are of the **numeric data type.** Later in the chapter, you will learn some built-in functions that allow you to convert integers to floating point numbers and vice versa as well as converting text values (strings) to numeric values.

You have seen how to declare a variable. At the same time that you declare a variable, you can give it an initial value. If this value is a number, the variable then becomes a numeric data type. The statements shown in Example 2.4 create numeric variables with initial values.

EXAMPLE 2.4

Declaring Variables As Numerics

a) `var myAge = 23;`

b) `var myScore = 86;`

c) `var myCost = 6.78;`

d) `var myAnswer = -45.879;`

Strings and Characters

A string is a sequence of keyboard characters including letters, digits, punctuation characters, and so forth. The string data type is the JavaScript data type for representing text. A variable is recognized as a string type if the value is enclosed in quotes. Unlike many programming languages, JavaScript allows the value of the string variable to be enclosed in either double quotes (" ") or single quotes (' '). The value of this feature is demonstrated in Example 2.5.

While many programming languages distinguish between the character data type which allows for a single character value (such as y or B or any single character) and the string data type which allows for long sequences of characters, JavaScript makes no such distinction. Any combinations of keyboard characters that are not numeric values are string values. Example 2.5 shows how to declare and initialize several string variables.

EXAMPLE 2.5

Declaring Variables As Strings

a) `var myName = "Georgie";`

b) `var myCar = 'red Mini Cooper';`

c) `var myChoice = "B";`

d) `var myUserName = "sun&rain#345";`

Note that strings can include spaces as well as a mix of uppercase and lowercase letters, special characters, and numbers.

What would happen if you wanted a string variable to hold a value that included quotes? For example, you might want your variable value to be Joe said, "Go, team!". But a string variable is already using the quotes to enclose the value of the text. We learned that JavaScript allows the use of either single or double quotes to enclose the value of a string variable. It's important to remember that once the program encounters an opening quote, it assumes that every character from then on, until another quote is encountered, is part of that string, But JavaScript also regards single quotes as completely different characters from double quotes. That's how we can use quotation marks inside a `string` variable value. So long as we enclose the entire value of the variable in one type of quotes and keep the quoted portion of the string enclosed in a different type of quotes, we are fine. The statements shown in Example 2.6 create `string` variables with quoted text.

EXAMPLE 2.6

Using Quotes Correctly

Part (a)

```
var Joe = 'Joe says, "Go team!" ';
```

When called to display the variable **Joe** in a web page, the text displayed is

```
                    Joe says, "Go team!"
```

Part (b)

```
var Joe = "Joe says, 'Go team!' ";
```

When called to display the variable **Joe** in a web page, the text displayed is

```
                    Joe says, 'Go team!'
```

Note the difference between the examples shown in Parts (a) and (b). Both examples are correct but the display is slightly different. In Part (a), the outer quotes which identify the beginning and end of the value of the variable are single and the inner quotes which are part of the value of the string are double. Therefore, double quotes display in the web page. In Part (b), the outer quotes are double and the inner quotes are single and single quotes appear in the web page. Below, in Part (c), we see an incorrect usage of quotes:

Part (c)

```
var Joe = "Joe says, "Go team!" ";
```

When called to display the variable **Joe** in a web page, the text displayed is

```
                    Joe says,
```

and the program would probably end with an error. In (c), double quotes were incorrectly used to indicate the beginning and end of the string's value as well as to enclose a quoted message as part of the string's value. JavaScript sees the first double quote as the beginning of the variable's value and, as soon as it encounters another double quote (after the comma), it assumes this is the end of the value of the variable. Then, it sees what's left of that statement (Go team!" ";) and, since to JavaScript, this is meaningless, the program will probably stop.

Named Constants

A **named constant** is, in general, a descriptive name given to a value that does not change throughout a program. JavaScript does not have named constants in the strictest sense, but you can declare a variable with a specific value and use it throughout a program. For example, if you write a program for a shopping cart that charges $5.00 for shipping to every customer, regardless of what the customer buys or where the customer lives, you might declare a named constant with the value of $5.00 as follows:

```
var SHIPPING = 5.00;
```

This tool is valuable when writing a program that uses a certain value frequently. By convention, for the variable name, named constants use all uppercase letters and underscores to separate words but this is not required.

The benefit of using a variable for a value that is constant throughout a program is that, should that value have to be changed at another time, it's easy to update. For example, if the company that offers a flat shipping rate decides to increase that rate to $6.00, the programmer simply goes to the single line where the constant was declared and changes it there. From then on, the new value appears everywhere in the program that references a shipping rate.

CHECKPOINT FOR SECTION 2.2

2.5 Explain the difference between a loosely typed language and a strongly typed language. Which one is JavaScript?

2.6 For the following situations, select an appropriate variable name and write variable declarations, including possible initial values:
a) a variable that stores the number of times a user tries to enter a password
b) a variable that stores the value of sales tax on a total purchase
c) a variable that stores the result of a mathematical calculation

2.7 For the following situations, select an appropriate variable name and write variable declarations, including possible initial values:
a) a variable that stores a player's username in an online game
b) a variable that stores a menu selection if the choices are A, B, C, or D
c) a variable that stores a greeting to be displayed when a user enters a website

2.8 You are programming a shopping cart. Create a named constant to hold the value of a 20% discount that is applied to all orders over $100.00.

2.3   Arithmetic Operators and Some Important Functions

The * symbol used to denote multiplication is an **arithmetic operator.** Almost all programming languages use at least four basic arithmetic operators—addition, subtraction, multiplication, and division. Some languages contain other arithmetic operators, such as exponentiation (taking a number to a power) and modulus. In JavaScript, a separate method called pow() is used for exponentiation, but JavaScript does have the modulus operator. Since the modulus operator may be unfamiliar, its description and how it is used is discussed next.

The Modulus Operator

The modulus operator (also called the mod operator) may seem odd at first, but as you start to write programs you will see its many uses. The **modulus operator** returns the remainder after dividing one number by another. In JavaScript, the symbol used to denote the modulus operator is the percent sign (**%**). Examples of the modulus operator are shown in Example 2.7.

Using the Modulus Operator

a) What is 15% 2?
15 divided by 2 = 7 with a remainder of 1 so 15% 2 = 1
This is read as "Fifteen mod 2 equals 1."

b) What is 39% 4?
39 divided by 4 = 9 with a remainder of 3 so 39% 4 = 3
This is read as "Thirty-nine mod 4 equals 3."

c) What is 21% 7?
21 divided by 7 is 3 with no remainder so 21% 7 = 0
This is read as "Twenty-one mod 3 equals 0."

The Hierarchy of Operations

Table 2.1 shows examples of the five arithmetic operators used in JavaScript.

But there's more to doing arithmetic than simply understanding these basic operations. The computer follows the same rules as a calculator; operations are performed in a specific order, based on these rules. We call these rules the **hierarchy of operations** or the **order of operations.** A programmer must understand these rules and write appropriate code; otherwise, the results may be disastrous. For example, imagine you want to calculate a discount offered for an item and then add a shipping cost. Example 2.8 demonstrates what might happen.

TABLE 2.1	Arithmetic Operators		
Operator	**Computer Symbol**		**Example**
Addition	+		2 + 3 = 5
Subtraction	–		7 – 3 = 4
Multiplication	*		5 * 4 = 20
Division	/		12 / 3 = 4
Modulus	%		14 % 4 = 2

EXAMPLE
2.8

When the Rules Are Ignored

Assume that a customer wants to buy a sweater that was originally priced at $100.00 and was discounted by $30.00. The store owner wants to get rid of stock so he decides to offer an additional 40% discount. The cost of a $100.00 item discounted $30.00 is $70.00. Reducing that amount by 40% is calculated by finding 40% of $70.00 and subtracting it from $70.00 or, more simply, finding 60% of $70.00. Mathematically, this can be expressed as follows:

```
0.6 * 100 - 30 = ?
```

When the program executes—or when you enter this into a calculator, the sweater will sell for $30.00. However, 60% of $70.00 is actually $42.00. By ignoring the rules governing the order of operations, the store owner loses a lot of money! Why?

The statement above is missing a set of parentheses. If the programmer had instead coded as follows:

```
0.6 * (100 - 30)
```

the result would have been accurate.

The following rules of arithmetic tell us the order in which arithmetic operations should be performed (i.e., their *hierarchy*):

   1. Perform the operations in parentheses (from the inside out, if there are parentheses within parentheses).
   2. Do multiplications, divisions, and modulus (from left to right if there is more than one).
   3. Do additions and subtractions (from left to right if there is more than one).

Unless you specify something different, the computer will apply the hierarchy of operations to any mathematical expression in a program. The best way to write a mathematical expression is to put parentheses around parts of the expression that you want evaluated together. You will not get an error if you use a set of parentheses where none is needed, but you may get incorrect results if you omit parentheses when they should be included. Examples 2.9 and 2.10 demonstrate how parentheses can make a big difference in the answer to even the simplest mathematical problems.

EXAMPLE
2.9

Using the Hierarchy of Operations

Given the following arithmetic expression: 6 + 8 / 2 * 4

a) Evaluate without parentheses:

```
6 + 8/2 * 4    = 6 + 4 * 4
               = 6 + 16
               = 22
```

b) Evaluate with parentheses:

$$6 + 8/(2 * 4) \quad = 6 + 8/8$$
$$= 6 + 1$$
$$= 7$$

c) Evaluate with different parentheses:

$$(6 + 8)/2 * 4 \quad = 14/2 * 4$$
$$= 7 * 4$$
$$= 28$$

d) Evaluate with two sets of parentheses:

$$(6 + 8)/(2 * 4) = 14/8$$
$$= 1\ 6/8$$
$$= 1.75$$

It's obvious that parentheses can make quite a difference in your results!

EXAMPLE 2.10

Using the Hierarchy of Operations Again

Given the following arithmetic expression: 20 % 3 + 5 * 4 – 3

a) Evaluate without parentheses:

$$20\ \%\ 3 + 5 * 4 - 3 \quad = 2 + 20 - 3$$
$$= 19$$

b) Evaluate with parentheses:

$$20\ \%\ (3 + 5) * 4 - 3 \quad = 20\ \%\ 8 * 4 - 3$$
$$= 4 * 4 - 3$$
$$= 16 - 3$$
$$= 13$$

c) Evaluate with three sets of parentheses:

$$(20\ \%\ 3) + (5 * (4 - 3)) = 2 + (5 * 1)$$
$$= 2 + 5$$
$$= 7$$

The Concatenation Operator

You've learned that there are five mathematical operators used by JavaScript. One of them—the + operator—serves two purposes. It adds numbers and is also used to join strings of text or characters. When acting in this capacity, it is called the **concatenation operator.** For example, if you had variables that stored a user's first name and last name, the concatenation operator could be used to display the person's full name in a web page, as shown in Example 2.11.

EXAMPLE 2.11

Using the Concatenation Operator

In the following short program, the user is prompted to enter a first name, a middle initial, and a last name which are stored in three variables. The concatenation operator, used in conjunction with HTML, displays the user's full name with a dot between the parts of the name. This is one way to create a username for a website or an email address.

```
1.   <html>
2.   <head>
3.       <title>Example 2.11</title>
4.   <script type="text/javascript">
5.       var first = prompt("Enter your first name:", " ");
6.       var middle = prompt("Enter your middle initial:", " ");
7.       var last = prompt("Enter your last name:", " ");
8.       document.write(first + "." + middle + "." + last + "<br />");
9.       document.write(first + " " + middle + ". " + last);
10.  </script>
11.  </head>
```

When executed, if the user enters Joe at the first prompt, M at the second prompt, and Harrison at the third prompt, the following is displayed:

```
Joe.M.Harrison
Joe M. Harrison
```

The concatenation operator, as used on line 8, joins the text from first with a dot and then with middle, another dot, and last. Note that no spaces are displayed on the first line of the output. If you want spaces between variables (as seen in the second line of the output), you must enter them as html, as shown on line 9.

Parsing Integers and Floating Point Numbers

You've learned that one difference between JavaScript and many other programming languages is that JavaScript does not differentiate between integers and floating point numbers when variables are declared. There's something else JavaScript doesn't do. When a user enters a number into a web page prompt, JavaScript takes in that number as text. For you to perform calculations or mathematical operations with that number, you must tell JavaScript that it is a number. There are two important built-in functions that do this: parseInt() and parseFloat(). When a variable name is placed inside the parentheses of these functions, the variable is then changed into an integer or a floating point number. Example 2.12 shows how to use these functions.

EXAMPLE
2.12

Using parseInt()

In the following short program, the user is prompted to enter an integer which will be stored in a variable named number. Then three displays are shown:

```
1.   <html>
2.   <head>
3.       <title>Example 2.12</title>
4.   <script type="text/javascript">
5.       var num = prompt("Enter a number:", 0);
6.       document.write(num + 2 + "<br />" );
7.       document.write((parseInt(num) + 2) + "<br />") ;
8.       document.write((num * 3) + "<br />");
9.   </script>
10.  </head>
```

When executed, if the user enters 7 at the prompt, the following is displayed:

```
72
9
21
```

The display can be explained. Line 5 prompts the user to enter a number. The entry, 7, is stored in the variable **num** as a text value. Thus, when line 6 is executed, the text value of **num** (7) is displayed, then it is concatenated with a 2, and then a line break. The display shows 72.

However, on line 7 the parseInt() function is used to change the data type of **num** to an integer. Now that **num** is an integer, the + operator becomes an addition operator, 2 is added to the value of **num**, and the result, 9, is displayed.

Now that **num** is officially an integer, it can be used as a number on line 8 and, when multipled by 3, the numeric result, 21, is displayed.

Example 2.12 uses the + operator in both its capacities—as an addition operator and as a concatenation operator. Clearly, when used to join to text variables, there is no confusion. JavaScript simply uses + as a concatenation operator and displays the values of the variables, one after the other. But it is up to you, as the programmer, to instruct the program to use + as an addition operator when necessary. You do this by ensuring that your numbers are processed as numbers, using parseInt() and parseFloat() and by enclosing numbers that you want added in parentheses.

Finally, you may be wondering about the difference between parseInt() and parseFloat() since JavaScript does not distinguish between integers and floating point numbers.

Assuming **str** is a string variable:

- parseInt(**str**) finds the first integer in the string (**str**), turns it into an integer value, and returns it. It only returns the first integer found in the string.
- parseFloat(**str**) finds the first floating point number in the string (**str**), turns it into a floating point value, and returns it. Unlike parseInt(), it also recognizes decimals.

If the first character in the string is not a number, both functions return the not-a-number value, NaN. Example 2.13 demonstrates the differences between parseInt() and parseFloat().

EXAMPLE 2.13

parseInt() or parseFloat()?

```
1.   <html>
2.   <head>
3.   <title>Example 2.13</title>
4.   <script type="text/javascript">
5.       var num = prompt("Enter a number:", 0);
6.       document.write("parseInt(): " + parseInt(num)+ "<br />");
7.       document.write("parseFloat(): " + (parseFloat(num)) + "<br />");
```

```
8.   </script>
9.   </head>
```

When executed, if the user enters 7 at the prompt, the following is displayed:

```
parseInt(): 7
parseFloat(): 7
```

However, if the user enters 7.893, the following is displayed:

```
parseInt(): 7
parseFloat(): 7.893
```

If the user enters 7.893Hello!, the text following the last number is ignored and the following is displayed:

```
parseInt(): 7
parseFloat(): 7.893
```

And finally, if the user enters Hello!7.893Hello!, since the first character is not a numeric, the following is displayed:

```
parseInt(): NaN
parseFloat(): NaN
```

If you ask the user for numeric input and you are sure that all you require throughout the program is an integer value, then parseInt() is the function for you. However, this will truncate any decimal part of the user's entry. If you think you may need that decimal part, then use parseFloat().

CHECKPOINT FOR SECTION 2.3 ✔

2.9 Find the value of each of the following expressions:
   a) 14 % 3
   b) 7 % 6
   c) (5 + (11 % 11)) * 5
   d) 8 + 25 % 3

2.10 If X = 2 and Y = 3, give the value of each of the following expressions:
   a) (2 * X - 1) % 2 + Y
   b) X * Y + 10 * X / (7 - Y)
   c) (4 + (12 % Y)) * (X + 1) / Y
   d) 4 * Y / X * 2

2.11 Which of the following shows what the code segment given below will display?
```
var name = "Morris"
var beastie = "cat"
document.write(name + "is a" + beastie + ".");
```
   a) Morrisis acat.
   b) Morris is a cat.

Fix the document.write() statement so it displays the proper spacing between words.

2.12 Describe the two ways the + symbol is used in JavaScript.

2.13 What is the main difference between parseInt() and parseFloat()?

2.14 Imagine you are writing a script to compute the sale cost of items in an online store. Create a script that allows the user to enter the percent of the discount (given as a percentage) and converts the percent to a decimal number. Then, after asking the user to enter the cost of an item, find its sale price and display it.

2.4 Relational Operators

If you were asked to find the address of your friend Marguerita Gonzalez in a list of all students at your school, you would immediately jump to the G's. A computer can't do that. It must compare the required name, letter by letter, to names in the list to find a match. In other words, it would compare Gonzalez to each name and decide if the names were the same. If not, the computer would ask if Gonzalez preceded the name in the comparison or followed it, alphabetically, before making another comparison. To do this, programmers use relational operators, coupled with properties of ASCII code. **Relational operators** allow a computer program to compare two things which can be values, variables, or expressions. But computers can only ask if one thing is larger, smaller, or the same as another. To compare alphabetical text and other keyboard symbols, the computer converts the text to numbers using **ASCII code** and compares the value of those numbers.

ASCII Code

All data, including text and other special characters, are stored in the computer's memory in binary form. These binary representations (sequences of 0s and 1s) can be translated to numbers in our decimal system. Thus, to make use of string variables, a scheme is used to associate each character with a number. The standard correspondence for a basic set of 128 characters is given by the American Standard Code for Information Interchange (ASCII). The acronym ASCII is pronounced "askey."

Under this coding scheme, each character is associated with a number from 0 to 127. For example, the uppercase (capital) letters have codes from 65 ("A") to 90 ("Z"); the digits have codes from 48 ("0") to 57 ("9"); and the blank (the keyboard's spacebar) code is 32. Table 2.2 lists the characters corresponding to ASCII codes from 32 to 127; codes 0 to 31 represent special symbols or actions, such as sounding a beep (ASCII 7) or issuing a carriage return (ASCII 13), and are not shown here.

Thus, a string is stored in the computer's internal memory as ASCII codes for its individual characters. For example, when program code corresponding to

```
var name = "Sam"
```

is executed, the ASCII codes for S, a, and m (83, 97, and 109, respectively) are stored in consecutive memory locations.

TABLE 2.2	The ASCII Codes from 32 to 127				
Code	**Character**	**Code**	**Character**	**Code**	**Character**
32	[blank]	64	@	96	`
33	!	65	A	97	a
34	"	66	B	98	b
35	#	67	C	99	c
36	$	68	D	100	d
37	%	69	E	101	e
38	&	70	F	102	f
39	'	71	G	103	g
40	(	72	H	104	h
41	)	73	I	105	i
42	*	74	J	106	j
43	+	75	K	107	k
44	,	76	L	108	l
45	–	77	M	109	m
46	.	78	N	110	n
47	/	79	O	111	o
48	0	80	P	112	p
49	1	81	Q	113	q
50	2	82	R	114	r
51	3	83	S	115	s
52	4	84	T	116	t
53	5	85	U	117	u
54	6	86	V	118	v
55	7	87	W	119	w
56	8	88	X	120	x
57	9	89	Y	121	y
58	:	90	Z	122	z
59	;	91	[	123	{
60	<	92	\	124	|
61	=	93	]	125	}
62	>	94	^	126	~
63	?	95	_	127	[delete]

Consider the string "31.5" and the real number 31.5. These expressions look similar, but from a programming standpoint, they are quite different:

■ The number 31.5 is stored in memory as the binary equivalent of 31.5. Moreover, since it's a number, it can be added to, subtracted from, divided by, or multiplied by another number.

- The string "31.5" is stored in memory by placing the ASCII codes for 3, 1, ., and 5 in consecutive storage locations.

Relational Operators

Sometimes finding the answer to a question is not as important as asking the right question. If you want to write a program that looks through a long list of names to find one that matches Marguerita Gonzalez, you could check each name on the list, asking the true/false question: "Is this name the same as Marguerita Gonzalez?" This would work but it would be incredibly inefficient and time-consuming. However, if you pick a name from the middle of the list and ask if Marguerita Gonzalez is bigger than this name, using the ASCII representation of the characters in the name, the answer would immediately reduce your work by half. If the answer to the question is true, you have eliminated the first half of the list and if the answer is false, you have eliminated the second half of the list. To ask this type of question, we use relational operators.

There are six relational operators, as listed in Table 2.3. Several of them are clear and uncomplicated but some of them are either specific to programming or have notation that may be unfamiliar. You probably know the **greater than** symbol (>) and the **less than** symbol (<) from math classes, but the other symbols deserve comment.

There are no single symbols on a keyboard to represent the concepts of less **than or equal to** and **greater than or equal to.** These concepts are represented by a combination of symbols: <= represents **less than or equal to** and >= represents **greater than or equal to.**

Similarly, there is no single symbol to represent the concept of **not equal to,** so again, a combination of two symbols is used. In JavaScript, the combination of symbols != represents the **not equal to** operator.

Finally, special attention needs to be paid to the equals sign. In programming, there is a distinction between setting one thing equal to the value of another and asking the question, "Does this thing have the same value as this other thing?" When we assign a value to a variable, we use the equals sign (=). In this case, the equals sign is used as an **assignment operator.** When we compare the value of one thing to another, we mean "Is the value of the thing on the left the same as the value of the thing on the right?" This is called a **comparison operator.** In JavaScript,

TABLE 2.3	**Relational Operators**
Relational Operator	**Definition**
<	Is less than
<=	Is less than or equal to
>	Is greater than
>=	Is greater than or equal to
==	Is equal to (Is same as)
!=	Is not equal to

the symbol == (a double equals sign) is used to compare the value of a variable to another variable, value, or expression.

When you use a mathematical operator in a statement, the result is a new value. For example, 3 + 5 equals 8 and the JavaScript statement myNum = 3 + 5; will put the value 8 into the variable myNum. That's not what happens with relational operators. Relational operators ask a question and the only possible answer to the question is yes or no or, in computer terms, true or false. Example 2.14 demonstrates the use of relational operators.

EXAMPLE 2.14

Using Relational Operators

a) 5 < 3 results in false because 5 is not less than 3.

b) 7 > 6 results in true because 7 is greater than 6.

c) 9 >= 9 results in true because >= asks the question, "Is the thing on the left greater than or equal to the thing on the left?" and 9, while not greater than 9, is equal to 9.

d) 18 != 6 results in true because 18 is not the same as 6.

e) 18 != 18 results in false because 18 is the same as 18 and, therefore, the statement, "18 is not the same as 18" is a false statement.

f) 12 == 12 results in true because 12 is the same as 12.

g) 12 == 45 results in false because 12 is not the same as 45.

Relational operators can be combined with other operators to create more complex conditions and questions. Example 2.15 demonstrates how to combine relational and mathematical operators using variables to represent values.

EXAMPLE 2.15

Using Relational Operators with Variables

For this example, the variables shown have the following values:

W = 2   X = 6   Y = 3   Z = 0

a) W < (X + Y) results in true because 2 is less than (6 + 3).

b) (Y * W) > X results in false because (3 * 2) is 6 and 6 is not greater than 6.

c) (Y + Z) >= (W - Z) results in true because (3 + 0) is greater than (2 - 0).

d) X != (W * Y) results in false because 6 is the same as (2 * 3) so it is false to say these things are not the same.

e) (Z/X) != Y results in true because (0/6) is not the same as 3.

f) (X - (W * Y)) == Z results in true because (6 - (2 * 3)) is the same as 0.

g) X == (X * Z) results in false because 6 is not the same as (6 * 0).

The program shown in Example 2.16 demonstrates the differences between the assignment operator and the comparison operator.

EXAMPLE
2.16

Comparing, Not Assigning

```
1.    <html>
2.    <head>
3.    <title>Example 2.16</title>
4.    <script type="text/javascript">
5.        var yourNumber = 8;
6.        var myNumber = 7;
7.        var answer = myNumber + yourNumber;
8.        document.write("the value of 'answer' is: " + answer + "<br />");
9.        document.write("the value of 'answer > mynumber' is: " ⌐
                    + (answer>myNumber) + "<br />");
10.   </script>
11.   </head>
12.   <body>
13.   </body>
14.   </html>
```

When executed, the following is displayed:

```
The value of 'answer' is 15
The value of 'answer > mynumber' is: true
```

Example 2.17 shows how to use relational operators with characters.

EXAMPLE
2.17

Using Relational Operators with Characters

For this example, the variables shown have the following values:

R = "R"   highA = "A"   lowa = "a"   star = "*"   x = "x"

a) **R** < **highA** results in `false` because uppercase R is 82 in ASCII and uppercase A is 65 in ASCII. 82 is not less than 65.

b) **lowa** > **highA** results in `true` because lowercase a is 97 in ASCII and uppercase A is 65 in ASCII. 97 is greater than 65.

c) **x** >= **star** results in `true` because lowercase x in ASCII is 120 and the asterisk (*) in ASCII is 42. 120 is greater than 42.

d) **highA** != **lowa** results in `true` because the ASCII values of uppercase A (65) and lowercase a (97) are not the same.

e) **R** != **R** results in `false` because the ASCII value of uppercase R is 82. Therefore, to say 82 is not the same as 82 is false.

Example 2.18 shows how to use relational operators with strings.

EXAMPLE
2.18

Using Relational Operators with Strings

For this example, the variables shown have the following values:

kangaroo = "joey"   **car** = "sedan"   **food** = "pie"
tree = "oak"   **boy** = "Joey"   **girl** = "Joan"

a) car < food results in false because the first letter of **car** is lowercase s which is 115 in ASCII and the first letter of food is lowercase p which is 112 in ASCII.

b) car > tree results in true because the first letter of **car** is lowercase s which is 115 in ASCII and the first letter of tree is lowercase o which is 111 in ASCII.

c) girl < boy results in true because the first letter of **girl** is uppercase J which is 74 in ASCII and is exactly the same as the first letter of **boy**. When the first letter of a string on one side of the expression matches the first letter of the string on the other side, the next letter is checked. In this case, the second letter of **girl** and **boy** are also the same. Both are lowercase o's. The next letter is then checked and now the answer is found. The third letter of **girl** is lowercase a (97 in ASCII) and the third letter of **boy** is e (101 in ASCII). Since 97 is less than 101, the statement is true.

d) car <= car results in true because, as we know, this relational operator returns true if either the value on the left is less than the value on the right or if they are the same.

e) kangaroo != boy results in true because, while the letters of each string are the same, the first letter of **kangaroo** is a lowercase j (106 in ASCII) and the first letter of **boy** is uppercase J (74 in ASCII). 106 is not the same as 74 so it is true that these variables do not hold the same values.

f) tree != tree results in false because both values are the same and, therefore, to say they are not the same is false.

CHECKPOINT FOR SECTION 2.4 ✓

2.15 Find the ASCII value of each of the following characters:

   a) Q   b) q   c) /   d) 4   e) &

2.16 If X = 2, Y = 3, and Z = 9, give the value of each of the following expressions:

   a) X > Y   b) Y <= Z   c) Y * Y != Z   d) X == Y

2.17 If K = 4, M = 7, and P = 2, give the value of each of the following expressions:

   a) K > M * P   b) (K * K)/P >= M
   c) K + 2 != K + P   d) M * M == M* (K + 3)

2.18 Describe the difference between the assignment operator (=) and the comparison operator (==).

2.19 If B = "B", b = "b", F = "+", G = "9", and H = "b", give the value of each of the following expressions:

   a) B > b   b) F <= G   c) B != G   d) b == H

2.20 If red = "red", green = "green", gold = "gold", and jewel = "golden", give the value of each of the following expressions:

   a) red > green   b) green <= gold
   c) gold != jewel   d) jewel == green

2.5 Logical Operators and the Conditional Operator

Logical operators are used to create compound conditions (also called complex conditions) from given simple conditions. A **compound condition** allows us to test for more than one thing at a time. For example, if you want to create a game where the user guesses a number between 1 and 100, you must check that the number entered is both greater than or equal to 1 and, at the same time, less than or equal to 100. In this case, both conditions must be true for the number to be valid. Another example is an adventure game that allows the user to achieve a higher level if he or she amasses 100 points or possesses a gold sword. In this case, only one of the two conditions has to be true for the game to proceed. In both examples, logical operators can be used to create these compound conditions—and many more complex ones.

Many logical operators are used by computer programmers and computer engineers. However, for our purposes we will discuss the three basic ones: AND, OR, and NOT.

The AND operator is used to create a compound condition in which *both* conditions must be true for the result to be considered true, as in the example of a guessing game where the number entered must be between 1 and 100, inclusive.

The OR operator is used to create a compound condition in which *either* of the conditions (or both of them) must be true for the result to be considered true, as in the example of an adventure game where there are two ways to proceed to the next level.

The NOT operator, unlike OR and AND, acts upon a single given condition. The resulting condition formed by using NOT is true if and only if the given condition is false. For example, NOT(A < 6) is true if A is not less than 6; it is false if A is less than or equal to 6. Thus, NOT(A < 6) is equivalent to the condition A >= 6. While this may seem to be silly at first, there are many times in programming where the NOT operator is extremely useful.

Logical Operators

Just as the plus sign (+) and the asterisk (*) represent mathematical operators and there are various symbols to represent relational operators, the logical operators are also represented in JavaScript by symbols, as follows:

- && represents the AND operator (two ampersands, with no space between)
- || represents the OR operator (two pipes—the symbol on your keyboard that is accessed by pressing SHIFT and the \ (next to each other with no space)
- ! represents the NOT operator

A Truth Table for the AND, OR, and NOT Operators

The result of any compound condition joined by a logical operator is either true or false. A compound condition involving the AND operator is false in all cases except when both parts of the condition are true. A compound condition involving

TABLE 2.4	Truth Table for Logical Operators			
X	Y	X || Y	X && Y	!X
true	true	true	true	false
true	false	true	false	false
false	true	true	false	true
false	false	false	false	true

the OR operator is true in all cases except when both parts of the condition are false. A condition involving the NOT operator is true if the expression is false and false if the expression is true.

The action of the operators || (OR), && (AND), and! (NOT) can be summarized by the use of a **truth table.** Let X and Y represent simple conditions. Then, for the values of X and Y given in the first two columns of Table 2.4, the resulting truth values of X || Y, X && Y, and !X are listed in the third, fourth, and fifth columns.

Boolean Logic and Boolean Operators

Since computers use a binary system (0s and 1s only), all computer programs must somehow manipulate this system to perform, as we know, incredibly complex tasks. In a computer, a 0 is often equated with false and a 1 with true. **Boolean logic** is a subset of algebra that is used to create true/false statements. Operators that return only true or false, like the AND, OR, and NOT operators, are, therefore, referred to as **boolean operators.** Computer programs perform complex calculations by linking multiple binary (or boolean) statements together.

Example 2.19 demonstrates how these operators work.

EXAMPLE 2.19

Using Logical Operators

For this example, suppose **num** = 1. Is each of the following expressions true or false?

a) ((2 * num) + 1 == 3) && (num > 2)

b) ((2 * num) + 1 == 3) || (num > 2)

c) !(2 * num == 0)

- In (a), the first simple condition is true because (2 * 1 + 1) is the same as 3, but the second condition is false (**num** is not greater than 2). Hence, the compound AND condition is false.

- In (b), the result is true even though, as in (a), one condition is true and one is false. However, the OR operator evaluates the whole expression to true so long as at least one of the two conditions is true.

- In (c), since 2 * **num** = 2, 2 * **num** is not equal to 0. Thus, the condition 2 * **num** = 0 is false, and the given condition is true.

Example 2.20 demonstrates how these operators work.

Using Logical Operators Again

For this example, suppose N = 6, P = 4, and S = 18. Is each of the following expressions true or false?

a) (N * P) > S) && (S > (P + N)

b) (S / N != 3) || (N * P < S)

c) !(2 * N + P == S - 2)

- In (a), both simple conditions are true (6 * 4 is greater than 18 and 18 is greater than 6 + 4). The AND operator evaluates to true when both conditions are true, so this expression evaluates to true.

- In (b), the result is false. Both simple conditions are false (18/6 equals 3 so it is false to say that it does not equal 3 and 6 * 4 is not less than 18). The OR operator evaluates to true so long as at least one of the two conditions is true. However, when both conditions are false, the OR operator evaluates to false.

- In (c), since 2 * 6 + 4 = 16 and 18 – 2 = 16, the expression is true. The NOT operator reverses the result and, therefore, NOT true is false. This expression evaluates to false.

The Order of Operations for Logical Operators

Just as there are rules governing the order in which arithmetic operators are performed, there are also rules about the order in which logical operators are performed. There is no order of operations for relational operators because the results of more than one relational operator in an expression will be the same, regardless of which is performed first.

If an expression has more than one logical operator, the NOT operator is performed first, then the AND operator, and finally the OR operator. In an expression with a combination of arithmetic, relational, and logical operators, if parentheses are present, we perform the operations within parentheses first. In the absence of parentheses, the arithmetic operations are done first (in their usual order), then any relational operation, and finally, NOT, AND, and OR, in that order. This hierarchy of operations is summarized in Table 2.5.

Logical operators allow us to create program code that uses more than a single condition in a decision. A **complex expression** is an expression that combines two or more possible conditions. For example, a business may send out a promotional discount code which can be used if the customer purchases over $50.00 of merchandise. Thus, the discount will only be applied if both conditions are true—the discount code entered by the customer matches the code sent out by the business *and* the purchase amount is over $50.00. The expression, "Is code correct **AND** is purchase amount over $50.00?" is one type of complex expression. Another business may offer customers either free shipping *or* a 10% discount on the purchase amount. The expression, "Do you want free shipping **OR** do you want a 10% discount?" is another type of complex expression.

TABLE 2.5	Hierarchy of Operations
Description	**Symbol**
Arithmetic operators are evaluated first in the order listed.	
First: Parentheses	( )
Second: Exponents	^
Third: Multiplication / Division / Modulus	*, /, %
Fourth: Addition / Subtraction	+ −
Relational operators are evaluated second. All relational operators have the same precedence.	
Less than	<
Less than or equal to	<=
Greater than	>
Greater than or equal to	>=
The same as, equal to	==
Not the same as	!=
Logical Operators are evaluated last in the order listed.	
First: NOT	!
Second: AND	&&
Third: OR	||

Example 2.21 shows how to use the hierarchy of operations with complex expressions.

EXAMPLE 2.21

Using the Hierarchy of Operations with Complex Expressions

Let **Q** = 3 and **R** = 5. Is the following expression true or false?

```
!Q > 3 || R < 3 && Q - R < 0
```

Remembering the hierarchy of operations and, in particular, the fact that among logical operators, ! is performed first, && is second, and || is last, let's insert parentheses to show explicitly the order in which the operations are to be performed:

```
(!(Q > 3)) || ((R < 3) && ((Q - R) < 0))
```

We evaluate the simple conditions first and find that **Q** > 3 is false, **R** < 3 is false, and (**Q** − **R**) < 0 is true. Then, by substituting these values (true or false) into the given expression and performing the logical operations, we arrive at the answer. We can show this with the following evaluation chart:

```
Given:  (!(Q > 3))    ||    ((R < 3)    &&    ((Q - R) < 0))
Step 1: (!(false))    ||    ((false)    &&    (true))
Step 2: true          ||    false
Step 3: true
```

This expression evaluates to true.

The Conditional Operator

JavaScript also contains another operator which works as shorthand for code that we will cover in Chapter 3. The **conditional operator** assigns a value to a variable based on some condition. The conditional operator uses two symbols and takes three operands. It's different enough from the operators we have discussed so far that it merits its own section.

An operand is acted upon by an operator. So far, all operators we have discussed except the NOT operator take two operands. For example:

- 5 + 3: the operator is + and the operands are 5 and 3.
- 16 >= 10: the operator is >= and the operands are 16 and 10.
- true && false: the operator is && and the operands are true and false.
- !true: the operator is ! and the single operand is true.

The conditional operator is written like this:

```
variableName = (condition) ? value1 : value2
```

An example might make this easier to understand. Imagine you want to test whether a character in a game has enough points to win a battle. If the character has at least 100 points, you want to set a variable called **battle** to "win" but if the character has fewer than 100 points, you want to set **battle** to "lose". Let's assume the character's points are stored in a variable named **points**. Then the conditional operator would be used as follows:

```
battle = (points >= 100) ? "win" : "lose";
```

This statement says, in words, "If the value of **points** is greater than or equal to 100, set **battle** to "win" but if **points** is less than 100, set **battle** to "lose".

Thus, the conditional operator works like this: The condition you are testing goes inside the parentheses followed by **?**. The next value is what will be stored in the variable on the left side if the condition is true. A colon (**:**) separates this value from the next value. The second value is what will be stored in the variable if the condition is false.

Example 2.22 demonstrates how to use the conditional operator.

EXAMPLE
2.22

Using the Conditional Operator

Imagine you are writing a program for an online business that provides an access code for free shipping to special customers. You want to check if users enter the correct code (FREESHIP). If the code is entered correctly, a message will tell the user he or she gets free shipping; otherwise the message will say "invalid code". The JavaScript code for this program snippet is as follows:

```
1.  <html>
2.  <head>
3.  <title>Example 2.22</title>
4.  <script type="text/javascript">
5.      var shipCode = prompt("Enter your access code:", " ");
6.      var message = " ";
```

```
7.          message = (shipCode == "FREESHIP")?"You are eligible ↵
                       for free shipping!":"invalid code";
8.          document.write(message);
9.      </script>
10.     </head>
11.     <body>
12.     </body>
13.     </html>
```

The conditional operator is used on line 7. The test condition is whether or not what is stored in **shipCode** is exactly the same as FREESHIP. If the answer to the condition is true the value stored in **message** will be "You are eligible for free shipping!"; if it is false the value stored in **message** will be "invalid code".

CHECKPOINT FOR SECTION 2.5 ✓

2.21 Replace the blank by one of the following words: arithmetic, relational, or logical.

   a) <= is a(n) _____ operator.

   b) + is a(n) _____ operator.

   c) && is a(n) _____ operator.

2.22 Let X = 1 and let Y= 2. Indicate whether each of the following expressions is true or false.

   a) X >= X || Y >= X

   b) X > X && Y > X

   c) X > Y || X > 0 && Y < 0

   d) !(! X == 0 && ! Y == 0)

2.23 Describe the function of each part of the conditional operator:

        variableName = (condition) ? value1 : value2

2.24 If K = 4, M = 7, and P = 2, what will be stored in **result**?

        result = (K > 12)? M : P;

2.25 If **myName** = "Lizzie", **yourName** = "Jimmy", what will be stored in **message** if the user enters Jimmy at the prompt.

        var name = prompt("Enter your name:", " ");
        var message = " ";
        message = (name == "Jimmy")? myName : yourName;

2.6 Putting It to Work

At this point, we will begin to develop the two websites discussed earlier in the text. Greg's Gambits is a game site. We will develop a game for the site here, and you will have a chance to create your own game in the exercises at the end of the chapter. Carla's Classroom is a teaching site for young children. We will develop a teaching unit for the site here, and you will have a chance to create your own unit in the end-of-chapter exercises.

Greg's Gambits: Creating Your Own Story

You probably played Mad Libs as a child—or perhaps as an adult. The game asks you to come up with words that are inserted into a story and, when read aloud, can be very funny. The players are asked to provide words by type—nouns, verbs, adjectives, adverbs, proper names, and more. Here, we will create a game that will be very similar. We'll call it Greg's Tales.

Developing the Program

To begin, we will create a tale (our story) and then identify the words in the tale that we want the user to replace with his/her own words. As an exercise, you can create your own tale, but for now we will use the following:

```
Once upon a time, about XXXXX (number) years ago, there was a XXXXX (boy/girl)
named XXXXX (name). XXXXX (name) lived in a small cabin in the woods just
outside XXXXX (city) limits. XXXXX (name) enjoyed walking in the woods every
day until . . . One day XXXXX (he/she) came upon a XXXXX (monster) sitting on
a log eating a XXXXX (food). The XXXXX (monster) jumped up, spilling his XXXXX
(drink). XXXXX (name) ran home as fast as XXXXX (he/she) could but the XXXXX
(monster) followed and . . . XXXXX (ending).
```

To code this game, we must decide on the variables we will use and the steps we should take to achieve the final goal. In very general pseudocode, this would be as follows:

- Declare variables
- Identify the part of speech for each variable (how the word will be described to the player)
- Request input for variables
- Output the story

We will add to this as we proceed. We will start with the variables needed and how we will describe these variables to the player.

Variable Name	Variable Type	Description
numYears	numeric	Enter a number > 0
gender	string	Is the person a boy or girl?
name	string	Proper name
city	string	City name
pronoun	string	Not entered by user—the pronoun depends on gender
monster	string	Type of monster
food	string	Type of food
drink	string	Type of drink

While we're in a creative mode, let's identify a few possible endings:

- Ending 1: "The XXXXX (monster) and XXXXX (name) became best friends and lived in XXXXX (name's) house happily ever after."

- Ending 2: "The XXXXX (monster) overpowered XXXXX (name) and gobbled down all the XXXXX (food) and XXXXX (drink) in XXXXX (name's) refrigerator."
- Ending 3: "XXXXX (name) screamed mean things at the XXXXX (monster), causing the XXXXX (monster) to turn and run back to the woods, never to be seen again."

Writing the Code

This page will be part of the Greg's Gambits site. We will create a new web page for each game. We will start with a simple web page and begin by declaring the necessary variables and displaying the game title and an explanation. The file corresponding to this code is named gregs_tales.html and is available in the Student Data Files.

```
1.  <!DOCTYPE html PUBLIC "-//W3C//DTD XHTML 1.0 Transitional//EN" ↵
    "http://www.w3.org/TR/xhtml1/DTD/xhtml1-transitional.dtd">
2.  <html xmlns="http://www.w3.org/1999/xhtml" lang="en" xml:lang="en">
3.  <head>
4.  <title>Greg's Gambits | Greg's Tales</title>
5.  <link href="greg.css" rel="stylesheet" type="text/css" />
6.  <script type="text/javascript">
7.  function startGame()
8.  {
9.      var gender = "boy";
10.     var city = " ";
11.     var monster = " ";
12.     var food = " ";
13.     var drink = " ";
14. }
15. </script>
16. </head>
17. <body>
18. <div id="container">
19. <img src="../images/superhero.jpg" class="floatleft" />
20. <h1><em>Greg's Tales</em></h1>
21. <h3>For this game, you will create a story by entering words as prompted. ↵
        The story will change each time you run this game, as you enter ↵
        different words.</h3>
22. <div id="nav">
23. <p><a href="index.html">Home</a>
24. <a href="greg.html">About Greg</a>
25. <a href="play_games.html">Play a Game</a>
26. <a href="sign.html">Sign In</a>
27. <a href="contact.html">Contact Us</a></p>
28. </div>
29. <div id="content">
30. <input type="button" value = "click to begin" onclick="startGame()" />
31. </div>
32. <div id="footer">Copyright &copy; 2013 Greg's Gambits<br />↵
        <a href="mailto:yourfirstname@yourlastname.com">↵
        yourfirstname@yourlastname.com</a></div>
33. </div>
34. </body>
35. </html>
```

The JavaScript and HTML code listed here shows just the beginning of the game. The web page itself must have a way for the user to begin the game. Note that on line 30, a button is displayed in the content area of the page. When the user clicks the button, something must happen. In this case, the caption on the button is its value ("click to begin") and when the user clicks, the JavaScript function named startGame() is called. This is an important piece of writing JavaScript—communicating between the program code and the web page. As soon as the button is clicked, the program control jumps to line 7 and the function, startGame(), begins. The code inside the curly brackets (currently lines 8 through 14) is executed. Of course, so far, the function does nothing more than initialize the variables we need. We will add to that code. You can add the following code to the gregs_tales.html file yourself and watch the game unfold.

The web page now looks like this:

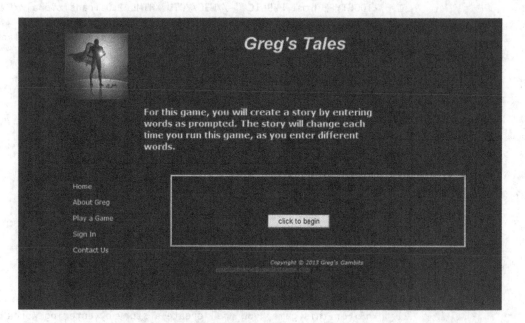

Next, we'll add the prompts. These will be placed after line 8. The **pronoun** variable will depend on the **gender** variable:

```
numYears = prompt("Enter a number greater than 0: ");
gender = prompt("Is the story about a boy or a girl? ");
name = prompt("Enter the hero's name: ");
city = prompt("Enter the name of a city: ");
monster = prompt("Enter a type of monster: ");
food = prompt("Enter a food you like: ");
drink = prompt("Enter a drink you like: ");
```

Let's deal with the **gender** variable. We need to account for the fact that a user might enter Boy, BOY, or boy, or any of many possibilities or even misspelled words. The same is true for girl. One thing we should be able to count on, though, is that if the player wants the hero of the story to be a boy, the first character of the entry will be b or B and if the user wants the hero to be a girl, the first character will be g or G. Later in the text, you will learn to account for all possible entries, but for now we will simply assume that the player has entered a value that either begins with b or g. Also, if the player selects a boy, the **pronoun** variable should be set to "he" and if the player selects a girl, the **pronoun** variable should be set to "she". We can code for that now, using the conditional operator. This code will test what the user enters for **gender** so we will put it below the prompt for **gender**. If the first character of the contents of **gender** is b or B, **gender** will be set to "boy" and **pronoun** will be set to "he". If the first character of **gender** is g or G, **gender** will be set to "girl" and **pronoun** will be set to "she".

The charAt() function

The first thing we must determine is whether the first character of **gender** is b or g. We can use a built-in JavaScript function to do this. The charAt() function returns the character at any specified location in a string. We want the character at the first location. The syntax of this function is as follows:

```
string.charAt(index)
```

The string we are interested in is **gender**. "**index**" refers to the location of the character of interest and, for us, the **index** is the first character in the string which is in location 0. We need a variable to hold the value that this function returns so we will use a new variable named **letter**. We store the result of the charAt() function in **letter**. Then we can use the conditional operator to set **gender** to either "boy" or "girl", depending on the value of **letter**. The code looks like this:

```
var letter = gender.charAt(0);
gender = (letter == "b" || letter == "B")? "boy" : "girl";
```

Next, we can use the conditional operator to set the variable pronoun to "he" or "she", depending on the status of gender, as follows:

```
pronoun = (gender == "boy")? "he" : "she";
```

Finishing the Code

We must add code to display the story, using the player's words, and the three possible endings. This code will go immediately after the last prompt, immediately before the start_game() function's ending brace:

```
document.getElementById("content").innerHTML = ("Once upon a time, about "
    + numYears + " years ago, there was a " + gender + " named " + name + ".
    " + name + " lived in a small cabin in the woods just outside " + city +
    " limits.</p><p>" + name + " enjoyed walking in the woods every day
    until...One day " + pronoun + " came upon a " + monster + " sitting
    on a log eating a " + food + ".</p><p>The " + monster + " jumped up,
    spilling his " + drink + ". " + name + " ran home as fast as " +
    pronoun + " could but the " + monster + " followed and...</p><h3>What
    happened? You decide!</h3><p>Ending 1: The " + monster + " and " + name +
    " became best friends and lived in " + name + "'s house happily ever
    after.</p><p>Ending 2: The " + monster + " overpowered " + name +
    " and gobbled down all the " + food + " and " + drink + " in " + name +
    "'s refrigerator.</p> <p>Ending 3: " + name + " screamed mean things at
    the " + monster + ", causing the " + monster + " to turn and run back to
    the woods, never to be seen again.</p>");
```

Now we can put it all together:

```
1.   <!DOCTYPE html PUBLIC "-//W3C//DTD XHTML 1.0 Transitional//EN" ↵
         "http://www.w3.org/TR/xhtml1/DTD/xhtml1-transitional.dtd">
2.   <html xmlns="http://www.w3.org/1999/xhtml" lang="en" xml:lang="en">
3.   <head>
4.   <title>Greg's Gambits | Greg's Tales</title>
5.   <link href="greg.css" rel="stylesheet" type="text/css" />
6.   <script type="text/javascript">
7.   function startGame()
8.   {
9.       var gender = "boy";
10.      var city = " ";
11.      var monster = " ";
12.      var food = " ";
13.      var drink = " ";
14.      numYears = prompt("Enter a number greater than 0: ");
15.      gender = prompt("Is the story about a boy or a girl? ");
16.      letter = gender.charAt(0);
17.      gender = (letter == "b" || letter == "B")?"boy":"girl";
18.      pronoun = (gender == "boy")?"he":"she";
19.      name = prompt("Enter the hero's name: ");
20.      city = prompt("Enter the name of a city: ");
21.      monster = prompt("Enter a type of monster: ");
22.      food = prompt("Enter a food you like: ");
23.      drink = prompt("Enter a drink you like: ");
24.      document.getElementById("content").innerHTML = ("Once upon a time, ↵
             about " + numYears + " years ago, there was a " + gender + ↵
             " named " + name + ". " + name + " lived in a small cabin in ↵
             the woods just outside " + city + " limits.</p> <p>" + name + ↵
             " enjoyed walking in the woods every day until...One day " ↵
             + pronoun + " came upon a " + monster + " sitting on a log ↵
             eating a " + food + ".</p> <p>The " + monster + " jumped up, ↵
             spilling his " + drink + ". " + name + " ran home as fast as " ↵
             + pronoun + " could but the " + monster + " followed and...</p> ↵
             <h3>What happened? You decide! </h3> <p>Ending 1: The " + ↵
             monster + " and " + name + " became best friends and lived in " ↵
             + name + "'s house happily ever after.</p> <p>Ending 2: The "↵
             + monster + " overpowered " + name + " and gobbled down all the " ↵
             + food + " and " + drink + " in " + name + "'s refrigerator.</p> ↵
             <p>Ending 3: " + name + " screamed mean things at the " + monster ↵
             + ", causing the " + monster + " to turn and run back to the ↵
             woods, never to be seen again.</p>");
25.  }
26.  </script>
27.  </head>
28.  <body>
29.  <div id="container">
30.  <img src="../images/superhero.jpg" class="floatleft" />
31.  <h1><em>Greg's Tales</em></h1>
32.  <h3>For this game, you will create a story by entering words as prompted. ↵
         The story will change each time you run this game, as you enter ↵
         different words.</h3>
33.  <div id="nav">
```

```
34.            <p><a href="index.html">Home</a>
35.            <a href="greg.html">About Greg</a>
36.            <a href="play_games.html">Play a Game</a>
37.            <a href="sign.html">Sign In</a>
38.            <a href="contact.html">Contact Us</a></p>
39.    </div>
40.    <div id="content">
41.            <p> </p>
42.            <input type="button" value = "click to begin" onclick="startGame()" />
43.    </div>
44.    <div id="footer">Copyright &copy; 2013 Greg's Gambits<br />
45.    <a href="mailto:yourfirstname@yourlastname.com"> ↵
                    yourfirstname@yourlastname.com</a>
46.    </div>
47.    </div>
48.    </body>
49.    </html>
```

Here are some sample outputs, given the inputs shown:

input:

numYears = 100, **gender** = boy, **name** = Joey, **city** = Paris, **monster** = troll, **food** = lasagna, **drink** = iced tea

output:

> Once upon a time, about 100 years ago, there was a boy named Joey. Joey lived in a small cabin in the woods just outside Paris limits.
>
> Joey enjoyed walking in the woods every day until... One day he came upon a troll sitting on a log eating a lasagna.
>
> The troll jumped up, spilling his iced tea. Joey ran home as fast as he could but the troll followed and ...
>
> **What happened? You decide!**
>
> Ending 1: The troll and Joey became best friends and lived in Joey's house happily ever after.
>
> Ending 2: The troll overpowered Joey and gobbled down all the lasagna and iced tea in Joey's refrigerator.
>
> Ending 3: Joey screamed mean things at the troll, causing the troll to turn and run back to the woods, never to be seen again.

input:

numYears = 500, **gender** = girl, **name** = Pamela, **city** = Chicago, **monster** = dragon, **food** = sushi, **drink** = lemonade output:

> Once upon a time, about 500 years ago, there was a girl named Pamela. Pamela lived in a small cabin in the woods just outside Chicago limits.
>
> Pamela enjoyed walking in the woods every day until... One day she came upon a dragon sitting on a log eating a sushi.
>
> The dragon jumped up, spilling his lemonade. Pamela ran home as fast as she could but the dragon followed and ...
>
> **What happened? You decide!**
>
> Ending 1: The dragon and Pamela became best friends and lived in Pamela's house happily ever after.
>
> Ending 2: The dragon overpowered Pamela and gobbled down all the sushi and lemonade in Pamela's refrigerator.
>
> Ending 3: Pamela screamed mean things at the dragon, causing the dragon to turn and run back to the woods, never to be seen again.

Carla's Classroom: A Spelling Lesson

Carla is an elementary school teacher who has commissioned you to create exercises for her class. At this point, although your programming skills are limited, you can develop some excellent exercises for young children. In this chapter, you will create a spelling test with a specific list of words; later in the text, you will learn how to enhance the test by allowing Carla to use any spelling words she wants. We'll call this exercise An Appetite for Spelling.

Developing the Program

We want to create a web page that presents students with a short spelling test. Before we begin to write the JavaScript code, we should design the page. We want a title and a brief explanation of the page. We want students to spell some words. But, because we can't ask them to spell a word if we show it to them, we'll need to represent each word with an image. For our purposes, we'll use pictures of food and, for this example, we will use five words. You can add more words later or, when you understand loops, you can enhance your project by allowing Carla to enter as many or as few words as she wants. Possible food words are avocado, bananas, celery, lemonade, and onions. Images of these foods are provided in the Student Data Files, or you can use your own images if you prefer.

To code this program, we must decide how we want the images, questions, and results displayed on the web page as well as which variables we will use and the steps we should take to achieve our final goal. General pseudocode for this program follows:

1. Explain the purpose of the program

2. Declare variables

3. Show a picture of a food

4. Request input—the spelling of the food

5. Check to see if the word is spelled correctly

6. Output the result (correct or incorrect)

7. Repeat Steps 3–6 for all the words

We will add to this as we proceed. First, we will determine the variables we need and how we will describe these variables to the player:

Variable Name	Variable Type	Description
word1	string	Name of a food
result1	string	Spelling is correct or incorrect

We need to display a food image and have the student, when ready, enter the spelling. Then we need to display a message stating whether the spelling is correct or incorrect. To accomplish this, we will use one button that the student will press when ready to answer the question and another button that the student will press to see if the answer is correct.

We will start with the web page. The following HTML code simply shows the web page with the first food displayed and the first question. You can find this page in the Student Data Files and add code as we progress to see the page as it actually works.

```
1.   <!DOCTYPE html PUBLIC "-//W3C//DTD XHTML 1.0 Transitional//EN" ↵
         "http://www.w3.org/TR/xhtml1/DTD/xhtml1-transitional.dtd">
2.   <html xmlns="http://www.w3.org/1999/xhtml" lang="en" xml:lang="en">
3.   <head>
4.   <title>Carla's Classroom | An Appetite for Spelling</title>
5.   <link href="carla.css" rel="stylesheet" type="text/css" />
6.   </head>
7.   <body>
8.   <div id="container">
9.       <img src="../images/write2.JPG" class="floatleft" />
10.      <h1><em>An Appetite for Spelling </em></h1>
11.      <p> </p>
12.      <div align="left">
13.      <blockquote>
14.          <p><a href="index.html"><img src =
                  "../images/owl_button.jpg"/>Home</a>
15.          <a href="carla.html"><img src = ↵
                  "../images/carla_button.jpg"/>Meet Carla</a>
16.          <a href="reading.html"><img src = ↵
                  "../images/read_button.jpg"/>Reading</a>
17.          <a href="writing.html"><img src =↵
                  "../images/write_button.jpg"/>Writing</a>
```

```
18.              <a href="math.html"><img src = ↵
                     "../images/arith_button.jpg" />Arithmetic</a><br />
19.          </p>
20.  </blockquote>
21.  </div>
22.  <div id="content">
23.  <p>For this exercise you will be shown some pictures and, for each ↵
             picture you will be asked to spell the word that describes ↵
             the picture. Type your answers in all lowercase letters.</p>
24.  <p>Question 1: What is this? <img src="../images/avocado.jpg"/></p>
25.  </div>
26.  <div id="footer">
27.      <h3>*Carla's Motto:Never miss a chance to teach -- and to learn!</h3>
28.  </div>
29.  </div>
30.  </body>
31.  </html>
```

The resulting output looks like this:

We need to add one button that allows the student to enter the answer and another button that allows the student to check the answer. The code for the buttons is simply this:

```
<input type="button" onclick = " " value="answer Question 1" />
<input type="button" onclick = " " value="check answer" />
```

The value attribute gives the text that will be displayed on the button. However, these buttons do not actually do anything. We want the first button, when clicked, to display a prompt box that will allow the student to enter the answer and the second button, when clicked, to display a message that will state whether or not the answer is correct. To achieve these things, we will use a function.

Functions

Functions play a significant role in any programming language. In languages other than JavaScript, it's possible to write some fairly complex programs without using functions that you create yourself. However, because of the nature of JavaScript, you will be required to use functions first (now) and understand their full impact and how to use them in more complex ways later. An entire chapter is devoted to functions (see Chapter 7).

In general terms, we need to use functions because web pages call on JavaScript code and JavaScript code sends information back to the web page. We put the code inside a function between the `<script></script>` tags and the web page uses the function's name to identify which part of the JavaScript code to execute. We used this concept in the `Greg's Tales` page when we called on the `startGame()` function.

In this situation, when the student clicks the button to answer the question, the JavaScript code that prompts for the answer must be called. After entering an answer, the student can click on the second button to check if the answer was correct. When the student clicks either button, the corresponding `onclick` event will call a JavaScript function that we will write. In the case of the first button, the function will prompt the student for the spelling of the word and check to see if the student spelled the word correctly. In the case of the second button, the `onclick` event will call on a function that will display whether or not the student's response is correct.

The `showPrompt1()` and `showResult1()` functions

We will name our first function `showPrompt1()`. When this function is called, two things should happen. The student should be prompted for an answer and the answer should be checked for accuracy. The code for these events is not difficult:

```
word1 = prompt("Enter your answer");
```

This line of code simply creates a prompt that asks the student to enter the spelling of the word and stores that answer in the variable **word1**.

To check the accuracy of the answer we can use the conditional operator as follows:

```
result1 = (word1 == "avocado")? "You're right!":"Sorry, incorrect";
```

We need to place this code inside our function. The format for creating a function in JavaScript is as follows:

```
function nameOfFunction()
    {
            JavaScript statements to be executed
    }
```

The word `function` is a keyword (like `var`) and indicates that this is a function. Some functions require arguments (values placed inside the parentheses) and some don't. For now, we don't need to put anything inside the parentheses of the two functions we are creating. All the statements that will be executed when the function is called are placed inside curly brackets. Thus, the following is the complete code for the function we are creating now to get the answer and check it:

```
function showPrompt1()
{
    word1 = prompt("Enter your answer");
    result = (word1 == "avocado") ? "You're right!" : "Sorry, that's incorrect";
}
```

Once we have created a function, to call that function we simply use its name. We add that to the onclick event in our button:

```
<input type="button" onclick = "showPrompt1()" value="answer Q. 1" />
```

The second button on the web page tells the student to click to see if the answer is correct. Therefore, once clicked, this button should call a function that will display the result of the spelling. That result has been determined previously in the showPrompt1() function and has been stored in the variable named **result1**. We can create a function named showResult1() which will display the result using an alert. The code for this function is as follows:

```
function showResult1()
{
    alert(result);
}
```

We call this function by inserting its name in the onclick event for the corresponding button:

```
<input type="button" onclick="showResult1()" value="check answer"/>
```

Putting It Together

The JavaScript code, placed in the <head> section, is shown below. The code for the buttons, placed in the <body> of the page, just below the Question, is also shown:

```
1.    <!DOCTYPE html PUBLIC "-//W3C//DTD XHTML 1.0 Transitional//EN" ↵
          "http://www.w3.org/TR/xhtml1/DTD/xhtml1-transitional.dtd">
2.    <html xmlns="http://www.w3.org/1999/xhtml" lang="en" xml:lang="en">
3.    <head>
4.    <title>Carla's Classroom | An Appetite for Spelling</title>
5.    <link href="carla.css" rel="stylesheet" type="text/css" />
4.      <script type="text/javascript">
5.      //declare and initialize variables
6.      var word1 = "avocado";
7.      var result = " ";
8.      // function to prompt for answer to Question 1
9.      function showPrompt1()
10.     {
11.         word1 = prompt("Enter your answer");
12.         result = (word1 == "avocado") ? "You're right!" : ↵
                "Sorry, that's incorrect";
13.     }
14.     //function to show result of answer
15.     function showResult1()
16.     {
```

```
17.          alert(result);
18.      }
19.      </script>
20.      . . . the rest of the head section code goes here
21.      </head>
22.      <body>
23.      <h2> An Appetite for Spelling </h2>
24.      . . . other HTML script goes here
25.      <p>For this exercise you will be shown some pictures and, for each ⏎
             picture you will be asked to spell the word that described the ⏎
             picture. Type your answers in all lowercase letters.</p>
26.      <p>Question 1: What is this? <img src="../images/avocado.jpg"/> </p>
27.      <input type="button" onclick="showPrompt1()" value="answer Q. 1" />
28.      <input type="button" onclick="showResult1()" value="check answer" />
29.      </div>
30.      . . . etc.
31.      </body>
32.      </html>
```

and now it looks like this:

Finishing Up

So far, the site tests the spelling of one word. But adding four more words or even forty more words is very simple. Later you will learn how to use the repetition structure to make this code more efficient, but for now we can simply copy and paste the code we use for one spelling word as many times as we want for more spelling words. It was with this in mind that the variables and functions were named with the number 1 at the end. By changing the 1 to 2 or 3 or 4 or 5, we can reuse the code. The finished website which tests all five spelling words is given here:

```
1.   <!DOCTYPE html PUBLIC "-//W3C//DTD XHTML 1.0 Transitional//EN" ↵
         "http://www.w3.org/TR/xhtml1/DTD/xhtml1-transitional.dtd">
2.   <html xmlns="http://www.w3.org/1999/xhtml" lang="en" xml:lang="en">
3.   <head>
4.   <title>Carla's Classroom | An Appetite for Spelling</title>
5.   <link href="carla.css" rel="stylesheet" type="text/css" />
6.   <script type="text/javascript">
7.   //declare and initialize variables
8.   var word1 = "avocado";
9.   var word2 = "bananas";
10.  var word3 = "celery";
11.  var word4 = "lemonade";
12.  var word5 = "onions";
13.  var result = " ";
14.  // Question 1
15.  function showPrompt1()
16.  {
17.      word1 = prompt("Enter your answer");
18.      result = (word1 == "avocado")? "You're right!" : ↵
             "Sorry, that's incorrect";
19.  }
20.  function showResult1()
21.  {
22.      alert(result);
23.  }
24.  //Question 2
25.  function showPrompt2()
26.  {
27.      word2 = prompt("Enter your answer");
28.      result = (word2 == "bananas")? "You're right!" :↵
             "Sorry, that's incorrect";
29.  }
30.  function showResult2()
31.  {
32.      alert(result);
33.  }
34.  //Question 3
35.  function showPrompt3()
36.  {
37.      word3 = prompt("Enter your answer");
38.      result = (word3 == "celery")? "You're right!" : ↵
             "Sorry, that's incorrect";
39.  }
40.  function showResult3()
41.  {
42.      alert(result);
43.  }
44.  //Question 4
45.  function showPrompt4()
46.  {
47.      word4 = prompt("Enter your answer");
48.      result = (word4 == "lemonade")? "You're right!" :↵
             "Sorry, that's incorrect";
49.  }
50.  function showResult4()
```

```
51.  {
52.      alert(result);
53.  }
54.  //Question 5
55.  function showPrompt5()
56.  {
57.      word5 = prompt("Enter your answer");
58.      result = (word5 == "onions")? "You're right!" :↵
             "Sorry, that's incorrect";
59.  }
60.  function showResult5()
61.  {
62.      alert(result);
63.  }
64.  </script>
65.  </head>
66.  <body>
67.  <div id="container">
68.  <img src="../images/write2.JPG" class="floatleft" />
69.  <h1><em>An Appetite for Spelling </em></h1>
70.  <div align="left">
71.  <blockquote>
72.      <p><a href="index.html"><img src = ↵
             "../images/owl_button.jpg"/>Home</a>
73.      <a href="carla.html"> <img src = ↵
             "../images/carla_button.jpg"/>Meet Carla</a>
74.      <a href="reading.html"><img src = ↵
             "../images/read_button.jpg"/>Reading</a>
75.      <a href="writing.html"> <img src =↵
             "../images/write_button.jpg"/>Writing</a>
76.      <a href="math.html"><img src = ↵
             "../images/arith_button.jpg" />Arithmetic</a><br />
77.      </p>
78.  </blockquote>
79.  </div>
80.  <div id="content">
81.  <p>For this exercise you will be shown some pictures and, for each ↵
             picture you will be asked to spell the word that describes ↵
             the picture. Type your answers in all lowercase letters.</p>
82.  <p>Question 1: What is this? <img src="../images/avocado.jpg"/> </p>
83.  <input type="button" onclick="showPrompt1()" value="answer Q. 1" />
83.  <input type="button" onclick="showResult1()" value="check answer" />
84.  <p>Question 2: What's this? <img src="../images/bananas.jpg" /></p>
85.  <input type="button" onclick="showPrompt2()" value="answer Q. 2" />
86.  <input type="button" onclick="showResult2()" value="check answer" />
87.  <p>Question 3: What's this? <img src="../images/celery.jpg" /></p>
88.  <input type="button" onclick="showPrompt3()" value="answer Q. 3" />
89.  <input type="button" onclick="showResult3()" value="check answer" />
90.  <p>Question 4: What's this? <img src="../images/lemonade.jpg" /></p>
91.  <input type="button" onclick="showPrompt4()" value="answer Q. 4" />
92.  <input type="button" onclick="showResult4()" value="check answer" />
93.  <p>Question 5: What's this? <img src="../images/onions.jpg" /></p>
94.  <input type="button" onclick="showPrompt5()" value="answer Q. 5" />
96.  <input type="button" onclick="showResult5()" value="check answer" />
97.  </div>
98.  <div id="footer">
99.  <h3>*Carla's Motto: Never miss a chance to teach -- and to learn!</h3>
100. </div>
```

```
101.    </div>
102.    </body>
103.    </html>
```

Here are some sample outputs, given the inputs shown:

input:

Clicked answer Q.1, entered avacada, clicked OK, and then clicked check answer:

output:

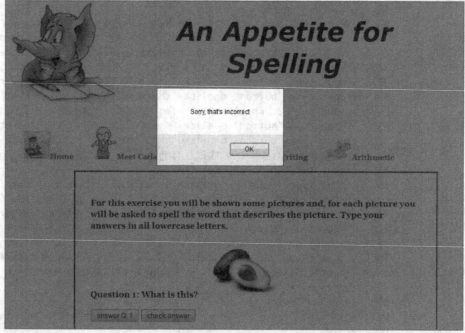

input:

Clicked answer Q.3, entered celery, clicked OK, and then clicked checkanswer:

output:

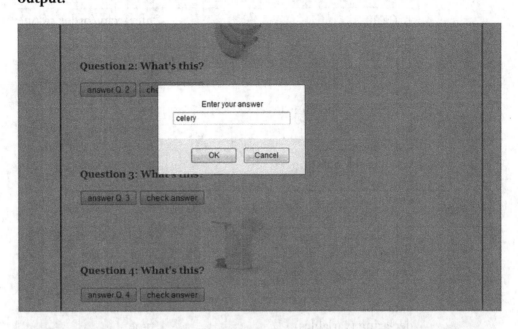

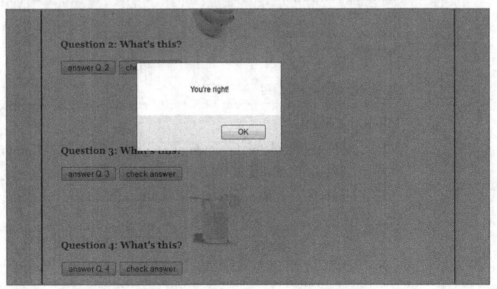

Chapter Review and Exercises

Key Terms

! (NOT)	hierarchy/order of operations
&& (AND)	initial value
|| (OR)	integers
arithmetic operator	keyword
ASCII code	logical operators
assignment operator	loosely typed language
boolean logic	modulus operator
boolean operators	named constant
CamelBack notation	numeric data type
characters	operations
charAt()	parseFloat()
comparison operator	parseInt()
complex/compound expressions	relational operator
compound condition	static typing
concatenation operator	strings
conditional operator	strongly typed language
data type	truth table
declaring (variables)	type
dynamic typing	var
floating point numbers	variable
function	

Review Exercises

Fill in the Blank

1. A variable is actually the name of a _____ in the computer's memory.

2. To declare a variable in JavaScript, you use the keyword _____.

3. A language that checks the type of a variable during runtime uses _____ typing.

4. The _____ operator can join strings or characters.

5. To assign a value to a variable based on a specific condition, you can use the _____ operator.

True or False

6. T/F A variable name can begin with a number.

7. T/F If you have more than one variable of the same type, you can declare all of them in a single statement.

8. T/F JavaScript allows the use of either double or single quotes to enclose the value of the text in a string variable.

9. T/F While mathematical operations must be done following the rules of the hierarchy of operations, logical operators have no such rules.

10. T/F Relational operators can be used to help put names in alphabetical order.

11. T/F If **X** = 0, determine whether each of the following expressions is true or false.
    a) `X >= 0`
    b) `2 * X + 1 != 1`

12. T/F If **boy** = "Adam", determine whether each of the following expressions is true or false.
    a) `boy == "adam"`
    b) `boy != "Adam"`
    c) `boy < "Ann"`
    d) `boy >= "Adalaide"`

13. T/F If **num1** = 1 and **num2** = 2, determine whether each of the following expressions is true or false.
    a) `(num1 == 1) || (num2 == 2) && (num1 == num2)`
    b) `((num1 == 1) || (num2 == 2)) && (num1 == num2)`
    c) `!(num1 == 1) && !(num2 == 2)`
    d) `!(num1 == 1) || !(num2 == 2)`

14. T/F Use the ASCII table to determine if the following statement is true or false:

    `"**?" < "***"`

15. T/F Use the ASCII table to determine if the following statement is true or false:

    `"** " < "***"`

Short Answer

16. Give the ASCII code for each of the following characters:
    a) "&"
    b) "2"
    c) " "

17. Given that **N** is a numeric variable, write expressions equivalent to the following without using the NOT operator:
    a) `!(N > 0)`
    b) `!((N >= 0) && (N <= 5))`

18. Given that **X** is a numeric variable, write expressions equivalent to the following using a single relational operator:
    a) `(X > 1) && (X > 5)`
    b) `(X = 1) || (X > 1)`

19. What (if anything) is wrong with each of the following variable names?
    a) `PlayerName`
    b) `2ndPlayer`
    c) `window_1`
    d) `little_doggie_in_the_doghouse`
    e) `joe.e.brown`
    f) `player_choice`

20. Create a string variable named **greeting** that will contain the following text:

    ```
    Mandy said, "Good morning!"
    ```

21. Give the results of the following operations:
    a) 38 % 7
    b) 14 % 4
    c) 3 % 3
    d) 15 % 14

22. For the following situations write variable declarations, including possible initial values:
    a) In an online game, the player is asked to decide whether or not to play the game again. The variable should hold the value of the player's choice.
    b) A math test requires the student to enter the answer to a division problem. The variable holds the answer to the problem.
    c) An online shopping site needs a variable to hold the value of the sales tax percent to be applied to an order.

For Exercises 23–30 assume all necessary HTML tags exist and the JavaScript code is correctly placed in the <head></head> section of a web page.

23. Given the following JavaScript code, what will be displayed on the web page after the document.write() statement?

    ```
    var num1 = 15;
    var num2 = 3;
    var answer = num1 / num2;
    document.write("answer is " + answer) ;
    ```

24. Given the following JavaScript code, what will be displayed on the web page after the document.write() statement?

    ```
    var firstName = "Batman";
    var secondName = "Robin";
    document.write(firstName + " and " + secondName);
    ```

25. Given the following JavaScript code, what will be displayed on the web page after the document.write() statement?

    ```
    var name = "Amanda";
    var num1 = "12";
    var num2 = "34";
    document.write("Your ID is: " + name + num1 + num2);
    ```

26. Given the following JavaScript code, what will be displayed on the web page after the document.write() statement?

    ```
    var num1 = "5";
    var num2 = "3";
    var num3 = num1 + num2;
    document.write("Your ID is: " + num3);
    ```

27. Given the following JavaScript code, what will be displayed on the web page after the document.write() statement if the user enters 8 at the prompt?

    ```
    var num = prompt("Enter a number:", 0);
    document.write(num + 4 + "<br />" );
    ```

```
document.write((parseInt(num) + 4)+ "<br />") ;
document.write(num * 4);
```

28. Given the following JavaScript code, what will be displayed on the web page after the document.write() statement if the user enters 8.25 at the prompt?

```
var num = prompt("Enter a number:", 0);
document.write(parseInt(num) + "<br />" );
document.write(parseFloat(num));
```

29. Given the following JavaScript code, what will be displayed on the web page after the document.write() statement if the user enters BFF2 at the prompt?

```
var num = prompt("Enter a number:", 0);
document.write(parseInt(num) + "<br />" );
document.write(parseFloat(num));
```

30. Given the following JavaScript code, what will be displayed on the web page after the document.write() statement if the user enters BFF2 at the prompt?

```
var result = "Yes!";
var num = prompt("What is 5 * 6?", 0);
result = (parseInt(num) == 30)? "Yes!":"Sorry, ↵
        wrong answer . . .";
document.write(result);
```

Programming Challenges

On Your Own

1. Create a web page that allows a user to create a username for a website. The user should be prompted to enter his or her first name, last name, and school's name. The program should create a username that consists of the user's initials concatenated with the first word of the school's name. For example, if Hector Lopez attends Universal Community College, his username would be HLUniversal. Save the web page with the filename username_XXX.html where XXX are your initials. Be sure to include an appropriate page title.

2. Create a web page that informs the user whether or not a person is old enough to vote. The user should be prompted to enter the age of the person in question. If the age is 18 or older, the output should read "You can vote." If the person is younger than 18, the output should read "You are too young to vote." Use the conditional operator in your JavaScript program. Save the web page with the filename voting_XXX.html where XXX are your initials. Be sure to include an appropriate page title.

3. Create a web page that displays the cost of a movie ticket for a customer. The user should be prompted for the age of the customer. The output should be a message telling the user what the customer's ticket will cost, based on the following criteria:
   - Under age 5 entry is free
   - Between ages 5 and 12 (inclusive) a child's ticket costs $5.00
   - Older than 12 an adult ticket costs $9.00

   Save the web page with the filename tickets_XXX.html where XXX are your initials. Be sure to include an appropriate page title.

VideoNote
Using the Conditional
Operator
On_Your_Own_4_
Alphabetize

4. Create a web page that alphabetizes two names. The user should be prompted to enter two names. The program will check to see which name comes first in the alphabet or if the two names are the same. The output should be the names listed in alphabetical order or, if the names are the same, a message stating that the names are identical. Save the web page with the filename names_XXX.html where XXX are your initials. Be sure to include an appropriate page title.

5. Create a web page that checks to see if the user enters a number within a given range. Write a program that uses two different methods to test if a number is between 1 and 50. One method must use the OR operator (||) and the other method must use the AND operator (&&). The web page should display the two equivalent expressions. Save the page with the filename expressions_XXX.html where XXX are your initials. Be sure to include an appropriate page title.

   Hint: X < 5 includes all numbers less than but not including 5. Therefore, 5 >= X is equivalent to X < 5 while 5 > X is not equivalent to X < 5.

6. Create a web page that identifies whether or not expressions are true or false. The page will display the following expressions. Under each expression there should be a button that the user can click to see if the left side of each expression is equivalent to the right side. If so, the value will be true. If not, the value will be false.
   - (X > 5) && (X < 10) == !(X <= 5) || !(X >= 10)
   - ![(X > Y) && (Y < Z)] == !(X > Y) || !(Y < Z)
   - (X == Y) || (X > Y) == (X == Y) && (X < Y)
   - ![(Z < X) || (Z < Y) == !(Z < X) && !(Z < Y)

   Use the following values for X, Y, and Z in your JavaScript program:

   X = 8, Y = 3, and Z = 5

   Save the web page with the filename true_false_XXX.html where XXX are your initials. Be sure to include an appropriate page title.

7. Create a web page that contains a simple math test. The page should have the following arithmetic problems. Add a button under each problem which, when clicked, will display a prompt for the user to enter the answer. Add a second button which, when clicked, will check to see if the user's answer is correct. The output should be either "correct" or "incorrect" displayed in an alert box.
   1. 5 + 9 = ??
   2. 4 * 6 = ??
   3. 25 - 14 = ??
   4. 48 / 3 = ??
   5. 26 % 6 = ??

   Save the web page with the filename math_XXX.html where XXX are your initials. Be sure to include an appropriate page title.

Case Studies

Greg's Gambits

Now you will add to the game created earlier in this chapter. You will create a second short story with variables that allow a player to make up alternate versions of the story.

Open the `index.html` page for `Greg's Gambits` and add a link, under the `Play A Game` link, that links to the page named `Greg's Tales`.

Open the `greg_tales.html` file and add your code to the code created earlier in this chapter. Create a second story which the player will help create by entering various words and numbers at prompts. Your story should include, at a minimum, the following variable types:

- one `numeric` variable that represents a number
- one `string` variable that represents a proper noun (a name)
- one `string` variable that represents a verb
- one `string` variable that represents a pronoun
- one `string` variable that represents an adjective

Save your page as `greg_tales2.html`. Test your story in a browser. Submit your work as instructed by your teacher.

Carla's Classroom

Now you will add to the spelling lesson created earlier in this chapter. You will create a new category of words.

Open the `index.html` page for `Carla's Classroom` and add a link, under the `Writing` link, that links to the page named `Carla's Classroom | An Appetite For Spelling`.

Open the `carla_spelling.html` file and add your code to the code created earlier in this chapter. Select one of the categories listed below and search the Internet or use your own images for pictures of items that can be used in a spelling test. Add code to this page that tests students' spelling of at least five words:

- Vehicles
- Animals
- Flowers and plants
- Furniture

Save your page as `carla_spelling2.html`. Test your page in a browser. Be sure to test both correct and incorrect spellings of each word. Submit your work as instructed by your teacher.

Lee's Landscape

Add a sign-up page to the `Lee's Landscape` website. The page should prompt the user to enter the following information and display it on the page:

- Name
- Street address
- City, state, zip code
- Daytime phone number
- Alternate phone number
- Email address

Include a check for the email address. This should prompt the user to re-enter the email address and check the second entry with the first to confirm they are the same. If they are different, output a message to that effect. Otherwise, no output is necessary. In a later chapter you will add more functionality to this feature to ensure that the user enters a correct email address.

Be sure to give this web page an appropriate page title; `Lee's Landscape ||`
`Signup` is suggested. Save this file with the filename `lee_signup.html`. Add a link to the `Lee's Landscape` home page to this new page.

Jackie's Jewelry

Add a sign-up page to the `Jackie's Jewelry` website. The page should prompt the user to enter the following information and display it on the page:

- Name
- Street address
- City, state, zip code
- Daytime phone number
- Alternate phone number
- Email address

Include a check for the email address. This should prompt the user to re-enter the email address and check the second entry with the first to confirm they are the same. If they are different, output a message to that effect. Otherwise, no output is necessary. In a later chapter you will add more functionality to this feature to ensure that the user enters a correct email address.

Be sure to give this web page an appropriate page title; `Jackie's Jewelry ||`
`Signup` is suggested. Save this file with the filename `jackie_signup.html`. Add a link to the `Jackie's Jewelry` home page to this new page.

Note: In this chapter, the assignment for the `Lee's Landscape` case and the `Jackie's Jewelry` case are the same. However, this will not be true in subsequent chapters.

Making Decisions: The Selection Structure

Chapter Objectives

Imagine going to a website that asks if you want to buy a sweater. If you say yes, you are sent to a checkout page where a size 4 red wool sweater, which costs $125.00 plus $8.00 shipping is charged to your credit card. If you say no, nothing happens. There are no options to see other merchandise, no options to contact the company, nothing. This website would be useless to anyone except someone who wanted a size 4 red wool sweater and didn't care what it cost. Without the ability to program decisions, computer programs would be able to do only one thing at a time. In this example, to buy a blue sweater would require a completely different web page. And to buy a red sweater in size 12 would also require a new web page. Luckily, we can program computers to make decisions so our shopping experiences as well as our gaming experiences and everything else we do on a computer can be varied and worthwhile. In this chapter, you will learn about the selection structure which allows a program to select one of several alternative groups of statements. These groups of statements, together with the condition that determines which of them is to be executed, make up a selection (or decision) control structure.

After reading this chapter, you will be able to do the following:

- Understand the single-, dual-, and multiple alternative selection structures
- Use if statements in a JavaScript program
- Use if...else statements in a JavaScript program
- Use nested selection structures
- Use if...else if statements in a JavaScript program
- Use the switch statement in a JavaScript program

3.1   What if? Types of Selection Structures

A **selection structure** consists of a test condition together with one or more groups (or blocks) of statements. The result of the test determines which of these blocks is executed. The three types of selection structures are as follows:

1. A **single-alternative** (or if...) **structure** contains only a single block of statements. If the test condition is met, the statements are executed. If the test condition is not met, the statements are skipped.

2. A **dual-alternative** (or if...else) **structure** contains two blocks of statements. If the test condition is met, the first block is executed and the program skips over the second block. If the test condition is not met, the first block of statements is skipped and the second block is executed.

3. A **multiple-alternative structure** (or if...else...if... or a switch **statement**) contains more than two blocks of statements. The program is written so that when the test condition is met, the block of statements that goes with that condition is executed and all the other blocks are skipped.

Figures 3.1, 3.2, and 3.3 show the flow of execution in each of the three types of selection structures.

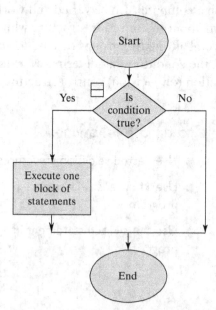

Figure 3.1   The single-alternative if... structure

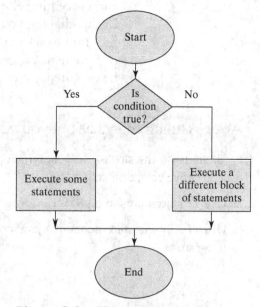

Figure 3.2   The dual-alternative if...else structure

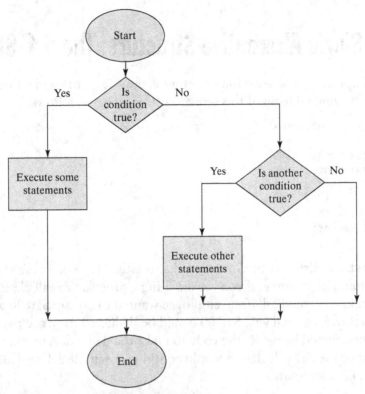

Figure 3.3 The multiple-alternative if...else if... structure

3.1 Define the term "selection structure."

3.2 What is the main difference between a single-alternative structure and a dual-alternative structure?

3.3 What is the main difference between a dual-alternative structure and a multiple-alternative structure?

3.4 Give an example of a situation in a program that would require a single-alternative structure.

3.5 Give an example of a situation in a program that would require a dual-alternative structure.

3.6 Give an example of a situation in a program that would require a multiple-alternative structure.

3.2 The Single Alternative Structure: The if Statement

The simplest type of selection structure is the if..., or single-alternative, structure. The general form of this selection structure is as follows:

```
if (test condition)
{
  statement;
  statement;
      .
      .
      .
  statement;
}
```

The **test condition** is an expression that is either true or false at the time of execution. For example, if you were writing a program to calculate an employee's paycheck, you could ask if the employee wanted to donate $10.00 to charity. If the employee entered yes, $10.00 would be deducted from the pay. Otherwise, no deduction would be made, the code to make the deduction would be skipped, and the rest of the pay calculation would continue. Example 3.1 provides an illustration of the if... structure.

EXAMPLE 3.1

What if?

The following script will display the greeting, It may snow today! if the temperature is below 32° Fahrenheit. If the temperature is 32° Fahrenheit or above, nothing will happen.

```
1.   <html>
2.   <head>
3.   <title>Example 3.1</title>
4.   <script>
5.   function getTemp()
6.   {
7.       var temp = prompt("What's the temperature today?", ↵
                  "degrees Fahrenheit");
8.       if (temp < 32)
9.       {
10.          document.write("<p>It may snow today!</p>");
11.      }
12.  }
13.  </script>
14.  </<head>
15.  <body>
16.  <h1>What's the Weather?</h1>
17.  <h3>Click the button! </h3>
18.  <p><input type="button" id="temperature" value="What is ↵
              today's temperature?" onclick="getTemp();" /></p>
19.  </body>
20.  </html>
```

When the user clicks the button, the getTemp() function is called. The user is prompted to enter the temperature. If the user enters a number less than 32, the message will appear. If the user enters a number equal to or greater than 32, nothing will happen. The test condition is on line 8. The statements that must be executed if the test condition is met are enclosed in curly brackets. In this example, there is only one statement. When there is only one statement to be executed if a condition is met, the curly brackets are not necessary but cannot hurt. If, however, there are two statements to be executed when the test condition is met, the curly brackets are essential. Copy this code, without the line numbers, to try it yourself.

A Note about the Test Condition

Look at Example 3.1. If the temperature is below 32°, the message will display. If it's warmer, nothing will happen. But what if it is exactly 32°? In this case, nothing will happen because the test condition specifies that the message should only be displayed if the temperature is less than 32°. At exactly 32°, it might snow. If you want the message to display when the temperature is exactly 32°, you would need to code the test condition slightly differently. In this case, it would be written: if (**temp** <= 32). When writing code that includes test conditions, you must be careful to think off all possibilities—greater than the test condition, less than the test condition, and exactly the same as the test condition.

A Note about the Curly Brackets

The question of when and where to include **curly brackets** ({ }) is important. A missing curly bracket can cause a program to crash, not run at all, or—and this may be the worst scenario—run with unexpected consequences. When either an opening or a closing bracket is omitted, you will probably be aware of it because your program will not run or will return errors. However, if you leave out a set of brackets where they are needed, you may not realize there is a problem until you run the program and don't get the results you expect. Example 3.2 will add one statement to the previous example to demonstrate when curly brackets must be included and when they are optional.

EXAMPLE 3.2

Brackets Make a Difference!

In this example, we will add another line of code to the `if` clause. Part (a) uses curly brackets to enclose both output statements and make them part of what happens when the test condition on line 8 is met.

Part (a)

```
1.   <html>
2.   <head>
3.   <title>Example 3.2, Part (a)</title>
4.   <script>
```

```
5.   function getTemp()
6.   {
7.       var temp = prompt("What's the temperature today?", ↵
                     "degrees Fahrenheit");
8.       if (temp < 32)
9.       {
10.          document.write("<p>It may snow today!</p>");
11.          document.write("<p>"Be sure to wear your boots ↵
                         and mittens.</p>");
12.      }
13.  }
14.  </script>
15.  </<head>
16.  <body>
17.  <h1>What's the Weather?</h1>
18.  <h3>Click the button! </h3>
19.  <p><input type="button" id="temperature" value="What is ↵
                today's temperature?" onclick="getTemp();" /></p>
20.  </body>
21.  </html>
```

The initial page looks like this:

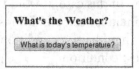

When the user enters 15 for the temperature the output looks like this:

> It may snow today!
>
> Be sure to wear your mittens and boots.

But if the user enters 45 for the temperature, nothing happens.

Part (b) does not use curly brackets and the consequences are shown in the output.

Part (b)

```
1.   <html>
2.   <head>
3.   <title>Example 3.2 Part(b)</title>
4.   <script>
5.   function getTemp()
6.   {
7.       var temp = prompt("What's the temperature today?", ↵
                     "degrees Fahrenheit");
8.       if (temp < 32)
9.          document.write("<p>It may snow today!</p>");
10.         document.write("<p>"Be sure to wear your boots ↵
                         and mittens.</p>");
11.  }
```

```
12.    </script>
13.    </<head>
14.    <body>
15.    <h1>What's the Weather?</h1>
16.    <h3>Click the button! </h3>
17.    <p><input type="button" id="temperature" value="What is ↵
               today's temperature?" onclick="getTemp();" /></p>
18.    </body>
19.    </html>
```

When the user enters 15 for the temperature, the output looks the same as for Part (a). However, if the user enters 45 for the temperature, this is the output:

Be sure to wear your mittens and boots.

What happened? The curly brackets enclose all the statements that should be executed if the test condition is met. In Part (a), this means that if the user enters a temperature below 32, both lines 10 and 11 in the Part (a) version (the two document.write() statements) should be executed. However, when the curly brackets are removed, as in Part (b), if a user enters a temperature below 32, the program executes line 9 of Part (b), the first document.write() statement. Then it moves to the next executable line of code which is line 10 (the second document. write() statement). This works fine if the temperature entered is lower than 32. However, when a user enters a higher temperature, the if clause is skipped. Without curly brackets, the default assumption is that the if clause has only one statement. So line 9 is skipped. However, line 10 is not part of the if clause. It is the next executable statement. This is why, no matter what temperature is entered, the second document.write() statement will always be executed.

If you aren't sure about whether or not to enclose statements in curly brackets, it's always better to err on the side of caution. Including curly brackets around a single statement in an if clause can't hurt the code but leaving curly brackets out can cause unwanted results.

CHECKPOINT FOR SECTION 3.2 ✓

3.7 Define the test condition in an if...clause.

3.8 What are the possible values of a test condition?

3.9 What will be displayed if the following code snippet is put into a program and run and the value of **age** is 10?

```
if (age > 16)
        document.write("<p>You are " + age + " years old.</p>");
        document.write("<p>You are eligible for a learner's permit.</p>");
```

3.10 Fix the code in Checkpoint 3.9 so nothing will display if a child is not older than 16.

3.11 Fix the code in Checkpoint 3.9 so children who are 16 or older can get a learner's permit.

3.3 The Dual Alternative Structure: `if...else` Statements

Sometimes you want code to execute if one thing happens and not execute if it doesn't. For example, if you were creating a game, you might want the player to receive a reward for amassing 20 points or more. If the player has 20 points or more, the reward is given. If not, nothing happens and the game proceeds. But often you will want something to happen if the condition is not met, as well as if it is met. Example 3.1 does nothing if the temperature entered is not less than 32. In this case, a user might think the program is not working if the button is clicked repeatedly and, because the entries are never less than 32, nothing happens. To avoid this you could add an `else` clause—statements that would execute if the test condition is not met. The general form of this selection structure is as follows:

```
if(test condition)
{
    statement;
    statement;
        .
        .
        .
    statement;
}
else
{
    statement;
    statement;
        .
        .
        .
}
```

Notice that multiple statements in both the `if` clause and the `else` clause must be contained within curly brackets. Example 3.3 adds a second option to the code of Example 3.2 to display an alternate message if the temperature is 32° or higher.

EXAMPLE 3.3

Using the `if...else` Structure

This example will display one set of statements if the temperature is less than 32°
and another set of statements if the temperature is equal to or greater than 32°.

```
1.    <html>
2.    <head>
3.    <title>Example 3.3</title>
4.    <script>
5.    function getTemp()
6.    {
7.        var temp = prompt("What's the temperature today?" , ⏎
                     "degrees Fahrenheit");
8.        if (temp < 32)
9.        {
10.           document.write("<p>It may snow today!</p>");
11.           document.write("<p>Be sure to wear your boots and mittens.</p>");
12.       }
13.       else
14.       {
15.           document.write("<p>It's too warm to snow today.</p>");
16.           document.write("<p>Boots are optional.</p>");
17.       }
18.   }
19.   </script>
20.   </head>
21.   <body>
22.   <h1>What's the Weather?</h1>
23.   <h3>Click the button! </h3>
24.   <p><input type="button" id="temperature" value="What is today's ⏎
              temperature?" onclick="getTemp();" /></p>
25.   </body>
26.   </html>
```

In this example, if the user enters a temperature less than 32, the display will be the
same as shown in Example 3.2:

> It may snow today!
>
> Be sure to wear your mittens and boots.

But if the user enters 32 or any number greater, the display will be as follows:

> It's too warm to snow today.
>
> Boots are optional.

Example 3.4 uses an `if...else` structure and includes statements that will be executed at the end, regardless of whether or not the condition is met.

Extra Credit

EXAMPLE 3.4

This example will display a student's exam grade. The exam has 21 questions. The basic score is based on the first 20 questions, with 5 points given for each correct answer. The last question is an extra credit option and worth 6 to 10 points. Another extra credit option gives the student up to 5 more points if he or she hands in a study guide with the exam. First, the instructor will enter the student's basic exam score and then enter the extra credit points earned. The program will calculate and display the student's final exam grade.

```
1.   <html>
2.   <head>
3.   <title>Example 3.4</title>
4.   <script>
5.   function getScore()
6.   {
7.      var basicScore = parseInt(prompt("What was the student's ⏎
                     initial score?"," "));
8.      var extraQuestion = prompt("Did the student do Q. 21 ⏎
                     (yes or no)?"," ");
9.      if (extraQuestion == "yes")
10.         var points = parseInt(prompt("How many points did the student ⏎
                     earn on Q. 21?"," "));
11.     else
12.         var points = parseInt(prompt("How many points did the student ⏎
                     earn for a study guide?"," "));
13.     var score = basicScore + points;
14.     document.write("<p>The student's score, with any extra credit, ⏎
                     is " + score + "%.</p>");
15.  }
16.  </script>
17.  </<head>
18.  <body>
19.  <h1>Student Score</h1>
20.  <p><input type="button" id="score" value="Enter the exam score?" ⏎
                 onclick="getScore();" /></p>
21.  </body>
22.  </html>
```

This example demonstrates several things:

- Lines 7 and 12 use the `parseInt()` function to ensure that the entries by the instructor are processed as numbers.

- Curly brackets are not used to enclose the statements in the `if` and the `else` clauses because both clauses consist of a single statement only. Curly brackets can be added but they are not necessary.

- Since each clause consists of one executable statement only, regardless of which statement occurs, lines 13 and 14 are always executed.

If you enter this code, the initial page looks like this:

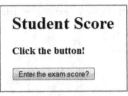

If a student gets 83% on the exam and earns 8 points for question 21, the output will look like this:

> The student's score, with any extra credit, is 91%.

If a student gets 83% on the exam, does not answer question 21, and hands in a study guide, the output will look like this:

> The student's score, with any extra credit, is 88%.

If a student earns 83% on the exam, does not answer question 21, and does not hand in a study guide, the output will look like this:

> The student's score, with any extra credit, is 83%.

But what if a student answers question 21 and also hands in a study guide? We will address this issue later in the chapter when we discuss compound conditions.

CHECKPOINT FOR SECTION 3.3

3.12 When are curly brackets required for if and else clauses?

3.13 Fix the following code snippet and add code so that a second message will display if the child is too young to get a learner's permit.

```
if (age > 16)
    document.write("<p>You are " + age + " years old.</p>");
    document.write("<p>You are eligible for a learner's ↵
                    permit.</p>");
```

3.14 Create a function that allows the user to enter two numbers. Then ask the user whether he or she wants to add or multiply the numbers. Include an if...else structure that will add or multiply the numbers. If the user does not want to add the numbers, the program will multiply them.

3.15 Add code to Checkpoint 3.14 that displays the result using one statement which is not inside the if...else structure. Add a second statement that tells the user what the numbers were and whether they were added or multiplied. *Hint:* Use a second selection structure.

3.4   Nested Selection Structures

Selection structures make it possible for you to code many alternative responses. For example, if you were programming a business site, you might want to calculate shipping costs based on several options. Shipping might be free if a consumer purchases more than a specified amount or enters a certain code. Shipping cost options might include ground, air, and special overnight service. Shipping costs might also depend on the distance a package has to travel and the weight of the package. For this type of situation, you would need to make many decisions. One customer might purchase $150.00 worth of merchandise and request free ground shipping. Another customer may purchase the same items and be willing to pay for a rush delivery. So once the cost of the merchandise is determined, there are more decisions to be made. One customer might live in the United States which would generate one shipping cost while another customer with the same shopping cart might live in Europe and the shipping cost would be different. To write code that allows for decisions that depend on the results of previous decisions, we can use **nested selection structures.** Figure 3.4 shows a portion of the decisions that would be required for the shipping costs example.

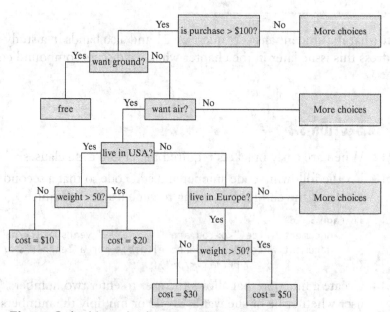

Figure 3.4   Nested selection structures

The general syntax for a multiple-alternative selection structure is as follows:

```
if (test condition1)
{
    if (test condition2)
    {
        block of statements to be executed if both condition1 and
        condition2 are true;
    }
    else
    {
        block of statements to be executed if condition1 is true
        but condition2 is not true;
    }
}
else
{
    block of statements to be executed if condition1 is false;
}
```

You can nest as many if... structures or if... else structures as you want. However, too many nested structures can be confusing. We will learn more efficient ways to deal with programs that require many decisions. There are some situations where a nested structure makes sense. Example 3.5 shows one such situation.

EXAMPLE 3.5

Nested Selection Structures

In this example, the user is asked if he or she wants to add or subtract two numbers. If the user decides to add the numbers, they are added. Since the result is the same, regardless of which number is added first, no further decisions are necessary. But if the user wants to subtract two numbers, the answer depends on which number is subtracted from the other. Therefore, a second selection structure is nested inside the else clause of the first selection structure.

```
1.   <head>
2.   <title>Example 3.5</title>
3.   <script>
4.   function getResult()
5.   {
6.       var x = parseInt(prompt("Enter x"," "));
7.       var y = parseInt(prompt("Enter y"," "));
8.       var add = prompt("Do you want to add the numbers (yes or no)?"," ");
9.       if (add == "yes")
10.      {
11.          var result = x + y;
12.          document.write("<p>I added the numbers " + x + ↵
                " and " + y + ".</p>");
13.          document.write("<p>The result is " + result + ".</p>");
14.      }
15.      else
```

```
16.        {
17.            var subtracty = prompt("Do you want to subtract x ↵
                       from y (yes or no)?"," ");
18.            if (subtracty == "yes")
19.            {
20.                var result = y - x;
21.                document.write("<p>I subtracted " + x + ↵
                      " from " + y + ".</p>");
22.                document.write("<p>The result is " + result + ".</p>");
23.            }
24.            else
25.            {
26.                result = x- y;
27.                document.write("<p>I subtracted " + y + ↵
                      " from " + x + ".</p>");
28.                document.write("<p>The result is " + result + ".</p>");
29.            }
30.        }
31.    }
32.    </script>
33.    </<head>
34.    <body>
35.    <h1>Add x and y or Subtract </h1>
36.    <h3>Click the button! </h3>
37.    <p><input type="button" id="numbers" value="Enter your numbers" ↵
                   onclick="getResult();" /></p>
38.    </body>
39.    </html>
```

CHECKPOINT FOR SECTION 3.4

3.16 Give one example, not used in this section, when you might use a nested
selection structure in a program.

3.17 Add selection structures as necessary to the following function so that, if the
user is exactly 16 years old, he or she is asked if today is his/her birthday and,
if it is, the message Happy Birthday! displays along with a message about a
learner's permit eligibility.

```
function getAge()
{
    var age = prompt("How old are you?"," ");
    if (age< 16)
    {
        document.write("<p>You are " + age + " years old.</p>");
        document.write("<p>You are not eligible for a ↵
                    learner's permit.</p>");
    }
    else
```

```
                    {
                        your code goes here
                        document.write("<p>You are " + age + " years old.</p>");
                        document.write("<p>You are eligible for a learner's ⏎
                                        permit.</p>");
                    }
                }
```

3.18 Create a function that allows the user to enter two numbers. Then ask the user whether he or she wants to multiply or divide the numbers. Include a nested if structure that will, if the user selects the option to divide, prompt the user for which number should be the divisor and which number should be the dividend. If the user wants to multiply the numbers, the program will multiply them. The program will then display either the quotient or the product. *Note:* In the expression a ÷ b = c, a is the dividend, b is the divisor, and c is the quotient. In the expression a x b = c, c is the product.

3.19 Fix the following code so that the message Your answer is incorrect displays whenever the user gives an incorrect answer.

```
var answer = parseInt(prompt("What is 3 plus 5?"," "));
if (answer == 8)
        document.write("Correct!</p>");
else
{
        if (answer == 15)
        {
                document.write("<p>Looks like you multiplied ⏎
                                instead of added</p>");
                document.write("<p>Your answer is incorrect</p>");
        }
}
```

3.5 Compound Conditions

The test condition in a selection structure can only have one of two possible outcomes: The condition is either true or false. That is always the case. However, you may have noticed that this limits the decisions we can allow users to make. Looking at Figure 3.4, you can see that programming all the possible shipping options would require many nested selection structures. There are better ways to do this! We will learn how to use selection structures with multiple alternatives in Section 3.6. But we can also ask questions that narrow down the choices by combining several options in one question. We do this by using **compound conditions** along with the relational and logical operators that we discussed in Chapter 2.

Combining Relational and Logical Operators

Let's return to the problem of calculating shipping costs by taking a closer look at Figure 3.4. The first decision the program must make is whether or not the customer has purchased more than $100.00 of merchandise. If this is true, the next decision is whether the customer wants ground shipping. If the purchase is not more than $100.00, the program will go to other options. If the purchase is $100.00 or more and the customer lives in the United States and is content to use ground shipping, then the shipping is free. But if the customer prefers air shipping, then several other questions must be answered. If the customer's package weighs more than 50 pounds, the shipping cost depends on whether or not he or she lives in the United States. Shipping costs vary depending on the weight of the merchandise as well as the shipping destination. Figure 3.5 demonstrates how we can use compound conditions to simplify the number of decision structures used in situations such as this.

Logical Operators Revisited

While there are many logical operators available, we only need to use three of them at this level, as discussed in Chapter 2. Recall that the AND operator is represented by a double ampersand (&&), the OR operator is represented by a double pipe (||), and the NOT operator is represented by an exclamation point (!).

A compound condition that uses the AND operator is true if and only if both conditions joined by && are true. A compound condition that uses the OR operator is

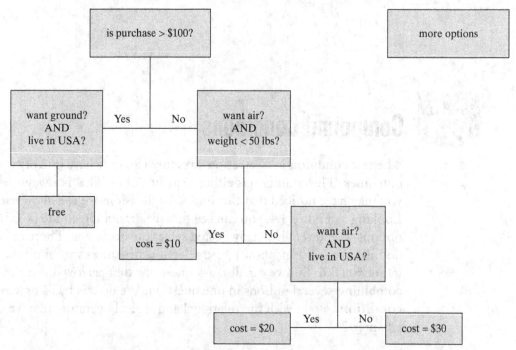

Figure 3.5 Using compound conditions

true unless both conditions joined by || are false. The NOT operator simply means that, if an expression is true, !(expression) is false and if an expression is false, !(expression) is true.

To demonstrate the use of logical operators and compound conditions, let's write the code for a payroll program that pays overtime wages if an employee has worked more than 40 hours in a week and earns less than $20.00 an hour. The code is shown in Example 3.6.

EXAMPLE 3.6

Overtime Pay

This example calculates the weekly pay of an employee. If an employee works less than 40 hours, the pay is simply the number of hours worked multiplied by the employee's hourly rate. Some employees are eligible to receive overtime pay for time worked over 40 hours. However, if an employee's pay rate is more than at least $20.00 an hour, he or she is not eligible for overtime pay. This may not be legal in all states, but it serves to illustrate the use of compound conditions. If an employee is eligible for overtime pay, it is calculated at 1.5 times the regular pay rate.

```
1.   <html>
2.   <head>
3.   <title>Example 3.6</title>
4.   <script>
5.   function paycheck()
6.   {
7.      var rate = parseInt(prompt("What is the employee's pay rate?"," "));
8.      var hours = parseInt(prompt("How many hours did the employee ⏎
                   work this week?"," "));
9.      if (hours > 40 && rate < 20)
10.     {
11.         var overtime = rate * 1.5 * (hours - 40);
12.         var regular = rate * 40;
13.         var pay = overtime + regular;
14.     }
15.     else
16.         var pay = rate * hours;
17.     document.write("<p>Your paycheck this week will be $ " + pay + ".</p>");
18.  }
19.  </script>
20.  </<head>
21.  <body>
22.  <h1>Calculating the Paycheck</h1>
23.  <h3>Click the button to calculate a paycheck with a compound condition</h3>
24.  <p><input type="button" id="paycheck" value="calculate the paycheck" ⏎
         onclick="paycheck();" /></p>
25.  </body>
26.  </html>
```

Line 9 shows the compound condition. It takes the place of a nested if...else structure and makes the program easy to run and simple to follow.

Example 3.7 provides another sample of logical operators and compound conditions.

Calculating Shipping Costs

In this example, we will add to the shipping cost program. Figure 3.5 shows options for customers who purchase more than $100.00 of merchandise. But the company may charge different shipping rates for other amounts. In the following example we use compound conditions to assign shipping costs to merchandise that totals $1.00 to $24.99, $25.00 to $49.99, $50.00 to $74.99, and $75.00 to $99.99. In this example, we will assume the customer has chosen ground shipping and lives in the United States. Similar code can be used for many other options.

```
1.   <html>
2.   <head>
3.   <title>Example 3.7</title>
4.   <script>
5.   function shipCost()
6.   {
7.       var price = parseInt(prompt("What is your merchandise total?"," "));
8.       if (price > 1.00 && price < 25.00)
9.           var ship = 5.00;
10.      if (price >= 25.00 && price < 50.00)
11.          var ship = 7.00;
12.      if (price >= 50.00 && price < 75.00)
13.          var ship = 9.00;
14.      if (price >= 75.00 && price < 100.00)
15.          var ship = 10.00;
16.      if (price >= 100.00)
17.          var ship = 0.00;
18.      document.write("<p>Your shipping cost will be $ " + ship + ".</p>");
19.  }
20.  </script>
21.  </<head>
22.  <body>
23.  <h1>Calculating Shipping Costs</h1>
24.  <h3>Click the button to calculate your shipping cost</h3>
25.  <p><input type="button" id="ship" value="calculate your shipping ⏎
                 charge" onclick="shipCost();" /></p>
26.  </body>
27.  </html>
```

This program works fine, but you may wonder if there is a better way to write code that includes many options. There is. We will discuss the options for this type of structure in Section 3.6.

The last example of compound conditions will use the OR operator. Example 3.8 builds on the code shown in Example 3.7 to add a free shipping option for customers who have a special code.

EXAMPLE 3.8

Adding the Free Shipping Option

We will add to Example 3.7 and provide free shipping for customers who enter a special code named FREESHIP. Only the shipCost() function on lines 5–19 from Example 3.7 are repeated here. By adding one line of code after line 6 and including a compound condition with an OR operator on line 16, we can provide free shipping to customers who use the FREESHIP code.

```
5.  function shipCost()
6.  {
    new line: var coupon = (prompt("Enter any code you have:", " ");
7.           var price = parseInt(prompt("What is your merchandise ⏎
                         total?"," "));
8.    if (price > 1.00 && price < 25.00)
9.        var ship = 5.00;
10.   if (price >= 25.00 && price < 50.00)
11.       var ship = 7.00;
12.   if (price >= 50.00 && price < 75.00)
13.       var ship = 9.00;
14.   if (price >= 75.00 && price < 100.00)
15.       var ship = 10.00;
16.   if (price >= 100.00 || coupon == "FREESHIP")
17.       var ship = 0.00;
18.   document.write("<p>Your shipping cost will be $ " + ⏎
                     ship + ".</p>");
19. }
```

Line 16 allows customers who purchase more than $100.00 of merchandise or who enter the correct code to get free shipping. Because the computer processes commands in order, it doesn't matter what the value of **ship** is when it reaches line 17. If the answer to the compound condition on line 16 is true, the value of **ship** becomes 0.00. It doesn't matter if the customer enters a free shipping code and purchases more than $100.00 of merchandise. Free, after all, is free.

A Note about Syntax

There is a point to make about writing compound conditions with if statements. The syntax is as follows:

```
if (condition 1 && condition 2)
```

You must write a complete condition each time. For example, the following would not work:

```
if (price > 5 && < 12)
```

Nor would this:

```
if (price > 5) && (price < 12)
```

The correct syntax is as follows:

```
if (price > 5 && price < 12)
```

The entire compound condition must be enclosed within the parentheses and, for each condition, the whole condition, including the variable, the relational operator, and the test, must be included.

Using AND and OR

Often students wonder if there are specific rules about when to use the AND operator and when to use the OR operator. Most of the time, either operator, so long as the conditions are written carefully, can work in a given situation. Let's say you want to narrow down a user's selections to the integers 6, 7, 8, and 9. You could use the AND operator to specify that any integer greater than 5 and less than 10 is acceptable. In JavaScript, that would be written as follows:

```
(num > 5 && num < 10)
```

This condition would only be true if **num** were 6, 7, 8, or 9. However, you could also say that any integer less than or equal to 5 or greater than or equal to 10 is false. In JavaScript, that would be written using both the NOT and OR operators as follows:

```
!(num <= 5 || num >= 10)
```

Either way would produce the same result. The reason one might be used in place of the other would depend on other elements of the program. Example 3.9 produces the same result using the AND operator in one case and the OR operator in another case.

EXAMPLE 3.9

Using Logical Operators with Compound Conditions

The following program does the same thing as the program shown in Example 3.6, but uses an alternate compound condition. The program is repeated here with the first alternative included as comments so you can compare the two:

```
1.   <html>
2.   <head>
3.   <title>Example 3.9</title>
4.   <script>
5.   function paycheck()
6.   {
7.       var rate = parseInt(prompt("What is the employee's pay rate?"," "));
8.       var hours = parseInt(prompt("How many hours did the employee ↵
                 work this week?"," "));
9.       //if (hours > 40 && rate < 20)
10.      //{
11.      //     var overtime = rate * 1.5 * (hours - 40);
12.      //     var regular = rate * 40;
13.      //     var pay = overtime + regular;
14.      //}
15.      //else
16.      //     var pay = rate * hours;
17.      if (hours <= 40 || rate>= 20)
18.          var pay = rate * hours;
19.      else
20.      {
21.          var overtime = rate * 1.5 * (hours - 40);
```

```
22.                var regular = rate * 40;
23.                var pay = overtime + regular;
24.        }
25.        document.write("<p>Your paycheck this week will be $ " + pay + ".</p>");
26.   }
27.   </script>
28.   </<head>
29.   <body>
30.   <h1>Calculating the Paycheck</h1>
31.   <h3>Click the button to calculate a paycheck with a compound condition</h3>
32.   <p><input type="button" id="paycheck" value="calculate the paycheck" ⏎
                          onclick="paycheck();" /></p>
33.   </body>
34.   </html>
```

In general, we can say that the following pairs of statements produce the same result:

1. if A is true AND B is true then do C
   else do D

2. if A is not true OR B is not true then do D
   else do C

CHECKPOINT FOR SECTION 3.5 ✓

3.20 What integer values of **num** would make the following statement true?

(**num** > 3) && (**num** < 8)

3.21 What values of **num** would make the following statement true?

(**num** < 12) || (**num** > 8)

3.22 Suppose the variable **num** = 4. Is each of the following expressions true or false?

a) ((2 * **num**) + 1 == 3) && (**num** > 2)
b) !(2 * **num** == 0) || (**num** + 1 == 5)

3.23 Write a program that will tell the user whether it is cold enough to wear a jacket. The user should be prompted to enter the temperature. The program will display Yes if the user enters a temperature below 50, No if the temperature entered is higher than 70, and Maybe if the temperature entered is between 50 and 70. The program should use a compound condition.

3.6 Multiple-Alternative Selection Structures

The if...else (dual-alternative) structure selects, based on the value of its test condition, one of two alternative blocks of statements. However, sometimes a program must handle decisions having more than two options. In these cases, we use a multiple-alternative selection structure. As you will see, this structure can be implemented in several different ways. To contrast the differences, we will use each method to solve the same problem (see Examples 3.10 and 3.15).

The if...else if... Structure

This structure depends on the sequential nature of computer programming and on the fact that decision structures only execute certain statements if the test condition is true; otherwise those statements are skipped. The general syntax for this structure is as follows:

```
if (test condition 1)
{
   statements to be executed;
}
else if (test condition 2)
{
   statements to be executed;
}
else
{
   statements to be executed if neither condition 1 nor
              condition 2 are true;
}
```

Notice that each clause (the if clause, the else if clause, and the final else clause) uses curly brackets to enclose the statements to be executed if the condition relating to that clause is true. It will make debugging much easier if you carefully line up the brackets as shown. As we learned, a missing bracket can cause frustrating logic errors!

You do not need to stop with a single else if clause. You can have as many else if clauses nested in an if...else if structure as you want. Too many nested clauses become unwieldy. We will cover another method that makes it possible to select from many alternatives in a less complicated way.

Using if...else if for a Rating System

As a web programmer, you want to create a way that users can rate your site. You offer the user a way to rate the site numerically from 1 to 10 but you want to assign a letter grade to the numerical rating. You need to create a program that will change the numerical rating entered by the user into a letter grade. Ratings will be assigned letter grades as follows:

- If the score is 10 the rating is "A".
- If the score is 7, 8, or 9 the rating is "B".
- If the score is 4, 5, or 6 the rating is "C".
- If the score is below 4 the rating is "D".

The following program uses if...else if statements to convert the numeric entry to a letter grade.

```
1.   <html>
2.   <head>
3.   <title>Example 3.10</title>
```

```
 4.  <script>
 5.  function rateIt()
 6.  {
 7.      var rate = parseInt(prompt("Rate the site from 1 to 10, ↵
                    with 10 as the best"," "));
 8.      var grade = " "
 9.      if (rate == 10)
10.          grade = "A";
11.      else if (rate >= 7 && rate <= 9)
12.          grade = "B";
13.      else if (rate >= 4 && rate < 7)
14.          grade = "C";
15.      else
16.          grade = "D";
17.      document.write("<p>You gave the site a rating of " + ↵
                    grade + ".</p>");
18.  }
19.  </script>
20.  </<head>
21.  <body>
22.  <h1>Rate the Site</h1>
23.  <h3>Rate the site from 1 to 10, with 10 as the best ever and ↵
                    1 as one of the worst</h3>
24.  <p><input type="button" id="rating" value="Enter your rating ↵
                    now" onclick="rateIt();" /></p>
25.  </body>
26.  </html>
```

Because each clause has only one executable statement, the curly brackets can be eliminated. But curly brackets are still required at the beginning and end of the rateIt() function.

Error Checking: Just the Beginning

In the examples so far, we have not discussed what would happen if the user does not enter one of the options specified. We have assumed that the user will enter a correct option. Such assumptions are fine when you are learning new concepts and syntax. But checking for errors—user errors and program-generated errors during execution—is a significant part of the programming process. In Example 3.10, what would happen if the user enters a number outside the range of 1 through 10? Or enters a letter instead of a number? Try it and you'll see that unless the digits 4, 5, 6, 7, 8, 9, or 10 are entered, the output will always be You gave the site a rating of D. This is because, if the first three conditions are not met, the program goes to the fourth condition by default. In this case, we can fix the problem by adding code at the end to cover all cases outside the range of 1 through 10. There are many techniques used to check for errors and, as you progress through this text, you will learn some of them. Example 3.11 shows the function that adds code to display an error message if an entry is invalid.

| EXAMPLE 3.11 | ## Using a Default Condition for Errors |

```
1.  function rateIt()
2.  {
3.      var rate = parseInt(prompt("Rate the site from 1 to 10, with ⏎
                          10 as the best"," "));
4.      var grade = " "
5.      if (rate == 10)
6.      {
7.          grade = "A";
8.          document.write("<p>You gave the site a rating of " + grade + ".</p>");
9.      }
10.     else if (rate >= 7 && rate <= 9)
11.     {
12.         grade = "B";
13.         document.write("<p>You gave the site a rating of " + grade + ".</p>");
14.     }
15.     else if (rate >= 4 && rate < 7)
16.     {
17.         grade = "C";
18.         document.write("<p>You gave the site a rating of " + grade + ".</p>");
19.     }
20.     else if (rate >= 1 && rate < 4)
21.     {
22.         grade = "D";
23.         document.write("<p>You gave the site a rating of " + grade + ".</p>");
24.     }
25.     else
26.         document.write("<p>Invalid entry</p>");
27. }
```

Now we can confirm that an invalid entry will not result in a D rating. In Chapter 4, when we cover loops, we will learn how to give a user the opportunity to fix such an error.

Before moving on to the next topic, we'll present another example that uses the if...else if structure. Example 3.12 shows how to code the results of a battle between a game player and an online adversary.

| EXAMPLE 3.12 | ## Using if...else if... in a Virtual Battle |

For this example, imagine that you are writing code for an online adventure game. At some point, the player will encounter an adversary who, for our purposes, is a troll. The two go to battle and the winner is determined as follows: If the player arrives with more points than a troll is assigned, the player wins. If the player arrives with fewer points than the troll but has acquired a gun or a sword in the game, the player also wins. And, if the player and the troll have the same number of points, the battle is declared a tie. A tie is also declared if the player cannot win but has wings or has acquired flying dust and flies away. In all other cases, the player loses. The program has assigned the troll 50 points. A few things have been added to this example to spice up the output a bit.

```
1.   <html>
2.   <head>
3.   <title>Example 3.12</title>
4.   <script>
5.   function fightTroll()
6.   {
7.      var trollPoints = 50;
8.      var points = parseInt(prompt("How many points do you have?" , " "));
9.      if (points < trollPoints)
10.     {
11.        var gun = prompt("Do you have a gun? (y/n)" , " ");
12.        if (gun == "n")
13.           var sword = prompt("Do you have a sword? (y/n)" , " ");
14.        if (gun == "n" && sword == "n")
15.           var wings = prompt("Do you have wings? (y/n)" , " ");
16.        if (wings == "n" && sword == "n" && gun == "n")
17.           var dust = prompt("Do you have flying dust? (y/n)" , " ");
18.        if (wings == "n" && sword == "n" && gun == "n" && dust == "n")
19.        {
20.           document.write("<h3>You lose...so sad</h3>");
21.           document.write("<img src = 'troll.jpg' />");
22.        }
23.        else if (gun == 'y' || sword == 'y')
24.        {
25.           document.write("<h3>You are the winner!</h3>");
26.           document.write("<img src = 'victor.jpg' />");
27.        }
28.        else if (dust == 'y' || wings == 'y')
29.        {
30.           document.write("<h3>You can fly away. The battle ⏎
                   is a tie.</h3>");
31.           document.write("<img src = 'flyaway.jpg' />");
32.        }
33.     }
34.     else
35.     {
36.        if (points == trollPoints)
37.        {
38.           document.write("<h3>It's a tie.</h3>");
39.           document.write("<img src = 'victor.jpg' />");
40.           document.write("<img src = 'troll.jpg' />");
41.        }
42.        else
43.        {
44.           document.write("<h3>You are the winner!</h3>");
45.           document.write("<img src = 'victor.jpg' />");
46.        }
47.     }
48.   }
49.   </script>
50.   </<head>
```

```
51.   <body>
52.   <h1>Battle with the Troll!</h1>
53.   <p><input type="button" id="battle" value="Push here to begin the battle" ↵
                           onclick="fightTroll();" /></p>
54.   </body>
55.   </html>
```

There are several aspects of this program that deserve some explanation. Line 11 prompts the player to declare whether or not he or she has a gun. Incidentally, it is convenient to use (y/n) as a prompt for "yes" or "no" responses and makes it less likely that a user will make a typo.

The if clause on lines 9–33 will be executed only if the player's points are less than the troll's. If the player has more points or the same number of points as the troll, the else clause on lines 34–47 is executed and it is determined if the battle goes to the player or is a tie by points.

However, if the player cannot win or tie by points, the if clause on lines 9–33 determines the outcome. Line 12 uses a simple if clause to prompt the player for a sword only if the player has no gun. While the player might have both a gun and a sword, for the sake of this battle, it is irrelevant. Line 14 asks the player if he or she has wings but only if the player has no gun and no sword. Line 16 begins an if clause that only is executed if the player so far has no possibility of winning by weapon and has no wings. Once it is determined that the player cannot win and cannot tie by flying away, lines 18–22 display the losing scenario. If the player has not automatically won or tied through points and has not lost, lines 23–27 determine if the player is a winner by possessing a weapon or, if not, if there is a tie (lines 28–32) by possessing the ability to fly away.

The inclusion of a few images with the text display makes the output more interesting. If you want to try this example, the images are in the Student Data Files. The initial display and the three possible outcomes are shown below.

The Switch Statement

To make it easier to code multiple-alternative structures, JavaScript contains a statement, called the **switch statement,** which is specifically designed for this purpose. This statement contains a single test expression that determines which block of code is to be executed. A typical switch statement looks like this:

```
switch(test expression)
{
case 1:
    execute code block 1
    break;
case 2:
    execute code block 2
    break;
    .
    ...all other cases and code to be executed
    .
case n:
    execute code block n
    break;
default:
    code to be executed is nothing matches the test condition
}
```

Here's how the switch statement works: The test expression is evaluated and its value is compared to the first case. If there is a match, the first block of statements is executed and the structure is exited. The **break** keyword forces the program to jump to the line of code following the ending curly bracket. If there is no match in the first case, the value of the test expression is compared to the second case value. If there is a match here, the second block of statements is executed and the structure is exited. This process continues until either a match for the test expression value is found or until the end of the cases is encountered. The programmer can either write a default statement—something that will happen if the test expression does not match any of the cases—or the programmer can allow no action to be taken. After either the default or the end of all the cases, the structure is exited.

The switch statement is ideal for many situations. It is often used to create menus. In a program where there are many options, it provides code that is much cleaner than using many if...else clauses. In fact, it would make the Rate the Site program we created in Example 3.10 much easier to code. We will redo that example later in this section.

The following examples show how to use a switch statement when the test condition is a string of text, a single character, or a number. Example 3.13 uses a switch statement to allow the user to change the background color of the web page.

EXAMPLE 3.13

Using a switch Statement for Page Color

```
1.   <html>
2.   <head>
3.   <title>Example 3.13</title>
4.   <script>
5.   function pageColor()
6.   {
7.        var color = prompt("enter a new background color:", " ");
8.        switch (color)
9.        {
10.            case "green":
11.                 document.body.bgColor="green";
12.                 break;
13.            case "blue":
14.                 document.body.bgColor="blue";
15.                 break;
16.            case "yellow":
17.                 document.body.bgColor="yellow";
18.                 break;
19.            case "lavender":
20.                 document.body.bgColor="lavender";
21.                 break;
22.            default:
23.                 document.write("Invalid entry");
24.        }
25.  }
26.  </script>
27.  </<head>
28.  <body>
29.  <h1>Change the page color</h1>
30.  <p>Select from blue, green, yellow, or lavender.</p>
31.  <p><input type="button" id="color" value="Enter a color" ↵
                     onclick="pageColor();" /></p>
32.  </body>
33.  </html>
```

This program prompts the user for a color. The value is stored in the variable, **color**. Then **color** serves as the test expression for each **case** in the **switch** statement. When a match is found, the statement that changes the background color of the web page is executed and the **break** statement causes the program execution to jump to line 25. You can see how easy it is to read this code compared to if it were coded with **if...else if** statements. It is also extremely easy to add more options, if you want to include other colors.

The **switch** statement is often used when the user is given a menu of choices. For example, the user might choose between playing a game again, resuming a game in progress, exiting a game, selecting a new game, and so on. Or, as shown in Example 3.14, the user may select which of several types of calculations to perform. The following program uses a **switch** statement to allow the user to find the area of a selected shape.

EXAMPLE 3.14

Using a `switch` to Find the Area of a Shape

```
1.   <html>
2.   <head>
3.   <title>Example 3.14</title>
4.   <script>
5.   function shapeShift()
6.   {
7.          var area = 0;
8.          var PI = 3.14159;
9.          var shape = prompt("Select a shape by entering the
                         corresponding letter", " ");
10.         switch (shape)
11.         {
12.         case "c":
13.                 var radius = parseInt(prompt("What is the radius of ⏎
                        the circle?", " "));
14.                 area = PI * radius * radius;
15.                 document.write("<p>The area of a circle with radius " ⏎
                        + radius + " is " + area +"</p>");
16.                 break;
17.          case "s":
18.                 var side = parseInt(prompt("What is the length of ⏎
                        one side of the square?", " "));
19.                 area = side * side;
20.                 document.write("<p>The area of a square with a side ⏎
                        of  " + side + " is " + area +"</p>");
21.                 break;
22.          case "t":
23.                 var base = parseInt(prompt("What is the length of ⏎
                        the base of this triangle?", " "));
24.                 var height = parseInt(prompt("What is the height of ⏎
                        this triangle?", " "));
25.                 area = 0.5 * base * height;
26.                 document.write("<p>The area of a triangle with a base ⏎
                        of " + base + " and a height of " + height + ⏎
                        " is " + area +"</p>");
27.                 break;
28.          default:
29.          document.write("Invalid entry");
30.          }
31.   }
32.   </script>
33.   </head>
34.   <body>
35.   <h1>Find the area of a shape</h1>
36.   <ul>
37.          <li> For a circle, enter c</li>
38.          <li> For a square, enter s</li>
39.          <li> For a triangle, enter t</li>
40.   </ul>
41.   <p><input type="button" id="shape" value="Begin calculation" ⏎
                       onclick="shapeShift();" /></p>
42.   </body>
43.   </html>
```

Notice that you can have as many statements as you want within each case option.

In JavaScript, each `case` in a `switch` statement can test for one thing at a time only. In other words, while an `if` clause can test for any number greater than 5 (i.e, `if (x > 5)`), the `switch` statement must test separately for each number greater than 5. However, there are ways to work around this. The program shown in Example 3.15 uses a `switch` statement to replace the `if...else if` statements shown in Example 3.10.

EXAMPLE 3.15

Using a switch Statement to Rate a Web Page

```
1.  <html>
2.  <head>
3.  <title>Example 3.15</title>
4.  <script>
5.  function rateIt()
6.  {
7.          var rate = parseInt(prompt("Rate the site from 1 to 10, ↵
                    with 10 as the best"," "));
8.          var grade = " "
9.          switch (rate)
10.         {
11.         case 10:
12.             grade = "A";
13.             document.write("<p>You gave the site a rating of " ↵
                    + grade + ".</p>");
14.             break;
15.         case 9:
16.         case 8:
17.         case 7:
18.              grade = "B";
19.             document.write("<p>You gave the site a rating of " ↵
                    + grade + ".</p>");
20.             break;
21.         case 6:
22.         case 5:
23.         case 4:
24.             grade = "C";
25.             document.write("<p>You gave the site a rating of ↵
                    " + grade + ".</p>");
26.             break;
27.         case 3:
28.         case 2:
29.         case 1:
30.             grade = "D";
31.             document.write("<p>You gave the site a rating of " ↵
                    + grade + ".</p>");
32.              break;
33.         default:
34.                 document.write("<p>Invalid entry</p>");
35.         }
36.  }
37.  </script>
38.  </<head>
39.  <body>
40.  <h1>Rate the Site</h1>
```

```
41.  <h3>Rate the site from 1 to 10, with 10 as the best ever and ↵
                     1 as one of the worst</h3>
42.  <p><input type="button" id="rating" value="Enter your rating now" ↵
                     onclick="rateIt();" /></p>
43.  </body>
44.  </html>
```

By simply eliminating the break statements after the case 9: and case 8: statements, if the user enters 8 or 9, the program automatically drops to the next executable statement (case 7:) and executes the statements in that case until it comes to the break statement on line 20. The same happens if a user enters a 5 or a 6; the next statements to be executed are lines 24 and 25 and the program ends because of the break statement on line 26. A similar situation occurs if the user enters a 3 or a 2.

When confronted with a situation that requires multiple decisions, it's your choice whether to use a switch, an if...else, or an if...else if structure. Evaluate which type of structure will provide the clearest and simplest solution. Sometimes, it's just a matter of personal preference but, by learning all the options available, you will become a better programmer.

CHECKPOINT FOR SECTION 3.6 ✓

3.24 Assume you have been asked to write a program for a professor who wants to reassign the letter grades given to students to numeric grades according to this rating system: A = 95, B = 85, C = 75, D = 65, F = 50. What type of decision structure would you use for this program?

3.25 Create the program described in Checkpoint 3.24 using an if...elseif structure.

3.26 Re-create the program described in Checkpoint 3.24 using a switch statement.

3.27 Add to the program created in Example 3.13 to allow the user to enter several more colors including red and black and any others you want.

3.28 Add to the program created in Checkpoint 3.27 to allow the user to change the text color on the web page.

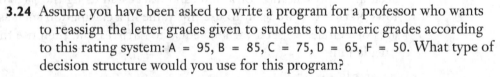

3.7 Putting It to Work

Now we'll combine everything we've learned to create a new game for Greg's Gambits and an arithmetic lesson for Carla's Classroom. You will have a chance to build on both of these sites in the end-of-chapter exercises.

Greg's Gambits: Madame Vadoma Knows All

Madame Vadoma knows all! In fact, the name Vadoma is a Romani name meaning "knowing one." She has a page on the Greg's Gambits site where she will answer any question a player asks. We will now create that page and, as we do, we will become privy to the secret of Madame Vadoma's skill. In this program, the player will type a question and Madame Vadoma will answer it. In the end-of-chapter exercises you will have a chance to create a second page, which will allow Madame Vadoma to provide the player with a prediction of what is in store for him or her.

In general terms, this program will have a button which the player will click to begin. A prompt will ask the player to type a question and Madame Vadoma will display the answer. The secret to Madame Vadoma's success is in her knowledge— and yours—of the Math.random() method. We'll discuss that method now. But first, we must learn a little about the JavaScript **Math object.**

The Math Object

The JavaScript Math object allows you to perform many mathematical tasks easily. Some of these tasks you can program yourself and others are complicated enough that you'll be glad they are available in JavaScript.

For example, in Example 3.14, we declared a constant named **PI** which we set equal to 3.14159. However, JavaScript already has a constant which is a more accurate representation of π and can be accessed using the Math object as follows: Math.PI. If we want to use this value in a calculation such as finding the area of a circle, we set a variable equal to Math.PI and then use the variable in the calculation:

```
var pie = Math.PI;
var area = pie * radius * radius;
```

JavaScript provides eight mathematical constants that can be accessed from the Math object: E, PI, square root of 2, square root of 1/2, natural log of 2, natural log of 10, base-2 log of e, and base-10 log of e. We probably won't use most of these in any of our programs.

However, the Math object also has methods available that can be very helpful. Table 3.1 provides a list of the methods that can be used with the Math object:

TABLE 3.1	The Math Object Methods
Method	**Description**
abs(x)	Returns the absolute value of x
acos(x)	Returns the arccosine of x, in radians
asin(x)	Returns the arcsine of x, in radians

Method	Description
atan(x)	Returns the arctangent of x as a numeric value between -PI/2 and PI/2
atan2(y,x)	Returns the arctangent of the quotient of its arguments
ceil(x)	Returns x, rounded up to the nearest integer
cos(x)	Returns the cosine of x (x is in radians)
exp(x)	Returns the value of E^x
floor(x)	Returns x, rounded down to the nearest integer
log(x)	Returns the natural logarithm (base E) of x
max(x,y,z,...,n)	Returns the number with the highest value
min(x,y,z,...,n)	Returns the number with the lowest value
pow(x,y)	Returns the value of x to the power of y
random()	Returns a random number between 0 and 1
round(x)	Rounds x to the nearest integer
sin(x)	Returns the sine of x (x is in radians)
sqrt(x)	Returns the square root of x
tan(x)	Returns the tangent of an angle

Many of these methods may be obscure to you now, but as you become familiar with them you will find them invaluable. The pow(**x,y**) method allows us to raise any number to any power. We can rewrite the code to calculate the area of a circle, replacing **radius * radius** with Math.pow(**radius**,2). This gives us **radius**². In this particular case, using the method is not really a time saver, but imagine a calculation that requires raising a number to the fifth or sixth power. It would be far easier to use Math.pow(**num**, 6) than to use **num * num * num * num * num * num**! Here is how this method would be used to calculate the area of a circle with a radius = **radius**:

```
var pie = Math.PI;
var area = pie * Math.pow(radius,2);
```

For Madame Vadoma's page, we only need to focus on two methods: Math. random()and Math.floor().

The Math.random() and Math.floor() Methods

The Math.random() method returns a number between 0 and 1. The syntax of its use in a program is as follows:

```
var num = Math.random();
```

In case you haven't guessed, Madame Vadoma isn't a real soothsayer. She will select her answers to the questions from answers that we have created. The answer she picks will be chosen at random, through the Math.random() method.

When a program encounters the expression `Math.random()` it generates a random number from 0.0 to 1.0, including 0.0 but not 1.0. Initially, this may seem unhelpful. After all, how many situations can you think of that can use a random number like 0.5024994240225955 or 0.843290654721918? While randomly generated numbers like these may have some esoteric uses, it is far more common to require integer random numbers in a specific range. For example, in simulating the roll of a single die (one of a pair of dice), the possible outcomes are 1, 2, 3, 4, 5, and 6. Therefore, we normally manipulate the generated number to turn it into an integer in the range we require. This may take several steps.

For the purposes of illustration, we will show random numbers generated to have four decimal places (the actual number of decimal places generated with this method in JavaScript is much more). For example, `Math.random()` might generate 0.3792 or 0.0578. If we multiply this random number by 10, we will generate numbers between 0 and 9.9999, as shown in the following:

- If `Math.random()` = 0.3234, then `Math.random()* 10` = 3.2340.
- If `Math.random()` = 0.0894, then `Math.random()* 10` = 0.8940.
- If `Math.random()` = 0.1737, then `Math.random()* 10` = 1.7370.
- If `Math.random()` = 0.9999, then `Math.random()* 10` = 9.9990.

We have increased the range from 0.000 up to, but not including, 10. We still, however, do not have integer values. But we do have the `Math.floor()` method, which takes a number and rounds it down to the nearest integer. Therefore, If we take the `floor()` of any random number, we will simply drop the decimal part, as you can see from the following:

- If `Math.random()` = 0.3234, then `Math.floor(Math.random() *10)` = 3.
- If `Math.random()` = 0.0894, then `Math.floor(Math.random() * 10` = 8.
- If `Math.random()` = 0.1737, then `Math.floor(Math.random() * 10` = 1.
- If `Math.random()` = 0.9999, then `Math.floor(Math.random() * 10` = 9.

We now have random numbers between 0 and 9. Finally, if we wish to generate a random number between 1 and 10, we can simply add 1 to the expression to get the following:

- If `Math.random()` = 0.3234, then `(Math.floor(Math.random() * 10)) + 1` = 4.
- If `Math.random()` = 0.0894, then `(Math.floor(Math.random() * 10)) + 1` = 9.
- If `Math.random()` = 0.1737, then `(Math.floor(Math.random() * 10)) + 1` = 2.
- If `Math.random()` = 0.9999, then `(Math.floor(Math.random() * 10)) + 1` = 10.

To use the random number generator in a program, you assign its value to an integer variable. To generate random numbers in any range desired, you change the multiplier and/or the number added, as needed. Example 3.16 demonstrates this.

EXAMPLE 3.16

Generating Random Numbers in a Given Range

If **newNum** is an integer variable, then the following happens:

- **newNum** = (Math.floor(Math.random() * 10)) + 1 will result in a random number between 1 and 10 (inclusive).
- **newNum** = (Math.floor(Math.random() * 100)) + 1 will result in a random number between 1 and 100 (inclusive).
- **newNum** = (Math.floor(Math.random() * 10)) + 4 will result in a random number between 4 and 13 (inclusive).
- **newNum** = (Math.floor(Math.random() * 2)) will result in either 0 or 1.
- **newNum** = (Math.floor(Math.random() * 2)) + 1 will result in either 1 or 2.
- **newNum** = (Math.floor(Math.random() * 6)) + 7 will result in a random number between 7 and 12 (inclusive).

After examining these examples, we can conclude that, to generate a sequence of N random integers beginning with the integer M, use the following:

```
Math.floor(Math.random() * N) + M
```

Developing the Program

First, we will create possible answers that Madame Vadoma will display after the player asks a question. For now, we will create 10 possible responses but, if you want to be creative, compose different responses or modify these. We will use the following responses:

1. Absolutely!
2. No way!
3. Probably . . .
4. Doubtful . . .
5. Could be . . .
6. Madame Vadoma cannot answer such a question.
7. You must find the answer within yourself.
8. Yes, of course!
9. You don't really believe this works, do you?
10. Madame Vadoma wonders about that too.

Next, we will create a page with a button to allow the user to begin. Then, we will prompt for the question. The program will generate a random number from 1 through 10. With a switch statement, the response that will be displayed is the one that corresponds to the generated random number.

Writing the Code

This page will be part of the Greg's Gambits site we have been developing. First, we will add a link on the play_games.html page to this page. It should look like this:

Next, we will create a page using the code below. You can create your own or add the necessary code to the file named gregs_fortune.html which is available in the Student Data Files.

First, add header elements with the following content:

Madame Vadoma Sees All!

Ask Madame Vadoma Anything That You Are Worried About

Next, add the image of Madame Vadoma (madame.jpg) and her name as well as a button for the player to click to begin. The code for this follows:

```
1.   <div id="content">
2.       <p class="floatright">Madame Vadoma<br /><br />
3.       <img src ="images/madame.jpg" /></p>
4.       <p> </p>
5.       <p><input type="button" value = "Ask your question" ⏎
         onclick="startFortune();" /></p>
6.       <p> </p>
7.   </div>
```

Put this in the content area on the page so that your page now looks like this:

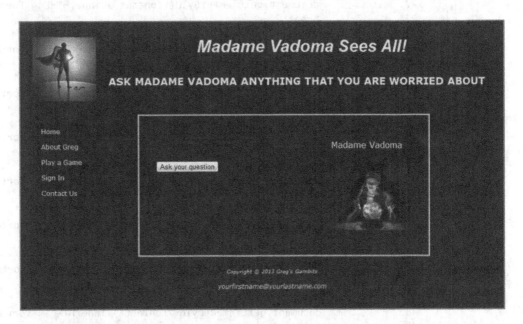

Now we will write the function called startFortune() that will generate a random number (1 through 10), prompt the player for a question, and use the generated random number to display an answer. We will use a switch statement to determine which answer will be displayed. The code follows:

```
1.  <script type="text/javascript">
2.  function startFortune()
3.  {
4.      var num = 0;
5.      var question = " ";
6.      var fortune1 = "Absolutely ";
7.      var fortune2 = "No way ";
8.      var fortune3 = "Probably...";
9.      var fortune4 = "Doubtful...";
10.     var fortune5 = "Could be...";
11.     var fortune6 = "Madame Vadoma cannot answer such a question. ";
12.     var fortune7 = "You must find the answer within yourself. ";
13.     var fortune8 = "Yes, of course! ";
14.     var fortune9 = "You don't really believe this works, do you? ";
15.     var fortune10 = "Madame Vadoma wonders about that too. ";
16.     num = (Math.floor(Math.random() * 10)) + 1;
17.     question = prompt("What is your question? ", " ");
18.     switch(num)
19.     {
20.        case 1:
21.            document.getElementById("content").innerHTML = fortune1;
22.            break;
23.        case 2:
24.            document.getElementById("content").innerHTML = fortune2;
25.            break;
```

```
26.          case 3:
27.                  document.getElementById("content").innerHTML = fortune3;
28.                  break;
29.          case 4:
30.                  document.getElementById("content").innerHTML = fortune4;
31.                  break;
32.          case 5:
33.                  document.getElementById("content").innerHTML = fortune5;
34.                  break;
35.          case 6:
36.                  document.getElementById("content").innerHTML = fortune6;
37.                  break;
38.          case 7:
39.                  document.getElementById("content").innerHTML = fortune7;
40.                  break;
41.          case 8:
42.                  document.getElementById("content").innerHTML = fortune8;
43.                  break;
44.          case 9:
45.                  document.getElementById("content").innerHTML = fortune9;
46.                  break;
47.          case 10:
48.                  document.getElementById("content").innerHTML = fortune10;
49.                  break;
50.      }
51.  }
52.  </script>
```

Note the use of the getElementById() method to place the result in the content area of the page. If the player asks "Will I get an A in this class?" and the random number generated is 10, the display will look like this:

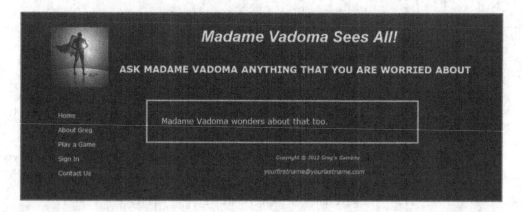

Putting It All Together

The following program puts it all together:

```
1.  <!DOCTYPE html PUBLIC "-//W3C//DTD XHTML 1.0 Transitional//EN" ↵
        "http://www.w3.org/TR/xhtml1/DTD/xhtml1-transitional.dtd">
2.  <html xmlns="http://www.w3.org/1999/xhtml" lang="en" xml:lang="en">
3.  <meta http-equiv="Content-Type" content="text/html; charset=utf-8" />
4.  <head>
```

```
5.    <title>Greg's Gambits | Madame Vadoma Sees All</title>
6.    <link href="greg.css" rel="stylesheet" type="text/css" />
7.    <script type="text/javascript">
8.    function startFortune()
9.    {
10.       var num = 0;
11.       var question = " ";
12.       var fortune1 = "Absolutely ";
13.       var fortune2 = "No way ";
14.       var fortune3 = "Probably...";
15.       var fortune4 = "Doubtful...";
16.       var fortune5 = "Could be...";
17.       var fortune6 = "Madame Vadoma cannot answer such a question. ";
18.       var fortune7 = "You must find the answer within yourself. ";
19.       var fortune8 = "Yes, of course! ";
20.       var fortune9 = "You don't really believe this works, do you? ";
21.       var fortune10 = "Madame Vadoma wonders about that too. ";
22.       num = (Math.floor(Math.random() * 10)) + 1;
23.       question = prompt("What is your question? ", " ");
24.       switch(num)
25.       {
26.          case 1:
27.             document.getElementById("content").innerHTML = fortune1;
28.             break;
29.          case 2:
30.             document.getElementById("content").innerHTML = fortune2;
31.             break;
32.          case 3:
33.             document.getElementById("content").innerHTML = fortune3;
34.             break;
35.          case 4:
36.             document.getElementById("content").innerHTML = fortune4;
37.             break;
38.          case 5:
39.             document.getElementById("content").innerHTML = fortune5;
40.             break;
41.          case 6:
42.             document.getElementById("content").innerHTML = fortune6;
43.             break;
44.          case 7:
45.             document.getElementById("content").innerHTML = fortune7;
46.             break;
47.          case 8:
48.             document.getElementById("content").innerHTML = fortune8;
49.             break;
50.          case 9:
51.             document.getElementById("content").innerHTML = fortune9;
52.             break;
53.          case 10:
54.             document.getElementById("content").innerHTML = fortune10;
55.             break;
56.       }
57.    }
58.    </script>
59.    </head>
60.    <body>
```

```
61.    <div id="container">
62.        <img src="../images/superhero.jpg" width="120" height="120" ↵
               class="floatleft" />
63.        <h1 id="logo"><em>Madame Vadoma Sees All!</em></h1>
64.        <h2 align="center">Ask Madame Vadoma anything that you are ↵
               worried about </h2>
65.        <p> </p>
66.        <div id="nav">
67.            <p><a href="index.html">Home</a>
68.             <a href="greg.html">About Greg</a>
69.             <a href="play_games.html">Play a Game</a>
70.             <a href="sign.html">Sign In</a>
71.             <a href="contact.html">Contact Us</a></p>
72.        </div>
73.        <div id="content">
74.            <input type="button" value = "Ask your question" ↵
                   onclick="startFortune();" />
75.            <p> </p>
76.        </div>
77.        <div id = "footer">Copyright &copy; 2013 Greg's Gambits <br />
78.            <a href="mailto:yourfirstname@yourlastname.com"> ↵
                   yourfirstname@yourlastname.com</a>
79.        </div>
80.    </div>
81.    </body>
82.    </html>
```

Finishing Up

Here is a sample question and a possible outcome:

input:

```
Will I buy a new car this year?
```

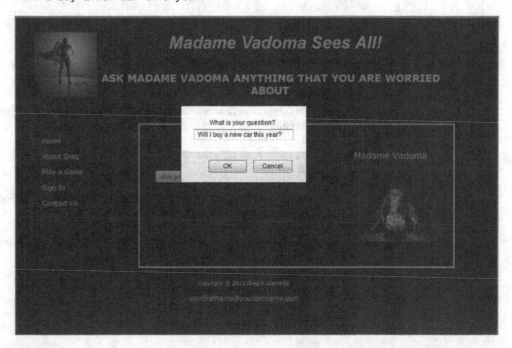

possible output:

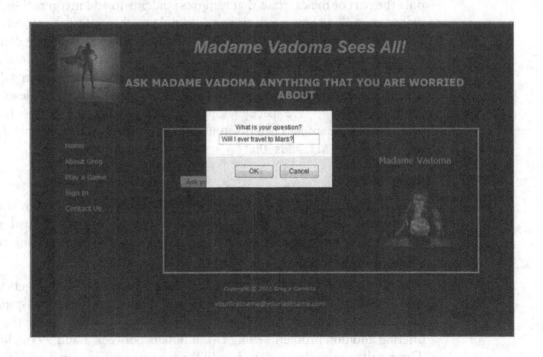

input:

Will I ever travel to Mars?

possible output:

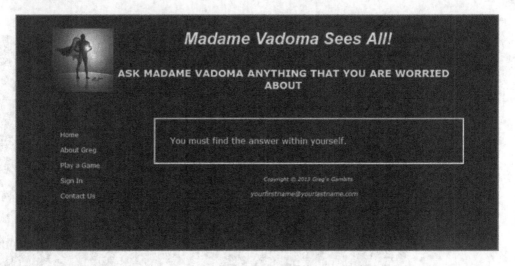

Carla's Classroom: **An Arithmetic Lesson**

We can use the skills we've learned to create a math exercise for Carla's Classroom that will adjust automatically to a child's ability. For this section, we will develop only the part of the exercise that requires students to add integers. Once this is complete, you will see how easy it is to add simple mathematical operations (subtraction, multiplication, division) and even more complex mathematical calculations. In this program, a student will attempt to solve easy addition problems. Once the student has completed a certain number of problems correctly, the program will increase the level of difficulty. For now we will restrict the number of each level of addition problems to five to save space; in Chapter 4, you will learn how to enhance this program so that the student can do an unlimited number of math problems. We'll call this exercise It All Adds Up.

Developing the Program

This program is a bit complicated; therefore, before we think about coding, we'll create some pseudocode to map out the flow of the program. We will program in three levels of difficulty: Level One (easy), Level Two (intermediate), and Level Three (advanced).

The Math.random() method will be used to generate random integers which the student will be asked to add for each problem. For Level One, the student will add two numbers between 1 and 10 (inclusive). Level Two will increase the difficulty by offering addition problems using two numbers between 1 and 99 (inclusive). Level Three will require the student to add three numbers between 1 and 99 (inclusive).

The return Statement

The return **statement** allows you to exit a function before all lines of code have been executed. We need to use this statement because each level will be exited if either the student answers three problems correctly or reaches the end of the problems in that level. The syntax for this statement is simple:

```
return;
```

The Counter

Counters are used frequently for many purposes in programming. We will rely on counters heavily in subsequent chapters, especially when we begin to use loops and repetition structures. For this program, we need a counter to record how many correct answers a student enters at each level. The counter must be an integer variable and can be increased or decreased throughout a program or part of a program. To increase a counter by one, we add one to the present value of the counter. The syntax for this, assuming we name our counter **count**, is as follows:

```
count = count + 1;
```

This may look strange if you just left an algebra class (how can something equal itself plus one?) but in programming, this statement means to take the value on the right-hand side of the expression (**count** + 1) and store it in the variable on the left-hand side (**count**). In this way, we increase the value of **count** by one.

Writing the Code

First, we'll have the student begin the math exercise by clicking a button in the content area of a web page. You can use the template provided in your Student Data Files to include the following code in the content area:

```
<p>This arithmetic test will increase in difficulty as you prove you are ready
for harder problems. As soon as you get 3 problems correct in Level One, you will
progress to Level Two and then to Level Three.</p>
<p><input type="button" onclick="addIt()" value="begin the test" /></p>
```

Your page will now look like this:

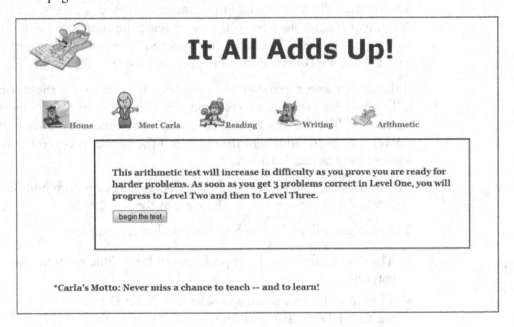

Save the page with the filename `carla_adding.html` and add a link to this page from the `math.html` page. The `math.html` page will now look like this:

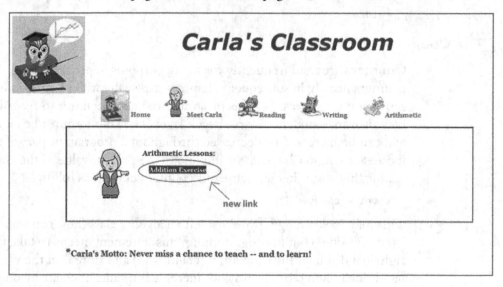

The Plan

When a student clicks the button, the function that will produce the simple addition problems will begin. For each addition problem we must generate two random numbers (between 1 and 10). Then the student will be prompted to add those numbers. The student's response will be compared to the correct response. If the response is incorrect, an alert will display that message and the next problem will be generated and shown to the student. But if the response is correct, we must keep track of that because, after three correct responses, the program will jump to the next level. For this we need a counter.

The counter will keep track of the number of correct answers. Each time the student answers a problem correctly, we increase the counter by one. After each problem, we test to see if the counter has reached 3. When this happens, the program will skip any statements in that function and move to the next level.

If the student gets three correct responses, the function for the second level is called. Now we generate two random numbers between 1 and 99 and repeat the process used for the first level: Ask the student to add the numbers, test if the answer is correct, increment the counter if the answer is correct, test to see if the counter has reached 3, and so on.

The third level, when reached, now generates three random numbers between 1 and 99 but is otherwise exactly the same as the first levels.

The program will end when one of the following happens:

- The student finishes all the problems of Level One without answering three correctly.
- The student answers three problems of Level One correctly but finishes answering all the Level Two problems without getting three right.

- The student answers three problems of Level One correctly, three of Level Two correctly, and completes all of Level Three without getting three right.

- The student answers three problems of Level One correctly, three of Level Two correctly, and three of Level Three correctly.

You may have noticed that, although this program may become lengthy, there will be much repetition. The function for Level One will be exactly the same as Level Two except for how the random numbers are generated. The function for Level Three will be exactly the same as Level Two except we will add a third random number. We'll put all of these functions within one main function. We'll develop the Level One function from the following pseudocode and use this as a template to develop the other two functions:

```
1.   Begin function levelOne()
2.     declare a counter variable = 0
3.     for each addition problem
4.         declare variable num1a = random number between 1 and 10
5.         declare variable num1b = random number between 1 and 10
6.         declare variable sum1 = num1a + num1b
7.         declare variable response = integer value of student's
                                      response to a prompt
8.         if the response is correct
9.             increase the counter by one
10.            tell student the answer is correct
11.        else if response is not correct
12.            tell student the answer is wrong
13.        if the counter = 3
14.            call the next level
15.            use a return statement to exit the program
```

Once we write the code that corresponds to this pseudocode, we can repeat the code on lines 4–15 as many times as we want. Each repetition will create a new addition problem for the student to solve.

The Code in Pieces

Level One Code   At the end of this section, we will put together the whole program, using more repetitions of the problems for each level. However, to save space, only the first repetition is shown here. The code that corresponds to the pseudocode shown above is as follows:

```
1.   function levelOne()
2.   {
3.         //problem 1
4.         var num1a = (Math.floor(Math.random() * 10)) + 1;
5.         var num1b = (Math.floor(Math.random() * 10)) + 1;
6.         var sum1 = num1a + num1b;
7.         var response = parseInt(prompt("What is the sum of " + num1a ↵
                         + " and " + num1b + " ?"));
8.         if (response == sum1)
9.         {
10.            count1 = count1 + 1;
11.            result = "correct!";
12.            alert(result);
```

```
13.             }
14.         else
15.         {
16.             result = "incorrect";
17.             alert(result);
18.         }
19.         if (count1 == 3)
20.         {
21.             levelTwo();
22.             return;
23.         }
 .          // insert code for more problems here
 .
 .
XX.    } //this bracket closes the levelOne() function after all the ⏎
                problems have been included
```

In this program, the variables for the random numbers, the counter, and the sum have been named with a "1" appended to the variable name. This was done to make it easier, later on, to identify which variables go with which levels. We will name the levelTwo() function variables **num2a**, **num2b**, **sum2**, and **count2** and use similar names for the levelThree() function. Because much of the code will be reused, it's advantageous to find ways to identify various elements easily in case debugging is necessary.

Finally, at the end of the last problem, if the student still has not answered three problems correctly, a message should display that tells the student that more practice is needed. The code for this should go under the last if clause that checks to see if the counter has reached 3 and is as follows:

```
else
{
    alert("You need more practice at this level.");
    return;
}
```

Level Two Code   The main difference between Level One and Level Two is that a new statement must be written to generate the numbers for each addition problem. We now want numbers between 1 and 99. The code to generate one addition problem at the second level is as follows:

```
1.    function levelTwo()
2.    {
3.        var count2 = 0;
4.        alert("you're at level 2");
5.        //problem 1
6.        var num2a = (Math.floor(Math.random() * 100)) + 1;
7.        var num2b = (Math.floor(Math.random() * 100)) + 1;
8.        var sum2 = num2a + num2b;
9.        var response = parseInt(prompt("What is the sum of " + num2a ⏎
                        + " and " + num2b + " ?"));
10.       if (response == sum2)
11.       {
12.           count2 = count2 + 1;
```

```
13.            result = "correct!";
14.            alert(result);
15.        }
16.     else
17.        {
18.            result = "incorrect";
19.            alert(result);
20.        }
21.     if (count2 == 3)
22.        {
23.            levelThree();
24.            return;
25.        }
```

Notice that a new counter is needed. The same variable could have been reused in this function but the counter still must be set back to 0 at the top of the new function. Remember that the only way a student would get to Level Two is if the counter in the level0ne() function reached 3. Unless the counter is reset to 0, the student would not get much use out of Level Two since he or she would begin with three correct responses already!

The only other changes in this function are the renaming of variables which is just a personal preference and the fact that, when the new **count2** reaches 3, the levelThree() function is called.

Just as with Level One, at the end of the last problem, if the student has not answered three problems correctly, a message should display that tells the student that more practice is needed. The code would be exactly the same as for Level One.

Level Three Code   For Level Three, a small amount of code is added to inform the student that he or she has successfully completed the sequence. Aside from this, the main difference between this code and the code for Level Two is that a third variable has been added which holds a third random number between 1 and 99. The student is then prompted to add three numbers instead of two. All the other programming logic remains the same as in the previous two levels.

```
1.   function levelThree()
2.   {
3.       var count3 = 0;
4.       alert("you're at level 3");
5.       //problem 1
6.       var num3a = (Math.floor(Math.random() * 100)) + 1;
7.       var num3b = (Math.floor(Math.random() * 100)) + 1;
8.       var num3c = (Math.floor(Math.random() * 100)) + 1;
9.       var sum3 = num3a + num3b + num3c;
10.      var response = parseInt(prompt("What is the sum of " + num3a ⏎
                        + ", " + num3b + ", and " + num3c + " ?"));
11.      if (response == sum3)
12.      {
13.          count3 = count3 + 1;
14.          result = "correct!";
15.          alert(result);
16.      }
```

```
17.        else
18.        {
19.            result = "incorrect";
20.            alert(result);
21.        }
22.        if (count3 == 3)
23.        {
24.            alert("That's all, folks! Proceed to multiplication ↵
                            now!");
25.            return;
26.        }
```

This time, if the student completes all the problems in Level Three and does not answer three correctly, the program will end and the message, to be added after the last Level Three problem should be as follows:

```
1.  else
2.  {
3.        alert("That's all, folks! But you need more practice ↵
                        at this level.");
4.        return;
5.  }
```

A Comment about Checking the Counter   You may wonder why this program checks the counter in the first two problems since it would be impossible for a student to get three right after only trying one or two problems. You can remove this check if you want. However, there are much easier and more efficient ways to handle this program using repetition structures. We will learn about them in Chapter 4 and will refine this program at that time. Because of the nature of repetition structures, it is simpler to code each repetition in the same way. It takes a computer a bare nanosecond to process the "Is the counter equal to 3?" command a few extra times and, by including it in all the problems, the rest of the code will be cleaner.

Putting It All Together

Now we will put the entire program together including the HTML script. You will have a chance to modify this code to create math exercises for subtraction, multiplication, and division in the end-of-chapter exercises or to add to the levels of difficulty for addition.

```
1.  <!DOCTYPE html PUBLIC "-//W3C//DTD XHTML 1.0 Transitional//EN" ↵
        "http://www.w3.org/TR/xhtml11/DTD/xhtml11-transitional.dtd">
2.  <html xmlns="http://www.w3.org/1999/xhtml" lang="en" xml:lang="en">
3.  <head>
4.  <title>Carla's Classroom | It All Adds Up</title>
5.  <link href="carla.css" rel="stylesheet" type="text/css" />
6.  <script type="text/javascript">
7.  function addIt()
8.  {
9.        var num1a = 0;
10.       var num1b = 0;
11.       var sum1 = 0;
```

```
12.        var count1 = 0;
13.        var response = " ";
14.        var result = " ";
15.        levelOne();
16.  function levelOne()
17.  {
18.  //problem 1
19.        var num1a = (Math.floor(Math.random() * 10)) + 1;
20.        var num1b = (Math.floor(Math.random() * 10)) + 1;
21.        var sum1 = num1a + num1b;
22.        var response = parseInt(prompt("What is the sum of " + num1a ↵
                         + " and " + num1b + " ?"));
23.        if (response == sum1)
24.        {
25.                count1 = count1 + 1;
26.                result = "correct!";
27.                alert(result);
28.        }
29.        else
30.        {
31.                result = "incorrect";
32.                alert(result);
33.        }
34.        if (count1 == 3)
35.        {
36.                levelTwo();
37.                return;
38.        }
39.  //problem 2
40.        var num1a = (Math.floor(Math.random() * 10)) + 1;
41.        var num1b = (Math.floor(Math.random() * 10)) + 1;
42.        var sum1 = num1a + num1b;
43.        var response = parseInt(prompt("What is the sum of " + num1a ↵
                         + " and " + num1b + " ?"));
44.        if (response == sum1)
45.        {
46.                count1 = count1 + 1;
47.                result = "correct!";
48.                alert(result);
49.        }
50.        else
51.        {
52.                result = "incorrect";
53.                alert(result);
54.        }
55.        if (count1 == 3)
56.        {
57.                levelTwo();
58.                return;
59.        }
60.                .
61.                .
62.  //add as many Level One problems as you want here
63.                .
64.                .
65.  //last Level One problem
```

```
66.        var numla = (Math.floor(Math.random() * 10)) + 1;
67.        var num1b = (Math.floor(Math.random() * 10)) + 1;
68.        var sum1 = numla + num1b;
69.        var response = parseInt(prompt("What is the sum of " + numla ↵
                        + " and " + num1b + " ?"));
70.        if (response == sum1)
71.        {
72.              count1 = count1 + 1;
73.              result = "correct!";
74.              alert(result);
75.        }
76.        else
77.        {
78.              result = "incorrect";
79.              alert(result);
80.        }
81.        if (count1 == 3)
82.        {
83.              levelTwo();
84.              return;
85.        }
86.        else
87.        {
88.              alert("You need more practice at this level.");
89.              return;
90.        }
91.    }
92.    function levelTwo()
93.    {
94.        var count2 = 0;
95.        alert("you're at level 2");
96.    //problem 1
97.        var num2a = (Math.floor(Math.random() * 100)) + 1;
98.        var num2b = (Math.floor(Math.random() * 100)) + 1;
99.        var sum2 = num2a + num2b;
100.       var response = parseInt(prompt("What is the sum of " + num2a ↵
                        + " and " + num2b + " ?"));
101.       if (response == sum2)
102.       {
103.             count2 = count2 + 1;
104.             result = "correct!";
105.             alert(result);
106.       }
107.       else
108.       {
109.             result = "incorrect";
110.             alert(result);
111.       }
112.       if (count2 == 3)
113.       {
114.             levelThree();
115.             return;
116.       }
117.    //problem 2
118.       var num2a = (Math.floor(Math.random() * 100)) + 1;
119.       var num2b = (Math.floor(Math.random() * 100)) + 1;
120.       var sum2 = num2a + num2b;
```

```
121.        var response = parseInt(prompt("What is the sum of " + num2a ↵
                       + " and " + num2b + " ?"));
122.        if (response == sum2)
123.        {
124.                count2 = count2 + 1;
125.                result = "correct!";
126.                alert(result);
127.        }
128.        else
129.        {
130.                result = "incorrect";
131.                alert(result);
132.        }
133.        if (count2 == 3)
134.        {
135.                levelThree();
136.                return;
137.        }
138.             .
139.             .
140. //add as many Level Two problems as you want here
141.
142.             .
143. //last Level Two problem
144.        var num2a = (Math.floor(Math.random() * 100)) + 1;
145.        var num2b = (Math.floor(Math.random() * 100)) + 1;
146.        var sum2 = num2a + num2b;
147.        var response = parseInt(prompt("What is the sum of " + num2a ↵
                       + " and " + num2b + " ?"));
148.        if (response == sum2)
149.        {
150.                count2 = count2 + 1;
151.                result = "correct!";
152.                alert(result);
153.        }
154.        else
155.        {
156.                result = "incorrect";
157.                alert(result);
158.        }
159.        if (count2 == 3)
160.        {
161.                levelThree();
162.                return;
163.        }
164.        else
165.        {
166.                alert("You need more practice at this level.");
167.                return;
168.        }
169. }
170. function levelThree()
171. {
172.        var count3 = 0;
173.        alert("you're at level 3");
174. //problem 1
175.        var num3a = (Math.floor(Math.random() * 100)) + 1;
```

```
176.        var num3b = (Math.floor(Math.random() * 100)) + 1;
177.        var num3c = (Math.floor(Math.random() * 100)) + 1;
178.        var sum3 = num3a + num3b + num3c;
179.        var response = parseInt(prompt("What is the sum of " + num3a ⏎
                          + ", " + num3b + ", and " + num3c + " ?"));
180.        if (response == sum3)
181.        {
182.            count3 = count3 + 1;
183.            result = "correct!";
184.            alert(result);
185.        }
186.        else
187.        {
188.            result = "incorrect";
189.            alert(result);
190.        }
191.        if (count3 == 3)
192.        {
193.            alert("That's all, folks! Proceed to multiplication now!");
194.            return;
195.        }
196.  //problem 2
197.        var num3a = (Math.floor(Math.random() * 100)) + 1;
198.        var num3b = (Math.floor(Math.random() * 100)) + 1;
199.        var num3c = (Math.floor(Math.random() * 100)) + 1;
200.        var sum3 = num3a + num3b + num3c;
201.        var response = parseInt(prompt("What is the sum of " + num3a ⏎
                          + ", " + num3b + ", and " + num3c + " ?"));
202.        if (response == sum3)
203.        {
204.            count3 = count3 + 1;
205.            result = "correct!";
206.            alert(result);
207.        }
208.        else
209.        {
210.            result = "incorrect";
211.            alert(result);
212.        }
213.        if (count3 == 3)
214.        {
215.            alert("That's all, folks! Proceed to multiplication now!");
216.            return;
217.        }
218.            .
219.            .
220.  //add as many Level Three problems as you want here
221.            .
222.            .
223.  //last Level Three problem
224.        var num3a = (Math.floor(Math.random() * 100)) + 1;
225.        var num3b = (Math.floor(Math.random() * 100)) + 1;
226.        var num3c = (Math.floor(Math.random() * 100)) + 1;
227.        var sum3 = num3a + num3b + num3c;
228.        var response = parseInt(prompt("What is the sum of " + num3a ⏎
                          + ", " + num3b + ", and " + num3c + " ?"));
```

```
229.      if (response == sum3)
230.      {
231.              count3 = count3 + 1;
232.              result = "correct!";
233.              alert(result);
234.      }
235.      else
236.      {
237.              result = "incorrect";
238.              alert(result);
239.      }
240.      if (count3 == 3)
241.      {
242.              alert("That's all, folks! Proceed to multiplication now!");
243.              return;
244.      }
245.      else
246.      {
247.              alert("That's all, folks! But you need more practice at ⏎
                            this level.");
248.              return;
249.      }
250. }
251. }
252. </script>
253. </head>
254. <body>
255. <div id="container">
256.      <img src="../images/writing_big.jpg" class="floatleft" />
257.      <h1 id="logo">It All Adds Up!</h1>
258.      <div align="left">
259.      <blockquote>
260.      <p><a href="index.html"><img src="images/owl_button.jpg" ⏎
                    width="50" height="50" />Home</a>
261.      <a href="carla.html"><img src="images/carla_button.jpg" ⏎
                    width="50" height="65" />Meet Carla </a>
262.      <a href="reading.html"><img src="images/read_button.jpg" /> Reading</a>
263.      <a href="writing.html"><img src="images/write_button.jpg" ⏎
                    width="50" height="50" />Writing</a>
264.      <a href="math.html"><img src="images/arith_button.jpg" /> ⏎
                    Arithmetic</a>
265.      <br /></p></blockquote>
266.      </div>
267.      <div id="content">
268.      <p>This arithmetic test will increase in difficulty as you ⏎
              prove you are ready for harder problems. As soon as ⏎
              you get 3 problems correct in Level One, you will ⏎
              progress to Level Two and then to Level Three.</p>
269.      <p><input type="button" onclick="addIt()" value="begin the test" /></p>
270.      </div>
271. </div>
272. <div id="footer"><h3>*Carla's Motto: Never miss a chance to ⏎
              teach -- and to learn!</h3>
273. </div>
274. </body>
275. </html>
```

Finishing Up

Here are some possible results after a student uses this page:

output:

The student completes Level One with three correct answers and begins Level Two:

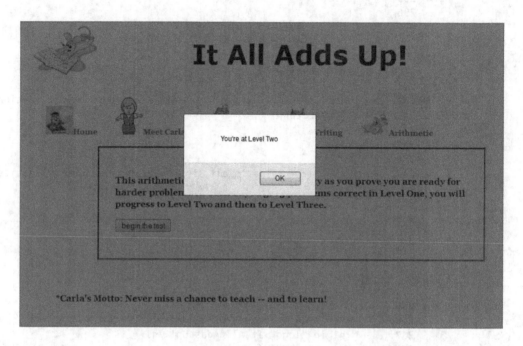

output:

The student completes Level One with three correct answers but does not get three correct answers on Level Two:

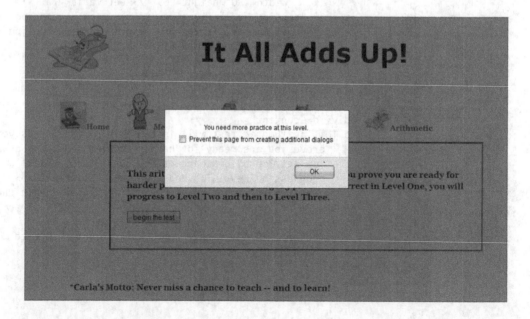

output:

The student completes all three levels successfully (i.e., answers three correctly at each level):

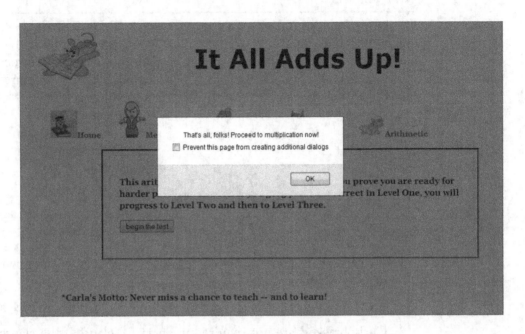

Chapter Review and Exercises

Key Terms

`break;`	`Math.floor()` method
compound conditions	`Math.random()` method
counters	multiple-alternative structure
curly brackets ({})	nested selection structure
dual-alternative structure	selection structure
`if...`	`return;` statement
`if...else`	single-alternative structure
`if...else if...`	`switch` statement
Math object	test condition

Review Exercises

Fill in the Blank

1. A selection structure needs a _____ _____ along with one or more blocks of statements.

2. An `if...else` clause is an example of a _____-alternative structure.

3. Curly brackets are not required in an `if...` clause if the clause contains only _____ _____.

4. A _____ statement can often be used to replace several `if...else if...` structures.

5. A _____ is used to keep track of how many times something has happened in a program.

True or False

6. T/F   An `if...else` structure needs only one test condition.

7. T/F   A multiple-alternative selection structure needs only one test condition.

8. T/F   The only possible values for a test condition are `true` and `false`.

9. T/F   Curly brackets must always be used to enclose statements in an `if...` clause even if there is only one statement.

10. T/F   The `return;` statement will cause a break in the execution of a clause in a selection structure.

11. T/F   An `if...else` structure cannot be nested within another `if...else` structure.

12. T/F   The test condition of an `else...` clause must be the same as the test condition of its `if...` clause.

13. T/F   All cases in a `switch` statement *must* include a `break;` statement.

14. T/F   If the test condition in an `if...` clause is `false`, the statements in that clause will be skipped.

15. T/F   A test condition can never contain compound conditions.

Short Answer

16. What is the result of the following statement, given that x = 4?

```
if(x == 5)
```

17. What will be displayed after the following code snippet is run, given that **Jody** = 18?

```
if(Jody > 18)
   document.write("You can vote");
if(Jody < 18)
   document.write("You're too young");
document.write("Bye bye");
```

18. What will be displayed after the following code snippet is run, given that **Jody** = 18?

```
if(Jody > 18)
   document.write("You can vote");
else if(Jody < 18)
   document.write("You're too young");
document.write("Bye bye");
```

19. What will be displayed after the following code snippet is run, given that rain = "yes"?

```
if(rain == "yes")
   document.write("Bring your umbrella");
else
{
   document.write("No umbrella needed");
   document.write("Bye bye");
}
```

20. What will be displayed after the following code snippet is run, given that **rain** = "yes"?

```
if(rain == "yes")
   document.write("Bring your umbrella");
else
   document.write("No umbrella needed");
   document.write("Bye bye");
```

21. A `switch` statement is often used to replace which of the following?
    a) Multiple `if...` statements
    b) A single `if...else if...` structure
    c) Multiple `if...else if...` statements
    d) Only (a) and (c)
    e) Any of the following: (a), (b), or (c)

22. What value is begin tested in the following code snippet?

```
switch(points)
{
        case 20:
                document.write("twenty");
                break;
        case 20:
                document.write("twenty");
                break;
        default:
                document.write("invalid entry");
}
```

23. Assume you want a user to enter a number between 10 and 20 (inclusive). Write the compound condition that should be entered in the following if... clause that will test for a number in this range, using the AND operator:

```
var num = parseInt(prompt("enter a number between 10 and 20"," "));
if(_____)
    document.write("good number");
else
    document.write("invalid number");
```

24. Assume you want a user to enter a number between 10 and 20 (inclusive). Write the compound condition that should be entered in the following if... clause that will test for a number in this range, using the OR operator:

```
var num = parseInt(prompt("enter a number between 10 and 20"," "));
if(_____)
    document.write("invalid number");
else
    document.write("good number");
```

25. Assume you want a user to enter a number between 10 and 20 (inclusive). Write the compound condition that should be entered in the following if... clause that will test for a number in this range, using the OR and NOT operators:

```
var num = parseInt(prompt("enter a number between 10 and 20"," "));
if(_____)
    document.write("good number");
else
    document.write("invalid number");
```

26. What will be displayed if the following code snippet is run, given that the user enters apple at the prompt?

```
var fruit = prompt("What do you want to eat? ", " ");
    switch (fruit)
    {
        case "apple":
          document.write("An apple a day is good for you.<br />");
        case "banana":
          document.write("Bananas are delicious.<br />");
        case "grapes":
          document.write("Who doesn't like grapes!<br />");
        default:
          document.write("You need to eat more fruit.<br />");
    }
```

27. Fix the code in Exercise 26 so that only the response that corresponds with the user's entry displays.

28. Add an if... clause to the program snippet you fixed in Exercise 27 so that, if the user enters apple, the program will prompt the user to enter a variety of apple, such as Granny Smith or McIntosh, and the output will use that apple variety to say "A _____ apple is good for you."

Exercises 29 and 30 refer to the following code:

```
var vacation = prompt("What do you want to do during Spring Break? ↵
                Type S for skiing, F for fishing, H for hiking,8
                J for learning JavaScript.", " ");
if (vacation == 'S')
   document.write("You should go to Aspen.<br />");
if (vacation == 'H')
   document.write("Be sure to buy good hiking boots.<br />");
if (vacation == 'F')
   document.write("Worms make good bait.<br />");
if (vacation == 'J')
   document.write("You're gonna have soooo much fun!<br />");
```

29. Rewrite the code as a series of if...else if...structures.

30. Rewrite the code using a switch statement.

Programming Challenges

On Your Own

1. Create a web page that acts as a temperature converter. The user should be given the option to enter the temperature in degrees Fahrenheit and the program will convert the temperature to degrees Celsius. Alternatively, the user can enter the temperature in degrees Celsius and the program will convert the temperature to degrees Fahrenheit. Save the page as temp.html and be sure to include an appropriate page title. The formulas for the conversions are as follows:

   - Celsius = 5/9 * (Fahrenheit - 32)
   - Fahrenheit = (Celsius * 5/9) + 32

2. Either create a new web page or add to the page you created in Programming Challenge 1. The page will act as a weather forecaster. The user will enter a temperature in either degrees Celsius or degrees Fahrenheit (your choice) and the program will display one of the following messages, depending on the temperature:

   - Less than 0^0F or -18^0C: Bundle up! It's really freezing out there!
   - $0^0 - 32^0$F or $-18^0 - 0^0$C: Pretty cold with a chance of snow.
   - $33^0 - 59^0$F or $-17^0 - 15^0$C: Don't forget your jacket. It's still chilly outside.
   - $60^0 - 80^0$F or $16^0 - 27^0$C: Perfect lovely weather...unless it rains.
   - $81^0 - 95^0$F or $28^0 - 35^0$C: Nice and warm. Go for a swim.

■ Greater than 95⁰F or 35⁰C: It's really hot! Probably best to stay in an air conditioned spot.

Save your page with the filename forecast.html and be sure to include an appropriate page title.

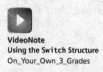

VideoNote
Using the Switch Structure
On_Your_Own_3_Grades

3. Create a web page that converts a student's course average to a letter grade. Save your page as grades.html and be sure to include an appropriate page title. The conversions are as follows:

■ Less than 60: F
■ 60 – 69.5: D
■ 69.6 – 79.5: C
■ 79.6 – 89.5: B
■ Greater than 89.5: A

4. Create a web page that calculates an employee's net pay. The program should prompt for an employee's hourly pay rate, number of hours worked per week, and number of dependents claimed. If the employee works more than 40 hours in a week, overtime is calculated at 1.5 times the regular hourly rate. Taxes are then deducted from the gross pay as follows:

■ No dependents: tax rate is 28%
■ 1 to 3 dependents: tax rate is 25%
■ 4 to 6 dependents: tax rate is 15%
■ More than 6 dependents: tax rate is 10%

Save your page as paychecks.html and be sure to include an appropriate page title.

5. Create a web page like the one created in Programming Challenge 4. However, this program will calculate taxes based on compound conditions as follows:

■ No dependents and gross pay is greater than $1000.00: tax rate is 33%
■ No dependents and gross pay is less than or equal to $1000.00: tax rate is 28%
■ 1 to 3 dependents and gross pay is greater than $1000.00: tax rate is 25%
■ 1 to 3 dependents and gross pay is less than or equal to $1000.00: tax rate is 22%
■ 4 to 6 dependents and gross pay is greater than $1000.00: tax rate is 22%
■ 4 to 6 dependents and gross pay is less than or equal to $1000.00: tax rate is 15%
■ More than 6 dependents and gross pay is greater than $1000.00: tax rate is 15%
■ More than 6 dependents and gross pay is less than or equal to $1000.00: tax rate is 10%

Save your page as paychecks2.html and be sure to include an appropriate page title.

6. Create a web page for a game site that allows the player to "purchase" various items, depending on the points the player amasses. The player should be

prompted to enter the number of points he or she has and then be allowed to select an item to purchase. If the player has enough points to cover the cost, a message will inform the player that the item has been added to his or her inventory. If the player does not have sufficient points to purchase the item, a message will appear saying that no purchase can be made. The items to be purchased should include the following but you can add your own items as well: a sword, a water skin to hold a gallon of water, a charm which allows the user to become invisible for five minutes, and a cell phone.

Save your page as `points.html` and be sure to include an appropriate page title.

7. Create a web page that allows the user to customize a web page by selecting a background color for the page, as shown in Example 3.13, as well as a color and font for the text. The following function shows you how to change font color and font family. Your page should offer the user more options than just the ones shown here.

```
<head>
<script type="text/javascript">
function customize()
{
       document.getElementById("p1").style.color="red";
       document.getElementById("p1").style.fontFamily="Arial";
}
</script>
</head>
<body>
<p id="p1">Hi there!</p>
<input type="button" onclick="customize()" value="customize" />
</body>
```

Save your page as `customize.html` and be sure to include an appropriate page title.

Case Studies

Greg's Gambits

Now you will add to Madame Vadoma's fortune telling abilities. On this new page Madame Vadoma will tell the player his or her fortune.

Open the `play_games.html` page and add a link, under the `Madame Vadoma Sees All!` link that links to the new page you will create. The new page title should be `Madame Vadoma Can Tell Your Fortune` and the filename should be `gregs_fortune2.html`.

Create this new page with the filename `gregs_fortune2.html`. You can use the page created earlier in the chapter as a template. The page title is `Madame Vadoma Can Tell Your Fortune` and this should also be the first header on the page.

In the content area, place a button that the player can click when he or she wants a fortune told.

Next, create at least 10 fortunes. You can create as many as you want but there should be at least 10. Here are a few sample fortunes to get you started:

- You will meet your soul mate very soon.
- You can get an A in this class if you work hard.
- A good job is in your future.
- No one likes a show-off.
- Don't believe everything you read.

Now create the JavaScript that will run when the player clicks the button. Use the Math.random() method to generate a random number between 1 and 10 (or 1 and however many fortunes you have created). Use a switch statement to display the fortune that corresponds to the random number that has been generated.

Test your page in at least two different browsers. Submit your work as instructed by your teacher.

Carla's Classroom

Now you will add to the addition exercise created earlier in this chapter. You will create pages with one or more of the following arithmetic exercises:

- Add two more levels of difficulty to the addition tests: adding floating point numbers (numbers with decimal parts) and adding fractions. Name this page adv_addition.html.
- Create three levels of multiplication problems: multiplying two single digit integers (from 1 to 10), multiplying two double-digit integers (from 1 to 99), and multiplying two double-digit floating point numbers. Name this page multiply.html.
- Create three levels of division problems using the three levels of difficulty as described for multiplication. Be sure to ensure that no division by zero error occurs. Name this page divide.html.

Each page you create should prompt the student to solve an arithmetic problem. There should be a minimum of five (preferably 10) problems at each level. Each problem should be created by generating two random numbers. The correct answer should be compared to the student's answer. If the answer is correct, a counter should be incremented. When the student has answered three problems correctly at any level, the program should progress to the next level. If a student goes through all the problems in one level without achieving three correct answers, the program should stop and a message should display telling the student that more practice is needed at that level. If the student successfully completes all levels, the message displayed should tell the student to move on to the next exercise.

Open the math.html file and add one or more links (depending on how many options you choose to program) under the Addition Exercises. The links should go to the new page or pages you create.

Use the carla_adding.html page that was created earlier in the chapter as a template to create these new arithmetic exercises for Carla's Classroom. In Chapter 4, we will learn how to generate as many problems as desired without repeating code. We will no longer be limited to five, six, ten, or any specific number of problems.

Test your page(s) in at least two different browsers. Be sure to test all possible combinations of both correct and incorrect responses at each level. Submit your work as instructed by your teacher.

Lee's Landscape

Add a page to the Lee's Landscape website that calculates the cost of various services offered. The page should display the services and their costs, as shown below. Then it will prompt the user to select a service along with one of the options shown and calculate the cost. If the user chooses to contract for the service for six months, there is a 10% discount. There is a 15% discount for a one-year contract and a 20% discount for a two-year contract.

Service	Options	
Lawn maintenance	Weekly: $15/service Twice a month: $25/service Monthly: $40/service	
Pest control	Monthly: $35/service Twice a year: $75/service Yearly: $150/service	
Tree and hedge trimming	Monthly: $25/service Twice a year: $75/service Yearly: $150/service	

The images used here are in the Student Data Files but you can use your own images too. Be sure to give this web page an appropriate page title, such as `Lee's Landscape | Our Services`. Save this file with the filename `lee_service.html`. Add a link to the `Lee's Landscape` home page to this new page. Test your page in at least two different browsers. Be sure to test all possible combinations of each service and contract. Submit your work as instructed by your teacher.

Jackie's Jewelry

Add a page to the `Jackie's Jewelry` website that calculates shipping costs for items purchased according to the rates given below. The page should prompt the user to enter the amount of the purchase and the country where the items will be shipped. It should also allow free shipping if the user has a special promo code called `FREEJACKIE`.

- User has `FREEJACKIE` promo code: free
- Purchase is greater than or equal to $100 and user lives in the United States: free
- Purchase is greater than or equal to $150 and user lives in Canada or Mexico: free
- User lives in the United States:
  - Purchase between $50.00–$99.99: shipping is $10.00
  - Purchase between $20.00–$49.99: shipping is $8.00
  - Purchase less than $20.00: shipping is $5.00
- User lives in Canada or Mexico:
  - Purchase between $50.00–$99.99: shipping is $15.00
  - Purchase between $20.00–$49.99: shipping is $12.00
  - Purchase less than $20.00: shipping is $10.00
- User lives outside the United States, Canada, and Mexico:
  - Purchase between $50.00–$99.99: shipping is $25.00
  - Purchase between $20.00–$49.99: shipping is $20.00
  - Purchase less than $20.00: shipping is $15.00

Be sure to give this web page an appropriate page title, such as `Jackie's Jewelry | Shipping`. Save this file with the filename `jackie_shipping.html`. Add a link to the `Jackie's Jewelry` home page to this new page. Test your page in at least two different browsers. Be sure to test all possible combinations of purchases, addresses, and promo code. Submit your work as instructed by your teacher.

4

Going Round and Round: The Repetition Structure

Chapter Objectives

In Chapter 3 you were asked to imagine what it would be like to go to a website that only offered one thing: a size 4 wool red sweater, costing $125.00 plus $8.00 shipping. If you didn't want this item, nothing would happen. Now imagine what it would be like if, while you could choose the size, color, and fabric of the sweater, you could only order one item. Not only would online shopping become an overwhelming chore but the business would barely make a profit. The same would be true if you could bold text only once in a document, play a computer game just once, or be unable to repeat any of the myriad tasks we normally expect to do on a computer. The fact that we can replay games, check the weather forecast on a website in as many locations as we want, or shop 'til we drop is because programmers understand and use the repetition structure.

Repetition structures are often called loops and we can use the terms interchangeably. In this chapter, you will learn about the repetition structure which allows a program to repeat a block of statements as many times as desired. Sometimes the number of repetitions is set by the programmer, sometimes it can be set by the user, and sometimes it depends on outside factors. But one thing is sure: Repetition structures (or loops) allow code blocks to be executed over and over again without having to write the same code many times. We will discuss the various types of loops and focus on one of the main uses for such a structure: to validate input. In Chapter 5, we will continue our discussion of repetition structures but focus on some advanced concepts and uses.

After reading this chapter, you will be able to do the following:

- Understand the basics of loops
- Understand how to write test conditions
- Understand the difference between pre-test and post-test loops
- Be able to create pre-test `while` loops
- Be able to create post-test `do...while` loops
- Understand and create sentinel-controlled loops
- Format output with the `toLowerCase()`, `toUpperCase()`, and `toFixed()` methods

- Understand and create counter-controlled loops
- Use shortcut operators to increment and decrement variables
- Understand the `for` loop and create the initial condition, test condition, and limit value
- Use loops for data validation

- Use the `NaN()` and `charAt()` methods
- Use the `length` property
- Understand ASCII and Unicode Standard code
- Use the `charCodeAt()` and `String.fromCode()` methods

Computers Don't Get Bored with Repetition

You have learned that all computer programs are created from three basic constructs: *sequence*, *decision*, and *repetition*. This chapter discusses repetition, which in many ways is the most important construct. We are lucky that computers don't find repetitious tasks boring.

The ability to repeat the same actions over and over is the most basic requirement in programming. When you go to any web page that allows you to purchase items, play a game, or search for information, you expect to be able to do whatever is available on the site more than once. Now we will examine how to write JavaScript programs that allow a task to be repeated as often as necessary.

Loop Basics

All programming languages provide statements to create a **loop.** The loop is the basic component of the **repetition structure.** This structure consists of a block of code, which under certain conditions, will be executed repeatedly. In this section, we will introduce some basic ideas about these structures. We will start with a simple illustration of a loop using pseudocode, as shown in Example 4.1.

Going Round and Round

The general form for a loop is as follows:

```
■ Begin the loop
■ Test to see if a certain condition has been met.
■ If the condition has been met:
■ { what is between the curly brackets only occurs if the condition has been met
    □ Do some stuff.
    □ Something changes the status of the test.
    □ Go back to the second line and start again.
■ }
■ If the condition is no longer true, go to the next line.
```

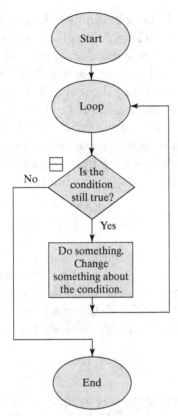

Figure 4.1   The most general flowchart depicting a loop structure

Figure 4.1 shows a flowchart representation of a repetition structure. This is the most generic type of loop; we will discuss other types in the following sections.

Iterations

We have said that the loop is the basic component of the repetition structure. The number of times a task is repeated is always a significant part of any repetition structure, but a programmer must be aware of how many times a loop will be repeated to ensure that the loop performs the task correctly. In computer lingo, a single pass through a loop is called a loop **iteration.** A loop that executes three times goes through three iterations. Example 4.2 demonstrates, with pseudocode, a loop that makes three iterations.

EXAMPLE 4.2

Going Round and Round and Round

```
1.  Set a variable equal to 1
2.  Begin the loop
3.  Test to see if the variable is less than 4.
4.  If the variable is less than 4:
5.  {
6.      Do some stuff.
7.      Increase the value of the variable by 1.
6.      Go back to line 3 and start again.
7.  }
8.  If the condition is no longer true, go to the next line.
```

The first time the program gets to line 3, the condition will be true because the variable is equal to 1 which is less than 4. So lines 5–7 will execute. Line 7 changes the value of the variable to 2. But, since 2 is still less than 4, the loop will enter another iteration (the second iteration). When it gets to line 7 the second time, the variable will be increased by 1 again, now making it equal to 3. When the program goes back to line 3, the condition is still true (3 is less than 4) and the loop begins its third iteration. Now line 7 increases the value of the variable to 4. When the program goes to line 3 again, the condition is no longer true since 4 is not less than 4. Execution then jumps to whatever is after line 8. So this program, if it were coded, would run through the statements inside the loop three times.

Writing Test Conditions

All programming languages provide statements to create a loop which contains a block of code. Under certain conditions these statements will be executed repeatedly. While there are numerous ways to write a condition that must be met, there are some basic concepts that need to be considered. Often a poorly conceived or incorrectly written **test condition** results in, at best, undesired results and, at worst, disastrous results.

Beware the Infinite Loop!

If a test condition can never be met by anything that happens within a loop, the loop will continue indefinitely. This is called an **infinite loop** and one needs little imagination to picture why this scenario can be a disaster. Example 4.3 is a pseudocode example of what could cause an infinite loop.

EXAMPLE 4.3

The Dangerous Infinite Loop

In this example, the test condition is impossible to achieve.

```
1.  Declare two integer variables, num1 and num2
2.  Begin the loop
3.  {
4.      Get a number from the user and store it in num1
5.      Set num2 = num1 + 1
6.      Display "Hello!"
7.  }
8.  Repeat until num1 > num2
9.  Display "The End"
```

After the loop is entered, the user is asked to enter a number on line 4 and it is stored in the variable **num1**. Line 5 sets **num2** equal to the value of **num1** plus one. Line 6 displays the word Hello. In this example, the condition is tested at the end of the loop (line 8). The test says that the loop should be repeated over and over (and over and over. . .) until **num1** is greater than **num2**. However, since, regardless of what value the user enters on any iteration for **num1**, line 5 always makes **num2** equal to that value plus one, and the loop will continue to repeat forever. The condition can never be met. When will it end? Never. The words The End will never be displayed but the word Hello will repeat endlessly on the screen.

Don't Let the User Get Trapped in a Loop

If the loop requires input from a user, it is important to make sure the user knows how to get out of the loop. For example, if you want your loop to end when the user enters a specific number or word, be sure to make that clear. Example 4.4 demonstrates, in pseudocode, how a loop might trap a user forever and how easy it is to avoid this situation.

EXAMPLE 4.4

Trapped in a Loop

In this example, the test condition is easy to meet if you know what it is!

```
1.  Declare a string variable, name
2.  Set the initial value of name to " "
3.  Begin the loop: test if name == "done"
4.  {
5.      Ask the user: "Enter your friend's name:"
6.      Store the entry in name
7.      Display name
8.  }
9.  Display "The End"
```

Unless the user happens to have a friend whose name is done, this loop will trap the user forever. Each time he or she enters a friend's name, the name will display and the user will be prompted for another name. It would be extremely frustrating to use this program!

Of course, this is easy to fix by simply telling the user how to get out of the loop. Change line 5 to read:

```
Ask the user: "Enter your friend's name or enter 'done' to quit:"
```

In the type of loops we used in Examples 4.3 and 4.4, the loop continues until the user ends it. Other loops end without user input. Regardless of what type of loop you write, you always want to avoid the possibility that the loop will continue without end. Therefore, you must ensure that the test condition can be met and, if the user must enter something special to end the loop, be sure to make that clear.

CHECKPOINT FOR SECTION 4.1

4.1 What is the basic component of the repetition structure?

4.2 Define the term **iteration**.

4.3 Define the term **test condition**.

4.4 What is wrong with the logic of the following pseudocode?

```
Set an integer variable named myage equal to 12
Set an integer variable named yourage equal to 14
Start a loop and test to see if myage < yourage
{
        Write to the screen "You are older than I am"
        Set yourage = myage + 1
}
End the loop
```

4.5 What is wrong with the logic of the following pseudocode?

```
Set an integer variable named mynum equal to 2
Start a loop and test to see if mynum != 0
{
        Write to the screen "Enter any number"
        Save the number entered in mynum
}
End the loop
```

4.6 What is the difference between an infinite loop and the loop shown in Example 4.4 that traps the user inside the loop?

4.2 Types of Loops

As you learn to write more complicated programs you will find that loops are one of your most indispensable tools. You'll use loops to load data, manipulate data, interact with the user, and much more. In fact, it would be difficult to imagine any program that does significant processing without loops. Just as one size does not fit all when it comes to choosing ingredients and pots and pans to cook dinner, loops also come in various types. One type of loop may work well for one specific program's need while another type fits a different program design. In this section, you will learn about several types of loops and how and why one may be chosen over another in a specific situation.

Pre-Test and Post-Test Loops

All repetition structures can be divided into two fundamental types: pre-test loops and post-test loops. In a pre-test loop, the test condition is tested before the loop is entered and in a post-test loop, the condition is tested after the **body** of the loop (the statements in the loop) have been executed. Example 4.5 depicts the flow of each type of loop and Figures 4.2 and 4.3 show a flowchart representation of the two types of loops.

EXAMPLE 4.5

Pre-Test and Post-Test Loops

a) The general form of a pre-test loop is as follows:

```
1.  Is some condition true? If yes, enter the loop: → Test here!
2.  {
3.        Do some stuff
4.  }
5.  Program continues
```

b) The general form of a post-test loop is as follows:

```
1.  Enter the loop:
2.  {
3.        Do some stuff
4.  }
5.  Is some condition true? If yes, go back to line 1 → Test here!
6.  Program continues
```

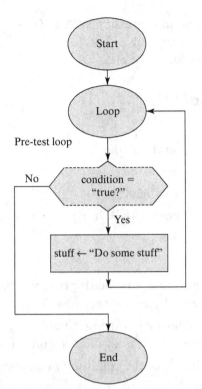

Figure 4.2 General flowchart of a pre-test loop

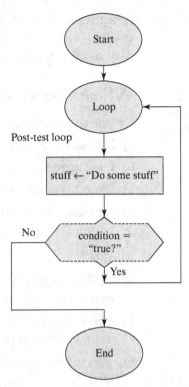

Figure 4.3 General flowchart of a post-test loop

Both types of loops have their uses. If you trace the flow of execution of a program in the flowcharts shown in Figures 4.2 and 4.3 you will see the main difference: The statements in the loop of a post-test loop are always executed at least once because the loop is entered before any test is made. However, if the test condition is not true, the statements in a pre-test loop will never be executed.

In general, there are two types of loops in JavaScript that test the condition before the loop is entered and one type that tests after the loop has completed one iteration. The two types of pre-test loops are `while` loops and `for` loops. The post-test loop is called a `do...while` loop. We will discuss each type in this chapter.

The Pre-Test `while` Loop

The general syntax for a `while` **loop** is as follows:

```
while (test condition)
{
    do some stuff
    change something about the test condition
}
```

Writing Test Conditions

Let's talk a bit about the test condition. Just as with a decision structure, the *test condition* in a loop must be something that is either `true` or `false`. A test condition can test if a value is greater than, less than, not equal to, or equal to something else. The value must be a variable but it can be compared to another variable, an actual value as, for example, 23 or "yes", or an expression such as (**x** + 4) or (**myAge** - 3). Compound test conditions can also be used but, for now, we'll stick with single conditions. Example 4.6 provides some samples.

Which Test Conditions Are Valid?

Are the following valid test conditions?

a) If **num1** is a numeric variable: **num1** >= 100;

b) If **myChoice** is a string variable: **myChoice** < 3;

c) If **num2** is a numeric variable: 14 > **num2**;

d) If **response** is a string variable: **response** != "no";

e) If **num3** is a numeric variable: **num3** = 15;

Answers:

a) This is a valid test condition. It asks the question, "Is **num1** greater than or equal to 100?" and will always be answered by either true or false.

b) This is not a valid test condition. Since **myChoice** is a string variable, it cannot be less than the integer 3. However, **myChoice** < "3"; is a valid test condition.

c) This is not a valid test condition. The left side of the condition must always be a variable.

d) This is a valid test condition. The answer to the question, "Is the value of response not the same as the string 'no'?" will always be either true or false.

e) This is also not a valid test condition. The statement **num3** = 15; does not ask a question. It is an assignment statement and assigns the value 15 to the variable **num3**. For this to be a valid test condition, the comparison operator (==) must be used. **num3** == 15; is, however a valid test condition.

In order to understand how a loop works, we'll go through some examples. First we'll use a **while** loop to generate a table on a web page and populate it with a list of names. Example 4.7 uses what is known as a sentinel controlled loop. We will discuss this type of loop in detail later in this section.

Generating and Filling a Table Using a **while** Loop

In this example, the user will enter the names of all the players in a game along with the number of points each player has accrued. The computer will display those names in an HTML table in one column and the points each player has in a second column. A game moderator might use this program to display contestants in a computer game. Since the number of players in the game can change as the game gains Internet popularity, the moderator will need the program to loop until the moderator is finished entering names. In this case, the test condition will be something that the game moderator will type in.

```
1.  <html>
2.  <head>
```

```
3.    <title>Example 4.7</title>
4.    <script>
5.    function getPlayers()
6.    {
7.          var player = prompt("Enter the name of a player:"," ");
8.          var points = prompt("Enter the points this player has:"," ");
9.          document.write('<table width="40%" border="1">');
10.         while (player != "done")
11.         {
12.               document.write('<tr>');
13.               document.write('<td width="50">' + player + '</td>');
14.               document.write('<td width = "50">' + points + '</td>');
15.               document.write('</tr>');
16.               player = prompt("Enter the name of a player or enter 'done' ↵
                                  when you're finished:"," ");
17.               points = prompt("Enter the points this player has or 0 if ↵
                                  finished:"," ");
18.         }
19.         document.write('</table>');
20.    }
21.    </script>
22.    </head>
23.    <body>
24.    <h1> </h1>
25.    <h1>Today's Players</h1>
26.    <h3>Click to enter players' names</h3>
27.    <p><input type="button" id="players" value="Enter today's players" ↵
                    onclick="getPlayers();" /></p>
28.    </body>
29.    </html>
```

We'll walk through the program, line by line, starting on line 5. We already know that the function getPlayers() is called when the user clicks the button on the page (lines 26–27). Line 6 contains the opening bracket of the function and it is closed on line 20. Now that our programs have become more complex and contain structures that use opening and closing brackets, it is essential that you use formatting to help ensure that open brackets have their closing partners in the correct place.

Lines 7 and 8 declare two variables to hold the values of the players' names and each player's points. We called these variables **player** and **points**. The two prompts on these lines allow the user to enter the first player's name and his or her points. Notice that we did not bother to turn **points** into a numeric variable even though a number will be entered. This program will not do any mathematical manipulation with these values so it's not necessary. Line 9 begins a table which will be displayed on the web page. This program generates a small table (40% of the window) and has borders around the cells.

The loop begins on line 10 and ends on line 18. Line 10 checks the value of **player**. Unless, by some very strange coincidence, the first player is named done, the test condition will be true. That is, the value of **player** will not be the same as done. Since the test condition is true, the loop is entered and control passes to line 11 (the opening bracket) and then to line 12. Line 12 begins a new row in the table. Line 13 does several things. It opens a table cell (document.write('<td width="50">'...) and concatenates this with the name of the first player which is stored in the variable,

player. Then it closes the cell (...'</td>');). Line 14 does the same thing but puts the value of **points** into the second cell of this row. Line 15 closes the row.

Lines 16 and 17 prompt the user for another player's name and points. The name that was previously stored in **player** is now gone, as is the original number of points. These prompts contain one more extremely important piece of information—how to end the loop. After entering another name and another number of points on lines 16 and 17, program control cycles back to line 10. Unless the user has entered done for the prompt on line 16, the test condition will again be true. The loop will continue for another iteration. Each iteration creates a new row, creates a first cell, puts the value of **player** into that cell, creates a second cell, puts the value of **points** into that cell, and ends the row. Finally, each iteration also prompts for a new value for both **player** and **points**. When the user enters done and control cycles back to line 10, the test condition will become false and control will jump to line 19.

You may have noticed that the user is also told to enter 0 for **points** when finished entering names. But the 0 doesn't come into play in this program at all. It really is unnecessary but, since the program is written to ask for both a player's name and the player's points, something must be entered. Psychologically, it would probably make the user feel better to enter 0 when finished entering information than some other number.

Once the loop is ended, control goes to line 19 which simply closes the table. The number of rows in this table strictly depends on how many names the user enters. Try it yourself, entering the following two lists of names and points and check that your display looks like the ones shown below.

a) Input: Joe, 20; Mary, 45; Pat, 62; done, 0

Joe	20
Mary	45
Pat	62

b) Input: Jane, 320; Mike, 456; Pamela, 167; Bobby, 88; Frank, 981; Annie, 2345; done, 0

Jane	320
Mike	456
Pamela	167
Bobby	88
Frank	981
Annie	2345

Example 4.8 will also prompt the user to enter information and will use a while loop to create a table on the web page, filling the table with the user-entered data. However, in this case the loop will complete a set number of iterations instead of allowing the user to determine when the loop should end. This type of loop is known as a counter controlled loop and will also be discussed further later in the section.

EXAMPLE
4.8

Using a while Loop for Exactly Ten Iterations

In this example, imagine an adventure game has begun. Each player is allowed to pick 10 items to start with. This program will display the choices available to the player and prompt the player, using a while loop, 10 times for each selection. By using the technique from Example 4.7 to create an HTML table one row at a time, within the loop, the player's selections are displayed as soon as each item is selected. Once the 10 selections have been made, the loop ends. In this case, the test condition has been defined before the program begins.

```
1.   <html>
2.   <head>
3.   <title>Example 4.8</title>
4.   <script>
5.   function getStuff()
6.   {
7.        document.write('<table width="40%" align = "center">');
8.        var num = 0;
9.        var item = " ";
10.       document.write('<h1> </h1>');
11.       while (num < 10)
12.       {
13.            item = prompt("What do you choose for item number " + (num + 1) ↵
                   + "?");
14.            document.write('<tr>');
15.            document.write('<td>item ' + (num + 1) + ' : ' + item + '</td>');
16.            document.write('</tr>');
17.            num = num + 1;
18.       }
19.       document.write('</table>');
20.  }
21.  </script>
22.  </head>
23.  <body>
24.  <table align ="center" width ="70%"><tr><td colspan ="2">
25.  <h1>Select Your Gear for the Game</h1>
26.  <p>You are allowed to pick up to 10 items from the following list before the ↵
                   game begins:</p>
27.  <table width = "60%">
28.  <tr><td colspan="2"><h3>Supplies Available</h3></td></tr>
29.  <tr><td>bag of food (1-day supply)</td><td>bottle of water (1-day supply) ↵
                   </td></tr>
30.  <tr><td>sword</td><td>shield</td></tr>
31.  <tr><td>kevlar vest</td><td>hunting knife</td></tr>
32.  <tr><td>bow with quiver of arrows</td><td>10 extra arrows</td></tr>
33.  <tr><td>backpack</td><td>slingshot</td></tr>
34.  <tr><td>box of 5 firestarters</td><td>pet goat</td></tr>
35.  <tr><td>falcon</td><td>falconer's gloves</td></tr>
36.  <tr><td>notebook</td><td>pen and pencil set</td></tr>
37.  <tr><td>walking stick</td><td>hammer</td></tr>
38.  <tr><td>shovel</td><td>1-person tent</td></tr>
39.  </table>
40.  <tr><td><p> </p>
41.  <p><input type="button" id="gear" value="Click to enter your selections" ↵
                   onclick="getStuff();" /></p>
```

```
42.    </td></tr>
43.    </table></body>
44.    </html>
```

The body of this web page (lines 23–43) simply lists all the items available to a player to choose from at the beginning of the game. The player is allowed to pick 10 of these items. The JavaScript function, getStuff(), on lines 5–20, is of most interest to us. In this while loop, a counter is used. The decisions about exactly what number the counter begins at, how it is changed within the loop, and how it is tested at the start of each iteration are all extremely important. They are explained here, in detail.

In this example, a string variable named **item** is declared on line 9 and given an initial value of an empty space. A numeric variable, **num**, is also declared and set equal to an initial value of 0 on line 8. The test condition for the loop on line 11 says to keep doing the loop while **num** is less than 10. This means that the loop will have 10 iterations: while **num** = 0, 1, 2, 3, 4, 5, 6, 7, 8, and 9. Keep this in mind as we walk through the code.

Line 12 prompts the user to enter one item. Let's look at this line:

```
item = prompt("What do you choose for item number " + (num + 1) + "?");
```

Because our counter starts at 0 but the first item is item number 1, we code the prompt to ask for item (**num** + 1). By putting this expression in parentheses, JavaScript knows that the + sign represents addition instead of concatenation. In this case, if **num** = 6, (**num** + 1) will display as 7. The prompt will say

```
What do you choose for item number 7?
```

If we left off the parentheses (and you can give it a try!), the display would be as follows:

```
What do you choose for item number 61?
```

Lines 14, 15, and 16 generate the next row of a table where the player's information will be displayed and also fills in that row with the player's selection. Once again, because the value of **num** is one less than the actual item number, in the display we must account for this by using (**num** + 1).

Line 17 assigns a new value to **num**. It increases the value of **num** by 1. Control then returns to the top of the while loop (line 11) where the new value of **num** is tested. The loop continues for 9 more times until, after the 10th item is entered by the player, the value of **num** becomes 10. At this point the test condition is now false because 10 is not less than 10. The loop ends and control drops to line 19 where the table is closed. The number of rows in this table will never be more than 10 or less than 10 because of how the test condition has been written. Try it yourself, entering the following list of items and check that your display looks like the one shown.

Input: bag of food; sword; backpack; kevlar vest; bottle of
water; box of 5 firestarters; slingshot; falcon;
falconer's gloves; shield

```
item 1 : bag of food
item 2 : sword
item 3 : backpack
item 4 : kevlar vest
item 5 : bottle of water
item 6 : box of 5 firestarters
item 7 : slingshot
item 8 : falcon
item 9 : falconer's gloves
item 10 : shield
```

Note: This code does not contain a way to check whether the player entered only items from the list given or that the items entered were spelled correctly. This type of error checking is extremely important but, for our purposes in this section, it is too advanced. We will add error checking as we continue in the text.

The Post-Test do...while Loop

The do...while **loop** is a variant of the while loop. This loop will execute the block of code at least once and then it will repeat the loop as long as the specified condition is true. The major difference between the do...while loop and the while loop is that, with a while loop, the condition must be met before the loop can begin. With a do...while loop, since the condition is tested at the end, the loop is entered, the block of statements are executed and then the condition is tested to see if the code should be executed again.

The general syntax for a do...while loop is as follows:

```
do
{
  do some stuff
  change something about the test condition
}
while (test condition)
```

Why Use One and Not the Other?

For many situations, either type of loop will work. In those cases, the decision about which type to use is up to the programmer and is simply a matter of preference. However, there are many situations where a loop should only execute if a given condition is true. In those cases, a pre-test loop must be used. Other situations may require that some code be executed at least once and, in those cases, a post-test loop is necessary.

Consider the following scenario: You are writing code for an online business. The user is on a page where he or she can select items for a shopping cart. If the user doesn't want to buy something, you don't want a loop that asks the user for the item number and then displays the price. This would be very frustrating for a user who has not yet decided to make a purchase! In this case, you would want to use a pre-test loop with a test condition that would only be `true` if the user answered "yes" to a question that might say, "Do you want to select an item to purchase?"

On the other hand, if you were an employer writing code to create paychecks for your employees, you would only run the program when you had at least one employee who needed a paycheck. In this case, you could use a post-test loop. You expect to have at least one employee so you need the loop to go through at least once. The test condition, at the end of the loop, might ask you if you want to enter another employee's information.

We will create this program in Example 4.9.

Using a do...while Loop for Payroll

Here, we will write a program that calculates the payroll for a small business. For the purposes of this example, we will assume everyone has the same tax rate of 15%. You will be asked to add code to this example as a Checkpoint exercise that will vary the tax rate based on the employee's number of dependents. This program will demonstrate how a post-test do...while loop is used. The test condition will be entered by the employer. Until the employer enters the word done when prompted for the employee's name at the end of the loop, the program will continue to loop.

The loop will generate a table with columns for each employee's name, gross pay, and net pay. An if...else structure is also nested inside the loop.

```
1.    <html>
2.    <head>
3.    <title>Example 4.9</title>
4.    <script>
5.    function getPay()
6.    {
7.        document.write('<table width="40%" align = "center">');
8.        var name = " ";
9.        var hours = 0;
10.       var rate = 0;
11.       var grossPay = 0;
12.       var netPay = 0;
13.       document.write('<tr><td>name</td><td>gross pay</td><td>net pay</td> ↵
                     </tr>');
14.       name = prompt("Enter the first employee's name:");
15.       do
16.       {
17.           hours = parseFloat(prompt("How many hours did " + name + " work ↵
                      this week?"));
18.           rate = parseFloat(prompt("What is " + name + "'s hourly pay rate?"));
19.           if (hours > 40)
20.               grossPay = (40 * rate) + ((hours - 40)*1.5*rate);
21.           else
22.               grossPay = hours * rate;
23.           netPay = grossPay * .85;
24.           document.write('<tr><td>' + name + '</td><td>$ ' + grossPay + ↵
                      '</td><td>$ ' + netPay + '</td></tr>');
```

```
25.            name = prompt("Enter another employee's name or enter 'done' ⏎
                    when finished:");
26.        }
27.        while  (name != "done")
28.        document.write('</table>');
29.    }
30.    </script>
31.    </head>
32.    <body>
33.    <table align ="center" width ="70%"><tr><td colspan ="2">
34.    <h1>Calculate Employees Paychecks</h1>
35.    <p>You can enter payroll information for all employees. Paychecks are ⏎
                    calculated as shown:</p>
36.    <table width = "70%">
37.    <tr><td>Gross pay for first 40 hours:</td><td>hourly rate * hours worked ⏎
                    </td></tr>
38.    <tr><td>Overtime:</td><td>overtime hours * 1.5 * hourly rate</td></tr>
39.    <tr><td>Tax rate for all employees: </td><td>15% of gross pay</td></tr>⏎
40.    </table>
41.    <p><input type="button" id="pay" value="Click to begin entering employees" ⏎
                    onclick="getPay();" /></p>
42.    </td></tr></table>
43.    </body>
44.    </html>
```

The body of this web page (lines 32–43) describes to the user how employee taxes are calculated. The JavaScript function, getPay(), which is called by pressing the button, is of most interest to us. Lines 7–13 set up the table that will display the output and initialize the necessary variables. Line 14 prompts the user to enter one employee's name before the loop is entered. In this example, it is assumed that, unless the employer wants to calculate someone's pay, the button would never be clicked and the function would never begin.

Lines 17 and 18 prompt the user to enter the employee's hours and hourly rate. The entries are converted to numeric values because they will be used in calculations. Lines 19–22 calculate each employee's gross pay, using an if...else structure to calculate overtime pay when appropriate. If the employee has worked more than 40 hours, the if clause is entered. The **grossPay** statement calculates regular pay for the first 40 hours and overtime at the time-and-a-half rate for all hours above 40. If the employee has not worked more than 40 hours, the else clause calculates **grossPay** as the number of hours worked multiplied by the hourly rate.

Line 23 calculates the net pay. This is, for our program, simply 85% of the gross pay since we have decided to give everyone a 15% tax rate. Line 24 displays this information in the three columns of a new row in the table that had previously been set up.

Finally, line 25 prompts the user to enter another employee's name or to indicate that there are no more employees. Unless the user enters the word done, the test condition in the while statement on line 27 will be true and program control will return to the do statement on line 15. Notice that the information in the next iteration of the loop goes with the name that has been entered at the end of the previous iteration.

Try this program, entering the following information, and check that your display looks like the one shown.

Input:

Employee's name	Hours Worked	Hourly Rate (dollars & cents)
Harvey Hardy	40	10.00
Louisa Lee	21	16.50
Elmer Erkenheimer	44	7.80
Millicent Murgatroyd	68	21.75

name	gross pay	net pay
Harvey Hardy	$ 400	$ 340
Louisa Lee	$ 346.5	$ 294.525
Elmer Erkenheimer	$ 358.8	$ 304.98
Millicent Murgatroyd	$ 1783.5	$ 1515.975

Note: This code does not contain any error checking. When you write code you should always include checks for errors. In this example, we would probably want to add code to ensure that the employer does not enter a numeric value for hours or rate that is less than 0 since no one can work a negative number of hours or get paid a negative number of dollars, under normal circumstances. Also, since there are only 168 hours in a 7-day period, we would want to make sure that no one was allowed to work more than 168 hours! However, while we are still learning the concepts, we can assume that all data entered will be valid data.

There are many ways to enhance this program. You will be given the opportunity to add two features to this program in the Checkpoint exercises.

Formatting the Output: The toFixed() Method

You may not like the fact that the values displayed in our payroll example either have no decimal places or have three decimal places. How can we change the display so that currency values display as currency? There are several ways to do this but one of the easiest is to use the toFixed() method. The general form of this method is as follows:

```
num.toFixed(x)
```

This will format the numeric variable, **num**, to **x** decimal places. By adding .toFixed(2) to the variables **grossPay** and **netPay** on line 24 of the code in Example 4.9, the output would now look like this:

name	gross pay	net pay
Harvey Hardy	$ 400.00	$ 340.00
Louisa Lee	$ 346.50	$ 294.52
Elmer Erkenheimer	$ 358.80	$ 304.98
Millicent Murgatroyd	$ 1783.50	$ 1515.97

Sentinel-Controlled Loops

Loops are often used to input large amounts of data. On each pass through the loop, one item of data (or one set of data) is entered into the program. The owner of a business who is converting her paper records to the cloud might use a loop to enter all her customers' names into a database and assign each an identification number. This can be used to greet each customer who visits the website and later linked to other information about each customer. The test condition for such a loop must cause it to be exited after all data has been entered. Often the best way to force a loop to end is to have the user enter a special item (a **sentinel value**) to act as a signal that input is complete. The sentinel item (which also may be called an **end-of-data marker**) should be chosen so that it cannot possibly be mistaken for actual input data. For example, using the businesswoman's website as an illustration, since all identi-fication numbers are positive integers, the sentinel value could be the number –9. No customer would have a negative identification number so when the value of –9 is encountered, the loop will end. We have already used **sentinel-controlled loops** in several examples in this chapter. Example 4.10 demonstrates another way to use one.

EXAMPLE 4.10

Using a Sentinel-Controlled Loop

Imagine you have been asked to write code that will allow a professor to enter all the names and student ID numbers for his classes. The professor wants to use it to assign usernames for each student that they can use when accessing a course web-site. However, each class has a different number of students so you decide to use a sentinel-controlled loop. This way, the professor can enter that sentinel value when he has finished entering data for each class and it will not matter if the class has 10 students or 20 or 300.

In this program, the username will be a concatenation of each student's first name with his or her student ID number.

```
1.   <html>
2.   <head>
3.   <title>Example 4.10</title>
4.   <script>
5.   function getClass()
6.   {
7.       document.write('<table width="40%" align = "center">');
8.       var fname = " ";
9.       var lname = " ";
10.      var id = " ";
11.      var username = 0;
12.      var course = " ";
13.      course = prompt("What is the name of this course?");
14.      document.write('<tr><td colspan =4 align = "center">' + course + ⏎
                 '</td></tr>');
15.      document.write('<tr><td>first name</td><td>last name</td> ⏎
                 <td>username</td></tr>');
16.      fname = prompt("Enter one student's first name:");
17.      lname = prompt("Enter the student's last name:");
18.      id = prompt("Enter the student's identification number:");
19.      do
```

```
20.          {
21.              username = fname + id;
22.              document.write('<tr><td>' + fname + '</td><td>' + lname ⏎
                     + '</td><td>' + id + '</td><td>' + username + '</td></tr>'); ⏎
23.              fname = prompt("Enter another student's first name or enter 'X' ⏎
                     when finished:");
24.              lname = prompt("Enter another student's last name or enter 'X' ⏎
                     when finished:");
25.              id = prompt("Enter another student's identification number or ⏎
                     enter -9 when finished:");
26.          }
27.      while  (id != -9)
28.      document.write('</table>');
29.  }
30.  </script>
31.  </head>
32.  <body>
33.  <table align ="center" width ="70%"><tr><td colspan ="2">
34.  <h1>Create Usernames</h1>
35.  <p>You can enter each student's name and ID number and <br /> this program ⏎
                     will create usernames for you</p>
36.  <tr><td><p> </p>
37.  <p><input type="button" id="username" value="Click to begin entering names" ⏎
                     onclick="getClass();" /></p>
38.  </td></tr>
39.  </table>
40.  </body>
41.  </html>
```

The sentinel in this program is the number -9. The loop continues until the user has entered -9 for a student identification number. Notice, though, that the user also is prompted to enter 'X' for the first and last names even though neither of these entries is evaluated in the test condition. The test condition could easily have be written as (**fname** != 'X') or (**lname** != 'X'). We include all the options because, when the user is done entering names, something must be entered in all three prompts and an 'X' is merely a placeholder. Other techniques can be used to avoid this as we will see later in the text.

If you try this code and enter the provided input, your output should look as shown below:

Input: Course Name: Introduction to JavaScript
              Students: Jacques Jolie, ID: 2345
                            Isabel Torres, ID: 6789
                            Kevin Patel, ID: 2037
                            Barbara Chen, ID: 6589
                            X X, ID: -9

Introduction to JavaScript			
first name	last name	ID number	username
Jacques	Jolie	2345	Jacques2345
Isabel	Torres	6789	Isabel6789
Kevin	Patel	2037	Kevin2037
Barbara	Chen	6589	Barbara6589

Formatting the Output: The toLowerCase() and toUpperCase() Methods

Example 4.10 did a decent job of creating usernames from input. Often, however, usernames are generated with only lowercase text. JavaScript has two methods that change all text in a string to either all lowercase (the toLowerCase() **method**) or all uppercase (the toUpperCase() **) method.** The general form of these methods are as follows:

- **stringVariable**.toLowerCase();
- **stringVariable**.toUpperCase();

You will be asked to use the toLowerCase() method as a Checkpoint exercise. Example 4.11 demonstrates how these two methods work.

Using the toLowerCase () and toUpperCase () Methods

The following code demonstrates how the toLowerCase() method changes all text to lowercase, regardless of whether or not it was originally all uppercase, all lowercase, or a combination, and how the toUpperCase() method does the same thing, but changes all text to uppercase.

```
1.   <html>
2.   <head>
3.   <title>Example 4.11</title>
4.   <script>
5.        var name = "MaryAnn";
6.        var greeting = "Welcome home, ";
7.        document.write('<p>' + greeting + name + '!</p>');
8.        document.write('<p>' + greeting.toUpperCase() + ⏎name.toLowerCase()
                        + '!</p>');
9.        document.write('<p>' + greeting.toLowerCase() + name. toUpperCase() ⏎
                        + '!</p>');
10.  </script>
11.  </head>
12.  <body>
13.  </body>
14.  </html>
```

The output of this code is as follows:

Welcome home, MaryAnn!

WELCOME HOME, maryann!

welcome home, MARYANN!

Counter-Controlled Loops

Many of the loops we have seen so far end when the user types a certain value. There are, of course, situations when you want a loop to execute a certain number of times without any user input. One way to construct such a loop is with a special type of pre-test loop known as a **counter-controlled loop**—a loop that is executed a fixed number of times, where that number is known prior to entering the loop for the first time.

A counter-controlled loop contains a variable (the **counter**) that keeps track of the number of passes through the loop (the number of loop iterations). When the counter reaches a preset value, the loop is exited. In order for the computer to execute the loop a certain number of times, it must keep track of how many times it goes through the loop.

Using a Counter

To keep track of how many times a loop has been executed using a counter, you must define, initialize, and either **increment** (to count up) or **decrement** (to count down) the counter. The code to keep a count like this may seem a bit strange at first, but it will quickly make sense. There are shortcuts to writing an increment or decrement that are normally used in JavaScript to make using counters easy. The steps to using a counter are described in the following list:

1. **Define a counter:** The counter is a variable. It is always an integer because it counts the number of times the loop body is executed and a computer cannot do something 1.25 times. Common variable names for counters are **counter, count, i**, or **j**. In some languages words like **count** or **counter** can be keywords. It is best to name your counter something very simple, like **i** or **j**.

2. **Initialize the counter:** Set the counter to a beginning value. Although a counter can begin at any integer value—often determined by other factors in the program—for now, we will usually set our counter equal to 0 or 1.

3. **Increment (or decrement) the counter:** The computer counts the way you did when you were very little. To count by ones, the computer takes what it had before and adds one. So the code for a computer to count by ones looks like **i + 1**, given that **i** is an integer variable. Then, to store the new value: Where the old value was you use the statement **i = i + 1**. This takes the old value, adds one to it, and stores the new value where the old value was.

Shortcut Operators

JavaScript has some shortcuts that allow you to increment or decrement a counter in one step instead of writing an entire expression. The most commonly used shortcut increments a variable by one and is simply **i++**. This is equivalent to the expression **i = i + 1**. Other shortcuts are shown in Table 4.1.

TABLE 4.1	Shortcut Operators		
Beginning Value of j	**Increment/Decrement Expression**	**Shortcut**	**Ending Value of j**
1	j = j + 1	j++	2
1	j = j − 1	j−−	0
5	j = j + 2	j+=2	7
5	j = j − 2	j−=2	3
4	j = j * 3	j*=3	12
4	j = j / 2	j/=2	2
1	j = j + 1	++j	2

As you look at the table, you might wonder what the difference is between **j++** and **++j**. On the table, the result is the same. The difference comes in when writing code. **++j** increments **j** before you use it, **j++** increments **j** after you use it. Examples 4.12 and 4.13 demonstrate the use of these operators and the difference between **j++** and **++j**.

EXAMPLE
4.12

Using Shortcuts

Use the following code to try variations of the shortcut operators shown in Table 4.1.

```
1.   <html>
2.   <head>
3.   <title>Example 4.12</title>
4.   <script>
5.        var j = 1; j++;
6.        document.write("<h3> if j = 1, then j++ is " + j + "!</p>");
7.        j = 1; j--;
8.        document.write("<h3> if j = 1, then j-- is " + j + "!</p>");
9.        j = 5; j+=2;
10.       document.write("<h3> if j = 5, then j+=2 is " + j + "!</p>");
11.       j = 5; j-=2;
12.       document.write("<h3>if j = 5, then j-=2 is " + j + "!</p>");
13.       j = 4; j*=3;
14.       document.write("<h3> if j = 4, then j*=3 is " + j + "!</p>");
15.       j = 4; j/=2;
16.       document.write("<h3> if j = 4, then j/=2 is " + j + "!</p>");
17.       j = 1; ++j;
18.       document.write("<h3> if j = 1, then ++j is " + j + "</p>");
19.       j = 8; --j;
20.       document.write("<h3> if j = 8, then --j is " + j + "!</p>");
21.  </script>
22.  </head>
23.  <body>
24.  </body>
25.  </html>
```

If you enter this code, your output should look as shown below. However, by varying the beginning values of **j** and by varying the increment, decrements, multiplicands, etc., you can see how these shortcuts work.

```
if j = 1, then j++ is 2

if j = 1, then j-- is 0

if j = 5, then j+=2 is 7

if j = 5, then j-=2 is 3

if j = 4, then j*=3 is 12

if j = 4, then j/=2 is 2

if j = 1, then ++j is 2

if j = 8, then --j is 7
```

Example 4.13 demonstrates the difference between putting the increment before the variable or after.

EXAMPLE 4.13

++counter or counter++?

```
1.   <html>
2.   <head>
3.   <title>Example 4.12</title>
4.   <script>
5.        var counterA = 8;
6.        var counterB = 0;
7.        document.write("<h3> counterA = " + counterA + "</h3>");
8.        counterB = counterA++;
9.        document.write("<h3> counterB = counterA++ so counterB now = ⏎
                  " + counterB + "</h3>");
10.       document.write("<h3> counterA++ = " + counterA + "</h3>");
11.       counterC = 8;
12.       counterD = 0;
13.       document.write("<h3> counterC = " + counterC + "</h3>");
14.       counterD = ++counterC;
15.       document.write("<h3> counterD = ++counterC so counterD now = ⏎
                  " + counterD + "</h3>");
16.       document.write("<h3> ++counterC = " + counterC + "</h3>");
17.  </script>
18.  </head>
19.  <body>
20.  </body>
21.  </html>
```

If you enter this code, your output should look as shown below. You will see that, while using the ++ operator before the variable results in the same value as using it after the variable (i.e. **j**++ == ++**j**), there is a significant difference in what happens when you use the operator in an expression. On line 8 the value of **counterA**++ is assigned to **counterB**. The output shows that **counterB** contains the value of **counterA** *before* it is incremented. But on line 14 the value of ++**counterC** is assigned to **counterD**. In this case, **counterD** takes the value of **counterC** *after* the increment.

```
counterA = 8

counterB = counterA++ so counterB now = 8

counterA++ = 9

counterC = 8

counterD = ++counterC so counterD now = 9

++counterC = 9
```

CHECKPOINT FOR SECTION 4.2

4.7 Add code to Example 4.7 that creates a title for the table that is generated and adds column headings. The title should be Game Players and the column headings should be Players and Points.

4.8 Redo Example 4.8 as a do...while post-test loop structure.

4.9 Add code to Example 4.9 so that the display outputs two more columns—one for regular pay and one for overtime pay as well as the net pay.

4.10 Add code to Example 4.9 that calculates each employee's taxes based on the criteria in the example but changes the tax rate according to the number of dependents an employee has. You will need to include a prompt for the number of dependents. Use the following tax rates:

0 dependents	tax rate = 28%
1–3 dependents	tax rate = 22%
4–6 dependents	tax rate = 17%
more than 6 dependents	tax rate = 12%

Hint: use a switch statement inside the loop.

4.11 Use the toLowerCase() method and what you know about JavaScript programming to change the format of the usernames generated in Example 4.10 so the text is all lowercase and there is an underscore between the student's first name and identification number. For example, for a student named Ivan Prokopenskaya whose identification number is 8823, his username should be ivan_8823.

4.12 Rewrite the following expressions using shortcut operators:
   a) myCounter = myCounter + 1;
   b) countdown = countdown – 5;
   c) multiply = multiply * 2;
   d) j = j + 3;

4.3 The for Loop

Most programming languages contain a statement that makes it easy to construct a counter-controlled loop. To create a built-in counter-controlled loop, we introduce the for loop. The for loop provides a shortened method to initialize the counter; to tell the computer how much to increase or decrease the counter for each pass through the loop; and to tell the computer when to stop.

The for Statement

The general form of the for loop in JavaScript is as follows:

```
for (counter = initialValue; test condition; increment/decrement)
{
    body of the loop;
}
```

The information inside the parentheses is actually three statements separated by semicolons. This kind of for statement will repeatedly execute the body of the loop starting with the counter equal to the specified initial value and incrementing or decrementing the counter by some specified value on each pass through the loop. We will discuss each part of the three statements in the for loop parenthetical expression in detail in this section.

The Initial Value

The first statement sets the counter to its **initial value.** The initial value can be any integer constant, such as 1, 0, 23, or –4. The initial value can also be another numeric variable. For example, if a variable named **lowNumber** was set equal to an integer prior to entering the for loop, the counter could be initialized to the value of **lowNumber**. The first statement in the for loop would then look like this: **counter = lowNumber**. Similarly, the counter could be set equal to an expression containing a numeric variable and a number, such as **counter = (lowNumber + 3)**. However, the counter itself must be a variable and the initial value must be a whole number.

- **counter** = 5 is a valid initialization of a counter.
- **counter** = **newNumber** is a valid initialization of a counter, if **newNumber** is a numeric integer variable.
- **counter** = (**newNumber** * 2) is a valid initialization of a counter.
- **counter** = (5/2) is not a valid initialization of a counter because 5/2 is not an integer.
- 23 = **counter** is not a valid initialization of a counter.

The Test Condition

The test condition is, perhaps, the most important statement of the three. It is essential to understand what the test condition represents, where the test is made, and what happens after the condition is tested. The test condition asks the question, "Is the counter within the range specified by this condition?" If the test condition is, for example, **counter** < 10, then the question asked is, "Is the value of the counter less than 10?" If the answer to that question is "yes" then the loop executes again. If the answer is "no" then the loop is exited. This means that when **counter** is equal to 10, the loop will be exited. However, if the test condition were **counter** <= 10, the question asked is, "Is the value of the counter less than or equal to 10?" In this case, the loop will not be exited until **counter** is at least 11.

Another important consideration about test conditions in any loop, including while and do...while loops as well as for loops, is when the check of the test condition occurs. As we have seen, the test condition is checked at the end of a loop in a post-test loop and at the beginning in a pre-test loop. This is clear from the language of those loops, but it is not so clear with a for loop. In a for loop, the test condition is checked at the beginning. If the initial value of the counter passes the test condition, the loop is entered once. After the loop body executes once, the counter is then either incremented or decremented and the test condition is checked again. So, after the initial execution of the loop, the test condition is checked each time after the body of the loop has completed.

The test condition can also be a number, another variable with a numeric value, or an expression containing variables and numbers. For example:

- **counter** < 5 is a valid test condition and a loop with this condition will execute until **counter** has the value of 5 or more.
- **counter** >= 6 is a valid test condition and a loop with this condition will execute until **counter** becomes 5 or less.
- **counter** >= **newNumber** is a valid test condition and will execute until **counter** becomes less than or equal to the value of **newNumber**.
- **counter** < (**newNumber** + 5) is a valid test condition. A loop with this condition will execute until **counter** becomes greater than or equal to the value of **newNumber** + 5.

The Increment/Decrement Statement

The increment or decrement statement uses the same shortcut notation shown in Table 4.1. Examples of valid increments and decrements include the following:

- **counter**++ increments **counter** by 1 on each pass
- **counter**-- decrements **counter** by 1 on each pass
- **counter**+=2 increments **counter** by 2 on each pass. For example, if **counter** = 0 initially, it will equal 2 on the next pass through the loop, 4 on the next pass, and so on. It is comparable to the following code: **counter** = **counter** + 2.
- **counter**-=3 decrements **counter** by 3. For example, if **counter** = 12 initially, it will equal 9 on the next pass through the loop, then 6, then 3 and so on, even including negative numbers. On the 5th pass, **counter** will equal 0 and it will equal -3 on the 6th pass. If you don't want this to happen, be careful how you write your test condition!

In general we can say

- **counter** +=X will increase **counter** by the value of X
- **counter**-=X will decrease **counter** by the value of X

after each pass through the loop.

The Careful Bean Counter

In Examples 4.14 through 4.19, we'll practice using the **for** statement and demonstrate the many ways counters can be use (or misused). One of the most common logical errors in a program is using a counter incorrectly. It is the programmer's decision to pick an initial value, an increment or decrement amount, and a test condition. Since these choices determine how many times the loop executes, it is very important to check your initial value and test condition value carefully to make sure your loop repeats exactly as many times as you need. With that in mind, we'll do some bean counting.

For the upcoming examples, you may want to use the jelly bean images included with the Student Data Files. Alternatively, you can substitute your own images or simply use the word BEAN instead of the image.

EXAMPLE
4.14

Count Out Five Beans

This example, and the next five examples, demonstrate how counters are used and what happens if the initial and test conditions are not chosen carefully. In this example, five beans will be displayed. The counter begins at 0 and the loop will continue for five iterations. A variable named **beans** is declared and initialized to 4. Since we want five beans to show up and the counter begins at 0, the test condition requires that the counter continue until it is greater than 4.

```
1.   <html>
2.   <head>
3.   <title>Example 4.14</title>
4.   <script>
5.   function countBeans()
6.   {
7.       var i = 0;
8.       var beans = 4;
9.       beanImage = ("<img src = 'blue_bean.jpg' >");
10.      document.write("<table align = 'center'><tr><td>");
11.      document.write("<h1> <br /> Here are your beans:</h1>");
12.      for (i = 0; i <= beans; i++)
13.          document.write(beanImage + "   ");
14.      document.write("</td></tr></table>");
15.  }
16.  </script>
17.  </head>
18.  <body>
19.  <table align ="center" width ="70%"><tr><td>
20.  <h1>Count Beans!</h1>
21.  <p><input type="button" id="beans" value="Click to count beans" onclick= ↵
                     "countBeans();" /></p>
22.  </td></tr></table>
23.  </body>
24.  </html>
```

For this first example, the entire code, including the HTML body, is shown. The next five examples will only show the changes in the countBeans() function. Line 9 declares a variable named **beanImage** which stores the HTML code to access the blue_bean.jpg image. We could have written the HTML code for this within the loop, but using a variable makes things a little neater.

Curly Braces: Do We Really Need Them?

Notice how the for loop works. Since there is only one statement in this loop, curly braces are not necessary. However, if the loop body contained more than one statement, we would have to enclose all the loop body's statements in curly braces. This is true for all loops as well as selection structures. When the structure has only one statement, curly braces are not needed. However, it does not hurt a program to include them so, to avoid unwanted results, until you become very familiar with programming, you may want to always use curly braces to set off one or many statements in your loops and selection structures.

On the first pass, line 12 sets the initial value of the counter (**i**) to 0. It had already been initialized to 0 when it was declared but a for loop requires that the counter be

initialized in its first statement. The next statement (i <= **beans**) is the test condition.
It says to continue with the body of the loop while i is less than or equal to **beans**.
The variable **beans** is initialized to 4 and never changes. The third statement in the
parentheses is not executed until after the loop body completes one iteration.

Line 13 is the body of the loop. It displays one bean image and two blank spaces.
After this is complete, the third statement in the for loop parentheses is executed—
the counter is incremented by 1.

The initialization statement only happens once, before the first pass through the
loop. The test condition is executed every time control returns to line 12. The
increment happens at the end of the loop body for each iteration.

Therefore, after the loop body has executed five times, the value of the counter is 4.
It is then incremented to 5. The test condition now fails and control jumps to line
14 where the table is closed and the program ends.

If you code and run this program, your display should look like this:

Here are your beans:

EXAMPLE
4.15

Count Out Five Beans Another Way

This example also displays five beans but uses a decrement for the
counter. In this case, the counter is initially set equal to the value of
the variable, **beans** and is decremented after each iteration. The loop
executes while the counter is 4, 3, 2, 1, and 0 but ends as soon as it becomes less
than 0. Therefore, it executes five times and five beans are displayed.

```
1.   function countBeans()
2.   {
3.        var beans = 4;
4.        beanImage = ("<img src = 'blue_bean.jpg' >");
5.        document.write("<table align = 'center'><tr><td>");
6.        document.write("<h1> <br /> Here are your beans:</h1>");
7.        for (var i = beans; i >= 0; i--)
8.             document.write(beanImage + "   ");
9.        document.write("</td></tr></table>");
10.  }
```

Another difference in this example from the previous one is that the counter was declared
as a variable in the for loop on line 7. In these little programs, either way works fine.

If you code and run this program, your display should look exactly like the one in
Example 4.14:

Here are your beans:

**EXAMPLE
4.16**

Too Many Beans

Let's say you want seven beans to display. Unless you're careful, you might not get what you want. Can you see why the following code displays more than seven beans?

```
1.   function countBeans()
2.   {
3.       var i = 0;
4.       beanImage = ("<img src = 'blue_bean.jpg' >");
5.       document.write("<table align = 'center'><tr><td>");
6.       document.write("<h1> <br /> Here are your beans:</h1>");
7.       for (i = 0; i <= 7; i++)
8.           document.write(beanImage + "   ");
9.       document.write("</td></tr></table>");
10.  }
```

If you code and run this program, your display should look exactly like the following (notice that there are eight beans, not seven!):

Here are your beans:

**EXAMPLE
4.17**

Not Enough Beans

If the initial condition and test condition are not chosen correctly, you could have the situation shown in this example. Seven beans are required. Can you see why the following code displays fewer than seven beans?

```
1.   function countBeans()
2.   {
3.       var i = 0;
4.       beanImage = ("<img src = 'blue_bean.jpg' >");
5.       document.write("<table align = 'center'><tr><td>");
6.       document.write("<h1> <br /> Here are your beans:</h1>");
7.       for (i = 1; i < 7; i++)
8.           document.write(beanImage + "   ");
9.       document.write("</td></tr></table>");
10.  }
```

If you code and run this program, your display should look exactly like the following (notice that there are only six beans, not seven!):

Here are your beans:

EXAMPLE
4.18

Using an Expression for the Test Condition

This example will display six beans. In this case, we use an expression for the test condition instead of a specified value.

```
1.   function countBeans()
2.   {
3.        var i = 0;
4.        var beans = 12;
5.        beanImage = ("<img src = 'blue_bean.jpg' >");
6.        document.write("<table align = 'center'><tr><td>");
7.        document.write("<h1> <br /> Here are your beans:</h1>");
8.        for (i = 0; i < (beans - i); i++)
9.             document.write(beanImage + "   ");
10.       document.write("</td></tr></table>");
11.  }
```

Let's take a look at line 8. The counter, **i**, is initialized to 0. The test condition says to do the loop body while the value of **i** is less than the value of (**beans** – **i**). The value of **beans** is 12 (line 4) and it never changes. However, on the first pass through the loop, (**beans** – **i**) is (12 – 0) or 12. On the second pass, **i** has been incremented to 1 so the value of (**beans** – **i**) is now 11. On the third pass, **i** is now 2 and (**beans** – **i**) is now 10. This continues until **i** has been incremented to 6 on the sixth pass. The value of (**beans** – **i**) is (12 – 6) or 6. This is the last pass. At the end of this pass, **i** is incremented to 7 so the value of (**beans** – **i**) Is (12 – 7) which is 5. 5 is less than the value of **i** (7) at this point so the loop ends. Six beans are displayed as shown:

Here are your beans:

EXAMPLE
4.19

Up and Down

This example is a variation of Example 4.18. Here, the counter is incremented while another variable is decremented. The changes in these values are used in the test condition.

```
1.   function countBeans()
2.   {
3.        var i = 0;
4.        var beans = 12;
5.        beanImage = ("<img src = 'blue_bean.jpg' >");
6.        document.write("<table align = 'center'><tr><td>");
7.        document.write("<h1> <br /> Here are your beans:</h1>");
8.        for (i = 0; i != beans; i++)
9.             document.write(beanImage + "   ");
10.            beans--;
11.       document.write("</td></tr></table>");
12.  }
```

In this example, the test condition says to continue the loop so long as the counter, **i**, is not the same as the value of the variable, **beans**. The value of **beans** is decremented by 1 during each iteration (line 10). The counter is incremented by 1 after each iteration. Since **beans** begins at 12 and keeps going down, while **i** begins at 0 and keeps going up, eventually the two values will meet. They meet when both are 6, after the sixth iteration and the loop ends. Six beans are displayed, as shown:

Here are your beans:

CHECKPOINT FOR SECTION 4.3

4.13 Change the code of Example 4.8 to use a for loop instead of a while loop.

4.14 Rewrite the following expressions using shortcut notation:

    a) **age = age + 2;**   c) **num = num * 3;**

    b) **counter = counter -1;**   d) **id = id + 5;**

4.15 What is the difference between **counter++** and **++counter**?

4.16 Fix the code in Example 4.16 so seven beans will display.

4.17 Fix the code in Example 4.17 so seven beans will display.

4.4 Data Validation

We have mentioned that it is important to make sure the user enters valid data when prompted for some input. This means, if asked for a number, a word will not do, nor will a letter of the alphabet. If prompted to select from a list of choices, we need to make sure the user doesn't choose something not on the list. However, up to now, we have written programs that just assume the user will enter what is called **valid data.** Now that we know how to write JavaScript loops, we can add **data validation** to our programs.

For example, you might write a program to accept orders for a small jewelry business. The customer would be asked to enter the number of beaded bracelets to be ordered—1, 2, 100, or even 0. To ensure that the user does not enter a negative number when entering a quantity of items to order, we use the code shown in Example 4.20.

EXAMPLE 4.20 Making Sure the Number Is Positive

```
var bracelets = parseInt(prompt("How many bracelets do you want?"," "));
while (bracelets < 0)
{
    bracelets = prompt("Please enter a positive number. How many bracelets ⏎
            you want?"," ");
}
document.write("You are ordering " + bracelets + " bracelets. Thank you!");
```

The loop will continue until the user enters a positive number.

However, other problems could exist. The user might enter a character like 'A' or 'm' instead of a number. The user might enter the number 4.67 or 9.5. If a user enters 9.5, does this mean the user hopes to buy nine and a half bracelets? Or did the user mean to type 10? or 95? The program code, as shown, would truncate the number 9.5 to 9 and the businessman would either lose a sale of one bracelet or 86 bracelets! We need to add code to ensure that the user enters a positive integer value. Let's first consider how to test for an entry that is not a number.

The isNaN() Method

The isNaN() **method** will **return** true if an expression or variable inside the parentheses is not a number. This requires a bit of explanation. A value that is a number is any positive or negative integer or floating point value. Thus, 6 is a number and -5.692 is also a number. But what does it mean to say the function will return true? Recall that we have said the only possible answers to a condition in a selection structure are either true or false. The same goes for the test condition in a loop—it is either true or false. But a condition does not have to be an expression (like x > 9). It can also be a method, like this one, which is either true or false. Thus, you can write a condition using a value that is either true or false. Example 4.21 shows the syntax for using the isNaN() function as a test condition in a loop.

EXAMPLE
4.21

Making Sure the Number Is a Number

```
while (isNaN(bracelets))
{
    bracelets = prompt("Please enter a number."," ");
}
```

This code will continue to prompt the user for a number so long as the user enters anything but a number. The test—isNaN(**bracelets**)—continues to be true while **bracelets** is not a number.

The final piece of this validation addresses the problem of checking to make sure that the user has entered an integer value.

EXAMPLE
4.22

Making Sure the Number Is a Positive Number

```
var bracelets = (prompt("How many bracelets do you want?"," "));
while (isNaN(bracelets) || (bracelets < 0))
{
    bracelets = prompt("Please enter a positive number. How many bracelets ⏎
             do you want?"," ");
}
document.write("You are ordering " + bracelets + " bracelets. Thank you!");
```

This code uses a compound condition. The condition will continue to be true so long as the user either does not enter a number or enters a number less than 0.

We can add this condition to the previous condition that ensures that the number entered is positive, as shown in Example 4.22.

Checking for Integers

JavaScript does not make a clear distinction between integer and floating point numbers. Therefore, if we, as programmers, want to ensure that a value is really an integer, we must write the code to do so. Otherwise, if an integer is needed, the parseInt() function will truncate the decimal part of a number. In the case of a user who accidently enters 9.5 instead of 95, as we mentioned above, the parseInt() function is not helpful.

So we need to think about what we know about integers and what we know about mathematical operators. We know that any integer divided by 1 will be the same as the original integer. But we also know what the mod operator (%) does: It gives the remainder after dividing one number by another. Thus, 16 % 3 = 1 because 16 divided by 3 is 5 with a remainder of 1. Similarly, 2.5 % 1 equals 0.5 because 2.5 divided by 1 equals 2 with a remainder of 0.5. And 6.2345692 % 1 equals 0.2345692 because, whenever a number with a decimal part is divided by 1, the remainder will be the decimal part. However, any number without a decimal part (i.e., an integer) will have a remainder of 0 when divided by 1.

We can use this fact to check if a number is an integer, as shown in Example 4.23.

EXAMPLE 4.23

Making Sure the Number is an Integer

```
var bracelets = parseInt(prompt("How many bracelets do you want?", " "));
var check = bracelets % 1;
while (check !=0)
{
    bracelets = prompt("Please enter a whole number. How many bracelets ↵
            do you want?"," ");
    var check = bracelets % 1;
}
document.write("You are ordering " + bracelets + " bracelets. Thank you!");
```

The test condition here asks if the remainder, after dividing the number by 1 is 0. If it is, then the number entered is an integer. If not, the loop continues to prompt the user for a valid integer.

Using Compound Conditions for Data Validation

We can put all these conditions together as a compound condition in a single test to ensure that the user enters a valid, positive integer. The complete short program is shown in Example 4.24.

EXAMPLE 4.24

Validating Positive Integer Entries

This code prompts the user to enter the number of bracelets he or she wishes to order. It checks for three things: Did the user enter a number? Is that number an integer? Is that number at least 0? We use a single loop with a compound condition with two OR statements to accomplish this task.

```
1.  <html>
2.  <head>
3.  <title>Example 4.24</title>
4.  <script>
5.  function getBracelet()
6.  {
7.       var bracelets = (prompt("How many bracelets do you want?"," "));
8.       var check = bracelets % 1;
9.       while ((isNaN(bracelets)) || (check != 0) || (bracelets < 0))
10.      {
11.          bracelets = prompt("Please enter a positive whole number. How many ↵
                 bracelets do you want?"," ");
12.          var check = bracelets % 1;
13.      }
14.      document.getElementById("theOrder").innerHTML ="<h3>You are ordering " ↵
             + bracelets + " bracelets.<br /> Thank you.</h3>";
15.  }
16.  </script>
17.  </<head>
18.  <body>
19.  <table align ="center" width ="70%" >
20.  <tr><td colspan ="2">
21.  <h1>Order Your Bracelets Now!</h1>
22.  <p><input type="button" id="bracelets" value="Order bracelets" onclick= ↵
             "getBracelet();" /></p>
23.  </td></tr>
24.  <tr><td id="theOrder"><p> </p></td></tr>
25.  </table>
26.  </body>
27.  </html>
```

Line 9 is the compound condition. Because we use the || operators, only one part of the condition needs to be true for the loop to be entered again. In other words, if a user enters a positive number for bracelets, isNaN(**bracelets**) will be false and (**bracelets** < 0) will also be false but (**check** != 0) will be true and the loop will be entered.

We should also briefly mention how the getElementById() method and the innerHTML property are used on line 14. We will use this method and this property often in future programs.

Line 24 identifies a particular cell in the HTML table with the id "theOrder". Line 14 accesses this cell with the getElementById() method; it puts the id of the element to be accessed inside the parentheses. The innerHTML property sets the new value of what goes into that element (here, it is the cell identified as "theOrder") to whatever is on the right side of the expression. In this case, we want to replace the empty contents of that cell with the information about how many bracelets have been ordered and then thank the user.

Before we finish this section, we will show another example of how to use data validation. Often users to a website are asked to enter their email addresses. At this point, it would be inefficient for a computer to send a test email to the address entered and wait for a response to verify the validity of that address. This is why websites often require users to confirm a site registration by email after accepting the user's entries. However, the computer can initially check to see if certain elements which are common to all emails are included in the user's entry. Therefore, it is possible to ensure that the email address a user enters has the correct email address form. Example 4.27 will demonstrate how to use a loop combined with what we have learned about JavaScript coding to validate the form of an email address. First, however, we need to discuss another JavaScript method and another JavaScript property, as shown in Examples 4.25 and 4.26.

The charAt() Method

The charAt() **method** returns the character at a specified index in a string. A string is a word or a phrase or any text that has been defined by being enclosed in quotes. Each character in the string has an **index** number. There are two important things to remember about the index of any string:

1. Every character counts. This includes punctuation, spaces, special characters such as '@' or '&'.

2. The **index** begins at 0. For example, the 'c' in the string cat has **index** = 0, the 'a' in cat has **index** = 1 and the 't' in cat has **index** = 2.

Thus, the charAt() method can be used to locate a particular character in a string, as shown in the Example 4.25.

EXAMPLE 4.25

Using the charAt() Method

Given the following string variables:

```
var myName = "Morty Mort, Jr."
var myAddress = "123 Duckwood Terrace";
```

(a) myName.charAt(0) = 'M';

(b) myName.charAt(3) = 't';

(c) myName.charAt(8) = 'r';

(d) myName.charAt(10) = ','

(e) myAddress.charAt(1) = '2';

(f) myAddress.charAt(3) = ' ';

(g) myAddress.charAt(8) = 'w';

(h) myAddress.charAt(14) = 'e'

if you have a numeric variable: var **j** = 4;

(i) myName.charAt(j) = 'y';

(j) myName.charAt(j + 2) = 'M';

(k) myAddress.charAt(j - 3) = '2';

(k) myAddress.charAt(j * 2) = 'w';

The length Property

The length **property** returns the length of a string of characters. When you append this property to a variable, the result is the number of characters in the variable, including all punctuation, special characters, and spaces.

There are two important things to remember about the length property:

1. Every character counts. This includes punctuation, spaces, special characters such as '@' or '&'.

2. The length of any string is simply how many characters are in the string. For example, the string "cat" has length = 3 and the string "Lee Clark owns a cat!" has length = 21.

Thus, the length property can be used to tell the programmer how many characters are in any string. If you want to check the entire string to see if a specific character is included in that string, the length property will tell you how many characters need to be checked or, in programming terms, how many times a loop must iterate to check every character.

Using the length Property

a) if **myName** = "Persephone", **myName**.length = 10

b) if **myName** = "Amy Ames", **myName**.length = 8

c) if **myAddress** = "New York, New York 10002", **myAddress**.length = 24

d) if **myAddress** = "the big oak tree", **myAddress**.length = 16

In Example 4.27, we use the charAt() method and the length property to write a program that will validate an email address.

Validating Email Addresses

In this example, the user will be asked to enter an email address and the program will verify that it's in the proper email address format. All email addresses include a username which can be anything, up to 64 characters. The username is followed by the @ sign. The domain follows the @ sign. While there are always exceptions, in general the domain consists of two parts. The first part identifies the host and a dot separates this part from the last part—normally, a three-character extension that identifies the type of host. For example, the .com extension normally identifies the host as a business and the .edu extension identifies the host as an educational institution. For our purposes, we will consider an email address as valid if it contains an @ sign somewhere in the address and if it contains a dot before the last three characters. We will also insist that the first character must be something other than the @ sign. While clearly there is still room for error (for example, A.b@c satisfies these criteria but is not a valid email address), this example demonstrates one way to validate user input.

```
1.    <html>
2.    <head>
3.    <title>Example 4.27</title>
4.    <script>
```

```
5.   function getEmail()
6.   {
7.        var atSign = "@";
8.        email = prompt("Enter your email address", " ");
9.        numChars = email.length;
10.       okSign = 1;
11.       for( j = 1; j < numChars; j++)
12.       {
13.            if (email.charAt(j) == atSign)
14.            {
15.                 okSign = 0;
16.            }
17.       }
18.       if (okSign == 0)
19.       {
20.            if (email.charAt(numChars - 4) != ".")
21.            {
22.                 document.getElementById("message").innerHTML = "<h3>You ⏎
                        entered " + email + ". This is not a valid email ⏎
                        address.</h3>";
23.            }
24.       else
25.       {
26.                 document.getElementById("message").innerHTML = "<h3>You ⏎
                        entered " + email + ". This is a valid email ⏎
                        address.</h3>";
27.            }
28.       }
29.       else
30.       {
31.            document.getElementById("message").innerHTML = "<h3>You entered " ⏎
                        + email + ". This is not a valid email address.</h3>";
32.       }
33.  }
34.  </script>
35.  </<head>
36.  <body>
37.  <table align ="center" width ="70%"><tr><td colspan ="2">
38.  <h1>Enter your contact information</h1>
39.  <tr><td><p> </p>
40.  <p><input type="button" id="email" value="Begin now" onclick= ⏎
                        "getEmail();" /></p>
41.  </td></tr>
42.  <tr><td id ="message"><p> </p></td></tr>
43.  </table>
44.  </body>
45.  </html>
```

Let's discuss this program in detail. The user enters an email address at the prompt on line 8 and this string is stored in a variable named **email**. Line 9 uses the length property to store the number of characters in the **email** string in a variable named **numChars**. Line 10 initializes a variable named **okSign** to 1. We have now set up the conditions needed to loop through the characters in the string to see if one of those characters is the @ sign.

The loop begins on line 11 and ends on line 17. We have used a for loop. The initial value of the variable j is set to 1. It will begin checking each character in the **email** string until it finds the @ sign. The variable j will represent the index value of any character in the string as it continues the loop's iterations. Recall that the first index value of the characters in a string is 0 but we have agreed that the @ sign cannot be the first character. This program assumes that the first character is not an @ sign but you could add code to check for that and you will be asked to do so as a Checkpoint exercise.

The test condition of the loop is j < numChars. This means that if the value of numChars is 10, the loop will continue for 9 iterations. Since the index of the first character in a string is 0, the index of the last character of a 10-character string is 9. In other words, the index of the last character is numChars - 1 and this is why we set the test condition to end when j is one less than numChars. Finally, we increment j by one for each iteration.

The if clause on lines 13–16 checks to see if a character is the @ sign. If it is, the okSign variable is changed to 0. This is known as a **flag.** It will be used later in the program to see if an @ sign has been found in the string.

After the loop has checked all the characters (except the first) for the @ sign, an if...else clause begins on line 17. This clause will be entered if the @ sign has been located; i.e., if okSign == 0. Lines 20 – 27 use a nested if...else clause to check to see if the character that is fourth from the end is a dot. If it is not a dot, the email address is pronounced invalid (line 22).

However, if this character is a dot, the email address is valid since we have already determined that it contains the required @ sign. This message is displayed on line 26.

The else clause of the outer if...else structure is on lines 29–32. This is the case when okSign does not equal 0 which means that we don't care if a dot exists in the right place. No @ sign has been found so the email address is not valid and that message is displayed on line 31.

This code can be refined to check for other requirements. For example, we could check to make sure there is no more than one @ sign in the string. However, while we are learning to use loops and adding more complexity to our code, for our present purposes, this program does the trick.

CHECKPOINT FOR SECTION 4.4

4.18 List the things that need to be validated in a program that requires the user to enter an integer between 1 and 20.

4.19 Write the code that is missing in the following program snippet that will check to make sure the value entered for **tShirts** is an integer:

```
var tShirts = parseInt(prompt("How many tee shirts do you want?"," "));
var check = ___???___;
while ( ___????___ )
```

```
        {
            tShirts = prompt("Please enter a whole number. How many tee shirts ↵
                do you want?"," ");
            var ___????___ ;
        }
        document.write("You want " + tShirts + " tee shirts.");
```

4.20 What is the value of the following, given the variables?

username = "jordy_345"   address = "Fort Walton Beach, FL"

a) **username**.charAt(5)   b) **username**.charAt(7)
c) **address**.charAt(4)   d) **address**.charAt(17)

4.21 What is the value of the following, given the variables?

username = "jordy_345"   address = "Fort Walton Beach, FL"

a) **username**.length   b) **address**.length

4.22 Add code to Example 4.27 to check that the first character in the **email** string is not the '@' sign.

4.5 Putting It to Work

In this section we will create a new game for Greg's Gambits and refine and expand the math exercises we developed for Carla's Classroom in Chapter 3. You will have a chance to build on both of these sites in the end-of-chapter Exercises.

Greg's Gambits: Encoding Secret Messages

We will use what we have learned in this chapter about repetition loops as well as the JavaScript methods and properties. This will be combined with some new material and what we have learned in previous chapters to create a page that will allow the player to generate secret messages through a form of encryption.

In general terms, this program will allow the player to enter an encrypted text message. The player will also be given the option to display the original message or keep it hidden. Note that, by "text" we do not mean the message must only contain alphabetic characters. Numbers, punctuation, and other keys on a normal keyboard are also allowed but the message will be stored as a string variable.

What Is Encryption?

Encryption is the process of transforming information using an algorithm to make it unreadable to other people except those possessing the special knowledge or **key** that has been used in the algorithm. The reverse process, (making the encrypted information readable again) is called **decryption.** Here, we will only encrypt the message; it will be up to you, as an Exercise, to code the decryption process.

The charCodeAt() and String.fromCharCode() Methods

We have used the charAt() method in this chapter. This method returns whatever character is at a specified place in a text string. We also know that the characters in a text string are identified by index numbers which start at 0. Thus, in a six-letter text string, such as kitten, the 'k' is at index 0 and the 'n' is at index 5. We must remember these facts when we use the charCodeAt() and String.fromCharCode() methods.

Unicode and ASCII Code   If you have previously taken a programming language course, you probably recall that each character that can be typed from a normal keyboard has a numeric representation, called the ASCII code. This code has 128 characters including 95 visible characters (keyboard characters) and 33 control characters. However, web pages normally use Unicode which provides a unique number for every character, no matter what the platform, no matter what the program, no matter what the language. The **Unicode Standard** has been adopted by major industry leaders and is required by modern standards including XML, Java, JavaScript, and more. You normally use Unicode in your web pages. Unicode includes all the ASCII characters. We will utilize that fact when we create our encoder.

The charCodeAt() Method   The charCodeAt() **method** returns the Unicode value of the character at the specified index in a string. Example 4.28 shows how to use this method to get the Unicode values of each character in a text string.

EXAMPLE 4.28

Getting Unicode Values in a Test String

The following code uses a loop to get the Unicode value of each letter in a string. You can copy this code into a web page and change the value of the variable **str** to see the Unicode values for any keyboard characters.

```
1.  <script>
2.  var str = "Kitten";
3.  document.write("for the string: " + str + "<br />");
4.  for (j = 0; j < str.length; j++)
5.  {
6.      document.write("Letter number " + (j+1) + " is " + str.charAt(j) + ". ");
7.      document.write("  The Unicode value is: " + str.charCodeAt(j) + "<br />");
8.  }
9.  </script>
```

If you run this code, the output will be as follows:

```
for the string: Kitten
Letter number 1 is K. The Unicode value is: 75
Letter number 2 is i. The Unicode value is: 105
Letter number 3 is t. The Unicode value is: 116
Letter number 4 is t. The Unicode value is: 116
Letter number 5 is e. The Unicode value is: 101
Letter number 6 is n. The Unicode value is: 110
```

The String.fromCharCode() Method   The String.fromCharCode() **method** converts Unicode values to characters. The syntax is always as shown below; a variable name cannot be substituted for the word String. This type of method is called a **static method.**

```
String.fromCharCode(UnicodeVal_1, UnicodeVal_2,...UnicodeVal_n)
```

Example 4.29 shows how to convert a list of Unicode values to their characters. You can copy this code into a web page and change the Unicode values to see different words or characters.

EXAMPLE 4.29

Getting Unicode Values in a Test String

```
1.  <script>
2.        document.write(String.fromCharCode(72,69,76,76,79));
3.        document.write(", ");
4.        document.write(String.fromCharCode(66,79,82,73,83));
5.  </script>
```

If you run this code, the output will be as follows:

```
HELLO, BORIS
```

Now that we have the tools we need to write the program we can begin to develop the plan.

Developing the Program

We need to create a page that will allow the user to enter a message to be encoded. The program will then encrypt the message and display the encrypted message. The initial page uses the same template we have used in the past for other Greg's Gambits games. The player can click a button when he or she is ready to enter a message. The hard part will be to develop the encryption algorithm.

While computers have developed extremely sophisticated encryption algorithms, we will use a very simple one. In fact, you may have done this by hand when you were a child. We will simply replace each letter of the alphabet with a different letter. One way to do this is to reverse the order of the alphabet. In other words, an A will become a Z, a B will become a Y, an F (the sixth letter) will become a U (the sixth letter from the end) and so on. In this encrypted code, the word ANNA would become ZMMZ and ZACK would become AZXP. We'll develop a simple encoding scheme for numbers and other characters.

The Unicode values for the printable ASCII characters are shown in Chapter 2 and are available in Appendix A. You can use this table to check that your program encodes messages correctly and, if you wish, to create more complex encoding algorithms. You will need to use it if you complete the more advanced program described in the Case Studies at the end of the chapter.

The web page will have a button that the player will click to begin. This will call the JavaScript function that will perform the encoding. The player will be prompted to enter a message which will be encoded and displayed. The player will also be asked whether or not the original message should also be displayed.

We need to change each letter in the message to a new character. To do this, we need to develop several algorithms. We can see, from the ASCII code table, that the Unicode values for the uppercase letters in the alphabet are 65 through 90. Lowercase letters are Unicode values 97 through 122. The 10 digits (0–9) are

Unicode values 48 through 57 and all other keys, including punctuation and special characters, are Unicode values 32 through 47, 58 through 64, and 123 through 126.

First, we will develop the algorithm to change A to Z, B to Y, C to X, and so on. In other words, we want to write an expression that will change 65 to 90, 66 to 89, 67 to 88, and so on. We can see that 65 + 90 = 155, 66 + 89 = 155, 67 + 88 = 155, etc. Thus, 155 − 65 = 90, which is what we want. In fact, for all Unicode values between 65 and 90, subtracting the original Unicode value from 155 will give us the Unicode value for the new character. The first algorithm, to convert uppercase letters, thus, is as follows:

```
newCode = 155 - oldCode
```

We can use similar reasoning to develop an algorithm to convert lowercase letters. For these letters, we want to convert Unicode 97 to 122, 96 to 121, 95 to 120, and so on. Since 122 + 97 = 219, 96 + 121 = 219, etc., the second algorithm will be

```
newCode = 219 - oldCode
```

Finally, we want to change numbers and other characters to something else. We'll use a very simple algorithm for this part. We'll just add 3 to whatever the Unicode value is. This will result in 2 (Unicode value 50) becoming 5 (Unicode value 53), the ampersand, & (Unicode value 38) becoming a closing parentheses,) (Unicode value 41) and the question mark, ? (Unicode value 63) becoming an uppercase A (Unicode value 65). For this page we will ignore the last four Unicode values (123, 124, 126, and 126) but you can add a new algorithm for these values if you want. The final algorithm for numbers, punctuation, and special characters is as follows:

```
newCode = oldCode + 3
```

Now we need to develop the logic that will implement these algorithms. We'll sketch it out with informal pseudocode before writing the code:

- First, prompt for the message.
- Next declare variables. We need string variables for the message and for the new (encrypted) message. We need numeric variables to hold our constants (155, 219, and 3) as well as a variable to hold the new Unicode value.
- The encoding will be done in a loop. The loop will go around as many times as there are characters in the message. For each character we will check if it is uppercase, lowercase, or another character. Depending on what type of character it is, we will convert its Unicode value to the new value, as determined by one of the three algorithms. At the end of each pass through the loop, the new character will be added to the new (encoded) message that we are building.
- At the end of the loop, the new message will have the same length as the old message but will contain all new values. Then we will display it on the web page.
- Last, we will prompt the user to decide if he or she wants the original message to be displayed. If the answer is yes, we will display the original message. If not, we will do nothing.

To accomplish this, we will use the JavaScript methods and properties that we already know and the new methods and properties that were described earlier in this section.

Writing the Code

This page will be part of the `Greg's Gambits` site we have been developing in previous chapters. First, add a link on the `play_games.html` page to this page. It should look like this:

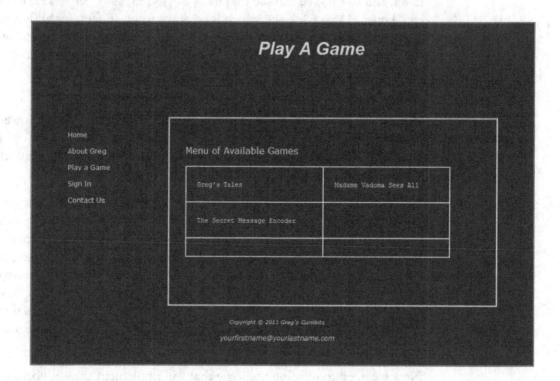

Next, we will create a page using the code below. You can create your own code or add the necessary code to the file named `gregs_encoder.html` which is available in your Student Data files.

First, add header elements with the following content:

The Secret Message Encoder

Add the following content to the `content` `<div>`. This includes a button to start play and a small table where the encoded message and original message will be displayed. The code for this part is as follows:

```
1.   <div id="content">
2.   <h2>Write A Message and Encode It</h1>
3.   <p><input type="button" id="encode" value="Enter your message" onclick= ↵
        "encodeIt();" /></p>
4.   <table cellpadding="2" width = "90%" align = "center" border="1">
5.   <tr> <td align="center" id="secret"><p>encoded message</p></td> </tr>
6.   <tr> <td align="center" id="message"> </td> </tr>
7.   </table>
8.   </div>
```

Put this in the content area on the page so that your page now looks like this:

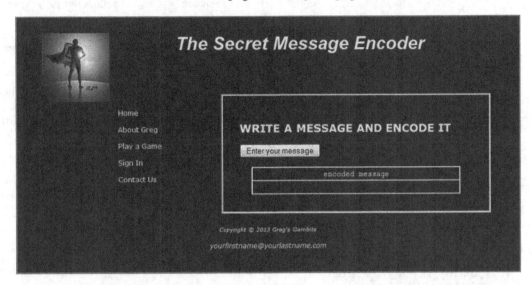

Now we will write the function called encodeIt() that will get the player's message, encode it, and display it. We will use the getElementById(), charCodeAt(), and String.fromCharCode() methods and the innerHTML and length properties. Here is the code:

```
1.    <script type="text/javascript">
2.    function encodeIt()
3,    {
4.         document.getElementById("message").innerHTML = ("<h2> </h2>");
5.         var msg = prompt("Enter your message." , " ");
6.         var newmsg = " ";
7.         var upCaseCode = 155;
8.         var newCode = 0;
9.         var lowCaseCode = 219;
10.        var specialCode = 3;
11.   //the loop encodes each letter in the message string
12.        for (var j = 0; j < msg.length; j++)
13.        {
14.        //check for upppercase letters and encode them
15.            if ((msg.charCodeAt(j)>=65) && (msg.charCodeAt(j)<=90))
16.            {
17.                newcode = (upCaseCode - msg.charCodeAt(j));
18.            }
19.            else
20.        //check for lowercase letters and encode them
21.                if ((msg.charCodeAt(j)>=97) && (msg.charCodeAt(j)<=122))
22.                {
23.                    newcode = (lowCaseCode - msg.charCodeAt(j));
24.                }
25.                else
26.        //check for numbers and special characters and encode them
27.                    if (((msg.charCodeAt(j) > 90) && ↵
                            (msg.charCodeAt(j) < 97)) || (msg.charCodeAt(j) < 65))
```

```
28.                              {
29.                                    newcode = (msg.charCodeAt(j) + specialCode);
30.                              }
31.          //add each encoded character to the new message
32.              newmsg = newmsg + " " + String.fromCharCode(newcode);
33.          }
35.          //display the encoded message on the web page
36.          document.getElementById("secret").innerHTML = ("<h2>" + newmsg + "</h2>");
37.          //decide if original message should be shown
38.          var choice = prompt("Do you want the original message displayed? Yes ↵
                            or No?", " ");
39.          if ((choice.charAt(0) == 'y') || (choice.charAt(0) == 'Y'))
40.          {
41.              document.getElementById("message").innerHTML = ("<h2>" + msg + ↵
                            "</h2>");
42.          }
43. }
44. </script>
```

Putting It All Together

Now we are ready to put it all together.

```
1.  <!DOCTYPE html PUBLIC "-//W3C//DTD XHTML 1.0 Transitional//EN" ↵
    "http://www.w3.org/TR/xhtml1/DTD/xhtml1-transitional.dtd">
2.  <html xmlns="http://www.w3.org/1999/xhtml" lang="en" xml:lang="en">
3.  <meta http-equiv="Content-Type" content="text/html;charset=utf-8"/>
4.  <head>
5.  <title>Greg's Gambits | Secret Message Encoder</title>
6.  <link href="greg.css" rel="stylesheet" type="text/css" />
7.  <script type="text/javascript">
8.  function encodeIt()
9.  {
10.      document.getElementById("message").innerHTML = ("<h2> </h2>");
11.      var msg = prompt("Enter your message." , " ");
12.      var newmsg = " ";
13.      var upCaseCode = 155;
14.      var newCode = 0;
15.      var lowCaseCode = 219;
16.      var specialCode = 3;
17.  //the loop encodes each letter in the message string
18.      for (var j = 0; j < msg.length; j++)
19.      {
20.  //check for upppercase letters and encode them
21.          if ((msg.charCodeAt(j)>=65) && (msg.charCodeAt(j)<=90))
22.          {
23.              newcode = (upCaseCode - msg.charCodeAt(j));
24.          }
25.          else
26.  //check for lowercase letters and encode them
27.          if ((msg.charCodeAt(j)>=97) && (msg.charCodeAt(j)<=122))
28.          {
29.              newcode = (lowCaseCode - msg.charCodeAt(j));
30.          }
31.          else
32.  //check for numbers and special characters and encode them
```

```
33.                    if ((((msg.charCodeAt(j)>90) && (msg.charCodeAt(j)<97)) || ↵
                          (msg.charCodeAt(j)<65))
34.                       {
35.                          newcode = (msg.charCodeAt(j) + specialCode);
36.                       }
37. //add each encoded character to the new message
38.       newmsg = newmsg + " " + String.fromCharCode(newcode);
39.       }
40. //display the encoded message on the web page
41.       document.getElementById("secret").innerHTML = ("<h2>" + newmsg + "</h2>");
42. //decide if original message should be shown
43.       var choice = prompt("Do you want the original message displayed? ↵
                          Yes or No?", " ");
44.       if ((choice.charAt(0) == 'y') || (choice.charAt(0) == 'Y'))
45.          {
46.             document.getElementById("message").innerHTML = ("<h2>" + msg + ↵
                          "</h2>");
47.          }
48. }
49. </script>
50. </head>
51. <body>
52. <div id="container">
53.       <img src="images/superhero.jpg" width="120" height="120" class= ↵
                          "floatleft" />
54.       <h1 id="logo"><em>The Secret Message Encoder</em></h1>
55.       <div id="nav">
56.          <p><a href="index.html">Home</a>
57.          <a href="greg.html">About Greg</a>
58.          <a href="play_games.html">Play a Game</a>
59.          <a href="sign.html">Sign In</a>
60.          <a href="contact.html">Contact Us</a></p>
61.       </div>
62.       <div id="content">
63.          <h2>Write A Message and Encode It</h1>
64.          <p><input type="button" id="encode" value="Enter your message" ↵
                          onclick="encodeIt();" /></p>
65.          <table cellpadding="2" width = "90%" align = "center" border="1">
66.          <tr><td align="center" id="secret"><p>encoded message </p></td></tr>
67.          <tr><td align="center" id="message"> </td></tr>
68.          </table>
69.       </div>
70.       <div id="footer">Copyright &copy; 2013 Greg's Gambits<br />
71.          <a href="mailto:yourfirstname@yourlastname.com"> ↵
                          yourfirstname@yourlastname.com</a>
72.       </div>
73. </div>
74. </body>
75. </html>
```

Finishing Up

Here are some sample messages and displays:

input: If the player enters the message Meet me at 9:00 at the oak tree! (and does not want the original message to be shown):

output:

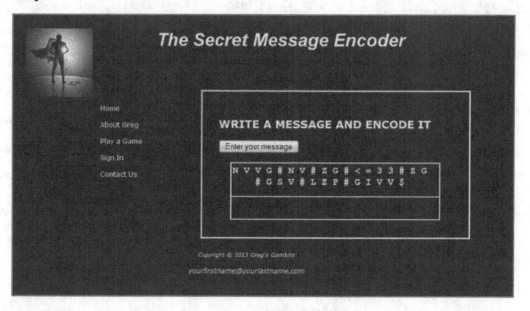

input: If the player enters the message Need more time! Be there at 9:30. (and wants the original message to be shown):

output:

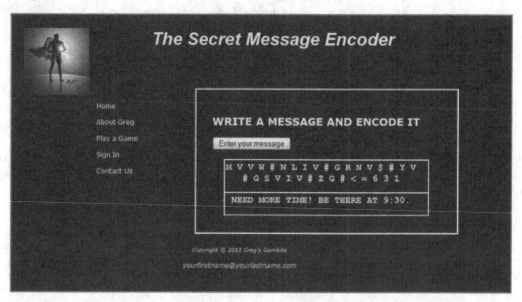

Carla's Classroom: Advanced Arithmetic Lessons

In Chapter 3, we developed a simple arithmetic exercise that allowed a student to advance through three levels of addition problems. However, because we didn't know how to use loops, we were limited to writing only five problems per level or as many as we had the patience to write code for. Now, however, we can create a program that will test for as many addition problems as we want; in fact, we could even make it limitless. Not only that, but our code will be shorter and cleaner. In this section, we will do just that. In Chapter 3's Case Studies, you were asked to add multiplication and division to Carla's Arithmetic Lesson. In this chapter's Case Studies you can improve on that code, using loops, to create a complete arithmetic exercise for Carla's students. We will add a feature that allows the student to decide if he or she wants to do as many problems as it takes to get five correct or if the student wants to stop after a pre-determined number of problems. We'll call this exercise `Become a Math Whiz!`.

Developing the Program

As always, it is important to create pseudocode to map out the flow of the program. We will use a lot of the code we developed in Chapter 3. The program in Chapter 3 contained four functions. The first function, `AddIt()`, called the `levelOne()` function. When a student succeeded at Level One, that function called the `levelTwo()` function and when `levelTwo()` was mastered, the `levelThree()` function was called. We'll continue to use that structure but, for now, we will develop the logic of the `levelOne()` function. From there, we can reuse most of the code, making necessary adjustments to the algorithms and variables, to create functions for `levelTwo()` and `levelThree()` as well as three functions for subtraction problems. We will spend a little extra time developing the first subtraction function because here we need to account for positive and negative numbers.

In general, the pseudocode for the first level function will be as follows:

- Create variables: a counter to count up to five correct answers, a string variable to hold the student's choice about how many problems to do, a numeric variable to hold the number of problems the student selects, and a second counter used to count the total number of problems attempted.

- Prompt the student for a decision about whether to keep doing problems until five answers are correct or to stop after a given number of problems.

- If student wants to select a number of problems, prompt the student for how many.

- Begin a loop that will either end after five correct answers or will end after the requested number of problems. The loop will use the `Math.random()` method to generate random integers for each addition problem. If a problem is answered correctly, one counter will be incremented. Regardless of the answer, a second counter will also be incremented to hold the number of problems the student attempted. When five problems have been answered correctly, if the student has chosen this option, this level will call the next level. If the student has chosen the other option, the next level will be called when the student has attempted the requested number of problems.

- We will also add code to display a message that will tell the student how many problems were attempted and how many were correct.

The most difficult part of this program is constructing the condition for the loop. We want the loop to continue under two conditions: if the student wants the default option (continue until five questions are answered correctly) or if the student has chosen the number of problems (continue until that number is reached). We will first look at the code and then explain some of the more complex statements.

Writing the Code

This page will be part of the Carla's Classroom site we have been developing in previous chapters. First, add a link on the math.html page to this page. The filename for this page should be carla_math_whiz.html. Your math.html page should look like this:

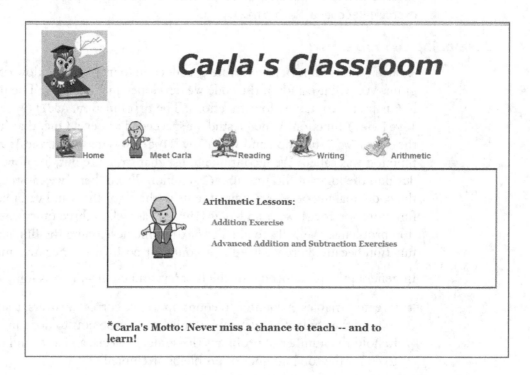

Next, we will create a page using the code below. You can create your own or add the necessary code to the file named carla_math_whiz.html which is available in the Student Data Files.

First, add header elements with the following content:

Become a Math Whiz!

Add the following content to the content <div>. This includes a button to begin addition problems and a button for subtraction problems. Also, add more explanation about how the program will work. The code for this part is as follows:

```
<p> There are two parts to this arithmetic test: addition and subtraction. ⏎
    Each part will increase in difficulty as you prove you are ready for ⏎
    harder problems. You may choose whether you want to move to another ⏎
    level after getting 5 questions correct or you may choose how many ⏎
    problems you want to attempt at any level</p>
<p><input type="button" onclick="addIt()" value="begin the addition test" /> </p>
<p><input type="button" onclick="subIt()" value="begin the subtraction ⏎
    test" /> </p>
```

Your page will now look like this:

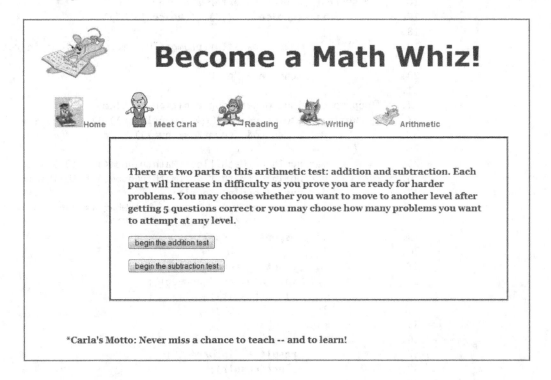

Save the page with the filename `carla_math_whiz.html`.

The plan is to write the code for Level One and reuse most of that code, with modifications, for all the other levels of addition and subtraction problems. We can also use the same code from Chapter 3 that we used to display a single addition problem but now put it in a loop. The code is given below and an explanation of the more complex statements follows:

The Code in Pieces

Level One Addition Code

```
1.  function levelOne()
2.  {
3.      var count1 = 1;
4.      var choice = "y";
5.      var num = 0;
6.      var countX = 1;
7.  //Prompt for default or enter number of problems for this level
8.      var choice = prompt("Do you want to continue only until you ⏎
            get 5 correct? Type 'y' for yes or 'n' for no:", " ");
9.  //if student chooses default
10.     if ((choice == "y") || (choice == "Y"))                 {
11.     {
12.         num = count1;
13.         choice = "y";
14.     }
```

```
15.        else
16.    //if student chooses to enter a number
17.            if ((choice != "y")||(choice !="Y"))              {
18.            {
19.                num = parseInt(prompt("How many problems in total do you ↵
                        want to try?", " "));
20.                choice = "n";
21.            }
22.    //loop to continue generating addition problems
23.        while ((((choice == "y") && (count1 < 6)) || ((choice == "n") ↵
                    && (countX <= num)))
24.        {
25.            var num1a = (Math.floor(Math.random() * 10)) + 1;
26.            var num1b = (Math.floor(Math.random() * 10)) + 1;
27.            var sum1 = num1a + num1b;
28.            var response = parseInt(prompt("What is the sum of " + num1a + ↵
                    " and " + num1b + " ?"));
29.            if (response == sum1)
30.            {
31.                count1 = count1 + 1;
32.                var result = "correct!";
33.                alert(result);
34.            }
35.            else
36.            {
37.                result = "incorrect";
38.                alert(result);
39.            }
40.            countX = countX + 1
41.        }
42.        alert("You completed " + (countX - 1) + " problems and got " ↵
                    + (count1 - 1) + " correct.");
43.    //Level One problems are done, call Level Two
44.        var move = prompt("Do you want to move to Level Two? Type 'y' for yes ↵
                    or 'n' to end this session", " ");
45.        if ((move == "y") || (move == "Y"))
46.        {
47.            levelTwo();
48.        }
49.        else
50.            alert("This session is ended.");
51.    }
```

Let's talk about this code. Line 8 prompts the student for a decision. If the student wants to receive problems until five answers are correct, the value of choice will be either "y" or "Y". Since we cannot assume that computer *users* understand what computer *programmers* know—the important difference between upper and lower case letters—we must account for both options.

The variable, **num**, on line 19 holds the number of problems the student wants if the default is not chosen on line 8. However, line 12 assigns **num** to the value of **count1** just to hold a value. The variable, **count1**, counts the number of correct responses. In this if statement, we set the value of choice to "y" in case a student has typed in an uppercase letter. It will make coding the condition easier later on.

Similarly, if the student does not type "y" or "Y" in answer to the prompt on line 8, any other letter defaults to the second option. We could add some code to check whether the student really meant to answer "no" to this question or just mistyped but, for our purposes, we will simply assume anything that is not a "y" or "Y" means "no." For this reason, we set the value of **choice** to "n" on line 20. We will need a definite value for **choice** when we write the condition for the loop.

The main part of this program is the loop that begins on line 23 and ends on line 41. As with the program we did in Chapter 3, the variables for the random numbers, the counter, and the sum have been named with a "1" appended to the variable name. This was done simply to make it easier, later on, to identify which of these variables go with which levels. We will name the levelTwo() function variables **num2a**, **num2b**, **sum2**, and **count2** and use similar names for the levelThree() function. Since much of the code will be copied and pasted from previous code, it is good to find ways to easily identify various elements in case debugging is necessary. The code to generate an addition problem, check the student's response, and display whether or not it is correct is on lines 24–39 and is copied directly from the program in Chapter 3. However, the condition in the while loop on line 23 deserves some explanation.

The loop should continue to generate addition problems under two possible conditions: if the student wants to continue until five answers are correct or if the student wants to continue for a predetermined number of problems. The first condition is identified with a compound condition that requires that **choice** be "y" and that the number of correct answers is less than 6 (i.e., up to 5). This condition is written as follows:

```
((choice == "y") && (count1 < 6))
```

Since we use the **&&** operator, the loop will continue only if both conditions are true. Because **choice** never changes in the loop, in effect, if this part of the condition is true, it is because the student has not yet reached five correct responses.

We also have declared a variable named **countX**. This variable will count all the problems given to any student. We will use it here, in the loop condition, and later to tell the student how many problems were attempted.

The second possible situation is if the student has picked a number of problems to receive. In this case, we have defined **choice** as "n" and the loop should continue until the selected number of problems have been given to the student. This condition is written as:

```
((choice == "n") && (countX <= num))
```

Since the loop can continue under either the first situation or the second, we combine these two compound conditions with an || operator. In the beginning, only one of the two compound conditions (either to the left of the || or to the right of the ||) will be true. This is fine because the || operator is true as long as either condition is true. As the loop continues to display addition problems, whichever side was initially true will eventually become false. Since the other side was already false, both compound conditions will now be false and the loop will end.

Line 40 increments **countX**. Regardless of whether a student wants to do a set number of problems or as many as it takes to get five correct, we want to count the number of problems offered. Once the loop ends, line 42 displays a message to the student about how many problems were attempted and how many of those were correct. Recall that **count1** keeps track of the number of problems answered correctly while **countX** keeps track of the number of problems offered. Since both **count1** and **countX** are incremented after a problem is displayed, after the loop is exited, their values will be one more than the number of problems answered correctly and given. This is why we must subtract 1 from both of these variables before displaying the results.

Finally, lines 44–51 give the student the option to continue to the next level or end.

Level Two and Level Three Addition Code We've already done the hard part! The next two levels use virtually the same code. The changes will be as follows:

- Change the variable names, if you wish (i.e., **count1** becomes **count2**, **num1a** becomes **num2a**, and so on).
- Change the statement that generates the random numbers to allow a range from 1 – 100 instead of 1 - 10.
- Add the third number to the Level Three addition problems.
- Change the prompts at the end to allow the student to move from Level Two to Level Three and simply end the program after Level Three.

Subtraction Most of the code for subtraction problems will be the same as for addtion. However, this is a program for elementary school children who do not, as yet, understand negative numbers. Therefore, we must add code to ensure that the problems offered do not result in a negative number. To do this, we will check to see if the first random number generated is greater than or equal to the second. If it is, the algorithm for subtraction will simply be the first number minus the second. If the first number is less than the second, then we must reverse the subtraction so the first number is subtracted from the second. For this program, we will only have two levels of subtraction and this piece of code can be reused for the second level. However, if Carla wants to teach negative numbers, we can create a third level which does not use this code and, therefore, will test for subtraction problems with negative numbers. All the other programming logic remains the same as with the addition problems. Here is the new code that will be inserted within the `while` loop after generating the two random numbers:

```
1.  if (num1a >= num1b)
2.  {
3.      var diff1 = num1a - num1b;
4.      var response = parseInt(prompt("How much is " + num1a + " minus " ↵
              + num1b + " ?"));
5.  }
6.  else
7.  {
8.      var diff1 = num1b - num1a;
9.      var response = parseInt(prompt("How much is " + num1b + " minus " ↵
              + num1a + " ?"));
10. }
```

In our subtraction code, we will use many of the same variable names that we used for the addition problems. Remember that we do not need to be concerned about any values from the addition problems being "left over" and popping up in the subtraction problems because any variables used within a function are not available to other functions. We will discuss this concept in greater detail when we discuss global and local variables, later in the text.

All code for the two subtraction levels should be placed under a function called subIt() which is called when the student clicks the button for subtraction. The entire code for the first level of subtraction problems now looks like this:

```
1.   function subIt()
2.   {
3.       levelOne()
4.       function levelOne()
5.       {
6.           var count1 = 1;
7.           var choice = "y";
8.           var num = 0;
9.           var countX = 1;
10.      //Prompt for default or enter number of problems for this level
11.          var choice = prompt("Do you want to continue only until you ⏎
                get 5 correct? Type 'y' for yes or 'n' for no:", " ");
12.      //if student chooses default
13.          if ((choice == "y") || (choice == "Y"))
14.          {
15.              num = count1;
16.              choice = "y";
17.          }
18.          else
19.      //if student chooses to enter a number
20.              if ((choice != "y")||(choice !="Y"))
21.              {
22.                  num = parseInt(prompt("How many problems in total do you ⏎
                        want to try?", " "));
23.                  choice = "n";
24.              }
25.      //loop to continue generating subtraction problems
26.              while ((((choice == "y") && (count1 < 6)) || ⏎
                    ((choice == "n") && (countX <= num)))
27.              {
28.                  var num1a = (Math.floor(Math.random() * 10)) + 1;
29.                  var num1b = (Math.floor(Math.random() * 10)) + 1;
30.      //check if num1a <= num1b
31.                  if (num1a >= num1b)
32.                  {
33.                      var diff1 = num1a - num1b;
34.                      var response = parseInt(prompt("How much is " + num1a ⏎
                            + " minus " + num1b + " ?"));
35.                  }
36.                  else
37.                  {
38.                      var diff1 = num1b - num1a;
39.                      var response = parseInt(prompt("How much is " + num1b ⏎
                            + " minus " + num1a + " ?"));
40.                  }
```

```
41.           if (response == diff1)
42.             {
43.                 count1 = count1 + 1;
44.                 var result = "correct!";
45.                 alert(result);
46.             }
47.           else
48.             {
49.                 result = "incorrect";
50.                 alert(result);
51.             }
52.             countX = countX + 1
53.         }
54.       alert("You completed " + (countX - 1) + " problems and got ↵
                  " + (count1 - 1) + " correct.");
55.     //Level One problems are done, call Level Two
56.         var move = prompt("Do you want to move to Level Two? Type 'y' for ↵
                  yes or 'n' to end this session", " ");
57.       if ((move == "y") || (move == "Y"))
58.         {
59.             levelTwo();
60.         }
61.       else
62.             alert("This session is ended.");
63.     }
64. }
```

Putting It All Together

Now we will put the entire program together including the three addition levels, the two subtraction levels, and the HTML script. You will have a chance to change this code to create math exercises for multiplication and division in the Review Exercises or to add to the levels of difficulty for addition and subtraction.

A Note about Code   This program is fairly long. Luckily, a computer ignores a lot of white space that humans use to make the code easier to read and debug. In this version of the code we will eliminate a lot of this extra space. For example, while an if clause that contains more than one statement must be enclosed in curly braces, the computer doesn't need each bracket—or even each statement—to be on a separate line. The semicolon indicates to a computer that a statement has ended. The computer doesn't care if a statement is on a line by itself or if there are two, three, or twenty statements on one line. So long as each statement ends with a semicolon, it will be executed properly. The code shown here eliminates many of the separate lines to save space in this text and also to show you what code can look like when the programmer is more experienced.

```
1. <!DOCTYPE html PUBLIC "-//W3C//DTD XHTML 1.0 Transitional//EN" ↵
       "http://www.w3.org/TR/xhtml1/DTD/xhtml1-transitional.dtd">
2. <html xmlns="http://www.w3.org/1999/xhtml" lang="en" xml:lang="en">
3. <head>
4. <title>Carla's Classroom | Become a Math Whiz!</title>
5. <link href="carla.css" rel="stylesheet" type="text/css" />
```

```
6.  <script type="text/javascript">
7.  function addIt()
8.  {
9.      levelOne();
10.         function levelOne()
11.         {
12.             var count1 = 1; var choice = "y"; var num = 0; var countX = 1;
13.     //Prompt for default or enter number of problems for this level
14.             var choice = prompt("Do you want to continue only until you ⏎
                    get 5 correct? Type 'y' for yes or 'n' for no:", " ");
15.     //if student chooses default
16.             if ((choice == "y") || (choice == "Y"))
17.             {num = count1; choice = "y"; }
18.     //if student chooses to enter a number
19.             else if ((choice != "y")||(choice !="Y"))
20.                 {num = parseInt(prompt("How many problems in total do you ⏎
                    want to try?", " ")); choice = "n";}
21.     //loop to continue generating addition problems
22.             while (((choice == "y") && (count1 < 6)) || ⏎
                    ((choice == "n") && (countX <= num)))
23.             {
24.                 var num1a = (Math.floor(Math.random() * 10)) + 1;
25.                 var num1b = (Math.floor(Math.random() * 10)) + 1;
26.                 var sum1 = num1a + num1b;
27.                 var response = parseInt(prompt("What is the sum of ⏎
                    " + num1a + " and " + num1b + " ?"));
28.                 if (response == sum1)
29.                     {count1 = count1 + 1;     var result = "correct!"; ⏎
                        alert(result);}
30.                 else
31.                     { result = "incorrect"; alert(result); }
32.                 countX = countX + 1
33.             }
34.             alert("You completed " + (countX - 1) + " problems and got ⏎
                    " + (count1 - 1) + " correct.");
35.     //Level One problems are done, call Level Two
36.             var move = prompt("Do you want to move to Level Two? Type 'y' ⏎
                    for yes or 'n' to end this session", " ");
37.             if ((move == "y") || (move == "Y"))
38.                 {levelTwo(); }
39.         else alert("This session is ended."); }
40.         function levelTwo()
41.         {
42.             var count2 = 1; var choice = "y"; var num = 0; ⏎
                    var countX = 1;
43.     //Prompt for default or enter number of problems for this level
44.             var choice = prompt("Do you want to continue only until you ⏎
                    get 5 correct? Type 'y' for yes or 'n' for no:", " ");
45.     //if student chooses default
46.             if ((choice == "y") || (choice == "Y"))
47.                 { num = count2; choice = "y"; }
48.     //if student chooses to enter a number
49.             else if ((choice != "y")||(choice !="Y"))
50.                 { num = parseInt(prompt("How many problems in ⏎
                    total do you want to try?", " ")); choice = "n";}
```

```
51.    //loop to continue generating addition problems
52.            while ((((choice == "y") && (count2 < 6)) || ↵
                   ((choice == "n") && (countX <= num)))
53.            {
54.                    var num2a = (Math.floor(Math.random() * 100)) + 1;
55.                    var num2b = (Math.floor(Math.random() * 100)) + 1;
56.                    var sum2 = num2a + num2b;
57.                    var response = parseInt(prompt("What is the sum of ↵
                        " + num2a + " and " + num2b + " ?"));
58.                    if (response == sum2)
59.                        {count2 = count2 + 1; var result = "correct!"; ↵
                            alert(result); }
60.                    else
61.                        {result = "incorrect"; alert(result); }
62.                    countX = countX + 1
63.            }
64.            alert("You completed " + (countX - 1) + " problems and got ↵
                " + (count2 - 1) + " correct.");
65.    //Level Two problems are done, call Level Three
66.            var move = prompt("Do you want to move to Level Three? Type 'y' ↵
                for yes or 'n' to end this session", " ");
67.            if ((move == "y") || (move == "Y"))
68.                { levelThree(); }
69.            else  alert("This session is ended.");
70.    }
71.    function levelThree()
72.    {
73.            var count3 = 1; var choice = "y"; var num = 0; var countX = 1;
74.    //Prompt for default or enter number of problems for this level
75.            var choice = prompt("Do you want to continue only until you ↵
                get 5 correct? Type 'y' for yes or 'n' for no:", " ");
76.    //if student chooses default
77.            if ((choice == "y") || (choice == "Y"))
78.                { num = count3; choice = "y"; }
79.    //if student chooses to enter a number
80.            else if ((choice != "y")||(choice !="Y"))
81.                { num = parseInt(prompt("How many problems in total do you ↵
                want to try?", " "));choice = "n"; }
82.    //loop to continue generating addition problems
83.            while ((((choice == "y") && (count3 < 6)) || ((choice == "n") ↵
                && (countX <= num)))
84.            {
85.                    var num3a = (Math.floor(Math.random() * 100)) + 1;
86.                    var num3b = (Math.floor(Math.random() * 100)) + 1;
87.                    var num3c = (Math.floor(Math.random() * 100)) + 1;
88.                    var sum3 = num3a + num3b + num3c;
89.                    var response = parseInt(prompt("What is the sum of " ↵
                        + num3a + ", " + num3b + ", and " + num3c + " ?"));
90.                    if (response == sum3)
91.                        { count3 = count3 + 1; var result = "correct!"; ↵
                            alert(result); }
92.                    else
93.                        { result = "incorrect"; alert(result); }
94.                    countX = countX + 1
95.            }
```

```
96.            alert("You completed " + (countX - 1) + " problems and got " ⏎
                   + (count3 - 1) + " correct.");
97.   //Level Two problems are done, end session or move to subtraction
98.            var move = prompt("Do you want to move to Subtraction? Type 'y' ⏎
                   for yes or 'n' to end this session", " ");
99.            if ((move == "y") || (move == "Y"))
100.               { alert("Click the Subtraction button to begin now"," "); }
101.           else alert("This session is ended.");
102.        }
103.   }
104.   function subIt()
105.   {
106.       levelOne()
107.       function levelOne()
108.       {
109.           var count1 = 1; var choice = "y"; var num = 0; var countX = 1;
110.   //Prompt for default or enter number of problems for this level
111.           var choice = prompt("Do you want to continue only ⏎
                   until you get 5 correct? Type 'y' for yes or ⏎
                   'n' for no:", " ");
112.           if ((choice == "y") || (choice == "Y"))
113.               { num = count1;  choice = "y"; }
114.           else if ((choice != "y")||(choice !="Y"))
115.               { num = parseInt(prompt("How many problems in total do ⏎
                   you want to try?", " ")); choice = "n"; }
116.   //loop to continue generating subtraction problems
117.           while ((((choice == "y") && (count1 < 6)) || ((choice == "n") ⏎
                   && (countX <= num)))
118.               {
119.                   var num1a = (Math.floor(Math.random() * 10)) + 1;
120.                   var num1b = (Math.floor(Math.random() * 10)) + 1;
121.                   if (num1a >= num1b)
122.                       { var diff1 = num1a - num1b;
123.                       var response = parseInt(prompt("How much is " ⏎
                           + num1a + " minus " + num1b + " ?")); }
124.                   else
125.                       { var diff1 = num1b - num1a;
126.                       var response = parseInt(prompt("How much is " + ⏎
                           num1b + " minus " + num1a + " ?")); }
127.                   if (response == diff1)
128.                       { count1 = count1 + 1; var result = "correct!"; ⏎
                           alert(result); }
129.                   else
130.                       { result = "incorrect"; alert(result); }
131.                   countX = countX + 1
132.               }
133.           alert("You completed " + (countX - 1) + " problems and got " ⏎
                   + (count1 - 1) + " correct.");
134.   //Level One problems are done, call Level Two
135.           var move = prompt("Do you want to move to Level Two? ⏎
                   Type 'y' for yes or 'n' to end this session", " ");
136.           if ((move == "y") || (move == "Y"))
137.               { levelTwo(); }
138.           else alert("This session is ended.");
139.       }
```

```
140.            function levelTwo()
141.            {
142.                    var count2 = 1; var choice = "y"; var num = 0; var countX = 1;
143.        //Prompt for default or enter number of problems for this level
144.                    var choice = prompt("Do you want to continue only until you ↵
                            get 5 correct? Type 'y' for yes or 'n' for no:", " ");
145.                if ((choice == "y") || (choice == "Y"))
146.                    { num = count2;  choice = "y"; }
147.                else if ((choice != "y")||(choice !="Y"))
148.                    {num = parseInt(prompt("How many problems in ↵
                        total do you want to try?", " "));choice = "n"; }
149.        //loop to continue generating subtraction problems
150.                while ((((choice == "y") && (count2 < 6)) || ((choice == "n") ↵
                        && (countX <= num)))
151.                {
152.                var num2a = (Math.floor(Math.random() * 100)) + 1;
153.                var num2b = (Math.floor(Math.random() * 100)) + 1;
154.                if (num2a >= num2b)
155.                    { var diff2 = num2a - num2b;
156.                    var response = parseInt(prompt("How much is " ↵
                        + num2a + " minus " + num2b + " ?")); }
157.                else
158.                    { var diff2 = num2b - num2a;
159.                    var response = parseInt(prompt("How much is " ↵
                        + num2b + " minus " + num2a + " ?")); }
160.                if (response == diff2)
161.                    { count2 = count2 + 1; var result = "correct!"; ↵
                            alert(result); }
162.                else
163.                    { result = "incorrect"; alert(result); }
164.                countX = countX + 1
165.                }
166.            alert("You completed " + (countX - 1) + " problems and got " ↵
                    + (count2 - 1) + " correct.");
167.        //Level Two problems are done, call Level Two
168.            alert("Congratulations! You have completed both levels of ↵
                    Subtraction. Your session is ended.");
169.        }
170.    }
171.    </script>
172.    </head>
173.    <body>
174.    <div id="container">
175.        <img src="images/writing_big.jpg" class="floatleft" />
176.        <h1 id="logo">Become a Math Whiz!</h1>
177.        <div align="left">
178.        <blockquote><p>
179.        <a href="index.html"><img src="images/owl_button.jpg"/> Home</a>
180.        <a href="carla.html"><img src="images/carla_button.jpg" /> ↵
                    Meet Carla </a>
181.        <a href="reading.html"><img src="images/read_button.jpg" /> Reading</a>
182.        <a href="writing.html"><img src="images/write_button.jpg" /> Writing</a>
183.        <a href="math.html"><img src="images/arith_button.jpg" /> ↵
                    Arithmetic</a><br /></p>
```

```
184.        </blockquote>
185.        </div>
186.        <div id="content">
187.        <p>There are two parts to this arithmetic test: addition and ↵
           subtraction. Each part will increase in difficulty as you prove you ↵
           are ready for harder problems. You may choose whether you want to ↵
           move to another level after getting 5 questions correct or you may ↵
           choose how many problems you ↵ want to attempt at any level.</p>
188.        <p><input type="button" onclick="addIt()" value="begin the addition ↵
               test" /> </p>
189.        <p><input type="button" onclick="subIt()" value="begin the subtraction ↵
               test" /> </p>
190.        </div>
191.   </div>
192.   <div id="footer">   <h3>*Carla's Motto: Never miss a chance to teach -- and ↵
               to learn!</h3>
193.   </div>
194.   </body> </html>
```

Finishing Up

Here are some possible results after a student uses this page:

output:

The student completes Level One addition, after attempting 10 problems and got 6 correct:

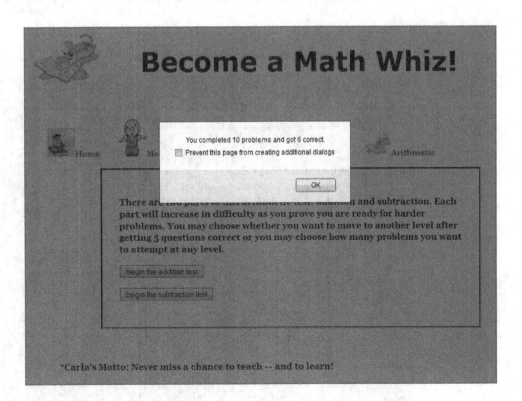

output:

The student completes Level Three and chooses to move to subtraction:

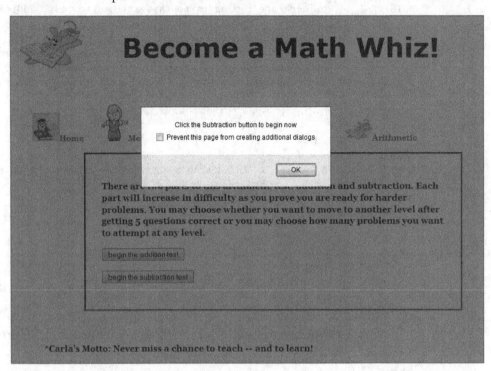

output:

The student completes both subtraction levels:

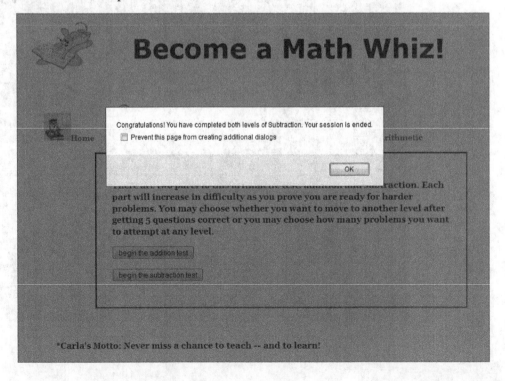

Chapter Review and Exercises

Key Terms

body (of a loop)	iteration
charAt() method	key (encryption)
charCodeAt() method	length property
counter	loop
counter-controlled loop	repetition structure
data validation	return true
decrement	sentinel value
decryption	sentinel-controlled loop
do...while loop	shortcut operators
encryption	static method
end-of-data marker	String.fromCharCode() method
flag	test condition
for loop	toFixed(x) method
increment	toLowerCase() method
index	toUpperCase() method
infinite loop	Unicode Standard
initial value	valid data
isNaN() method	while loop

Review Exercises

Fill in the Blank

1. The basic component of the repetition structure is the _____.

2. A loop that executes three times is said to have performed three _____.

3. The type of loop in which the body of the loop is always executed at least once is a _____ - test loop.

4. In the statement for(x = 1; x < 10; x++) the test condition is _____.

5. The _____ method can be used to set a number to a specified number of decimal places.

True or False

6. T/F   An infinite loop occurs when, in a post-test loop, the test condition can never be met.

7. T/F   In a pre-test loop, the loop body is always executed at least once.

8. T/F   The value of a test condition can only be true or false.

9. T/F   Compound conditions can be used in if...else structures but not in repetition structures.

10. T/F   The following is a valid test condition: 21 < myAge, where myAge = 23.

11. T/F   The do...while loop is a post-test loop.

12. T/F   In a sentinel-controlled loop, the sentinel value must be an integer.

13. T/F   The toLowerCase() method cannot be used if any of the characters in the string is initially entered in lowercase.

14. T/F   Counters can count up or down but only by ones.

15. T/F   The expression j+=2; will add 2 to the variable j.

Short Answer

16. How many times will the alert display?

```
var x = 5;
var y = 1;
while (x < y)
{
    alert("Good morning!");
    x--;
}
```

    a) 5   b) 4   c) 1   d) none

17. How many times will the alert display?

```
var x = 1;
var y = 5;
while (x < y)
{
    alert("Good morning!");
    x++;
}
```

    a) 5   b) 4   c) 1   d) none

18. How many times will the alert display?

```
var x = 5;
var y = 1;
do
{
    alert("Good morning!");
    x--;
}
while (x < y)
```

    a) 5   b) 4   c) 1   d) none

19. How many times will the alert display?

```
var x = 1;
var y = 5;
do
{
    alert("Good morning!");
    x++;
}
while (x < y)
```

    a) 5   b) 4   c) 1   d) none

20. Rewrite the following expressions using shortcut operators.
    a) `w = w + 1`   b) `x = x - 2`
    c) `y = y * 5`   d) `z = z - 1`

21. If **R** = 8, what are the values of **R** and **S** after the following statement?

    `S = R++;`

22. If **R** = 8, what are the values of **R** and **S** after the following statement?

    `S = ++R;`

23. What is the value of **myCity** if **city** = "Los Angeles"?

    `myCity = city.length;`

24. Rewrite the following code using a for loop:

```
m = 1;
while (m < 20)
{
    alert("Hi, friend!");
    m = m+=2;
}
```

25. Rewrite the following code using a for loop:

```
p = 100;
while (p >= 0)
{
    alert("Counting down in..." + p + "seconds!");
    p-=5;
}
```

26. Fill in the missing statements or expressions in the following code that checks to ensure that a user enters an integer value at the prompt:

```
var purchase = parseInt(prompt("How many do you want?"," "));
var check = _____;
while (_____)
{
    purchase = parseInt(prompt("Enter a whole number:", " "));
    _____;
}
```

27. Fill in the missing statements or expressions in the following code that checks whether the user enters an odd or an even number at the prompt:

```
var myNumber = parseInt(prompt("Enter a whole number:"," "));
var check = _____;
if (_____)
    alert("Even number");
else
    alert("Odd number");
```

28. Fill in the missing statements or expressions in the following code that checks whether the user enters an odd or an even number at the prompt:

```
var myNumber = parseInt(prompt("Enter a whole number:"," "));
var check = _____;
```

```
if (_____)
   alert("Odd number");
else
   alert("Even number");
```

29. What is the value of the following, given that **myName** = "M. Nguyen III"?

    a) myName.charAt(3)   **b) myName**.charAt(10)

30. Add the condition needed to allow the player of a guessing game to make another guess for a secret number. Another guess is allowed if the player has previously guessed incorrectly and has not used 10 guesses.

```
var secret = Math.floor(Math.random()*10));
var numGuess = 1;
var newGuess = parseInt(prompt("Take a guess: ", " "));
while (_____)
{
   alert("incorrect");
   newGuess = parseInt(prompt("Guess again: ", " "));
   numGuess++;
}
```

Programming Challenges

On Your Own

1. Create a web page that will display a countdown to a rocket blasting off. Use a button to start the countdown. The countdown sequence should display on the web page and should display BLASTOFF! at the end. You can, if you wish, add a rocket image. Save the page as `blastoff.html` and be sure to include an appropriate page title.

2. Create a web page that asks the user for a password. The password must have exactly eight characters and may not include spaces. All other keyboard characters are allowed. A loop should prompt the user to re-enter another password until both these conditions are met. Save your page with the filename `password.html` and be sure to include an appropriate page title.

3. Create a web page that allows the user to evaluate his or her car's performance on various trips. The user should be allowed to enter as many data sets as desired. For each set the following information will be entered: the name of the trip, the number of miles driven, and the number of gallons of gas used. The output should be put into a JavaScript-generated table and look like this:

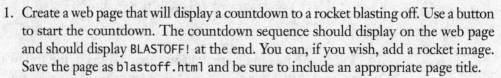

Trip Name	Miles Driven	Gallons Used	Miles per Gallon
Disney World	560	20	28 mpg
...	...	...	...
...	...	...	...
New York City	152	8	19 mpg

Save your page as `mpg.html` and be sure to include an appropriate page title.

4. The factorial of a number, N, is defined as follows:

   `N! = 1 * 2 * 3 * 4 *.....* N`

   For example, 4! = 4 * 3 * 2 * 1 and 7! = 7 * 6 * 5 * 4 * 3 * 2 * 1

   Create a web page that allows the user to enter a positive integer and the page will display the factorial of that number. *Hint:* Use a variable, **factorial**, with an initial value of 1. Then use a loop to multiply **factorial** by successive integers up to the value entered by the user. Save your page as factorial.html and be sure to include an appropriate page title.

5. A biologist has determined that the approximate number of bacteria in a culture after a given number of days is given by the following formula:

   bacteria = initialBacteria * $2^{(days/10)}$

   where **initialBacteria** is the number of bacteria present at the beginning of the observation period. Let the user input the value for **initialBacteria**. Then compute and display the number of bacteria in the culture over 10 days. Do this in a loop that also generates the output in a table on the web page as shown:

   Initial Bacteria present:

Day	Bacteria
1	
.	
.	
.	
10	

   Save your page as bacteria.html and be sure to include an appropriate page title.

6. Create a web page that uses a loop to allow a teacher to enter the following information for all students in a class: student's name, midterm exam grade, final exam grade, homework grade, attendance grade. The program should calculate each student's numeric total grade based on the following formula:

   grade = (midterm*0.3)+(final*0.4)+(homework*0.2)+(attendance*0.1)

   Display the results in a JavaScript-generated table as shown:

Name	Attendance	Homework	Midterm	Final	Course Grade
Bianca	90	85	78	92	86.2
.	.	.	.	.	.
.	.	.	.	.	.
.	.	.	.	.	.
Walter	70	50	83	74	71.5

   Save your page as points.html and be sure to include an appropriate page title.

7. Create a web page that allows a player to enter a message. When a button is clicked, all the text on the page (except the text on the button), including the player's message, will be displayed in reverse. For example, if the page had a

heading that says **Mirror Image**, after the button is clicked, the header will say **egamI rorriM**. The player should also be able to return the page to normal. *Hint:* What would happen if you reversed a word that had been reversed? Save your page as mirror.html and be sure to include an appropriate page title.

Case Studies

Greg's Gambits

Here you will add to the encryption page created earlier in this chapter. The encryption system that has been written in this chapter would be pretty easy for someone to figure out. Now you will create a more sophisticated encryption algorithm.

Open the play_games.html page and add a link, under the The Secret Message Encoder link that links to the new page you will create. The new page should have Unbreakable Secret Message Encoder as a page title and the filename should be gregs_encoder2.html.

You can use the page created earlier in the chapter as a template. The page title, Unbreakable Secret Message Encoder, should also be the first header on the page. In the content area, place a button that the player can click when he or she is ready to encrypt a message.

In the chapter example, we used the following algorithms to encode text:

- uppercase letters: **newcode = (upCaseCode - msg**.charCodeAt(**j**);
- lowercase letters: **newcode = (lowCaseCode - msg**.charCodeAt(**j**);
- numbers and special characters: **newcode = (msg**.charCodeAt(**j**) + **specialCode**;

where **newcode** was the new character in the encoded message, **msg** was the message the user entered, **j** was the index of the character in question, **upCaseCode** = 155, **lowCaseCode** = 219, and **specialCode** = 3.

Now you will generate a random number that will move the value of the **newcode** up (or down) by a certain number of characters. By generating a new random number each time a message is encrypted, the code will be a lot more difficult to break. In a real encryption program, this number would be sent to both the player who is encrypting the message and the person who is receiving the message so it can be decrypted. It would be the key. But anyone else who sees the secret message and does not have the key will not know how to decrypt it. On our page we will just ask the player if he wants to see the random number that has been used in the encryption. If yes, then display that number along with the encryption algorithm. Use the table of Unicode values to ensure that you do not generate any characters outside the range of acceptable ASCII keyboard strokes.

For example, you might use the following for encoding uppercase values: There are 26 letters in the alphabet and uppercase values range from 65 to 90 while lowercase values range from 97 to 122. You might decide to change an uppercase A to its lowercase value plus a random number between 2 and 26. If the random number was 5, this would encode A to Unicode 97 (lowercase a) plus 5 or Unicode 102 which is lowercase f. Using this scheme, the word CAT would become hfy. You need to consider, of course, what would happen to an uppercase Z? The Unicode value for z is 122; therefore, 122 + 5 = 127 which is not included in the ASCII values we can use. You will need to add code to account for this situation. How you do this is up to you. You could simply define all characters that are greater than 126 to be a specific character. Or you could alter your algorithm to change the addition to subtraction in this case. You may think of another clever way to control this situation.

For this program, create new algorithms for uppercase and lowercase letters as well as digits and punctuation. Test your page in at least two different browsers. Submit your work as instructed by your teacher.

Carla's Classroom

Now you will add to the addition and subtraction exercises created earlier in this chapter by creating multiplication and division exercises.

Each page or exercise you create should prompt the student to answer an arithmetic question. The student should be given the option to continue until five questions are answered correctly or to stop after a desired number of questions. As with the addition and subtraction exercises created in the chapter, each question should be created by generating two random numbers. The correct answer should be compared to the student's answer. There should be two counters: one to count the number of correct answers and one to count the number of problems attempted. At the end of each level, the student should receive a message stating how many questions were attempted and how many were correct. At the end of each level the student should be prompted to continue to another level, if one is available, or to end the program.

Open the math.html file and add one or more links (depending on how many options you choose to program) under the Advanced Addition and Subtraction Exercises. The links should go to the new page or pages you create.

Use the carla_math_whiz.html page that was created earlier in the chapter as a template. You can create one or both of the following arithmetic exercises:

- Create two levels of multiplication. The first level should multiply whole numbers between 1 and 10 and the second level should multiply numbers between 10 and 100. You can add this code to the carla_math_whiz.html page created earlier in the chapter or, if you only do this part, name this page adv_multiplication.html.
- Create two levels of division problems. The first level should divide whole numbers between 1 and 100 but only generate problems that result in integer quotients. The second level should also include integers between 1 and 100 but allow for decimal responses (i.e., 11/2 = 5.5). You need to make sure your code checks for the following:
  - For the first level, the dividend must be bigger than or equal to the divisor; i.e., in the expression **a** ÷ **b**, **a** must be larger than (or equal to) **b**.
  - For the second level, instruct the student to display the answer only to two decimal places and be sure your result is also truncated after two decimal places.

You can add this code to the `carla_math_whiz.html` page created earlier in the chapter or, if you only do this part, name this page `adv_division.html`.

Test your page(s) in at least two different browsers. Be sure to test all possible combinations of correct and incorrect responses at each level. Submit your work as instructed by your teacher.

Lee's Landscape

In this exercise, you will use the table of services from the `Lee's Landscape | Services` page that you created in Chapter 3. On this new page, the customer will order services. The page should prompt the user to enter an amount he or she wishes to spend. Then the customer can order services from the table of services (copied from Chapter 3, below, for your convenience). The program should keep a running total of how much the customer has spent afterw each entry. If the customer tries to go over his initial spending limit, the customer should be alerted to this fact; the last item ordered should be deleted from the list; and the customer prompted to either order something more affordable or stop ordering. The final output should be a table that lists the services the customer has ordered, the prices, and a grand total.

Service	Options	
Lawn maintenance	Weekly: $15/service Twice a month: $25/service Monthly: $40/service	
Pest control	Monthly: $35/service Twice a year: $75/service Yearly: $150/service	
Tree and hedge trimming	Monthly: $25/service Twice a year: $75/service Yearly: $150/service	

The images used here are available in the Student Data Files. Of course, you can substitute your own images if you wish. Be sure to give this web page an appropriate page title; `Lee's Landscape | Order Services` is suggested. Save this file with the filename `lee_order.html`. Add a link to the `Lee's Landscape` home page (if you created one in a previous chapter) to this new page. Test your page in at least two different browsers. Be sure to test all possible combinations of each service and contract. Submit your work as instructed by your teacher.

Jackie's Jewelry

Add a page to the Jackie's Jewelry website that allows a customer to select free samples. Jackie offers eight possible samples from which a customer can pick and gives free samples as follows:

- If the purchase is any amount up to (and including) $50.00, one sample is given.
- If the purchase is between $50.01 and 100.00, two samples are given.
- If the purchase is over $100.00, three samples are given.

Later in the text you will create a shopping cart for Jackie. However, at this point, you can simply prompt the customer to enter the amount of his or her purchase. The program should then tell the customer how many samples can be chosen and ask the customer to pick from the following list. Then the program should display the samples the customer will receive.

Available Samples

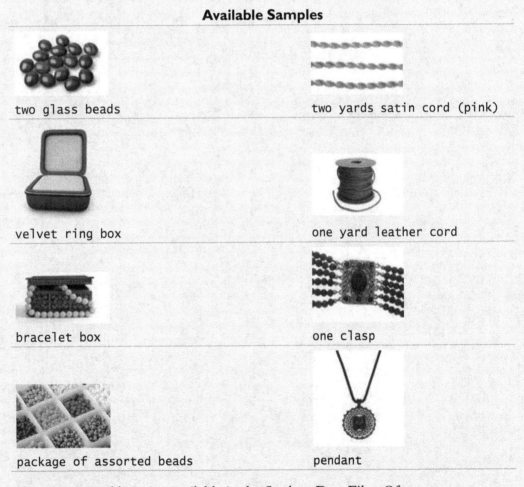

two glass beads	two yards satin cord (pink)
velvet ring box	one yard leather cord
bracelet box	one clasp
package of assorted beads	pendant

The images used here are available in the Student Data Files. Of course, you can substitute your own images if you wish. Be sure to give this web page an appropriate page title; Jackie's Jewelry | Samples is suggested. Save this file with the filename jackie_samples.html. Add a link to the Jackie's Jewelry home page to this new page. Test your page in at least two different browsers. Submit your work as instructed by your teacher.

5

Advanced Decisions and Loops

Chapter Objectives

By now, you probably realize the power of using decisions and loops in your programs. You may be thinking about how to make the programs we have designed so far more complex, more efficient, and more interesting. In this chapter, we'll incorporate what we've learned so far and do just that—create more advanced programs.

We have covered the basics of programming in the first chapters, but JavaScript has a lot more to offer and there's a great deal more to learn. Before we move on to advanced topics like functions and arrays, we will learn to use loops and decisions nested inside other loops and decisions. We'll learn to compute sums and averages which are used for a lot more than math problems. We'll learn to exit a loop early. These concepts all build on what we have learned, so, while there are no new basic concepts, we will practice combining and using what we know through longer examples that use the three basic programming structures.

After reading this chapter, you will be able to do the following:

- Use loops to compute sums and averages

- Understand how to use loops to find odd or even numbers

- Understand how to use loops to find the largest and smallest in a list

- Understand how to identify an integer

- Understand how and when to use the break; statement

- Understand how and when to use the continue; statement

- Create nested for loops

- Create nested loops using both pre- and post-test loops

- Nest loops and if...else structures

- Draw shapes and patterns with JavaScript

- Use various mouse events

Some Simple Schoolroom Statistics

In this section, we'll review some ways to use JavaScript that we touched on earlier in the text and perhaps even used without making a big deal about it. These are tools you will find useful in many programs. We'll learn how to compute simple statistics by finding sums and averages, how to identify odd and even numbers and use this to compute the middle value in a list of numbers, and how to determine if a number is an integer or a floating point number. We will use these in the examples throughout this chapter.

It All Adds Up

Often, a program requires that we keep a running total as a loop continues through its iterations. For example, a shopping cart may need to display subtotals as a customer adds items. A game may need to keep track of points a player accrues. A teacher who wants a program to calculate student averages will need to sum up the grades to compute that average.

Elementary school students learn to add a list of numbers. For example, if a professor is getting married and his students want to donate money toward a gift, the way to determine how much money was donated would be to add the donations, as follows:

```
5.00 + 7.00 + 3.00 + 5.00 + 10.00 + 6.00 + 4.00 = 40
```

However, this method is not effective in a computer program. The program that took in these seven amounts separately would need a separate variable for each amount. If we did not store each amount in a variable, then the program could only be used once. A calculator could do this for us. In "real life" if an eighth student wanted to add a donation, we could just add the new amount to the total. In a program, once it was written, there would be no way to accept any new amounts. But a computer program should be written so that it can be used many times. It should be flexible enough to allow for seven amounts or seventy. And we certainly don't want separate variables for many amounts. To create a sum of any number of numbers, one version of the JavaScript pseudocode would look like this:

```
Declare variables to hold a number and the sum
Initialize the variables to 0
Start a loop
    Prompt the user for a number and tell the user what to enter
    when done
    Store that number in a variable
    Create the sum: sum = old sum + new number
End the loop
```

The **sum** is initially 0. Let's say the first number the user enters is 5. The first time through the loop, the **sum** equals 0 plus the value of the first number which is 5. Then the loop goes through the second iteration. Let's say the user enters 7. Now

sum = old **sum** (5) plus the new number (7). The **sum** now is 12. If the user enters 3 at the third prompt, the **sum** will be the old **sum** (12) plus the new number (3). Now **sum** = 15. And so on. When creating a sum, the variable that holds the total as the program progresses is called the **accumulator** because it accumulates all the values. This is how a computer sums numbers. Example 5.1 demonstrates how this is used in a simple program.

EXAMPLE 5.1

Summing Up

The following program will allow Professor Henrietta Crabtree to enter all the scores for her class on her first exam. The scores will be summed until Henrietta stops entering scores. We will add to this program when we learn to calculate an average in the next example. This program allows Henrietta to enter numbers until she enters the sentinel value. We choose -999 as the sentinel because, for this situation, it is virtually impossible for a student to get a score of -999 on an exam. The sentinel value should be chosen so that it would never be part of the valid input.

```
1.   <html>
2.   <head>
3.   <title>Example 5.1</title>
4.   <script>
5.   function getSum()
6.   {
7.      var score = 0; var sum = 0;
8.      while (score != -999)
9.      {
10.         sum = sum + score;
11.         score = parseInt(prompt("Enter a score or enter -999 ↵
                     when you're finished:"," "));
12.      }
13.      document.write("the sum of these scores is: " + sum + ".");
14.   }
15.   </script>
16.   </<head>
17.   <body>
18.   <h1>Exam 1 Scores</h1>
19.   <h3>Click to enter students' scores</h3>
20.   <p><input type="button" id="scores" value="Enter the scores" ↵
                     onclick="getSum();" /></p>
21.   </body> </html>
```

This code accepts numbers and will continue until the number entered is -999. The **sum** continues to add the new values to its previous total in the loop. One point in particular needs to be mentioned. We do not want -999 to be part of this sum. In this case, by putting the computation for **sum** on line 10, before the prompt for the next number, we ensure that -999 does not get included in the **sum**. On the last two iterations the user enters the last score on line 11. Let's imagine the last student got an 85 on the test. The condition on line 10 is checked and, since 85 != -999, the loop continues. Now 85 is added to the previous **sum** (line 11). The user is prompted again for another score on line 12 and enters -999. Now, when the condition is checked again, it becomes false and the loop is exited. In this manner, -999 is not included in the **sum**. If lines 10 and 11 were written in reverse order, -999 would be included in the **sum**.

So far, this code isn't much good for anything except as an adding machine. We will add to the code in the next example so that it can use the data to find the average grade on Henrietta's exam.

Computing Averages

Once you know the sum of a list of numbers, it is simple to find the average value, so long as you know how many numbers were in the list. But in programming, we may not know in advance how many numbers will be in the sum. To find the average value when a user enters a bunch of numbers, we need to sum the numbers and we also need to count the numbers. We have previously used a counter in many programs as a test condition. In Example 5.2, we will add to the code in Example 5.1 and find the average of the scores on Henrietta Crabtree's exam using a counter to keep track of how many scores Henrietta enters.

EXAMPLE 5.2

The Average Value

By adding just a few lines of code to Example 5.1 we can compute the average of the exam scores that Henrietta enters, regardless of whether she enters 3 scores or 300. We use a new variable, a counter, to count each score entered. At the end, this counter holds the number of scores entered so the average is simply the sum divided by the number of scores. We also add a variable to hold the average. Following is just the JavaScript code since the rest of the page is the same as the previous example.

```
1.   <script>
2.   function getAverage()
3.   {
4.       var score = 0; var sum = 0; var count = 0; var average = 0;
5.       while (score != -999)
6.       {
7.           sum = sum + score;
8.           count++;
9.           score = parseInt(prompt("Enter a score or enter -999 ↵
                           when you're finished:"," "));
10.      }
11.      average = sum/(count - 1);
12.      document.write("<p>The sum of these scores is: " + sum ↵
                               + ".</p>");
13.      document.write("<p>The average of these scores is: " ↵
                               + average + ".</p>");
14.  }
15.  </script>
```

Line 4 adds two numeric variables, **count** and **average**, to the list of variables and both are initialized to 0. The code on line 8 keeps track of how many scores have been entered by adding 1 to the value of **count** with each iteration. The important thing to note is this: If Henrietta enters four scores and then enters -999 to quit, the counter will have the value of 5 when the loop is exited. We need to consider this when computing the average. Since the last entry, -999, will always increment the counter by one more than the actual number of exam scores, we need to subtract this before calculating the average (line 11).

Normally, whenever writing a program that uses division, we would need to check for a division by zero error. This type of error can cause serious problems and we always want to make sure that our programs never end up with a zero in the divisor. However, in this program the only way such a situation could arise would be if the user entered -999 at the very first prompt. Still, when we put this code together with the next few examples, we will add code to check for the possibility that the divisor is zero.

The Range

We can now use the previous program and add to it to find the range of values from lowest to highest. This requires a little more programming, as shown in Example 5.3. Then we can finish off our statistical analysis of Professor Crabtree's exam.

EXAMPLE 5.3

The Highest and the Lowest

In this example, we will add code to find the lowest and the highest score entered. This gives us the range of scores. We add two more variables—one to keep track of the highest score entered (**high**) and one to keep track of the lowest score entered (**low**). We'll also restrict the value of the average to be an integer. In this example, we need to change the code a bit by prompting for a value before entering the loop. We need to do this to initialize our highest and lowest values with the first score entered. Since we are now generating more information from the data entered and will, after the next example, have several statistics to display, the function that is called is now renamed to getStats(). The only change in the HTML page is that the function called by the button is now getStats(). The code is as follows:

```
1.    <script>
2.    function getStats()
3.    {
4.        var score = 0; var sum = 0; var count = 1; var average = 0;
5.        var high = 0; var low = 0;
6.        score = parseInt(prompt("Enter a score or enter -999 ↵
                    when you're finished:"," "));
7.        low = score;
```

```
 8.          high = score;
 9.          while (score != -999)
10.          {
11.              sum = sum + score;
12.              count++;
13.              score = parseInt(prompt("Enter a score or ↵
                     enter -999 when you're finished:"," "));
14.              if (score > high)
15.                  high = score;
16.              if ((score < low) && (score != -999))
17.                  low = score;
18.          }
19.          average = parseInt(sum/(count - 1));
20.          document.write("<p>The number of scores entered is: " ↵
                     + (count - 1) + ".</p>");
21.          document.write("<p>The sum of these scores is: " ↵
                     + sum + ".</p>");
22.          document.write("<p>The average of these scores is: " ↵
                     + average + ".</p>");
23.          document.write("<p>The lowest score is: " + low + ".</p>");
24.          document.write("<p>The highest score is: " + high + ".</p>");
25.  }
26.  </script>
```

The two new variables, **high** and **low**, are declared on line 5. Line 6 now prompts the user for the first score. Now, in case Henrietta finds herself in the program by accident, she can enter -999 at this time and the loop will never execute. However, the main reason to enter a value before the loop begins is to give an initial value to **high** and **low**. From now on, every time a new score is entered it will be compared to **high** (line 14) and to **low** (line 16). If the new score is higher than the first score, that value will replace the value presently in **high** (line 15). If the score is lower than **low**, the lower score will replace what is in **low** (line 17). The one exception is the sentinel value. Clearly, -999 will be lower than any exam score so we ensure that it is not allowed to replace the value of **low** by using the compound condition on line 16. At the end of the loop, **low** will hold the lowest score and **high** will hold the highest score. This is the range of scores on the exam and these values are displayed on lines 23 and 24.

At this point, if the program is run and the following values are entered, the output should be as shown below.

Input: 93, 84, 72, 79, 62, 96, 77, 82, 98, 65, -999

Output:

```
The number of scores entered is: 10.

The sum of these scores is: 808.

The average of these scores is: 80.

The lowest score is 62.

The highest score is 98.
```

Odd and Even

There are many situations where you may find it necessary to identify whether a number is odd or even. In Chapter 9, we will need this information to find the median value in a list of numbers. The median value is defined as the value where half the numbers are higher than that number and half are lower. If the list contains an odd number of entries, the median value is simply the exact middle. But if the list contains an even number of entries, the median value is the average of the two middle numbers. This is just one instance where a programmer needs to identify whether a number is odd or even. Example 5.4 provides a practical application.

EXAMPLE 5.4

Right or Wrong? Odd or Even?

In our example where we are building statistics for Professor Crabtree, we will imagine that she had created an exam with two types of questions. She is interested in finding out whether her students are simply memorizing information or are able to apply information using logical reasoning and critical thinking skills. Therefore, she has designed her exam so that all the odd numbered questions are based on facts from the book. Students who have memorized these facts can answer these questions easily. The even numbered questions, on the other hand, require logical thinking to apply knowledge in order to get the correct answer. Now Professor Crabtree wants to identify how many odd-numbered questions a student got wrong and compare that number to how many even numbered-questions that student got wrong. She will use this information to help her identify a student's learning style.

In this example we will write the code for a single student's exam results. Later in the chapter you will add to this example so that Professor Crabtree can compile statistics on all odd and even questions for her class.

In this example we will assume the exam has twenty questions and we will use a for loop. The following code can be inserted into the getStats() function from the previous example or used, as shown, as a stand-alone function. Since the HTML web page is the same as for the previous examples, that code is not included.

```
1.   <script>
2.   function getStats()
3.   {
4.   var question = " "; var count = 0;
5.   var oddCount = 0; var evenCount = 0;
6.   var name = " ";
7.   name = (prompt("What is this student's name?"," "));
8.   alert("At each prompt enter 'y' if the student got the ↵
                    question correct or 'n' for incorrect");
9.   for (count = 1; count < 21; count++)
10.  {
11.       question = (prompt("Question " + count + ": ", " "));
12.       if ((question == "n") && ((count % 2) == 0))
13.           evenCount++;
```

```
14.         if ((question == "n") && ((count % 2) != 0))
15.           oddCount++;
16.  }
17.         document.write("<p>Results for " + name + ":</p>");
18.         document.write("<p>Out of the 20 questions on this ↵
                        exam: </p>");
19.         document.write("<p>The number of odd questions missed is: "↵
                        + oddCount);
20.         document.write("<p>The number of even questions missed is: "↵
                        + evenCount);
21.  }
22.  </script>
```

In this program we use five variables: **question**, **oddCount**, **evenCount**, **count**, and **name**. The student's name is stored in **name**. The variable **question** holds a character variable—either 'y' for a correct response or 'n' for an incorrect answer. The two variables, **oddCount** and **evenCount** keep track of how many odd and even questions were missed.

The counter, **count**, keeps track of the loop iterations and allows the loop to prompt for responses to the 20 exam questions. It is also used to identify which question each iteration refers to and is used to distinguish between odd-numbered questions and even-numbered questions. This is how it is accomplished: If any integer is an even number, it is evenly divisible by 2. Therefore, any even integer divided by 2 will have a remainder of 0. We use the **modulus operator** to test for a remainder of 0 on lines 12 and 14. If the remainder is 0, we know this is an even-numbered question but if the remainder is anything but 0, it is an odd-numbered question. Note that any integer divided by 2 will always give a remainder of 0 or 1. We could have checked for a remainder of 1 instead of 0; whichever way the code is written is a matter of programmer preference.

The compound condition on lines 12 and 14 ensure that **evenCount** will be incremented only when an even-numbered question is incorrect and **oddCount** will be incremented only when an odd-numbered question is incorrect.

At this point, if the program is run and the following values are entered, the output should be as shown below:

Input: Student's name is Sonny Nguyen
            Questions missed: 1, 3. 7, 8, 12, 15, 17, 19

Output:

Results for Sonny Nguyen

Out of the 20 questions on this exam:

The number of odd questions missed is: 6

The number of even questions missed is: 2

Integer Accuracy: Math Methods

We use the parseInt() method frequently for many purposes. It is extremely useful to change strings to numbers when data is entered. However, it is not particularly accurate. Regardless of what floating point number is entered, the parseInt() method simply lops off anything after the decimal point. Thus, parseInt(89.001) results in the integer 89 and parseInt(89.999) also results in 89. For a student who is desperately seeking an A, this does not seem fair. In the first case, the student is 1/1000th of a point above an 89, which is normally considered to be a B+. In the second case, the student is only 1/1000th of a point away from an A. While there is some disagreement in the world of mathematics about how to treat a number like 89.5, mathematicians do agree that a number greater than X.5 should be rounded up to the next integer while anything less than X.5 should be rounded down.

The Math.round() Method

JavaScript allows us to write code that will treat rounding floating point numbers to integers reasonably through the use of the **Math.round() method.** Two other methods, Math.floor() and Math.ceil(), also give us more control over how we deal with converting floating point numbers to integers.

The Math.round() method will round off numbers mathematically. Math.round(89.001) will result in 89 and Math.round(89.999) will result in 90. Math.round() will round any decimal part that is equal to or greater than 0.5 up to the next integer. Thus, Math.round(89.5) will become 90 while Math.round(89.499) results in 89.

The Math.floor() and Math.ceil() Methods

The **Math.floor() method** takes any floating point number and rounds it down; just as with parseInt(), Math.floor() cuts off the decimal part of the number. The **Math.ceil() method,** on the other hand, will always round up. In other words, both Math.ceil(89.001) and Math.ceil(89.999) result in 90.

These three methods allow us to decide exactly what we want to accomplish when we change a floating point number to an integer. The following example demonstrates how these three methods work and how results will differ, depending on which method is used.

In example 5.5 we only display the code for this function. In Example 5.6, we will put it all together to create a program to help Professor Crabtree with her exam grades.

EXAMPLE 5.5

Dealing with Integers

```
1.   <script>
2.   function floatToInteger()
3.   {
4.        var floatNum = 0; var newValue = 0;
5.        floatNum = prompt("Enter any number or enter -99 to ⏎
                      quit:", "");
```

```
 6.          while (floatNum != -99)
 7.          {
 8.              document.write("<p>You originally entered: " ↵
                     + floatNum + "</p>");
 9.              newValue = parseInt(floatNum);
10.              document.write("<p>The result of parseInt(X) is: " ↵
                     + newValue + "</p>");
11.              newValue = Math.floor(floatNum);
12.              document.write("<p>The result of Math.floor(X) is : " ↵
                     + newValue + "</p>");
13.              newValue = Math.ceil(floatNum);
14.              document.write("<p>The result of Math.ceil(X) is : " ↵
                     + newValue + "</p>");
15.              newValue = Math.round(floatNum);
16.              document.write("<p>The result of Math.round(X) is : " ↵
                     + newValue + "</p>");
17.              floatNum = prompt("Enter any number or enter -99 ↵
                     to quit:", "");
18.          }
19.      }
20.  </script>
```

If the program is run and the following values are entered, the outputs should be as shown below. Try this program yourself with various values.

Input: 3.467	Input: 16.53
You originally entered: 3.467	You originally entered: 16.53
The result of parseInt(X) is: 3	The result of parseInt(X) is: 16
The result of Math.floor(X) is : 3	The result of Math.floor(X) is : 16
The result of Math.ceil(X) is : 4	The result of Math.ceil(X) is : 17
The result of Math.round(X) is : 3	The result of Math.round(X) is : 17

Input: 79.01	Input: 79.88
You originally entered: 79.01	You originally entered: 79
The result of parseInt(X) is: 79	The result of parseInt(X) is: 79
The result of Math.floor(X) is : 79	The result of Math.floor(X) is : 79
The result of Math.ceil(X) is : 80	The result of Math.ceil(X) is : 80
The result of Math.round(X) is : 79	The result of Math.round(X) is : 80

EXAMPLE 5.6

Professor Crabtree's Exam Results

Now we'll combine the features from Examples 5.1 through 5.5 to create a program for Professor Crabtree to analyze the results of her exam. The whole program will do the following:

■ Allow Professor Crabtree to enter scores for all students

■ Compute the class average as an integer value using the Math.round() method

■ Find the range of grades

■ Allow Professor Crabtree to select students, one at a time, to determine how many odd-numbered (memorization) questions were missed and how many even-numbered (logical reasoning) questions were missed.

The entire program is as follows:

```
1.   <!DOCTYPE HTML PUBLIC "-//W3C//DTD HTML 4.0 Transitional//EN">
2.   <html>
3.   <head>
4.   <title>Example 5.6</title>
5.   <script>
6.   function getStats()
7.   {
8.        var score = 0; var sum = 0; var count = 1; var average = 0;
9.        var high = 0; var low = 0;
10.       score = parseInt(prompt("Enter a score or enter -999 ↵
                          when you're finished:"," "));
11.       low = score;
12.       high = score;
13.       while (score != -999)
14.       {
15.            sum = sum + score;
16.            count++;
17.            score = parseInt(prompt("Enter a score or enter ↵
                              -999 when you're finished:"," "));
18.            if (score > high)
19.                high = score;
20.            if ((score < low) && (score != -999))
21.                low = score;
22.       }
23.       average = Math.round(sum/(count - 1));
24.       document.write("<p>The number of scores entered is: " + ↵
                          (count - 1) + ".</p>");
25.       document.write("<p>The average of these scores is: " + ↵
                          average + ".</p>");
26.       document.write("<p>The lowest score is: " + low + ".</p>");
27.       document.write("<p>The highest score is: " + high + ".</p>");
28.   }
29.   function getStudent()
30.   {
31.       var question = " ";
32.       var name = " ";
33.       name = (prompt("What is this student's name?"," "));
34.       var oddCount = 0; var evenCount = 0; var count = 0;
35.       alert("At each prompt enter 'y' if the student got the ↵
                          question correct or 'n' for incorrect");
36.       for (count = 1; count < 21; count++)
37.       {
38.            question = (prompt("Question " + count + ": ", " "));
39.            if ((question == "n") && ((count % 2) == 0))
40.                evenCount++;
41.            if ((question == "n") && ((count % 2) != 0))
42.                oddCount++;
43.       }
44.       document.write("<p>Results for " + name + ":</p>");
```

```
45.        document.write("<p>Out of the 20 questions on this ↵
                            exam: </p>");
46.        document.write("<p>The number of odd questions missed is: " ↵
                            + oddCount);
47.        document.write("<p>The number of even questions missed is: " ↵
                            + evenCount);
48.    }
49.    </script>
50.    </head>
51.    <body>
52.    <table align ="center" width ="70%"><tr><td colspan ="2">
53.    <h1>Exam 1</h1>
54.    <h3>Get a summary of exam results</h3>
55.    <p><input type="button" id="scores" value="Class results" ↵
                            onclick="getStats();" /></p>
56.    <h3>Get an individual student's results</h3>
57.    <p><input type="button" id="studentscores" value="Student ↵
                            results" onclick="getStudent();" /></p>
58.    </td></tr></table></body>
59.    </html>
```

Notice that we use two buttons in this program. One calls the function that computes the exam statistics for the class—getStats(). The other calls the function getStudent() that allows Professor Crabtree to get individual results for a selected students. Note: It does not matter in which order these functions are entered into the <head> section of the page. Each function is activated only when it is called by the button on the web page.

This program runs fine so long as Professor Crabtree enters the information required as explained by the prompts and the alert. But what if she types a 'g' instead of a 'y' or 'n'? What if she accidentally types a letter instead of a number? These options must be addressed by the professional programmer. You will be asked to add error checking and data validation to this program in the Checkpoint exercises. Example 5.7 will add some data validation to the previous example and get you started on completing the related Checkpoint exercises.

EXAMPLE 5.7

Validating Professor Crabtree's Input

This program will check to make sure the professor enters valid numbers for the scores in the getStats() function. The code for this part of the function is as follows:

```
1.  function getStats()
2.  {
3.      var score = 0; var sum = 0; var count = 1; var average = 0;
4.      var high = 0; var low = 0;
```

```
5.        score = parseInt(prompt("Enter a score or enter -999 ⌐
                  when you're finished:"," "));
6.        while (isNaN(score))
7.        {
8.            score = parseInt(prompt("Enter a valid score or ⌐
                  enter -999 when you're finished:"," "));
9.        }
10.  . . . The rest of the function remains the same...
.
.
.
last line     }
```

Lines 6–9 are the new error checking lines of code. The JavaScript **isNaN()**
method is true if the value in the parentheses is not a number. So, if the user enters
a character or string the condition in the while statement will be true and the user
will be repeatedly prompted until a valid number is entered. Once a valid number is
entered, isNaN(score) becomes false and the loop is exited.

CHECKPOINT FOR SECTION 5.1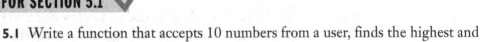

5.1 Write a function that accepts 10 numbers from a user, finds the highest and
lowest numbers and then displays the results.

5.2 Write a function that accepts integers, one at a time, from a user, determines
whether the number is odd or even, and displays the result to the user. The
display should tell the user what number was entered and whether it is odd or
even. Use a loop to allow the user to do this as often as desired.

5.3 Write a function that allows the user to pick what decimal value he or she
wants to use as the limit for rounding down. For example, the user might
want all numbers with decimal parts greater than 0.3 to round up to the next
integer. Use the Math.round() method. The program should display the
original number and the rounded number. Do this in a loop so the user can
continue to enter as many numbers as desired.

5.4 Add error checking to the program in Example 5.6 that ensures no division
by zero error will occur when the average exam score is calculated in the
getStats() function.

5.5 Add validation to the getStudent() function to make sure the user only
enters an 'n' or a 'y' at the prompt.

5.6 Add validation to the getStudent() function to allow the user to enter either
uppercase or lowercase responses of 'n' or 'y' at the prompt.

5.2 To Continue or Not to Continue?

We have learned that a loop ends when the test condition is no longer true. For many situations, this is good enough. For example, if you want to use a loop to enter the names of all the players in a game, you can end, using a predetermined sentinel value, when there are no more names to enter. Or, if you want a loop to allow a customer to pick three samples, you end the loop after it has made three iterations. But what if you want a loop to allow a player to make 10 moves unless the player's points drop below 100? You could use a compound condition, as we have done in the past, requiring the loop to end when either the number of moves exceeds 10 or the number of points is less than 100. There are some times, however, when you might prefer not to use a compound condition to break out of a loop. For these situations, JavaScript provides a way to allow you to exit a loop early.

Another possible scenario is when you want an iteration to be skipped but don't want to end the loop. JavaScript provides a statement that allows you to skip an iteration without completely exiting the loop. We will discuss both these statements—break and `continue`—in this section.

The break Statement

We used the **break statement** when we discussed the `switch structure` in Chapter 3. The break statement is extremely important in a `switch` structure. Example 5.8 is given to refresh your memory of why `breaks` must be included in a `switch` structure. Such is not the case with loops.

EXAMPLE 5.8

Using breaks in a `switch` structure

The following program is shown in two forms. The first does not include the break statement in any of the cases. The second includes `break` statements.

Part (a)

```
<html>
<head>
  <title>Example 5.8a</title>
<script>
function spellIt()
{
    var letter = prompt("Pick a letter between a and d", " ");
    switch (letter)
    {
    case "a":
        document.write("<p>" + letter + " is for aardvark.</p>");
    case "b":
        document.write("<p>" + letter + " is for baboon.</p>");
```

```
        case "c":
            document.write("<p>" + letter + " is for canary.</p>");
        case "d":
            document.write("<p>" + letter + " is for donkey.</p>");
        default:
            document.write("<p>" + letter + " is not an option. </p>");
    }
}
</script>
</<head>
<body>
<h1>Learn your letters</h1>
<p><input type="button" value="Begin" onclick="spellIt();" /></p>
</body>
</html>
```

The following outputs result, given the inputs shown:

input = "a"	input = "b"	input = "c"
a is for aardvark	b is for baboon.	c is for canary.
a is for baboon.	b is for canary.	c is for donkey.
a is for canary.	b is for donkey.	c is not an option.
a is for donkey.	b is not an option.	
a is not an option.	**input = "d"**	**input = "ZZZ"**
	d is for donkey.	ZZZ is not an option.
	d is not an option.	

Part (b)

```
<html>
<head>
  <title>Example 5.8b</title>
<script>
function spellIt()
{
    var letter = prompt("Pick a letter between a and d", " ");
    switch (letter)
    {
    case "a":
        document.write("<p>" + letter + " is for aardvark.</p>");
        break;
    case "b":
        document.write("<p>" + letter + " is for baboon.</p>");
        break;
    case "c":
        document.write("<p>" + letter + " is for canary.</p>");
        break;
    case "d":
        document.write("<p>" + letter + " is for donkey.</p>");
        break;
    default:
        document.write("<p>" + letter + " is not an option. </p>");
    }
}
```

```
</script>
</<head>
<body>
<h1>Learn your letters</h1>
<p><input type="button" value="Begin" onclick="spellIt();" /></p>
</body>
</html>
```

The following outputs result, given the inputs shown:

input = "a"	input = "b"	input = "c"
a is for aardvark.	b is for baboon.	c is for canary.

	input = "d"	input = "ZZZ"
	d is for donkey.	ZZZ is not an option.

As you can see from part (a), without a break statement, as soon as the appropriate case is identified, the program executes that code and continues to execute all the subsequent code, regardless of whether or not the condition is met. The break statement as in part (b), is necessary to jump out of the switch structure when the proper code segment has been executed.

It's clear that the break statement is important, as shown above. It can also be used in a loop to force the loop to end. However, it is far better to create compound conditions to force a loop to end whenever possible. It's simply better programming! But if you find your conditions become too complex or you require a loop to end in a situation that cannot be accounted for in a compound condition, it's nice to know you have the break statement as an option. Example 5.9 demonstrates how to use the break statement in a loop.

EXAMPLE 5.9

You Can't Shop 'til You Drop

In this program, we will imagine that many of the customers at the online Jackie's Jewelry website have complained because they are surprised, at the end of their order, by the cost of shipping. Jackie has asked you to modify a program that allows customers to order merchandise so that, when a given limit has been reached, the loop that receives each new item will end and the customer will get a message saying that the next item will raise the shipping cost. Until that limit is reached, the customer should be allowed to continue ordering items until he or she is done.

The following program would only be part of a whole shopping cart. However, this program demonstrates several of the important concepts of this chapter, including nesting selection structures inside loops and using the break statement to exit a loop early. Notice that we have condensed some of the lines of code by putting more than one statement on a single line, as, for example, declaring and initializing three variables on line 8.

The body of this page includes nine sale items. The images used in this page (lines 56–64) are available in the Student Data Files. They can be used to re-create this page and to create the Jackie's Jewelry Case Study at the end of the chapter.

```
1.   <html>
2.   <head>
3.   <title>Example 5.9</title>
4.   <script>
5.   function getOrder()
6.   {
7.         document.write('<table width="60%" align = "center">');
8.         var count = 1; var num = 0; var cost = 0;
9.         var item = " ";
10.        document.write('<tr><td><img src="images/jewel_box1.jpg" /> ↵
                         </td></tr>');
11.        while (item != "X")
12.        {
13.              item = prompt("Enter the letter of item number " + ↵
                     count + " or enter 'X' when finished."," ");
14.              num = parseInt(prompt("How many do you want (enter 0 ↵
                     if done)?", " "));
15.              document.write('<tr>');
16.              switch (item)
17.              {
18.                    case "A":
19.              case "B":
20.                    cost = cost + (num * 5.95);
21.                    break;
22.              case "C":
23.                    cost = cost + (num * 8.95);
24.                    break;
25.              case "D":
26.                    cost = cost + (num * 12.95);
27.                    break;
28.              case "E":
29.                    cost = cost + (num * 14.95);
30.                    break;
31.              case "F":
32.                    cost = cost + (num * 18.95);
33.                    break;
34.              case "G":
35.                    cost = cost + (num * 15.95);
36.                    break;
37.              case "H":
38.              case "I":
39.                    cost = cost + (num * 21.95);
40.                    break;
41.              }
42.              count++;
43.              if ((item != "X") && (cost <= 100))       {
44.                    document.write("<td>You ordered " + num + ↵
                         " of item " + item + " <br /> The total ↵
                         cost so far is $ " + cost.toFixed(2) ↵
                         + "</td>");
45.                    document.write('</tr>');        }
46.              if (cost > 100)       {
47.                    alert("Your purchase will put your order over ↵
                         $100 and shipping costs triple.");
```

```
48.                 break;      }
49.         }
50.         document.write('</table>');
51.     }
52.     </script>
53.     </<head>
54.     <body>
55.     <table align ="center" width ="70%" ><tr><td colspan ="3">
56.         <h1>Order Your Jewelry Now!</h1>
57.         <tr><td><img src = "ring1.jpg" alt ="ring1" /> <br /> ↵
                        A: ring 1, cost: $ 5.95 </td>
58.         <td><img src = "ring2.jpg" alt ="ring2" /> <br /> ↵
                        B: ring 2, cost: $ 5.95 </td>
59.         <td><img src = "ring3.jpg" alt ="ring3" /> <br /> ↵
                        C: ring 3, cost: $ 8.95 </td></tr>
60.         <tr><td> <img src = "bracelet1.jpg" alt = "bracelet1" /> ↵
                        <br /> D: bracelet 1, cost: $ 12.95 </td>
61.         <td> <img src = "bracelet2.jpg" alt = "bracelet2" /> ↵
                        <br /> E: bracelet 2, cost: $ 14.95 </td>
62.         <td> <img src = "bracelet3.jpg" alt = "bracelet3" /> ↵
                        <br /> F: bracelet 3, cost: $ 18.95 </td></tr>
63.         <tr><td><img src = "pendant1.jpg" alt ="pendant1" />
                        <br /> G: pendant 1, cost: $ 15.95 </td>
64.         <td><img src = "pendant2.jpg" alt ="pendant2" /> ↵
                        <br /> H: pendant 2, cost: $ 21.95 </td>
65.         <td><img src = "pendant3.jpg" alt ="pendant3" /> ↵
                        <br /> I: pendant 3, cost: $ 21.95 </td></tr>
66.         <tr><td colspan="3"><p><br /><input type="button" id="order" ↵
                    value="Place your order" onclick="getOrder();" />
67.         </p></td></tr>
68.     </table> </body></html>
```

This program appears long but the getOrder() function can be condensed to the following pseudocode:

■ Declare and initialize variables
■ Start a while loop
  □ Prompt the customer for the item desired and how many will be bought
  □ Use a switch structure to identify the cost of that item, calculate the cost of the number of that item ordered and keep a running sum of the total cost.
  □ Check if the total cost will put the customer over the cheaper shipping rate
  □ If this is true, break out of the loop and inform the customer that another item will triple the shipping cost
  □ Continue with the loop until the customer is done shopping

With that in mind, we'll discuss some of the significant statements. Since the cost of items A and B is the same, as is the case with items H and I, we do nothing when either A or H is selected. This allows the switch structure to drop to the next case. In other words, the same calculation is used for either item A or B and the same calculation is used for items H and I.

Two numeric variables, **num** and **count**, are used for different purposes in this program. The first, **num**, holds the value of how many of an item a customer wants. The second, **count**, holds the value of how many distinct items the customer has purchased.

After an item has been selected and the total cost is calculated, line 43 checks to see if the customer's order is complete. If the order total so far is less than the amount that would put the total over the lower shipping rate, line 44 outputs a summary of the purchase and total cost. If the order total at this point is more than $100.00, the `if` clause on lines 46–49 executes. The customer is alerted to the fact that the last purchase goes over the $100.00 limit and ordering ends. The break statement is used on line 48 to jump out of the loop, even though the customer has not entered the sentinel condition (X).

In this example, the program ends in one of two ways: Either the customer must stop shopping because the total purchase is too close to the higher shipping cost or because the customer has finished ordering. Either way, the end is rather abrupt. We will add Example 5.10 to this program to ensure that the jewelry business owner does not lose the business of a customer who wants to keep buying items even with the higher shipping cost. Since you now know what most of the program does so far, you can focus on the added features in the next example.

If you enter the code shown in Example 5.9, using the images in the Student Data Files, your initial page should look like this:

If the customer tries to buy one ring (item C) and eight pendants (item H), the result will be as follows:

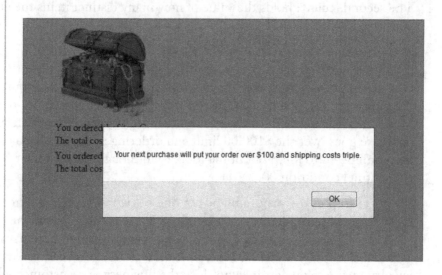

But if the customer orders one ring (item C), three bracelets (item D) and two pendants (item G), the result will be as follows:

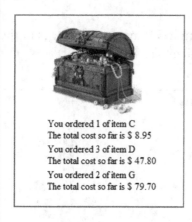

Let the Customer Shop!

EXAMPLE
5.10

In this example we will add to Example 5.9 to allow the customer to continue to shop, even if it means paying extra for shipping. Much of this code is a repeat of the code in Example 5.9; therefore, to save space, we will not repeat the original web page lines or all the cases in the switch structure.

```
1.    <html>
2.    <head>
3.    <title>Example 5.10</title>
4.    <script>
5.    function getOrder()
```

```
6.   {
7.        document.write('<table width="60%" align = "center">');
8.        var count = 1; var num = 0; var cost = 0; var sub = 0;
9.        var item = " "; var choice = " ";
10.       document.write('<tr><td><img src="images/jewel_box1.jpg" /> ⌐
                    </td></tr>');
11.      shop();
12.      function shop()
13.      {
14.           while (item != "X")
15.           {
16.                item = prompt("Enter the letter of item number " ⌐
                   + count + " or enter 'X' when finished.", " ");
17.                num = parseInt(prompt("How many do you want ⌐
                   (enter 0 if done)?", " "));
18.                document.write('<tr>');
19.                sub = cost;
20.                switch (item)
21.                {
22.     ...the contents of the switch are the same as Example 5.2
23.                }
24.                count++;
25.                if (item != "X")
26.                {
27.                     document.write("<td>You ordered " + num ⌐
                        + " of item " + item + " <br /> The total ⌐
                        cost so far is $ " + cost.toFixed(2) ⌐
                        + "</td>");
28.                     document.write('</tr>');
29.                }
30.                else
31.                     break;
32.                if ((cost > 100) && (choice == " "))
33.                {
34.                     alert("Your next purchase will put your ⌐
                        order over $100 and shipping costs triple.");
35.                     choice = prompt("Do you want to continue ⌐
                        shopping anyway? Enter 'y' or 'n':" , " ");
36.                }
36.                if (choice == "y")
37.                     shop();
38.                if (choice == "n")
39.                {
40.                     document.write("<td>Your last item has ⌐
                        been removed. Your present total is $ " ⌐
                        + sub.toFixed(2) + "</td>");
41.                     break;
42.                }
43.           }
44.           document.write('</table>');
45.      }
46.  }
47.  </script>
48.  </<head>
49.  <body>
```

```
50.    <table align ="center" width ="70%" ><tr><td colspan ="3">
51.    <h1>Order Your Jewelry Now!</h1>
52.    ... the body of this page is the same as Example 5.2
53.    </table></body></html>
```

We will discuss each addition made here to the program of Example 5.9 and explain how it works.

On line 8 we add a new numeric variable, **sub** and set its initial value to 0. The purpose of this variable is to hold the value of the total cost of the purchase prior to the last item bought. This is used later, when we want to display the cost to the user before the purchase that puts him or her over the $100.00 mark. Therefore, before a new cost is calculated in each iteration, **sub** takes on the old value of **cost** (line 19). We have also added a new character variable, **choice**, on line 9. This variable will allow the customer to decide whether or not to continue shopping after the $100.00 level has been reached.

In this new version we create a new function called shop(). The initial function that is called by the button, getOrder(), calls the function shop() after it completes some tasks that should only be done once, regardless of what happens during a customer's order. getOrder() sets up the table for the output, initializes the variables, and then calls the new shop() function.

The new function is where the shopping takes place. As shown in Example 5.9, a loop allows the customer to select as many items as desired and a running total of the cost is maintained. In our new version, as soon as the customer enters X for the item letter, the loop ends (lines 30 and 31). We use the break statement here to end the loop.

Lines 32–42 now deal with what happens when a customer orders more than $100.00 worth of merchandise. The first time the customer's order is more than $100.00 the value of **choice** will be a space, as it was initialized. Therefore, the compound condition on line 32 will be true. Regardless of what the user enters after this first time, the compound condition will always be false because **choice** will not be an empty space. We are assured that the customer will only be alerted to the fact that the order is over $100.00 once, even if the customer chooses to shop for hundreds more items.

Lines 36 and 37 deal with one of the **choice** options—when the customer wants to continue shopping. This is where the new function, shop(), comes into play. If **choice** is "y" the shop() function is called and control goes back into the loop that continues to prompt the user for items, keep a total of the cost, and display that information. From now on, the only way the user can stop shopping is by entering the sentinel value, X.

Lines 38–42 deal with the second **choice** option—when the customer chooses to end shopping. In this case, the customer is told that the cost of the last item was subtracted from the present total. In fact, the program does not need to subtract anything since **sub** holds the value of the previous total before the offending item was added. However, since the customer does not know what is happening in the code, we need to assure him or her that the last item is no longer part of the order nor will it be charged. At this point, the break statement is used again to jump out of the loop and end the shopping spree.

When the page is loaded, it will look exactly like the one shown in Example 5.9. If the customer initially tries to buy one ring (item C) and 8 pendants (item H), the result will also be the same as shown in Example 5.9. However, when the customer clicks OK at the alert, then enters "y" at the next prompt, and orders 2 bracelets (item E) before quitting, the output will be as follows:

You ordered 1 of item C
The total cost so far is $ 8.95
You ordered 8 of item H
The total cost so far is $ 184.55
You ordered 2 of item E
The total cost so far is $ 214.45

On the other hand, if the customer initially tries to buy one ring (item B), three bracelets (item F), and then tries to order two pendants (item H) but chooses not to go over the $100.00 limit, the end result will be as follows:

You ordered 1 of item B
The total cost so far is $ 5.95
You ordered 3 of item F
The total cost so far is $ 62.80
You ordered 2 of item H
The total cost so far is $ 106.70
Your last item has been removed. Your present total is $ 62.80

There are some things missing from this program. There is no data validation. You will have the chance to add data validation in the Checkpoint exercises for this section. You will also have a chance to enhance and expand this program for the Jackie's Jewelry website that we are building in the Programming Challenges Case Studies.

The continue Statement

The **continue statement** will allow you to skip an iteration in a loop. When the break statement is used in a loop, the loop ends early. But the continue statement allows you to skip the loop body once (or more, depending on the conditions) but return and complete more iterations. Example 5.11 shows how this works.

Counting by Threes

This example demonstrates the use of the `continue` statement with a simple `for` loop that goes through 101 iterations, from 0 to 100. It counts by threes; in other words, if the number is evenly divisible by 3, it displays that number. If the number is not evenly divisible by 3, it skips the display statement in the loop.

```
1.   <html>
2.   <head>
3.   <title>Example 5.11</title>
4.   <script>
5.   function getThrees()
6.   {
7.       var i = 0;
8.       for (i = 0; i <= 100; i++)
9.       {
10.          if ((i/3) != parseInt(i/3))
11.          {
12.              continue;
13.          }
14.          document.write(i + "   ");
15.      }
16.  }
17.  </script>
18.  </head>
19.  <body>
20.  <table align ="center" width ="70%"><tr><td colspan ="2">
21.  <h1>Count By Threes</h1>
22.  <p><input type="button" id="scores" value="Count by Threes from 0
         to 100" onclick="getThrees();" /></p>
23.  </td></tr></table></body></html>
```

The test to see if a number is divisible evenly by 3 is on line 10. If this is the case, the rest of the statements in the loop are skipped and **i** is incremented to the next value. For the first time, **i** = 1 and 1 is not divisible by 3 so the `document.write` statement on line 14 is not executed. The same is true on the next iteration when **i** = 2. But when **i** = 3, 3 ÷ 3 = 0 which is an integer. So line 14 is executed. This process continues until **i** becomes 101 and the loop ends. If you code this program, your output should look like this (although you may see more numbers on one line, depending on your screen resolution and default text size):

```
0    3    6    9    12   15   18   21   24   27   30   33   36   39   42   45
48   51   54   57   60   63   66   69   72   75   78   81   84   87   90   93
96   99
```

Example 5.12 uses the `continue` statement with a slightly more complex program.

The Retake Group

Professor Crabtree wasn't happy with the results of her exam. She decides to give her students a second chance. However, the students who did well do not have to retake the exam. This program uses the `continue` statement to allow Professor

Crabtree to enter each student's name and exam score. If the score is below 95, the student will have to retake the exam. That student's name will appear on a list. If the student scored 95 or above, no retake is necessary. The continue statement will be used to skip adding a student's name to the retake list if the student's score is 95 or above. The code for this program is as follows:

```
1.   <html>
2.   <head>
3.   <title>Example 5.12</title>
4.   <script>
5.   function getGroup()
6.   {
7.        var i = 0; var score = 0; var name = " "; students = 0;
8.        document.write("<table width = '60%' align = 'center'> ↵
             <tr><td>Students who must retake the exam</td></tr>");
9.        students = parseInt(prompt("How many students took this ↵
             exam? ", " "));
10.       for (i = 0; i < students; i++)
11.       {
12.            name = prompt("Enter the student's name: "," ");
13.            score = parseInt(prompt("Enter the student's score: " ↵
                 , " "));
14.            if (score >= 95)
15.                 continue;
16.            document.write("<tr><td>" + name + "</td></tr>");
17.       }
18.       document.write("</table>");
19.  }
20.  </script>
21.  </head>
22.  <body>
23.  <table align ="center" width ="70%"><tr><td colspan ="2">
24.  <h1>Students who must do the retake</h1>
25.  <p><input type="button" id="scores" value="Get List of Retake ↵
             Students" onclick="getGroup();" /></p>
26.  </td></tr></table></body></html>
```

If you create and run this program with the following input, your output should be as shown below.

input: Eight students took the exam

Student		Student	
Name	Score	Name	Score
Joe Jones	73	Mary Mead	84
Kim Kang	96	Tim Teague	63
Maria Montas	98	Pat Smith	70
Harvey Howe	95	Juan Vasquez	94

output:

Students who must retake the exam

Joe Jones

Mary Mead

Tim Teague

Pat Smith

CHECKPOINT FOR SECTION 5.2

5.7 Add code to Example 5.9 and/or Example 5.10 to change all entries for the **item** variable to uppercase.

5.8 Add code to Example 5.9 and/or Example 5.10 to account for **item** entries that are not within the range specified (i.e., A though I). (*Hint:* use Unicode values.)

5.9 Add code to Example 5.9 and/or Example 5.10 to validate the entries for the **choice** variable.

5.10 Redo Example 5.11 so that the program counts by five's.

5.11 Give an example of a scenario where a loop might need a break statement.

5.12 Give an example of a scenario where a loop might need a continue statement.

5.3 Nested for Loops

We have nested a loop inside another loop and a selection structure inside a loop. When we talk about **nested loops,** the larger loop is called the **outer loop;** the one lying within it is called the **inner loop.** Sometimes it is very difficult to follow the logical sequence of steps that occurs when nested loops are implemented. Therefore, we will spend quite a bit of time developing short programs with nested loops and will step through each line of each program carefully. Now, more than ever, it is important to be able to walk through (**desk check**) what the program does at each step, often using pencil and paper to carefully record the values of each variable and the output at each step.

Desk Checking

While it has always been important to walk through programs by hand to check that the results you get when you run the program are what you expected, it becomes almost imperative that you do this with complicated programs involving nested loops. This means that you sit in front of your computer, pencil and paper in hand. As you go through the program, line by line, you should write down the value of each variable at each line as well as any output which will be displayed. Examples 5.13 and 5.14 demonstrate how to do this.

EXAMPLE 5.13

Desk Checking Nested For Loops

Here is a very short program. It should be simple to figure out what it does. However, it isn't as easy as it looks. Below is a detailed demonstration of how to desk check this program to ensure that the output looks like it should.

```
1.  function getLoops()
2.  {
3.      var x = 0; var y = 0; var z = 0;
4.      for (x = 1; x < 4; x++)
5.      {
6.          document.write("<h3>Pass " + x + "</h3>");
7.          for (y = 1; y < 10; y+=3)
8.          {
9.              z = x + y;
10.             document.write("<p>"+ x +" + "+ y +" = "+ z +"</p>");
11.         }
12.     }
13. }
```

Pass	value of x	value of y	value of z	output
Outer pass 1	1	0	0	
Inner pass 1	1	1	2	1 + 1 = 2
Inner pass 2	1	4	5	1 + 4 = 5
Inner pass 3	1	7	8	1 + 7 = 8
loop ends, test fails	1	10	8	
Outer pass 2	2	10	8	
Inner pass 1	2	1	3	2 + 1 = 3
Inner pass 2	2	4	6	2 + 4 = 6
Inner pass 3	2	7	9	2 + 7 = 9
loop ends, test fails	2	10	9	
Outer pass 3	3	10	9	
Inner pass 1	3	1	4	3 + 1 = 4
Inner pass 2	3	4	7	3 + 4 = 7
Inner pass 3	3	7	10	3 + 7 = 10
loop ends, test fails	3	10	10	

Notice the values of the variables. At the end of each time the inner loop stops the variables retain their last values. These are reset at the beginning of the next time the inner loop begins. The display, if you were to run this program, should look like this:

Pass 1

$1 + 1 = 2$

$1 + 4 = 5$

$1 + 7 = 8$

Pass 2

$2 + 1 = 3$

$2 + 4 = 6$

$2 + 7 = 9$

Pass 3

$3 + 1 = 4$

$3 + 4 = 7$

$3 + 7 = 10$

EXAMPLE 5.14

Desk Checking Nested Post-Test and Pre-Test Loops

In this example, we nest a pre-test while loop inside a post-test do...while loop. The program may appear deceptively short but it takes some serious concentration to understand what is happening. We will use desk checking at the end to explain the results.

```
1.   function getLoops()
2.   {
3.       var y = 3; var count1 = 1; var count2 = 1;
4.       do
5.       {
6.           var x = count1 + 1; count2 = 1;
7.           document.write("<h3>Pass Number: " + count1 + "</h3>");
8.           while(count2 <= y)
9.           {
10.              var z = y * x;
11.              document.write("<p> x = " + x + ", y = " + y + ↵
                             ", z = " + z + "</p>");
12.              x++;
13.              count2++;
14.          }
15.          count1++;
16.      }
17.      while(count1 < y)
18.  }
```

Pass	value of x	value of y	value of z	value of count1	value of count2	output
line 7 (Outer pass 1)	2	3	?	1	1	Pass Number 1
line 11 (Inner pass 1)	2	3	6	1	1	x=2, y=3, z=6
line 14 (end Inner pass 1)	3	3	6	1	2	
line 11 (Inner pass 2)	3	3	9	1	2	x=3, y=3, z=9
line 14 (end Inner pass 2)	4	3	9	1	3	
line 11 (Inner pass 3)	4	3	12	1	3	x=4, y= 3, z=12
line 14 (end Inner pass 3)	5	3	12	1	4	

Pass	value of x	value of y	value of z	value of count1	value of count2	output
Inner pass test condition fails, control goes to line 15						
line 15	5	3	12	2	4	
line 7 (Outer pass 2)	3	3	12	2	1	Pass Number 2
line 11 (Inner pass 1)	3	3	9	2	1	x=3, y=3, z=9
line 14 (end Inner pass 1)	4	3	9	2	2	
line 11 (Inner pass 2)	4	3	12	2	2	x=4, y=3, z=12
line 14 (end Inner pass 2)	5	3	12	2	3	
line 11 (Inner pass 3)	5	3	15	2	3	x=5, y=3, z=15
line 14 (end Inner pass 3)	6	3	15	2	4	
Inner pass test condition fails, control goes to line 15						
line 15	6	3	15	3	4	
Outer pass test condition fails, program ends						

The display, if you were to run this program, should look like this:

Pass Number: 1

x = 2, y = 3, z = 6

x = 3, y = 3, z = 9

x = 4, y = 3, z = 12

Pass Number: 2

x = 3, y = 3, z = 9

x = 4, y = 3, z = 12

x = 5, y = 3, z = 15

Different Ways to Nest Loops

Example 5.15 puts nested loops to good use in a business situation.

EXAMPLE 5.15

Getting Subtotals Using Nested for Loops

In this example, a business owner wants to enter each day's receipts over a period of several weeks and wants weekly subtotals. In this program, we will only display the results of two weeks' receipts but the program can be used for any number of weeks by merely changing the test condition in the outer loop. The code is as follows:

```
1.   <html>
2.   <head>
3.   <title>Example 5.15</title>
4.   <script>
5.   function getReceipts()
6.   {
7.        var week = 0; var day = 0; var subtotal = 0;
8.        var count = 0; receipt = 0; total = 0;
9.        for (week = 1; week < 3; week++)
10.       {
11.            document.write("<h3>Week " + week + "</h3>");
12.            count = 1; subtotal = 0;
13.            for (day = 1; day < 8; day++)
14.            {
15.                 receipt = parseFloat(prompt("Enter the receipts ↵
                         for day " + day + ": " , ""));
16.                 document.write("amount for day " + count + ": $ " ↵
                         + receipt.toFixed(2) + "<br />");
17.                 subtotal = subtotal + receipt;
18.                 count++;
19.            }
20.            document.write("<p>Week " + week + " subtotal is $ " ↵
                    + subtotal.toFixed(2) + "</p>");
21.            total = total + subtotal;
22.       }
23.       document.write("<p>The total amount for these weeks is $ " ↵
                    + total.toFixed(2) + "</p>");
```

```
24.     }
25.   </script>
26.   </<head>
27.   <body>
28.   <table align ="center" width ="70%"><tr><td>
29.   <h1>Subtotals</h1>
30.   <h3>Click to enter receipts</h3>
31.   <p><input type="button" id="nesting" value="Enter receipts" ⏎
                        onclick="getReceipts();" /></p></td></tr>
32.   </table></body></html>
```

We'll go through the function that generates the prompts for the business owner to enter information, the calculations, and the displays (lines 5–24) in detail.

Lines 7 and 8 declare and initialize the necessary variables. The variable **week** is a counter which is used in the outer for loop to allow the program to work for as many weeks as desired. The variable **day** is also a counter. It keeps track of how many times the inner for loop goes around. The variable **subtotal** keeps track of the sum of daily receipts for each of the seven entries per week. The variable **total** sums up all the subtotals. The variable **receipt** will hold each entry as the business owner puts them in and the variable **count** is used only in the output to identify each day's receipts.

The outer loop begins on line 9 and ends on line 22. It sets the initial value (**week** = 1), tells us how many times this loop will go around (**week** < 3) and increments **week** (**week**++) at the end of each iteration. For this program, since **week** starts at 1 and will end when **week** becomes 3, it will only have two iterations. However, if the owner wants to enter data for 4 weeks, this is easily accomplished by changing the test condition to **week** < 5. Similarly, for 52 weeks, all that is needed is to change the test condition to **week** < 53.

For each of the outer loop's iterations, a heading is displayed (line 11) and **count** is set to 1. This assures that each week will display values for day 1, day 2, and so on until day 7.

The inner loop begins on line 13 and ends on line 19. Here, the initial condition is that **day** = 1. The test condition is **day** < 8 which allows the loop to go around seven times—one for each day of a week. The first thing it does, on line 15, is to get the value of that day's receipts from the user. That value is stored in the variable **receipt**. It is then displayed under the heading (line 16). A subtotal is kept by adding that day's receipts to the previous **subtotal** (line 17). The counter is then incremented and the next day's receipt is input, displayed, and added to the subtotal. This continues for seven iterations and then the inner loop ends.

Line 20 is the next part of the outer loop. It displays the **subtotal** for that week. Line 21 keeps a running total of all the subtotals by adding that week's **subtotal** to whatever was previously stored in **total**. At this point, the outer loop counter, **week**, is incremented and, if the test condition is still valid, the process starts again.

The second time around, **week** = 2 so the outer loop begins again. A new heading, identifying this as week 2 is displayed. The variable **count** is set back to 1 on line 12.

Since **count** is only used to display which day of the week is input each time, it must be set back to 1 before entering the inner loop each time. The variable **subtotal** is also reset to 0. This must be done so, when the inner loop calculates a new **subtotal** it is not adding to the previous **subtotal**. Now the inner loop goes to work again, taking in seven more values, displaying them, and finding a new subtotal.

When the inner loop ends a second time, the outer loop takes over again, displays the new **subtotal** and adds it to the previous **total**. In this code, at this time, **week** is incremented to 3 and it fails the outer loop's test condition so the outer loop ends.

Control then goes to line 23 which is outside both loops. This line displays the grand total and the program ends. If the business owner's receipts for two weeks are as given and this program was run, the output would look as shown below.

Week One Receipts (in dollars and cents):

| 234.67 | 543.32 | 665.89 | 1235.23 | 234.43 | 555.21 | 447.88 |

Week Two Receipts (in dollars and cents):

| 337.87 | 654.78 | 879.34 | 987.87 | 567.44 | 1145.63 | 653.49 |

Week 1

amount for day 1: $ 234.67
amount for day 2: $ 543.32
amount for day 3: $ 665.89
amount for day 4: $ 1235.23
amount for day 5: $ 234.43
amount for day 6: $ 555.21
amount for day 7: $ 447.88

Week 1 subtotal is $ 3916.63

Week 2

amount for day 1: $ 337.87
amount for day 2: $ 654.78
amount for day 3: $ 879.34
amount for day 4: $ 987.87
amount for day 5: $ 567.44
amount for day 6: $ 1145.63
amount for day 7: $ 653.49

Week 2 subtotal is $ 5226.42

The total amount for these weeks is $ 9143.05

Which Way Should Loops Be Nested?

There really is no answer to this question. You can nest a pre-test loop inside a post-test loop or nest a for loop inside a while loop or nest several while loops inside a for loop or any other combination. The programming problem that you are faced with will often determine how you write the code. If there is no clear reason to select one option over another, the choice is yours.

Example 5.16 ends this section with a war game.

EXAMPLE 5.16

The Game of War

As a child you probably played the card game called War. In this game, each of two players is dealt a card. The player with the higher card keeps both cards. The game ends when one player holds all the cards. There are many variations of this game; in one, a tie results in the game starting over. The game can go on and on but in our example, we will simplify it. You will be able to add a lot more functionality as you learn more JavaScript but for now our game will do this: The computer will deal each player a random card from 1 to 13. This is because there are thirteen possible values of cards in a deck. The 52 cards results from four of each value (hearts, spades, diamonds, and clubs). You can add all 52 cards later as an Exercise. Also, to keep the code simple, we will consider a player to have won when his or her score reaches 10. The code for this simplified game of War is as follows:

```
1.    <html>
2.    <head>
3.    <title>Example 5.16</title>
4.    <script>
5.    function goToWar()
6.    {
7.        var name1 = " "; var name2 = " ";
8.        name1 = prompt("Enter your name: ", " ");
9.        name2 = prompt("Enter your name: ", " ");
10.       var playerOne = 0; var playerTwo = 0; var oneCard = 0;
11.       var twoCard = 0; var count = 1;
12.       document.write("<table width = 40% align='center'> ↵
              <tr><td colspan = '2'><h3>The Game of War</h3> ↵
              </td></tr>");
13.       while ((playerOne < 10) && (playerTwo < 10))
14.       {
15.           oneCard = Math.floor(Math.random() * 13 + 1);
16.           twoCard = Math.floor(Math.random() * 13 + 1);
17.           if(oneCard > twoCard)
18.               playerOne++;
19.           else
20.               if(twoCard > oneCard)
21.                   playerTwo++;
22.           document.write("<tr><td colspan = '2'> </td></tr>↵
              <tr><td colspan = '2'>Deal Number" + ↵
              count + ": </td></tr>");
```

```
23.              document.write("<tr><td>" + name1 + "'s card: " ↵
                         + oneCard + " -- Score: " + playerOne ↵
                         + "</td>");
24.              document.write("<td>" + name2 + "'s card: " + twoCard ↵
                         + " -- Score: " + playerTwo + "</td></td>");
25.         count++;
26.       }
27.       if ((playerOne == 10) && (playerTwo != 10))
28.              document.write("<tr><td colspan = '2'><h3>The winner ↵
                         is " + name1 + "!</h3></td></tr>");
29.       if ((playerTwo == 10) && (playerOne != 10))
30.              document.write("<tr><td colspan = '2'><h3>The winner ↵
                         is " + name2 + "!</h3></td></tr>");
31.       document.write("</table>");
32.   }
33.   </script>
34.   </<head>
35.   <body>
36.   <table align ="center" width ="70%"><tr><td>
37.       <h1>Play a Card Game: War</h1>
38.       <h3>Click to begin the game</h3>
39.       <p><input type="button" id="war" value="begin the game" ↵
                         onclick="goToWar();" /></p></td></tr>
40.   </table></body></html>
```

After the players are prompted for their names (lines 8 and 9) and the variables are declared and initialized (lines 7, 10, and 11), the output table is set up (line 12). Then the loop begins (line 13) and continues until one player reaches a score of 10. The compound condition uses an AND (&&) condition to ensure that the loop condition will fail as soon as one of the players' scores is 10.

The loop generates two random numbers between 1 and 13 (lines 15 and 16) and assigns each value to one of the players. The first player (**name1**) is assigned the value of **oneCard** and the second player (**name2**) is assigned the value of **twoCard**. Next, if statements are nested within the loop to check which card is higher. There are three counters in this program. The first, **playerOne**, keeps track of the first player's score. The second, **playerTwo**, keeps track of the second player's score. The third, **count**, keeps track of how many times two cards have been dealt.

If **oneCard** is higher than **twoCard**, the first player's score is incremented (line 18). If **twoCard** is higher than **oneCard**, the second player's score is incremented. If the random numbers generated are the same and there is a tie, no one's score is incremented.

Lines 23 and 24 simply output the results of this deal. Then **count** is incremented. Notice that, since **count** was initialized to 1 on line 11, the first time the loop executes, this is deal number 1. The counter is incremented at the end of the loop, in readiness for the next deal.

Finally, when one of the players reaches a score of 10, the loop ends, the winner is decided (line 27 or line 29), and the winner is displayed (line 28 or line 30). The table is closed on line 31 and the game is over.

CHECKPOINT FOR SECTION 5.3 ✓

5.13 What is desk checking and why is it important?

5.14 What is wrong with the following nested loops?

```
for(x = 1; x < 10; x++)
{
    for(x = 0; x < 5; x++)
    {
        document.write("Hi there!");
    }
}
```

5.15 True or False: A do...while loop cannot be nested inside a for loop.

5.16 What would you need to do to allow the business owner from Example 5.15 to find subtotals of the business receipts for a whole year?

5.17 Create a JavaScript program that tosses a coin and allows the user to toss the coin as often as desired. A zero should represent heads and a 1 should represent tails. The result of each toss should be displayed.

5.4 Drawing Shapes and Patterns with Loops

The last thing we'll do before continuing to develop our Greg's Gambits and Carla's Classroom sites is to use loops to draw shapes and patterns on a web page. This can be used to add decoration but can also be used to generate information. The following examples demonstrate some different uses for drawing patterns with JavaScript.

Drawing Shapes

We can use loops to create geometric shapes on a web page. The shapes can be outlined in various keyboard symbols or filled in. Image files can also be displayed repeatedly by using a loop to create a nice border around some text. Example 5.17 demonstrates how to draw a geometric shape.

EXAMPLE 5.17

Drawing a Square, a Rectangle, and a Right Triangle

The following program gives the user the option to draw one of three shapes: a square, a rectangle, or a right triangle. In this program the user can also choose the symbol used for the drawing.

```
1.   <html>
2.   <head>
3.   <title>Example 5.17</title>
4.   <script>
5.   function getSquare()
6.   {
```

```
 7.          var side = 0; row = 1; col = 1; symbol = "* ";
 8.          symbol = prompt("Pick a keyboard symbol for your square, ↵
                        such as a * or # ", " ");
 9.          side = prompt("How big is the side of your square? The ↵
                          value must be a positive number: "," ");
10.          side = parseInt(side);
11.          while (side < 1)
12.          {
13.              side = prompt("How big is the side of your square? The ↵
                          value must be a positive number: "," ");
14.              side = parseInt(side);
15.          }
16.          for (row = 1; row <= side; row++)
17.          {
18.              for (col = 1; col <= side; col++)
19.                  document.write(symbol + " ");
20.              document.write("<br />");
21.          }
22.      }
23.      function getRectangle()
24.      {
25.          var width = 0; var length = 0; row = 1;
26.          col = 1; symbol = "* ";
27.          symbol = prompt("Pick a keyboard symbol for your rectangle, ↵
                          such as a * or # ", " ");
28.          width = prompt("What is the width? The value must be a ↵
                          positive number: "," ");
29.          width = parseInt(width);
30.          while (width < 1)
31.          {
32.              width = prompt("What is the width? The value must be a ↵
                          positive number: "," ");
33.              width = parseInt(width);
34.          }
35.          length = prompt("What is the length? The value must be ↵
                          a positive number: "," ");
36.          length = parseInt(length);
37.          while (length < 1)
38.          {
39.              length = prompt("What is the length? The value must be ↵
                          a positive number: "," ");
40.              length = parseInt(length);
41.          }
42.          for (row = 1; row <= width; row++)
43.          {
44.              for (col = 1; col <= length; col++)
45.                  document.write(symbol + " ");
46.              document.write("<br />");
47.          }
48.      }
49.      function getTriangle()
50.      {
51.          var row = 1; var base = 1; var symbol = "* "; var col = 0;
52.          symbol = prompt("Pick a keyboard symbol for your triangle, ↵
                          such as a * or # ", " ");
```

```
53.        base = prompt("How big is the base of your triangle? The ↵
                            value must be a positive number: "," ");
54.        base = parseInt(base);
55.        while (base < 1)
56.        {
57.            base = prompt("How big is the base of your triangle? ↵
                            The value must be a positive number: "," ");
58.            base = parseInt(base);
59.        }
60.        for (row = 1; row <= base; row++)
61.        {
62.            for(col = 1; col <= row; col++)
63.                document.write(symbol + " ");
64.            document.write("<br />");
65.        }
66.    }
67. </script>
68. </<head>
69. <body>
70. <table align ="center" width ="70%"><tr><td colspan ="2">
71. <h1>Shapes</h1>
72. <h3>Pick a Shape</h3>
73. <p><input type="button" id="square" value="Draw a square" ↵
                        onclick="getSquare();" />    
74.    <input type="button" id="triangle" value="Draw a triangle" ↵
                        onclick="getTriangle();" />    
75.    <input type="button" id="rectangle" value="Draw a rectangle" ↵
                        onclick="getRectangle();" /></p>
76. </td></tr></table>
77. </body></html>
```

In this program, we identify the number of symbols going horizontally with the variable **row** and the number going vertically with the variable **col**. For a square, since the length and width are the same, we only need one variable (**side**). The code to draw a square is on lines 5–22. A nested loop is used to display a **symbol** and a space as many times as the value of **side** across. This is the inner loop and it displays one row of symbols. It is repeated for as many columns are the value of **side**; this is the outer loop. The rectangle code is on lines 23–48 and it does almost the same thing but in this case the variable **width** represents how many symbols are in each row and the variable **length** represents how many rows are needed.

Drawing a triangle is a bit trickier. The code for this is on lines 49–66. Here we draw only a right triangle but you can expand on this in the Review Exercises. The outer loop sets up how high the triangle will be. In this case, it means that **base** holds the value of the base of the triangle but also informs the program of how high the triangle will be. Therefore, the outer loop goes around for that number of times. The inner loop draws a single **symbol** on the first row, two **symbols** on the second row, and so on until it has drawn as many **symbols** as are in the **base**.

You may notice that we repeat almost the exact same code each time we validate whether the input is a positive number. This code is on lines 10–15 for the square, lines 29–34 for the rectangle, and lines 54–59 for the right triangle. In Chapter 7, we will learn how to eliminate duplication of code. Don't despair—once you learn more programming, many of the tedious and repetitive tasks can be dispensed with using a lot fewer lines of code and a lot less typing!

If you enter and run this code, using the inputs given with a # as the symbol, your displays should look like those shown below:

input: side = 4	**input:** width = 4, length = 9	**input:** base = 6
# # # #	# # # # # # # # #	#
# # # #	# # # # # # # # #	# #
# # # #	# # # # # # # # #	# # #
# # # #	# # # # # # # # #	# # # #
		# # # # #
		# # # # # #

Using Loops to Create Patterns

Example 5.18 shows how we can use loops to create patterns and borders to make web pages more interesting or to enhance messages and information visually.

EXAMPLE 5.18

Putting Yourself in a Box

The following program allows the user to enter a name and have the name displayed with symbols around it as a border.

```
1.   <html>
2.   <head>
3.   <title>Example 5.18</title>
4.   <script>
5.   function getName()
6.   {
7.       var name = " "; count = 0; symbol = "* ";
8.       symbol = prompt("Pick a keyboard symbol to border your ↵
                        name, such as a * or # ", " ");
9.       name = prompt("What is your name? "," ");
10.      for (count = 1; count <= (name.length + 4); count++)
11.          document.write(symbol + " ");
12.      document.write("<br />");
13.      document.write(symbol + " " + symbol + " " + name + " " ↵
                        + symbol + " " + symbol);
14.      document.write("<br />");
15.      for (count = 1; count <= (name.length + 4); count++)
16.          document.write(symbol + " ");
17.  }
18.  </script>
19.  </<head>
20.  <body>
21.  <table align ="center" width ="70%"><tr><td colspan ="2">
22.  <h1>Name in a Box</h1>
23.  <p><input type="button" id="name" value="Put your name in ↵
                        a box" onclick="getName();" /> </p>
24.  </td></tr></table>
25.  </body></html>
```

This code uses a loop to display as many symbols as there are characters (including spaces and punctuation) in the user's name. We use the JavaScript length property on line 10 as part of the test condition in the loop. The loop continues until **count** is greater than the number of characters in the name, but we add 4 to that number to account for the fact that we want to use two symbols on each side of the name. After a line of symbols is displayed through the first for loop on lines 10 and 11, we display a line break (line 12) and a line that shows the user's name, bordered on each side by two symbols (line 13). Then the for loop is repeated to display a line of symbols under the user's name.

The box around the name will often not be perfect. This is because different characters take up different amounts of space and the display will depend on the font the user's computer defaults to as well as the choice of symbol. To use this in a professional program, more code would be added to ensure that the display always looked exactly as desired.

If you enter and run this code, using the inputs given with a # as the symbol, your displays should look like those shown below:

input: name = Maura

```
# # # # # # # #
  # # Maura # #
# # # # # # # #
```

input: name = Howard. Q. Jones

```
# # # # # # # # # # # # # # # # # #
# # Howard Q. Jones # #
# # # # # # # # # # # # # # # # # #
```

Example 5.19 is similar but uses a small image file to surround the name as a border.

EXAMPLE 5.19

A Prettier Border

The code to enclose a name in an image border is almost the same as the code for Example 5.18. We use a small image file named border.jpg which is available in the Student Data Files. Since the web page is the same as for the previous example, only the function code is given here:

```
1.  function getName()
2.  {
3.      var name = " "; count = 0;
4.      name = prompt("What is your name? "," ");
5.      for (count = 1; count <= (name.length + 4); count++)
6.          document.write("<img src = 'images/border.jpg' />  ");
7.      document.write("<br />");
8.      document.write("<h1> <img src = 'images/border.jpg' /> ↵
                "+ "<img src = 'images/border.jpg' /> " + ↵
                "  " + name + "  " + "<img src = ↵
                'images/border.jpg' />  " + "<img src = ↵
                'images/border.jpg' /> </h1> ");
9.      document.write("<br />");
10.     for (count = 1; count <= (name.length + 4); count++)
11.         document.write("<img src = 'images/border.jpg' />  ");
12. }
```

If you enter this code and save the border.jpg file in an images folder, then run it using the name Lynne as your input, the output will look like the one shown. Notice that your border may be a bit off center and you may have to play around a little with the image size and font size to make a perfect display.

The mouse Events

Most of the time, in this text, we have created our own JavaScript code to instruct a computer to do what we want the web page to do. However, there are ways to use JavaScript that don't require us to write code; someone has already done it for us. JavaScript code snippets have been written that execute when something—an event—occurs on a web page. An event can be any of several occurrences. A user can scroll up or down, click on a link, enter a value into a form box or, as we will discuss in this section, move or click the mouse.

JavaScript **events** trigger actions in a browser. In this text we have used the onclick event often. Each **event attribute** must include JavaScript instructions. The event attribute tells the browser what *can* be done and you describe the specific way that it *should* be done. The following examples will demonstrate several **mouse events**—things that can happen when the user manipulates the mouse.

In Example 5.20, we will use a little JavaScript within the HTML page to create a **rollover effect.** We do this in preparation for later examples and exercises.

EXAMPLE
5.20

Creating a Rollover

As the user rolls the mouse over an image, the image will change to another image. When the mouse is rolled off the image, the first image is returned.

```
1.   <html>
2.   <head>
3.   <title>Example 5.20</title>
4.   </head>
5.   <body>
6.   <table align ="center" width ="70%"><tr><td colspan ="2">
7.   <h1>The Rollover</h1>
8.   <h3>To change the image, roll your mouse over it</h3>
9.   <table align="center" width = "70%"><tr><td id = "photo" name = "photo">
10.  <a href = '#' onmouseover = "document.photo.src = 'troll.jpg';" ↵
                 onmouseout = "document.photo.src = 'wizard.jpg';"> ↵
                 <img src = "wizard.jpg" alt = "the winner" name = "photo" /></a>
11.  <tr><td><h3>Change me!</h3></td></tr>
12.  </table></body></html>
```

In this example the JavaScript is within the HTML page, not in the <head> section. All the code is on line 10. Line 9 identifies the element we are changing with id = "photo". From now on, the placement of the image will go into the cell with id = "photo".

As you probably know, images on a web page are not really inserted; rather a link to the image is created. Thus, line 10 begins with a link (`<a href ='#'`). The # sign is a dummy link source. The images in this code are not outside the web page site. Next comes the **onmouseover** event. The script that will be executed when the user moves a mouse over the initial image is in double quotes. The event that will happen is that the element on the page with the `id` of `photo` will have a new image. The source (`src`) of this image is, in this case, simply the name of the image file. If the image had been stored elsewhere (say, in an `images` folder), the exact path to the image would have to be included. Because we began the statement with double quotes, anything that needs quotes within the statement must be enclosed in single quotes; thus, the path to the image is in single quotes. And, since `document.photo. src = 'troll.jpg'` is a JavaScript statement, it must be terminated with a semicolon. Then the double quotes are closed. That's the first part of the rollover.

The next part tells the browser what to do when the mouse is moved off the image. This is the **onmouseout** event. In this case, the first image is replaced using the same JavaScript statement as for the `onmouseover` event but changing the image filename back to the original.

Finally, we need the HTML code for the original image that is displayed when the page is first loaded. Notice that the `</a>` tag is closed here.

If you enter and run this code using the `troll.jpg` and `wizard.jpg` image files from the Student Data Files, first you will see the following:

If you run your mouse over the wizard you will see the following:

And, finally, if you move your mouse off the image, you will see the following:

Additional mouse events are shown in Table 5.1. They work in all elements except base, bdo, br, frame, frameset, head, html, iframe, meta, param, script, style, and title.

TABLE 5.1	JavaScript Mouse Events	
Attribute	**Value**	**Description: what it does**
onclick	JavaScript	what happens when the mouse is clicked
ondblclick	JavaScript	what happens when the mouse is double-clicked
onmousedown	JavaScript	what happens when a mouse button is pressed
onmousemove	JavaScript	what happens when the mouse pointer moves
onmouseout	JavaScript	what happens when the mouse pointer moves off an element
onmouseover	JavaScript	what happens when the mouse pointer moves over an element
onmouseup	JavaScript	what happens when the mouse button is released

In Example 5.21 we will use the **ondblclick** event to allow the user to change an image.

EXAMPLE
5.21

Changing the Image

When the user double-clicks the mouse, the image changes.

```
1.   <head>
2.   <title>Example 5.21</title>
3.   </head>
4.   <body>
5.   <table align ="center" width ="70%"><tr><td colspan ="2">
6.   <h1>Change the Image</h1>
7.   <h3>To change the image, double-click on it</h3>
```

```
8.    <table align="center" width = "70%"><tr><td id = "photo" ↵
              name = "photo">
9.    <a href = '#' ondblclick = "document.photo.src = 'troll.jpg';"> ↵
              <img src = "wizard.jpg" alt = "the winner" ↵
              name = "photo" /></a>
10.   </td></tr>
11.   <tr><td><h3>Change me!</h3></td></tr>
12.   </table></body></html>
```

If you enter and run this code, first you will see the following:

If you double click on the wizard you will see the following:

In Example 5.22, we will use JavaScript code to allow us more control over how our images are displayed and exchanged. This code will be valuable when we design the game for the Greg's Gambits section in this chapter.

EXAMPLE 5.22

Writing Code to Change the Image

This code changes the image of a wizard to that of a troll and allows the user to do this repeatedly, by answering a question in a prompt.

```
1.    <html>
2.    <head>
3.    <title>Example 5.22</title>
```

```
4.    <script>
5.    function getSwap()
6.    {
7.          var again = "y"; var pic = "troll";
8.          while (again == "y")
9.              {
10.                 if (pic == "wizard")
11.                 {
12.                         document.getElementById('photo').innerHTML = ↵
                                    "<img src='troll.jpg' />";
13.                     pic = "troll";
14.                     var again = prompt("See new image? y/n?", " ");
15.                 }
16.                 if (pic == "troll")
17.                 {
18.                         document.getElementById('photo').innerHTML = ↵
                                    "<img src='wizard.jpg' />";
19.                     pic = "wizard";
20.                     var again = prompt("See new image? y/n?", " ");
21.                 }
22.             }
23.    }
24.    </script>
25.    </head>
26.    <body>
27.    <table align ="center" width ="70%"><tr><td colspan ="2">
28.    <h1>Swapping Images</h1>
29.    <p><input type="button" id="swap" value="Push me to change ↵
                            the image" onclick="getSwap();" /></p>
30.    <table align="center" width = "70%">
31.    <tr><td id = "photo" name = "photo">
32.    <img src = "troll.jpg" alt = "troll" name = "myPhoto" />
33.    </td></tr></table></body></html>
```

In this example, the page begins displaying the troll image. When the button is clicked, the getSwap() function is called from the <head> section. The variable, **pic**, is initially set to "troll" so the corresponding if clause is executed. This clause changes the image to the wizard image and sets the value of **pic** to "wizard". It also prompts the user to switch images again. If the user says yes, since **pic** is now "wizard", the if clause that corresponds to **pic** = "wizard" is executed and the image is swapped to the troll image. Once again, the value of **pic** is changed and the user is prompted to decide whether to make the swap again.

CHECKPOINT FOR SECTION 5.4 ✓

5.18 Use a loop to create the following display on a web page:

```
           *
          ***
         *****
        *******
```

5.19 Add code to Example 5.17 to draw a triangle that is the reverse of the one in Example 5.17.

5.20 Modify Example 5.20 to use the `onmousedown` event to change the image on the web page.

5.21 Add code to Example 5.21 to allow a third image to be swapped. You can use any image from the Student Data Files or one of your own.

5.5 Putting It to Work

Now we will create a new game for `Greg's Gambits` and focus on grammar in `Carla's Classroom`.

Greg's Gambits: The Battle between Wizard and Troll

The traditional Scissors, Paper, Rock game is frequently used in introductory programming classes. We will use the concepts behind this game and combine it with what we have learned about swapping images to stage a battle for the `Greg's Gambits` site between the player (our hero, the wizard) and the evil troll. In our game, the troll will have a secret arsenal of weapons. The player will be allowed to choose which of three weapons he or she wants to use in the ensuing fight. The computer will generate, using random numbers, which weapon the troll selects and, based on comparing the two weapons, the program will declare a winner. Later, you can add more weapons and provide your player with avatar choices.

Before we begin to write the program we will add a link to this game on the `play_games.html` page. We'll call our new game `greg_battle.html`. Add this link on the `play_games.html` page so that it looks like this:

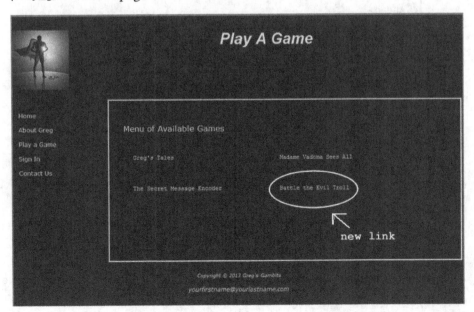

Developing the Program

For this game we will need room for the initial display and instructions as well as the battle itself—so we will use two pages. The first page will give the instructions, present the avatars, and display the weapons. From this page the player will push a button to begin the battle. The entire battle will consist of a number of rounds of fighting. On the second page, for each round of the battle, the user will be prompted to select a weapon. Then the program will randomly select a weapon for the troll, decide on the winner, based on criteria that we will write, and display the winner. To add complexity to the program, we will give each combatant an initial number of points. Each time a winner is declared, the loser gives the winner 10 points. The game ends when one player has all the points and the other has none.

We will also use a button to link to the second page and a similar button to return to the initial page. We can use a template that we have used in the past for other Greg's Gambits games for both pages.

The Button As a Link

A button can be turned into a link to another page with the following code:

```
<input type="button" id="whatever" value="This button will take you to another
web page" onclick = "location.href = 'URL_of_requested_page.html'"; />
```

EXAMPLE
5.23

A Button As a Link

The following two very short and simple web pages are linked by buttons. The filename of the first page is page_one.html and the filename of the second page is page_two.html.

The first page:

```
<html>
<head>
<title>Example 5.23: Page One</title>
</head>
<body>
<h3>See what's on the next page...</h3>
<p><input type="button" id="pageOne" value="This button will take ⌐
                you to the next page"
onclick = "location.href = 'page_two.html'"; /></p>
</body>
</html>
```

The second page:

```
<html>
<head>
<title>Example 5.23: Page Two</title>
</head>
<body>
<h3>You can go back too...</h3>
<p><input type="button" id="pageTwo" value="This button will take ⌐
                you back to the previous page"
```

```
onclick = "location.href = 'page_one.html'"; /></p>
</body>
</html>
```

If you create these two pages, they will look like the ones shown below. Clicking either button will take you to the other page:

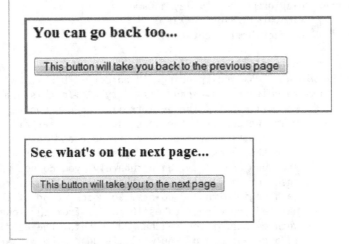

Notice how the onclick event now works. The entire instruction is enclosed in double quotes. The URL of the page we are linking to is enclosed in single quotes.

The Web Pages

We need to pay a little extra attention to the web pages we will use for this program. Since we need two pages for this game, we'll link the two with buttons.

The first page will give the user instructions about the battle and will link to the next page where the battle will actually take place. Therefore, the first page is merely an information page and no JavaScript program will run in the <head> section. We will give this page the filename greg_battle.html and the page title will be Greg's Gambits | Battle the Evil Troll. We'll add the title to the page and put the instructions, along with images depicting our hero (the player who will be a wizard) and his foe (the evil troll), as well as the three weapon choices. The arsenal available to both combatants will be a set of magic rocks, a sword, and a crossbow and arrow. These images are available in the Student Data Files. The code for this page is as follows:

```
1.   <html>
2.   <head>
3.   <title>Greg's Gambits | Battle the Evil Troll</title>
4.   <link href="greg.css" rel="stylesheet" type="text/css" />
5.   <style type="text/css">
6.   <!--
7.        .style1 {font-size: 18px}
8.   -->
9.   </style>
10.  </head>
11.  <body>
12.  <div id="container">
```

```
13.        <img src="images/superhero.jpg" class = "floatleft" />
14.        <h1 align="center"><em>Battle the Evil Troll</em></h1>
15.        <div style ="clear:both;"></div>
16.        <div id="nav">
17.        <p><a href="index.html">Home</a>
18.        <a href="greg.html">About Greg</a>
19.        <a href="play_games.html">Play a Game</a>
20.        <a href="sign.html">Sign In</a>
21.        <a href="contact.html">Contact Us</a></p>
22.        </div>
23.        <div id="content">
24.        <table width = "85%" cellpadding="5" border = "0">
25.            <tr><td colspan = 4><span class="style1">In this game ↵
                   you will battle the evil troll. You can choose ↵
                   your  weapon from the three shown -- a set of ↵
                   magic rocks that are a lot stronger and heavier ↵
                   than they look, an extremely sharp sword, or a ↵
                   crossbow and arrow. Unfortunately, you do not know↵
                   ahead of time what weapon the troll will use. You↵
                   each begin with 100 points. For each round of the↵
                   battle, the winner takes 10 points from the loser.↵
                   When either of you reaches 200 points, the battle↵
                   is over and one of you will lie dead. The winner ↵
                   is determined by the list shown below. Push the ↵
                   button when you are ready to begin the battle and ↵
                   ... Good luck!</span></td></tr>
26.            <tr><td width = 20%><p><img src="images/wizard.jpg" />↵
                   </p> <p><span class="style1">Wizard</span></p></td>
27.            <td width=20%><p><img src="images/troll.jpg" /></p> ↵<p><span
                   class="style1">Troll</span></p></td>
28.            <td width = 10%> </td>
29.            <td width = 50%> <span class="style1"><p>Weapons</p> ↵
                   <p><img src="images/rock.jpg" width="100" ↵
                   height="70" /> magic rocks</p> <p><img src = ↵
                   "images/sword.jpg" width = "100" height = "70" /> ↵
                   sword</p> <p><img src = "images/arrow.jpg" width = ↵
                   "100" height = "70" /> bow & arrow</span> ↵
                   </p></td></tr>
30.            <tr><td colspan = 4><span class="style1">Note: <br /> ↵
                   The rocks can deflect the arrow.<br /> ↵
                   The sword beats the rocks. <br /> ↵
                   The arrow beats the sword.</span></td></tr>
31.        </table>
32.        <input type="button" id="battle" value="Begin the battle!" ↵
                   onclick = "location.href = 'battleground.html'"; />
33.        </div>
34.        <div id="footer">Copyright &copy; 2013 Greg's Gambits<br />
35.            <a href="mailto:yourfirstname@yourlastname.com">↵
                   yourfirstname@yourlastname.com</a>
36.        </div>
37.    </div></body></html>
```

Notice that we added a new style in the <head> section to make the text on this page stand out. The new button on line 32 is used as a link to the next page. This page should now look like this:

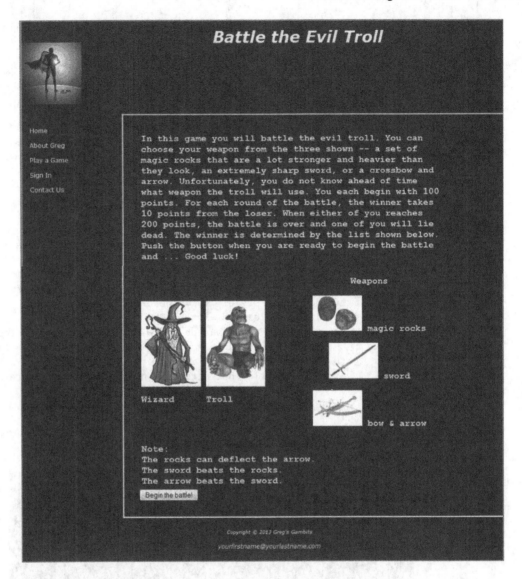

Next, we'll create the actual battle. For this we need a new page. The filename for this page will be battleground.html and the page title will be Greg's Gambits | The Battleground. If you want to create this page yourself, you can use the previous page as the template. The JavaScript code for the program exists in the <head> section and the execution of the program is behind-the-scenes. But, until now, we have only displayed one or two results on a page. For the battle, we will need to display several things as the battle progresses. Before the battle begins, the page will show images of the hero (the wizard) and the opponent (the troll). It will also need an area to display each combatant's weapon choice for each round of play, the results of each round of play, and the point tally as the battle continues. Since these items will be displayed as the program executes, we need to identify the areas where each will go so we can use the getElementById() method with the innerHTML property to send the results out. We'll put our battleground in a table and identify areas with cell ids. The HTML code for the battleground should be inside the content `<div>` and is as follows:

```
1.   <div id="content">
2.   <table width = "85%" cellpadding="5" cellspacing="0" border = "0">
3.       <tr><td><img src="images/wizard.jpg" /></td>
4.       <td><img src="images/troll.jpg" /></td></tr>
5.       <tr><td><span class="style1">Wizard uses: </span></td>
6.       <td><span class="style1">Troll uses: </span></td></tr>
7.       <tr><td id = "playerWeapon" span class="style1">Weapon ↵
                goes here</span></td>
8.       <td id = "trollWeapon" span class="style1">Weapon ↵
                goes here</span></td></tr>
9.       <tr><td colspan = 2><span class="style1">The winner ↵
                is:</span></td></tr>
10.      <tr><td colspan = 2 id="winner" align = "center" class = ↵
                "style1">  </td></tr>
11.      <tr><td><span class="style1">Wizard points: </span></td>
12.      <td><span class="style1">Troll points:</span></td></tr>
13.      <tr><td class="style1" id = "heroPts">100</td>
14.      <td class="style1" id = "trollPts">100</td></tr>
15.      <tr><td><input type="button" id = "battle" value="Let the ↵
                battle begin!" onclick = "battleIt()"; /> </td>
16.      <td><input type="button" id="return" value="Return to ↵
                battle instructions" onclick = "location.href↵
                = 'greg_battle.html'"; />
17.      </td></tr></table>
18.  </div>
```

Before the game begins, the battleground now looks like this:

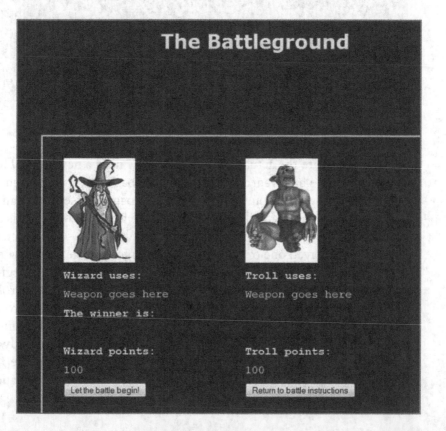

We are now ready to write the code for the battle.

Writing the Code

The battle must do several things. As our programs become longer and more complex, it becomes even more important to plan them carefully before beginning to write code. We will start with a general plan and add to it as we develop the program.

First, we must set the displays in the cells on the web page to their default values. While we already typed in the default settings, if we do not include this in the battle function, each time a new battle begins, the results of the last battle will be displayed on the screen. We set the default values with the following code:

```
1.  document.getElementById("trollPts").innerHTML = (trollPts);
2.  document.getElementById("heroPts").innerHTML = (heroPts);
3.  document.getElementById("playerWeapon").innerHTML = ("Your weapon: ");
4.  document.getElementById("trollWeapon").innerHTML = ("The troll's weapon: ");
5.  document.getElementById("winner").innerHTML = (" ");
```

The values for **trollPts** and **heroPts** are set to initial values when we create those variables.

Next, we must create a loop that will do the following until either the wizard or the troll wins enough fights to win the battle:

- The player has to pick a weapon and that weapon must be displayed on the web page
- The troll has to pick a weapon and that weapon must be displayed on the web page
- The winner of the round must be decided and the winner displayed on the web page
- The points must be adjusted and displayed

When either the player or the troll gets a certain number of points, the battle (and the loop) ends and the winner of the battle should be displayed.

We'll do each of these things separately. We've already decided to call the function battleIt() (see line 15 of the HTML code for the greg_battle.html page). First, let's decide on the variables we will need. Following is the list of necessary variables along with their initial values:

```
var heroPlay = 0; This identifies the hero's weapon choice as a number
var heroPts = 100; The initial hero (player) points when player begins the battle
var trollPts = 100; The initial troll points when player begins the battle
var trollPlay = 0; This identifies the troll's weapon choice as a number
var rocks = "magic rocks"; This stores the description of one weapon (rocks)
var sword = "the sword"; This stores the description of one weapon (sword)
var arrow = "bow and arrow"; This stores the description of one weapon (crossbow & arrow)
var heroChoice = " "; This holds the description of the weapon the hero chooses
var trollChoice = " "; This holds the description of the weapon the troll chooses
```

The code for the player to select a weapon and display that weapon is as follows:

```
heroPlay = parseInt(prompt("What weapon do you choose? Enter 1 for magic ↵
rocks (enter 1), 2 for the sword, or 3 for the bow and arrow: (Enter 4 to ↵
leave the game at any time)" , " "));
```

Notice that we have also included an option for the player to leave the game early. If this option is chosen, the following code will break out of the loop and end the program:

```
if (heroPlay == 4) break;
```

The troll's weapon will be selected by generating a random number between 1 and 3 and assigning a weapon to each number. As the prompt for the player's choice shows, a 1 means the troll chooses the magic rocks, a 2 means the sword is chosen, and a 3 means the troll selects the bow and arrow. The code for this is as follows:

```
trollPlay = Math.floor(Math.random() * 3 + 1);
```

Right now we know that the player has either chosen a 1, a 2, or a 3 and the same is true for the troll. However, we want to display the actual weapon and not a number. The code to assign one of the variables that holds the text value of the weapon to both player and hero is as follows:

```
if (trollPlay == 1)
    trollChoice = rocks;
if (trollPlay == 2)
    trollChoice = sword;
if (trollPlay == 3)
    trollChoice = arrow;
if (heroPlay == 1)
    heroChoice = rocks;
if (heroPlay == 2)
    heroChoice = sword;
if (heroPlay == 3)
    heroChoice = arrow;
```

We can now display the weapon choices on the web page using the cell ids for this information and the following code:

```
document.getElementById("playerWeapon").innerHTML = ("Your ↵
            weapon: " + heroChoice);
document.getElementById("trollWeapon").innerHTML = ("The ↵
            troll's weapon: " + trollChoice);
```

We are now in a position to find the winner of a given round. You may recall that the previous web page with the instructions stated that rocks deflect the arrow, the sword beats the rocks, and the arrow beats the sword. For our purposes, this means that 1 beats 3, 2 beats 1, and 3 beats 2. Those are all the combinations we need to determine the winner. We will also assume that if both the player and the troll have the same weapon, the round will be considered a tie and there will be no winner. This also means no points will change in the event of a tie.

We could write out the winning possibilities, one at a time. There are three ways for the troll to win and three ways for the player to win plus three ways for a tie. For each winning combination, it would be necessary to write lines of code to display the image of the winner, to increase the winner's points, to decrease the loser's points, and to display the two new values for player and troll points. Each time we would repeat, almost verbatim, these five lines of code. That's a lot to type! However, we don't need to do that. We can use compound conditions to lighten our load considerably.

We know that these are winning combinations:

For the hero: hero chooses rocks (1) and troll chooses bow and arrow (3)
                 hero chooses sword (2) and troll chooses rocks (1)
                 hero chooses bow and arrow (3) and troll chooses sword (2)

For the troll: troll chooses rocks (1) and hero chooses bow and arrow (3)
                 troll chooses sword (2) and hero chooses rocks (1)
                 troll chooses bow and arrow (3) and hero chooses sword (2)

A tie: troll chooses rocks (1) and hero chooses rocks (1)
                 troll chooses sword (2) and hero chooses sword (2)
                 troll chooses bow and arrow (3) and hero chooses bow and arrow (3)

In English, this means that IF the hero chooses rocks AND the troll chooses the arrow OR the hero chooses the sword AND the troll chooses rocks OR the hero chooses the arrow AND the troll chooses the sword, THEN the hero will win. If the hero wins, we want to display the hero's image in the winner area on the page, we want to increase the hero's points by 10 and decrease the troll's points by 10 and we want to display the new point values in the heroPts and trollPts areas on the page. By writing all the conditions for the hero to win in one statement, using several compound conditions, we can save ourselves a lot of time and space. The code for three possible wins for a troll is almost the same and the code for the three tie possibilities is even simpler. The code to determine the winner and display the results is as follows:

```
1.   if (((trollPlay == 1) && (heroPlay == 3)) || ((trollPlay == 2) ↵
                && (heroPlay == 1)) || ((trollPlay == 3) ↵
                && (heroPlay == 2)))
2.   {
3.        document.getElementById("winner").innerHTML = ("<img src = ↵
                'images/troll.jpg' />");
4.        trollPts = trollPts + 10;
5.        heroPts = heroPts - 10;
6.        document.getElementById("trollPts").innerHTML = (trollPts);
7.        document.getElementById("heroPts").innerHTML = (heroPts);
8.   }
9.   if (((heroPlay == 1) && (trollPlay == 3)) || ((heroPlay == 2) ↵
                && (trollPlay == 1)) || ((heroPlay == 3) ↵
                && (trollPlay == 2)))
10.  {
11.       document.getElementById("winner").innerHTML = ("<img src = ↵
                'images/wizard.jpg' />");
12.       trollPts = trollPts - 10;
13.       heroPts = heroPts + 10;
14.       document.getElementById("trollPts").innerHTML = (trollPts);
15.       document.getElementById("heroPts").innerHTML = (heroPts);
16.  }
17.  if (((heroPlay == 1) && (trollPlay == 1)) || ((heroPlay == 2) ↵
                && (trollPlay == 2)) || ((heroPlay == 3) && ↵
                (trollPlay == 3)))
18.  {
19.       document.getElementById("winner").innerHTML = ("This round ↵
                is a tie. New weapons must be chosen...");
20.  }
```

We have now written almost the entire program. We'll add an alert box after both combatants have chosen their weapons as a way to slow down the execution of the code and give the player a chance to look at the screen and see what weapon he is up against. The code for the alert will be inserted right before we determine the winner and is as follows:

```
alert("This round of the battle begins now!");
```

All the code we have written so far should go into a while loop that will continue to execute until either the player breaks out by entering 4 when prompted for a choice of weapon or when either of the combatants reach a predetermined number of points. We have arbitrarily chosen 200 points to win but this can be changed at any time. The while statement will look like this:

```
while ((trollPts < 200) && (heroPts < 200))
```

Finally, after the loop is exited we need to display the winner, if there is one, or a good-bye message if the player has opted to end the battle early. Here is the code:

```
1.   if (heroPlay == 4)
2.       document.getElementById("winner").innerHTML = ("It's true: ↵
                    when you run, you live to fight another day. See ↵
                    you again soon!");
3.   if (trollPts >= 200)
4.       document.getElementById("winner").innerHTML = ("The battle ↵
                    has been fought valiently but the troll has beaten ↵
                    you. Go home and nurse your wounds.");
5.   if (heroPts >= 200)
6.       document.getElementById("winner").innerHTML = ("The battle ↵
                    has been fought valiently and you have prevailed! ↵
                    Congratulations!");
```

Putting It All Together

Now we are ready to put it all together. The code for the entire battle is as follows:

```
1.   <html>
2.   <head>
3.   <title>Greg's Gambits | The Battleground</title>
4.   <link href="greg.css" rel="stylesheet" type="text/css" />
5.   <script type="text/javascript">
6.   function battleIt()
7.   {
8.       var heroPlay = 0; var trollPlay = 0;
9.       var heroPts = 100; var trollPts = 100;
10.      var rocks = "magic rocks"; var sword = "the sword";
11.      var arrow = "bow and arrow";
12.      var heroChoice = " "; var trollChoice = " ";
13.      document.getElementById("trollPts").innerHTML = (trollPts);
14.      document.getElementById("heroPts").innerHTML = (heroPts);
15.      document.getElementById("playerWeapon").innerHTML = ("Your weapon: ");
16.      document.getElementById("trollWeapon").innerHTML = ("The ↵
                    troll's weapon: ");
17.      document.getElementById("winner").innerHTML = (" ");
18.      //loop repeats until troll or player get 130 points
19.       while ((trollPts < 130) && (heroPts < 130))
```

```
20.          {
21.                      // get player's weapon
22.                      heroPlay = parseInt(prompt("What weapon do you choose? ↵
                                       Enter 1 for magic rocks (enter 1), 2 ↵
                                       for the sword, or 3 for the bow and ↵
                                       arrow: (Enter 4 to leave the game at ↵
                                       any time)" , " "));
23.                      if (heroPlay == 4) break;
                         // get troll's weapon
24.                      trollPlay = Math.floor(Math.random() * 3 + 1);
25.                      // assign weapon to player and troll
26.                      if (trollPlay == 1)
27.                          trollChoice = rocks;
28.                      if (trollPlay == 2)
29.                          trollChoice = sword;
30.                      if (trollPlay == 3)
                             trollChoice = arrow;
31.                      if (heroPlay == 1)
32.                          heroChoice = rocks;
33.                      if (heroPlay == 2)
34.                          heroChoice = sword;
35.                      if (heroPlay == 3)
36.                          heroChoice = arrow;
37.                      //display weapon selections
38.                      document.getElementById("playerWeapon").innerHTML =↵
                                       ("Your weapon: " + heroChoice);
39.                      document.getElementById("trollWeapon").innerHTML = ↵
                                       ("The troll's weapon: " + trollChoice);
40.                      alert("This round of the battle begins now!");
                         //find the winner
41.                      if (((trollPlay == 1)&&(heroPlay == 3)) || ((trollPlay↵
                                       == 2)&&(heroPlay == 1)) || ((trollPlay↵
                                       == 3)&&(heroPlay == 2)))
42.                      {
43.                          document.getElementById("winner").innerHTML = ↵
                                       ("<img src='images/troll.jpg' />");
44.                          trollPts = trollPts + 10;
45.                          heroPts = heroPts - 10;
46.                          document.getElementById("trollPts").innerHTML = (trollPts);
47.                          document.getElementById("heroPts").innerHTML = (heroPts);
48.                      }
49.                      if (((heroPlay == 1)&&(trollPlay == 3)) || ((heroPlay ↵
                                       == 2)&&(trollPlay == 1)) || ((heroPlay ↵
                                       == 3)&&(trollPlay == 2)))
50.                      {
51.                          document.getElementById("winner").innerHTML = ↵
                                       ("<img src='images/wizard.jpg' />");
52.                          trollPts = trollPts - 10;
53.                          heroPts = heroPts + 10;
54.                          document.getElementById("trollPts").innerHTML = (trollPts);
55.                          document.getElementById("heroPts").innerHTML = (heroPts);
56.                      }
57.                      if (((heroPlay == 1)&&(trollPlay == 1)) || ((heroPlay ↵
                                       == 2)&&(trollPlay == 2)) || ↵
                                       ((heroPlay == 3)&&(trollPlay == 3)))
58.                      {
```

```
59.                      document.getElementById("winner").innerHTML =↵
                            ("This round is a tie. New weapons must↵
                            be chosen...");
60.               }
61.           }
62.       //display the final winner
63.       if (heroPlay == 4)
64.           document.getElementById("winner").innerHTML = ("It's ↵
                            true: when you run, you live to fight↵
                            another day. See you again soon!");
65.       if (trollPts >= 130)
66.           document.getElementById("winner").innerHTML = ("The ↵
                            battle has been fought valiently but ↵
                            the troll has beaten you. Go home and↵
                            nurse your wounds.");
67.       if (heroPts >= 130)
68.           document.getElementById("winner").innerHTML = ("The↵
                            battle has been fought valiently and ↵
                            you have prevailed! Congratulations!");
69.   }
70.   </script>
71.   <style type="text/css">
72.   <!--
73.   .style1 {font-size: 18px}
74.   -->
75.   </style>
76.   </head>
77.   <body>
78.   <div id="container">
79.   <img src="images/superhero.jpg" width = "120" height = "120" ↵
                            class = "floatleft" />
80.   <h1 align="center">The Battleground</h1>
81.   <div style ="clear:both;"></div>
82.   <div id="nav">
83.       <p><a href="index.html">Home</a>
84.       <a href="greg.html">About Greg</a>
85.       <a href="play_games.html">Play a Game</a>
86.       <a href="sign.html">Sign In</a>
87.       <a href="contact.html">Contact Us</a></p>
88.   </div>
89.   <div id="content">
90.       <table width = "85%" cellpadding = "5" border = "0">
91.       <tr><td><img src = "images/wizard.jpg" /></td>
92.       <td><img src = "images/troll.jpg" /></td></tr>
93.       <tr><td><span class="style1">Wizard uses: </span></td>
94.       <td><span class="style1">Troll uses: </span></td></tr>
95.       <tr><td id = "playerWeapon" span class = "style1">Weapon ↵
                            goes here</span></td>
96.       <td id = "trollWeapon" span class = "style1">Weapon goes ↵
                            here</span></td></tr>
97.       <tr><td colspan = 2><span class = "style1">The winner ↵
                            is:</span></td></tr>
98.       <tr><td colspan = 2 id = "winner" align = "center" class =↵
                            "style1"> </td></tr>
99.       <tr><td><span class = "style1">Wizard points: </span></td>
100.      <td><span class = "style1">Troll points:</span></td></tr>
```

```
101.          <tr><td class = "style1" id = "heroPts">100</td>
102.          <td class = "style1" id = "trollPts">100</td></tr>
103.          <tr><td><input type = "button" id = "battle" value = "Let ⏎
                              the battle begin!" onclick = ⏎
                              "battleIt()"; /> </td>
104.          <td><input type = "button" id = "return" value = "Return ⏎
                              to battle instructions" onclick = ⏎
                              "location.href = 'greg_battle.html'"; /></td>
105.          </table>
106.    </div>
107.    <div id="footer">Copyright &copy; 2013 Greg's Gambits<br />
108.          <a href = "mailto:yourfirstname@yourlastname.com"> ⏎
                              yourfirstname@yourlastname.com</a>
109.    </div>
110.    </div></body></html>
```

Finishing Up

Here are some sample displays as the game is being played:

output: The player and troll have chosen the same weapon and the battle is about to begin (the troll's weapon shown is from a previous round of play and is not part of this new round):

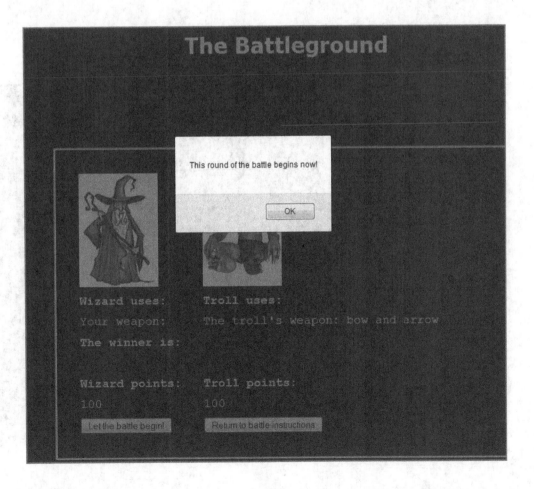

output: The player and troll have chosen the same weapon and a tie is declared:

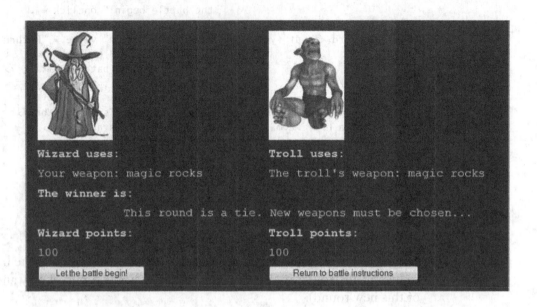

output: The player is winning:

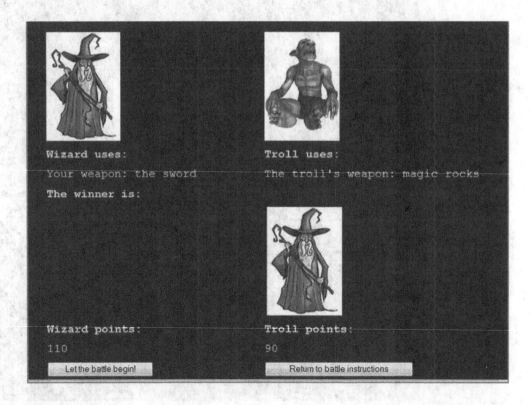

output: The troll is winning:

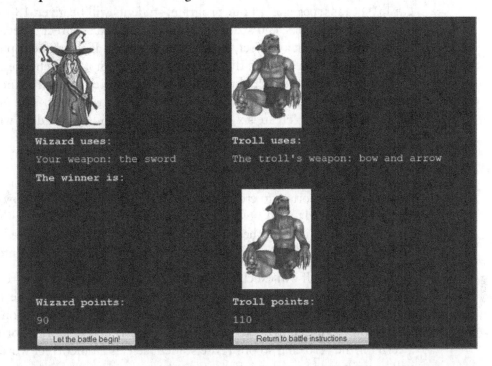

output: This player has chosen to leave the game while he is ahead by 20 points:

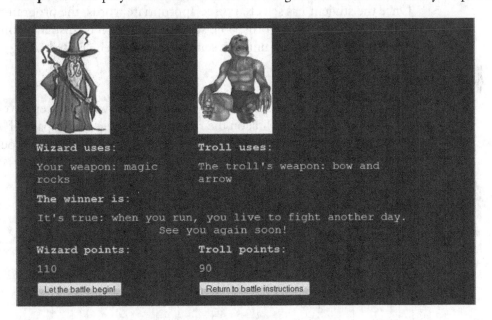

Carla's Classroom: A Grammar Lesson

This time we will develop a program that will help Carla's students identify parts of a sentence. We'll restrict ourselves to identifying sentence subjects, verbs, and objects. We can return to this project later, when we learn about arrays, to increase the levels of difficulty. The program will be included as a Reading page on the Carla's Classroom site. In our program, students will be given 18 words consisting of six nouns, six verbs, and six words that can be used as direct objects. The students will be asked to pick a subject, a verb, and an object. If the student picks an incorrect word for each category, the student will be prompted to choose again. Once the student has correctly selected three words (one subject, one verb, and one object), the program will display a sentence created from those words. The program will allow the student to create six sentences so, at the end, the student will have created a little story that will be displayed on the web page.

Developing the Program

As always, it is important to create some pseudocode to map out the flow of the program. In general, we need to add a table to the initial web page and fill it with the 18 words. We also need a button to allow the student to begin the exercise and we need to include table cells with ids that will be used later to identify where to display each sentence.

The program itself will execute six times—once for each sentence. Therefore, a large outer loop will repeat for six iterations. For each iteration, the student will be prompted to select a subject, a verb, and an object from the words on the page. An inner loop will check to make sure the student has picked a noun for the subject, a verb for the verb, and so on. If the student selects an incorrect word, the student will be prompted to pick a different word.

Once the student has selected three appropriate words, the program will construct a sentence from those words. The sentence will then be displayed on the web page and the loop will repeat until six sentences have been created.

Writing the Code

This page will be part of the Carla's Classroom site we have been developing in previous chapters. First, add a link on the reading.html page to this page. The filename for this page should be carla_grammar.html. Your reading.html page should look like this:

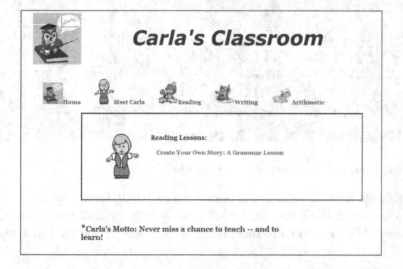

Next, we will create a page using the code below. You can create your own or add the necessary code to the file named carla_grammar.html which is available in the Student Data Files.

First, add header elements with the following content:

Create Your Story

A Grammar Lesson

You can add the following style to the <head> section of the page:

```
<style type="text/css">
    <!--
    .style2 {font-size: 24px; font-style: italic; line-height: 80%; }
    -->
</style>
```

And add the following HTML to the top of the page:

```
<h2>Create Your Story </h2>
<h2 class="style2">A Grammar Lesson</h2>
```

The page title should be Carla's Classroom | Create Your Story.

Add the following content to the content <div>. This includes a nested table with the words we are offering the students, a button to begin the exercise, and six table cells for the output. Here is the code:

```
<div id="content">
<table width = "95%" align="center">
    <tr><td><table width= "60%" align = "center">
    <tr><td colspan = 6>Here are your words: </td></tr>
    <td>teacher</td><td>jumps</td><td>down</td><td>boy</td> ↵
                <td>flies</td><td>out</td></tr>
    <tr><td>dog</td><td>me</td><td>loves</td><td>girl</td> ↵
                <td>stands</td><td>underwater</td></tr>
    <tr><td>bike</td><td>rides</td><td>up</td><td>cat</td> ↵
                <td>swims</td><td>fast</td></tr>
    <tr><td colspan = 6> <input type="button" id="sentence" ↵
                value="begin" onclick="getSentence();" />
    </td></tr></table></tr></td>
<tr><td><p>My Story</p></td></tr>
<tr><td id = "sentence1">sentence 1</td></tr>
<tr><td id = "sentence2">sentence 2</td></tr>
<tr><td id = "sentence3">sentence 3</td></tr>
<tr><td id = "sentence4">sentence 4</td></tr>
<tr><td id = "sentence5">sentence 5</td></tr>
<tr><td id = "sentence6">sentence 6</td></tr>
</table>
</div>
```

Your page will now look like this:

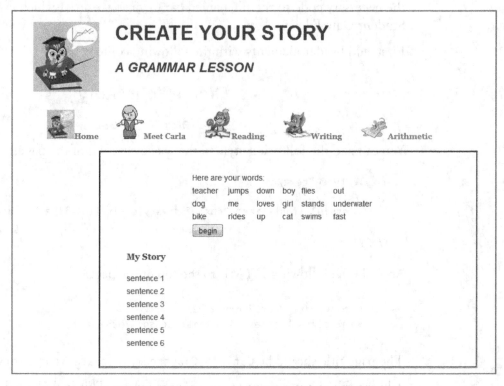

Save the page with the filename `carla_grammar.html`.

When the student clicks the button, the program will begin. We'll break up the code into manageable pieces and then put it all together.

The Code in Pieces

The Function and the Outer Loop We will call our function `getSentence()`. For this program we need the following variables:

Variable Name	Variable Type	Purpose	Initial Value
mySub	String	holds student's subject choice	" "
myVerb	String	holds student's verb choice	" "
myObj	String	holds student's object choice	" "
idNum	String	holds id of cell for output	" "
newSentence	String	holds sentence created	" "
sentence	Boolean	true when three words are correct	false
subject	Boolean	true when subject choice is correct	false
verb	Boolean	true when verb choice is correct	false
object	Boolean	true when object choice is correct	false
i	numeric	counter	0

The variables are declared and initialized when the function call is made. Then the outer loop begins. We know the student will create six sentences so we know this loop must repeat six times. Therefore, we will use a for loop with **i** as the counter. We also need to prompt the student to select a subject, verb, and object. The code to begin the function, declare and initialize the variables, begin the outer loop, and do the first prompts is as follows:

```
function getSentence()
{
    var mySub = " "; var myVerb = " "; var myObj = " ";
    var sentence = false; var idNum = " ";
    var i = 0; var subject = false; var verb = false;
    var object = false; var newSentence = " ";
    for(i = 1; i < 7; i++)
    {
        mySub = prompt("Please pick a word from the list as ↵
                    the subject: ", " ");
        myVerb = prompt("Please pick a word from the list as ↵
                    the verb: ", " ");
        myObj = prompt("Please pick a word from the list as ↵
                    the object: ", " ");
    }
}
```

Check for Valid Selections   Next, we need to check to make sure the student has chosen correct words for each part of the sentence. We will use an inner while loop to do this. For each of the three parts of speech, if the student's selection is valid, we will set the corresponding Boolean variable to true. If the selected word is invalid, the student will be prompted to pick another word. In this way, this loop will continue until the student has selected three valid words. At that time, the three corresponding Boolean variables will all be true. When these three variables are true, the variable **sentence** will be set to true. Therefore, the test condition for this while loop will be to continue while **sentence** is false. The code for this inner loop is as follows:

```
while(sentence != true)
{
    if((mySub=="teacher")||(mySub=="boy")||(mySub=="dog")|| ↵
                (mySub=="girl")||(mySub=="bike")||(mySub=="cat"))
        { subject = true;  }
    else
        mySub = prompt("Please pick a different word for the ↵
                    subject: ", " ");
    if((myVerb=="jumps")||(myVerb=="rides")||(myVerb=="loves")|| ↵
                (myVerb=="stands")||(myVerb=="flies")|| ↵
                (myVerb=="swims"))
        {  verb = true;      }
    else
        myVerb = prompt("Please pick a different word for the verb: ", " ");
    if((myObj=="up")||(myObj=="out")||(myObj=="me")||(myObj=="underwater")|| ↵
                (myObj=="down")|| (myObj == "fast"))
        {   object = true; }
    else
        myObj = prompt("Please pick a different word for the object: ", " ");
    sentence = true;
}
```

Notice that each if...else clause uses the OR operator (||) multiple times. This is a long and tedious method of checking all the correct possibilities. We will see how to make this more efficient—as well as more robust—when we learn to use arrays. For now, we are limited to six sentences and, therefore, six words for each part of speech. Once the student has correctly picked a subject, a verb, and an object, the variable **sentence** is set to true, the condition in the while loop becomes false and the inner loop ends.

Displaying the Story   The final part of the program resides inside the outer loop but is executed after the inner loop ends. It resets the required variables to their original values and displays one sentence in one of the designated cells. The code for this part is shown below with an explanation following:

```
1.  if((subject == true) && (verb == true) && (object == true))
2.  {
3.      newSentence = "The " + mySub + " " + myVerb + " " + ⏎
             myObj + ".";
4.      idNum = "sentence" + i;
5.      document.getElementById(idNum).innerHTML  = newSentence;
6.  }
7.  sentence = false; subject = false;
8.  verb = false; object = false;
```

We'll discuss some of this code in detail. The first line, the if statement, will only execute if the student has chosen an appropriate word for each part of speech. Since the only way out of the inner loop is if these three variables have been switched to true, this check might be redundant but it does serve as an added piece of validation and can be used later if we decide to enhance the program in other ways. For example, we could allow subject words to be used as objects or add other features to the program.

Line 3 creates a new sentence by concatenating some text with the value of the three variables, **mySub**, **myVerb**, and **myObj**. Since all the words used as subjects of a sentence are nouns (i.e., no proper nouns), adding the word "The" at the beginning of the sentence makes sense. We also need to add spaces between words and punctuation at the end.

Line 4 uses a new feature. We want the first sentence to display in the cell with id = sentence1. The second sentence goes into the cell with id = sentence2, the third into the cell with id = sentence3 and so on up to the sixth sentence which goes into the cell with id = sentence6. So we see that the only difference between cell ids is the number at the end of the id. We also see that these numbers correspond to the iteration of the outer loop. In other words, on the first pass, i (the outer loop counter) is 1, on the second pass i is 2, and so on up to the last pass where i is 6. It is possible to concatenate text and a variable to create a new string variable and that is what we do on line 4. On the first pass, **idNum** will have the value of sentence1, on the second pass **idNum** will have the value of sentence2 and on the sixth pass **idNum** will be sentence6. Since **idNum** will always have the value of the appropriate cell id, we can use it on line 5 to identify the cell where the new sentence created on that pass should be displayed.

Lines 7 and 8 return the four Boolean variables to their initial setting of false in preparation for the next pass.

Putting It All Together

Now we will put the entire program together. You are welcome to change the word choices if you want.

```
1.    <html>
2.    <head>
3.    <title>Carla's Classroom | Create Your Story</title>
4.    <link href="carla.css" rel="stylesheet" type="text/css" />
5.    <style type="text/css">
6.    <!--
7.    .style2 {font-size: 24px; font-style: italic; line-height: 80%;  }
8.    -->
9.    </style>
10.   <script>
11.   function getSentence()
12.   {
13.       var mySub = " "; var myVerb = " "; var myObj = " ";
14.       var sentence = false; var idNum = " ";
15.       var i = 0; var subject = false; var verb = false;
16.       var object = false; var newSentence = " ";
17.       for(i = 1; i < 7; i++)
18.       {
19.           mySub = prompt("Please pick a word from the list as↵
                          the subject: ", " ");
20.           myVerb = prompt("Please pick a word from the list as↵
                          the verb: ", " ");
21.           myObj = prompt("Please pick a word from the list as↵
                          the object: ", " ");
22.           while(sentence != true)
23.           {
24.               if((mySub == "teacher")|| (mySub == "boy") ||↵
                      (mySub == "dog") || (mySub == "girl")↵
                      || (mySub == "bike") || ↵
                      (mySub == "cat"))
25.                   { subject = true;            }
26.           else
27.                   mySub = prompt("Please pick a different↵
                          word for the subject: ", " ");
28.               if((myVerb == "jumps") || (myVerb == "rides") ||↵
                      (myVerb == "loves") || (myVerb == ↵
                      "stands") || (myVerb == "flies") ||↵
                      (myVerb == "swims"))
29.                   { verb = true;  }
30.           else
31.                   myVerb = prompt("Please pick a different ↵
                          word for the verb: ", " ");
32.               if((myObj == "up") || (myObj == "out") ↵
                      || (myObj == "me") || (myObj == ↵
                      "underwater") || (myObj == "down") ||↵
                      (myObj == "fast"))
33.                   { object = true;       }
34.           else
```

```
35.                              myObj = prompt("Please pick a different ⏎
                                      word for the object: ", " ");
36.                    sentence = true;
37.                 }
38.             if((subject == true) && (verb == true) && (object == true))
39.                 {
40.                     newSentence = "The " + mySub + " " + myVerb + " " + myObj + ".";
41.                     idNum = "sentence" + i;
42.                     document.getElementById(idNum).innerHTML  = newSentence;
43.                 }
44.             sentence = false; subject = false;
45.             verb = false; object = false;
46.         }
47.  }
48. </script>
49. </head>
50. <body>
51. <div id="container">
52. <img src="images/owl_reading.jpg" class="floatleft" />
53. <h2>Create Your Story </h2>
54. <h2 class="style2">  A Grammar Lesson</h2>
55. <div align="left"><blockquote>
56.     <p><a href="index.html"><img src="images/owl_button.jpg" ⏎
                            width="50" height="50" />Home</a>
57.     <a href="carla.html"><img src="images/carla_button.jpg" ⏎
                            width="50" height="65" />Meet Carla </a>
58.     <a href="reading.html"><img src="images/read_button.jpg" ⏎
                            width="50" height="50" />Reading</a>
59.     <a href="writing.html"><img src="images/write_button.jpg" ⏎
                            width="50" height="50" />Writing</a>
60.     <a href="math.html"><img src="images/arith_button.jpg" ⏎
                            width="50" height="50" />Arithmetic</a>
61.     <br /></p></blockquote></div>
62.     <div id="content">
63.     <table width = "95%" align="center">
64.         <tr><td><table width= "60%" align = "center">
65.         <tr><td colspan = 6>Here are your words: </td></tr>
66.         <td>teacher</td><td>jumps</td><td>down</td><td>⏎
                    boy</td><td>flies</td><td>out</td></tr>
67.         <tr><td>dog</td><td>me</td><td>loves</td><td>girl</td>⏎
                    <td>stands </td><td>underwater</td></tr>
68.         <tr><td>bike</td><td>rides</td><td>up</td><td>cat</td> ⏎
                    <td>swims</td><td>fast</td></tr>
69.         <tr><td colspan = 6> <input type="button" id = "sentence" ⏎
                    value="begin"onclick="getSentence();" /><td></tr>
70.     </table></tr></td>
71.     <tr><td><p>My Story</p></td></tr>
72.     <tr><td id = "sentence1">sentence 1</td></tr>
73.     <tr><td id = "sentence2">sentence 2</td></tr>
74.     <tr><td id = "sentence3">sentence 3</td></tr>
75.     <tr><td id = "sentence4">sentence 4</td></tr>
76.     <tr><td id = "sentence5">sentence 5</td></tr>
77.     <tr><td id = "sentence6">sentence 6</td></tr>
78.     </table>
79.     </div>
80.     <div id="footer">
```

```
81.        <h3><span class="style1">*</span>Carla's Motto: Never miss ↵
                       a chance to teach -- and to learn!</h3>
82.        </div>
83.  </div></body></html>
```

Finishing Up

Here are some possible results after a student uses this page:

output: This is what the whole page will look like:

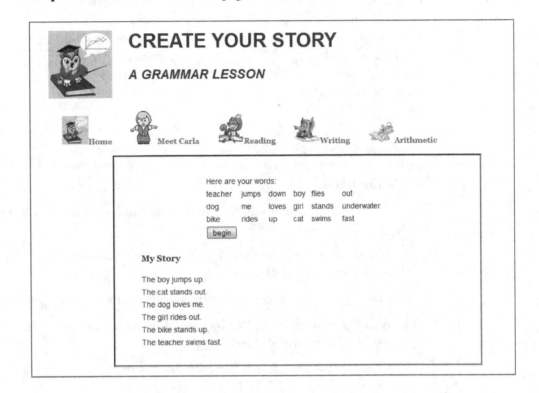

output:

Here is another possible story:

> **My Story**
>
> The teacher stands up.
> The boy rides fast.
> The girl rides fast.
> The cat loves me.
> The dog loves me.
> The bike stands up.

output:

And here is a third possible story:

> **My Story**
>
> The bike flies up.
> The boy swims underwater.
> The girl swims underwater.
> The cat loves me.
> The girl rides fast.
> The boy jumps out.

Chapter Review and Exercises

Key Terms

accumulator

break statement

continue statement

desk check

event attributes

inner loop

isNaN() method

event

Math.ceil() method

Math.floor() method

Math.round() method

modulus operator

mouse events

nested loops

ondblclick event

onmouseout event

onmouseover event

outer loop

rollover effect

Review Exercises

Fill in the Blank

1. The variable that holds the total of a sum of values in a loop is called the _____.

2. The Math method that turns any floating point number into an integer, following normal mathematical rules, is _____.

3. The _____ statement allows a program to skip the loop body.

4. Walking through code, line by line, using pencil and paper to keep track of the results of each line is called _____.

5. A loop that is nested inside another loop is the _____ loop.

True or False

6. T/F   If **number** is an even integer, the result of the following statement will be true.

    number = number % 2

7. T/F   If **num** = 4.6, the result of **x** = Math.floor(**num**) is 5.

8. T/F   While it is often necessary to use break statements in a loop, they are rarely used in a switch structure

9. T/F   A continue statement may allow a loop body to be skipped several times, depending on the loop test condition.

10. T/F   A for loop cannot be nested inside any type of loop except another for loop.

11. T/F   The choice of which type of loop to nest inside another loop is determined by the needs of the specific programming problem or the programmer's preferences.

12. T/F   If a button is used as a link, it can only be used to link to a page within the same site.

13. T/F   JavaScript events can trigger actions in a browser.

14. T/F   The onmouseup event is triggered when a user releases the mouse button.

15. T/F   In a nested loop, if the outer loop uses a counter, the inner loop must also use a counter.

Short Answer

16. Write a function that will add all the integers from 1 to 10.

17. Write a function that will find the average of six numbers entered by the user.

18. Write a function that will determine if a number entered by the user is even or odd. Use a loop to allow the user to enter as many numbers as desired and be sure to use an appropriate sentinel value for the user to end the program.

19. Write a function that allows the user to enter any real number. The output should be "positive" if the number is greater than or equal to 0 and "negative" if the number is less than 0. Use a loop to allow the user to enter as many numbers as desired and be sure to use an appropriate sentinel value for the user to end the program.

20. Write a function that uses the Math.round() method to round any number with a decimal part less than or equal to 0.6 down. For example, the result of using the program with the number 3.6 should be 3 but the result of 3.69 should be 4. Use a loop to allow the user to enter as many numbers as desired and be sure to use an appropriate sentinel value for the user to end the program.

21. Write a function that will display every number evenly divisible by 7 from 1 to 500; i.e., a program that will count by sevens.

22. What will the following program display?

```
function loopIt()
{
    var i = 0; var j = 0; var x = 0;
    for (i = 0; i < 3; i++)
    {
        x = i;
        for (j = 1; j < 5; j++)
        {
            x = x * j;
            document.write(x + " ");
        }
        document.write("<br />");
    }
}
```

23. What will the following program display?

```
function loopIt()
{
    var k = 0; var m = 0; var p = 0;
    while (k < 6)
    {
        m = k;
        for (p = 0; p < 4; p++)
        {
```

```
                    m = m + p;
                    document.write(m + " ");
                }
                document.write("<br />");
                k = k + 2;
            }
        }
```

24. Rewrite the loop of Exercise 5.22 using a do...while loop for the outer loop and a while loop for the inner loop.

25. Rewrite the loop of Exercise 5.23 using a for loop for the outer loop and a while loop for the inner loop.

26. What is wrong with the following nested loops?

```
for (var i = 0; i < 6; i++)
{
    for (var i = 3; i < 12; i++)
    {
        document.write("Ooops! <br />");
    }
}
```

27. How many times will "Hello there!" be displayed after the following code runs?

```
function loopIt()
{
    var x = 0; var y = 0;
    while (x < 3)
    {
        y = 1;
        while(y < 2)
        {
            document.write("Hello there <br /> ");
            y++;
        }
        x++;
    }
}
```

28. Write a function that will draw a shape on a web page. The shape should look like this:

```
**********
*        *
**********
*        *
**********
```

29. Write a function that will draw a shape on a web page. The shape should look like this:

```
******
*  *  *
*  *  *
*  *  *
*  *  *
******
```

30. Find any two images (you can use your own or use the images in the Student Data Files) and create a rollover effect on a web page.

Programming Challenges

On Your Own

1. Mathematicians disagree on how to round numbers when the decimal part is exactly 0.5. JavaScript, as well as many other programming languages, round up at this point with the Math.round() method. However, some mathematicians disagree. They believe a number ending in 0.5 should be rounded in a way that the result is even. In other words, 4.5 would be rounded *down* to 4 but 5.5 would be rounded *up* to 6. The reasoning behind this solution is that by always rounding up, an upward bias is created. This solution rounds up half the time and down the other half and, theoretically, might get rid of some of the bias. Regardless of whether or not you agree with the reasoning or even this method, for this program, create a web page that will round numbers up if the integer part of the number is odd and will round down if the integer part is even. The code should use a loop to allow the user to enter as many floating point numbers as desired and the display should show both the original number and the rounded number. Save the page as roundit.html and be sure to include an appropriate page title.

2. Rewrite the game of War from Example 5.16 so that the cards are more like a real deck of cards with four suits: hearts, diamonds, spades, and clubs. This means for each of the random numbers generated from 1 to 13, a second random number from 1 to 4 will assign the card a suit. Also, add the following enhancement to the display: a 1 should display as an Ace, an 11 as a Jack, a 12 as Queen, and a 13 as a King. Your program must check to make sure no two cards are exactly the same and that a tie occurs when the two cards have the same number value even if they are different suits. Save your page as war_enhanced.html and be sure to include an appropriate page title.

3. Create a web page that displays three designs and allow the user to select a design and a message to go with the design. Then prompt the user for the necessary information to create that design, as well as the message, and display it. If you want, you can restrict the number of characters allowed in the user's message so the design displays nicely. The designs, with sample messages, are shown below. Save your page as designs.html and be sure to include an appropriate page title.

```
                                      *                     *
                                    ***                   *   *
  * * * * * * *                    *****                 *       *
* Welcome Home! *                 *******               *  Sam  *
  * * * * * * *                    **ENTER**             *       *
                                  ***********             *     *
                                 *************               *
```

4. Create a web page that allows the coach of a town's soccer league to enter the ages of all the children who have registered for soccer this year. Children between the ages of 4 and 15 are allowed to sign up for soccer but there can

be a lot of variation in the number of children who sign up each year and their ages. Eventually the children will be placed into one of three leagues: Junior, Intermediate, and Senior. The Junior League is for children ages 4–7, the Junior League is for children ages 8–11, and the Senior League is for children ages 12–15. The coach wants to know how many children will be in each group. Your program should allow the coach to enter the ages of as many children as desired and should keep track of how many are in each group. The final display should tell the coach how many children signed up and how many will be in each group. Save your page as soccer.html and be sure to include an appropriate page title.

5. Create a small guessing game using nested loops. The user should be allowed to choose when to finish one round of play and whether or not to start another. The inner loop should generate a random number between 1 and 100. Allow the user to choose how many guesses will be permitted. For each number, display whether the user's number is greater than, less than, or equal to the random number. If the user guesses correctly, the game should display the winner's status and give the choice to play another round. If an incorrect guess is entered, the user should be given a hint. The game ends when either the user has used up all his guesses or has guessed correctly. If the user has used up all the guesses but has not been correct, the program should display the correct number. Be sure to generate a new random number for each round of play. Save your page as guess_it.html and be sure to include an appropriate page title.

VideoNote
Using Nested Structures
and the Math.random()
Function
On_Your_Own_6_CoinToss

6. Create a web page that will allow the user to toss a coin as often as desired. Use the Math.random() function to determine the result, where 0 = heads and 1 = tails. If the user's guess matches the computer's toss, the user wins. Use the coin images in the Student Data Files to display the winning result. Save your page as coin_toss.html and be sure to include an appropriate page title.

7. Create a web page that allows the user to enter as many numbers as desired and separates them into even and odd. Then find and display the sum and average of all the even numbers and the sum and average of all the odd numbers. Save your page as odd_even.html and be sure to include an appropriate page title.

Case Studies

Greg's Gambits

Create the Game of 21 for the Greg's Gambits site. In the real Game of 21, a dealer deals each player as well as the dealer two cards each. The goal is to get as close to 21 when the value of the cards is summed without going over 21. This game will be a simplified version. There will only be two players—the player and the dealer. We will also assume that the dealer has as many cards as necessary and will not worry about duplicates (such as two Queen of Hearts or two Three of Diamonds). In this game, each player begins with a score of 0. The computer will generate two random numbers between 2 and 11 for the player (the player's cards) and two for the computer (the dealer's cards). An ace should have the value of 11; therefore there is no 1. Face cards (Jack, Queen, King) all have the value of 10. The player will be shown his two cards but will not see the dealer's cards. Then the player will be asked, in a loop, whether he or she wants another card. The player's card values should be summed up. When the player no longer wants more cards, the player's sum will be compared to the sum of the dealer's two cards. The winner is assigned points equal to the numeric value of his or her hand. The winner of each deal is determined as follows:

- If one sum is greater than 21, the other player automatically wins the round.
- If both are over 21, no one wins the round.
- If neither sum is over 21, the player with the sum closer to 21 wins the round.
- If both have the same sum, it is a tie and no one wins the round.

The winner's sum is added to a total of his or her points. The game ends when either the player or the dealer has at least 200 points.

Open the play_games.html page and add a link to this page. The filename should be game21.html and the page title should be Greg's Gambits | Game of 21. Test your page in at least two different browsers. Submit your work as instructed by your teacher.

Carla's Classroom

Now you will add to the Grammar Lesson created earlier in this chapter by including indirect objects to the sentences the student can create and thus make the composed stories more interesting.

Display a list of words on the initial web page. Allow the student to select a word and let the student decide which of the following parts of a sentence that word will be: subject, verb, direct object, or indirect object. Subjects and indirect objects will all be nouns. Check to make sure the chosen category is allowed for that word. If the student chooses to make a noun a subject, add "the" to the word. If the student chooses to use a noun as an indirect object, prompt the user to select one of the prepositions listed. Then add the preposition and the word "the" to the noun. This will now be the indirect object of the sentence. When a complete sentence has been created (i.e., subject-verb-direct object or subject-verb-indirect object), that sentence should be displayed on the web page. If you wish, you can restrict the story to six sentences (or however many you want) or allow the student to create as long a story as desired.

The following words are suggestions but you can create your own list if you prefer. Be sure to mix up the order of the words on the initial web page.

Create a link to this page on the Reading page of the Carla's Classroom site, under the Grammar Lesson page. This page should have the filename grammar_extended.

html and the page title, as well as the heading, should be Carla's Classroom | An Advanced Grammar Lesson. Test your page in at least two different browsers. Submit your work as instructed by your teacher.

Nouns		Verbs	Direct Objects	Prepositions
boy	pool	loves	me	in
girl	store	swims	up	on
cat	table	rides	out	to
dog	bed	eats	fast	with
teacher	book	runs	underwater	off
bike	cake	jumps	down	under
		reads		
		hides		

Lee's Landscape

Create a web page for the Lee's Landscape business that allows Lee to calculate how much money he has spent on payroll for one month, with subtotals for each week. Lee should enter the names of his 10 employees and each one's gross salary (pre-tax) for each week in the month. For this program, we will assume the month has four weeks. The output should be a table which lists each name and salary for a week, then a subtotal, then the following week, for four weeks. At the end the grand total should be displayed. The table will look similar to the following. Some suggested employee names are provided, or you can create your own.

	Employee	Salary
	Week 1	
Week 1	1. Maria Montas	$ 456.78
	.	.
	.	.
	.	.
	10. Abe Abrams	
		subtotal:$ XXXXX.XX
Week 2	1. Maria Montas	
	.	.
	.	.
	.	.
	10. Abe Abrams	
		subtotal:$ XXXXX.XX
Week 3		and so on...
		Grand Total for month: $ XXXXXX.XX

Possible employee names:

Maria Montas	Pedro Perez	Kim Kang	Gregor Gorchevsky
Bob Barnaby	Charles Chan	Wanda Williams	Pammy Popper
Lucy Lacey	Abe Abrams		

The filename for this page should be month_payroll.html and the page title should be Lee's Landscape | Monthly Payroll. Be sure to test your program in at least two browsers. Submit your work as instructed by your teacher.

Jackie's Jewelry

Use Example 5.10 from this chapter to create a new page on the Jackie's Jewelry website. Your new page should include a chart for shipping costs which are based on the total cost of a customer's order. The chart is given below.

As the customer continues to order merchandise, a 6.5% sales tax should be added to each subtotal. Shipping costs are based on the total purchase price, including sales tax. In other words, a customer who orders $50.00 worth of merchandise must still pay the shipping costs for merchandise between $50.01 and $100.00 because $50.00 in merchandise will cost the customer $53.25 after including the tax.

As the customer's purchase cost reaches any of the limits for a higher shipping cost, the program should alert the customer of the increase and ask if the customer wants to continue shopping or remove the last item and stop. Remind customers that orders over $200.00 qualify for free shipping.

Shipping Costs	
cost of items including tax	shipping
less than $50.00	$ 5.00
$50.01 - $100.00	$ 8.00
$100.01 - $150.00	$12.00
$150.01 – 200.00	$15.00
over $200.00	free

You can use the jewelry images from the Student Data Files or find your own. Remember that if you use images from the Internet, you must be sure that the images do not have copyright restrictions. Save your page with the filename purchases.html and the page title should be Jackie's Jewelry | Shop. Test your page in at least two different browsers. Submit your work as instructed by your teacher.

6 Forms and Form Controls

Chapter Objectives

Today, using the Internet is as much a part of our daily lives as using a refrigerator to keep food fresh or using a car to travel from one place to another. And it wasn't more than a decade ago that most web pages were static informational pages. But now most websites—and definitely all business sites—include ways for the user to interact with the page. And the people who create these sites want to know what works and what doesn't; they want return customers and consumers. There are many ways to achieve both of these things, but one of the most popular and easiest methods is to use forms or form elements. Web users can click radio buttons, checkboxes, or menu items. They can send messages with textboxes. And all this can be done, if necessary by using JavaScript, without involving a server. While JavaScript form results can go through a server, it is not necessary. This is a plus because it bypasses a lot of security issues. In this chapter, we will learn to use the various form elements and learn how information can be returned to the website developer (you) with and without using a server.

After reading this chapter, you will be able to do the following:

- Create a form
- Understand the `mailto` action
- Understand what CGI scripts are and how they work
- Have `form` results returned to you by email
- Create and use the following `form` elements: radio buttons, checkboxes, textboxes, and textarea boxes

- Create hidden fields and passwords on a form
- Create and use the `<select></select>` and `<option></option>` tag pairs
- Use the results of a form in a JavaScript program
- Use the submit and reset buttons
- Use various form control enhancements

6.1   What Is a Form?

What exactly is a form? Here's one:

An HTML form is a way to enclose a section of a page with a name and use that name to access the form or the elements in the form, similar to creating a <div></div>. However, the elements in a form are treated differently from other HTML elements. Forms are created in the <body> of the web page so you may wonder why they are included in a JavaScript text. And you may already have created and used forms in an HTML page. There are not too many differences between this type of form and one enhanced with JavaScript. However, a JavaScript form relies on one or more **event handlers,** such as onclick() or onsubmit(). Some action is evoked when the user does something in the form, like clicking a button. The event handlers are placed with the rest of the attributes in the HTML **<form> </form> tags** and are invisible to browsers that don't support JavaScript. However, we will use the form results to enhance our JavaScript programs.

Forms are often used to obtain information from a user and return it to the developer, but the results of the user's actions on a form can also be used in JavaScript programs. In this chapter, we will use forms for both purposes. We will revisit some programs we created earlier in the text and see how they can be enhanced and made more user-friendly by using forms and form elements.

The Most Basic Form

A form is an HTML object. The object is created by using an opening `<form>` tag and a closing `</form>` tag. There are methods, events, attributes, and properties that can be used by the form object but, regardless of which ones you use in any situation, the most important is the name. A form is used to collect user input and, without a name, there is no way to access the form and retrieve this input.

A web page can contain multiple forms but they cannot be nested inside each other. Normally form elements are placed within a form. These include, but are not limited to, radio buttons, checkboxes, menu selections, textboxes, and more. We will discuss each of these elements later in the chapter.

The `<form>` `</form>` Tag Pair

Each form usually includes certain other properties which will be discussed in more detail. If the results of the form are to be submitted to a server or to someone's email, this is indicated in the opening `<form>` tag by the method and action properties. Example 6.1 shows how to create a blank form.

EXAMPLE 6.1

Creating a Form

The following program shows how and where to create a simple blank form.

```
1.   <html>
2.   <head>
3.   <title>Example 6.1</title>
4.   </head>
5.   <body>
6.        <form name="myfirstform" action="mailto:liz@forms.net" ⏎
                     method="post" enctype="text/plain">
7.        form elements go here
8.             .
9.             .
10.            .
11.        </form>
12.  </body></html>
```

In this example the form is opened in the `<body>` of the page and closed right before the ending `</body>` tag. However, a form can be opened and closed anywhere within a web page. Notice the properties that are defined in the example:

- **name** defines the name of this form and will be used to access the information on the form.

- **action** returns the value of this attribute. In this form, the action will be to send an email to the following imaginary email address: liz@forms.net.

- **method** specifies how to send the results. In this case, results will be sent as an HTTP post transaction.

- **enctype** specifies how the data from the form should be encoded before sending it. In this case, the data will use plain text.

The submit and reset Buttons

The form in Example 6.1 specifies that the results of the form would be sent to an email address, which would happen when the user clicked a **submit button.** If the form is used to return data to a server or an email address, a submit button is required. Another button that should be included on every form is a **reset button.** This will allow the user to clear his or her entries. You wouldn't want to create a form that didn't allow the user to fix errors or have a change of heart.

Both of these buttons are automatically created by using type = "submit" or type = "reset". The way to create these buttons is shown in Example 6.2.

Submitting and Resetting

The following code shows how to create submit and reset buttons:

```
1.   <html>
2.   <head>
3.   <title>Example 6.2</title>
4.   </head>
5.   <body>
6.       <form name="myfirstform" action="mailto:liz@forms.net"
                      method="post" enctype="text/plain">
7.       <h3>The contents of the form would go here</h3>
8.       <input type="reset" value="ooops! Clear my form please">
9.       <input type="submit" value ="I'm done! Send my info">
10.      </form>
11.  </body></html>
```

Notice lines 8 and 9. The "reset" type automatically clears all the user's entries on the form. The "submit" type automatically submits the user's information using the attributes defined in the <form> tag. The **value attribute** of either of these buttons allows you to customize the message the user sees on the button but the results, when clicked, will always be that the form will be cleared (the reset button) or the information will be submitted (the submit button). If you create this empty form, your page should look like this:

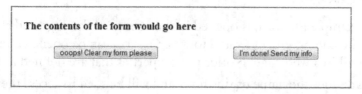

Returning Form Submissions

There are three basic ways that the data entered into a form is returned to the developer or programmer: The data can be sent to a server and stored in a database for analysis or other uses; the data can be sent directly to a person identified on the form by email; or the data can be returned to a JavaScript program to be used within the program. Most HTML texts discuss one of the first two methods when covering forms. We will focus on the third method.

The Common Gateway Interface (CGI)

The **Common Gateway Interface,** usually called **CGI,** is a standard method used by web server software. It allows web pages to be generated as executable files. These files are called **CGI scripts.** They are programs that are usually written in a scripting language. The server ordinarily has a folder named **cgi-bin** at the base of its directory tree and it treats all executable files in that folder as CGI scripts. If form data is to be sent to a script on a web server, the syntax in the opening <form> tag would be as follows, assuming the script is named data.php:

```
<form name = "myform" method = "post" id = "myform" ↵
          action = "cgi-bin/data.php">
```

This requires that the programmer has access to a web server. The data would be passed into the program (here, named data.php) using certain specific environment variables.

Since we cannot be sure that all students have access to a server with any specific CGI script, we will not use this method in our examples in this chapter. However, if you were creating websites for a large business, you would use the business's web server to return your form data and, by that time, you would surely be able to write your own CGSI scripts and thus control exactly how the users' data is processed.

Returning Form Data by Email

A second method to receive a user's data is to have each submission returned to the developer through an email message. This method is simple and can be used by anyone with an email account but, as you can probably imagine, it's not ideal. If you expect your form to be used by 100 people, then you would receive 100 emails. There are certainly better ways to process large amounts of information! On the other hand, you might want to respond specifically to certain types of form data. For example, a website might have a form for complaints and the company would want each complaint answered individually. Thus, generating emails from these forms would be appropriate. We will use this method in some examples and in the Case Studies at the end of the chapter.

If form data is to be sent to the developer (or, for example, the customer service manager), the syntax would be as follows, assuming the Customer Service Manager is named Liz Loverly and her email is liz.loverly@jackiejewels.net:

```
<form name = "complaints" method = "post" id = "complaints" ↵
          action = "mailto:liz.loverly@jackiejewels.net">
```

This method generates an email message to liz.loverly@jackiejewels.net from whatever email program the user employs. One nice feature is that it allows the user to see exactly what will be sent. However, the company may want the email to be sent automatically, without forcing the user to go through the secondary step of actually sending the email. This requires the use of server-side technologies that are not covered in this text.

Returning Form Data to a Program

In this chapter, we will use most of the form data in our JavaScript programs. This means we'll use selections a user makes on the form in whatever program we write instead of asking the user to type a selection from a prompt. In this case, we do not need to include a method or an action. We use the form elements to allow the user to enter information without worrying about whether the user has misspelled a word or has entered an invalid selection.

CHECKPOINT FOR SECTION 6.1 ✓

6.1 Can a single web page have multiple forms?

6.2 What are the two buttons that are normally included on all forms?

6.3 Create a reset button that will say "let me start over".

6.4 Create a submit button that will say "send it off!".

6.5 Create the code for a simple form named "problems" that sends the form data back to the following email address: john.doe@nowhere.com.

6.6 What is a CGI script and where would it reside?

6.2 Form Controls

You are probably familiar with the many types of form controls. In this section, we will discuss radio buttons, checkboxes, textboxes and textarea boxes. Each serves its purpose and it is important to learn how to use all of them.

These controls are considered objects and, as such, support the standard properties and events. The standard properties that we will use most often and are W3C compliant are the id and innerHTML. The standard events are those we have already used, including mouse events and keyboard events.

Radio Buttons

The radio button is an object in an HTML form. This means it has properties and events. Properties that are specific to radio buttons are shown in Table 6.1.

The main thing to remember about **radio buttons** is that, when confronted with a list of radio buttons options, only one may be selected. This is a significant difference from checkboxes in which the user is allowed to select as many options as he or she wants. We'll use examples from previous chapters to show how each of these controls work in specific situations.

The syntax for each radio button is as follows:

```
<input type = "radio" name = "radio_button_name" id = "radio_button_id" ⏎
            value = "radio_button_value">
```

TABLE 6.1	Properties of the Radio Button

Property	Description
checked	sets or returns the checked state of the button
defaultChecked	returns the default value of the checked attribute
disabled	sets or returns whether or not the button is disabled
form	returns a reference to the form where the button is
name	sets or returns the name of the button
type	returns the type of the form element
value	sets or returns the value assigned to the button

Example 6.3 demonstrates how to use radio buttons.

EXAMPLE 6.3

Using Radio Buttons

The following code creates a form that uses radio buttons to allow the user to select a favorite color. Styles have been added to show the colors in the text.

```
1.   <html>
2.   <head>
3.   <title>Exercise 6.3</title>
4.   <style type="text/css">
5.   <!--
6.         .style5 { color: #0000FF; font-weight: bold; }  // blue
7.         .style6 { color: #FF0000; font-weight: bold; }  // red
8.         .style7 { color: #00CC33; font-weight: bold; }  // green
9.         .style8 { color: #660066; font-weight: bold; }  // purple
10.        .style9 { color: #FF9900; font-weight: bold; }  // orange
11.  -->
12.  </style>
13.  </head>
14.  <body>
15.  <form name="buttons" >
16.      <h2>What color do you like best?</h2>
17.      <input type="radio" name="color" id="blue" value="blue">
18.      <span class="style5"> Blue</span><br />
19.      <input type="radio" name="color" id="red" value="red">
20.      <span class="style6">Red</span><br />
21.      <input type="radio" name="color" id="green" value="green">
22.      <span class="style7">Green</span><br />
23.      <input type="radio" name="color" id="purple" value="purple">
24.      <span class="style8">Purple</span><br />
25.      <input type="radio" name="color" id="orange" value="orange">
26.      <span class="style9">Orange</span>
27.  </form></body></html>
```

If you look at lines 17, 19, 21, 23, and 25 you will see that the name attribute of all the radio buttons is the same; it is "color". This is important; it defines a group of buttons and thus requires that only one of them can be selected at any time. If your buttons each had different names, the point of using radio buttons would be lost because each would be in its own group and all of them could be selected. The id of each button, however, is unique, as is the value. These are the properties that would be used to identify which of the buttons named color, was selected.

If you code and run this program, your output would look like the one shown below. You should test it to ensure that, when a second button is selected, the first one chosen is deselected. In the example, the user has selected Green.

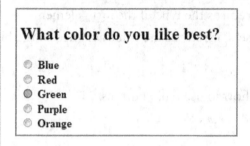

In Example 6.4, we will revise code from an example used in a previous chapter. Our earlier example allowed a player to select his or her avatar. We allowed the player to click a button which displayed the avatar choices and then the player was prompted to select one. This required the player to type the name of the avatar. This scenario can cause many problems. The player might misspell the avatar's name or enter a value that is not an option. We can use radio buttons to do everything in one step and, at the same time, prevent errors.

EXAMPLE 6.4

Selecting an Image with Radio Buttons

In this example, we will ask a player to select an avatar from a group of choices. The selection is made by checking a radio button. This page uses the greg.css stylesheet. The code for this part of the page follows:

```
1.   <html>
2.   <head>
3.   <title>Example 6.4</title>
4.   <link href="greg.css" rel="stylesheet" type="text/css" />
5.   <script>
6.   function pickAvatar(picked)
7.   {
8.       var avatar = document.getElementById(picked).value;
9.       document.getElementById('myavatar').innerHTML = avatar;
10.  }
11.  </script>
12.  </head>
13.  <body>
14.  <div id="container">
```

```
15.   <table width = "80%" align = "center">
16.        <tr><td colspan = "5" class="nobdr"><h1>Select Your ⏎
                    Avatar:</h1></td></tr>
17.        <td class="nobdr"> <img src="images/bunny_ch01.jpg" /></td>
18.        <td class="nobdr"> <img src="images/elf_ch01.jpg" /> </td>
19.        <td class="nobdr"> <img src="images/ghost_ch01.jpg" /></td>
20.        <td class="nobdr"><img src="images/princess_ch01.jpg" /></td>
21.        <td class="nobdr"><img src="images/wizard_ch01.jpg" /></td>
22.        </tr> <tr>
23.        <td class="nobdr"><input type="radio" name="avatar" id="bunny" ⏎
                    value="Bunny" onclick="pickAvatar('bunny')"/></td>
24.        <td class="nobdr"><input type="radio" name="avatar" id="elf" ⏎
                    value="Elf" onclick="pickAvatar('elf')"/></td>
25.        <td class="nobdr"><input type="radio" name="avatar" id="ghost" ⏎
                    value="Ghost" onclick="pickAvatar('ghost')"/> </td>
26.        <td class="nobdr"><input type="radio" name="avatar" id="princess" ⏎
                    value="Princess" onclick="pickAvatar('princess')"/></td>
27.        <td class="nobdr"><input type="radio" name="avatar" id="wizard" ⏎
                    value="Wizard" onclick="pickAvatar('wizard')"/> </td></tr>
28.   </table>
29.   <p>The avatar you selected is:<span id="myavatar">kitty</span></p>
30.   </div></body></html>
```

There are a few things to focus on in this code. First, we have not created a form. Since there is only one set of radio buttons which will be used in the JavaScript code, we do not need a form; we are just using one type of form control.

For simplicity, the information is in a table. Since we are building on the greg.css page that we have been using throughout the chapter, a new class has been created on the style sheet to remove the unattractive border around each image. The new class is named nobdr and is seen on each <td></td> on on the web page.

Lines 17–21 create cells on a table row and one image of one avatar is placed in each cell. Lines 23–27 create the row of radio buttons. Each button has the name = "avatar" and this creates a group of buttons and restricts the player to selecting only one. However, the value and id of each button identifies as a unique avatar. The onclick() method is used so that, as soon as a player clicks one button, the JavaScript function, pickAvatar(), is called. Here we do something new. So far we have called functions but never sent in any values to those functions. The functions have worked completely separately from the method that calls them. In this case, we tell the function some information when we call it. For example, if the player selects a ghost, when the pickAvatar() function is called, the Ghost id ('ghost') is sent to the function. We will discuss what it means to send and return values in detail in Chapter 7. For now, it is sufficient to know that, when the pickAvatar() function begins to work, it knows that it is working with the radio button with id = "ghost".

The function begins on line 6. Notice that the function declaration is pickAvatar(picked). The word picked, in the parentheses, means that, when the function is called, a value will be sent in and picked will hold that value. If the player selects the Wizard the function call would be onclick = pickAvatar('wizard') and picked will now hold the value 'wizard'. But if the

Bunny is selected, the function call would be `onclick = pickAvatar('bunny')` and `picked` would now have the value `'bunny'`.

Line 8 now sets the value of a variable named **avatar** to the value of the button with the `id` that was sent in to `picked`. In this case, the `id` is `"ghost"` and the value is `Ghost`. Now line 9 sends that value back to the element with the `id = 'myavatar'`. In this example, that element is on line 29. The default value, `Bunny`, is replaced by the new value of **avatar** which, in this case, is `Ghost`.

If you enter this code and run it, your initial display will look as follows. The output below shows what is displayed if an Elf is selected.

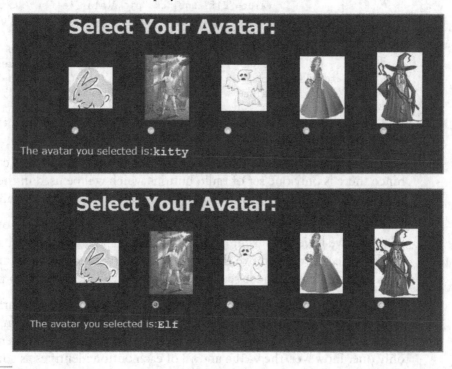

Checkboxes

The **checkbox** is also an object in an HTML form. It supports the same properties and events as the radio button, shown in Table 6.1. However, when the user sees a list of options that are checkboxes, any number of these checkboxes may be selected.

The syntax for each checkbox is as follows:

```
<input type="checkbox" name = "box_name" id = "box_id" ↵
        value = "box_value">
```

The checked Property

It is often necessary to identify which checkboxes have been selected. Or you may want the set of checkboxes to initially display with one or more checkboxes already checked. The **checked property** can either set or return the checked state of a checkbox. The state of the `checked` property is either `true` or `false`.

You can set a checkbox to become checked by setting the checked property to true in a function and, by the same logic, can uncheck it. Example 6.5 shows how to use the checked property with a group of checkboxes.

However, the checked property is also used to return the state of a checkbox to a function and we will use this property in future examples to identify one or more checked boxes.

EXAMPLE
6.5

Using the checked Property

```
1.  <html>
2.  <head>
3.  <title>Example 6.5</title>
4.  <script>
5.      function checkIt()
6.      {     document.getElementById("tibet").checked = true     }
7.      function uncheckIt()
8.      {     document.getElementById("tibet").checked = false     }
9.  </script>
10. </head>
11. <body>
12. <h2>Where do you live? </h2>
13. <input type="checkbox" name="country" id="argentina" value="Argentina" ⌐
                    >Argentina<br />
14. <input type="checkbox" name="country" id="china" value="China">China<br />
15. <input type="checkbox" name="country" id="france" value="France">France<br />
16. <input type="checkbox" name="country" id="italy" value="Italy">Italy<br />
17. <input type="checkbox" name="country" id="spain" value="Spain">Spain<br />
18. <input type="checkbox" name="country" id="tibet" value="Tibet">Tibet<br />
19. <input type="checkbox" name="country" id="usa" value="United States">United ⌐
                    States<br />
20. <p><button onclick="checkIt()">Check Tibet</button>
21. <button onclick="uncheckIt()">Uncheck Tibet</button></p>
22. </body></html>
```

If you code this program and run it, the output will be as follows:

initially: **after clicking the Check**   **after clicking the**
                                   Tibet button: **Uncheck Tibet button:**

Example 6.6 demonstrates how to use checkboxes and the checked property to identify more than one selected checkbox.

| EXAMPLE 6.6 | ## Using Checkboxes |

In this example we will assume that a restaurant offers diners the ability to order a meal through an online form. The user can select a single main course using radio buttons and then select two side dishes by checking two items in the checkbox list.

```
1.   <html>
2.   <head>
3.   <title>Example 6.6</title>
4.   <script>
5.   function pickEntree(picked)
6.   {
7.       var entree = document.getElementById(picked).value;
8.       document.getElementById('main_dish').innerHTML = entree;
9.   }
10.  function pickSides()
11.  {
12.      var flag = false;
13.      var i =0;
14.      var side1 = "";
15.      var side2 = "";
16.      for (i = 1; i <= 7; i++)
17.      {
18.          if ((document.getElementById(i).checked == true) && ↵
                            (flag == false))
19.          {
20.              side1 = document.getElementById(i).value;
21.              flag = true;
22.          }
23.          else if ((document.getElementById(i).checked == true) ↵
                            && (flag == true))
24.              side2 = document.getElementById(i).value;
25.      }
26.      document.getElementById('side_one').innerHTML = side1;
27.      document.getElementById('side_two').innerHTML = side2;
28.  }
29.  </script>
30.  </head>
31.  <body>
32.  <table align = "center" width = "60%">
33.  <form name="menu">
34.  <tr><td colspan = "2"><h2><br />Select Your Meal</h2></td></tr>
35.  <tr><td>Pick your main course:<br />
36.      <input type="radio" name="entree" id="steak" value="Rib-Eye Steak" ↵
                    onclick="pickEntree('steak')">Rib-Eye Steak<br />
37.      <input type="radio" name="entree" id="chicken" value="Fried ↵
                    Chicken" onclick="pickEntree('chicken')">Fried ↵
                    Chicken<br />
38.      <input type="radio" name="entree" id="veggie" value="Veggie Platter" ↵
                    onclick="pickEntree('veggie')">Vegetarian Fried Tofu<br />
```

```
39.              <input type="radio" name="entree" id="fish" value="Broiled Salmon" ⏎
                         onclick="pickEntree('fish')">Broiled Salmon<br /></td>
40.    <td> Pick two side dishes<br />
41.              <input type="checkbox" name="sides" id="1" value="French Fries" ⏎
                         >French Fries<br />
42.              <input type="checkbox" name="sides" id="2" value="Baked ⏎
                         Potato">Baked Potato<br />
43.              <input type="checkbox" name="sides" id="3" value="Cole ⏎
                         Slaw">Cole Slaw<br />
44.              <input type="checkbox" name="sides" id="4" value="Garden ⏎
                         Salad">Garden Salad<br />
45.              <input type="checkbox" name="sides" id="5" value="Mixed ⏎
                         Vegetables">Mixed Vegetables<br />
46.              <input type="checkbox" name="sides" id="6" value="Macaroni ⏎
                         and Cheese">Macaroni and Cheese<br />
47.              <input type="checkbox" name="sides" id="7" value="Applesauce"> ⏎
                         Applesauce<br /></td></tr>
48.    <tr><td><input type="reset" value="ooops! Let me change my ⏎
                         selections"> </td>
49.    <td><input type ="button" onclick="pickSides()" value = "Enter my ⏎
                         side dish selections" "></button></td></tr>
50.    <tr><td colspan = "2">
51.        <h2>Entree selected:<span id="main_dish"> </span></h2>
52.        <h2>First side dish:<span id="side_one"> </span> </h2>
53.        <h2>Second side dish: <span id="side_two"> </span> </h2>
54.    </td></tr>
55.    </table></form></body></html>
```

The radio buttons are on lines 36–39. The checkboxes begin on line 41. Notice that all the checkboxes have the same name but different ids. For this program, since we want to discover which two have been picked later, the ids have been given the names 1 through 7. You will see the benefit of this when the pickSides() function is called. Each checkbox also has a value that will be used in the display.

After the customer makes the side dish selections, the button on line 49 calls the JavaScript program that will find which two have been chosen and will display the selections on the page. This button is simply a button. It is not an input button or a checkbox or a radio button. Its only purpose is to call the JavaScript function, pickSides(). We will call it an **OK button.**

We will discuss the pickSides() function now because it is a bit complex. The function begins on line 10. There is no need to send a value to this function, as we do with the pickEntree() function. The first thing the function does is to declare four variables. The counter, i, is familiar to us. The variables **side1** and **side2** will hold the values of the two side dishes selected, once they are identified. The **flag**, on line 12, is a Boolean variable. It will be either true or false. It initially begins as false but is set to true as soon as one side dish selection is identified.

The loop, on lines 16–25, runs through the seven checkboxes. Line 18 is the beginning of a selection structure. If the checkbox identified by the id which corresponds to the current value of i is checked and **flag** is still false, this means that the customer has picked this particular side dish and that it has not previously been identified. In this case, we set **side1** equal to the value of that checkbox. Then we set the **flag** to true to indicate that one side has been identified. If the checkbox we are looking at now has previously been identified (i.e., **flag** will be true), the if clause is not entered and control passes to the else...if clause.

Now the program (line 23) looks to see if that checkbox has been checked, again using the checked property. It also checks to see if the **flag** is true. If the **flag** is true, this means that a previous checkbox has been selected and has been assigned to **side1** and this is the second checkbox that has been selected. Thus, line 24 sets the **side2** to the value of this checkbox.

Finally, lines 26 and 27 display the values of **side1** and **side2** in their appropriate places on the web page.

If this program is coded and run, the outputs will look as shown below, given the selections made by two different diners:

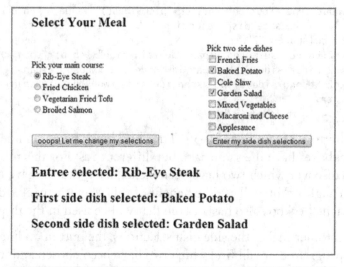

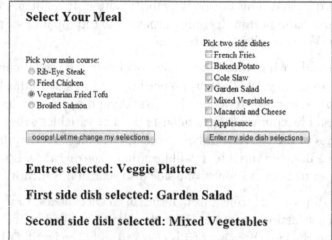

Textboxes

The **textbox** is an input element that allows the web developer to display a small area for a user to enter some information. We can use the information entered in our programs. The textbox has several properties that are not available to radio buttons or checkboxes. We can set the **size** of the box (i.e., its width) and the **maxlength** which configures the maximum number of characters that will be accepted by the textbox. We can also place an initial value in the box, if desired. The syntax for a textbox is as follows:

```
<input type="text" name = "box_name" id = "box_id" size = "20" ⏎
        maxlength = "25" value = "my box!">
```

Example 6.7 shows how various textboxes can be configured to accept a user's full name.

EXAMPLE 6.7

A Few Textboxes

```
1.   <html>
2.   <head>
3.   <title>Example 6.7</title>
4.   </head>
5.   <body>
6.   <h2> Enter the requested information</h2>
7.       <p>This box uses the default values for size and maxlength ⏎
                  and has no initial value:
8.          <br /><input type="text" name="fullname" id="fullname" ></p>
9.       <p>This box is 30 spaces wide and limits the user to 25 ⏎
                  characters in his or her name:
10.         <br /><input type="text" name="fullname" size = "30" maxlength ⏎
                  = "25" id="fullname"></p>
11.      <p>This box is 60 spaces wide, allows the user to enter up to ⏎
                  100 characters and shows an initial value ⏎
                  of a name: <br />
12.         <input type="text" name="fullname" size = "60" maxlength = ⏎
                  "100" id="fullname" value="Hermione Priscilla ⏎
                  Throckmorton-Nabolonikoff" ></p>
13.  </body></html>
```

If you create this page, it will initially look like this:

Enter the requested information

This box uses the default values for size and maxlength and has no initial value:

[   ]

This box is 30 spaces wide and limits the user to 25 characters in his or her name:

[   ]

This box is 60 spaces wide, allows the user to enter up to 100 characters and shows an initial value of a name:

[Hermione Priscilla Throckmorton-Nabolonikoff   ]

If you enter the ridiculously long name, `Hermione Priscilla Throckmorton-Nabolonikoff`, in the first box, it will accept the entire name but only the last part of the name will be displayed. If you enter the same name in the middle box, it will cut off your entry after the first 25 characters, as shown:

Enter the requested information

This box uses the default values for size and maxlength and has no initial value:

| ockmorton-Nabolonikoff |

This box is 30 spaces wide and limits the user to 25 characters in his or her name:

| Hermione Priscilla Throck |

This box is 60 spaces wide, allows the user to enter up to 100 characters and shows an initial value of a name:

| Hermione Priscilla Throckmorton-Nabolonikoff |

The Label, Fieldset, and Legend Elements

We now have discussed three form controls and we see how they are often used together in a single form. Three elements can make our forms look neater, more aesthetic, and clearer to understand: **label, fieldset** and **legend.**

When you create a textbox, the **<label></label> tags** allow you to enter a label for your textbox. In Example 6.7 we used a sentence to describe what was in each textbox. However, we probably would have wanted a label next to the textbox to explain to the user what to enter. The opening <label> tag goes right before the desired label and the closing </label> tag goes after the label or after the <input> statement.

If a group of form controls are enclosed in **<fieldset></fieldset> tags**, the browser will put a border around these elements. Adding the **<legend></legend> tags** will allow the browser to include a label for this grouping. Example 6.8 shows how these elements can be used as well as how textboxes are used and accessed by the JavaScript program.

Using Labels, Fieldsets, and Legends

The following program adds to the menu example we created earlier. We now ask the customer to enter his or her name and provide a contact phone number. We add labels to the textboxes and enclose each group in fieldset tags with legends. We have added two functions to display the results of the textboxes when the final meal selections have been made.

```
1.   <html>
2.   <head>
3.   <title>Example 6.8</title>
4.   <script>
5.   function pickEntree(picked)
6.   {
```

```
7.          var entree = document.getElementById(picked).value;
8.          document.getElementById('main_dish').innerHTML = entree;
9.  }
10. function customerInfo(cName)
11. {
12.         var dinerName = document.getElementById(cName).value;
13.         document.getElementById('cust_name').innerHTML = dinerName;
14. }
15. function customerPhone(cell)
16. {
17.         var phone = document.getElementById(cell).value;
18.         document.getElementById('cell_phone').innerHTML = phone;
19. }
20. function pickSides()
21. {
22.         var flag = false;
23.         var i =0;
24.         var side1 = "";       var side2 = "";
25.         for (i = 1; i <= 7; i++)
26.         {
27.             if ((document.getElementById(i).checked == true) ↵
                        && (flag == false))
28.             {
29.                 side1 = document.getElementById(i).value;
30.                 flag = true;
31.             }
32.             else if ((document.getElementById(i).checked == true) ↵
                        && (flag == true))
33.                 side2 = document.getElementById(i).value;
34.         }
35.         document.getElementById('side_one').innerHTML = side1;
36.         document.getElementById('side_two').innerHTML = side2;
37. }
38. </script>
39. </head>
40. <body>
41. <form name="menu">
42. <h2><br />Select Your Meal</h2>
43. <div style="width: 80%;">
44. <div style="width: 40%; float: left;">
45. <fieldset><legend>Your Information</legend>
46.     <h3>Enter the following information:</h3>
47.     <label>Your name:<br /></label>
48.     <input type="text" name="dinername" id="dinername" ↵
                    size = "30" value = ""/>
49.     <input type ="button" onclick="customerInfo('dinername')" ↵
                    value = "ok"></button>
50.     <p>We will call your cell phone when your order is ready.<br />
51.     <label>Phone:<br /> </label>
52.     <input type="text" name="phone" id="phone" size="30" ↵
                    value = ""/></label>
53.     <input type ="button" onclick="customerPhone('phone')" ↵
                    value = "ok"></button><br />
54. </fieldset>
55. </div>
56. <div style=" width: 30%; float: left;">
57. <fieldset><legend>Main Course</legend>
```

```
58.          <h3>Pick your main course:</h3>
59.          <input type="radio" name="entree" id="steak" value="Rib-Eye Steak" ⏎
                        onclick="pickEntree('steak')"> Rib-Eye Steak<br />
60.          <input type="radio" name="entree" id="chicken" value="Fried Chicken" ⏎
                        onclick="pickEntree('chicken')"> Fried Chicken<br />
61.          <input type="radio" name="entree" id="veggie" value="Veggie ⏎
                        Platter" onclick="pickEntree('veggie')"> ⏎
                        Vegetarian Fried Tofu<br />
62.          <input type="radio" name="entree" id="fish" value="Broiled ⏎
                        Salmon" onclick="pickEntree('fish')"> ⏎
                        Broiled Salmon<br /><br />
63.   </fieldset>
64.   </div>
65.   <div style="width: 30%; float: left;">
66.   <fieldset><legend>Side Dishes</legend>
67.          <h3>Pick two side dishes</h3>
68.          <input type="checkbox" name="sides" id="1" value="French ⏎
                        Fries" >French Fries<br />
69.          <input type="checkbox" name="sides" id="2" value="Baked ⏎
                        Potato">Baked Potato<br />
70.          <input type="checkbox" name="sides" id="3" value="Cole ⏎
                        Slaw">Cole Slaw<br />
71.          <input type="checkbox" name="sides" id="4" value="Garden ⏎
                        Salad">Garden Salad<br />
72.          <input type="checkbox" name="sides" id="5" value="Mixed ⏎
                        Vegetables">Mixed Vegetables<br />
73.          <input type="checkbox" name="sides" id="6" value="Macaroni ⏎
                        and Cheese">Macaroni and Cheese<br />
74.          <input type="checkbox" name="sides" id="7" value= ⏎
                        "Applesauce">Applesauce<br />
75.          <input type ="button" onclick="pickSides()" value = "Enter ⏎
                        my side dish selections" "></button>
76.   </fieldset>
77.   </div> </div> <div style="clear:both;"></div>
78.   <div ><input type="reset" value="ooops! I made a mistake. Let ⏎
                        me start over."><br /></div>
79.   <div>
80.          <h3>Your meal:</h3>
81.          <h3>Your name: <span id = "cust_name"> </span></h3>
82.          <h3>Your contact phone: <span id = "cell_phone">   </span></h3>
83.          <h3>Entree selected: <span id = "main_dish">  </span></h3>
84.          <h3>First side dish selected: <span id = "side_one">   </span></h3>
85.          <h3>Second side dish selected: <span id = "side_two">   </span></h3>
86.   </div>
87.   </form></body></html>
```

Most of this code is copied from Example 6.6. However, this code is changed to use <div></div> tags instead of a table for the page layout. There are three groups of form elements which display side by side. The new group uses two textboxes for the customer to enter a name and a phone number. They are on lines 45–54. The <fieldset></fieldset> tag pair begins on line 45 and ends on line 54. It creates a border around these two textboxes and the other information included in this fieldset. The <label></label> tags put a title for the fieldset within the border.

Each textbox is followed by a button that, when clicked, calls a JavaScript function. The onclick() method sends the id of the textbox to the function (lines 49 and

53) so the customerInfo() function (lines 10–14) and the customerPhone() function (lines 15–19) know what element to access. If, for example, the customer enters Louis Lin in the textbox for a name, the value cName identifies that textbox in the function. Line 12 says

```
var dinerName = document.getElementById(cName).value;
```

The computer will go to the element with id = 'cName' and get its value. Then it assigns the value (Louis Lin, in this case) to the variable dinerName.

The next line, line 13, is

```
document.getElementById('cust_name').innerHTML = dinerName;
```

Now the computer puts the value of dinerName into the element with id = 'cust_name'. In our program, this element is part of the <div></div> that begins on line 79. It is where the customer's name will be displayed.

The same process occurs for the phone number, where the function is called on line 53 and the value of the phone number is sent, through the id = 'phone', to the function customerPhone() (lines 15–19). The value of the phone textbox is stored in the variable phone (line 17) and sent to the web page (line 18).

If this program is coded and run, the following output will occur, given that the customer's name is Jackie Jackson, the phone number is 555-3455, and Jackie wants to eat salmon with a side of cole slaw and a baked potato:

Select Your Meal

Your Information	Main Course	Side Dishes
Enter the following information:	**Pick your main course:**	**Pick two side dishes**
Your name:	○ Rib-Eye Steak	☐ French Fries
Jackie Jackson [ok]	○ Fried Chicken	☑ Baked Potato
	○ Vegetarian Fried Tofu	☑ Cole Slaw
We will call your cell phone when your order is ready.	● Broiled Salmon	☐ Garden Salad
Phone:		☐ Mixed Vegetables
555-3455 [ok]		☐ Macaroni and Cheese
		☐ Applesauce
		[Enter my side dish selections]

[ooops! I made a mistake. Let me start over.]

Your meal:

Your name: Jackie Jackson

Your contact phone: 555-3455

Entree selected: Broiled Salmon

First side dish selected: Baked Potato

Second side dish selected: Cole Slaw

Textarea Boxes

With a **textarea box,** a space can be designated for a user to enter text. While a textbox only allows the width to be specified, both height and width can be specified in a textarea box. The textarea tags are **<textarea></textarea>** and the **cols** and **rows properties** determine the size of the box. These boxes are normally used to allow a web site visitor to include comments or questions when returning a form. The syntax for a text is as follows:

```
<textarea name = "box_name" id = "box_id" cols = "20" ⌐
            rows = "5">Default text if desired</textarea>
```

When a user enters more text than can fit in the area that has been created, a textarea box allows more text to be entered and displays a scroll bar.

Example 6.9 shows how various textarea boxes can be configured to accept comments from a website visitor:

EXAMPLE 6.9

Textarea Boxes

```
1.   <html>
2.   <head>
3.   <title>Example 6.9</title>
4.   </head>
5.   <body>
6.   <h2> Enter your comments or questions below</h2>
7.   <p>This box uses the default values for rows and columns and ⌐
                      has no initial value: <br />
8.   <textarea name = "the_box" id = "the_box"></textarea> </p>
9.    <p>This box is set to 3 rows and 15 columns and has text that ⌐
                      appears initially: <br />
10.   <textarea name = "the_box" id = "the_box" rows = "3" cols = ⌐
                      "15">Hi!</textarea> </p>
11.   <p>This box is set to 7 rows and 80 columns and has initial text: <br />
12.   <textarea name = "the_box" id = "the_box" rows = "10" cols = "50">Enter ⌐
                      your comments or questions here</textarea> </p>
13.   </body></html>
```

If you create this page, it will initially look like this:

If the user types the following text into all three textarea boxes, the scrollbars will appear in the first two boxes when the initial room is filled up. The final display is as shown.

Input text: I have been extremely pleased with your products. Whenever I order from your company, the order is filled correctly and shipped to me in record time. If I do not want an item that I ordered, returns are easy and painless. It is wonderful that you offer free shipping and pay for shipping on returns. Congratulations on your customer service and excellent products!

The email action

So far we have used the information from form controls in JavaScript programs which displayed the results on the web page. However, in some cases, it is valuable to generate an email to be sent to the web developer or to the business that runs the web page with a single user's information. The email action is placed in the opening `<form>` tag, as we have mentioned earlier. We can also add a subject line to the generated email and a copy to be sent to another recipient. The syntax for these options are as follows:

This will generate an email sent to whoever@wherever.net with the subject line Whatever:

```
<form name="myform" method="post" enctype="text/plain" ⏎
action ="mailto:whoever@wherever.net?Whatever">
```

This will generate an email sent to whoever@wherever.net with the subject line Whatever and will send a copy to whatshisname@whereisit.net:

```
<form name="myform" method="post" enctype="text/plain" action = ⏎
"mailto:whoever@wherever.net?Whatever&cc=whatshisname@whereisit.net">
```

In Example 6.10, we will put it all together to allow a customer to send a dinner order to a restaurant by email along with any comments or special requests. The example will show why the name and value attributes are important in each form control. Since the JavaScript code is the same as Example 6.8 as is much of the code to create the form controls, we have truncated some of the code to save space.

EXAMPLE 6.10

Using a Textarea Box and Sending Information

The following code adds a textarea box for comments to the menu selection example (Example 6.6) we have previously developed. It also adds a submit button and an action in the form which contains the email address of the restaurant manager. When the submit button is clicked, it calls on the form action to create the email that will be sent to the restaurant. We have also added a subject line to the email that is sent. Then, if this were a real-life situation, the restaurant staff could package the meal and call the customer when it is ready to be picked up.

```
1.   <html>
2.   <head>
3.   <title>Example 6.10</title>
4.   <script>
5.   function pickEntree(picked)
6.       //{   the pickEntree() function code is here       }
7.   function customerInfo(cName)
8.       //{   the customerInfo() function code is here       }
9.   function customerPhone(cell)
10.      //{   the customerPhone() function code is here       }
11.  function pickSides()
12.      //{   the pickSides() function code is here       }
13.  </script>
14.  </head>
15.  <body>
16.  <form name="order" method="post" id="dinner" enctype="text/plain" ⏎
                 action ="mailto:manager@mealstogo.net?Dinner Order">
17.  <h2><br />Select Your Meal</h2>
18.  <div style="width: 80%;">
19.  <div style="width: 40%; float: left;">
20.  <fieldset><legend>Your Information</legend>
21.  <h3>Enter the following information:</h3>
22.  <label>Your name:<br /></label> <input type="text" name = ⏎
                 "dinername" id="dinername" size = "30" value = ""/>
23.  <input type ="button" onclick="customerInfo('dinername')" ⏎
                 value = "ok"></button>
24.  <p>We will call your cell phone when your order is ready.<br />
25.  <label>Phone:<br /> </label><input type="text" name="phone" ⏎
                 id="phone" size="30" value = ""/></label>
```

```
26.    <input type ="button" onclick="customerPhone('phone')" value = ⌐
                       "ok"></button><br /></fieldset></div>
27.    <div style=" width: 30%; float: left;">
28.    <fieldset><legend>Main Course</legend>
29.    <h3>Pick your main course:</h3>
30.    <input type="radio" name="entree" id="steak" value="Rib-Eye Steak" ⌐
                       onclick="pickEntree('steak')">Rib-Eye Steak<br />
31.        //all the other radio buttons for entrees go here
32.    <div style="width: 30%; float: left;">
33.    <fieldset><legend>Side Dishes</legend>
34.    <h3>Pick two side dishes</h3>
35.    <input type="checkbox" name="sides" id="1" value="French Fries"> ⌐
                       French Fries<br />
36.        //all the other checkboxes for side dishes go here
37.    <input type ="button" onclick="pickSides()" value = "Enter my ⌐
                       side dish selections" "></button>
38.    </fieldset></div>
39.    </div><div style="clear:both;"></div>
40.    <div><input type="reset" value="ooops! I made a mistake. Let ⌐
                       me start over."><br /></div>
41.    <div style="width: 40%; float: left;"><h3>Your meal:</h3>
42.    <p>Your name: <span id = "cust_name"> </span> <br />
43.        //all other results of selections are displayed here
44.    </div>
45.    <div style="width: 40%; float: left;">
46.    <h3>Comments or questions:</h3>
47.    <textarea name = "dinnerorder" id="dinner" rows="6" cols="40"> ⌐
                       Enter your comments or questions here</textarea>
48.    </div><div style="clear:both;"></div>
49.    <div>
50.    <input type = "submit" value="submit my order"><br />
51.    </div>
52.    </form></body></html>
```

The first line that contains something new is line 16. This is where we added the email action to the **<form></form> tag.** The email in this case will be sent to manager@mealstogo.net. We have added a subject line to be inserted into the email which says Dinner Order. When the new submit button on line 50 is clicked, the email will be generated.

The new textarea box is created on line 47. It is 6 rows long and 40 columns wide and allows the customer to enter any special requests. These need not be displayed again on the page since the customer has the ability to edit his or her own comments right in the textbox. However, those comments will be included in the email.

If the customer's information is as follows, the email that is generated will be as shown:

A customer named Howard Higgins (cell phone 555-6789) orders a Rib-Eye Steak with French Fries and Applesauce. However, he requests that the steak be medium-rare and wants extra ketchup. The email that is generated to the manager looks like this:

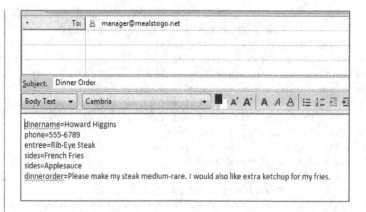

It is important to note that each control is identified in the email by its name. Therefore, you should use names that actually mean something to you. The customer's selection, however, is listed by the form control's value.

A second customer named Lily Field (cell phone (200) 555-4466) orders Fried Chicken with a Garden Salad and a Baked Potato. She wants the chicken broiled instead of fried, wants salad dressing on the side, and requests real butter instead of margarine for her potato. In fact, Lily's comments far exceed the space allotted in the textarea box but, while the whole message is not displayed on the web page, it will be included in its entirety in the email that is generated to the manager, as shown:

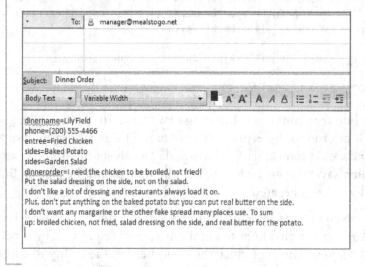

CHECKPOINT FOR SECTION 6.2 ✓

6.7 What is wrong with the following code that creates a group of three radio buttons?

```
<fieldset><legend>Pick your major</legend>
    <input type="radio" name="math" id="math" value=⏎
                        "Mathematics"> Mathematics<br />
```

```
              <input type="radio" name="history" id="history" value= ⏎
                              "History"> History<br />
              <input type="radio" name="physics" id="physics" value ⏎
                             ="Physics"> Physics<br />
        </fieldset>
```

6.8 Create a function that will set the following checkbox to a checked state:

```
     <input type="checkbox" name="box" id="agree" value="OK">I agree!>
```

6.9 What is the difference between a textbox and a textarea box?

6.10 Create a textbox for a user's first name and one for the user's last name. Write a function that, when called in the HTML page, will display the user's first and last names back to the web page.

6.11 Create an opening form tag that is configured to send the form results to the email address given below, with a copy to the second email address and a subject line that is `Here is the requested information.`

email 1: `lily.field@flowers.net`

email 2: `howard.higgins@flowers.net`

6.12 If form results are sent to the web developer by email, which of the control attributes are used and what is the purpose of each?

6.3   Hidden Fields and Passwords

No matter where you go on the web, if you want to view a site's information, get on your college's website, buy something online, or sometimes for no apparent reason, you are asked to establish a username and password. Passwords are, in the minds of many, synonymous with security while others debate just how secure a **password** really is. Regardless of your opinion on this subject, passwords are unavoidable in today's world and web sites that you create for any business or school will most likely require them. And one thing that is true of all passwords: once created, they should not be displayed when a user visits a site and enters the password. We'll learn how to create a form element that accepts a password without displaying what the user types on the screen.

Another form control that can be created and used but remains invisible to the user is the **hidden object.** This is an input field which the user will not see. However, the field can be accessed by a server as well as by a JavaScript program. There are many reasons why a web site developer might want to store information in a hidden input field. We will cover a few of them in this section.

The Hidden Form Element

Imagine you are developing a business website. On one page, the customer signs in with his or her username. You may want to use that name in an area on every subsequent page. You can store that username in a hidden field and carry it from page to page. You can also use the information in a hidden field when you communicate with the server. The properties of a hidden object are the same as the ones we have used previously: name, type, id, and value. The general syntax for a hidden field is as follows:

```
<input type = "hidden" name = "field_name" id = "field_id" ⏎
              value = "field_value" />
```

To illustrate how the hidden field is used we will return to the menu we created in Example 6.10. In that example, the customer selects an entrée and two side dishes and, along with the customer's name, phone contact, and comments, that information is sent by email to the manager. Let's now assume that the restaurant has forms for a diner to select breakfast, lunch, or dinner. The manager wants to know which meal is being referred to in the email. The customer does not need to see this information so we can put it in a hidden field and, when the email is sent to the manager, the first line will identify which meal the information is about.

Since all the code is the same as the previous example, in Example 6.11 we will only display a small part of the code.

EXAMPLE 6.11

Using a Hidden Object

```
1.   <html>
2.   <head>
3.   <title>Example 6.11</title>
4.   <script>
5.   function customerInfo(cName)
6.   {
7.        var dinerName = document.getElementById(cName).value;
8.        document.getElementById('cust_name').innerHTML = dinerName;
9.   }
10.  function customerPhone(cell)
11.  {
12.       var phone = document.getElementById(cell).value;
13.       document.getElementById('cell_phone').innerHTML = phone;
14.  }
15.  //functions to pick the entrée and sides go here
16.  </script>
17.  </head>
18.  <body>
19.  <form name="order" method = "post" id = "dinner" ⏎
                action="mailto:manager@mealstogo.net?subject=Dinner ⏎
                Order" enctype="text/plain" >
20.  <input type ="hidden" name ="meal" id ="dinner" value = "dinner choice" />
21.  <h2><br />Select Your Meal</h2>
22.  <div style="width: 80%;"><div style="width: 40%; float: left;">
23.  <fieldset><legend>Your Information</legend>
24.  <h3>Enter the following information:</h3>
25.  <label>Your name:<br /></label>
26.      <input type="text" name="dinername" id="dinername" ⏎
                      size = "30" value = ""/>
```

```
27.        <input type ="button" onclick="customerInfo('dinername')" ⏎
                     value = "ok"></button>
28.        <p>We will call your cell phone when your order is ready.<br />
29.    <label>Phone:<br /> </label>
30.        <input type="text" name="phone" id="phone" size="30" ⏎
                     value = ""/></label>
31.        <input type ="button" onclick="customerPhone('phone')" ⏎
                     value = "ok"></button><br /></fieldset></div>
32.    the rest of the HTML page goes here
33.    <div><input type = "submit" value="submit my order"><br />
34.    </div></form></body></html>
```

The hidden field is on line 20. It identifies the information (the id) as "dinner" and the value that will be sent when this field is accessed is "dinner choice". If we use the entire page we created in the previous example and add line 20 after the form description, the form that the customer sees will not change at all. However, if a customer named Robbie Roberts (phone 555-4958) orders a Rib-Eye Steak with French Fries and Applesauce, and asks for his steak to be cooked well done, the body of the email that will be generated and sent to the manager would look like this:

```
meal=dinner choice

dinername=Robbie Roberts

phone=555-4958

entree=Rib-Eye Steak

sides=French Fries

sides=Applesauce

dinnerorder=Make my steak well done.
```

The Password Form Element

The **password form element** is a single-line input field in a form. The content of the field will be **masked.** This means that, instead of whatever the user types into the field, a character such as an asterisk or small dot will appear instead. The password object uses the same properties as the other input fields we have discussed but may contain several other properties you may want to use (see Table 6.2).

A password field can be accessed by using document.getElementById(). The general syntax of a password field is as follows:

```
<input type = "password" and then set desired properties />
```

Example 6.12 shows how to create a password box and returns the number of characters allowed in the field, the number of characters the user entered, and the actual password (unmasked). Later, this information can be used to check that the user enters a valid password but for now we will simply assume that's the case.

TABLE 6.2	Properties of the Password Element
Property	**Description**
defaultValue	returns or sets the default value of a password field
disabled	sets or returns whether or not the field is disabled
form	returns a reference to the form where the field is
name	sets or returns the name of the password field
maxLength	sets or returns the maximum number of characters allowed
readOnly	sets or returns whether or not the field is read-only
type	returns the type of the form element
value	sets or returns which type of form element the field is
size	sets or returns the width of the field (i.e., number of characters)

EXAMPLE 6.12

The Password Box

```
1.   <html>
2.   <head>
3.   <title>Example 6.12</title>
4.   <script>
5.   function getPasswordInfo(pword)
6.   {
7.       var pwordSize = 0; var userWord = " "; var wordLength = 0;
8.       pwordSize = document.getElementById(pword).size;
9.       document.getElementById('field_size').innerHTML = pwordSize;
10.      userWord = document.getElementById(pword).value;
11.      document.getElementById('pword').innerHTML = userWord;
12.      wordLength = userWord.length;
13.      document.getElementById('word_size').innerHTML = wordLength;
14.  }
15.  </script>
16.  </head>
17.  <body>
18.  <h2> Enter a password that is between 4 and 8 characters, using ⏎
                only digits (0 - 9) and letters. </h2>
19.      <p><input type="password" name="user_pwrd" id="passwrd" />
20.      <input type ="button" onclick="getPasswordInfo('passwrd')" ⏎
                value = "ok"></button></p>
21.      <p>Password information:<br />
22.  Number characters allowed: <span id = "field_size"> ⏎
                  </span> <br />
23.  Number characters entered: <span id = "word_size"> ⏎
                  </span><br />
24.      Password entered: <span id = "pword"> </span></p>
25.  </body></html>
```

In this example the password box is defined on line 19. No size is set but the box has a name and an id. Line 20 is a button that, when clicked, calls the getPasswordInfo() JavaScript function. Notice that we send in the id of the password box when we call this function. In this example, the function does three things. First, it finds the size of this box. Since no size was defined, the default size is stored in the variable **pwordSize** on line 8 and sent back to the web page on line 9. Then, lines 10 and 11 get the actual password that the user entered, store it in the variable **userWord**, and display it on the web page. Finally, using the length property, the number of characters in the password is determined (line 13), stored in **wordLength**, and displayed (line 14). If a user enters ange1888 for a password, the page will look like this:

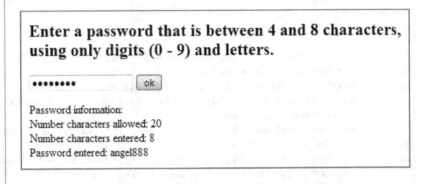

The substr() Method

The **substr()method** will extract the characters from a string, beginning at the character you specify and continuing through as many characters as you want. It returns the new **substring**. The method requires that you enter two numbers, separated by commas, within the parentheses. The first number identifies which character you want the new substring to begin with. The second number identifies how many characters you want in your new substring. Note that the first character is considered character 0. We will discuss why this is so in Chapter 8.

For example, if you wanted to extract the last four characters from a string that contained six characters, the first number entered in the parentheses would be 2 and the second number would be 4.

String	Character Number							
	0	1	2	3	4	5	...	n
cat	c	a	t					
A table	A		t	a	b	l	e	
Jones-Smith	J	o	n	e	s	-	...	h

Example 6.13 verifies the validity of a password and continues to prompt the user until an appropriate password is entered.

EXAMPLE 6.13

Using the substr() Method

This example demonstrates how to use the substr() method to extract the first character, the last character, and some middle characters from a string.

```
1.  <html>
2.  <head>
3.  <title>Example 6.13</title>
4.  <script>
5.  function checkIt(phrase)
6.  {
7.      var userWord = ""; var charOne = ""; var charEnd = "";
8.      var middle = ""; wordLength = 0;
9.      userWord = document.getElementById(phrase).value;
10.     document.getElementById('user_word').innerHTML = userWord;
11.     wordLength = userWord.length;
12.     document.getElementById('word_size').innerHTML = wordLength;
13.     charOne = userWord.substr(0,1);
14.     document.getElementById('first_char').innerHTML = charOne;
15.     charEnd = userWord.substr((wordLength - 1),1);
16.     document.getElementById('last_char').innerHTML = charEnd;
17.     middle = userWord.substr(3,4);
18.     document.getElementById('the_middle').innerHTML = middle;
19.  }
20.  </script>
21.  </head>
22.  <body>
23.  <h3> Enter a word or a phrase:</h3>
24.      <p><input type="text" name="user_word" id="the_word" />
25.      <input type ="button" onclick="checkIt('the_word')" ↵
                     value = "ok"></button></p>
26.      <p>Word/Phrase information:<br />
27.      You entered: <span  id = "user_word"> </span> <br />
28.      It has this many characters: <span  id = "word_size"> ↵
                       </span> <br />
29.      The first character is: <span id = "first_char">  ↵
                     </span> <br />
30.      The last character is: <span id = "last_char">  ↵
                     </span> <br />
31.      The 4th, 5th, 6th, and 7th characters are: <span id = ↵
                     "the_middle"> </span> <br /></p>
32.  </body></html>
```

Lines 22–32 are the body of this page. This is where the user initially enters a word or phrase and, by clicking the OK button (line 25), the JavaScript function checkIt() is called. The id of the textbox that contains the word or phrase, 'the_word', is sent to the checkIt() function.

The checkIt() function does several things. It gets the text that the user entered and displays it on the web page (lines 9 and 10). Then it determines the length of the word (i.e., how many characters the word or phrase contains, including punctuation, spaces, or special characters) and stores this information in the **wordLength** variable. This is done on line 11. Line 12 sends that information back to the web page.

Line 13 uses the substr() method to extract the first character from the string. Note that the first character is identified as the character in space 0. The fact that we only want a single character is shown by the second argument in the method, the 1.

To get the last character in the string, we use the length of the phrase that we have previously stored in the variable **wordLength**. Line 15 says to store this character in a variable named **charEnd**. The first argument in the substr() method tells the program where to start extracting characters. We know the number of characters in the string because it is stored in **wordLength**. However, the characters in the string are numbered from 0 to the end. Thus, in a string with 5 characters, the last character is character #4. In a string of 187 characters, the last character is character #186. In other words, the last character is the number of characters in the string minus 1 or, in our code, **wordLength** - 1. Therefore, this becomes the first argument in the code that extracts the last character in the user's entry. The second argument, a 1, says only to extract one character. The value of the last character in the string is stored in the variable **charEnd**. The next line, line 16, sends this information back to the web page.

Finally, on lines 17 and 18, we extract the fourth, fifth, sixth, and seventh characters in the string. The arguments in the substr() method are 3 (because 3 identifies the fourth character in a string and this is where we want to begin to extract characters) and 4 (because we want to extract four characters, beginning at the fourth character in the string). The value of this little substring is stored in the variable named **middle** and, on line 18, sent back to the web page.

If a user enters the phrase Life is good! in the textbox, the output will look like this:

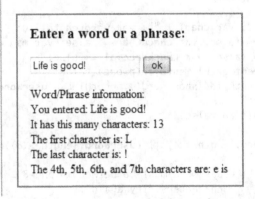

If a user enters the name Hermione in the textbox, the output will look like this:

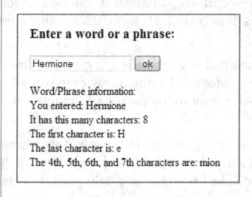

Enter a word or a phrase:

Hermione   [ok]

Word/Phrase information:
You entered: Hermione
It has this many characters: 8
The first character is: H
The last character is: e
The 4th, 5th, 6th, and 7th characters are: mion

Now we will put it all together in Example 6.14 to write a program that allows the user to enter a password and validates that password.

EXAMPLE 6.14

Validating a Password

In this example, we will put the password box together with our programming skills to require that a user's password is within our specifications. Here, we will insist that the password is between four and eight characters long, begins with a letter, includes at least one digit (which may not be the first character) and includes at least one of the following special characters but no other special characters. In other words, the user can use the letters of the alphabet, the 10 digits, and one of the following but nothing else: $, * , or #. The code is given and the detailed explanation follows.

```
1.   <html>
2.   <head>
3.   <title>Example 6.14</title>
4.   <script>
5.   function checkPassword(pword)
6.   {
7.       var userWord = ""; var char1 = ""; var wordLength = 0;
8.       var checkLength = false; var checkChar = false; var msg = "";
9.       var checkDigit = false; var checkSpecial = false;
10.      userWord = document.getElementById(pword).value;
11.      document.getElementById('show_word').innerHTML = userWord;
12.  //check length of word
13.      while (checkLength == false)
14.      {
15.          if ((userWord.length < 4) || (userWord.length > 8))
16.          {
17.              msg = "The password must be between 4 and 8 ⏎
                          characters. Try again";
18.              document.getElementById('error_msg').innerHTML = msg;
19.              userWord = document.getElementById(passwrd).value;
20.          }
21.          else
```

```
22.                          checkLength = true;
23.                 }
24.    //check first character
25.           char1 = userWord.substr(0,1);
26.           while (checkChar== false)
27.           {
28.                 if ((char1 < 65) || ((char1 > 90) && (char1 < 97)) || ↵
                                    (char1 > 122))
29.                 {
30.                     msg = "The first character must be a letter of ↵
                                    the alphabet. Try again";
31.                     document.getElementById('error_msg').innerHTML = msg;
32.                     userWord = document.getElementById(passwrd).value;
33.                 }
34.                 else
35.                     checkChar = true;
36.           }
37.    //check for digit
38.           wordLength = userWord.length;
39.           for (i = 1; i <= (wordLength - 1); i++)
40.           {
41.                 if ((userWord.charCodeAt(i) >= 47) && ↵
                                    (userWord.charCodeAt(i) <= 58))
42.                 {
43.                     checkDigit = true;
44.                     break;
45.                 }
46.           }
47.           if (checkDigit == false)
48.           {
49.                 msg = "You must have at least one number in the ↵
                                    password. Try again";
50.                 document.getElementById('error_msg').innerHTML = msg;
51.                 userWord = document.getElementById(passwrd).value;
52.           }
53.    //check for special character
54.           for (i = 1; i <= (wordLength - 1); i++)
55.           {
56.                 if ((userWord.charCodeAt(i) == 35) || ↵
                                    (userWord.charCodeAt(i) == 36) || ↵
                                    (userWord.charCodeAt(i) == 37))
57.                 {
58.                     checkSpecial = true;
59.                     break;
60.                 }
61.           }
62.           if (checkSpecial == false)
63.           {
64.                 msg = "You must have one special character ($, %, or #) ↵
                                    in the password. Try again";
65.                 document.getElementById('error_msg').innerHTML = msg;
66.                 userWord = document.getElementById(passwrd).value;
67.           }
68.           if ((checkLength == true) && (checkChar == true) && ↵
                                    (checkDigit == true) && ↵
                                    (checkSpecial == true))
```

```
69.        {
70.                msg = "Congratulations! You have successfully entered ⏎
                           a valid password.";
71.                document.getElementById('error_msg').innerHTML = msg;
72.        }
73.  }
74.  </script>
75.  </head>
76.  <body>
77.  <h3> Enter a password in the box below. Your password must:</h3>
78.  <ul>
79.        <li>contain between 4 and 8 characters</li>
80.        <li>begin with a letter of the alphabet (upper or ⏎
                     lowercase)</li>
81.        <li>contain at least one digit (0 - 9)</li>
82.        <li>contain one of the following special characters: dollar ⏎
                     sign ($), percent sign (%), or pound sign (#)</li>
83.  </ul>
84.  <p><input type="password" name="user_pwrd" id="passwrd" size = ""/>
85.  <input type ="button" onclick="checkPassword('passwrd')" ⏎
                     value = "ok"></button></p>
86.  <p><span id="error_msg"> </span><br /></p>
87.  <p>Password information:<br />
88.  Password entered: <span  id = "show_word"> </span> </p>
89.  </body></html>
```

This code is rather long and complex so we'll discuss it one part at a time. The <body> of the page begins on line 76. Line 84 defines a password box with id = "passwrd". From now on, whenever the program rechecks the password, it will be identified by this id. Line 85 is the button the user will click each time a new password is entered. Line 86 defines a space where the error messages will be displayed as the password is being validated. In this program, we include two lines (87 and 88) that display the unmasked password entry. In a real program, these lines would probably be deleted but, until we are sure the program is working correctly, it's wise to leave them in as a way to check that what we enter is actually what is being validated.

Now we will discuss the JavaScript program. The function, checkPassword() is accessed when the user clicks the OK button after entering a password on line 85. When the function is called, the id, "passwrd", of the password box is passed to the checkPassword() function. Lines 7, 8, and 9 in the function declare and initialize the variables that will be used. The variable **userWord** will store the untested password that is passed to the function. The variable **msg** will store whatever message is necessary to display to the user as the password is validated. There are four Boolean variables (**checkLength, checkChar, checkDigit**, and **checkSpecial**) which are used to tell when each of the options has been validated. Line 10 gets the value of the user-entered password from the password box and stores that value in **userWord**. Line 11 displays what the user entered (unmasked) on the web page in the <span> with id = "show_word". This line would, ordinarily, be commented out or deleted when the page goes live.

The first validation check begins on line 13 and ends on line 23. It checks to see if the password is between four and eight characters. The flag, **checkLength**, initially is false. The while loop that begins on line 13 will repeat until **checkLength** is set to true. If the password is less than four characters or more than eight characters (line 15) a message is displayed to the user (lines 17 and 18) that a new password must be entered. Line 19 retrieves the new password and the loop executes again. When the user's entry is finally between four and eight characters, the if clause on lines 15–20 is skipped and the else clause is executed. This sets the flag, **checkLength**, to true and the while loop to check the length of the password ends. The program is ready to check the next requirement.

Lines 25–36 check to see if the first character in the password is a letter. The substr() method is used on line 25 to set a variable, **char1**, equal to the value of the first character in the password. A while loop is created that will continue its iterations until the second flag, **checkChar**, becomes true. Inside this loop line 28 checks to see whether the first character is between A - Z or a - z. The Unicode values for these characters are used. If the first character is not a lowercase or uppercase letter, a message is displayed and the user is asked to enter a new password. If the first character is a letter, the if clause on lines 28–33 is skipped. The else clause on lines 34–35 sets the flag, **checkChar**, to true. The second condition has been met and we are ready to check the third requirement.

Next, we check whether at least one character in the password is a digit. The flag for this part is **checkDigit**. The length property is used on line 38 to set a variable, **wordLength**, to the number of characters in the password. A for loop is used (lines 39–46) to check each character in the password, beginning at the second character (the first character must be a letter!) and going up through the last character. The beginning value of the counter, **i**, therefore, is 1 since character 0 must be a letter. The ending value is (**wordLength** - 1) because, in a word of length = 9, the last character is in the spot identified as 8. For each character the if clause checks to see if it is between the Unicode values for 0 - 9. As soon as any character is identified as a digit, the **checkDigit** flag is set to true and the loop ends. This is accomplished with the break statement on line 44. If the loop continues through all its iterations without encountering a number, **checkDigit** will remain false and the if clause on lines 47–52 will be executed. This will prompt the user to reenter a password which contains at least one digit. But if any character which is a number has been found, **checkDigit** will be true, the if clause will be skipped, and the program will be ready for its final requirement.

The last condition for a valid password is that one of three special characters must be included. These characters have Unicode values 35, 36, and 37. The flag for this part is the variable **checkSpecial**. The logic is almost the same as for the previous part. Each character, from the second through the last, is checked in the for loop on lines 54–61. The if statement on line 56 checks to see if each specific character is either a #, $, or %. As soon as any character is identified as one of these, the flag, **checkSpecial**, is set to true and the loop ends. If the loop continues to the end and no special character is found, the if clause on lines 62–67 is executed and the user is prompted to enter a new password.

These four checks will end when the user has complied with all four requirements. When that happens, the four flags (**checkLength**, **checkChar**, **checkDigit**, and **checkSpecial**) will all be true. Thus, a valid password has been created and line 70 displays the congratulatory message. And the program ends!

If the user enters how (three characters) or howardhillsborough (more than eight characters), the output will be as follows:

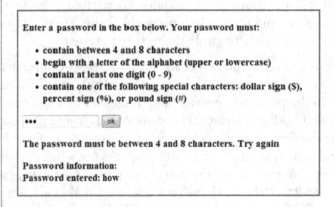

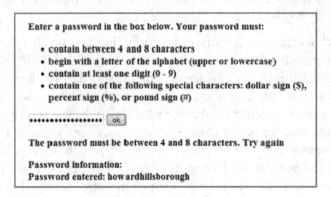

If the user enters 4puppy$$ (begins with a number) or cat#dog (no digit) the output will be as follows:

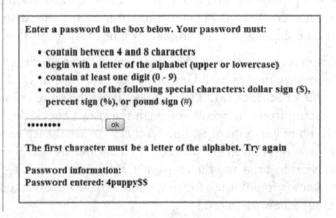

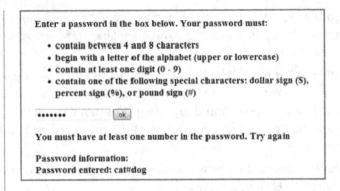

If the user enters my1stcar (no special character) or Bst2pw$d (a valid password) the output will be as follows:

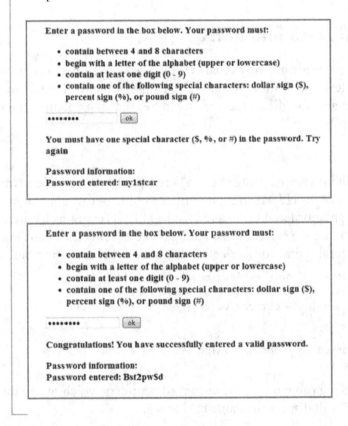

CHECKPOINT FOR SECTION 6.3

6.13 Give one example of when a hidden field might be used in a form.

6.14 Add a hidden field to the menu program of Example 6.11 that will be sent with the email to the restaurant manager. The value should be "add lemon wedge with salmon, ketchup with fries, dressing with salad".

6.15 Write a line of code that will extract the fifth and sixth characters from a string variable, **username**, to a variable named **middle**.

6.16 Write code to extract the last character from a string variable, **username**. Store this substring in a variable named **endChar**. (*Hint:* you will also have to use the `length` property.)

6.17 Write code to "unmask" the first and last characters from a password that has been stored in a variable named **pword**. Display the results to the user with an alert box. The alert box should say "Your password is X***…***Y" where X and Y are the first and last characters of the password and all the middle characters are *s.

6.18 Write code to check if a password, stored in a variable named **pword**, contains the character & (Unicode value = 38).

6.4   Selection Lists and More

There is one more form control that is often used—the selection list—which allows the user to select one or more options from a list or menu. We will discuss this one in this section and also discuss several attributes that can enhance the way the user uses the controls.

Selection Lists

A **selection list** is created using the **\<select>\</select> container tags.** It acts similar to \<ul>\</ul> HTML tags; it defines a container which will house options. Then, just as an unordered or ordered list in HTML contains list items, configured with \<li>\</li> tags, a selection list configures the items with **\<option>\</option> tags.** The general syntax for a selection list, where N is some number is as follows:

```
<select size = "N" name = "list_name" id = "list_id">
    <option value ="option1 value">some text </option>
    <option value ="option2 value">some text </option>
            ......
            ......
    <option value ="optionN value">some text </option>
    </select>
```

The \<option> tag can contain the **selected property** which, when included and set to "selected" will display the value in that tag.

Example 6.15 demonstrates what a very plain selection list looks like. There are four items in the list. One has been chosen as the default selection but will change when the user makes another selection.

EXAMPLE 6.15

A Simple Selection List

```
1.    <html>
2.    <head>
3.    <title>Example 6.15</title>
4.    </head>
```

```
 5.    <body>
 6.    <h3>What color do you like best?</h3>
 7.    <select name="color" size = "5" id="color">
 8.        <option value = "favorite color: periwinkle"> periwinkle ⏎
                              </option>
 9.        <option value = "favorite color: fawn"> fawn</option>
10.        <option value = "favorite color: melon" selected = "selected">⏎
                              melon</option>
11.        <option value = "favorite color: mocha"> mocha</option>
12.        <option value = "favorite color: raspberry"> raspberry</option>
13.    </select>
14.    </body></html>
```

The page initially looks like this:

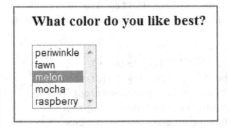

But after selecting raspberry, it looks like this:

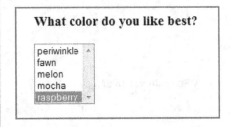

The selection box can be configured so that more than one selection can be made. It can also be created so that only one (or as many as desired) options presents initially and then shows a drop-down box that holds all the selections. You have probably seen this type of selection box on a website when you are asked to select your state from a list of U.S. states or your language from a list of many languages.

The size Attribute

The size attribute shows how many of the options will be visible. If size is set to 1 a drop-down list will automatically be created to show all the options. If the size is set to fewer than the number of options, a scroll bar is automatically added to allow the user to see all the options.

Example 6.16 creates two selection lists to demonstrate various uses of the size attribute. To save space, several option choices are on each line.

Using the `size` Attribute

```
1.    <html>
2.    <head>
3.    <title>Example 6.16</title>
4.    </head>
5.    <body>
6.    <h3>Where do you live?</h3>
7.    <select name="country" size = "1" id="country">
8.        <option>Australia</option> <option>Canada</option>
9.        <option>England</option> <option>France</option>
10.       <option>Germany</option> <option>Haiti</option>
11.       <option>India</option> <option>Japan</option>
12.       <option>Malaysia</option> <option>New Zealand</option>
13.       <option>Taiwan</option> <option>United States</option>
14.       <option>Venezuela</option> <option>Yugoslavia</option>
15.   </select>
16.   <h3>Where do you live?</h3>
17.   <select name="country" size = "5" id="country">
18.       <option>Australia</option> <option>Canada</option>
19.       <option>England</option> <option>France</option>
20.       <option>Germany</option> <option>Haiti</option>
21.       <option>India</option> <option>Japan</option>
22.       <option>Malaysia</option> <option>New Zealand</option>
23.       <option>Taiwan</option> <option>United States</option>
24.       <option>Venezuela</option> <option>Yugoslavia</option>
25.   </select>
26.   <body></html>
```

The page initially looks like this:

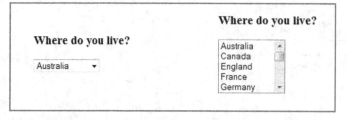

The drop-down menu shows all the items and scrolling to the end of the items with the scroll bar shows the last five items:

The multiple Attribute

When a selection list is created, by default the user is only allowed to select one item. However, the **multiple attribute** allows you to configure a selection box so the user is permitted to select more than one of the options. Sometimes this attribute may be useful but the user must hold down a particular key to select multiple items so it may be more complicated than it's worth.

As shown in Example 6.17, adding the multiple attribute to the <select> tag allows the user to select more than one option from a selection list. However, instructions on which button or key must be pressed at the same time should be included.

EXAMPLE 6.17

Using the multiple Attribute in a Selection List

```
1.   <html>
2.   <head>
3.   <title>Example 6.17</title>
4.   </head>
5.   <body>
6.   <h3>Select three favorite foods:</h3>
7.   <select multiple = "multiple" name="food" size = "10" id="food">
8.        <option>meatloaf</option>
9.        <option>macaroni and cheese</option>
10.       <option>pizza</option>
11.       <option>fish and chips</option>
12.       <option>fried chicken</option>
13.       <option>hamburgers and fries</option>
14.       <option>potato curry</option>
15.       <option>spaghetti</option>
16.       <option>sushi</option>
17.       <option>burritos</option>
18.  </select>
19.  <h3>You must hold down the CTRL key on a Windows computer <br />
20.  or the Command button on a Mac to select multiple options.</h3>
21.  </body></html>
```

The page will look like this if pizza, potato curry, and sushi are selected:

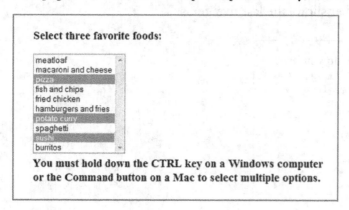

Enhancements for Form Elements

The tabindex Attribute

When a page contains several form controls, it is convenient to be able to tab from one to the next. The default action for the tab (I← →I) key is to move to the next form control. However, if you want to change the tab order you can do this with the **tabindex attribute.** By setting a tabindex value on each control, you can ensure that, when the user uses the tab to move to the next control, it will go to the control you have selected, regardless of where it exists on the form. If two form controls go to the same index value, the one that is coded first in the web page will be visited first.

The index value begins at 1 which may be surprising since we have seen other situations where values normally begin at 0. It may be hard to envision a use for this attribute but it might be fun to include the tabindex value on a game page to keep a player going back and forth between two controls.

The accesskey Attribute

The **accesskey attribute** allows you to assign a keyboard character as a hot key that the user can press to move the cursor immediately to a specific form control. The accesskey property can also be used to access any element with a specified access key. The following is the general syntax for any element:

```
element.accesskey = key_you_choose;
```

The syntax for a form control such as an input box is as follows:

```
<input type = "text" name = "box_name" id = "box_id accesskey = "b" />
```

However, the accesskey attribute is not supported by all browsers and requires that you add instructions. The user must press the ALT key along with the specified access key. Also, it is important to avoid using combinations that are already used by the operating system, like ALT + f which will display the file menu.

The onfocus Event

The **onfocus event** happens when an element gets focus. If the element is an input box, this means it gets focus when the cursor is clicked into the box. There are many events that can occur when an element is accessed and we have used some of them. Here, we will use the onfocus event to add a little pizazz to a form. The general syntax for using the onfocus event in an HTML document is as follows:

```
<element onfocus = "JavaScript code" >
```

The general syntax for using the onfocus event in JavaScript is as follows:

```
object.onfocus = "JavaScript code";
```

An Introduction to the this Keyword

The **this keyword** is one of the most powerful JavaScript keywords and perhaps one of the hardest to define. The this keyword always refers to the function or element that you are referring to. It appears in multiple situations which we will discuss and use more often in upcoming chapters. For now, we will learn how it is used in Example 6.18. Consider this example an introduction to using the this keyword in more complex situations. The syntax of the this keyword is as follows:

```
<input type="text" name="box_name" id="box_id" onfocus = ⌐
"setFunction(this.id)" />
```

In this case, the this keyword, combined with .id, identifies the id of this textbox. We could also have specified the exact id of this textbox but there are many situations when using the this keyword is preferable. It will give you much more control over your programs and allow one function or event to be used in various situations where the exact id (or whatever property the this keyword refers to) is not known.

The next example combines the use of the onfocus event, the this keyword, and the tabindex attribute to create a form that is a little silly and makes the form a little more fun. We will use some of the enhancements in the next section and in the Review Exercises.

EXAMPLE 6.18

Having Fun with a Form

This example creates a form that asks a user to enter some information about him or herself. However, by using the tabindex attribute, the user will be taken to boxes out of order. By using the onfocus event, each box will change color when the user begins typing in that box. Several styles have been added to the <head> section to add a new text color to the page and to center the form elements. Each textbox requires a different background color. These color functions are called when a box gets focus. We need to send the id of the box in focus to the function. Instead of coding each id individually, we have used the this keyword to identify the id of the box. Functions and styles that are short have been put on one line to save space.

```
1.   <html>
2.   <head>
3.   <title>Example 6.18</title>
4.   <script>
5.   function setYellow(x)
6.   {        document.getElementById(x).style.background="yellow";   }
7.   function setKhaki(x)
8.   {        document.getElementById(x).style.background="khaki";    }
9.   function setGreen(x)
10.  {        document.getElementById(x).style.background="green";    }
11.  function setOrange(x)
12.  {        document.getElementById(x).style.background="orange";   }
13.  function setRed(x)
14.  {        document.getElementById(x).style.background="red";      }
15.  function setPurple(x)
16.  {        document.getElementById(x).style.background="purple";   }
17.  function getFname(firstname)
18.  {
19.       var fName = document.getElementById(firstname).value;
20.       document.getElementById('first_name').innerHTML = fName;
21.  }
22.  function getLname(lastname)
23.  {
24.       var lName = document.getElementById(lastname).value;
25.       document.getElementById('last_name').innerHTML = lName;
26.  }
27.  function getNname(nickname)
28.  {
29.       var nName = document.getElementById(nickname).value;
30.       document.getElementById('nick_name').innerHTML = nName;
31.  }
32.  function getCar(car)
33.  {
34.       var dreamCar = document.getElementById(car).value;
35.       document.getElementById('dream_car').innerHTML = dreamCar;
36.  }
37.  function getMeal(meal)
38.  {
39.       var favMeal = document.getElementById(meal).value;
40.       document.getElementById('favorite_meal').innerHTML = favMeal;
41.  }
42.  function getVacation(vacation)
43.  {
44.       var vacationSpot = document.getElementById(vacation).value;
45.       document.getElementById('vacation_spot').innerHTML = vacationSpot;
46.  }
47.  </script>
48.  <style type="text/css">
49.       body        {        margin: 5%;           }
50.       p           {        font-weight: bold;        color: #006A9D;       }
51.       label       {        font-weight: bold;        color: #006A9D;       }
52.       h3          {        color: #006A9D;       }
53.  </style>
54.  </head>
55.  <body>
56.  <h3><br />Fun with the Form</h3>
```

```
57.  <p>Enter your information in the boxes. After you are satisfied ↵
                with each entry, press the OK button to see the ↵
                information displayed below. Use the TAB key to ↵
                move from box to box and don't be surprised by ↵
                where the TABs take you.</p>
58.  <div style="width: 90%;">
59.  <div style="width: 33%; float: left;">
60.  <fieldset><label>First name:<br /></label>
61.      <input type="text" name="firstname" id="firstname" size = ↵
                "30" value = "" tabindex = "1" onfocus = ↵
                "setYellow(this.id)" />
62.      <input type ="button" onclick="getFname('firstname')" value ↵
                = "ok" tabindex = "1" /></button><br /><br />
63.  </fieldset></div>
64.  <div style="width: 33%; float: left;">
65.  <fieldset><label>Dream car:<br /></label>
66.      <input type="text" name="car" id="car" size = "30" value ↵
                = "" tabindex = "4" onfocus = "setKhaki(this.id)" />
67.      <input type ="button" onclick="getCar('car')" value = "ok" ↵
                tabindex = "4" /> </button><br /><br />
68.  </fieldset></div>
69.  <div style="width: 33%; float: left;">
70.  <fieldset><label>Dream vacation:<br /></label>
71.      <input type="text" name="vacation" id="vacation" size = "30" ↵
                value = "" tabindex = "6" onfocus = ↵
                "setGreen(this.id)" />
72.      <input type ="button" onclick="getVacation('vacation')" value ↵
                = "ok" tabindex = "6" /></button><br /><br />
73.  </fieldset></div>
74.  <div style="width: 33%; float: left;">
75.  <fieldset><label>Nickname:<br /></label>
76.      <input type="text" name="nickname" id="nickname" size = ↵
                "30" value = "" tabindex = "3" onfocus = ↵
                "setOrange(this.id)" />
77.      <input type ="button" onclick="getNname('nickname')" value ↵
                = "ok" tabindex = "3" /></button><br /><br />
78.  </fieldset></div>
79.  <div style="width: 33%; float: left;">
80.  <fieldset><label>Favorite meal:<br /></label>
81.      <input type="text" name="meal" id="meal" size = "30" value ↵
                = "" tabindex = "5" onfocus = "setRed(this.id)" />
82.      <input type ="button" onclick="getMeal('meal')" value = ↵
                "ok" tabindex = "5" /></button><br /><br />
83.  </fieldset></div>
84.  <div style="width: 33%; float: left;">
85.  <fieldset><label>Last name:<br /></label>
86.      <input type="text" name="lastname" id="lastname" size = ↵
                "30" value = "" tabindex = "2" onfocus = ↵
                "setPurple(this.id)" />
87.      <input type ="button" onclick="getLname('lastname')" value ↵
                = "ok" tabindex = "2" /></button><br /><br />
88.  </fieldset></div>
89.  <div style="clear:both;"></div>
90.  <div> <input type="reset" value="ooops! I made a mistake. Let ↵
                me start over." /><br /></div>
91.  <div>
```

```
92.  <h3>Your information:</h3>
93.  <p>First name: <span id = "first_name"> </span> <br />
94.  Last name: <span id = "last_name"> </span> <br />
95.  Nickname: <span id = "nick_name"> </span> <br />
96.  Dream car: <span id = "dream_car"> </span> <br />
97.  Favorite meal: <span id = "favorite_meal"> </span> <br />
98.  Vacation desired: <span id = "vacation_spot"> </span>
99.  </p></div>
100. </body></html>
```

If you create this program, the output will initially look like this:

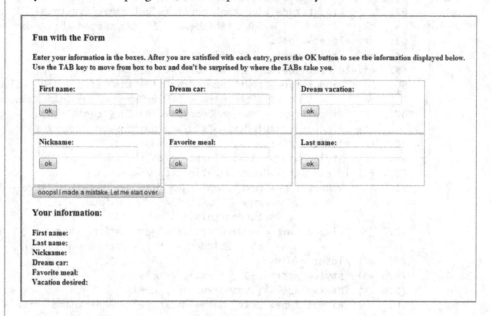

If the user enters the first name Mortimer, presses the OK button, and tabs to the next field, the page will look like this:

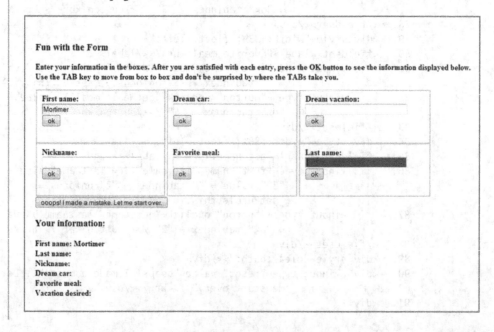

Notice that the tabindex property moved to the box with tabindex = "2" even though this is not the next box. Also, as soon as the user clicks the name box, the SetYellow(this.id) function is called. The id sent to this function is the id of the box which calls the function. In this case, this.id refers to the id of the name box which happens to be "firstname". After the user clicks OK the getFname() function is called, using the actual id of the box this function needs. The getfName() function displays the user's first name on the bottom of the page. Then, when the TAB is pressed, the user is moved to the next box and, since the last name box now has focus, the onfocus event changes its color to purple.

Finally, if the user enters the following information, clicks OK after each entry, and TABs through the boxes, the page will look like this:

Input: Mortimer Mahoney, aka mortyma, loves macaroni and meatballs, wants to drive a Mustang, and dreams of vacationing in Madagascar

Output:

An Image As an OK Button

We can add another feature to a web page to make it more interesting. Instead of using the default button for the player to click when an entry is finalized, we can design our own button. To do this, we create the image and, instead of using an input box, we insert the image between <a href> and </a> tags. Rather than linking to another web page or another place on a web page, we use the anchor tag to link to a JavaScript program. The general syntax is as follows:

```
<a href="JavaScript:function_name()"> <img src = "image_name.gif"></a>
```

If we substitute the following code for the default OK buttons in Example 6.18, using the ok.gif image that is supplied in the Student Data Files, the display of the program is changed to the one shown in Example 6.19. The exact same functions will be executed when the user clicks the new image. Since the code is identical to that in Example 6.18 except for the substitution, only the new code for the first textbox as shown.

EXAMPLE 6.19

An Image As an OK Button

```
1.  <fieldset>
2.  <label>First name:<br /></label>
3.  <input type="text" name="firstname" id="firstname" size = "30" value = "" ⏎
            tabindex = "1"  onfocus = "setYellow(this.id)" />
4.  <a href = "JavaScript:getFname('firstname')"> <img src = "ok.gif"></a>
5.  <br /><br /></fieldset>
```

Line 4 is where the image has been used as a button. If the substitutions are made for all the textboxes, the output, after the user has entered the first two pieces of information is as shown:

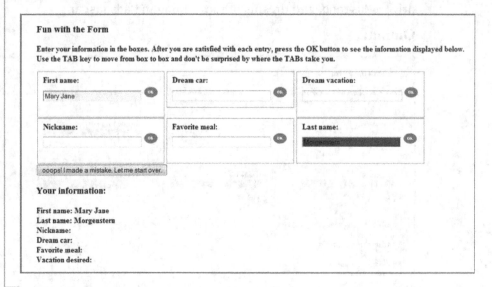

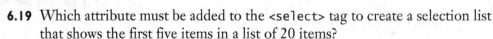

CHECKPOINT FOR SECTION 6.4 ✓

6.19 Which attribute must be added to the `<select>` tag to create a selection list that shows the first five items in a list of 20 items?

6.20 Which attribute must be added to the `<select>` tag to allow a user to select five items from a list of 20 items?

6.21 What value would you enter for the `size` attribute in a selection list if you wanted the items in the list to display as a drop-down menu?

6.22 Give one example of a place where it might be valuable to use the `tabindex` property in a form with several controls.

6.23 Give one example of when a hot key, using the `accesskey` property, might be useful.

6.24 Create a selection list that contains six types of cars but only the first two initially are revealed. A scroll bar should allow the user to view the rest of the items in the list.

6.5 Putting It to Work

Now we will create a Sign In page for the Greg's Gambits site for a player to create a user profile and a Progress Report form for the Carla's Classroom site for Carla to send assessments to her students' parents.

Greg's Gambits: Player Information and Inventory

The page we will create will be accessed from the Sign In link on Greg's home page. The page will allow a player to enter some personal information as well as information that should be saved and updated each time the player visits the site. Later, we will learn how to update this information dynamically as a game progresses. This requires the use of PHP and will be discussed in Chapters 11 and 12.

Now our page will allow the player to enter his or her real name, a username, the chosen avatar, and the items in the player's inventory (weapons and supplies) as well as the number of points amassed. We will use the form elements that we have discussed in this chapter and use JavaScript to allow the player to make changes to previous entries.

The page title should be Greg's Gambits | Player Inventory and the filename is signin.html.

Developing the Program

First we will design the form. The elements for each entry should be appropriate for that entry:

- Player's name: a textbox
- Username: a textbox
- Avatar: radio buttons (since only one avatar may be chosen)
- Player's points: a textbox
- Weapons: checkboxes (since more than one weapon can be in the inventory)
- Supplies: checkboxes (since a player normally has several supplies)

The Web Page Design For this page we will use one of the previous pages as a template. The new content will go into the content <div>. We'll include three textboxes for the player's name, username, and points. We can reuse code from Chapter 1 to display the possible avatars and use radio buttons to allow the user to select an avatar. We did this earlier in the text, but in this chapter, we'll use a JavaScript program to display the chosen avatar and its image in the inventory display area. We will also use checkboxes to allow the user to select three weapons and five items from a list of supplies. The HTML code for this, including calls to functions that we have not yet written, is as follows:

```
1.  <div id="content">
2.  <h2><br />Tell Greg About You</h2>
```

```
3.   <div><div><form name = "inventory">
4.   <fieldset><h3>Enter the following information:</h3>
5.   <p><label>Your name:<br /></label>
6.       <input type="text" id="realname" size = "40" value = ""/>
7.       <input type ="button" onclick="getRealName('realname')" ⏎
                 value = "ok"> </button></p>
8.   <p><label>Your username:<br /> </label>
9.       <input type="text" id="username" size="40" value = ""/>
10.      <input type ="button" onclick="getUsername('username')" ⏎
                 value = "ok"> </button></p>
11.  <p><label>Points to date:<br /></label>
12.      <input type="text" id="points" size = "10" value = ""/>
13.      <input type ="button" onclick="getPoints('points')" ⏎
                 value = "ok"> </button></p>
14.  </fieldset></div><div style="clear:both;"></div>
15.  <div> <table width = "100%" border = "2"> <br />
16.      <tr><td colspan = "5" class = "nobdr"><h3>Your Avatar </h3></td></tr>
17.      <tr><td class="nobdr"><img src="images/bunny.jpg" /></td>
18.      <td class="nobdr"> <img src="images/elf.jpg" /> </td>
19.      <td class="nobdr"> <img src="images/ghost.jpg" /></td>
20.      <td class="nobdr"><img src="images/princess.jpg" /></td>
21.      <td class="nobdr"><img src="images/wizard.jpg" /></td></tr>
22.      <tr><td class="nobdr"><input type = "radio" name = "avatar" ⏎
                 id = "bunny" value = "Bunny" onclick= ⏎
                 "pickAvatar('bunny')"/></td>
23.      <td class="nobdr"><input type = "radio" name = "avatar" ⏎
                 id = "elf" value = "Elf" ⏎
                 onclick="pickAvatar('elf')"/></td>
24.      <td class="nobdr"><input type = "radio" name = "avatar" ⏎
                 id = "ghost" value = "Ghost" ⏎
                 onclick="pickAvatar('ghost')"/> </td>
25.      <td class="nobdr"><input type = "radio" name = "avatar" ⏎
                 id = "princess" value = "Princess" ⏎
                 onclick="pickAvatar('princess')"/></td>
26.      <td class="nobdr"><input type = "radio" name = "avatar" ⏎
                 id = "wizard" value = "Wizard" ⏎
                 onclick="pickAvatar('wizard')"/> </td></tr>
27.      </table><div style="width: 50%; float: left;"><fieldset>
28.  <h3>Select three weapons to help you in your quest</h3>
29.      <input type="checkbox" name="weapons" id="w0" ⏎
                 value="Sword" />Sword<br />
30.      <input type="checkbox" name="weapons" id="w1" ⏎
                 value="Slingshot" />Slingshot<br />
31.      <input type="checkbox" name="weapons" id="w2" ⏎
                 value="Shield" />Shield<br />
32.      <input type="checkbox" name="weapons" id="w3" value="Bow ⏎
                 and 10 Arrows" />Bow and 10 Arrows<br />
33.      <input type="checkbox" name="weapons" id="w4" value="3 Magic ⏎
                 Rocks" />3 Magic Rocks<br />
34.      <input type="checkbox" name="weapons" id="w5" value= ⏎
                 "Knife" />Knife<br />
35.      <input type="checkbox" name="weapons" id="w6" ⏎
                 value="Staff" />Staff<br />
36.      <input type="checkbox" name="weapons" id="w7" value="Wizard's ⏎
                 Wand" />Wizard's Wand<br />
```

```
37.        <input type="checkbox" name="weapons" id="w8" value="Extra ↵
                  Arrows" />10 Extra Arrows<br />
38.        <input type="checkbox" name="weapons" id="w9" value="Cloak of ↵
                  Invisibility" />Cloak of Invisibility<br />
39.        <input type ="button" onclick="pickWeapons()" value = "Enter ↵
                  my selections" /></button></fieldset></div>
40. <div style="width: 50%; float: left;"><fieldset>
41. <h3>Select five items to carry with you on your journeys</h3>
42.        <input type="checkbox" name="supplies" id="s0" value="3-Day ↵
                  Food Supply" />3-Day Food Supply<br />
43.        <input type="checkbox" name="supplies" id="s1" value= ↵
                  "Backpack" />Backpack<br />
44.        <input type="checkbox" name="supplies" id="s2" value="Kevlar ↵
                  Vest" />Kevlar Vest<br />
45.        <input type="checkbox" name="supplies" id="s3" value="3-Day ↵
                  Water Bottle" />3-Day Supply of Water<br />
46.        <input type="checkbox" name="supplies" id="s4" value="Box of 5 ↵
                  Firestarters" />Box of 4 Firestarters<br />
47.        <input type="checkbox" name="supplies" id="s5" value= ↵
                  "Tent" />Tent<br />
48.        <input type="checkbox" name="supplies" id="s6" value="First ↵
                  Aid Kit" />First Aid Kit<br />
49.        <input type="checkbox" name="supplies" id="s7" value="Warm ↵
                  Jacket" />Warm Jacket<br />
50.        <input type="checkbox" name="supplies" id="s8" value="3 Pairs ↵
                  Extra Socks" />3 Pairs Extra Socks<br />
51.        <input type="checkbox" name="supplies" id="s9" value="Pen and ↵
                  Notebook" />Pen and Notebook<br />
52.        <input type ="button" onclick="pickSupplies()" value = "Enter ↵
                  my selections" /></button></fieldset></div>
53. </div><div style="clear:both;"></div>
54. <div ><br />
55.        <input type="reset" value="ooops! I made a mistake. Let me ↵
                  start over."><br />
56. </div><div style="width: 90%; float: left;">
57. <h3>Your information<br />
58. Your name: <span  id = "real_name"> </span> <br /><br />
59. Username: <span  id = "user_name"> </span> <br /><br />
60. Player points: <span id = "user_points"> </span> <br /><br />
61. Avatar: <span  id = "myavatar"> </span> <span id = "avatar_img"> ↵
                   </span><br /> <br />
62. Weapons:<br />
63.     <span id = "weapon_one"> </span> <br />
64.     <span id = "weapon_two"> </span><br />
65.     <span id = "weapon_three"> </span> <br /><br />
66. Supplies:<br />
67.     <span id = "supply_one"> </span> <br />
68.     <span id = "supply_two"> </span><br />
69.     <span id = "supply_three"> </span> <br />
70.     <span id = "supply_four"> </span><br />
71.     <span id = "supply_five"> </span> </h3></div>
72. </div></form><div style="clear:both;"></div>
```

The images you need to create this page are in the Student Data Files. Notice that each avatar image has been named specifically. The reason for this will be clear when we create the function to display both the text value of the avatar and its image. The web page now looks like this:

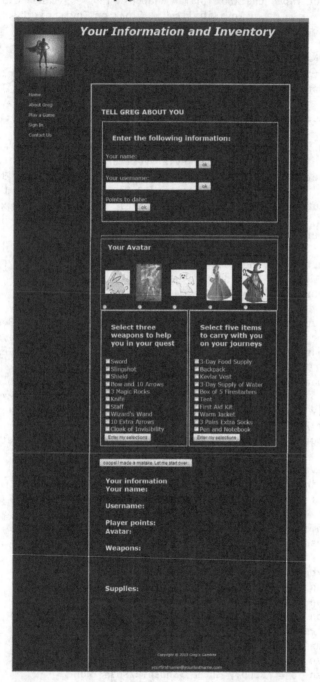

Writing the Code

Now we must begin to write the JavaScript that will extract the data from the form controls and display it on the bottom of the page. In Chapter 12, we will learn how to extract that information and send it, using PHP, to a database that maintains information about all the players to the site.

Some of the functions (those that get the player's name, username, and number of points) are relatively simple and virtually the same as those we wrote for the dinner menu earlier in this chapter. The same is true for the radio button that identifies the avatar, but we will add code to send the avatar image along with its text value to the inventory area. Identifying the three weapons and five supply items are more complex and will be explained in detail.

The Textbox Functions   The functions to get the player's name, username, and points are as follows:

```
1.   function getRealName(realname)
2.   {
3.       var real = document.getElementById(realname).value;
4.       document.getElementById('real_name').innerHTML = real;
5.   }
6.   function getUsername(username)
7.   {
8.       var user = document.getElementById(username).value;
9.       document.getElementById('user_name').innerHTML = user;
10.  }
11.  function getPoints(points)
12.  {
13.      var pts = document.getElementById(points).value;
14.      document.getElementById('user_points').innerHTML = pts;
15.  }
```

The Radio Buttons Function   The function to get the player's avatar and display it, along with the avatar image, is as follows:

```
1.   function pickAvatar(picked)
2.   {
3.       var avatar = document.getElementById(picked).value;
4.       document.getElementById('myavatar').innerHTML = avatar;
5.       document.getElementById('avatar_img').innerHTML = ("<img src ⌐
                            = 'images/" + avatar + ".jpg' />");
6.   }
```

The line in this code that is of interest to us is line 5. When we saved the avatar images, we made sure to save them with filenames that describe them exactly. The text value for a bunny avatar, for example, is bunny. This value is stored in the variable, **avatar**. The bunny image is also named bunny.jpg. The same is true for the ghost (image name is ghost.jpg), princess (image name is princess.jpg) and so on. Because this is the case, we can concatenate whatever value is in the variable, **avatar**, with .jpg on line 5 and use the innerHTML property to display the image corresponding with the value of **avatar** to the web page.

The Checkbox Functions   Previously, we created a function to extract two selections from a list of checkboxes. Now we must extract three items from the list of possible weapons and five from the supply list. We will use different logic to achieve these things. The function that identifies the three weapons is given, with an explanation following. The function for the supply list is almost the same, but expanded to account for the fact that we need to find five items.

```
1.   function pickWeapons()
2.   {
3.       var i = 0; var j = 0; var k = 0;
4.       var weapon1 = ""; var weapon2 = ""; var weapon3 = "";
5.       for (i=0; i <= 9; i++)
6.       {
7.           if (document.getElementById('w'+ i).checked == true)
8.           {
9.               weapon1 = document.getElementById('w'+ i).value;
10.              document.getElementById('weapon_one').innerHTML = weapon1;
11.              break;
12.          }
13.      }
14.      for (j=(i+1); j <=9; j++)
15.      {
16.          if (document.getElementById('w'+ j).checked == true)
17.          {
18.              weapon2 = document.getElementById('w'+ j).value;
19.              document.getElementById('weapon_two').innerHTML = weapon2;
20.              break;
21.          }
22.      }
23.      for (k=(j+1); k <=9; k++)
24.      {
25.          if (document.getElementById('w'+ k).checked == true)
26.          {
27.              weapon3 = document.getElementById('w'+ k).value;
28.              document.getElementById('weapon_three').innerHTML = weapon3; ↵
                 break;
29.          }
30.      }
31.  }
```

Notice that, in the loops that cycle through the checkboxes, each box is identified by its id. The boxes have been named 'w' (for weapons) or 's' (for supplies) and a number. The numbers begin at 0 so that they will correspond with a loop that begins at 0. We concatenate the letter 'w' in this function with the number in the counter (i on line 7) to create the id of any given checkbox.

There is a problem: If the program cycles through all the checkboxes, once it finds one checked box (on line 8), it assigns the value of that box to the variable weapon1. Now we need to look through the rest of the checkboxes to find weapon2 and weapon3. Instead of using a flag, as we did in the menu program, we use a second loop that begins where the first loop left off. Once a checked box has been identified in the first loop, the first weapon's value is stored in weapon1 (line 9) and this value is sent to the web page (line 10). Then the break statement forces this loop to end. Now the second loop begins with a new counter (line 14). We do not want this loop to look through the values previously checked so we begin this loop at the value right after the first loop ended. In this case, the new loop begins at i + 1. If the first checked box was the box with id = 4, the second loop begins at the box with id = 5.

The second loop does exactly the same thing as the first loop. However, when it encounters a second checked checkbox, this value is assigned to weapon2, the value is sent to the web page, and the loop ends. If, for example, the second checkbox that was selected has id = 7, we only need to check the final two checkboxes in the list to find the third weapon.

Now we begin a third loop (line 23) which starts at the id value immediately following the one that has been identified as **weapon2**. This loop uses **k** as a counter and **k** begins at **j** + 1. The last items in the list are checked here. When a third checkbox that has been selected is identified, its value goes into **weapon3** (line 27) and the value displayed on the web page (line 28). There is no reason to break out of this loop because we have identified three weapons and displayed them so the function ends.

In a real program, we would add code to ensure that the player has not selected more than three weapons. However, this is enough for now and, regardless of how many weapons the player checks, only the first three selected will be displayed.

The code for the function that identifies and displays the supplies selected is almost the same. We only need to add two more loops, with new counters, to identify a fourth and fifth selection. The new counters are **m** and **p**. These letters have been selected simply because the lowercase l looks very much like a lowercase i and the lowercase o can be easily confused with the number 0. Any counters that you like would, of course, be fine.

Putting It All Together

We are ready to put it all together. We did not include error checking in this program. If you were coding this for an active site, you would have to include error checking. Error checking should be done for the following situations; you may be able to think of others. In Chapter 7, when we discuss JavaScript source files, you will learn to include error checking without increasing the size of your main program and without duplicating code. For now, consider these situations and think about how you could check for errors:

- a name or username that exceeds a predetermined length (do you want a user to have a 4,567-character username?)

- a value entered for Points that is not a number, is a negative number, or is outside a range that is appropriate for your game site

- too many or too few items selected from the two checkbox fields

For now, we will assume the player enters valid information. The code for the whole page, therefore, is as follows:

```
1.   <html><head>
2.   <title>Greg's Gambits | Player Inventory</title>
3.   <link href="greg.css" rel="stylesheet" type="text/css" />
4.   <script>
5.   function pickAvatar(picked)
6.   {
7.       var avatar = document.getElementById(picked).value;
8.       document.getElementById('myavatar').innerHTML = avatar;
9.       document.getElementById('avatar_img').innerHTML = ("<img src ↵
                  = 'images/"+ avatar + ".jpg' />");
10.  }
```

```
11.   function getRealName(realname)
12.   {
13.       var real = document.getElementById(realname).value;
14.       document.getElementById('real_name').innerHTML = real;
15.   }
16.   function getUsername(username)
17.   {
18.       var user = document.getElementById(username).value;
19.       document.getElementById('user_name').innerHTML = user;
20.   }
21.   function getPoints(points)
22.   {
23.       var pts = document.getElementById(points).value;
24.       document.getElementById('user_points').innerHTML = pts;
25.   }
26.   function pickWeapons()
27.   {
28.       var i = 0; var j = 0; var k = 0;
29.       var weapon1 = ""; var weapon2 = ""; var weapon3 = "";
30.       for (i = 0; i <= 9; i++)
31.       {
32.           if (document.getElementById('w'+i).checked == true)
33.           {
34.               weapon1 = document.getElementById('w'+i).value;
35.               document.getElementById('weapon_one').innerHTML = weapon1;
36.               break;
37.           }
38.       }
39.       for (j = (i+1); j <=9; j++)
40.       {
41.           if (document.getElementById('w'+j).checked == true)
42.           {
43.               weapon2 = document.getElementById('w'+j).value;
44.               document.getElementById('weapon_two').innerHTML = weapon2;
45.               break;
46.           }
47.       }
48.       for (k = (j+1); k <=9; k++)
49.       {
50.           if (document.getElementById('w'+k).checked == true)
51.           {
52.               weapon3 = document.getElementById('w'+k).value;
53.               document.getElementById('weapon_three').innerHTML = weapon3; ⏎
                      break;
54.           }
55.       }
56.   }
57.   function pickSupplies()
58.   {
59.       var i = 0; var j = 0; var k = 0; var m = 0; var p = 0;
60.       var supply1 = ""; var supply2 = ""; var supply3 = "";
61.       var supply4 = ""; var supply5 = "";
62.       for (i = 0; i <= 9; i++)
63.       {
64.           if (document.getElementById('s'+i).checked == true)
65.           {
66.               supply1 = document.getElementById('s'+i).value;
```

```
67.                        document.getElementById('supply_one').innerHTML = supply1;
68.                        break;
69.                    }
70.            }
71.        for (j = (i+1); j <=9; j++)
72.            {
73.                    if (document.getElementById('s'+j).checked == true)
74.                    {
75.                        supply2 = document.getElementById('s'+j).value;
76.                        document.getElementById('supply_two').innerHTML = supply2;
77.                        break;
78.                    }
79.            }
80.        for (k = (j+1); k <=9; k++)
81.            {
82.                    if (document.getElementById('s'+k).checked == true)
83.                    {
84.                        supply3 = document.getElementById('s'+k).value;
85.                        document.getElementById('supply_three').innerHTML = supply3;
86.                        break;
87.                    }
88.            }
89.        for (m = (k+1); m <=9; m++)
90.            {
91.                    if (document.getElementById('s'+m).checked == true)
92.                    {
93.                        supply4 = document.getElementById('s'+m).value;
94.                        document.getElementById('supply_four').innerHTML = supply4;
95.                        break;
96.                    }
97.            }
98.        for (p = (m+1); p <=9; p++)
99.            {
100.                    if (document.getElementById('s'+p).checked == true)
101.                    {
102.                        supply5 = document.getElementById('s'+p).value;
103.                        document.getElementById('supply_five').innerHTML = supply5; ⏎
                               break;
104.                    }
105.            }
106.  }
107.  </script></head>
108.  <body>
109.  <div id="container">
110.  <img src="images/superhero.jpg" class="floatleft" />
111.  <h1 align="center"><em>Your Information and Inventory</em></h1>
112.  <div style ="clear:both;"></div>
113.  <div id="nav">
114.        <p><a href="index.html">Home</a>
115.        <a href="greg.html">About Greg</a>
116.        <a href="play_games.html">Play a Game</a>
117.        <a href="sign.html">Sign In</a>
118.        <a href="contact.html">Contact Us</a></p>
119.        </div>
120.  <div id="content">
121.  <h2><br />Tell Greg About You</h2>
122.  <div>
```

```
123.    <div><form name = "inventory"><fieldset>
124.        <h3>Enter the following information:</h3>
125.        <p><label>Your name:<br /></label>
126.        <input type="text" id="realname" size = "40" value = ""/>
127.        <input type ="button" onclick="getRealName('realname')" value = "ok">↵
                            </button></p>
128.        <p><label>Your username:<br /> </label>
129.        <input type="text" id="username" size="40" value = ""/></label>
130.        <input type="button" onclick="getUsername('username')" value = "ok"> ↵
                            </button></p>
131.        <p><label>Points to date:<br /></label>
132.        <input type="text" id="points" size = "10" value = ""/>
133.        <input type ="button" onclick="getPoints('points')" value = "ok"> ↵
                            </button></p>
134.        </fieldset></div><div style="clear:both;"></div>
135.        <div> <table width = "100%" border = "2"> <br />
136.        <tr><td colspan = "5" class = "nobdr"><h3>Your Avatar </h3></td></tr>
137.        <tr><td class="nobdr"><img src="images/bunny.jpg" /></td>
138.        <td class="nobdr"> <img src="images/elf.jpg" /> </td>
139.        <td class="nobdr"> <img src="images/ghost.jpg" /></td>
140.        <td class="nobdr"><img src="images/princess.jpg" /></td>
141.        <td class="nobdr"><img src="images/wizard.jpg" /></td></tr>
142.        <tr><td class="nobdr"><input type = "radio" name = "avatar" ↵
                            id = "bunny" value = "Bunny" ↵
                            onclick="pickAvatar('bunny')"/></td>
142.        <td class="nobdr"><input type = "radio" name = "avatar" ↵
                            id = "elf" value = "Elf" ↵
                            onclick="pickAvatar('elf')"/></td>
143.        <td class="nobdr"><input type = "radio" name = "avatar" ↵
                            id = "ghost" value = "Ghost" ↵
                            onclick="pickAvatar('ghost')"/> </td>
144.        <td class="nobdr"><input type = "radio" name = "avatar" ↵
                            id = "princess" value = "Princess" ↵
                            onclick="pickAvatar('princess')"/></td>
145.        <td class="nobdr"><input type = "radio" name = "avatar" id =↵
                            "wizard" value = "Wizard" onclick = ↵
                            "pickAvatar('wizard')"/></td></tr>
146.        </table>
147.    <div style="width: 50%; float: left;"><fieldset>
148.        <h3>Select three weapons to help you in your quest</h3>
149.        <input type="checkbox" name = "weapons" id="w0" ↵
                            value = "Sword" />Sword<br />
150.        <input type="checkbox" name = "weapons" id="w1" ↵
                            value = "Slingshot" />Slingshot<br />
151.        <input type="checkbox" name = "weapons" id="w2" ↵
                            value = "Shield" />Shield<br />
152.        <input type="checkbox" name = "weapons" id="w3" value = "Bow ↵
                            and 10 Arrows" />Bow and 10 Arrows<br />
153.        <input type="checkbox" name = "weapons" id="w4" value = ↵
                            "3 Magic Rocks" />3 Magic Rocks<br />
154.        <input type="checkbox" name = "weapons" id="w5" ↵
                            value = "Knife" />Knife<br />
155.        <input type="checkbox" name = "weapons" id="w6" value = ↵
                            "Staff" />Staff<br />
156.        <input type="checkbox" name = "weapons" id="w7" value = ↵
                            "Wizard's Wand" />Wizard's Wand<br />
157.        <input type="checkbox" name = "weapons" id="w8" value = ↵
                            "Extra Arrows" />10 Extra Arrows<br />
```

```
158.        <input type="checkbox" name = "weapons" id="w9" value = "Cloak of ↵
                        Invisibility" /> Cloak of Invisibility<br />
159.        <input type ="button" onclick="pickWeapons()" value = "Enter my ↵
                        selections" /></button>
160.  </fieldset></div>
161.  <div style="width: 50%; float: left;"><fieldset>
162.        <h3>Select five items to carry with you on your journeys</h3>
163.        <input type="checkbox" name="supplies" id="s0" value="3-Day ↵
                        Food Supply" />3-Day Food Supply<br />
164.        <input type="checkbox" name="supplies" id="s1" value= ↵
                        "Backpack" />Backpack<br />
165.        <input type="checkbox" name="supplies" id="s2" value= ↵
                        "Kevlar Vest" />Kevlar Vest<br />
166.        <input type="checkbox" name="supplies" id="s3" value="3-Day ↵
                        Water Supply" />3-Day Supply of Water<br />
167.        <input type="checkbox" name="supplies" id="s4" value= "Box of 5 ↵
                        Firestarters" />Box of 5 Firestarters<br />
168.        <input type="checkbox" name="supplies" id="s5" value= "Tent" /> ↵
                        Tent<br />
169.        <input type="checkbox" name="supplies" id="s6" value="First Aid Kit" /> ↵
                        First Aid Kit<br />
170.        <input type="checkbox" name="supplies" id="s7" value="Warm Jacket" /> ↵
                        Warm Jacket<br />
171.        <input type="checkbox" name="supplies" id="s8" value="3 Pairs ↵
                        Extra Socks" />3 Pairs Extra Socks<br />
172.        <input type="checkbox" name="supplies" id="s9" value="Pen and ↵
                        Notebook" />Pen and Notebook<br />
173.        <input type ="button" onclick="pickSupplies()" value = ↵
                        "Enter my selections" /></button>
174.  </fieldset></div>
175.  </div><div style="clear:both;"></div>
176.  <div> <br /><input type="reset" value="ooops! I made a mistake. ↵
                        Let me start over."><br /></div></form>
177.  <div style="width: 90%; float: left;">
178.        <h3>Your information<br />
179.        Your name: <span  id = "real_name"> </span> <br /><br />
180.        Username: <span  id = "user_name"> </span> <br /><br />
181.        Player points: <span  id = "user_points"> </span><br />
182.        Avatar: <span  id = "myavatar"> </span> <span id = ↵
                        "avatar_img"> </span><br /> <br />
183.        Weapons:<br />
184.        <span id = "weapon_one"> </span> <br />
185.        <span id = "weapon_two"> </span><br />
186.        <span id = "weapon_three"> </span> <br /><br />
187.        Supplies:<br />
188.        <span id = "supply_one"> </span> <br />
189.        <span id = "supply_two"> </span><br />
190.        <span id = "supply_three"> </span> <br />
191.        <span id = "supply_four"> </span><br />
192.        <span id = "supply_five"> </span> </h3></div>
193.  </div><div style="clear:both;"></div>
194.  <div id="footer">
195.        Copyright &copy; 2013 Greg's Gambits<br />
196.        <a href="mailto:yourfirstname@yourlastname.com"> ↵
                        yourfirstname@yourlastname.com</a>
197.  </div>
198.  </div></body></html>
```

Finishing Up

Here are some sample displays as various players enter information:

input: Ken Kang goes by the username casper because he is a ghost and he has 4,895 points. He chooses Magic Rocks, a knife, and an invisibility cloak for his weapons and he wants to bring food, water, a tent, firestarters, and a pen and notebook with him on his journey.

output:

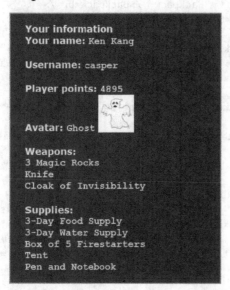

```
Your information
Your name: Ken Kang

Username: casper

Player points: 4895

Avatar: Ghost

Weapons:
3 Magic Rocks
Knife
Cloak of Invisibility

Supplies:
3-Day Food Supply
3-Day Water Supply
Box of 5 Firestarters
Tent
Pen and Notebook
```

input: Alicia Alba likes to be called PerkyPrincess and chooses the princess as an avatar. She has 12,345 points. Her weapons of choice are a sword, a shield, and a slingshot and she chooses food, water, a warm jacket, a first aid kit, and a backpack to bring on her journey.

output:

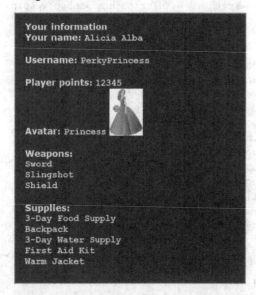

```
Your information
Your name: Alicia Alba

Username: PerkyPrincess

Player points: 12345

Avatar: Princess

Weapons:
Sword
Slingshot
Shield

Supplies:
3-Day Food Supply
Backpack
3-Day Water Supply
First Aid Kit
Warm Jacket
```

Carla's Classroom: Carla's Progress Report Form

In this section, we will develop a form that Carla will use to send progress reports to her students' parents or guardians. The form will generate an email message sent to Carla which she can forward to the parent or file for her own records.

Developing the Program

There are three steps involved in developing this program. First, we will design the page, deciding on what types of reporting Carla wants. Then, we will decide which form elements are best for each option and design a page that includes those elements. Finally, we will write the JavaScript code needed to retrieve the data, display it on the page, and send it as an email.

Carla's Categories   Carla wants to send the following information to her students' parents:

- Homework average
- Exam average
- Attendance
- Arithmetic progress
- Reading progress
- Writing progress
- An overall grade

She also needs to include the student's name and wants an area to include her own comments.

The Page Design   We decide on the following form elements for each item:

- Student name: a textbox
- Homework average: a textbox
- Exam average: a textbox
- Attendance: radio buttons with options for Excellent, Satisfactory, Needs Improvement
- Arithmetic progress: radio buttons with options for Excellent, Satisfactory, Needs Improvement
- Reading progress: radio buttons with options for Excellent, Satisfactory, Needs Improvement
- Writing progress: radio buttons with options for Excellent, Satisfactory, Needs Improvement
- An overall grade: radio buttons with options for A, B, C, D, and F
- Comments: a textarea box

- A reset button
- A submit button which will create an email to be sent to Carla

After we design the page we will write the functions to retrieve the data.

Creating the Form

Let's first place a link to this page on Carla's home page. Open the `carla.html` file and replace the default code in the content area as shown below. Line 3 refers to a survey you can create in the Programming Challenges at the end of the chapter. Line 4 creates a link to the new page we are creating.

```
1.   <div id="content">
2.   <p><img src="images/carla_pic.jpg" class="floatleft" /> Who is Carla? ↵
         Carla is a teacher who cares about her students!</p>
3.   <p>Help Carla improve! Take the Rate Carla survey now.</p>
4.   <p><a href= "carla_progress.html">Carla's Progress Report Form</a></p>
5.   </div>
```

The filename of the new page will be `carla_progress.html`. At this point, your `carla.html` page will look like this:

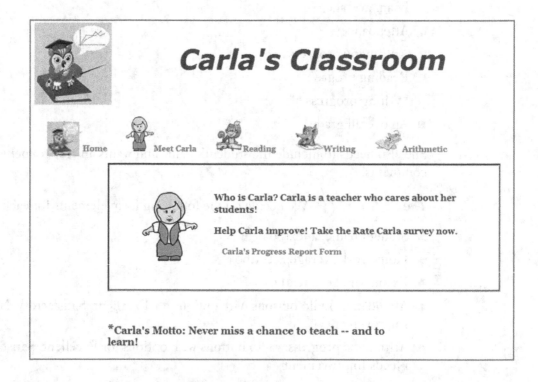

For our new Progress Report page we will use one of the previous pages as a template. However, since this page is part of the `Carla's Classroom` website but is not used by students to link to classroom exercises, we can dispense with the navigation links at the top and the image of Carla in the content area. The form will go into the content `<div>`. We'll include three textboxes for the student's name, homework average, and test average. We will also use radio buttons to allow Carla to check off one of three descriptions of the student's progress in arithmetic, reading, and writing, as well as the student's attendance. These four radio button groups can be neatly displayed in a table. We will also use radio buttons for the overall grade and a textarea box for Carla to enter her comments about each student. The page title should be `Carla's Classroom | Progress Report Form`. The HTML code for this, including calls to functions that we have not written, is as follows:

```
1.    <html>
2.    <head>
3.    <title>Carla's Classroom | Progress Report Form</title>
4.    <link href="carla.css" rel="stylesheet" type="text/css" />
5.    </head>
6.    <body>
7.    <form>
8.    <div id="container">
9.        <img src="images/owl_reading.jpg" class="floatleft" />
10.       <h2 id="logo"><em>Carla's Progress Report</em></h2>
11.   </div><div style="clear:both;"></div>
12.   <div id="content">
13.       <p><label>Student's name:</label>
14.       <input type="text" name = "Student Name: "id="stu_name" ⏎
                      size = "40" value = ""/>
15.       <input type ="button" onclick="getName('stu_name')" ⏎
                      value = "ok"></button></p>
16.       <p><label>Homework average:</label>
17.       <input type="text" name = "Homework Average: " id="hw_avg" ⏎
                      size="8" value = ""/>
18.       <input type ="button" onclick="getHW('hw_avg')" value = "ok"> ⏎
                      </button>     
19.       <label>Test average:</label>
20.       <input type="text" name = "Test Average:" id="test_avg" ⏎
                      size="8" value = ""/>
21.       <input type ="button" onclick="getTest('test_avg')" value = ⏎
                      "ok"></button></p>
22.   <table width = "100%">
23.       <tr><td><h4>attendance</h4></td><td><h4>arithmetic</h4></td>
24.       <td><h4>reading</h4></td><td><h4>writing</h4></td></tr>
25.       <tr><td><input type = "radio" name = "Attendance: " id = "a1" ⏎
                      value = "excellent" onclick = ⏎
                      "getAttendance('a1')"/>Excellent</td>
26.       <td><input type = "radio" name = "Arithmetic: " id = "m1" ⏎
                      value = "excellent" onclick = ⏎
                      "getArithmetic('m1')"/>Excellent</td>
27.       <td><input type = "radio" name = "Reading: " id = "r1" ⏎
                      value = "excellent" onclick = ⏎
                      "getReading('r1')"/>Excellent</td>
28.       <td><input type = "radio" name = "Writing: " id = "w1" ⏎
                      value = "excellent" onclick = ⏎
                      "getWrite('w1')"/>Excellent</td></tr>
29.       <tr><td><input type = "radio" name = "Attendance: " id = "a2" ⏎
                      value = "satisfactory" onclick = ⏎
                      "getAttendance('a2')"/>Satisfactory</td>
```

```
30.        <td><input type = "radio" name = "Arithmetic: " id = "m2" ↵
                       value = "satisfactory" onclick = ↵
                       "getArithmetic('m2')"/>Satisfactory</td>
31.        <td><input type = "radio" name = "Reading: " id = "r2" ↵
                       value = "satisfactory" onclick = ↵
                       "getReading('r2')"/>Satisfactory</td>
32.        <td><input type = "radio" name = "Writing: " id = "w2" ↵
                       value = "satisfactory" onclick = ↵
                       "getWrite('w2')"/>Satisfactory</td></tr>
33.        <tr><td><input type = "radio" name = "Attendance: " id = "a3" ↵
                       value = "needs improvement" onclick = ↵
                       "getAttendance('a3')"/>Needs Improvement</td>
34.        <td><input type = "radio" name = "Arithmetic: " id = "m3" ↵
                       value = "needs improvement" onclick = ↵
                       "getArithmetic('m3')"/>Needs Improvement</td>
35.        <td><input type = "radio" name = "Reading: " id = "r3" ↵
                       value = "needs improvement" onclick = ↵
                       "getReading('r3')"/>Needs Improvement</td>
36.        <td><input type = "radio" name = "Writing: " id = "w3" ↵
                       value = "needs improvement" onclick = ↵
                       "getWrite('w3')"/>Needs Improvement</td></tr>
37.    </table>
38.    <p><label>Overall Semester Grade:</label>     
39.    <input type = "radio" name = "grade" id = "A" value = "A" ↵
                       onclick="getGrade('A')"/> A   
40.    <input type = "radio" name = "grade" id = "B" value = "B" ↵
                       onclick="getGrade('B')"/> B   
41.    <input type = "radio" name = "grade" id = "C" value = "C" ↵
                       onclick="getGrade('C')"/> C   
42.    <input type = "radio" name = "grade" id = "D" value = "D" ↵
                       onclick="getGrade('D')"/> D   
43.    <input type = "radio" name = "grade" id = "F" value = "F" ↵
                       onclick="getGrade('F')"/> F   </p>
44.    <p><textarea name="comments" id="comments" rows="5" cols="50"> ↵
                       Comments</textarea>
45.    <input type ="button" onclick="getComments('comments')" ↵
                       value = "ok"></button></p>
46.    <div><h3><u>Student Report</u><br />
47.        Student name: <span  id = "sName"> </span> <br />
48.        Homework Average: <span  id = "hw"> </span> <br />
49.        Test Average: <span  id = "test"> </span> <br />
50.        Attendance: <span  id = "att"> </span><br />
51.        Arithmetic: <span id = "math"> </span> <br />
52.        Reading: <span id = "read"> </span><br />
53.        Writing: <span id = "writng"> </span> <br />
54.        Overall Semester Grade: <span id="overall"> </span><br />
55.        Comments: <span id = "mycomments"> </span><br />
56.    </div><div style="clear:both;"></div>
57.    <p><input type="reset" value="Start over">   
58.    <input type = "submit" value ="Submit report"></p>
59.    </form></div>
60.    </div></body></html>
```

Your page will now look like this:

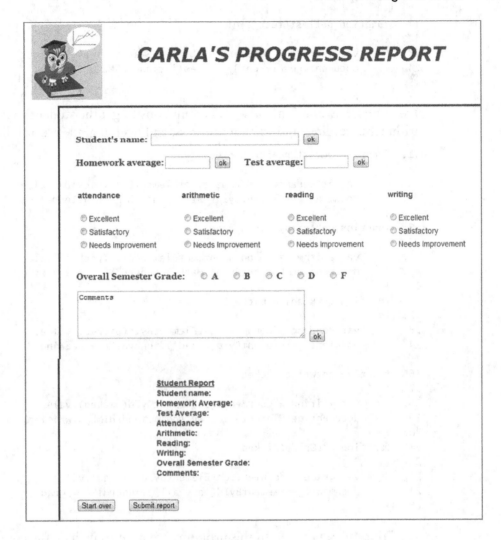

Now we will write the functions that will will create the report and generate the email.

Writing the Code

The Textbox Functions The functions to get the student's name, homework average, and test average are as follows:

```
1.   function getName(stu_name)
2.   {
3.        var studentName = document.getElementById(stu_name).value;
4.        document.getElementById('sName').innerHTML = studentName;
5.   }
6.   function getHW(hw_avg)
7.   {
8.        var hwAvg = document.getElementById(hw_avg).value;
9.        document.getElementById('hw').innerHTML = hwAvg;
10.  }
```

```
11.  function getTest(test_avg)
12.  {
13.       var testAvg = document.getElementById(test_avg).value;
14.       document.getElementById('test').innerHTML = testAvg;
15.  }
```

The Radio Buttons Functions   The functions to get the student's attendance, arithmetic, reading, and writing progress, and overall grade are as follows:

```
1.   function getAttendance(picked)
2.   {
3.        var attendance = document.getElementById(picked).value;
4.        document.getElementById('att').innerHTML = attendance;
5.   }
6.   function getArithmetic(picked)
7.   {
8.        var arithmetic = document.getElementById(picked).value;
9.        document.getElementById('math').innerHTML = arithmetic;
10.  }
11.  function getReading(picked)
12.  {
13.       var reading = document.getElementById(picked).value;
14.       document.getElementById('read').innerHTML = reading;
15.  }
16.  function getWrite(picked)
17.  {
18.       var writing = document.getElementById(picked).value;
19.       document.getElementById('writng').innerHTML = writing;
20.  }
21.  function getGrade(picked)
22.  {
23.       var grade = document.getElementById(picked).value;
24.       document.getElementById('overall').innerHTML = grade;
25.  }
```

The Textarea Function   In this program, we want to include the comments in our summary report at the end of the page. Therefore, we need a function to get the contents of the textarea box. The code for that function is as follows:

```
1.   function getComments(comments)
2.   {
3.        var carlaComments = document.getElementById(comments).value;
4.        document.getElementById('mycomments').innerHTML = carlaComments;
5.   }
```

Generating the Email   We add the following code to the opening <form> tag so that, when Carla clicks the submit button, an email is generated which she can send to herself. She can, at that time, add a parent's email address and send the email to herself and the parent. Notice that we have included "Student Progress Report" as the subject line.

```
<form name="progress" action="mailto:carla@carlaschool.net?subject=
Student Progress Report" method="post" enctype="text/plain">
```

Putting It All Together

Now we will put the entire program together.

```
1.   <html>
2.   <head>
3.   <title>Carla's Classroom | Progress Report Form</title>
4.   <link href="carla.css" rel="stylesheet" type="text/css" />
5.   <script>
6.   function getName(stu_name)
7.   {
8.        var studentName = document.getElementById(stu_name).value;
9.        document.getElementById('sName').innerHTML = studentName;
10.  }
11.  function getHW(hw_avg)
12.  {
13.       var hwAvg = document.getElementById(hw_avg).value;
14.       document.getElementById('hw').innerHTML = hwAvg;
15.  }
16.  function getTest(test_avg)
17.  {
18.       var testAvg = document.getElementById(test_avg).value;
19.       document.getElementById('test').innerHTML = testAvg;
20.  }
21.  function getAttendance(picked)
22.  {
23.       var attendance = document.getElementById(picked).value;
24.       document.getElementById('att').innerHTML = attendance;
25.  }
26.  function getArithmetic(picked)
27.  {
28.       var arithmetic = document.getElementById(picked).value;
29.       document.getElementById('math').innerHTML = arithmetic;
30.  }
31.  function getReading(picked)
32.  {
33.       var reading = document.getElementById(picked).value;
34.       document.getElementById('read').innerHTML = reading;
35.  }
36.  function getWrite(picked)
37.  {
38.       var writing = document.getElementById(picked).value;
39.       document.getElementById('writng').innerHTML = writing;
40.  }
41.  function getGrade(picked)
42.  {
43.       var grade = document.getElementById(picked).value;
44.       document.getElementById('overall').innerHTML = grade;
45.  }
46.  function getComments(comments)
47.  {
48.       var carlaComments = document.getElementById(comments).value;
49.       document.getElementById('mycomments').innerHTML = carlaComments;
50.  }
51.  </script>
52.  </head>
53.  <body>
54.  <form name = "progress" action = ↵
                 "mailto:carla@carlaschool.net?subject=Student ↵
                 Progress Report" method = "post" enctype = "text/plain">>
55.  <div id="container">
56.       <img src="images/owl_reading.jpg" class="floatleft" />
```

```
57.          <h2 id="logo"><em>Carla's Progress Report</em></h2>
58.     </div><div style="clear:both;"></div>
59.     <div id="content">
60.          <p><label>Student's name:</label>
61.          <input type="text" name = "Student Name: "id="stu_name" ↵
                        size = "40" value = ""/>
62.          <input type ="button" onclick="getName('stu_name')" ↵
                        value = "ok"></button></p>
63.          <p><label>Homework average:</label>
64.          <input type="text" name = "Homework Average: " id="hw_avg" ↵
                        size="8" value = ""/>
65.          <input type ="button" onclick="getHW('hw_avg')" value = "ok">↵
                        </button>     
66.          <label>Test average:</label>
67.          <input type="text" name = "Test Average:" id="test_avg" ↵
                        size="8" value = ""/>
68.          <input type ="button" onclick="getTest('test_avg')" value = "ok"> ↵
                        </button></p>
69.     <table width = "100%">
70.          <tr><td><h4>attendance</h4></td><td><h4>arithmetic</h4></td>
71.          <td><h4>reading</h4></td><td><h4>writing</h4></td></tr>
72.          <tr><td><input type = "radio" name = "Attendance: " id = "a1" ↵
                        value = "excellent" onclick = ↵
                        "getAttendance('a1')"/>Excellent</td>
73.          <td><input type = "radio" name = "Arithmetic: " id = "m1" ↵
                        value = "excellent" onclick = ↵
                        "getArithmetic('m1')"/>Excellent</td>
74.          <td><input type = "radio" name = "Reading: " id = "r1" ↵
                        value = "excellent" onclick = ↵
                        "getReading('r1')"/>Excellent</td>
75.          <td><input type = "radio" name = "Writing: " id = "w1" ↵
                        value = "excellent" onclick = ↵
                        "getWrite('w1')"/>Excellent</td></tr>
76.          <tr><td><input type = "radio" name = "Attendance: " id = "a2" ↵
                        value = "satisfactory" onclick = ↵
                        "getAttendance('a2')"/>Satisfactory</td>
77.          <td><input type = "radio" name = "Arithmetic: " id = "m2" ↵
                        value = "satisfactory" onclick = ↵
                        "getArithmetic('m2')"/>Satisfactory</td>
78.          <td><input type = "radio" name = "Reading: " id = "r2" ↵
                        value = "satisfactory" onclick = ↵
                        "getReading('r2')"/>Satisfactory</td>
79.          <td><input type = "radio" name = "Writing: " id = "w2" ↵
                        value = "satisfactory" onclick = ↵
                        "getWrite('w2')"/>Satisfactory</td></tr>
80.          <tr><td><input type = "radio" name = "Attendance: " id = "a3" ↵
                        value = "needs improvement" onclick = ↵
                        "getAttendance('a3')"/>Needs Improvement</td>
81.          <td><input type = "radio" name = "Arithmetic: " id = "m3" ↵
                        value = "needs improvement" onclick = ↵
                        "getArithmetic('m3')"/>Needs Improvement</td>
82.          <td><input type = "radio" name = "Reading: " id = "r3" ↵
                        value = "needs improvement" onclick = ↵
                        "getReading('r3')"/>Needs Improvement</td>
83.          <td><input type = "radio" name = "Writing: " id = "w3" ↵
                        value = "needs improvement" onclick = ↵
                        "getWrite('w3')"/>Needs Improvement</td></tr>
```

```
84.  </table>
85.  <p><label>Overall Semester Grade:</label>     
86.  <input type = "radio" name = "grade" id = "A" value = "A" ↵
                        onclick="getGrade('A')"/> A   
87.  <input type = "radio" name = "grade" id = "B" value = "B" ↵
                        onclick="getGrade('B')"/> B   
88.  <input type = "radio" name = "grade" id = "C" value = "C" ↵
                        onclick="getGrade('C')"/> C   
89.  <input type = "radio" name = "grade" id = "D" value = "D" ↵
                        onclick="getGrade('D')"/> D   
90.  <input type = "radio" name = "grade" id = "F" value = "F" ↵
                        onclick="getGrade('F')"/> F   </p>
91.  <p><textarea name="comments" id="comments" rows="5" cols="50"> ↵
                        Comments</textarea>
92.  <input type ="button" onclick="getComments('comments')" ↵
                        value = "ok"></button></p>
93.  <div><h3><u>Student Report</u><br />
94.      Student Name: <span  id = "sName"> </span> <br />
95.      Homework Average: <span   id = "hw"> </span> <br />
96.      Test Average: <span  id = "test"> </span> <br />
97.      Attendance: <span  id = "att"> </span><br />
98.      Arithmetic: <span id = "math"> </span> <br />
99.      Reading: <span id = "read"> </span><br />
100.     Writing: <span id = "writng"> </span> <br />
101.     Overall Semester Grade: <span id="overall"> </span><br />
102.     Comments: <span id = "mycomments"> </span><br />
103. </div><div style="clear:both;"></div>
104. <p><input type="reset" value="Start over">   
105. <input type = "submit" value ="Submit report"></p>
106. </form></div>
107. </div></body></html>
```

Finishing Up

Here are two sample Summary Reports (at the bottom of the web page) and corresponding emails that are generated after Carla enters information for these students:

Student 1:

> **Student Report**
> **Student Name:** Jacob Jacobs
> **Homework Average:** 78
> **Test Average:** 74
> **Attendance:** needs improvement
> **Arithmetic:** satisfactory
> **Reading:** satisfactory
> **Writing:** needs improvement
> **Overall Semester Grade:** C
> **Comments:** Jacob has missed 9 days of school this quarter. Please contact me if he has any special health issues. Otherwise, he could be an excellent student if he applied himself.

To: carla@carlaschool.net

Subject: Student Progress Report

Body Text | Cambria | A A A A A A 三 三 三 三 三 三 三 三 三

Student Name: =Jacob Jacobs
Homework Average: =78
Test Average:=74
Arithmetic: =satisfactory
Reading: =satisfactory
Attendance: =needs improvement
Writing: =needs improvement
grade=C
comments=Jacob has missed 9 days of school this quarter. Please contact me if he has any special health issues. Otherwise, he could be an excellent student if he applied himself.

Student 2:

Student Report
Student Name: Nanette Nance
Homework Average: 42
Test Average: 96
Attendance: excellent
Arithmetic: excellent
Reading: excellent
Writing: satisfactory
Overall Semester Grade: B
Comments: Clearly, Nanette could be a superb student but she consistently does not do homework. Her test scores demonstrate that she has great ability. I hope you and I can work together to help her reach her potential by completing her homework.

To: carla@carlaschool.net

Subject: Student Progress Report

Body Text | Variable Width | A A A A A A 三 三 三 三 三 三 三 三 三

Student Name: =Nanette Nance
Homework Average: =42
Test Average:=96
Attendance: =excellent
Arithmetic: -excellent
Reading: =excellent
Writing: =satisfactory
grade=B
comments=Clearly, Nanette could be a superb student but she consistently does not do homework. Her test scores demonstrate that she has great ability. I hope you and I can work together to help her reach her potential by completing her homework.

Chapter Review and Exercises

Key Terms

`<fieldset></fieldset>` tags	masked
`<form></form>` tags	`maxlength` property
`<label></label>` tags	`method` property
`<legend></legend>` tags	`multiple` attribute
`<option></option>` tags	`name` property
`<select></select>` container tags	OK button
`<textarea></textarea>` tags	`onfocus` event
`accesskey` attribute	password form object
`action` property	radio button
CGI scripts	reset button
`cgi-bin`	`rows` property
checkbox	`selected` property
`checked` property	selection list
`cols` property	`size` property
Common Gateway Interface (CGI)	submit button
`email action`	`substr()` method
`enctype` property	substring
event handlers	`tabindex` attribute
fieldset element	textarea box
hidden object	textbox
label element	`this` keyword
legend element	`value` attribute

Review Exercises

Fill in the Blank

1. The `<form></form>` tag pair goes in the _____ (`<head></head>`/`<body></body>`) section of the web page.

2. The type of form control that allows a user to pick only one option is a _____.

3. The type of `<input>` box that will mask the characters typed in by a user is a _____ box.

4. The _____ method is used to extract specific characters from a string.

5. The _____ keyword is used to refer to a function or element that the user is referring to.

True or False

6. T/F   CGI scripts reside on the client's server.

7. T/F   Form data can be returned to a web page through a JavaScript program.

8. T/F   Both checkboxes and selection lists allow users to select more than one option.

9. T/F   The property that ensures that only one radio button can be selected from a list of radio buttons is the id.

10. T/F   If the size property of a selection list is set to "1" only one option is allowed in the list.

11. T/F   If the tabindex property is not specified the form will not work.

12. T/F   To extract the second character from a string variable named **word** and store it in a variable named **character**, you would use the code:

    character = **word**.substr(2, 1)

13. T/F   The substr() method can only be used to extract letters from a string. Spaces, digits, and special characters are ignored.

14. T/F   The unmask attribute will display a password as it is entered instead of masking the characters with *s or another symbol.

15. T/F   The <fieldset></fieldset> tags are used to put a border around a group of form controls.

Short Answer

16. Create the code to open a form which will return the data to the following email address including a copy to the second address listed and will contain the given subject line:

email:	janey.doe@ourcollege.edu
copy:	john.deer@ourcollege.edu
subject line:	Video Game Survey Results

17. Create a function that will send the value of a selected radio button to an area on your web page. The name of the radio button group is "cars". The value of the selected button is "red Porsche". The id of this button is "Porsche". The element on the web page that should receive the information has id = "mycar".

18. Create a selection list that allows the user to pick as many options from the list as desired. The list should ask the user to pick the courses he or she wants to take next semester and should include the following subjects: English, Calculus, World History, Psychology, Sociology, Spanish, and Computer Programming.

19. Create the selection list described in Exercise 18 but set it so the first item listed is "none" and only the first two items ("none" and the first subject) are initially visible.

20. Given the string "We love JavaScript", stored in a variable named **message**, use the substr() method in a function to extract the characters Java and store the substring in a variable named **coffee**.

21. Add code to Exercise 20 that will display the following sentence in an area on the web page with `id = "beverage"`:

    `"I need a cup of java every morning."`

    Use the variable **coffee** in your statement for the word `java` but be sure to change the first character to lowercase.

22. Create a function to validate a password entered by a user in a password box with `id = "pword"` that must contain exactly eight characters and must begin with a digit.

23. Add to the code created in Exercise 22 to ensure that all of the last seven characters (after the first which is a digit) are lowercase letters.

24. Create a web page with six textboxes. They can contain any information you want but one suggestion is shown below. The user should begin at the last textbox and, using the `tabindex` property, should work his way to the first box.

    Suggested information for the six boxes:

    Box 1: favorite teacher   Box 2: favorite book
    Box 3: favorite color   Box 4: favorite song or music group
    Box 5: favorite movie   Box 6: user's name

25. Add to the code of Exercise 24 so that when any textbox gets the focus, the box changes color.

26. Add to the code of Exercise 24 so that the user's entries are displayed on a web page, starting with the information entered in Box 6 and ending with the information in Box 1.

27. Create a function that will verify that a user enters a 10-digit phone number in a textbox in the following format: (XXX)XXX-XXXX (where X is a digit).

28. Create a function that will verify that a user enters a five-digit zip code into a textbox which has `id = "zip"`.

29. Create function that will take a user's last name (stored in a variable named **lName**) and first name (stored in a variable named **fName**) and generate a username of the form `lastname*first_initial` which is stored in a variable named **username**.

30. Create a function that will verify the user's entry of his city, state, and zip code. The entry should be of the format:

    `MyCity, 2-character_code_for_state 5-digit_zip_code`

    The address is entered in a textbox with `id = "address"`.

    The function should verify the following:

    - The city name is followed by a comma.
    - The state is two characters and both are uppercase.
    - The zip code consists of five digits.

Programming Challenges

On Your Own

VideoNote
Using and Validating Form
Controls
On_Your_Own_2_Signin

1. Create a web page that will take a survey of music preferences. List five types of music and have the user rate each type from 1 to 5 with 1 being the favorite and 5 being the least liked. Include options for the user's age (you can make these age ranges, such as under 20, 20–30, and so on) and gender. The survey should be returned to you by email. Save the page as `music.html` and be sure to include an appropriate page title.

2. Create a sign-in page for a website. The page should obtain the following information: the user's first and last names, street address, city, state, zip code, email address, and phone number. The phone number should be entered in the form (XXX)XXX-XXXX (where X is a digit). Validate the phone number entry to ensure that the user has entered 10 digits with the area code in parentheses and the three-digit extension separated from the last four digits by a hyphen. Save your page as `sign_in2.html` and be sure to include an appropriate page title.

3. Add a username and password to Programming Challenge 2. The username should be between 4 and 20 characters. The password should be between 4 and 12 characters, contain at least one digit, and contain at least one uppercase and one lowercase character. Select four special characters and require that the password contain at least one of them. Save your page as `sign_in3.html` and be sure to include an appropriate page title.

4. Add a feature to Programming Challenge 3 that will change the color of each textbox when the user enters his or her information. Save your page as `sign_in4.html` and be sure to include an appropriate page title.

5. Change the page you created in Programming Challenge 2 or 3 so a selection list is used for the user's state of residence. Add a radio button that the user will click "yes" or "no" when asked if the business can contact the user by email, phone, or snail mail. Save your page as `sign_in5.html` and be sure to include an appropriate page title.

6. Create a web page similar to the menu program of Example 6.11 but use a luncheon menu. Include choices for sandwiches (at least three), sides (at least three), and a drink order. Save your page as `lunch.html` and be sure to include an appropriate page title.

7. Create a web page that gives the user two drop-down menus of color names. When the user selects a color from one menu, the background color of the page turns to that color. When the user selects a color from the other menu, the text on the web page changes to that color. Save your page as `colors.html` and be sure to include an appropriate page title.

Case Studies

Greg's Gambits

Create a tic-tac-toe game for two players using form elements. The game should be called Tic Tac Toe and should be part of the Greg's Gambits site. The players enter Xs or Os. When an X is clicked, the box should turn yellow. When an O is clicked, the box should turn orange. You can, of course, use any two colors you want. An image has been provided for you to use as a button or you can create your own button. The page should look similar to the one shown below.

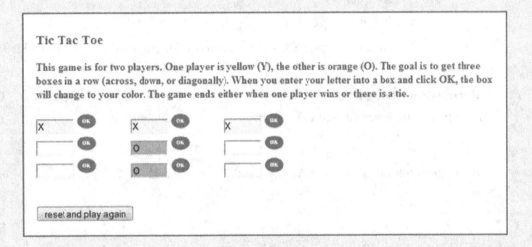

Open the play_games.html page and add a link to this page. The filename should be tictactoe.html and the page title should be Greg's Gambits | Tic Tac Toe. Test your page in at least two different browsers. Submit your work as instructed by your teacher.

Carla's Classroom

Now you will add to the carla.html page by creating a link to a Rate Your Teacher page that you will create. Carla wants her students to have a chance to rate her so she has asked you to create this form. Put a link in the carla.html page created in the Putting It to Work section in this chapter on the text "Help Carla improve! Take the Rate Carla survey now." to this new page. The filename of the new page will be rate_carla.html.

Your page should include a textbox for a student to enter his or her name, if desired. There should be places for the student to rate Carla for her instruction in arithmetic, reading, and writing. You can do this using radio buttons with numerical ratings (i.e., 1 to 5 or number grades such as 100%, 90%, 80% and so on) or category ratings (i.e., excellent, satisfactory, etc. or A, B, C, D, F). Include a textarea box for optional comments for each category.

You also should include ratings for Carla's personality and teaching methods. Some suggested options are fairness, willingness to listen, clarity of explanations, testing methods, and so on. Use your creativity to develop categories for the ratings and for the form elements used for each category.

The form should be submitted to Carla via email at carla@carlaschool.net with Rate Carla as the subject line.

This page should have Carla's Classroom | Rate Carla as the page title and an appropriate heading on the web page. Test your page in at least two different browsers. Submit your work as instructed by your teacher.

Lee's Landscape

Create a Customer Satisfaction Survey for the Lee's Landscape business site. The survey should include the following information:

Information Requested	Form Element Type	Options
How many times have you used Lee's services?	radio buttons	1 2–5 more than 5
Which of the following services have you used?	checkboxes	lawn care pest control tree removal landscaping
Overall satisfaction with service	radio buttons	Excellent Good Fair Poor
Customer name	textbox	optional
Customer contact information	textbox	optional
Comments	textarea box	optional

The filename for this page should be customer_satisfaction.html and the page title should be Lee's Landscape | Customer Satisfaction. Be sure to test your program in at least two browsers. Submit your work as instructed by your teacher.

Jackie's Jewelry

Create a User Information form for the Jackie's Jewelry website. The form should include the following information:

Information Requested	Form Element Type	Options
User's real name	textbox	limit to 50 characters
User's address	textboxes	street city state zip code

Information Requested	Form Element Type	Options
User's email address	textbox	Be sure to verify that the email contains an @ sign, a host, a dot, and an extension
password	textbox	Verify: 6-10 characters, only uppercase and lowercase letters and digits (no special characters)
User's age	radio buttons	create age ranges
User's interests: types of materials preferred for jewelry	checkboxes	gold silver platinum wood beads
User's interests: types of jewelry user likes	checkboxes	necklaces bracelets rings ankle bracelets hair jewelry

Save your page with the filename customer_info.html and the page title should be Jackie's Jewelry | Customer Information. Test your page in at least two different browsers. Submit your work as instructed by your teacher.

Keeping it Neat: Functions and JavaScript Source Files

Chapter Objectives

You may wonder why this chapter is about functions when we have been using functions from the beginning of the text. It's because there's much more to learn! Until now, we have used functions without regard to why and how they work. In this chapter, we'll learn a lot more about creating and using functions.

You probably know that there are three ways to create styles in an HTML page: You can include external style sheets with your web page; you can include your styles in the <head> section; or you can write styles right in the HTML script. These methods are known as linked (or external), embedded, or inline. The same is true for JavaScript. Most of the code we have written so far has been included in the <head> section. However, the other options are also available. JavaScript can be linked to a web page as a separate file (external) or included in the HTML page (inline). This valuable tool can help keep code shorter and neater. Learning to create and use JavaScript source files is an important part of this chapter.

After reading this chapter, you will be able to do the following:

- Understand arguments and parameters
- Understand the scope of a variable
- Pass arguments to functions
- Understand what it means to pass by value
- Understand what it means to pass by reference
- Understand when and how a function will return a value
- Understand a JavaScript object

- Use the Date object
- Use the setTimeout() method (function)
- Create a JavaScript source file
- Use the new keyword, the visibility property, and the replace()method (function)
- Write JavaScript code that uses functions and objects in the web page and in a JavaScript source file

7.1 Functions

A function is code that will be executed by an event or when it is called. We've often used built-in JavaScript functions without realizing it. We've called them methods. Each time we create a program, first we create at least one function. So we know there are two types of functions—those that are already part of the JavaScript language and those we create. In this section, we'll talk about the two types of functions and introduce two new concepts: arguments and parameters.

Built-In Functions

Most programming languages typically provide a wide assortment of **built-in functions.** These are often referred to as a library. Someone has already written the code to do something and, by calling on the function, we reap the benefit because we don't have to write that code ourselves. For example, we have used the toUpperCase() function. This changes any text in a given string variable to all uppercase. We could, at this point, easily write this code ourselves. We would simply write code to switch the ASCII code value for each lowercase letter to its corresponding uppercase ASCII code value. The pseudocode for this function might look something like this:

```
function upperCase()
    set a variable, x, to the length of the string
    in a loop that starts at 0 (the first letter of the string)
    and goes up to x - 1 (the last letter of the string)
        check if the letter is between unicode values 65 - 90
            if so, leave it as is (it is already uppercase)
            if not, replace with unicode value that is the (present unicode
            value - 32) (this corresponds to
            the same letter but uppercase)
    That's all
```

This code would not be difficult for an experienced programmer to write quickly but using the built-in toUpperCase() function saves time which can be better spent on solving more complex programming problems.

In this text, you have already seen many examples of built-in functions or, as we have often called them, methods. The following functions (see Table 7.1) are some JavaScript global functions. A **global function** can be used with all the built-in JavaScript objects:

TABLE 7.1	Some JavaScript Global Functions
Function	**Description**
isFinite()	determines whether a value is a finite, legal number
isNan()	determines whether a value is an illegal number
parseFloat()	returns a floating point number
parseInt()	returns an integer
String()	converts an object's value to a string

Built-in functions can be viewed as subprograms, which contain one or more parameters and return (export) at least one value. We will discuss parameters and return values in the next section. For now, we simply define a parameter as the value or values inside the parentheses. When a built-in function is called, the function name is assigned a value (of the type specified for that function). A built-in function is called by using the function name anywhere in the program that a constant of its type is allowed.

For example, the parseInt() function is of type integer—it is assigned an integer value when it is called. parseInt() may be used (called) anywhere in a program that a constant of this type is allowed. Thus, all of the following are valid calls to the parseInt() function (assuming of course that **num** is a variable of numeric type):

- X = parseInt(10.76);
- document.write(parseInt(2*(**num** + 1));
- displayNumber(parseInt(**num**));

User-Defined Functions

Until now, we have written JavaScript functions that are, in effect, individual mini-programs. We have written functions that play games or give math tests. The built-in functions discussed above don't do anything like that. Instead, they return a single value to the program. For example, if you use the statement

```
age = parseInt(34.56);
```

you expect that **age** will have the value 34 after the statement is executed. In other words, you set the value of a variable equal to the result of calling the function when the value you send it is 34.56. We can create that type of function ourselves. This type of **user-defined function** is valuable because it can be used in a program to get a single value without rewriting code. Example 7.1 shows how to create and use a function named quotient().

EXAMPLE 7.1

Creating a Simple Function

The following function takes two numbers and divides the first by the second. Then it sends the result back to whatever statement in the main program called it.

```
1.   <html>
2.   <head>
3.   <title>Example 7.1</title>
4.   <script>
5.   function quotient(x,y)
6.   {
7.        illegal = "Illegal division operation";
8.        if (y != 0)
9.            return x/y;
10.       else
11.           return illegal;
12.  }
```

```
13.   function clickIt()
14.   {
15.         document.write(quotient(60, 5));
16.   }
17.   </script>
18.   </head>
19.   <body>
20.   <input type ="button" onclick="clickIt()" value = "How much ⏎
                              is 60 divided by 5?"></button>
21.   </body></html>
```

The function quotient() does a single thing. It divides one number by another
and sends back the result of the division to whatever called it. In this example, we
send in two hard-coded values (60 and 5) but we could also send in variables and
whatever we sent in for the first number would become the **x** value while the second
variable would become the value of **y**. We could, instead of displaying the result on
a new page, store the result in a new variable and use it in a program. Example 7.2
demonstrates more uses of this simple function.

**EXAMPLE
7.2**

Using a User-Defined Simple Function

This example shows how the function we created, quotient() is used instead of a
variable when displaying its value on a web page, using the innerHTML property.

```
1.    <html>
2.    <head>
3.    <title>Example 7.2</title>
4.    <script>
5.    function quotient(x,y)
6.    {
7.          illegal = "Illegal division operation";
8.          if (y != 0)
9.                return x/y;
10.         else
11.               return illegal;
12.   }
13.   function clickIt()
14.   {
15.         var divTop = parseFloat(prompt("Enter the divisor:"));
16.         var divBottom = parseFloat(prompt("Enter the dividend:"));
17.         document.getElementById('division').innerHTML = (divTop + ⏎
                                   " divided by " + divBottom);
18.         var division;
19.         division = quotient(divTop, divBottom);
20.         if (isNaN(division))
21.               division = "illegal division operation";
22.         else
23.               division = division.toFixed(2);
24.         document.getElementById('result').innerHTML = division;
25.   }
```

```
26.   </script>
27.   </head>
28.   <body>
29.       <input type ="button" onclick="clickIt()" value = "Enter ↲
                           a division problem"></button>
30.       <h2><span  id = "division"> </span></h2>
31.       <h2>The result is: <span id = "result"> </span></h2>
32.   </body></html>
```

Line 19 uses the `quotient()` function to get the result of the division by sending in the two numeric values for the divisor and dividend. **divTop** and **divBottom** are received by the function `quotient()` and stored as **x** and **y** within the function. The result is computed and returned to the function that called `quotient()`.

If the user enters the numbers 56 and 7 at the prompts, the result will look like this:

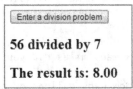

But if the user enters 56 and 0 at the prompts, the result will be as follows:

> Enter a division problem
>
> **56 divided by 0**
>
> **The result is: Illegal division operation**

Once the function is created, it can be reused for various purposes throughout a program, just as we can use the `parseInt()` function or the `toUpperCase()` function anywhere we need an integer or a value changed to uppercase. Example 7.3 uses the `quotient()` function in three different ways in one program.

EXAMPLE 7.3

Using One Function for Various Purposes

The following program uses the `quotient()` function in three different little programs. First, it does a division problem, as shown in Example 7.1. Then, it allows a user to find the miles per gallon on a given road trip. Finally, it allows a user to determine his or her Body Mass Index (BMI).

```
1.    <html>
2.    <head>
3.    <title>Example 7.3</title>
4.    <script>
5.    function quotient(x,y)
6.    {
7.        illegal = "Illegal division operation";
8.        if (y != 0)
```

```
9.              return x/y;
10.         else
11.             return illegal;
12.   }
13.   function divideIt()
14.   {
15.       var divTop = parseFloat(prompt("Enter the divisor:"));
16.       var divBottom = parseFloat(prompt("Enter the dividend:"));
17.       document.getElementById('division').innerHTML = (divTop + ↵
                      " divided by " + divBottom);
18.       var division = quotient(divTop, divBottom);
19.       if (isNaN(division))
20.           division = "illegal division operation";
21.       else
22.           division = division.toFixed(2);
23.       document.getElementById('result').innerHTML = division;
24.   }
25.   function getMileage()
26.   {
27.       var miles = parseFloat(prompt("How many miles did you drive  ↵
                      on this trip?"));
28.       var gallons = parseFloat(prompt("How many gallons of gas ↵
                      did you use?"));
29.       var trip = quotient(miles, gallons);
30.       if (isNaN(trip))
31.       {
32.           trip = "illegal division operation";
33.           document.getElementById('mileage').innerHTML = ("Cannot ↵
                      complete the calculation. " + trip);
34.       }
35.       else
36.       {
37.           trip = trip.toFixed(1);
38.           document.getElementById('mileage').innerHTML = ("Your ↵
                      mileage for this trip was " + trip + " mpg.");
39.       }
40.   }
41.   function getBMI()
42.   {
43.       var feet = parseFloat(prompt("How tall are you? Enter your ↵
                      height in feet first:"));
44.       var inches = parseFloat(prompt("How many inches over " + feet ↵
                      + " feet are you?"));
45.       var height = (feet * 12 + inches);
46.       var hInches= height * height;
47.       var weight = parseFloat(prompt("What is your weight in pounds? ↵
                      You may include a partial pound, like 128.5 ↵
                      lbs, for example."));
48.       document.getElementById('height').innerHTML = ↵
                      (height.toFixed(2));
49.       document.getElementById('weight').innerHTML = ↵
                      (weight.toFixed(2));
50.       var bmi = (quotient(weight, hInches) * 703);
51.       if (isNaN(bmi))
52.       {
53.           bmi = "illegal division operation";
```

```
54.              document.getElementById('bmi').innerHTML = ("cannot ⏎
                         complete the calculation. " + bmi);
55.          }
56.      else
57.      {
58.              bmi = bmi.toFixed(2);
59.              document.getElementById('bmi').innerHTML = (" " + bmi);
60.      }
61.  }
63.  </script>
64.  </head>
65.  <body>
66.      <h2>Using the quotient() function</h2>
67.      <div style="width: 80%;">
68.      <div style="width: 50%; float: left;">
69.          <fieldset><legend>Division Problem</legend>
70.          <input type ="button" onclick="divideIt()" value = ⏎
                     "Enter a division problem" />
71.          <h2><span  id = "division"> </span></h2>
72.          <h2>The result is: <span id = "result"> </span></h2>
73.          </fieldset></div>
74.      <div style=" width: 50%; float: left;">
75.          <fieldset><legend>Gas Mileage</legend>
76.          <input type ="button" onclick="getMileage()" value ⏎
                     = "Find the gas mileage" />
77.          <h2><span  id = "mileage"> </span></h2>
78.          </fieldset></div>
79.      <div style="clear:both;"></div></div> <br />
80.      <div style="width: 80%;">
81.          <fieldset><legend>BMI (Body Mass Index) Calculator ⏎
                     </legend>
82.          <p>The formula to calculate your BMI is your weight in ⏎
                     pounds (lbs) divided by your height in inches ⏎
                     (in) squared and multiplied by a conversion ⏎
                     factor of 703. But don't worry about doing ⏎
                     the math! If you enter your weight (lbs) and ⏎
                     height (in feet and inches), the program will ⏎
                     calculate your BMI.</p>
83.          <input type ="button" onclick="getBMI()" value = ⏎
                     "Calculate your BMI (Body Mass Index)" />
84.          <h3>Your height (in inches): <span id = "height"> ⏎
                      </span></h3>
85.          <h3>Your weight (in pounds): <span id = "weight">   ⏎
                     </span></h3>
86.          <h3>Your BMI: <span id = "bmi"> </span></h3>
87.          </fieldset></div>
88.  </body></html>
```

The quotient() function is called three times—on lines 18, 29, and 50. Each time different variables are passed to the function and each time the result is used for a different purpose. We will discuss the passing of values from a program to a function in greater detail later in this chapter.

If this page was coded and run with the input shown, the display would be as given below.

Input:

Division problem: the numbers entered are 348 and 23

Mileage problem: the trip was 568 `miles` and used 18 `gallons` of gas

BMI problem: the user is 5'8" `tall` and weighs 173.5 `lbs`.

Output:

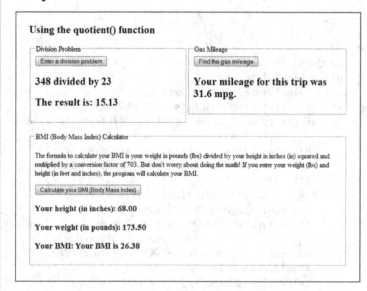

CHECKPOINT FOR SECTION 7.1

7.1 List three global JavaScript functions.

7.2 Create `document.write` statements that will output the floating point value for each of the following:
a) 6.83
b) (**age** - 2.385) where **age** is a number
c) the value of **score** after the user responds to the following prompt:
```
score = prompt("What is your score?");
```

7.3 When a built-in function is called, the function name is assigned a _____.

7.4 Which of the following is not a valid call to the `parseInt()` function, given that **num** is a numeric variable?
a) **num** = parseInt(43.67);
b) **num** = parseInt(43);
c) document.write(parseInt(**num** - 3));
d) all are valid calls

7.5 What does the following function do?
```
function product(a, b)
{
    return a * b;
}
```

7.2 The Scope of a Variable

In many programming languages a program begins with what we call a **driver program** or the **main program (or main function).** This driver program often does little except call other functions as needed. In most of the JavaScript programs that we have written, however, an event on the web page triggers a call to a JavaScript function. Often, for one reason or another, the code in the function calls another JavaScript function. Different events on the web page drive the execution of the program as much as the actual JavaScript code. Therefore, in JavaScript we often don't have a main function. For this reason, a discussion of the scope of a variable in JavaScript is a bit different from the discussion of scope in other languages.

When a variable is input, processed, or output, we say that it has been **referenced.** In general, the **scope of a variable** refers to the part of the program in which a given variable can be referenced. If a variable is defined outside of all functions then the variable will exist from that point until the end of the program. Such a variable is said to have **global scope.** On the other hand, any variable defined within a function will only exist while the function is running. Such a variable is said to have **local scope.** The consequences of using a variable that is global can be serious so it is important that you understand the distinction and are aware of the scope of the variables you use.

Global Variables

When a variable is declared outside a function but then referenced within the function, it brings its value with it to the function. This may, at first, seem to make things easier but, in fact, it is a dangerous situation. We will learn a far better way to send information to a function in the next section.

Example 7.4 demonstrates how using a global variable can have undesirable results.

EXAMPLE 7.4

Beware the Global Variable

The following code declares one variable, **age**, which is used in two functions:

```
1.   <html>
2.   <head>
3.   <title>Example 7.4</title>
4.   <script>
5.   function getAges()
6.   {
7.        var age = 0;
8.      age = parseInt(prompt("How old is your grandmother?"));
9.       pet();
10.    function pet()
11.    {
12.        age = parseInt(prompt("How old is your puppy?"));
```

```
13.                 document.getElementById('puppy').innerHTML = (age + 10);
14.        }
15.                 document.getElementById('granny').innerHTML = (age + 10);
16.    }
17.    </script>
18.    </head>
19.    <body>
20.        <input type ="button" onclick="getAges()" value = "Find the ⏎
                         age in 10 years"></button><br />
21.        <h3>Your granny's age in 10 years: <span id = "granny"> ⏎
                          </span></h3>
22.        <h3>Your puppy's age in 10 years: <span id = "puppy"> ⏎
                          </span></h3>
23.        </body></html>
```

If you code and run this program, entering 105 for your grandmother's age and 5 for your puppy's age, your output would look like the one shown below. This is because the value of **age** on line 8 is 105 but it is changed on line 12 to 5. Since **age** has global scope within the getAges() function, it displays this value as requested on line 13 but retains this value even after the pet() function is exited and this is what is displayed when line 15 is executed.

Find the age in 10 years

Your granny's age in 10 years: 15

Your puppy's age in 10 years: 15

JavaScript is a loosely typed language which means it is often forgiving of what would be considered a sin in a strictly typed language. For example, variables can be created "on the fly"; and even created without using the keyword var. In Example 7.5, we show how we can accomplish this with no apparent consequences. This means the program will work. But it is not good programming practice.

EXAMPLE 7.5

Living Dangerously: Declaring Variables "On the Fly"

In this example we add a line to the previous program. Inside the pet() function, a new numeric variable, **num**, is used in two ways. To save space, since the HTML page is not changed, we only show the new code:

Part (a)

```
1.    function getAges()
2.    {
3.        var age = 0;
4.        age = parseInt(prompt("How old is your grandmother?"));
5.        pet();
```

```
6.        function pet()
7.        {
8.                age = parseInt(prompt("How old is your puppy?"));
9.                num = 2;
10.   document.getElementById('puppy').innerHTML=(age+10+num);
11.          }
12.   document.getElementById('granny').innerHTML=(age+10+num);
13.   }
```

If this program were run, using the same input as the previous example, the output would be as follows:

```
┌──────────────────────────────────────────────┐
│   ┌─────────────────────────┐                │
│   │ Find the age in 10 years │                │
│   └─────────────────────────┘                │
│                                                │
│   Your granny's age in 10 years: 17           │
│                                                │
│   Your puppy's age in 10 years: 17            │
│                                                │
└──────────────────────────────────────────────┘
```

This is because the variable **num** is used globally. But if the var keyword is is used when **num** is first initialized on line 9, it becomes a local variable. This means it cannot be used outside of the function where it is created, pet(), and the new output will not show any results for granny's age.

Part (b) shows the code for the function with **num** defined locally within the function:

```
1.    function getAges()
2.    {
3.          var age = 0;
4.          age = parseInt(prompt("How old is your grandmother?"));
5.          pet();
6.          function pet()
7.          {
8.              age = parseInt(prompt("How old is your puppy?"));
9.              var num = 2;
10.             document.getElementById('puppy').innerHTML = (age + 10 ⌐
                            + num);
11.          }
12.          document.getElementById('granny').innerHTML = (age + 10 + num);
13.   }
```

The output will look as follows and, if you use a JavaScript debugger, line 12 will show the error message, "**num** is not defined."

```
┌──────────────────────────────────────────────┐
│   ┌─────────────────────────┐                │
│   │ Find the age in 10 years │                │
│   └─────────────────────────┘                │
│   Your granny's age in 10 years:              │
│                                                │
│   Your puppy's age in 10 years: 15            │
│                                                │
└──────────────────────────────────────────────┘
```

Example 7.5(b) shows code that runs but does not produce the expected outcome. In a short program like this one, the problems are clear and are immediately obvious. But when you write a longer program with many possible outputs, an error like this may not be easy to spot. The fact that JavaScript allows you to declare variables anywhere and does not require that you specify a data type does not mean that you should do this. To avoid this type of situation, you should always declare all variables with the var keyword and be aware of the scope of each variable. The best way to fix the problem is to make all the variables have local scope.

Local Variables

When a variable is declared within a function, its value can only be referenced inside that function. The problem with the programs in Examples 7.4 and 7.5 can be avoided by making all variables local, as we do in Example 7.6.

EXAMPLE 7.6   Using Local Variables

This example changes only one line of Example 7.4 but it significantly changes the output. Only the JavaScript functions are given here, since the HTML script does not change:

```
1.   function getAges()
2.   {
3.       var age = 0;
4.       age = parseInt(prompt("How old is your grandmother?"));
5.       pet();
6.       function pet()
7.       {
8.           var age = parseInt(prompt("How old is your puppy?"));
9.           document.getElementById('puppy').innerHTML = (age +10);
10.      }
11.      document.getElementById('granny').innerHTML = (age + 10);
12.  }
```

The only change in this example is on line 8. By using the var keyword, the variable **age** is now made into a new variable within the pet() function. Its scope is local; in other words, its value can only be referenced within pet(). The variable **age**, declared on line 4, is now referenced only by the getAges() function. Thus, if this program were coded and run, with the input as before where granny's age is 105 and the puppy's is 3, the output would be what is desired:

Find the age in 10 years

Your granny's age in 10 years: 115

Your puppy's age in 10 years: 15

In this example, we have two variables named **age**. It is not, however, good programming practice to give variables the same name in different functions. This example was solely for demonstration purposes. The only exception to this rule, in general, is when it comes to naming counters. People often name counters **i** or **j** or **count** and, since counters are normally set to an initial value before they are used, using the same name for counters in several functions is rarely problematic.

CHECKPOINT FOR SECTION 7.2 ✔

Refer to the following code to answer Checkpoints 7.6 through 7.12:

```
1.   function xx()
2.   {
3.    var one = 1;
4.    yy();
5.    function yy()
6.    {
7.        var two = 2;
8.        three = one + two;
9.        document.write("in function yy(), one = " + one + ↵
                         "<br />");
10.       document.write("in function yy(), two = " + two + ↵
                         "<br />");
11.       document.write("in function yy(), three = " + three + ↵
                         "<br />");
12.   }
13.   four = one + three;
14.   document.write("in function xx(), one = " + one + "<br />");
15.   document.write("in function xx(), three = " + three + ↵
                     "<br />");
16.   document.write("in function xx(), four = " + four + ↵
                     "<br />");
17.   }
```

7.6 What will be displayed after line 9 is executed?

7.7 What will be displayed after line 10 is executed?

7.8 What will be displayed after line 11 is executed?

7.9 What will be displayed after line 14 is executed?

7.10 What will be displayed after line 15 is executed?

7.11 What will be displayed after line 16 is executed?

7.12 What are the values of **one**, **three**, and **four** at the end of the program?

7.3 Sending Information to a Function

When data is passed between functions, programming languages use arguments and parameters to transfer the data. Let's assume we have a program in a business site that prompts the user for an item and its price. Then the price of the item is passed to a function which computes a discount. In this example, let's assume that items costing more than $100.00 will receive a 20% discount, items costing between $50.00 and $99.99 will receive a 15% discount, and items costing less than $50.00 qualify for a 10% discount. We would probably have variables to identify the original price and the discount rate which we'll now call **originalPrice** and **discountRate**. These values must be sent from one function to another.

We will call the function that does the actual computation **salePrice()**. This function would do a simple calculation, multiplying **originalPrice** by (1 - **discountRate**). However, the original price of each item will be different, as will the discount rate. Each time we call the **salePrice()** function, we send over the values we want it to use in its calculation. We put those values inside the parentheses. These are called the **arguments.**

When we create the **salePrice()** function, we list variables that it will accept from the function call inside the parentheses. In this example, we need to send two numeric values to the **salePrice()** function so the function name must have two numeric variables in its parentheses. These are called the **parameters.** These parameters are placed in the parentheses, separated by commas. The value of each argument in the function call is passed to a corresponding parameter in the function name.

Passing Arguments to Parameters

The names of the variables listed in the function call and those in the function name don't need to be the same. In fact, in most cases, it is better if they are not the same for reasons that will soon become clear. However, the names of the variables listed in the function call statement and those in the function name *must* agree in number, in type, and in the order in which they are given. In our general example, we are sending (or **passing**) two values (stored in variables named **originalPrice** and **discountRate**) so there must be two variables listed in the function name. Also, if a certain variable in the call statement is of one type, then the corresponding variable in the function name must be of the same type. In this case, our two variables are of numeric type so the variables in the function name's parentheses must also be numeric.

Let's assume we use the following code for the function name:

```
function salePrice(oldPrice, rate)
```

This means the **salePrice()** function must have two numeric variables passed to it when it is called. The *order* in which the variables are sent to a function is extremely important. When this function is called, it must be called like this:

```
salePrice(originalPrice, discountRate);
```

If we had reversed the order of the variables, the function would use the value of **discountRate** wherever **oldPrice** is referenced and the value of **originalPrice** wherever **rate** is referenced. Our results would be completely wrong. We will take a closer look at what this means in Example 7.7.

Arguments in a call statement may be constants, variables, or general expressions, but parameters that appear in the function name *must* be variables. This means you can *send* data to a function that is stored as a variable or is a constant or an expression. These values will be passed into the variables listed as parameters in the function.

We have used these concepts in the past but have not actually created functions with parameters. The ability to accept arguments sent during a function call makes our functions far more useful. Example 7.7 provides a few examples.

EXAMPLE 7.7

Let's Validate

The following example uses a function to validate user input. This example follows the general discussion in the beginning of the section. A user is asked to enter an item and its original cost. Then a sale price is calculated with the discount rate dependent on the cost of the item. However, before the sale price is calculated, a function is called to ensure that the user has not entered a negative number for the cost. The function, checkNum() has one parameter, a numeric variable. The call to the function sends in one argument, also a numeric variable.

```
1.   <html>
2.   <head>
3.   <title>Example 7.7</title>
4.   <script>
5.   function getDiscount()
6.   {
7.       var item = " "; var rate = 0; var salePrice = 0; var cost = 0;
8.       item = prompt("What is the item you want to buy?");
9.       cost = parseFloat(prompt("How much does this item cost?"));
10.      checkNum(cost);
11.      if (cost < 50)
12.      {
13.          rate = .10;
14.          salePrice = cost * (1 - rate);
15.      }
16.      else
17.          if (cost < 100)
18.          {
19.              rate = .15;
20.              salePrice = cost * (1 - rate);
21.          }
22.          else
23.          {
24.              rate = .20;
25.              salePrice = cost * (1 - rate);
26.          }
27.      document.getElementById('item').innerHTML = item;
28.      document.getElementById('orig_price').innerHTML = ("$ " + ↵
                              cost.toFixed(2));
29.      document.getElementById('discount').innerHTML = ((rate * 100) ↵
                              + "%");
30.      document.getElementById('result').innerHTML = ("$ " + ↵
                              salePrice.toFixed(2));
```

```
31.  }
32.  function checkNum(num)
33.  {
34.      if (num < 0)
35.          alert("Invalid entry");
36.  }
37.  </script>
38.  </head>
39.  <body>
40.      <input type ="button" onclick="getDiscount()" value = "How ⤸
                      much will you save? Find out now" /><br />
41.      <h3>You plan to purchase: <span id = "item"> </span></h3>
42.      <h3>The original cost is: <span id = "orig_price"> ⤸
                       </span></h3>
43.      <h3>The discount rate is: <span id = "discount"> ⤸
                       </span></h3>
44.      <h3>You pay: <span id = "result"> </span></h3>
45.  </body></html>
```

The function to check that the cost entered is not less than 0 is on lines 32–36. As soon as the user enters the cost of the item (line 9), the checkNum() function is called. One argument, **cost**, is sent to the function and its value is stored in the parameter, **num**.

This program works well. If the user enters valid input, as shown in the sample output below, all is fine. This output corresponds to input of a sweater that originally costs $68.95.

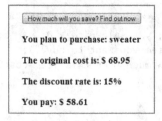

If the user enters a cost of -20, the alert appears:

Unfortunately, after clicking OK on the alert, the following also appears:

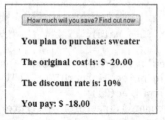

We must make sure the program does not continue with the calculation if the entry is invalid. We accomplish this with the return statement.

The *return* Statement

The return **statement** allows functions to send a value back to the expression or statement that called them. If no return statement is used in a function, an undefined value will be returned.

A return statement can only return a single value. Example 7.8 adds a return statement to the checkNum() function of the previous example as well as some code to clean up the output in the case of an invalid cost entry (i.e., a negative amount).

EXAMPLE 7.8

Using the return Statement

To save space we will only show the JavaScript code; the HTML script remains the same as for the previous example.

```
1.   <script>
2.   function getDiscount()
3.   {
4.        var item = " "; var rate = 0; var salePrice = 0; var cost = 0;
5.        item = prompt("What is the item you want to buy?");
6.        cost = parseFloat(prompt("How much does this item cost?"));
7.        cost = checkNum(cost);
8.        if (cost < 50 && cost > 0)
9.        {
10.            rate = .10;
11.            salePrice = cost * (1 - rate);
12.        }
13.           else if (cost >= 50 && cost < 100)
14.           {
15.                rate = .15;
16.                salePrice = cost * (1 - rate);
17.           }
18.              else if (cost >= 100)
19.              {
20.                   rate = .20;
21.                   salePrice = cost * (1 - rate);
22.              }
23.                 else
24.                 {
25.                      rate = 0;
26.                      salePrice = 0;
27.                 }
28.        document.getElementById('item').innerHTML = item;
29.        document.getElementById('orig_price').innerHTML = ("$ " + ↵
                              cost.toFixed(2));
30.        document.getElementById('discount').innerHTML = ((rate * 100) ↵
                              + "%");
31.        document.getElementById('result').innerHTML = ("$ " + ↵
                              salePrice.toFixed(2));
32.   }
33.   function checkNum(num)
34.   {
35.        if (num < 0)
```

```
36.          {
37.               alert("Invalid cost entered");
38.               num = 0;
39.          }
40.      return num;
41.  }
42.  </script>
```

The checkNum() function has been edited to add two features. If the value of **num** is less than 0, **num** is set equal to 0 on line 38. The return statement on line 40 sends the value of **num** back to the function that called it. In this case, if the argument (**cost**) is not less than 0, nothing is changed. For example, if the user enters a value of 43.89, **num** will equal 43.89 which is greater than 0. The if clause on lines 35–39 will never be executed and the return statement will return the original value. However, if the user enters a value of -83.65, the if clause will send out the alert and set **num** to 0. This is the value that will be returned to the calling statement.

Line 7 is where the checkNum() function is called. Notice that it sets the value of **cost** to whatever the checkNum() function returns. Therefore, if **cost** is less than 0, the value of **cost** after this statement is executed will be the return value of the checkNum() function; in this case, it will be 0. If the value of **cost** is initially greater than or equal to 0, after line 7 is executed, the value of **cost** will not be changed.

Code has also been added so that, if **cost** equals 0 after its value has been checked, the display will not calculate a sale price for that item. Now if the user tries to buy a sweater for $–68.95, the display will be an alert with the message "Invalid cost entered" and the output will be as follows:

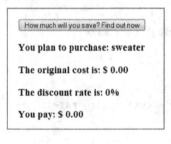

Passing Values: A Complex Issue

At this point, we will backtrack a bit to make sure the concept of passing variables is clear. You know that, when you declare a variable this means a location in the computer's memory is identified and, whenever the name of that variable is used in the program, the computer goes to that location to retrieve the value. If a variable named **numMice** is assigned the value of 12, then the statement document. write(**numMice**); will result in 12 being displayed on a web page.

And if you create a new variable, named **numDogs** and set it equal to **numMice**, then n**umDogs** has the value of 12 also. However, there are now two areas in the computer which have the value of 12—one referenced by **numMice** and the other referenced by **numDogs**. In other words, we have made a copy of **numMice** and given it a new name. Anything we do to **numMice** to change its value will not affect the value of **numDogs**. This is, in effect, the process that happens when a variable is **passed by value.** The function that received the variable makes a new copy of that variable and manipulates the new copy. That's one way to pass variables in a program.

The second way is called passing by reference. When a variable is **passed by reference,** what is sent to the function is actually the location in the computer's memory of the variable. The variable in the function probably has a different name from the variable that was passed in but the new variable points to the same location as the original variable. From that point on, any changes made to the new variable change the value in the location and, therefore, change the original variable also.

How a variable is passed to a function can have profound effects on a program so this topic must be treated with respect. We will discuss both methods in this section.

■ **Value parameters** have this property: Changes to their values in the function *do not* affect the value of the corresponding (argument) variables in the calling function. These parameters can only be used to import data.

■ **Reference parameters** have this property: Changes in their values *do* affect the corresponding arguments in the calling function. They can be used to **import data** into and **export data** from a function.

Each programming language uses its own rules and protocols when it comes to passing variables by reference or by value. With JavaScript, it is both simpler and more complex than in other languages.

In JavaScript, **primitive types** are manipulated by value, and reference types, as the name suggests, are manipulated by reference. Numbers, Booleans, and (normally) strings are considered primitive types in JavaScript. Objects, on the other hand, are considered **reference types.** Arrays (see Chapter 8) and functions, which are specialized types of objects, are also reference types.

Passing by Value

When data is passed to a function by value, a copy of the value is made and that value is passed to the corresponding parameter in the called function. The best way to truly understand the difference between passing by reference and passing by value is through examples.

When passing a numeric variable which is considered a primitive type, the value is passed in by value. This means that any changes to that variable while in the function are completely separate from anything that happens outside the function as shown in Example 7.9.

EXAMPLE
7.9

Passing Number Variables by Value

```
1.   <html>
2.   <head>
3.   <title>Example 7.9</title>
4.   <script>
5.   function getValue()
6.   {
7.       var numMice = 12;
8.       document.getElementById('first').innerHTML = (numMice);
9.       changeValue(numMice);
10.      document.getElementById('third').innerHTML = (numMice);
11.  }
12.  function changeValue(x)
13.  {
14.    x = 5;
15.    document.getElementById('second').innerHTML = (x);
16.  }
17.  </script>
18.  </head>
19.  <body>
20.      <input type ="button" onclick="getValue()" value = "Can you ↵
                        change the number? Try it"><br />
21.      <h3>The value of numMice is: <span id = "first">   ↵
                        </span></h3>
22.      <h3>The value of x, in the changeValue() function is: <span ↵
                        id = "second"> </span></h3>
23.      <h3>The value of numMice after calling the changeValue() ↵
                        function is: <span id = "third"> ↵
                         </span></h3>
24.  </body></html>
```

If this program is coded and run the output will be as follows:

```
Can you change the number? Try it

The value of numMice is: 12

The value of x, in the changeValue() function is: 5

The value of numMice after calling the changeValue() function is: 12
```

In this program, line 7 declares a variable, **numMice**, and sets its initial value to 12. That value is displayed (line 8). Line 9 calls the changeValue() function and sends in one argument, **numMice**. The parameter, **x**, on line 12, now contains the value of **numMice**. At this point, $x = 12$. However, line 14 changes the value of **x** to 5 and line 15 displays this value on the web page. Then control returns to line 10. Since **numMice** was passed to changeValue() by value, it retains its original value and line 10 displays this value (12) on the web page.

Is passing by value a good thing? Sure it is, if you want to manipulate a variable in a function but want it to remain unchanged in the main program. For example, if you were creating a game, you might want to do some calculations of a player's points and send messages to the player about what might result in various scenarios but want to keep the actual point value for this player the same in the main program. You could use a function to do all the manipulations but, when the program returned to the main area, the player's points remain secure. But what if you wanted to use the results of some manipulation in the function that is called when control returns to the main program? We can do this using a return statement, as shown in Example 7.10.

EXAMPLE
7.10

Returning an Updated Value

The following code returns the new value of **numMice** after it has been changed in the changeValue() function. Since the HTML script has not changed, only the JavaScript is given below.

```
1.   <script>
2.   function getValue()
3.   {
4.        var numMice = 12;
5.        document.getElementById('first').innerHTML = (numMice);
6.        numMice = changeValue(numMice);
7.        document.getElementById('third').innerHTML = (numMice);
8.   }
9.   function changeValue(x)
10.  {
11.       var x = 5;
12.       document.getElementById('second').innerHTML = (x);
13.       return x;
14.  }
15.  </script>
```

Line 6 sets the value of **numMice** to its value after it is manipulated in the changeValue() function. However, the return statement on 13 is required. This tells the function to send the new value of **x** back to the original call statement. Any time **numMice** is used after line 6, until it is changed again, its value will be the new value of 5. If this program is coded and run the output will be as follows:

| Can you change the number? Try it |

The value of numMice is: 12

The value of x, in the changeValue() function is: 5

The value of numMice after calling the changeValue() function is: 5

While strings are not primitive values, JavaScript passes string variables to functions by value as shown in Example 7.11.

EXAMPLE
7.11

Passing String Variables by Value

This little program prompts the user for a name and an email address. A function, checkEmail() has one parameter, a string variable. The single argument, a string variable, is passed to the function. The checkEmail() function only ensures that the value the user has entered has a dot, the @ sign, and three characters at its end. It does not, of course, check to make sure the user has typed in a working address. If the value entered by the user is invalid, the function requires a valid email address to be entered before returning the good address to the main function.

```
1.    <html>
2.    <head>
3.    <title>Example 7.11</title>
4.    <script>
5.    function getInfo()
6.    {
7.         var name = prompt("What's your name?");
8.         var email = prompt("What is your email address?");
9.         email = checkEmail(email);
10.        document.getElementById('first').innerHTML = name;
11.        document.getElementById('second').innerHTML = email;
12.    }
13.    function checkEmail(address)
14.    {
15.        var flag = true; var atSign = "@"; var address; ↵
                            var okSign = true;
16.        while (flag)
17.        {
18.            var numChars = address.length;
19.            for( j = 1; j < (numChars -5); j++)
20.            {
21.                if (address.charAt(j) == atSign)
22.                    okSign = false;
23.            }
24.            if ((address.charAt(numChars-4)!=".") || (okSign==true))
25.            {
26.                alert("Not a valid email address");
27.                address = prompt('Enter a valid email address ↵
                            or enter "quit" to exit the program');
28.                if (address == "quit")
29.                {
30.                    address = "unavailable";
31.                    flag = false;
32.                }
33.            }
34.            else
35.                flag = false;
36.        }
37.        return address;
38.    }
39.    </script>
40.    </head>
41.    <body>
```

```
42.        <input type ="button" onclick="getInfo()" value = "Enter ⏎
                            your information"><br />
43.        <h3>Your name is: <span id = "first"> </span></h3>
44.        <h3>Your email address is: <span id = "second">   ⏎
                            </span></h3>
45.  </body></html>
```

If an invalid email address is entered, the checkEmail() function (lines 13–38) will continue to prompt the user for a valid email address. This code added a feature to allow the user to refuse to enter an email address. Whichever option the user chooses—to enter a valid address or to quit—the value is returned to the calling program.

If the program is coded with the following input, the output will be as shown below:

Input: Henry Higglesby, first email: henryh@mymail, second email: henryh@ mymail.com

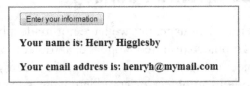

Your name is: Henry Higglesby

Your email address is: henryh@mymail.com

Input: Henry Higglesby, first email: henryh.com, second email: quit

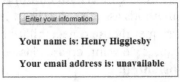

Your name is: Henry Higglesby

Your email address is: unavailable

CHECKPOINT FOR SECTION 7.3

7.13 Given the following code snippet, identify the argument(s) and the parameter(s):

```
var x = checkIt(age);
function checkIt(num)
{
      var num;
      if (num > 0)
           return true;
}
```

Use the following function to answer Checkpoints 7.14–7.16

```
function addIt(a, b)
{
      return a+b;
}
```

7.14 What, if anything, is wrong with this call to the function?

```
var z = addIt(z);
```

7.15 What, if anything, is wrong with the following call to the function?

```
var x = "car"; var y = 3;
var z = addIt(x,y);
```

7.16 What, if anything, is wrong with this call to the function?

```
var z = addIt(6,8);
```

7.17 How many values can be returned by a function?

7.18 What is the difference between passing by value and passing by reference?

7.4 Objects and Object-Oriented Concepts

JavaScript is an object-oriented language, but we have not made a big deal about this so far in this book. In an object-oriented language, an object (or, more precisely, the class that the object comes from) is basically a bit of reusable software. Programmers who write code in an object-oriented language, such as C++, often create their own classes and use objects based on those classes in their programs. Without going into too much detail, one can conceive of an **object** as something in a program that has properties and methods associated with it. In JavaScript, we rarely create our own objects but we frequently use objects that have been created for us. In this sense, and because we can, if we want, create classes and new objects, JavaScript can be considered **object-oriented.**

The Math Object

Consider an object we have used often in the text—the **Math object.** The Math object allows you to perform many mathematical tasks. Some of the properties and methods of the Math object are shown in Table 7.2.

More JavaScript Objects

Other JavaScript objects are listed in Table 7.3. We have used some already and we will use some later in the text. You can use others as you create more advanced programs.

You can think of an object as a new variable type. When we declare a variable to be of numeric type, we know some things about it. We know it must be a number; it can be negative or positive; it can be an integer or have a decimal part. These are its properties (or attributes). We also know some things we can do to it and things that it can do. We can add, subtract, multiply, and do other mathematical operations on a numeric variable. We can't do these things with a string variable because these methods are available to the numeric type and not to the string type.

TABLE 7.2	Properties and Methods of the Math Object

Some Properties of the Math Object

Property	Description
LN10	returns the natural logarithm of 10 (≈ 2.302)
PI	returns π (≈ 3.14)
E	returns Euler's number (≈ 2.718)
SQRT2	returns $\sqrt{2}$ (≈ 1.414)
SQRT1_2	returns $\sqrt{1/2}$ (≈ 0.707)

Some Methods of the Math Object

Method	Description
abs(x)	returns the absolute value of x
floor(x)	returns the integer value of x, rounded down
random()	returns a random number between 0 and 1
pow(x,y)	returns the value x^y
round(x)	Rounds x to the nearest integer
sqrt(x)	returns the square root of x

TABLE 7.3	Some JavaScript Objects

JavaScript Object	Description
Array	allows you to store multiple values with a single variable name
Boolean	allows you to convert a non-Boolean value to a Boolean (true/false) value
Date	used to work with dates and times
Math	allows you to perform mathematical tasks
Number	used for primitive numeric values
String	allows you to manipulate and store text

The same is true with objects. The Math object can round off the number 6.57 by using the round() method but the Boolean object cannot use the round() method. However, the Boolean object has its own methods. In this sense, we can think of an object as a variable type.

With the numeric or string types, you do not need to specify which method or attribute you want to use; these are inherent in the type. But when you use an object, you must include the method or property you want. For example, x = Math.round(46.7) will result in a very different value for x than x = Math.sqrt(46.7).

Passing by Reference

When a value is passed to an object, it is passed by reference. Passing by reference can sometimes improve the performance of a program. A function can only return a single value. Therefore, if you have a function that needs to change the value of several variables or, as we will now discuss, objects, when a value is passed by reference, its value is automatically changed, without using the `return` statement. However, passing by reference is also dangerous because values manipulated inside the called function are changed outside the program.

We have been passing values to functions by reference without even realizing it. The methods that go with various objects are, of course, just functions. We will see a few examples of using JavaScript objects and passing by reference now. Later in the text, after learning about arrays, we will revisit the concepts of objects and passing by reference.

The `Boolean` Object

We know that a variable of Boolean type has only two possible values: `true` or `false`. The `Boolean` object is used to convert a non-Boolean value to a Boolean value. When we set a variable equal to `true` (or `false`) we are creating a Boolean variable. However, we can also create a **Boolean object** which will return `true` or `false` for a non-Boolean value. Sometimes we either want the `return` value to be `true` or `false` or we want to determine if a value has the Boolean equivalent of `true` or `false`.

The new Keyword   Whenever we create a new instance of a JavaScript object we do so by using the **new keyword**. When an instance of an object is created, it has all the properties and methods associated with that type of object. For example, when we create a new instance of a `Boolean` object, it will have only two possible values—`true` or `false`. Example 7.12 demonstrates how to create instances of the Boolean object and what is returned in various situations.

Creating Objects and Passing Variables

This example creates several instances of the `Boolean` object and then converts a value to the Boolean type. We then check to see if that value results in one of the two possible `Boolean` values: `true` or `false`.

```
1.   <html>
2.   <head>
3.   <title>Example 7.12</title>
4.   <script>
5.   function begin()
6.   {
7.        var one = 0; var two = 1; var three = "_"; var four = NaN;
8.        var bool1 = new Boolean(one);
9.        var bool2 = new Boolean(two);
10.       var bool3 = new Boolean(three);
11.       var bool4 = new Boolean(four);
```

```
12.         document.getElementById('1').innerHTML = (one + " results ⏎
                              in Boolean " + bool1);
13.         document.getElementById('2').innerHTML = (two + " results ⏎
                              in Boolean " + bool2);
14.         document.getElementById('3').innerHTML = (three + " results ⏎
                              in Boolean " + bool3);
15.         document.getElementById('4').innerHTML = (four + " results ⏎
                              in Boolean " + bool4);
16.  }
17.  </script>
18.  </head>
19.  <body>
20.      <input type ="button" onclick="begin()" value = "Check ⏎
                              Boolean values"><br />
21.  <h3><span id = "1"> </span></h3>
22.  <h3><span id = "2"> </span></h3>
23.  <h3><span id = "3"> </span></h3>
24.  <h3><span id = "4"> </span></h3>
25.  </body></html>
```

This program creates four variables (**one**, **two**, **three**, and **four**) with various values.
Then, on lines 8–11, four instances of the Boolean **object** are created. The values
of each of the four variables are sent to the function that creates a new instance
of the Boolean object. The object turns the value into a Boolean value. But, since
variables are passed by reference, the value of the initial variable remains the same.
For instance, while **one** has the value of 0, the value of **bool1** which is the result of
changing **one** to a Boolean value has the value false. Line 12 displays the values
of both **one** and **bool1** on the web page. If this program is coded and run the output will show that **one** still retains its initial value even though the Boolean object,
bool1, now has the value of false. The output also shows us that a 0 results in a
Boolean false, a 1 is a Boolean true, an underscore is a Boolean true, and NaN is a
Boolean false.

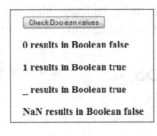

The Date Object

The **Date object,** one of the most versatile objects, is used for many different
purposes because it has many methods. With the Date object we can get the
value of a date in years, hours, minutes, seconds, even milliseconds, and beyond.
We can set aspects of the date. We can work with time zones and convert dates
to readable strings. Table 7.4 shows some of the methods associated with the
date object.

TABLE 7.4	Some Methods of the Date Object

Some Methods of the Date() Object

Method	Description
getDate()	returns the day of the month (numerical, from 1 to 31)
getDay()	returns the day of the week (from 0 to 6)
getFullYear()	returns the year in four digits
getHours()	returns the hour (from 0 to 23)
getMinutes()	returns the minutes (from 0 to 59)
getMonth()	returns the month (from 0 to 11)
getTime()	returns the number of milliseconds since midnight January 1, 1970
getTimezoneOffset()	returns the time difference, in minutes, between the local time and Greenwich Mean time (GMT)
setDate()	sets the day of the month of a Date object
setFullYear()	sets the year, using four digits, of a Date object
setHours()	sets the hour of a Date object
setMonth()	sets the month of a Date object
setTime()	sets a date and time by adding or subtracting a number of milliseconds that you specify to or from midnight, January 1, 1970
toString()	converts a Date object to a string
toTimeString()	converts the time portion of a Date object to a string

Example 7.13 shows how to use the date object to learn what day it is now and to change the date to something in the past and something in the future.

EXAMPLE 7.13

Creating and Using the Date Object

```
1.   <html>
2.   <head>
3.   <title>Example 7.13</title>
4.   <script>
5.   function begin()
6.   {
7.        var now = new Date(); var before = new Date();
8.        var later = new Date();
9.        before.setFullYear(1812, 2, 3);
10.       later.setFullYear(2095,6,15);
11.       document.getElementById('now').innerHTML = ("Today's date: " ↵
                            + now);
12.       document.getElementById('before').innerHTML = ("In the past ↵
                            it was: " + before);
```

```
13.        document.getElementById('later').innerHTML = ("One day it ↵
                                will be: " + later);
14.    }
15.    </script>
16.    </head>
17.    <body>
18.        <input type ="button" onclick="begin()" value = "Does ↵
                                anyone know what day it is?"><br />
19.        <h3><span id = "now"> </span></h3>
20.        <h3><span id = "before"> </span></h3>
21.        <h3><span id = "later"> </span></h3>
22.    </body></html>
```

This program creates four instances of the Date object. Today's date is displayed (line 11). It will be different for you because you will be running the program on a different date. The second instance is stored in a variable named **before** and will display as shown below. The three arguments sent to the Date object are 1812 for the year, 2 for the month, and 3 for the day. Since the months go from 0 to 11, month 2 is the third month, March. However, the days go from 1 to 31 so day 3 is the third of the month. The third instance of the Date object is stored in the variable **later** and the arguments send 2095 for the year, 6 for the month (i.e., the seventh month or July) and 15 for the day. The display, therefore, is as follows:

Does anyone know what day it is?

Today's date: Sat May 26 2012 18:34:51 GMT-0400 (Eastern Daylight Time)

In the past it was: Tue Mar 03 1812 18:34:51 GMT-0500 (Eastern Standard Time)

One day it will be: Fri Jul 15 2095 18:34:51 GMT-0400 (Eastern Daylight Time)

The setTimeout() Function

It's easy to create a timer in JavaScript. The **setTimeout() function** takes two arguments. The first is a JavaScript statement and the second is the number of milliseconds the function should wait. Thus, the general syntax is as follows:

```
var timer = setTimeout(expression, milliseconds);
```

The timer and the Date() object have many uses. We will use both of them in Example 7.14.

EXAMPLE 7.14

Creating a Clock with the Date Object

This program will display today's date and begin a clock that counts the passing seconds. It has a function to display minutes and seconds with two digits; i.e., if minutes is 6, it will display as 06. It also includes a timer so the clock will wait half a second before displaying any change.

```
1.    <html>
2.    <head>
3.    <title>Example 7.14</title>
```

```
4.   <script>
5.   function startClock()
6.   {
7.       var today = new Date();
8.       var hour = today.getHours();
9.       var min = today.getMinutes(); var sec = today.getSeconds();
10.      var timer;
11.      min = checkTime(min);
12.      sec = checkTime(sec);
13.      document.getElementById('now').innerHTML = ("Today's date: " ↵
                            + today);
14.      document.getElementById('clock').innerHTML = (hour + ":" + ↵
                         min + ":" + sec);
15.      timer = setTimeout('startClock()',500);
16.  }
17.  function checkTime(i)
18.  {
19.      if (i < 10)
20.          i = "0" + i;
21.      return i;
22.  }
23.  </script>
24.  </head>
25.  <body>
26.      <input type ="button" onclick="startClock()" value = "Does ↵
                          anyone know what day it is?"><br />
27.      <h3><span id = "now"> </span></h3>
28.      <h3><span id = "clock"> </span></h3>
29.  </body></html>
```

The setTimeout() function is used on line 15 to force a delay of half a second (500 milliseconds) before the startClock() function is called again. By calling startClock() over and over, the time display changes as every second passes. This creates our clock.

Notice that the checkTime() function accepts one argument—either **min** or **sec**—to ensure that all minute and second displays contain two digits. This illustrates an important feature of passing arguments to parameters. The checkTime() function is used twice. It doesn't matter whether we send in **min** or **sec**; the function works for both situations. The beauty of creating functions that can be used in many different situations is how extensive complex programs can be written with efficient, elegant code.

If you create and run this program your output will differ from the one shown, of course, but should be similar, with the clock ticking away as the seconds pass.

Does anyone know what day it is?

Today's date: Sat May 26 2012 19:08:47 GMT-0400 (Eastern Daylight Time)

19:08:47

7.19 A JavaScript object is basically a bit of _____ code.

7.20 What does the Math object do?

7.21 How are values passed to an object—by value or by reference?

7.22 Create code to set the date in a program to May 27, 1852.

7.23 Write code to set a timer to display a clock that counts off the seconds from the current time on a web page.

7.5 JavaScript Source Files

Styles are used in a web page to create presentational aspects: colors, fonts, element placement, and much more. As mentioned, styles can be included in the HTML code (**inline** styles). Or styles can go in the <head> section, inside <style></style> tags (**embedded** styles). When creating a large website you will want your pages to have a consistent look and feel, so you probably will use an external style sheet. The <head> section contains a link to this sheet. The style sheet has the extension .css and is a plain text file. If every page contains the same formatting for headers or margins or font types and colors, an external style sheet is the most efficient option. This way, if you decide to make one change to one tag, you can change it on the external style sheet and the change will be implemented throughout the website.

There is a similar situation with JavaScript. Sometimes we have placed JavaScript inline with the web page. Most often, in this book, our JavaScript code has gone in the <head> section inside <script></script> tags. But it's also possible to create an external page with JavaScript code that can be linked to the web page, in the <head> section and used by as many pages as you want. An external JavaScript file is called a **JavaScript source file.** It is written as a plain text file, and it has the extension .js.

Work Smarter, Not Harder

Many of the programs we have written have left off some important code. When a user inputs a value, it almost always needs to be validated. If the user is asked for his age, not only must the entry be a number, but also it should be a number that makes sense. No one can possibly be 2,387 years old. If a user is asked to enter his or her name, chances are the name is not more than, at the most, 50 characters long.

You may also have noticed that some code we write is remarkably similar to other code written in a different program, serving a different purpose. But the logic of the code may be essentially the same.

We also know that a JavaScript object is, basically, a reusable bit of code. If we use the sqrt() method of the Math object, we are actually calling on written code that will calculate the square root of any valid number.

We can do that too! Now that we understand how values are passed to functions, we can write functions that perform a single task but that can be used for various purposes. For example, we can write code to validate a range of numbers that works exactly the same, whether we want to ensure that a game player's age is between 18 and 118, or that a teacher enters test scores between 0 and 100, or that a customer wants to buy more than 0 widgets but less than 1,000.

If we create carefully written functions that can be used in many different situations, we can reuse the code in multiple pages. And if we store those functions in a single file, we are creating our own library of functions. We can give this page a filename and use the **.js extension.** Then we can include a link to this page on all our web pages in the <head> section and these functions are available to any JavaScript code anywhere on the web page at any time. Instead of rewriting lines of code, we merely need to call the function, sending in the appropriate arguments. This is the value of external JavaScript Source (.js) files.

Creating and Accessing a JavaScript Source (.js) File

A JavaScript source file is a simple text file. Code is written in the file without tags or headings. Text that is not valid JavaScript code is simply ignored by the browser. While a link to a .js file can be placed in the <head> or the <body> section, we will follow our convention and place most of the JavaScript in the <head> section. This way any code we write in the <head> section will have access to the .js file.

Note: Do not use <script></script> tags in a .js file!

The syntax for linking to an external JavaScript source file is as follows:

```
<script type="text/javascript" src="filename.js"></script>
```

Of course, if your .js file was inside a folder, you would include the whole path to the file as part of the src.

You can put all the JavaScript code for a single web page inside a source file. In that case, the link to the single .js file, as shown above, would be sufficient. But in this book we plan to use source files to supplement our code. We will create multiuse functions in the source file and always include the source file so that we don't have to rewrite that code if it is needed in a particular situation. But the JavaScript code that is specific to each web page will still go in the <head> section. In other words, we are creating a **library of functions** that we need most often, just as programmers before us have created libraries in most common languages, including JavaScript.

Therefore, we still need to use a second set of <script></script> tags in the <head> section for whatever code we write for a particular page. In this case, the syntax in the <head> section would be as follows:

```
<html>
<head>
<title> Page Title </title>
<link href="filename.css" rel="stylesheet" type="text/css" />
<script type="text/javascript" src="filename.js"></script>
<script>
    JavaScript code goes here
</script>
</head>
```

Example 7.15 shows how to create and use a source file that includes a single function.

EXAMPLE 7.15

A Source File to Check Spelling

This example creates a source file which we will call mySource.js. It contains one function that will check whether a word is spelled correctly. The word entered by the user and the correct spelling of the word are sent to the function in the source file by the JavaScript code in the web page. Below the source file is the code for the web page that uses this function.

Source file: mySource.js

```
1.  function checkWord(x,y)
2.  {
3.      var x; var y; var spell = true;
4.      if (x != y)
5.      spell = false;
6.      return spell;
7.  }
```

Web page file: ex_7_15.html

```
1.  <html>
2.  <head>
3.  <title>Example 7.15</title>
4.  <script type="text/javascript" src="mySource.js"></script>
5.  <script>
6.    function shipIt()
7.  {
8.      var shipCode = "FREEBIE";
9.      var userCode = prompt("Enter your code:");
10.     if (checkWord(shipCode, userCode))
11.         document.getElementById('result').innerHTML = ↵
                              ("Shipping is free!");
12.     else
13.         document.getElementById('result').innerHTML = ↵
                              ("Sorry, your code is not valid");
14. }
15. </script>
16. </head>
17. <body>
```

```
18.          <input type ="button" onclick="shipIt()" value = "Enter ↵
                           free shipping code"><br />
19.          <h3><span id = "result"> </span></h3>
20.     </body></html>
```

The JavaScript function shipIt() is called when the button is clicked. It initializes a variable with the value of the free shipping code ("FREEBIE") and then prompts the user to enter his or her code. Then it calls a function named checkWord(). The if statement on line 10 means that if the checkWord() function returns true, line 11 is executed. If checkWord() returns false, the else statement on line 13 is executed.

When checkWord() is called, the computer will look through the <head> section for a function named checkWord(). Since none is found, it then goes to the .js file and looks for checkWord() there. The variables, **shipCode** and **userCode**, are passed into the parameters of checkWord()—**x** and **y**. The function evaluates **x** and **y**, checking to see if they match. If they don't, the variable **spell** is changed to false but if they do, **spell** remains as it was initialized, true. This is what is returned to the shipIt() function and the program continues.

JavaScript Source Files Cascade

Styles cascade. This means that if you have an inline style, an embedded style, and an external style, the style closest to the element that uses it prevails. The same is true with JavaScript. Inline code is implemented first. If a function is called, the computer will first look for it where it is called. If it is called from the <head> section, the computer will look through code in the <head> section for a function with that name. If none is found, it will go to the attached source file and look for the function there.

This means that if you know you have a function named checkWord() in your source file but you want to write code for a function that does something else, it is possible to write another checkWord() function, place it in the <head> section, and have it take precedence over the function of the same name in the source file. Of course, it is preferable to find a new name for your new function.

Example 7.16 builds on Example 7.15. We'll assume that the business owner who has hired you to write this program knows what happens in Example 7.15 and wants the customer to be allowed more chances to enter a correct code. While the checkWord() function worked fine in the source file, it did not give the customer a chance to correct a misspelled or mistyped word. You decide to add a function in the <head> section which you also name checkWord() and which will add the new feature the employer wants. In real life you would probably avoid naming the new function the same as one in the source file but here we will do that for demonstration purposes. There may be times when you unintentionally name a function in the <head> section the same as a function in your source file so it's helpful to understand what happens in that situation.

Two Functions, One Function Name: What Happens?

In this example, the source file has not changed from what was presented in the previous example nor has the HTML code in the web page changed so only the new JavaScript code is given:

```
1.    <script type="text/javascript" src="mySource.js"></script>
2.    <script>
3.    function shipIt()
4.    {
5.         var shipCode = "FREEBIE";
6.         var userCode = prompt("Enter your code:");
7.         if (checkWord(shipCode, userCode))
             document.getElementById('result').innerHTML = ↵
                            ("Shipping is free!");
8.         else
9.             document.getElementById('result').innerHTML = ↵
                            ("Sorry, your code is not valid");
10.   }
11.   function checkWord(one, two)
12.   {
13.        var one; var two; var code = true; var i;
14.        for (i = 1; i < 4; i++)
15.        {
16.            code = true;
17.            if (one != two)
18.            {
19.                code = false;
20.                two = prompt("Invalid code but try again or ↵
                            enter Q to quit:");
21.                if (two == "Q")
22.                    break;
23.            }
24.        }
25.        return code;
26.   }
27.   </script>
```

In this case, when the program calls the checkWord() function, the computer finds the function first in the <head> section and uses this version. If a customer enters the wrong code first, the display will be as follows:

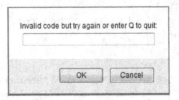

Example 7.17 shows a more complex function in an external source file that can be used in various situations.

EXAMPLE
7.17

Building a Table

This example uses the same source file we created previously and adds a new function. We won't use the checkWord() function that is still in our source file in this program but that doesn't matter. It will be there if we need it in the future. Since a JavaScript source file is a simple text file, it uses very little room in a computer's memory and can be loaded into memory in almost no time when a website is called up.

This new function, buildTable(), will build a table interactively. The user will be prompted to enter the size of the table (the number of rows and columns) as well as several other options: whether the cells should be empty, filled with random numbers, or filled by the user as each cell is created. We'll also allow the user to enter the filename of a style sheet so the table can appear as desired. Other options can be added later, as necessary. For now, we can think about using this table for a game in Greg's Gambits or for an exam in Carla's Classroom.

Source file: mySource.js

```
1.   function checkWord(x,y)
2.   {
3.       var x; var y; var spell = true;
4.       if (x != y)
5.           spell = false;
6.       return spell;
7.   }
8.   function buildTable(rows, cols, fill, style)
9.   {
10.      var rows; var cols; var fill; var ranNum;
11.      var i; var j; var style;
12.      document.write("<link href='"+style+"' rel='stylesheet' ↵
                             type='text/css' />");
13.      document.write("<div id='content'><p> </p>");
14.      document.write("<table width = '60%' border='1' align='center' ↵
                             cellpadding='5' cellspacing='5'>");
15.      ranNum = (rows + 1) * (cols + 1);
16.      for (i = 0; i < rows; i++)
17.      {
18.          document.write("<tr>");
19.          for (j = 0; j < cols; j++)
20.          {
21.              if (fill == "empty")
22.                  document.write("<td width = '"+(1/cols)+"%'> ↵
                         <h1> <br /></h1></td>");
23.              if (fill == "random")
24.              {
25.                  entry = parseInt(Math.random()*ranNum)+1;
26.                  document.write("<td width = '"+(1/cols)+"%'> ↵
                         <h1>"+entry+"</h1></td>");
27.              }
28.              if (fill == "prompt")
29.              {
30.                  entry = prompt("Enter a value for the cell in ↵
                         row "+(i+1)+", column "+(j+1));
```

```
31.                        document.write("<td width='"+(1/cols)+"%'> ↵
                              <h2>"+entry+"</h2></td>");
32.                    }
33.                }
34.            document.write("</tr>");
35.        }
36.        document.write("</table> </div>");
37. }
```

Web page file: ex_7_17.html, The first example uses the Greg's Gambits styles

```
1.  <html>
2.  <head>
3.  <title>Example 7.17</title>
4.  <link href="greg.css" rel="stylesheet" type="text/css" />
5.  <script type="text/javascript" src="mySource.js"></script>
6.  <script>
7.  function buildIt()
8.  {
9.      var numRows; var numCols; var table;
10.     var filler; var filename;
11.     numRows = parseInt(prompt("How many rows do you want in ↵
                        your table?"));
12.     numCols = parseInt(prompt("How many columns do you want in ↵
                        your table?"));
13.     filler = prompt("Do you want to leave the table cells empty? ↵
                        Type y for yes, n for no.");
14.     if (filler == "y")
15.         filler = "empty";
16.     else
17.     {
18.         filler = prompt("Do you want the cells filled with ↵
                            random numbers? Type y for yes, ↵
                            n for no");
19.         if (filler == "y")
20.             filler = "random";
21.         else
22.             filler = "prompt";
23.     }
24.     filename = prompt("Enter the filename of the style sheet ↵
                        to use with this table:");
25.     table = buildTable(numRows, numCols, filler, filename);
26. }
27. </script>
28. </head>
29. <body>
30. <div id="container">
31.     <img src="images/superhero.jpg" class="floatleft" />
32.     <h1 id="logo">Table Builder</h1>
33.     <p><input type ="button" onclick="buildIt()" value = ↵
                        "Build a table"></p>
34. </body></html>
```

Let's start by looking at the web page file. In this example, we used the Greg's Gambits style but could, just as easily, insert line 33 (the button that calls the function) on any web page to create a page with a different look. The button, when clicked, calls the `buildIt()` function in the <head> section of the page. Here, the important attributes of the table are input by the user: the number of rows and columns; whether or not the cells will be filled by the program (empty or random numbers) or entered by the user; and the name of the style sheet to be used on the page that will contain the table. This occurs on lines 11–24.

Then the `buildTable()` is called on line 25. The arguments passed to the table are the number of rows (**numRows**), the number of columns (**numCols**), how the cells should be filled (**filler**) and the filename of the style sheet (**filename**).

Control is then passed to the source file which has four parameters. The value of **numRows** is now passed to **rows**, **numCols** to **cols**, **filler** to **fill**, and **filename** to **style**. The building of the table begins on line 12 where a link is made to a style sheet using the value of **style** for the name of the stylesheet file. Line 13 creates a <div> area for content and line 14 opens a new table.

The variable **ranNum** creates a range to use if the user has requested that the cells be filled with random numbers. Any range could be used but this program chose to use the product of (**rows** +1)*(**cols** + **1**).

Line 16 begins the loop that will create the table. For a table, we need a nested loop. The outer loop has as many iterations as there are rows. Before we begin the inner loop, a new row is created on line 18. For each row, the inner loop has as many iterations as there are columns. The inner loop begins on line 19.

The first `if` statement, on line 21, checks to see if the user has selected to leave the cells empty. If so, line 22 creates a cell and puts an empty space into it. The width of the cell is a percentage of number of cells in each row (i.e., 1/**cols**). If there are five columns, then, to make each cell even, each cell should be 20% of the table width or 1/5. If there are 10 columns, then each cell will be 10% (or 1/10) of the table width.

If the user has not chosen to leave the cells empty, line 23 checks to see if the user wants random numbers to fill the cells. If this is true, the variable **entry** on line 25 creates a random number in the range of 1 through the value of **ranNum**. Line 26 creates a new cell and fills it with this random number.

If **fill** does equal "random" or "empty" then the user wants to enter the values for each cell as it is created. The clause on lines 28–32 accomplishes this. Now the variable **entry** is set to whatever the user types at each iteration (line 30) and the cell is created with this value on line 31.

The inner loop ends on line 33. Next, the row is closed (line 34) and the outer loop is executed again, creating a new row and filling all the cells in that row. When the outer loop has completed all its iterations, the loop ends and the table is closed on line 36. The function ends and control returns to the web page for any more coding. In this case, we do nothing else.

If the user wants to create a page with Greg's styles that has a 4 × 4 table, filled with random numbers, the output will look like this:

But if the user wants to create a 3 × 5 table, using Carla's styles, and filling each cell with an arithmetic problem, the output will look like this:

3+4	3+4	2+2	6+3	5+5
3+2	9+7	7+6	3+3	8+5
9-2	6-3	8-8	7-1	5-4

Creating a Library of Functions

Now we will add to our source file with functions that we have used in the past or may use in the future. These functions can serve many purposes so we will write them in the most general form. This is just a sampling of the type of functions you may want to keep in your own JavaScript source file. Or you may want to create several source files, organizing them by topics. Simply by including a link to the file in the <head> section, they will always be at your fingertips, ready to use when needed. Example 7.18 gives four functions, often used in programs, and written in a general manner. These will be added to our mySource.js file and included in future examples and exercises.

Functions for a Source File

(a) A function to check if a number is within a given range:

```
1.  function checkRange(x,low,high)
2.  {
3.      var x; var low; var high;
4.      var result = true;
5.      if (x < low || x > high)
6.          result = false;
7.      return result;
8.  }
```

(b) A function to check if a character is in a specific spot in a string:

```
1.  function charAtPlace(x, y, z)
2.  {
3.      var x; var y; var z; var result = false;
4.      if (x.charAt(y-1) == z)
```

```
5.          result = true;
6.      return result;
7.  }
```

(c) A function to check if a character is in a specific word:

```
1.  function checkForChar(x, y)
2.  {
3.      var x; var y; var i; var lgth; var result = false;
4.      lgth = x.length;
5.      for (i=0; i < lgth; i++)
6.      {
7.          if (x.charAt(i) == y)
8.              result = true;
9.      }
10.     return result;
11. }
```

(d) A function to get a percent of a number:

```
1.  function checkPercent(x, y, z)
2.  {
3.      var x; var y; var z; var percent;
4.      percent = (y/100)*x;
5.      if (z == "y")
6.          return (x - percent);
7.      else
8.          return percent;
9.  }
```

CHECKPOINT FOR SECTION 7.5

7.24 Describe three ways to include JavaScript in a web page.

7.25 If a web page has a function named checkIt() in the <head> section and a function named checkIt() in the linked source file, which will be used by a call to checkIt() inside the <script></script> tags in the <head> section?

7.26 What is wrong with a file named source.js that looks like this:

```
<script>
function addIt(x, y)
{
    var x; var y;
    return x + y;
}
</script>
```

7.27 Given the following function which is in a source file?

```
function showName(a, b, c)
{
    var a; var b; var c;
    c = b + ", " + a;
    return c;
}
```

What is wrong with the following call to the function? (The call is in <script></script> tags in the <head> section of the page.)

```
fullName = showName("Jane","Jones");
```

7.6 Putting It to Work

Now we will create the game of Hangman for the Greg's Gambits site and a reading comprehension lesson for the Carla's Classroom site.

Greg's Gambits: Hangman

Our new page will be accessed from the Play A Game link on Greg's home page. The page will be the game of Hangman, familiar to many schoolchildren. In our game, the computer will generate one of 10 words which will be displayed by underscores representing each letter in the word. The player will guess letters and, for each correct guess, the corresponding underscore will be replaced by that letter. For each incorrect guess, a stick figure will be drawn, piece by piece, attached to a hangman's noose. The game ends when the player correctly guesses the word or the player has made enough incorrect guesses to hang the man at the gallows. If the player wins, we will display both a message and an image of the word to replace the hangman's gallows.

The page title will be Greg's Gambits | Hangman and the filename is gregs_hangman.html.

Developing the Program

First, place a link to this game on the menu of games. Add a link to this game on the play_games.html page so that, if you have completed the previous Putting It To Work exercises, your play_games.html page will look like this:

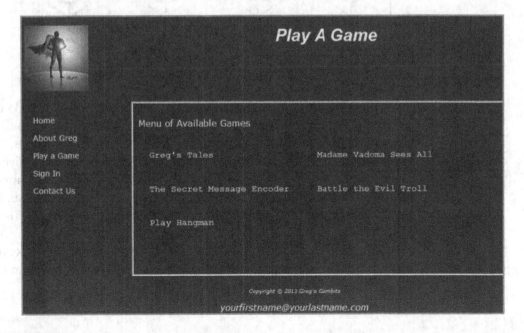

The Man in the Noose   As the player guesses letters for the hidden word, each incorrect guess must result in something added to the man hanging from the noose. Because your computer has no artistic ability, we achieve this by replacing one image with another, each image exactly the same as the previous one with one added feature. Eleven images have been created for you and are available in the Student Data Files. The images have been named hangman0.gif, hangman1.gif, hangman2.gif, and so on. This will make it possible to replace the images by identifying the name as part text and part variable where the variable will be a counter. The initial image will be an empty noose. The 10 images look like this:

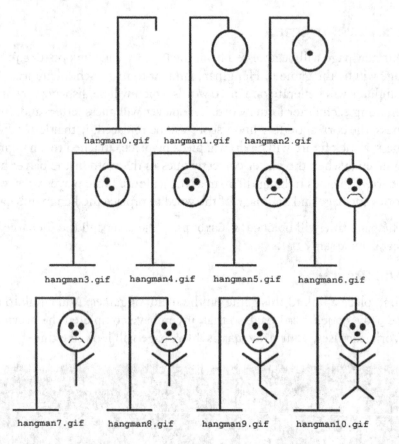

The Secret Words   We also need a way to generate secret words. When we learn to use arrays (in Chapter 8) or, even better, PHP (in Chapter 12) to pull information from a database, we can write programs that have extensive options. For now, we will generate nine possible words. Since we want the program to display a picture of the word if the player guesses correctly, we'll make a similar connection between the image filenames and the words in the game as with the hangman images. In this case, we will generate a random number between one and nine. This number will identify which word will be used and the number will also identify the image that corresponds to that word. Thus, all our images will be named picX.jpg where X is a number between one and nine. The images we use for this program are in the Student Data Files and are shown below:

pic1.jpg
ghost

pic2.jpg
horse

pic3.jpg
insect

pic4.jpg
celery

pic5.jpg
pelican

pic6.jpg
jewelbox

pic7.jpg
castle

pic8.jpg
monster

pic9.jpg
bunny

Writing the Code

The general flow of the game will be as follows:

A word will be picked, using the `Math.random()` method to generate a number between one and nine. We'll use a `switch` statement to match the random number with a word.

Next, we will display an underscore (_) and a space to represent each letter by finding the length of the word, using the `length` property, and displaying "_ " in a loop for as many times as there are letters in the word. At this point, we will also display the image of an empty noose.

The game will be played within a `while` loop. When the player clicks the button to begin the game, he will be prompted to enter a letter. The word must be checked to see if this letter is in that word. If it is, a function will be called to replace the display with this letter in place of its corresponding underscore (or underscores if the letter is in more than one place in the word). When this is complete, a function will be called to check if replacing this letter results in a match between the letters guessed by the player and the secret word.

If there is a match, the noose will be replaced by an image that corresponds to the word and the player will get a `"You win!"` message. If there is no match, the noose image will be replaced by the next noose image which contains one more piece of the picture of the man being hanged. A message will be displayed that says, `"not a winner yet"`.

The `while` loop continues until either the entire word is guessed or until the last image of a complete hangman has been displayed, depending on which comes first. Since this code is a bit complex in some places, we'll discuss it in pieces.

The *startHangman()* *Function*   The main function is as follows:

```
 1.  function startHangman()
 2.  {
 3.       var nooseCount = 0;
 4.       var wordNum = Math.floor((Math.random()*9)+1);
 5.       var picture = "pic" + wordNum + ".jpg";
 6.       switch(wordNum)
 7.       {
 8.           case 1:
 9.               word = "ghost"; break;
10.           case 2:
11.               word = "horse"; break;
12.           case 3:
13.               word = "insect"; break;
14.           case 4:
15.               word = "celery"; break;
16.           case 5:
17.               word = "pelican"; break;
18.           case 6:
19.               word = "jewelbox"; break;
20.           case 7:
21.               word = "castle"; break;
22.           case 8:
23.               word = "monster"; break;
24.           case 9:
25.               word = "bunny"; break;
26.       }
27.       var newWord = ""; var win = false;
28.       var lgth = word.length;
29.       var guessLetter; var goodGuess = false;
30.       for (var i = 0; i < lgth; i++)
31.           newWord = newWord + "_ ";
32.       document.getElementById("noose").innerHTML = ("<img src ↵
                          ='images/hangman0.gif' />");
33.       document.getElementById("game").innerHTML = newWord;
34.       while (win == false && nooseCount < 10)
35.       {
36.           goodGuess = false;
37.           guessLetter = prompt("Guess a letter");
38.           for (var j = 0; j < lgth; j++)
39.           {
40.               if (guessLetter == word.charAt(j))
41.               {
42.                   goodGuess = true;
43.                   var offSet = 2*j;
44.                   newWord = setCharAt(newWord, offSet, ↵
                          guessLetter);
45.               }
46.           }
47.           document.getElementById("game").innerHTML = newWord;
48.           win = checkWord(word, newWord);
49.           if (win == true)
50.           {
51.               document.getElementById("result").innerHTML = ↵
                          ("You win!");
```

```
52.                  document.getElementById("noose").innerHTML = ↵
                         ("<img src = '" + picture + "' />");
53.          }
54.          else if (win == false)
55.          {
56.                  document.getElementById("result").innerHTML = ↵
                         ("not a winner yet");
57.              if (goodGuess == false)
58.                  nooseCount = nooseCount + 1;
59.                  document.getElementById("noose").innerHTML = ↵
                         ("<img src ='images/hangman" + ↵
                         nooseCount + ".gif' />");
60.          }
61.      }
62.  }
```

Lines 1–29 are self-explanatory. The rest of the code deserves some discussion. Lines 30 and 31 create a string that consists of the number of underscores and spaces that correspond to the number of characters in the selected word. Line 32 displays the initial noose and line 33 displays the string of underscores and spaces that was just created.

The while loop that begins on line 34 will continue until one of the two test conditions are met. Either the variable **win** is false which, as we will see, means the letters guessed have not completely matched the secret word, or **nooseCount** is less than 10. There are nine possible hangman images which add limbs and facial features to the image of the poor hanged man. When the entire man is displayed, **nooseCount** will equal 9 and the game will end.

Line 37 prompts the player for a letter. Line 38 begins the loop that checks to see if this letter matches a letter in the secret word. Therefore, it has as many iterations as there are characters in the word, stored in the variable **lgth** which was determined on line 28. If a match is found, we know where it is. The charAt() method identifies where the character is in the word, using the counter **j** as the identifier of the index value of that character. A Boolean variable, **goodGuess**, which was initially set to false is now set to true. This variable will be used later to decide whether or not to change the hangman image. If the player has guessed a letter that is in the word, no new hangman image will display. Line 44 calls a new function, setCharAt() which will create a new display, using underscores and spaces for letters that have not yet been guessed, but replacing an underscore and a space with the correctly guessed letter. The setCharAt() function takes three arguments and we send in the value of **newWord** (the masked word), **offSet**, and the letter that has been guessed, **guessLetter**. The variable **offSet** is used to identify where the guessed letter should be placed.

Here is what **offSet** does: Imagine the secret word is table. Initially, the screen display is as follows:

_ _ _ _ _

If the player guesses 'b' then a b must be replace the third underscore. We have identified the 'b' as index value 2 because in table, b is charAt(2). But in **newWord**, the 'b' is actually at index 4 because each letter is represented by an underscore and a space. Thus, **j** = 2 so **offSet** = 2*2 or 4 and **offSet** can be used to identify the actual index of the character to be replaced.

We will discuss how the setCharAt() function works in more depth later. The next thing the startHangman() function does, after replacing a correct guess in the displayed word (line 47), is to check whether this action has created a winner or not. Line 48 calls the checkWord() function. The function is similar to one we have saved previously in our source file but adds a new feature. Once the word has been checked, **win** is either **true** or **false**. If it is true, lines 49–53 display the winning message and change the image of the noose to the image that represents the secret word.

If **win** is **false** (lines 54–60), a message is sent to the screen and the noose image is updated. The **nooseCount** variable is also updated because a false guess represents one more increment in the number of false guesses allowed.

The setCharAt() Function   The function that replaces the secret word with a player's correct guess is as follows:

```
1.    function setCharAt(str,index,chr)
2.    {
3.        if(index > str.length-1)
4.            return str;
5.        return str.substr(0,index) + chr + str.substr(index+1);
6.    }
```

This function has three parameters: **str**, **index**, and **chr**. The startHangman() function sends in three arguments: **newWord**, **offSet**, and **guessLetter**. Lines 3 and 4 of the function check to see if **index** (which represents the index value of the character which is to be replaced) is greater than the length of the word. If that is true, the character is not in the word and the entire word is returned, unchanged. However, if that is not true, we need to replace an underscore with the character that has been guessed which is represented by **chr** in the function. It does this as follows:

The first part of what is returned, **str**.substr(0, **index**) identifies the substring that starts at character 0, goes up to the value of **index**, and extracts that part of the word. If the original word was jewelbox and the guessed letter was a 'w', **index** would be the value of **offSet**. Since w is the third letter, it would be found when **j** = 2 so **offSet** would be 2*2 or 4. The value of **str** the first time this function is called would be " _ _ _ _ _ _ _ _". The substring that is extracted by **str**.substr(0, **index**) would be characters 0 through 4 or "_ _ ".

This substring is then concatenated with **chr** which, in this example is a 'w' so up to this point we have " _ _ w ". The last part of this statement concatenates what we have so far with what is left in the original **str**. The part of the statement **str**.substr(**index**+1) extracts the substring that starts at space 5 (**index** + 1) and goes to the end. Thus, the value returned is " _ _ w _ _ _ _ _".

The next time a correct letter is guessed, the value of **newWord** is " _ _ w _ _ _ _ _" so if a 'b' is entered, the new value of **offSet** will be 10 (the index of a 'b' in jewelbox is 5 and 5*2 = 10). Thus, the first part of the return statement, str.substr(0, **index**), will extract the substring from character 0 through character 10 (" _ _ w _ _ "), concatenate that with the 'b' to get " _ _ w _ _ b " and then concatenate this with what is left to get " _ _ w _ _ b _ _". This is how, each time a correct letter is guessed, an underscore is replaced with that letter.

The replace() Method and Regular Expressions   JavaScript has a way to search for a specified value—what is called a **regular expression**—and return a new string where the specified value is replaced. This is the **replace() method** and the syntax used to replace a character or string with another character or string is as follows:

```
var newString = str.replace(/value_to_replace/g,new_value);
```

By placing the original string between slashes (/ /) and including a g, the replacements will be global. Therefore, everywhere the value identified to be replaced is found, the new value will replace it. The original string remains unchanged. We will use this method to clean up the word that results from a player guessing a correct letter. Since we originally displayed the secret word with a space and an underscore to represent each letter, each time a character is replaced, an extra space may be left over.

The checkWord() function that we created earlier in the chapter simply compares two words and returns true if they are the same. In this program, after the user has made correct guesses, we need to clean out extra spaces before we can compare the secret word with the word resulting from the player's guesses. We will use the replace()method to clean up the word.

The Revised checkWord() Function   The code for our new and improved checkWord() function is as follows:

```
1.   function checkWord(word, otherWord)
2.   {
3.        var cleanWord;
4.        cleanWord = otherWord;
5.        cleanWord = otherWord.replace(/ /g, "");
6.        if (word == cleanWord)
7.             return true;
8.        else
9.             return false;
10.  }
```

Before comparing the two strings, line 5 replaces all the spaces in the string that has been sent in with nothing. In this way, the two words can be correctly compared.

Putting It All Together

We are ready to put it all together. The code for the whole page is as follows:

```
1.   <html>
2.   <head>
3.   <title>Greg's Gambits | Hangman</title>
4.   <link href="greg.css" rel="stylesheet" type="text/css" />
5.   <script>
```

```
 6.  function startHangman()
 7.  {
 8.      var nooseCount = 0;
 9.      var wordNum = Math.floor((Math.random()*9)+1);
10.      var picture = "pic" + wordNum + ".jpg";
11.      switch(wordNum)
12.      {
13.          case 1:
14.              word = "ghost"; break;
15.          case 2:
16.              word = "horse"; break;
17.          case 3:
18.              word = "insect"; break;
19.          case 4:
20.              word = "celery"; break;
21.          case 5:
22.              word = "pelican"; break;
23.          case 6:
24.              word = "jewelbox"; break;
25.          case 7:
26.              word = "castle"; break;
27.          case 8:
28.              word = "monster"; break;
29.          case 9:
30.              word = "bunny"; break;
31.      }
32.      var newWord = ""; var win = false; var goodGuess = false;
33.      var lgth = word.length; var guessLetter;
34.      for (var i = 0; i < lgth; i++)
35.          newWord = newWord + "_ ";
36.      document.getElementById("noose").innerHTML = ("<img src ↵
                          ='images/hangman0.gif' />");
37.      document.getElementById("game").innerHTML = newWord;
38.      while (win == false && nooseCount < 10)
39.      {
40.          goodGuess = false;
41.          guessLetter = prompt("Guess a letter");
42.          for (var j = 0; j < lgth; j++)
43.          {
44.              if (guessLetter == word.charAt(j))
45.              {
46.                  goodGuess = true;
47.                  var offSet = 2*j;
48.                  newWord = setCharAt(newWord, offSet, ↵
                          guessLetter);
49.              }
50.          }
51.          document.getElementById("game").innerHTML = newWord;
52.          win = checkWord(word, newWord);
53.          if (win == true)
54.          {
55.              document.getElementById("result").innerHTML = ↵
                          ("You win!");
56.              document.getElementById("noose").innerHTML = ↵
                          ("<img src = '" + picture + "' />");
```

```
57.                  }
58.              else if (win == false)
59.              {
60.                      document.getElementById("result").innerHTML = ⏎
                                ("not a winner yet");
61.                      if (goodGuess == false)
62.                          nooseCount = nooseCount + 1;
63.                      document.getElementById("noose").innerHTML = ⏎
                          ("<img src ='images/hangman" + ⏎
                          nooseCount + ".gif' />");
64.              }
65.          }
66.  }
67.  function checkWord(word, otherWord)
68.  {
69.      var cleanWord;
70.      cleanWord = otherWord;
71.      cleanWord = otherWord.replace(/ /g, "");
72.      if (word == cleanWord)
73.          return true;
74.      else
75.          return false;
76.  }
77.  function setCharAt(str,index,chr)
78.  {
79.      if(index > str.length-1)
80.          return str;
81.      return str.substr(0,index) + chr + str.substr(index+1);
82.  }
83.  </script>
84.  </head>
85.  <body>
86.      <div id="container">
87.          <img src="images/superhero.jpg" class="floatleft" />
88.          <h1 id="logo"><em>The Game of Hangman</em></h1>
89.          <h2 align="center">Greg Challenges You to a Game ⏎
                        of Hangman</h2>
90.          <div id="nav">
91.              <p><a href="index.html">Home</a>
92.              <a href="greg.html">About Greg</a>
93.              <a href="play_games.html">Play a Game</a>
94.              <a href="sign.html">Sign In</a>
95.              <a href="contact.html">Contact Us</a></p>
96.          </div>
97.          <div id="content">
98.              <p><input type="button" value = "Start the ⏎
                        game" onclick="startHangman();" /></p>
99.              <div id = "noose" class = "floatright">
100.                 <img src ="images/hangman10.gif" />
101.             </div>
102.             <div id = "game"><p> </p></div>
103.             <div id = "result"><p> </p></div>
104.         </div>
105.         <div id="footer">
106.             Copyright &copy; 2013 Greg's Gambits<br />
```

```
107.                          <a href="mailto:yourfirstname@yourlastname.com"> ↵
                                  yourfirstname@yourlastname.com</a>
108.              </div>
109.          </div>
110.  </body></html>
```

Finishing Up

If you enter this code, your page will first look like this:

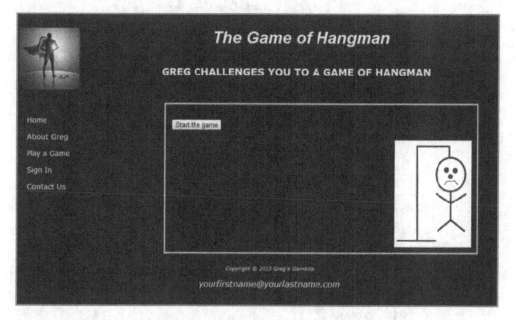

After clicking the Start the game button, the display will be as follows, although the word generated may be different so there will be a different number of underscores and spaces:

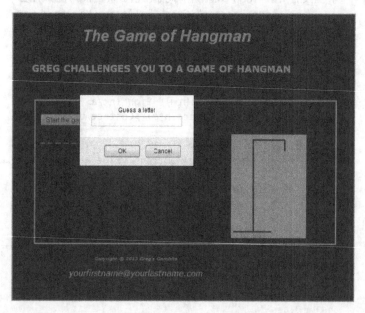

input: In this case, the secret word is insect. If the player guesses n, g, f, s, k, m, r, t and c, given this particular game, the output will be as follows:

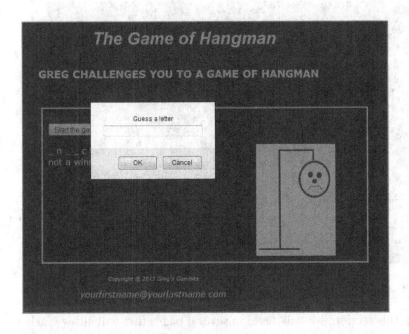

Input: If the player guesses more incorrect letters, the completed game will look like this:

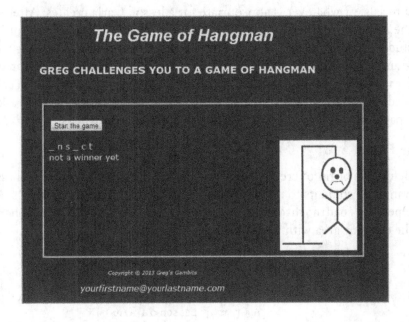

But if the player enters all the correct letters in another round of play, the display will be as follows:

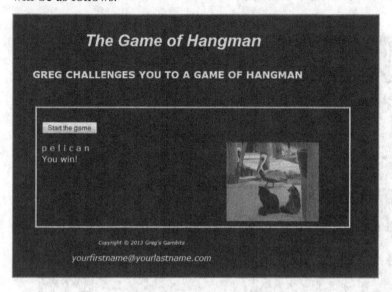

Carla's Classroom: Reading Comprehension

In this section, we will develop several pages that will allow Carla to assign reading comprehension exercises to her students. We will generate the pages that will allow Carla to build as many reading comprehension lessons as she wishes but we will only do one completely.

Developing the Program

For this program, we will use several web pages. One page will allow Carla to add reading material as often as she wants. The page can link to essays, short stories, tutorials, or whatever is appropriate for a lesson Carla creates. After a student reads the material, the student will be required to answer questions about it. When the student is ready, he or she can click a link to the questions. Here is where our programming comes in. The questions will be on a page that Carla can create. We will create a page that allows Carla to create questions as they apply to each piece of reading material. Later, as a Programming Challenge, you will be asked to generate a page that a student will access to enter his or her answers.

Creating the First Page

Before we begin to create the page that will display the stories and essays that Carla wants her students to read, let's place a link to this page on Carla's Reading page. Open the reading.html file and add a link to the Reading Comprehension page in the content area with the following:

```
1.   <div id="content">
2.       <p><img src="images/carla_pic.jpg" class="floatleft" /> ↵
                     Reading Lessons: </p>
3.       <p><a href = "carla_grammar.html">Create Your Own Story: ↵
                 A Grammar Lesson</a></p>
```

```
4.        <p><a href = "carla_comprehension.html">Reading ⏎
                  Comprehension Exercises</a></p>
5.   </div>
```

If you have been creating all Carla's Classroom pages in the text so far, the only new content is on line 4. At this point, your reading.html page will look like this:

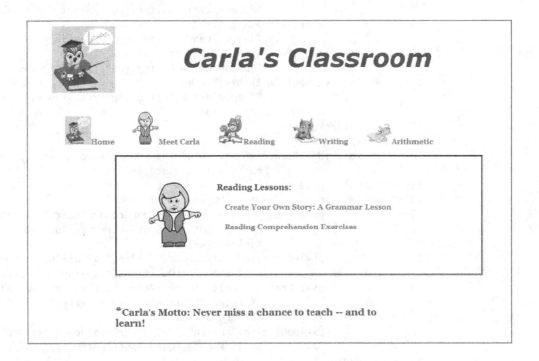

Now we'll create the page that students will click to begin their reading comprehension exercises. You will find four small text files in the Student Data Files. Each is a short story. We will only create content for one of the stories, but Carla can use the pages we design to create content for all these stories and as many others as she wants. First, we will create the carla_comprehension.html page that will link from the reading.html page. Next to the link to each story will be a button that the student will click when he or she is ready to answer questions about the story. We will also create a page that is password-protected so only Carla can access it. When she does, she will be able to enter questions about a particular story or edit questions she has already entered. The HTML code for the initial page, using any of the Carla's Classroom pages as a template, is as follows:

```
1.   <html>
2.   <head>
3.   <title>Carla's Classroom | Reading Lessons</title>
4.   <link href="carla.css" rel="stylesheet" type="text/css" />
5.   </head>
6.   <body>
```

```
7.    <div id="container">
8.        <img src="images/owl_reading.jpg" class="floatleft" />
9.        <h1><em>Carla's Classroom</em></h1>
10.       <p> </p>
11.       <div align="left">
12.       <blockquote>
13.           <p><a href="index.html"><img src = ↵
                      "images/owl_button.jpg" />Home</a>
14.           <a href="carla.html"><img src = ↵
                      "images/carla_button.jpg" />Meet Carla </a>
15.           <a href="reading.html"><img src = ↵
                      "images/read_button.jpg" />Reading</a>
16.           <a href="writing.html"><img src = ↵
                      "images/write_button.jpg" />Writing</a>
17.           <a href="math.html"><img src = ↵
                      "images/arith_button.jpg" />Arithmetic</a> ↵
                      <br /></p>
18.       </blockquote>
19.       </div>
20.       <div id = "content" style="width: 700px; margin-left: auto; ↵
                      margin-right: auto;">
21.           <p>Select a Story</p>
22.       <div style = "width: 300px; float: left;">
23.           <p><a href = "carla_stories/Leopard_spots.rtf">How the ↵
                      Leopard Got its Spots <br />by Rudyard ↵
                      Kipling</a></p>
24.           <p><input type="button" id="kipling" value="questions" ↵
                      onclick = "getQuestions('kipling');" /></p>
25.           <p><a href = "carla_stories/Peter_Rabbit.rtf">The Tale ↵
                      of Peter Rabbit <br />by Beatrix ↵
                      Potter</a></p>
26.           <p><input type="button" id="potter" value="questions" ↵
                      onclick = "getQuestions('potter');" /></p>
27.       </div>
28.       <div style = "width: 300px; float: right;">
29.           <p><a href = "carla_stories/RipVanWinkle.rtf">Rip ↵
                      Van Winkle <br />by Washington Irving</a></p>
30.           <p><input type="button" id="irving" value="questions" ↵
                      onclick = "getQuestions('irving');" /></p>
31.           <p><a href = "carla_stories/little_Cloud.rtf">A Little ↵
                      Cloud<br />by James Joyce</a></p>
32.           <p><input type="button" id="joyce" value="questions" ↵
                      onclick = "getQuestions('joyce');" /></p>
33.       </div>
34.       <div style="clear:both;"></div>
35.       </div>
36.       <div id="footer">
37.           <h3>* Carla's Motto: Never miss a chance to teach -- ↵
                      and to learn!</h3>
38.       </div>
39.   </div>
40.   </body></html>
```

Your page will now look like this:

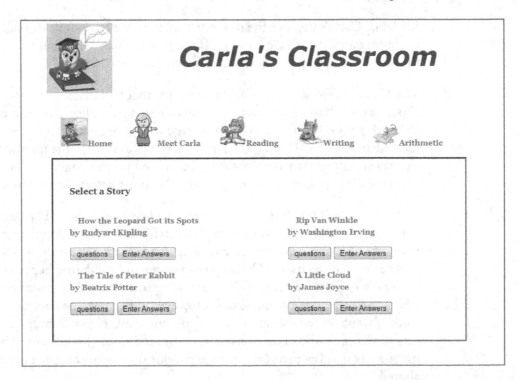

Now we will create the page Carla will use when she generates reading comprehension pages for her students. We will only create one page using The Tale of Peter Rabbit but you will see how Carla can use our program to customize questions for each story or text that she assigns to her students.

Writing the Code

We'll write the page used by Carla to enter questions she wants students to answer about the selected story. For now, we will fill in our own questions for just one story. You can complete the other stories if you want. You will create a second page that students can use to enter their answers in the Case Study for Carla's Classroom.

The pages with the questions for each story are only edited by Carla. However, they will be viewed by the students so we'll used Carla's style sheet and put the questions within a content <div>.

Password Protection   Some of Carla's students are computer-savvy, so we will add a password feature to the page Carla uses to create her questions. We do not need to validate the creation of the password; Carla can make it anything she wants, without restrictions. But we have to check that the person using the page knows the password. At this point, Carla has told us she wants the password to be carlaIsTheBest so that's what we will hard code into the page. Before anyone can enter any questions, the person must enter the password. We'll use the checkWord() function in our source file to check that the password entered matches the one "on file." For Carla's site, use the `mySource.js` page we have built throughout this chapter but rename it `carlaSource.js`. If the word entered matches Carla's password, the web page will allow questions to be entered or changed.

The First Web Page: We will create a page that will be used for two purposes. First, Carla will use it to enter questions about a story. For this example, we use `The Tale of Peter Rabbit` but the same page can be reused for any story, by editing the title in the HTML file. Also, if Carla wants to change the questions at any time, she can simply rewrite the questions, by pulling up this page. The page will include a feature we have not mentioned so far: a button that can be hidden when needed.

Use the `visibility` Property to Create a Hidden Button   The page we create will be seen in two situations. First, Carla will use it to develop a page of comprehension questions. And the students will also use it to access these questions. We first verify that the user is Carla by requesting and validating her password. Then, if it really is Carla, she can click a second button that will take her to a new page where she will enter her questions. However, if this page has been created and a student wants to see the questions, we do not want to give him or her the opportunity to change Carla's questions. Therefore, if a student accesses the page, we will use the **visibility property** to hide the button that allows the questions to be altered.

The `visibility` property sets or returns whether an element should be visible; it allows us to show or hide an element. A similar property is the **display property.** However, if the `display` propert is set to `"none"`, the entire element will be hidden, while setting the `visibility` property to `"hidden"` means that the contents of the element will be invisible, but the element stays in its original position and size. This keeps content from jumping around on a page.

Here is the syntax to hide an object:

```
object.style.visibility = "hidden";
```

In this case, the object is a button.

The code for this first page, therefore, is as follows:

```
1.    <html>
2.    <head>
3.    <title>Reading Lesson: Beatrix Potter</title>
4.    <link href="carla.css" rel="stylesheet" type="text/css" />
5.    <script type="text/javascript" src="carlaSource.js"></script>
6.    <script>
7.    function signIn()
8.    {
9.        var carla; var entry; var password; var student; var status;
10.       var key1 = "carlaIsTheBest";
11.       var key2 = "ready";
12.       status = prompt("Are you a student? Type y or n");
13.       if (status == 'n')
14.       {
15.           password = prompt("Enter the password:");
16.           carla = checkWord(password, key1);
```

```
17.              if (carla)
18.                  alert ("Click the button to begin entering ↵
                                 questions.");
19.              else
20.                  alert("Bye bye");
21.          }
22.          if (status != 'n')
23.          {
24.              document.getElementById("create").style.visibility = ↵
                                 "hidden";
25.              entry = prompt("Are you ready for questions? Type ↵
                                 'ready' or 'no'");
26.              student = checkWord(entry, key2)
27.              if (student)
28.                  alert ("Click the button to view your questions.");
29.              else
30.                  alert("Bye bye");
31.          }
32.      }
33.  </script>
34.  </head>
35.  <body>
36.  <div id="container">
37.          <img src="images/owl_reading.jpg" class="floatleft" />
38.          <h2>Carla's Classroom <br />
39.          Reading Comprehension</h2>
40.          <div id = "content" style="width: 700px; margin-left: auto; ↵
                                 margin-right: auto;">
41.              <p>The Tale of Peter Rabbit by Beatrix Potter</p>
42.              <div style = "width: 300px; float: left;">
43.                  <p><input type="button" id="potter" value="signin" ↵
                                 onclick="signIn();" />
44.                  <p> <span id = "create"> <input type = "button" id ↵
                                 = "create" value = "Enter the questions" ↵
                                 onclick = "location.href = ↵
                                 'questions_potter.html'"; /></span>
45.                  <span id = "view"> <input type = "button" id ↵
                                 = "view" value = "View the questions" ↵
                                 onclick="location.href = ↵
                                 'questions_potter.html'"; /></span></p>
46.              </div>
47.          <div style="clear:both;"></div>
48.  </div>
49.          <div id="footer">
50.              <h3>* Carla's Motto: Never miss a chance to teach -- ↵
                                 and to learn!</h3>
51.          </div>
52.  </div>
53.  </body></html>
```

There are a few lines in this code to discuss. Line 16 uses the checkWord() function from the attached source file named carlaSource.js. The arguments sent in are the password the user entered (**password**) and the password Carla selected (**key1**). The function returns either true or false so if the password entered is correct, the value of the variable **carla** will be true. This is tested on line 17. If **carla** is true, the `Enter the questions` button will remain visible and Carla is alerted to the fact that she can go ahead and enter her questions.

However, if the value of **carla**, after the `checkWord()` function has checked the password, is `false`, the `Enter the questions` button is hidden (line 24). This ensures that no one but Carla can alter the questions.

It may happen that a student accessed the page but isn't ready to submit answers to the questions. This option is offered on line 25. Here we use the `checkWord()` function again but only to check whether or not the student has said he or she is `"ready"` to view the questions.

Finally, whether Carla is ready to enter questions or a student is ready to answer questions, both of those buttons use the **location.href property** to send the user to a new page (lines 44 and 45).

If you enter this code, the page will look like this:

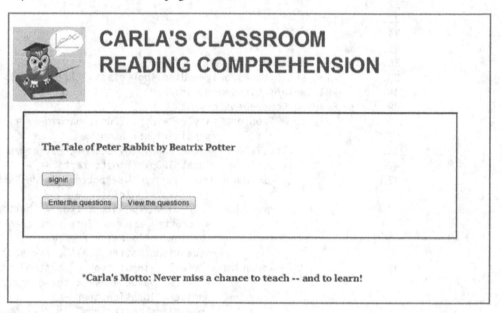

Building the Page with Questions   The page where Carla will enter her questions is very simple. A prompt asks her how many questions she wants to enter, up to 10 questions. A single statement, in a loop, fills the areas on the page with her questions. The code is as follows:

```
1.  <html>
2.  <head>
3.  <title>Reading Lesson Questions: Beatrix Potter</title>
4.  <link href="carla.css" rel="stylesheet" type="text/css" />
5.  <script>
6.  function startIt(story)
7.  {
8.      var numRows = parseInt(prompt("How many questions are there ⏎
                          for this story?"));
9.      for (var i = 0; i < numRows; i++)
```

```
10.                    document.getElementById('div'+i).innerHTML = ((i + 1) ↵
                                + ". " + (prompt("Enter question ↵
                                number " + (i + 1) + ":")));
11.    }
12.    </script>
13.    </head>
14.    <body>
15.    <div id="container">
16.        <img src="images/owl_reading.jpg" class="floatleft" />
17.        <h2>Carla's Classroom<br /> Reading Comprehension</h2>
18.        <div id = "content" style="width: 700px; margin-left: auto; ↵
                                margin-right: auto;">
19.            <h3>The Tale of Peter Rabbit by Beatrix Potter</h3>
20.            <div style = "width: 300px; float: left;">
21.                <p><input type = "button" id = "potter" ↵
                                value = "questions" onclick = ↵
                                "startIt('potter');" />
22.                <p><span  id = "div0"> </span></p>
23.                <p><span  id = "div1"> </span></p>
24.                <p><span  id = "div2"> </span></p>
25.                <p><span  id = "div3"> </span></p>
26.                <p><span  id = "div4"> </span></p>
27.                <p><span  id = "div5"> </span></p>
28.                <p><span  id = "div6"> </span></p>
29.                <p><span  id = "div7"> </span></p>
30.                <p><span  id = "div8"> </span></p>
31.                <p><span  id = "div9"> </span></p>
32.            </div>
33.        <div style="clear:both;"></div>
34.    </div>
35.        <div id="footer">
36.            <h3>* Carla's Motto: Never miss a chance to teach ↵
                                -- and to learn!</h3>
37.        </div>
38.    </div>
29.    </body></html>
```

Line 10 is the essence of the program:

```
document.getElementById('div'+i).innerHTML = ((i + 1) + ". " +
    (prompt("Enter question number " + (i + 1) + ":")));
```

This one line does many things. The id of each line is identified by the prefix div plus the value of the variable, i. Therefore, the first question goes in the <span> with id = 'div0', the next question in the <span> with id = 'div1' and so on. The number of each question is displayed first by adding 1 to the value of i (since i starts at 0 but we want to start at Question 1). This is concatenated with a dot and a space and the question Carla enters at the prompt. The counter is used one more time, in the prompt display where Question 1 is identified as (i + 1) when i = 0, Question 2 as (i + 1) when i = 1, and so on.

What the Student Sees   Once Carla has created her questions, she will save the file with the filename questions_potter.html. The completed page will be what is seen by a student when clicking the View the questions button.

Putting It All Together

The complete code has been shown in each of the previous subsections. Here are views of what will be seen in various situations:

When Carla opens the `comprehension_begin.html` page and signs in, using her password, she will be taken to an empty page to enter her questions:

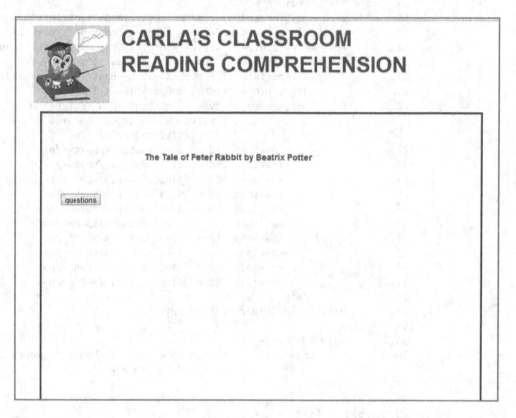

Next, Carla is prompted to enter the number of questions she wants to enter. This value is used in the loop as the limit condition.

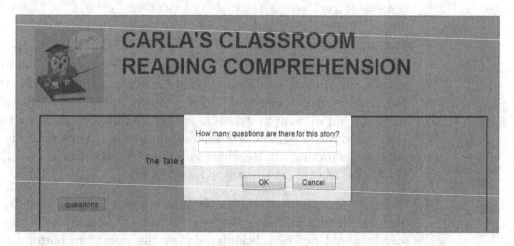

And, after entering six questions, this is what the page will look like:

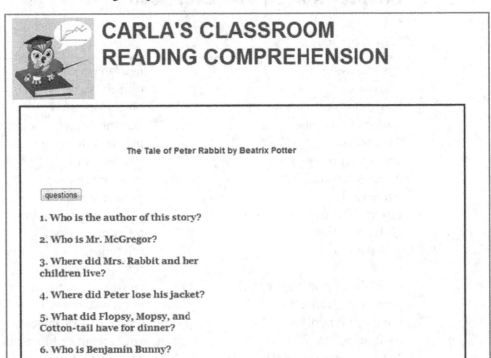

Finishing Up

After creating this page, Carla can save it with the original filename and so, when a student accesses the page, the student will see the same thing as shown in the display above.

Chapter Review and Exercises

Key Terms

.js extension	new keyword
arguments	object
Boolean object	object-oriented
built-in functions	parameters
Date object	pass by reference
display property	pass by value
driver program	passing values
embedded	primitive types
export data (from a function)	reference parameters
global function	reference types
global scope	referenced
inline	regular expression
input data (from a function)	replace() method
JavaScript source files	return statement
library of functions	scope (of a variable)
local scope	setTimeout() function
location.href property	user-defined function
main program (main function)	value parameters
Math object	visibility property

Review Exercises

Fill in the blanks

1. A _____ is a collection of built-in functions that are often included with a programming language.

2. The part of a program in which a given variable can be referenced is known as the variable's _____.

3. The variables listed in a function's name when the function is created are the _____.

4. Arguments, in a call to a function, may be constants, _____, or expressions.

5. When a variable is passed by _____, a new copy of that variable is created.

True or False

6. T/F   A function can be used in a program to get a single value without rewriting code.

7. T/F   A variable that is created and initialized outside all functions is a local variable.

8. T/F   The number of arguments in a function call must always match the number of parameters in the function definition.

9. T/F   The names of arguments in a function call must always be the same as the names of the parameters in the function definition.

10. T/F   While parameters may be constants, variables, or expressions, arguments can only be variables.

11. T/F   A return statement can only return a single value.

12. T/F   When a variable is passed by value to a function, changes to the value in that function do not affect the value of the argument in the function that called it.

13. T/F   Numbers and Booleans are considered primitive types.

14. T/F   Objects are always considered primitive types.

15. T/F   When two variable names point to the same memory location, an error is generated.

Short Answer

16. Which of the following is not a valid function call?
    a) **x** = parseFloat(**y**);
    b) document.write(parseFloat(**y**));
    c) parseFloat(**y**) = x;

17. Create a function named subtract() that accepts two numeric arguments and returns the value of the first subtracted from the second.

    Use the following code for Review Questions 18 and 19:

```
1.  function apples()
2.  {
3.     var number = 0;
4.     number = parseInt(prompt("How many apples do you have?"));
5.     oranges();
6.     document.write("You have " + number + " apples <br />");
7.     function oranges()
8.     {
9.        number = parseInt(prompt("How many oranges do you have?"));
10.       document.write("You have " + number + " oranges <br />");
11.    }
12. }
```

18. What would the output be if the user said he had 5 apples and 12 oranges?

19. How should the program be changed so the output is correct?

20. Which types of parameters can be used to import data into and export data from a function? Are these value or reference parameters?

    Use the following code for Review Questions 21 and 22:

```
1.  var sandwich = "tuna"; var drink = "iced tea";
2.  var meal = menu(sandwich, drink)
3.  document.write(meal);
4.  function menu(a, b)
5.  {
6.     menu = "Lunch is a " + a + " sandwich, " + b + ", and chips.";
```

```
7.    return menu;
8. }
```

21. Identify the arguments and the parameters in the code.

22. What will be displayed after this code snippet is entered into a program and run?

23. Write code to create a variable named **result** that is a Boolean object.

24. Create an instance of the Date object named **longAgo** and set it to the following date: April 23, 1725.

25. In the following statement, what is the length of time specified?

```
timer = setTimeout('startIt()', 3000);
```

26. Create a JavaScript source file that contains a function that will multiply two numbers and return the product as well as a function that will add two numbers and return the sum. Save the file as arithmeticSource.js.

27. Create a web page with a clock that will update the time display every five seconds.

28. What is wrong with the following text that is the content of a .js source file?

```
<script>
function addItUp(r, s, t)
{
    return (r + s + t);
}
</script>
```

29. Example 7.18 creates a .js file that contains four functions. Add two more functions to this file so it can be useful in several situations. Select two of the following three options:

    - a function to concatenate two strings with or without a space or other punctuation between them
    - a function to set a timer which accepts two parameters: the JavaScript instruction about what to do when the timer begins and the time delay
    - a function to select one of a list of Math objects to use

30. What will be displayed after the following code is entered and run if the user enters "9 am" at the first prompt and "N-215" at the second prompt? If you think there is an error, describe how you would fix it.

```
function examTime()
{
    var time = prompt("What time is the exam?");
    var room = prompt("What room is the exam in?");
    showIt(time, room);
}
function showIt(a, b)
{
    document.write("Your exam is in room " + a + " at " + b);
}
```

Programming Challenges

On Your Own

1. Create a web page with JavaScript code that will prompt the user to select one of three options. The JavaScript code should include four functions. The main function describes the selections, prompts the user for two numbers, and prompts the user to select one of the options. Depending on the user's choice, one of the following three functions will be called:

   a) A function will find the value of x^y where x and y are the numbers input by the user.

   b) A function will find the area of a right triangle and return the area. The formula for the area of a right triangle is as follows:

   ```
   Area = ½ base * height
   ```

   The two numbers input by the user represent base and height.

   c) A function will find the distance between two points. The first point will be assumed to start at the origin and will have coordinates (0, 0). The two numbers input by the user represent the coordinates of the second point. The formula for the distance between two points is as follows:

   ```
   Distance = √a² + b² where a = (x₁ - x₂) and b = (y₁ - y₂).
   ```

   In this program, $x_1 = 0$, $y_1 = 0$, x_2 and y_2 are the numbers input by the user.

   The output should display on the web page as one of the following statements:

   ```
   The value of x^y is result.
   The area of a right triangle with base = x and height = y is result
   The distance from the origin to a point at coordinates (x, y) is result
   ```

   Save the page as mathFacts.html and be sure to include an appropriate page title.

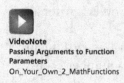

VideoNote
Passing Arguments to Function Parameters
On_Your_Own_2_MathFunctions

2. Create a web page that has JavaScript code for a main function and two other functions. The main function should prompt the user for a positive integer between 1 and 20 (inclusive). Include validation to make sure the number is an integer in that range. Then pass the number to each of the following functions:

   a) A function to check if the number is prime. A prime number is a number that is divisible by 1 and itself only. The function should return either true (if the number is prime) or false (if the number is not prime).

   b) A function to get the factorial of the number. For any positive integer, except 0, the factorial of a number is defined as N! and is calculated as follows:

   ```
   N! = N * (N - 1) * (N - 2) * (N - 3) * ... *1
   ```

   The results that should display on the web page are as follows:

   ```
   N is/is not a prime number.
   N! = result
   ```

   Save your page as moreMath.html and be sure to include an appropriate page title.

3. Create a page that allows the user to play a game with the computer. In this game, the player will roll two dice and the computer will roll two dice. The Math.random() method will be used to generate each roll of a die, from 1 to 6. The sum of the computer's roll should be compared to the sum of the player's roll and whoever has the greater sum is the winner of that round. The sum of the winner's roll for that round should be added to his or her point total. Use functions to call for each roll of two dice and the sum, for keeping track of the points, and to allow the player to continue or quit after a round of play. The following are the game rules:

- If one player rolls doubles (i.e., two fours or two sixes, etc.) and is a winner for that round, he or she should get double points.
- If one player rolls doubles but is not a winner, nothing special happens.
- If the two sums for any round are a tie, no one gets any points.
- The game ends when either player reaches at least 100 points or when the human player wants to quit.

Save your page as dice.html and be sure to include an appropriate page title.

4. Add wagering to the page created in Programming Challenge 3. Allow the human player to choose how much money he or she wishes to wager on a roll. Instead of the sum of the face value of the two dice accruing to a winner, the dollar amount in the kitty for each roll will go to the winner. After the player "bets" on a roll, the computer should, using a random number, generate one of three responses: either the computer matches the bet, folds (wagers nothing and the round goes to the player) or raises the bet. If the computer raises the bet, the player can either match the raise, fold and his initial wager is added to the computer's total, or match and raise the bet. In the last case, the process begins again. Save your page as wagers.html and be sure to include an appropriate page title.

5. Create a web page that uses JavaScript to generate a table with three rows and four columns. Each cell should be filled with a simple math problem. After a cell is created, two functions should be called to fill the cell:

- One function should generate a random number between 1 and 20 (inclusive). This function should be called twice and it returns a number each time.
- A second function should generate one of four operations at random, using a random number from 1 to 4 where 1 = add, 2 = subtract, 3 = multiply, and 4 = divide. The result should be returned to the main function.

Use the results of these three calls to fill each cell as follows:

```
cellContents = randomNumber1 + operation + randomNumber2;
```

Save your page as math_ops.html and be sure to include an appropriate page title.

6. Use the page generated in Programming Challenge 5 and add a way for a student to enter answers to the math problems. The answers should display on the web page in spaces numbered 1 - 12. Save your page as math_answers.html and be sure to include an appropriate page title.

Case Studies

Greg's Gambits

For the Greg's Gambits site, select one (or both!) of the following options:

1. Create a dice-rolling game as described in Programming Challenges 3 and 4. Put a link on the play_games.html page to this page. The filename of this page should be betTheRoll.html and the page title should be Greg's Gambits | Rolling Dice. Test your page in at least two different browsers. Submit your work as instructed by your teacher.

2. Re-do the Hangman game from the Putting It To Work section of this chapter. However, instead of using JavaScript code to display and replace the secret word on the web page, use HTML <div>s to display a space and an underscore for each letter in the secret word at the beginning. Then, as the player guesses various letters, write code that will replace a <div> that corresponds with a letter that was guessed correctly. Put a link on the play_games.html page to this page. The filename of this page should be hangman2.html and the page title should be Greg's Gambits | Hangman 2. Test your page in at least two different browsers. Submit your work as instructed by your teacher.

Carla's Classroom

Now add to the carla_comprehension.html page by including links to a page that students will use to enter their answers to the questions about the story. We created the page that Carla uses to put in the questions and linked this page from the carla_comprehension.html page (see Putting It To Work). Now you will add a button that the students will use when they are ready to answer questions about a story. Then you will create that page. The page should prompt the students to enter answers to each question. Include a textbox at the top of the page for the student to enter his or her name. At the end, the Reading Comprehension page should look like the one shown below and the Enter Answers button should link to the page you create. Complete this for The Tale of Peter Rabbit story. The filename of the new page will be potter_answers.html.

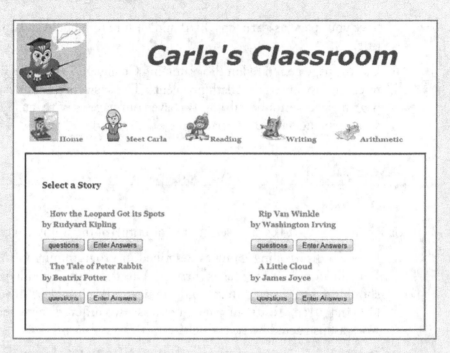

This page should have `Carla's Classroom | Reading Comprehension Answers` as the page title and an appropriate heading on the web page. Test your pages in at least two different browsers. Submit your work as instructed by your teacher.

Lee's Landscape

Create a new page for the `Lee's Landscape` business site. Lee wants to inform his customers about the many gardening issues he can help with. You will create pages that are only available to Lee so he can enter information about a particular subject. Each page should include at least one sample image and areas for Lee to enter text. There will be four pages. Each page will contain functions that are called from an external JavaScript source file. When Lee has completed entering the information, he can link these pages from his home page. The general outline for each page follows.

There should be a button which Lee will click to get started. The button will call a function that will call three more functions on an external source file. One function will prompt Lee to enter a title for the page (one of the topics listed below). Another function will prompt Lee to enter information. The first time this function is called Lee will enter information about the topic in general and the second time it is called he will enter information about how his business handles the issue. A third function will prompt Lee to enter the path to an image that he wants displayed on the page. Finally, a fourth function, when he is done, will set the `visibility` property of the button to make it `"hidden"`.

The four topics are `Pest Control`, `Weeds`, `Landscaping`, and `Fruit and Flowers`. Several images have been provided for you in the Student Data Files but, as always, you can find your own images. Be aware of copyright issues and always give credit to any site you use for your images.

A sample of what one page might look like is shown below. You may need to do some research on the web to find out information about the four topics so you can create information about Lee's services.

The filename for the source file should be `leeSource.js`. Each page should be named as follows:

Pest Control: `pest.html`
                                page title: `Lee's Landscape | Pest Control`

Weeds: `weeds.html`
                                page title: `Lee's Landscape | Weeds`

Landscaping: `landscaping.html`
                                page title: `Lee's Landscape | Landscaping`

Fruit and Flowers: `fruit_flowers.html`
                                page title: `Lee's Landscape | Fruit and Flowers`

Sample page, with dummy text:

Be sure to test your program in at least two browsers. Submit your work as instructed by your teacher.

Jackie's Jewelry

Create a new page for the `Jackie's Jewelry` business site. This project will be similar to the one created for `Lee's Landscaping`. Jackie wants to provide some background information about the jewelry she sells and she also wants to expand into jewelry making classes. Create one page that allows Jackie to enter information about various types of beads. One page will be about African beads and beading techniques and another will be about Native American beads and techniques. A third page will allow Jackie to enter a schedule of planned classes. Each of the pages about beads should include at least one sample image and areas for Jackie to enter text. The third page should allow Jackie to build the content using a function similar to the `buildTable()` function presented earlier in the chapter. This way Jackie can update the pages as her schedule changes. When Jackie has completed entering all the information, she can link these pages from her home page. Each page should also include a button which Jackie will click to get started. Once the information is entered to Jackie's satisfaction, a function will set the `visibility` property of the button to make it `"hidden"`.

A sample of what one page might look like is shown below. You may need to search the web to find information about various types of beading. Image files that may be used are available in the Student Data Files or you can find your own images. Be aware of copyright issues and always give credit to any site you use for your images. The three pages should be named as follows:

African Beads: `african_beads.html`
                                   page title: `Jackie's Jewelry | African Beading`

Native American Beads: `native_am_beads.html`
                                   page title: `Jackie's Jewelry | Native American Beads`

Class Schedule: `classes.html`
                                   page title: `Jackie's Jewelry | Schedule of Classes`

Sample page, with dummy text:

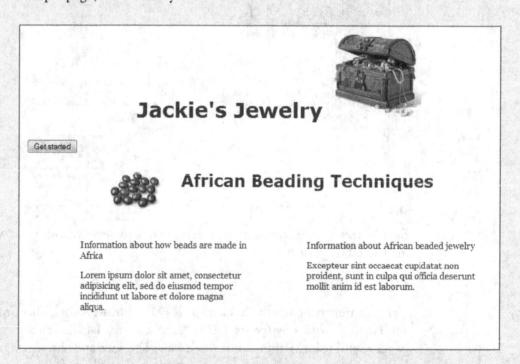

Test your page in at least two different browsers. Submit your work as instructed by your teacher.

CHAPTER

8

Arrays

Chapter Objectives

Until now we have associated a single value with a single variable. This is an important programming concept and it is almost impossible to conceive of a program that does not use variables. Sometimes, however, you may need multiple variables to hold the values of similar items. For example, if you needed to store information about 10 players in a game or 25 students in a class, each person would have a variable associated with his or her name or information. But all these variables would have much in common; they are of the same type and they hold related values. That's where arrays come in. An array is a collection of variables of the same type that is referenced by the same name. Sounds confusing? How can we distinguish one player in a game from another if all the variables have the same name? Each element of the array uses a number, called an index, to identify it. That's the short answer. This chapter explains how arrays work and provides the long answer to the question posed.

After reading this chapter, you will be able to do the following:

- Describe a one-dimensional array and how to declare an array

- Understand the Array object including its properties and methods

- Load arrays directly (in the program) and interactively (by user entry)

- Display the contents of an array and display specified array elements

- Understand how to use parallel arrays

- Add new elements to an array with the push() method

- Join two arrays with the concat() method

- Understand and create two-dimensional arrays

8.1   One-dimensional Arrays

A **one-dimensional array** is a list of related data of the same type (for example, integers or strings) referred to by a single variable name with an **index number** to identify each item. If, for example, you have a list of players in an online game, you could identify each one by a separate variable name such as the following:

```
var player1 = "Marie";
var player2 = "Luis";
var player3 = "Winnie";
... and so on
```

But what would you do if you had 200 players and more people joined the game daily? Using an array named, for example, **players[]**, where each player is identified by an index number facilitates manipulating the players in the game, including adding, deleting, or searching for a specific player. In this section, we will discuss how to set up and manipulate arrays, and we will present several advantages of using them.

Creating an Array in JavaScript

In JavaScript, an array is created using the **var keyword,** followed by the array name. However, instead of putting a specific value on the right side of the expression, an array is declared using the JavaScript keyword **new Array().** The number of elements in the array may be specified inside the parentheses but it is not required. For example, an array named **players[]** that contains places for 200 players in a game is created as follows:

```
var players = new Array(200);
```

Since an array stores many data values under the same variable name, we must be able to refer to the individual elements contained within it. Each element is an item in the array and has its own value. To indicate a particular element the array name is followed by an index number enclosed in brackets.

It's important to note how arrays store elements. The name of the array is similar to the name of a variable. In the sample array declaration shown above, an array named **players[]** was created and will contain the names of 200 players in a game. Therefore, the array will have 200 names. Each name is an element and the array must indicate which particular element the program refers to at any time. This is done by using the index number placed within brackets (**[]**). The first element of an array is referred to with the index number 0. An array with 200 elements will have index numbers that range from 0 to 199. This is a significant to remember, especially when you manipulate arrays.

Since the first element of an array is referenced with an index value of 0, if you want to refer to the third name in the list of elements—that is, the third element of the array named **players[]**—you would use the expression **players[2]**, where 2 is the **subscript** or index number that references the third element of the array. We read this expression as "**players** sub 2," and the value 2 is called the subscript—or index number—for this array element. Because array indexes begin with 0, the first element of **players[]** is **players[0]**, the second element is **players[1]**, and the third element is **players[2]**.

An array element such as **players[2]** is treated by the program as a single (or simple) variable, and may be used in input, assignment, and output statements in the usual way. Thus, to display the value of the second player's name, we use the following statement:

```
document.write(players[1]);
```

There are several ways to load the values of the array elements. Example 8.1 demonstrates one way; we will learn the others later in this chapter.

EXAMPLE 8.1

Creating an Array

Here is how to create an array in JavaScript with three elements, which contain the values "coffee", "tea", and "juice":

```
1.  <script type="text/javascript">
2.  var beverages = new Array(3);
3.  beverages [0] = "coffee";
4.  beverages [1] = "tea";
5.  beverages [2] = "juice";
6.  </script>
```

Note that there are three elements in this array. Line 2 declares the array, **numbers[]**, as an array with three elements. The number of elements is in the parentheses after the Array keyword. However, the indexes of the array elements are 0, 1, and 2.

In Example 8.1 we created an array with three elements. However, it is not necessary to specify how many elements will be in an array when it is declared. By leaving the parentheses empty, the number of elements is unlimited.

In Example 8.2, we use an array named **numbers** with three elements that are declared and initialized. We add a variable named **result** to demonstrate how the elements of an array can be manipulated in JavaScript expressions exactly as variables are.

EXAMPLE 8.2

Manipulating Array Elements

```
1.  <html>
2.  <head>
3.  <title>Example 8.2</title>
4.  <script type="text/javascript">
5.      var numbers = new Array(3);
6.      numbers[0] = 4;
7.      numbers[1] = 5;
8.      numbers[2] = 6;
9.      var result = 0;
10.     result = numbers[0] + numbers[1];
11.     document.write("a) result = " + result + "<br />");
12.     result = numbers[1] * numbers[2];
13.     document.write("b) result = " + result + "<br />");
14.     result = numbers[2] % numbers[0];
```

```
15.          document.write("c) result = " + result + "<br />");
16.    </script>
17.    </head>
18.    <body>
19.    </body></html>
```

The statement on line 10 adds the values of **numbers[0]** and **numbers[1]**, and stores the answers in the variable **result**. The statement on line 12 multiplies the values of **numbers[1]** and **numbers[2]**, and stores the answers in the variable **result**. The statement on line 14 takes the modulus of **numbers[2]** and **numbers[0]**, and stores the answers in the variable **result**. Thus, if this program were entered in a web page and run, the display would be as follows:

> a) result = 9
>
> b) result = 30
>
> c) result = 2

The Array Object

Because arrays are objects, they have associated methods and properties. We will use some of them throughout the rest of the text and will briefly discuss some of them here.

A Note About Array Names

We can refer to an array by its name with or without the brackets. For example, we can refer to the array **numbers** created in Example 8.2 as either **numbers[]** or **numbers**. If brackets are not included, the context will make it clear whether we are referring to a single variable name or an array name.

The length Property

It is not required that the programmer limit the size of an array when it is created. In Example 8.1, we created an array with three elements. However, at any time, we could add one or more elements. Since the size of an array in JavaScript is fluid, it is helpful to have a property that allows you to check the size of an array at any time. The **length property** allows you to do just that. The syntax is simply **array_name.length** and Example 8.3 demonstrates how to use it.

EXAMPLE 8.3

Using the length Property

The following code creates an array with two elements, checks the size of the array, and then adds two more elements and checks the new size. The output is shown below the code.

```
1.    <html>
2.    <head>
3.    <title>Example 8.3</title>
4.    <script type="text/javascript">
5.        var food = new Array();
```

```
6.        food[0] = "pizza";
7.        food[1] = "hamburger";
8.        document.write("Original length: " + food.length + "<br />");
9.        food[2] = "chips";
10.        food[3] = "cake";
11.        document.write("New length: " + food.length);
12.  </script>
13.  </head>
14.  <body>
15.  </body></html>
```

The output is as follows:

> Original length: 2
> New length: 4

Some Methods of the Array Object

There are many methods associated with the **Array object.** Table 8.1 provides descriptions of what some of these methods can accomplish. We will discuss several of these methods in more depth throughout the chapter.

TABLE 8.1	Methods of the Array Object
Method	**Description**
concat()	joins two or more arrays, and returns a copy of the joined arrays
join()	joins all elements of an array into a string
push()	adds new elements to the end of an array, and returns the new length
reverse()	reverses the order of the elements in an array
shift()	removes the first element of an array, and returns that element
sort()	sorts the elements of an array
splice()	adds/removes elements from an array
toString()	converts an array to a string, and returns the result
unshift()	adds new elements to the beginning of an array, and returns the new length

CHECKPOINT FOR SECTION 8.1

8.1 Array elements must be of the same _____.

8.2 What is the syntax for creating a new array in JavaScript?

8.3 Write the JavaScript code to create an array named **byFives()** which has five elements containing the following sequence of numbers: 5, 10, 15, 20, 25.

8.4 Add code to the following to check the length of the array named `mycars()`:

```
<html>
<body>
<script type="text/javascript">
var mycars = new Array();
mycars[0] = "sedan";
mycars[1] = "pickup truck";
mycars[2] = "SUV";
????????????????
</script>
</body>
</html>
```

8.2 Populating Arrays

We have learned one simple way to populate an array: The array is declared and then each array element is assigned a value. This is exactly how you would assign values to a long list of variables that were of the same data type. This method is time consuming and tedious and not often used. Arrays save space and time; therefore, we use much more efficient methods to populate them.

Loading Arrays Directly

We've seen how to load each element of an array separately. The value of an array is that it holds many related items using a single name (the array name) and identifies each value by the array index number. There are various uses for such a list of related values. Imagine that a college wants to associate each of its students with an ID number. An array can hold hundreds (or thousands) of values. Normally, ID numbers are created in such a way to ensure that no number is used more than once. Example 8.4 demonstrates how to load an array directly with 200 ID numbers, beginning with ID2000 and ending with ID2199.

EXAMPLE 8.4

Loading Arrays Directly with a Loop

To load 200 elements of an array with consecutive numbers, we can use a loop with a counter. The counter can perform double duty—it can function as both counter and array index.

In this example, we are asked to load the array with ID numbers that are a combination of characters (ID) and numbers (from 2000 through 2199). We will need to concatenate the string value with the numeric value. The following code will do this. We will add to this code to display the results in an upcoming example.

```
1.  <script type="text/javascript">
2.  var idNums = new Array();
3.  var i=0;
```

```
4.    for (i=0; i<=199; i++)
5.    {
6.          idNums[i] = ID + (2000 + i);
7.    }
8.    </script>
```

The single line of code inside the for loop beats loading 200 elements separately!

Arrays can also be populated in a single statement that both creates and fills the array. Instead of specifying the contents of each element, one statement can be used to load multiple elements simultaneously. This is convenient when the values of the elements are known, there are not many elements in the array, and when, because of the type of values, a loop cannot be used. Example 8.5 demonstrates how this is done.

Loading Arrays Directly in One Statement

Imagine you want to create a web page that allows the user to design the page by selecting a color scheme. The user may pick a background color, text color, and perhaps other things, such as a border color. You could use an array to store the names of five colors. The values are known in advance and there is no reason to write a separate statement for each array element. Instead, you can declare the array and load the values in one statement as shown:

```
1.    <script type="text/javascript">
2.    var colors = new Array("red","blue","yellow","green","pink");
3.    </script>
```

At the end of this statement, the **colors[]** array contains the following values:

colors[0] = "red"	**colors[1]** = "blue"	**colors[2]** = "yellow"
colors[3] = "green"	**colors[4]** = "pink"	

Loading Arrays Interactively

Often, a programmer does not know the values to be stored in an array. For example, an array that stores the names of all students in a class will change for each teacher, class, and semester. The user must enter these values. We can easily use a loop to prompt the user to enter the values. There are several possible scenarios, including the following.

First, the number of elements in the array is fixed. A business might want an array of images to display on a web page but wants the images to change with the seasons or perhaps with items that are offered on sale. The business owner might want 10 images to cycle through—no more and no less—but wants to have the option to change the images. In this case, we can use a loop to ask the user to enter values and the loop would be controlled by a predetermined counter value.

Second, the number of elements in the array is fluid. A teacher may want to enter the students' names for each class but the number of students in each class per semester will change. In this case, we can prompt the user to enter the number of students in a particular class and the loop would be controlled by a counter set equal to this value.

Third, the user wants the flexibility to stop entering values at any time. In this case, we can use a loop to prompt for user entries and a sentinel value would identify when the loop will end.

In Example 8.6, the user (a classroom teacher) will load the names of her students into an array named **names[]**. Because each class has a different number of students, she must be prompted to enter the number of students in the class. That number will be used to count how many loop iterations are needed. However, we must remember that the names of 25 students will be stored in the array from **names[0]** to **names[24]**. The following code considers that by initializing the counter to 0 and making the loop test condition end at one less than the number of elements in the array which is the highest index value.

EXAMPLE 8.6

Loading Arrays Interactively

```
1.   <html>
2.   <head>
3.   <title>Example 8.6</title>
4.   <script type="text/javascript">
5.       var names = new Array();
6.       var numStud = prompt("How many students are in class: ");
7.       numStud = parseInt(numStud);
8.       var i = 0;
9.       for (i = 0; i <= numStud - 1; i++)
10.      {
11.          names[i]= prompt("Enter the student's name: ");
12.      }
13.  </script>
14.  </head>
15.  <body>
16.  </body></html>
```

Look at line 9 and notice that the test condition in this loop is set to one less than the number of students in the class. This is because, for an array of 20 students, the index values of the elements in the array are 0 through 19.

Displaying Arrays

A document.write statement, added to the loop, is the simplest way to display the contents of an array. This is demonstrated in Example 8.7. It is also possible to display one or several elements of an array only. We do this exactly as we would display the value of a variable except that the element of interest must be identified by its name and index. Later in the chapter, we will learn to store images in an array and use them on a web page to create a slide show. For now, Example 8.7 demonstrates how to display the contents of an array.

EXAMPLE 8.7

Displaying Arrays

By adding one output line to the code in Example 8.6, we can see the contents of the array after the teacher has entered the student names. The line of code added is on line 12. It deserves a bit of explanation. We want to display the name of each student. Student #1 is stored in **names[0]** and Student #8 is stored in **names[7]**. If we use the counter variable **i** to identify both the student's place in the list and the value stored in that place, we must be diligent. Recall that the variable **i** starts at 0 and ends at one less than the number of students in the array. Therefore, we identify the first student's name entered by the teacher as **i + 1** and identify the index of that student as **i**.

```
1.  <html>
2.  <head>
3.  <title>Example 8.7</title>
4.  <script type="text/javascript">
5.        var names = new Array();
6.        var numStud = prompt("How many students are in the class? ");
7.        numStud = parseInt(numStud);
8.        var i = 0;
9.        for (i = 0; i <= numStud - 1; i++)
10.       {
11.             names[i]= prompt("Enter the student's name: ");
12.             document.write("Name of student " + (i + 1) + ": " + ↵
                              names[i] + "<br />");
13.       }
14.  </script>
15.  </head>
16.  <body>
17.  </body></html>
```

Try entering this code into a web page. If you enter the following values at the prompts, your display should look like the display shown below.

Input: Number of students in the class: 5

   Students: Andy Arnold, Davey Drew, Kim Kurtz, Sam Sanchez, and Zack Zell

Output:

Name of student 1: Andy Arnold
Name of student 2: Davey Drew
Name of student 3: Kim Kurtz
Name of student 4: Sam Sanchez
Name of student 5: Zack Zell

8.5 What is the difference between loading arrays directly and interactively?

8.6 Write JavaScript code to create and load an array named **music[]** that contains five elements with the following values: "jazz", "blues", "classical", "rap", and "opera".

8.7 Write JavaScript code to create and load an array named **twos[]** which contains 20 elements with numbers from 2 to 40, counting by twos. Use a loop to load this array.

8.8 Given: an array named **rain[]** that contains the rainfall amounts in inches in a certain state over a one-year period (12 months), as shown below. Use a loop to display the rainfall amounts for the 12 months of that year.

```
<script type="text/javascript">
var rain = new Array(3,4,3,5,6,7,8,2,9,3,4,5);
fill in the loop here
</script>
```

8.3 Parallel Arrays

We often use parallel arrays in programming. These are arrays of the same size in which elements with the same subscript are related. For example, suppose we wanted to modify the program of Example 8.7 so that the teacher can keep records of grades for each student. If we store the grades for each student in an array named **grades[]**, then **names[]** and **grades[]** are considered **parallel arrays.** For each **k**, **names[k]** and **grades[k]** would refer to the same student so they are related data items. Example 8.8 illustrates this concept.

EXAMPLE 8.8

Parallel Arrays Save Time and Work

This program inputs the names of students in a class and their grades for the semester into two parallel arrays (**names[]** and **grades[]**). It determines which student has the highest grade (**high**).

```
1.   <html>
2.   <head>
3.   <title>Example 8.8</title>
4.   <script type="text/javascript">
5.       var names = new Array();
6.       var grades = new Array();
7.       var high = 0; var index = 0; var k = 0;
8.       while (names[k] != "*")
9.       {
10.          names[k]= prompt("Enter the student's name or enter ⏎
                     an asterisk (*) when you are done: ");
11.          if (names[k] == "*")
12.              break;
```

```
13.              grades[k]= prompt("Enter the student's grade: ");
14.              grades[k] = parseFloat(grades[k]);
15.              document.write("Name of student " + (k + 1) + ": " + ⏎
                          names[k] + " grade: " + grades[k] + "<br />");
16.              if (grades[k] > high)
17.              {
18.                  index = k;
19.                  high = grades[index];
20.              }
21.              k = k + 1;
22.          }
23.          document.write("The highest grade in the class is: " + ⏎
                          grades[index] + "<br />");
24.          document.write(names[index] + " is the high-achieving student! ⏎
                          <br />");
25.      </script>
26.      </head>
27.      <body>
28.      </body></html>
```

This program contains features that are new to this chapter and some that we have previously discussed. An explanation of these features may be helpful.

The program does two things simultaneously. It loads an array of strings (students' names) and an array of numbers (students' grades). Because each class has a different number of students, a sentinel (the asterisk, "*") allows the user to determine when the array is complete. This makes the program useful for a class or a group of people. Line 8 determines the test condition—when an asterisk has been entered—and the if clause on lines 11 and 12 force the loop to end when this condition is met.

Thus, the while loop body performs the following functions:

- Each student's name is entered and stored in the **names[]** array (line 10).
- There is a check at this point (lines 11 and 12) to see if the user is finished entering values. If so, there is no need for a grade to be entered so the loop is exited before asking for another value for the **grades[]** array.
- That student's grade is entered and stored in the corresponding element of the **grades[]** array (line 13). This makes the arrays parallel. If we want to access the record of the student whose name is in **names[5]**, that record will be a parallel element of the **grades[]** array; i.e., **grades[5]**. On line 14, the value entered as a grade is turned into a numeric value. Since the program looks for the highest value, the grades must be numeric values so they can be compared.
- Each student's name and grade are displayed on the screen (line 15).
- Now the program begins to check for the highest grade. On line 7, several numeric variables are declared and initialized to 0. The variable **high** will hold the temporary high score while the program runs. The variable **index** will hold the index value of the student whose place in the **names[]** array and, of course, the parallel place in the **grades[]** array is highest. Lines 16–20 check to find the high scorer. If a grade is higher than what is stored in **high**, that student

is identified as the high scorer and that grade becomes the new value of **high**. On the first pass through the loop, it really doesn't matter what score the first student has; it will almost always be greater than the value of **high** which, at first, is 0. So the new value of **high** is the first score. Let's, for example, assume the first score is 78. Now the index value is set to 0 because **k** = 0 on the first iteration and **high** = 78. For each subsequent pass, the new score is compared to **high** and, if the new score is greater than 78, **high** takes on the new value and **index** takes on the value of whatever **k** is at that point. If, for example, the next 3 scores are 65, 72, and 88, on the fourth pass **k** = 3. After lines 16–20 are executed, **high** = 88 and **index** = 3. If no one else scores higher than 88, these will be the values of **high** and **index** when the loop ends.

- Line 21 simply increments **k**, the counter, and line 22 ends the loop.
- Line 23 displays the highest grade and line 24 identifies the student who got that high grade. Since **index** identifies the subscript of the array element with the high score and this is in an array that is parallel to the student **names** array, the program can identify both the student's name and grade using that **index** value.

If this program was run with the input shown, the output will be as follows:

Input: (entered in the order shown)		Output:
Student Name	**Student Score**	Name of student 1: Andy Arnold grade: 67
Andy Arnold	67	Name of student 2: Davey Drew grade: 82
Davey Drew	82	Name of student 3: Kim Kurtz grade: 96
Kim Kurtz	96	Name of student 4: Sam Sanchez grade: 94
Sam Sanchez	94	Name of student 5: Zack Zell grade: 77
Zack Zell	77	The highest grade in the class is: 96
		Kim Kurtz is the high-achieving student!

Why Use Arrays?

There are many advantages to using arrays. As you have seen, arrays can reduce the number of variable names needed in a program because we can use a single array instead of a collection of simple variables to store related data. Arrays can help you create more efficient programs. Once data is entered into an array, it can be processed many times without having to be input again. Example 8.9 illustrates this.

EXAMPLE 8.9

Arrays Make Less Work for Programmers

In this example, we assume a teacher enters the scores of all students into an array. Now the teacher wants to know the class average and wants to determine how many students scored above the average and how many scored below. Without arrays the program would require that all the scores were entered and averaged and then each score would have to be compared individually to the average to see if it was above or below. However, by storing the scores in an array, the process is facilitated, as shown by the following program:

```
1.   <html>
2.   <head>
3.   <title>Example 8.9</title>
4.   <script type="text/javascript">
5.        var scores = new Array();
6.        var sum = 0; var average = 0;
7.        var count1 = 0; var count2 = 0; var count = 0;
8.        while (scores[count1] != 999)
9.        {
10.               scores[count1]= prompt("Enter the student's grade ⏎
                        or enter 999 when you are done: ");
11.               scores[count1] = parseFloat(scores[count1]);
12.               if (scores[count1] == 999)
13.                   break;
14.               sum = sum + scores[count1];
15.               count1 = count1 + 1;
16.        }
17.        average = sum / count1;
18.        for (count = 0; count < count1; count++)
19.        {
20.             if (scores[count] > average)
21.                   count2 = count2 + 1;
22.        }
23.        document.write("The average is: " + average.toFixed(2) + "<br />");
24.        document.write("The number above the average is: " + count2 + "<br />");
25.        document.write("The number below the average is: " + (count1 - ⏎
                        count2) + "<br />");
26.   </script>
27.   </head>
28.   <body>
29.   </body></html>
```

This program handles several tasks at once.

- The while loop on lines 8–16 does the following:
    □ Line 10 prompts the user for a test score. Because the number of scores is not determined by the program, the user can stop at any time by entering the sentinel value, 999. One counter, count1, is used as the index of the scores[] array. At the end of the loop, count1 will have the value of the highest index in the array. This means that count1 also holds the number of elements in the array. Why, you may wonder, is the highest index value also the number of elements in the array when you know that array indexes go from 0 to some number (call it X), but the number of elements in the array is actually X + 1? This is because the last index value (the last value of count1) is used to store the sentinel entry, 999. We need to be aware of this.
    □ Since values entered to prompts are stored as text and this program needs to manipulate numbers, line 11 changes the value of each score entered to a numeric value.

- □ Lines 12 and 13 check to see if the sentinel value has been entered. If so, the loop ends.
- □ Line 14 keeps a running sum of all the scores. We need this later, to compute the average score.
- □ Line 15 increments `count1`.
- □ Line 17 computes the average. Notice that the **sum** includes the sum of all values of the array except 999 since the `break` statement is executed before that value can be included in the **sum**. Also, as noted, `count1` holds the number of all elements in the array except the last element so the **average** is simply the sum of all the values divided by the number of elements in the array.
- □ The next loop, the `for` loop on lines 18–22, uses a new counter, `count`, to cycle through the array again. This time each element is compared to the value of **average**. Notice that the test condition in this loop uses the value of `count1` to limit the number of iterations in the loop. For example, assume `scores[]` holds four elements, including 999, which are 30, 40, 50, and 999. These elements are stored as follows:

  `scores[0]` = 30, `scores[1]` = 40, `scores[2]` = 50, and `scores[3]` = 999. The value of `count1` is 3. But we only want to compare the first three elements. The `for` loop will end when the new counter, `count`, reaches one less than the value of `count1` and thus it will not compare **average** to the last element of the array.
- □ The `if` clause on lines 20 and 21 simply checks each element to see if its value is greater than the average. If it is, a third counter, `count2`, is incremented. Thus, at the end of the loop, all the valid scores in the array have been checked and we have a count of how many are above the average.

- ■ Line 23 displays the average.
- ■ Line 24 displays the number above the average (`count2`).
- ■ Line 25 displays the remaining numbers, after subtracting the number above from the total.

It would have been simple to add code to check if a number was below the average or if a number was exactly equal to the average but, in the interest of saving time and space, this program stops here. You are asked to add this code in Checkpoint 8.12.

If this program is coded and run with the given input, the output will be as shown below:

Input: 67, 89, 93, 59, 98, 77, 82, 72, 84, 94, 88, 999

Output:

```
The average is: 82.09
The number above the average is: 6
The number below the average is: 5
```

✓

8.9 What makes two arrays parallel?

8.10 Imagine you are writing a program for an adventure game. Describe a situation in which you might use parallel arrays and describe what values each array would hold.

8.11 Which of following pairs of arrays would be considered parallel? Briefly explain your answers.

a) an array named **colors[]** that holds the values of 10 different color shades and an array named **sizes[]** that holds the values of 10 different font sizes

b) an array named **patients[]** that holds the values of the names of patients in a doctor's office and an array named **pharmacies[]** that holds the values of the pharmacy each patient uses for prescriptions.

c) an array named **cards[]** that holds the name of each client's credit card in an online business and an array named **expires[]** that holds the expiration date of each credit card.

8.12 Add code to Example 8.9 that will check how many scores are within a one-point range of the average. For example, if the average score is 86.5, your program should check to find out how many scores are between 86.0 and 87.0. You will have to alter some of the code that checks for scores above the average and how the results are displayed to take this new information into account.

8.4 Using Array Methods

Several JavaScript methods can be used to make manipulating arrays relatively easy. We will discuss four of them in this section. The push() method allows you to add a new item or several items to the end of an array and returns the new array length. The unshift() method adds a new item or items to the beginning of an array and returns the new length. The concat() method is used to join two arrays. Finally, the splice() method adds items to an array or removes items from an array.

The push() Method

If you owned a jewelry business and used arrays to hold your collections, when you designed a new piece of jewelry, you would want to add it to its appropriate array (bracelet, necklace, earrings, etc.). If you used parallel arrays to store the names and grades of students in your classroom, as a new student is enrolled in your class, you would want to add that student to the appropriate array. Or you might have forgotten to include one item when loading an array. The **push()method** makes it easy to add an item (or several items) to an array.

If you have an array named **myArray[]** which already has been filled with five names, the syntax to add another name is as follows:

```
myArray.push("newName");
```

The syntax to add several names is as follows:

```
myArray.push("newName1", "newName2", "newName3", ...);
```

You may consider it useless to have a method that only adds an element to the end of an array. In the case of an inventory, the items may be listed alphabetically. Or they may be parallel arrays arranged by price. Adding an element to the end of an array (or to the beginning as we will see in the discussion of the unshift() method) might be counterproductive. However, it is easy to sort arrays. In Chapter 9, we will learn several ways to sort arrays. Often, a sort routine is called immediately following any change in an array.

The length Property Can Be Used to Find the Length of an Array

The push() method will add items to the end of an array and return the new length of the array. However, if you want to see the new length, you must ask for it. The syntax to get the length of an array uses the length property like this:

```
var x = myArray.length;
```

This statement will set the variable **x** equal to the number of elements in the array, **myArray[]**.

In Example 8.10, we will assume that Jackie, of the Jackie's Jewelry website, sells hand-carved wood pendants, which she hangs on satin ribbons. She offers several ribbon color choices and displays them when a customer selects a pendant. Until recently, she was able to obtain ribbons in five colors but her supplier now offers two additional options. She wants to add these options to the array and uses the push() method as shown in the following code. This code includes how the array was originally loaded and, for demonstration purposes, displays, along with the old array, the old length of the array, the new array elements, and the new length.

EXAMPLE 8.10

Adding Color Choices to an Array at the End

```
1.   <html>
2.   <head>
3.   <title>Example 8.10</title>
4.   <script type="text/javascript">
5.   function getColors()
6.   {
7.       var ribbons = new Array("black", "white", "brown", "blue", "red");
8.       var r = ribbons.length; var i = 0;
9.       document.write("<table align = 'center'><tr><td>");
10.      document.write("<br /> Old colors:</td></tr><tr><td>");
11.      for (i = 0; i <= (r - 1); i++)
12.          document.write(ribbons[i] + " ");
13.      document.write("</td></tr><tr><td>Original length: " + r + ↵
                                "</td></tr><tr><td>");
14.      ribbons.push("purple","green");
15.      r = ribbons.length;
16.      document.write("New colors:</td></tr><tr><td>");
17.      for (i = 0; i <= (r - 1); i++)
18.          document.write(ribbons[i] + " ");
```

```
19.     document.write("</td></tr><tr><td>New length: " + r + ↵
                              "</td></tr>");
20.     document.write("</table>");
21.   }
22.   </script>
23.   </head>
24.   <body>
25.   <button onclick="getColors()">See ribbon colors</button>
26.   </body></html>
```

If you enter this code, the output will look like this:

> Old colors:
> black white brown blue red
> Original length: 5
> New colors:
> black white brown blue red purple green
> New length: 7

The unshift() Method

The **unshift()method** inserts the array element values at the beginning of the array instead of at the end. It also returns the length of the changed array. Note, however, that this method does not work properly in all versions of all browsers. It inserts the values but the return value of the length is undefined.

Example 8.11 does the exact same thing as the previous example but uses the unshift() method. Two new colors, purple and green, will be added to the beginning of the array. The code is the same as the previous example except for the changes on line 14.

EXAMPLE 8.11

Adding Color Choices to an Array in the Beginning

```
1.    <html>
2.    <head>
3.    <title>Example 8.11</title>
4.    <script type="text/javascript">
5.    function getColors()
6.    {
7.       var ribbons = new Array("black", "white", "brown", "blue", "red");
8.       var r = ribbons.length; var i = 0;
9.       document.write("<table align = 'center'><tr><td>");
10.      document.write("<br /> Old colors:</td></tr><tr><td>");
11.      for (i = 0; i <= (r - 1); i++)
12.         document.write(ribbons[i] + " ");
13.      document.write("</td></tr><tr><td>Original length: " + r + ↵
                              "</td></tr><tr><td>");
```

```
14.      ribbons.unshift("purple","green");
15.      r = ribbons.length;
16.      document.write("New colors:</td></tr><tr><td>");
17.      for (i = 0; i <= (r - 1); i++)
18.          document.write(ribbons[i] + " ");
19.      document.write("</td></tr><tr><td>New length: " + r + "</td></tr>");
20.      document.write("</table>");
21.  }
22.  </script>
23.  </head>
24.  <body>
25.  <button onclick="getColors() ">See ribbon colors</button>
26.  </body></html>
```

If you enter this code, the output will look like this:

> Old colors:
>
> black white brown blue red
>
> Original length: 5
>
> New colors:
>
> red purple green black white brown blue
>
> New length: 7

The splice() Method

The **splice()method** allows you to insert or delete one or more array element values in the array. To do this, you must include several parameters. You must define at what position to add or remove an item or items; this is the index parameter. If removing items, you must stipulate the number of items to be removed. If adding items, this parameter must be set to 0. Finally, you need to include the items to be added, if there are any. We will demonstrate the use of this method with two examples—one in which items are added and another in which items are deleted. Following is the general syntax for using the splice() method:

```
arrayName.splice(index,howmany,newItem1,......,newItemX);
```

The syntax to delete the first three items in an array is as follows:

```
arrayName.splice(0,3);
```

The 0 means to start at the first element (the index value of this element is 0) and the 3 means to delete the three items, beginning at the item with index = 0.

The syntax to add two items in the middle of an array, starting at the fifth element, is as follows:

```
arrayName.splice(4,0,newItem1,newItem2);
```

The 4 means to start at the fifth element (the index value of this element is 4) and the 0 means that no items will be deleted. However, newItem1 and newItem2 will be added, in the fifth and sixth places of the array. All remaining elements in the array will be pushed to the end.

Example 8.12 uses the splice() method to add four colors to our array of ribbon colors.

EXAMPLE 8.12

Adding Color Choices to an Array in the Middle

In this example, we will place the new colors between white and brown in the original array, starting at index = 2.

To save space, since only one line of code is changed, we will only show that line. The code is exactly the same as for the previous example but line 14 is now as follows:

```
14.    ribbons.splice(2,0,"mauve","teal","ecru","buttercup");
```

If you enter this code, the output will look like this:

Old colors:
black white brown blue red
Original length: 5
New colors:
black white mauve teal ecru buttercup brown blue red purple green
New length: 9

In Example 8.13, we will begin with the array filled with the nine elements from the end of the previous example and use the splice() method to delete white and mauve from the list.

EXAMPLE 8.13

Deleting Color Choices from an Array

```
1.    <html>
2.    <head>
3.    <title>Example 8.13</title>
4.    <script type="text/javascript">
5.    function getColors()
6.    {
7.        var ribbons = new Array("black", "white", "mauve", "teal", ↵
                    "ecru", "buttercup", "brown", "blue", "red");
8.        var r = ribbons.length; var i = 0;
9.        document.write("<table align = 'center'><tr><td>");
10.       document.write("<br /> Old colors:</td></tr><tr><td>");
11.       for (i = 0; i <= (r - 1); i++)
12.           document.write(ribbons[i] + " ");
13.       document.write("</td></tr><tr><td>Original length: " + r + ↵
                    "</td></tr><tr><td>");
14.       ribbons.splice(1,2);
15.       r = ribbons.length;
16.       document.write("New colors:</td></tr><tr><td>");
17.       for (i = 0; i <= (r - 1); i++)
18.           document.write(ribbons[i] + " ");
19.       document.write("</td></tr><tr><td>New length: " + r + "</td></tr>");
20.       document.write("</table>");
```

```
21.    }
22.    </script>
23.    </head>
24.    <body>
25.    <button onclick="getColors()">See ribbon colors</button>
26.    </body></html>
```

If you enter this code, the output will look like this:

> Old colors:
>
> black white mauve teal ecru buttercup brown blue red
>
> Original length: 9
>
> New colors:
>
> black teal ecru buttercup brown blue red
>
> New length: 7

We'll put these methods to good use in Example 8.14. We can use them to update an inventory page for an online business.

EXAMPLE 8.14

Updating the Inventory

This program will allow Jackie to enter her inventory of rings, bracelets, and pendants. She will also be allowed to add or delete items. First, we will show and explain only the code for the rings. You can add code for the inventory of bracelets in Checkpoint 8.17 and for the inventory of pendants in the end-of-chapter Exercises.

```
1.    <html>
2.    <head>
3.    <title>Example 8.14</title>
4.    <script type = "text/javascript">
5.    function getRings()
6.    {
7.         var rings = new Array();
8.         document.getElementById('ring_inventory').innerHTML = ("");
9.         var r = parseInt(prompt("How many rings are in the inventory now?"));
10.        var i = 0;
11.        for (i = 0; i <= (r - 1); i++)
12.             rings[i] = prompt("Enter ring # " + (i + 1) +":");
13.        displayRings(rings);
14.        addRings(rings);
15.        deleteRings(rings);
16.    }
17.    function displayRings(rings)
18.    {
19.         var r = rings.length; var i = 0;
20.         for (i = 0; i <= (r - 1); i++)
21.             document.getElementById('ring_inventory').innerHTML = ↵
                                ("<h3>" + rings + "</h3>");
22.    }
23.    function addRings(rings)
24.    {
```

```
25.          var r = rings.length; var i = 0;
26.          var numAdd = parseInt (prompt("If you want to add to the ↵
                                 inventory, enter the number of rings ↵
                                 you want to add (or enter 0):"));
27.          for (i = 0; i <= (numAdd - 1); i++)
28.          {
29.              if (numAdd == 0)
30.                  break;
31.              var newRing = prompt("Enter a ring to add:");
32.              rings.push(newRing);
33.          }
34.          displayRings(rings);
35.  }
36.  function deleteRings(rings)
37.  {
38.          var r = rings.length; var i = 0; var j = 0;
39.          var numSubt = parseInt(prompt("If you want to subtract from ↵
                                 the inventory, enter the number of rings you ↵
                                 want to subtract (or enter 0):"));
40.          for (i = 0; i <= (numSubt - 1); i++)
41.          {
42.              if (numSubt == 0)
43.                  break;
44.              var oldRing = prompt("Enter a ring to delete:");
45.              for (j = 0; j <= (r - 1); j++)
46.              {
47.                  if (rings[j] == oldRing)
48.                      rings.splice(j,1);
49.              }
50.          }
51.          displayRings(rings);
52.  }
53.  </script>
54.  <style type="text/css">
55.  <!--
56.          body { margin: 20pt; padding: 5%; width: 80%; }
57.          .div_width { width: 33%; float: left; }
58.  -->
59.  </style>
60.  </head>
61.  <body>
62.  <div id="container">
63.          <img src="images/jewel_box1.jpg" class="floatleft" />
64.          <h1 align="center">Jackie's Jewelry Inventory</h1>
65.          <div style ="clear:both;"></div>
66.  <div = "content" width = "800">
67.          <div class="div_width" id="rings">
68.              <input type="button" value="Enter your inventory of ↵
                                 rings" onclick="getRings()"; />
69.          <h2>Ring Inventory</h2>
70.          <div id = "ring_inventory"></div>
71.      </div>
72.      <div class="div_width" id="bracelets">
73.              FILL IN THIS CODE AS A CHECKPOINT EXERCISE
74.      </div>
75.      <div id="pendants" >
76.              FILL IN THIS CODE AS AN END OF CHAPTER EXERCISE
```

```
77.        </div>
78.    </div>
79.    </div>
80.    </body></html>
```

The body of the page, lines 61–80, set up a web page with buttons for Jackie to use when handling her inventory. In this page (for demonstration purposes only) the button will prompt Jackie to enter her initial inventory. Later in the text, when we learn to use PHP, the inventory could be pulled from a database and this page used to edit the inventory only. For now, the function getRings() will first prompt Jackie to enter the inventory.

The getRings() function declares a new array named **rings**. The function prompts Jackie for the number of items in the inventory (**numRings**) and uses a loop on lines 11 and 12 to get each item and store it in the array. Then the displayRings() function is called. We must pass in the one argument, **rings**. The displayRings() function accepts one parameter. In this example, since the array **rings** is passed from one function to another, we have used **rings** for the name of the argument and for each function's parameter.

The displayRings() function displays the list of items in the inventory. First, we need to ascertain how many elements are in the array. We use the length property on line 19 to get the number of elements in the array. This value will change every time this function is called because we will reuse the function to display the array each time Jackie updates it. Lines 20 and 21 use a loop to display the values in the array. If an array has 10 elements, these elements are stored in index values **[0]** through **[9]**. This is why the loop begins at **i** = 0 and continues until **i** is one less than the number of elements, **r**.

Once the displayRings() function has competed its task, control returns to line 14 in the getRings() function. Now the addRings() function is called.

This function also accepts one argument, **rings**. Here, on line 25, again we ascertain the length of the array using the local variable, **r**. Now Jackie is prompted to decide if she wants to add elements to her inventory. The number of elements she wants to add is stored in the variable **numAdd**. The loop on lines 27–33 does two things. It either jumps to the next part of the code if Jackie has nothing to add to this inventory or it adds as many elements as Jackie wants to add to the inventory. Therefore, it will have as many iterations as the number of elements Jackie wants to add. The counter, **i**, begins at 0 and goes up to one less than **numAdd**. You may wonder why we simply don't start the counter at 1 and loop up to the value of **numAdd**. This is because we need to deal with the possibility that Jackie has chosen not to add anything to her inventory at this time. In this case, **numAdd** = 0. Lines 29 and 30 take care of this option by breaking out of the loop if **numAdd** = 0. However, if **numAdd** is not 0, Jackie is prompted, on line 31, to enter a new element which is stored in **newRing**. Then line 32 uses the push() method to add this new value to the inventory. The process repeats for as many elements as Jackie wants to add to her inventory. After all the new elements have been added, the displayRings() function is called again, passing in the new array. The displayRings() function now overwrites the initial array with the new array. At the end of displayRings()

control is passed back to addRings(). Since this is the end of the addRings() function, control is now passed back to the calling function, getRings().

The next line in getRings() calls the deleteRings() function, passing in the newest version of the **rings** array. The deleteRings() function on lines 36–52 is similar to the addRings() function but a bit more complex. Line 38 determines the length of the **rings** array at this point. Jackie is then prompted (line 39) to say how many, if any, rings she wants to delete from the inventory. The loop on lines 40–50 will do the same things as the loop in the addRings() function but takes a bit more work. First, the loop will have as many iterations as Jackie wants to delete items. If she does not want to delete any items, the value **numSubt** will be 0 and the if statement on lines 42–43 will break out of the loop; there will be no changes in the array.

However, if Jackie does want to delete one or more items, we need to find those items. Line 44 prompts Jackie for the value of an item to be deleted and stores this value in **oldRing**. The inner loop on lines 45–49 identifies which element in the **rings** array corresponds to this value. The loop will check each item in the array by going from index **0** through the last index in the array (**r - 1**). As soon as a match is found (lines 47–48), the splice() method is used to delete that item.

The inner loop checks each item in the array to find one item Jackie wants to delete. The outer loop repeats this process for as many items as Jackie wants to delete. After this process is complete, the displayRings() function is called again and the revised inventory replaces the old inventory. Control goes from displayRings() to the function that called it—deleteRings() in this case—and from there, back to getRings() where the program ends.

In this program, we have not included any validation nor have we created a pretty inventory display. When JavaScript displays an array, the items are displayed as simple text with a comma between each item. Some data validation is left to you as an end-of-chapter Exercise. You can then create a more pleasing web page display, if you wish.

The following images show the initial page and the sequence of events for certain entries:

- **Initial inventory:** gold band, silver band, silver ring with turquoise inlay, gold with ruby stone
- **Items added:** gold ring with silver etching, wood band
- **Items deleted:** gold with ruby stone

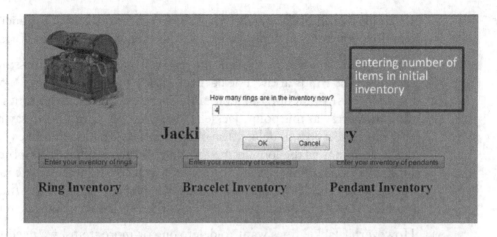

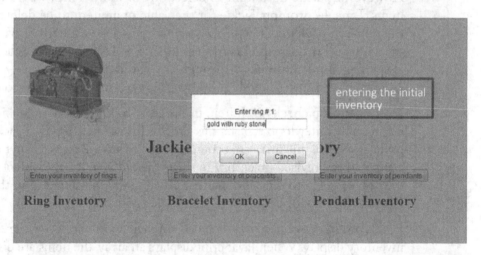

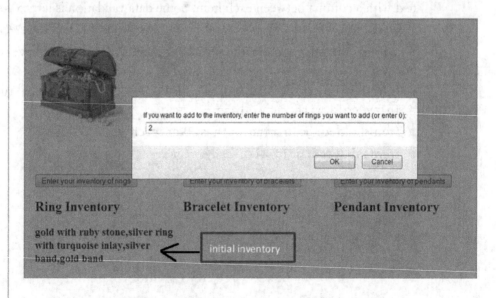

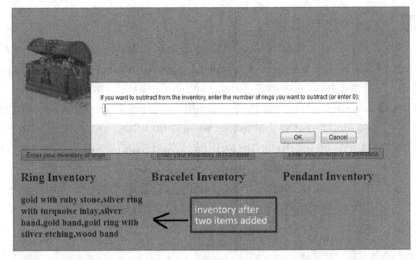

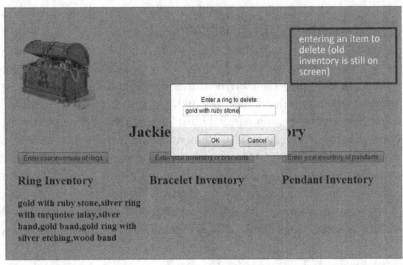

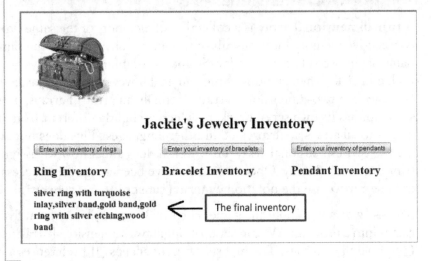

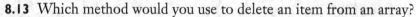

8.13 Which method would you use to delete an item from an array?

8.14 Write a statement that will add the following two elements to the end of an array named **games**: "hangman" and "hide-and-seek".

8.15 Write a statement that will add the colors "magenta" and "lime" to an array named **colors**. The items should be in the fourth and fifth places in the array.

8.16 Add code to the deleteRings() function of Example 8.14 to alert Jackie if a ring she wants deleted does not exist in the inventory.

8.17 Add code to Example 8.14 that will allow Jackie to enter her inventory of bracelets and to add or subtract from that inventory.

8.5 Multi-Dimensional Arrays

So far, in the arrays you have seen the value of an element has depended upon a single factor. For example, if one element in an array holds a game player's point score, the value of this number depends on which player is being processed. While parallel arrays are valuable for accessing parallel information, they have limitations. Sometimes it's convenient to use arrays whose elements are determined by two or more factors. For example, we might have several games (and, therefore, several different scores) associated with each player. In this case, the value we look for would depend on two factors—the particular person *and* the particular game in which we are interested. In these situations, we use **multi-dimensional arrays.** This text covers two-dimensional arrays only. Advanced programming allows for the use of arrays with more dimensions.

Introduction to Two-Dimensional Arrays

A **two-dimensional array** is a collection of elements of the same type stored in consecutive memory locations, all of which are referenced by the same variable name using two subscripts. In JavaScript, two-dimensional arrays are a valuable tool, especially when creating some games. However, because JavaScript arrays are objects, a two-dimensional array is actually an array of arrays. Therefore, each subscript has its own set of brackets, which is slightly different from how two-dimensional arrays are expressed in other languages. This does not affect how we use the two-dimensional array. However, it does affect how we assign values to a two-dimensional array. Once the values have been assigned, to access any element of the array we use the notation **myArray[subscript 1][subscript 2]**.

Suppose we want to input the game scores of 30 game players from five different games into a program. We can set up a single two-dimensional array named **scores[] []** to hold these results. The first subscript of **scores[][]** references a particular player; the second subscript references a particular game. For example, the array element **scores[0][0]** contains the score of the first player in the first game and the array element **scores[8][1]** contains the score of the ninth player in the second game.

Player	Game 1	Game 2	Game 3	Game 4	Game 5
EdEvil	235	29	333	486	0
DorianDragon	782	45	314	0	568
puppypal	398	66	327	517	462
.	.	.	.	.	.
.	.	.	.	.	.
.	.	.	.	.	.
crusher	441	0	388	452	609

Figure 8.1 The two-dimensional array named scores[][]

This situation may be easier to understand if you picture the array elements in a rectangular pattern of horizontal rows and vertical columns. The first row gives the scores of the first player, the second row gives the scores of the second player, and so forth. Similarly, the first column gives the scores of all players in the first game, the second column gives all scores in the second game, and so forth (see Figure 8.1). The entry in the box at the intersection of a given row and column represents the value of the corresponding array element.

- **scores[1][4]** represents the score of player 2, DorianDragon, in Game 5 which is 56
- **scores[2][1]**, represents the score of player 3, puppypal, in Game 2 which is 66

Declaring and Filling Two-Dimensional Arrays

To declare a two-dimensional array, we can use the **new keyword** to create the array and identify how many rows there will be. Next, we can use the new keyword to specify how many columns will be in each row. JavaScript allows us to create an array where each row has a different number of elements and that option does have its uses. However, for our purposes, we will only use arrays where each row has the same number of columns. Therefore, it is easier to use a for loop to specify how many columns will be in each row. Example 8.15 shows both ways to declare two-dimensional arrays.

Creating Two-Dimensional Arrays

a) Using the new keyword to create an array in which each row has a different number of columns:

```
var myarray = new Array(3); //allocates 3 rows to the array
myarray[0] = new Array(4); //allocates 4 columns for 1st row
myarray[1] = new Array(2); //allocates 2 columns for 2nd row
myarray[2] = new Array(6); //allocates 6 columns for 3rd row
```

b) Using a for loop to create a two-dimensional array in which each row has the same number of columns:

```
var myarray = new Array(25); //allocates 25 rows to the array
for (i = 0; i < 25; i++)
{
    myarray[i] = new Array(5); //allocates 5 columns each row
}
```

There are several ways to load the elements of the array. Example 8.16 demonstrates how to load the array directly and how to load using prompts for user input.

EXAMPLE 8.16

Filling Two-Dimensional Arrays

a) The following shows filling a two-dimensional array directly at the same time the array is created:

```
var myarray = [  [0, 1, 2, 3],      //fills the 1st row
                 [4, 5, 6, 7],      //fills the 2nd row
                 [8, 9, 10, 11] ];  //fills the 3rd row
```

This code creates a two-dimensional array named **myarray[]** which has three rows and four columns. The column entries for each row are contained in brackets (**[]**) and entries for each row are separated by commas. The entire array is also contained in an outer set of brackets.

b) The following shows using a for loop to load a two-dimensional array with user input. The array is named **myarray[]**; it consists of six rows with five columns in each row.

```
var myarray = new Array(6); //allocates 6 rows to the array
for (i = 0; i < 6; i++)
{
    myarray[i] = new Array(5); //allocates 5 columns each row
}
for (i = 0; i < 6; i++)
{
    for (j = 0; j < 5; j++)
    {
        myarray[i][j] = prompt("Enter value for row " ⏎
            + i + ", column " + j +":");
    }
}
```

We will develop a game using a two-dimensional array in the next section. In preparation, Example 8.17 demonstrates how to create a two-dimensional array and fill the contents of an HTML table with user input.

EXAMPLE 8.17

Displaying Array Elements on a Web Page

In this program, a two-dimensional array is created and initialized to hold the contents of each cell of a table on the web page. The cells are then loaded with values input by the user. The significant lines of the code are explained following the code.

```
1.   <html>
2.   <head>
3.   <title>Example 8.17</title>
4.   <script type="text/javascript">
5.   function setup()
6.   {
7.       cells = new Array([document.getElementById("cell00"), ⏎
             document.getElementById("cell01"), ⏎
```

```
                    document.getElementById("cell02")], ↵
              [document.getElementById("cell10"), ↵
               document.getElementById("cell11"), ↵
               document.getElementById("cell12")], ↵
              [document.getElementById("cell20"), ↵
               document.getElementById("cell21"), ↵
               document.getElementById("cell22")] );
8.          placeValues();
9.    }
10.   function placeValues()
11.   {
12.        for (var rows = 0; rows < 3; rows++)
13.        {
14.             for (var cols = 0; cols< 3; cols++)
15.                  cells[rows][cols].innerHTML = prompt("Enter a value:");
16.        }
17.   }
18.   </script>
19.   <style type="text/css">
20.   <!--
21.   table { border: solid #4f81bd; }
22.   body { margin: 10ex; color: #4f81bd; font-weight: bold; }
23.   td    {
24.        font-size: 18px; color: #4f81bd; font-weight: bold; margin: 10%;
25.        padding: 5px; line-height: 120%; width: 75pt; height: 25pt;
26.        text-align: center;
27.   }
28.   -->
29.   </style>
30.   </head>
31.   <body onload ="setup()">
32.   <h1>Loading a 2-Dimensional Array</h1>
33.   <table id = "myTable" border = "1">
34.        <tr>
35.        <td> <span id = "cell00" />cell 00 </td>
36.        <td> <span id = "cell01" />cell 01 </td>
37.        <td> <span id = "cell02" /> cell 02 </td>
38.        </tr><tr>
39.        <td> <span id = "cell10" />cell 10 </td>
40.        <td> <span id = "cell11" />cell 11 </td>
41.        <td> <span id = "cell12" />cell 12 </td>
42.        </tr><tr>
43.        <td> <span id = "cell20" />cell 20 </td>
44.        <td> <span id = "cell21" />cell 21 </td>
45.        <td> <span id = "cell22" />cell 22 </td>
46.        </tr>
47.   </table>
48.   </body></html>
```

Let's analyze this program. We'll start at the end and work our way back.

■ Lines 33–47 create a simple 3 × 3 table on the web page. Each cell has been assigned an id which, in this case, is the word "cell" followed by its location (row and column) in the cell. The id could, of course, be anything you want but it seems to make the most sense to identify each cell by its location. The initial contents of each cell have simply been set to its location but, of course, these values can be anything you want. Using id values such as the location of the cell will also help in future programs when you can concatenate the first part of a cell id with a counter variable in a loop.

- As soon as the page loads (line 31) the setup() function is called. This function, on lines 5–9, creates a two-dimensional array named **cells[][]** with three rows and three columns. Each element in the array is loaded with the getElementById() method. This method accesses the first element with the specified id. Thus, the statement

```
document.getElementById("cell00")
```

loads the first element of the array with the contents of the element with id = "cell00"; in this case, that is the first cell of our table. From now on, the contents of the first array element (**cells[0][0]**) will be whatever is in the first cell of the table.

- Line 8 calls the placeValues() function. This function allows the user to place whatever values he or she wants in each cell in the table.

- The placeValues() function is on lines 10–17. The function uses nested loops to fill the table with user input.

- Line 15 uses the inner.HTML property which sets or returns the inner HTML of an element. Whatever the user enters at the prompt will be sent to the corresponding table cell.

The page initially looks like this:

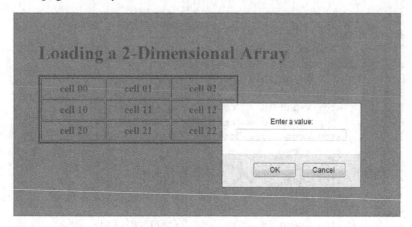

After entering the following values, the page looks like this:

Input: A, B, C, D, E, F, G, H, I

CHECKPOINT FOR SECTION 8.5 ✓

8.18 Given the following two-dimensional array:

```
var tests = [ [95, 89, 72, 83], [94, 95, 86, 77],
              [88, 99, 100, 61], [76, 65, 78, 83] ];
```

What are the values of the following elements?

a) **tests[0][3]**

b) **tests[2][2]**

c) **tests[3][1]**

8.19 Create a two-dimensional array named **mixedArray** which has four rows and the following number of columns in each row:

Row 1 has two columns.
Row 2 has five columns.
Row 3 has one column.
Row 4 has eight columns.

8.20 Use a for loop to create a two-dimensional array named **myArray** that has 100 rows and three columns. Fill the array with its row values; i.e., row 1 would contain all 1s, row 2 would contain all 2s, and so on.

8.21 Load the array you created in Checkpoint 8.20 with Xs in the first column, Ys in the second column, and Zs in the third column.

8.22 Redo Checkpoint 8.20 to allow user input to load the array. *Hint:* first write the program with five rows (or any lower value) so you can test it without entering 100 values.

8.6 Putting It to Work

In this section, we will develop a game to add to Greg's Gambits and a writing lesson for Carla's Classroom.

Greg's Gambits: The Game of 15

In this game, the screen loads with a 4 × 4 table. The cells are filled, at random, with the numbers from 1 to 15 and an empty cell. The player, by moving numbers around, must put the numbers in order. We'll call this game Greg's 15. Figure 8.2 shows sample beginning and ending screens:

Beginning Screen				Winning Screen			
4	7	15	8	1	2	3	4
2		11	3	5	6	7	8
13	9	1	12	9	10	11	12
10	6	14	5	13	14	15	

Figure 8.2 The Game of 15

Developing the Program

This program is complex but we have already done some of the work in Example 8.17 In that example, we created a 3 × 3 table and populated it with values from a two-dimensional array. Now we need to add code to do several things:

- change the 3 × 3 table to a 4 × 4 table
- change the array from three rows and columns to four
- populate the table cells initially with random values from 1 to 15 and one empty space
- add functionality to allow the player to move contents of one cell to another
- add validation to ensure that player moves are legal
- add a check to indicate when the player has won the game

Setting the Stage   Let's begin by creating the web page that will hold this game. We'll use the template for the Greg Gambits site and put a table in the center box (the "content" <div>). Recall from Example 8.17 that, to manipulate values in cells in a table, each cell must have its own id. As we create the page, we will include ids for each cell. We will also add instructions about how to play the game.

```
1.  <!DOCTYPE html PUBLIC "-//W3C//DTD XHTML 1.0 Transitional//EN" ↵
    "http://www.w3.org/TR/xhtml1/DTD/xhtml1-transitional.dtd">
2.  <html xmlns="http://www.w3.org/1999/xhtml" lang="en" xml:lang="en">
3.  <head>
4.  <title>Greg's Gambits | Greg's 15</title>
5.  <link href = "greg.css" rel = "stylesheet" type = "text/css" />
6.  </head>
7.  <body>
8.  <div id="container">
9.  <img src="images/superhero.jpg" class="floatleft" />
10. <h1><em>Greg's 15</em></h1>
11. <p> </p>
12. <div id="nav">
13. <p><a href="index.html">Home</a>
14. <a href="greg.html">About Greg</a>
15. <a href="play_games.html">Play a Game</a>
16. <a href="sign.html">Sign In</a>
17. <a href="contact.html">Contact Us</a></p>
18. </div>
19. <div id="content">
20. <p>You can move any number into an empty spot by moving up, down, ↵
        right, or left. Diagonal moves are not allowed. The object is ↵
        to get all the numbers into correct order, from 1 through 15 ↵
        with the empty space at the end. </p>
21. <table width = "60%" align = "center" >
22.    <tr>
23.      <td height = "60"> <span id = "cell00" /> </td>
24.      <td> <span id = "cell01" /> </td>
25.      <td> <span id = "cell02" /> </td>
```

```
26.          <td> <span id = "cell03" /> </td>
27.      </tr> <tr>
28.          <td height = "60"> <span id = "cell10" /> </td>
29.          <td> <span id = "cell11" /> </td>
30.          <td> <span id = "cell12" /> </td>
31.          <td> <span id = "cell13" /> </td>
32.      </tr> <tr>
33.          <td height = "60"> <span id = "cell20" /> </td>
34.          <td> <span id = "cell21" /> </td>
35.          <td> <span id = "cell22" /> </td>
36.          <td> <span id = "cell23" /> </td>
37.      </tr> <tr>
38.          <td height = "60"> <span id = "cell30" /> </td>
39.          <td> <span id = "cell31" /> </td>
40.          <td> <span id = "cell32" /> </td>
41.          <td> <span id = "cell33" /> </td>
42.      </tr>
43.  </table>
44.  </div>
45.  <div id="footer">Copyright &copy; 2013 Greg's Gambits<br /> ↵
            <a href="mailto:yourfirstname@yourlastname.com"> ↵
            yourfirstname@yourlastname.com</a></div>
46.  </div>
47.  </body></html>
```

The web page now looks like this:

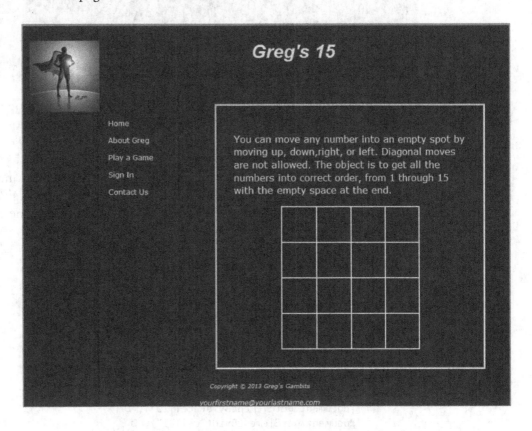

Since this page is part of the Greg's Gambits site that we have been developing, we will save it with the filename greg_game_15.html and create a link on the menu of games page. If you create this link, your menu site will look like this:

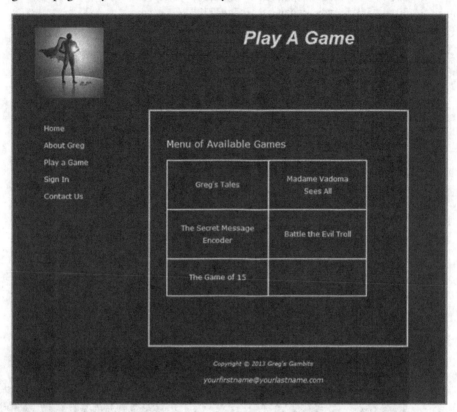

Creating the Array with the setup() Function　Now we'll focus on the JavaScript code to create the game. First, we will use the same setup() function that we used in Example 8.17 to create the two-dimensional array and link the elements to the cells in the table with the getElementById() method. We can also use the same placeValues() function that we have created. However, instead of initially putting in specific values, we need to generate random values from 1 through 15. We also must be sure that no numbers are repeated and we need to leave one cell empty.

The setup() function looks like this:

```
function setup()
    {
        cells = new Array([document.getElementById("cell00"), ↵
        document.getElementById("cell01"), ↵
        document.getElementById("cell02"), ↵
        document.getElementById("cell03")], ↵
        [document.getElementById("cell10"), ↵
        document.getElementById("cell11"), ↵
        document.getElementById("cell12"), ↵
        document.getElementById("cell13")], ↵
        [document.getElementById("cell20"), ↵
        document.getElementById("cell21"), ↵
        document.getElementById("cell22"), ↵
```

```
                document.getElementById("cell23")], ⏎
                [document.getElementById("cell30"), ⏎
                document.getElementById("cell31"), ⏎
                document.getElementById("cell32"), ⏎
                document.getElementById("cell33")]);
          placeValues();
      }
```

We also need to add a call to the setup() function in the <body> tag:

```
<body onload = "setup()">
```

Populating the Array with the Math.random() Function   The placeValues()
function will generate the random numbers needed to be placed initially in the
table. The code for this function is given and an explanation of how it works follows
the code.

```
 1.   function placeValues()
 2.   {
 3.          var numbers = new Array();
 4.          var randomLoc;
 5.          var temp;
 6.          for (var i = 0; i < 16; i++)
 7.                  numbers[i] = i;
 8.          for ( i= 0; i < 16; i++ )
 9.          {
10.                  randomLoc = Math.floor(Math.random() * 15 + 1 );
11.                  temp = numbers[i];
12.                  numbers[i] = numbers[randomLoc];
13.                  numbers[randomLoc] = temp;
14.          }
15.          i = 0;
16.          for (var rows = 0; rows < 4; rows++)
17.          {
18.                  for (var cols = 0; cols< 4; cols++)
19.                  {
20.                      if (numbers[i] != 0)
21.                          cells[rows][cols].innerHTML = numbers[i];
22.                      else
23.                          cells[rows][cols].innerHTML = "";
24.                          ++i;
25.                  }
26.          }
27.   }
```

The function first creates a new array called **numbers**. The for loop on lines 6 and
7 initializes the values of the elements in **numbers** to numbers 0 though 15. Now we
have an array that contains each element needed to fill the table.

The for loop on lines 8–14 is of special interest. It has 16 iterations. For each
iteration, it generates a random number between 0 through 15. Recall that these
numbers are both the subscripts of the new array (**numbers**) as well as the initial
value of each element of **numbers**. Thus, each time a random number is generated,
the value of the element identified by the random number subscript is exchanged
with the value of the element that has the counter (i) subscript. At the end of the

loop, the 16 numbers are in some random order. You may wonder what might happen if a particular number between 0 and 15 was never generated by the random number generator. This would not matter; it would simply mean that the cell corresponding to that element would contain its original value. But other cells would be different (unless there was a bizarre situation where the sequence of random numbers was 0, 1, 2, 3, . . . through 15!).

The next for loop on lines 16–26 places the new values on the table. Line 15 sets **i** back to 0. Two new variables are used: **rows** for the outer loop and **cols** for the inner loop. For the first row (**rows** = 0), the four cells are checked in the inner loop. If a value in **numbers[i]** is 0, the element in the **cells** array and the corresponding table cell is filled with empty text. If not, that element in **cells** and its corresponding table cell is filled with the value of **numbers[i]**.

The Code to Exchange Cell Values   The game is played when a player clicks on a number which is either above, below, to the left or to the right of the empty cell. Then the contents of that cell move to the empty cell's place and the first cell becomes empty. We will do this by creating a function that will be called whenever a cell is clicked (so we will call it doClick()). The function must be called from every cell in the table so doClick() calls must be added to the HTML code.

Imagine you are playing the game and you click on a cell. For example, assume you click the number in the third row, second column. This cell has id = "cell21". The doClick() function must check to see if any cell above, below, left, or right of this cell is empty. If none of those cells is empty, an exchange cannot take place and a message should be sent to the player explaining that this is an illegal move. If doClick() is called from "cell21" we must check the contents of "cell20", "cell22", "cell11", and "cell31".

But what if you click the number in "cell00"? This cell has nothing above it or to its left. A similar situation occurs in all cells in the first and last rows and first and last columns. We need a way to identify the possibility that cells do not completely surround the chosen cell. The doClick() function will identify whether or not a swap can take place, using all the given criteria. If a swap is possible, another function, which we will name swap() will be called to do the actual exchange. We will also call a function named checkWinner() to see if this exchange has won the game.

Part (a)

First we add a call to the doClick() function in each table cell:

```
1.   <table width = "60%" align = "center" >
2.      <tr>
3.          <td height = "60"> <span onclick = "doClick(0,0)" ↵
                             id = "cell00" /> </td>
4.          <td> <span onclick = "doClick(0,1)" id = "cell01" /> </td>
5.          <td> <span onclick = "doClick(0,2)" id = "cell02" /> </td>
6.          <td> <span onclick = "doClick(0,3)" id = "cell03" /> </td>
7.      </tr> <tr>
8.          <td height = "60"> <span onclick = "doClick(1,0)" ↵
                             id = "cell10" /> </td>
```

```
9.          <td> <span onclick = "doClick(1,1)" id = "cell11" /> </td>
10.         <td> <span onclick = "doClick(1,2)" id = "cell12" /> </td>
11.         <td> <span onclick = "doClick(1,3)" id = "cell13" /> </td>
12.     </tr> <tr>
13.         <td height = "60"> <span onclick = "doClick(2,0)" ↵
                              id = "cell20" /> </td>
14.         <td> <span onclick = "doClick(2,1)" id = "cell21" /> </td>
15.         <td> <span onclick = "doClick(2,2)" id = "cell22" /> </td>
16.         <td> <span onclick = "doClick(2,3)" id = "cell23" /> </td>
17.     </tr> <tr>
18.         <td height = "60"> <span onclick = "doClick(3,0)" ↵
                              id = "cell30" /> </td>
19.         <td> <span onclick = "doClick(3,1)" id = "cell31" /> </td>
20.         <td> <span onclick = "doClick(3,2)" id = "cell32" /> </td>
21.         <td> <span onclick = "doClick(3,3)" id = "cell33" /> </td>
22. </tr>
23. </table>
```

Note that the doClick() function takes two arguments: the row number and the column number.

Part (b)

Here is the function with an explanation of the code:

```
1.  function doClick(row, col)
2.  {
3.      var top = row - 1;
4.      var bottom = row + 1;
5.      var left = col - 1;
6.      var right = col + 1;
7.      swapped = false;
8.      if (top != -1 && cells[top][col].innerHTML == "")
9.          swap(cells[row][col], cells[top][col]);
10.     else if (right != 4 && cells[row][right].innerHTML == "")
11.         swap(cells[row][col], cells[row][right]);
12.     else if (bottom != 4 && cells[bottom][col].innerHTML == "")
13.         swap(cells[row][col], cells[bottom][col]);
14.     else if (left != -1 && cells[row][left].innerHTML == "")
15.         swap(cells[row][col], cells[row][left]);
16.     else
17.         alert("Illegal move.");
18.     checkWinner();
19. }
```

Each time a player clicks a cell, the function is called, receiving the location of that cell (through its row and column identities, sent to the variables **row** and **col** as numbers). For example, if the player clicks the cell in row 1, column 2, its location is (0,1) and the function is called as doClick(0,1) (see line 4 of the HTML code in Part (a)).

Line 3 of the function code in Part (b) identifies a variable, **top**, as equal to **row** - 1. This variable is used to check if the cell clicked is in the top row. If the cell is in the second, third, or fourth row of the table, the **row** variable will be 1, 2, or 3 and **top** will be 0, 1, or 2 which are all valid row numbers. However, if the cell is in the first row of the table, then **top** will equal 0 - 1 or **top** = -1. This fact is used to identify a cell in the top row. It is also used to identify the location of the row directly below the cell that was clicked.

Similar logic is used to identify the bottom row as well as the leftmost and right-most columns. Variables named **bottom**, **left**, and **right** indicate when a cell is a border cell (lines 4–6). These variables also identify the row and column values of the cells above, to the left, and to the right of the clicked cell.

Line 7 sets the value of a variable named **swapped** to false. This will be used later to check whether or not a click has generated an exchange.

The check for the "illegal move" alert or for an exchange of cell contents begins on line 8 and ends on line 17.

Line 8 checks to see if the cell is not a top row cell (**top** != -1) and if the cell directly above the chosen cell is empty (**cells[top][col]**). If both these conditions are true, we know that the cell above the clicked cell is empty and a legal exchange can be made. The swap() function is called. The code for this function is shown below. It takes two arguments. One argument is the contents of the clicked cell which is identified in the **cells** array as **cells[row][col]** and the second argument is the array element at the location that is, at present, empty. This element is **cells[top][col]**.

If either of these conditions is false, the program continues to the next if clause on lines 10–11. Now the program checks to see if **right** != 4. The variable **right** will only equal 4 if the clicked cell is in the fourth column of the table (**col** = 3). So, if **right** = 4, a right-side border cell has been clicked and it cannot be swapped with a cell to its right. However, if **right** != 4 and the cell to its right, **cells[row][right]** is empty, a swap should be made. The swap() function is called, sending as its two arguments the clicked cell, **cells[row][col]**, and the cell to its right, **cells[row][right]**.

If either of the conditions on line 10 is false, program exection continues to lines 12–13 where a check is made to see if the clicked cell is not a bottom row cell and if the cell directly under the clicked cell is empty. If a legal exchange can be made, the swap() function is called.

But if either of those conditions is false, the program continues to the last if clause which checks, in a manner similar to the other conditions, whether the clicked cell is not a left-border cell and whether the cell to its left is empty. As before, if both conditions are true (the cell is not a left-border cell and its left-side neighbor is empty), the swap() function is called.

After testing the four conditions we have checked all possible conditions that allow for a legal swap: the cell above, below, to the left, or to the right of the clicked cell is within the table and is empty. If the program has not made a swap by the end of line 15, then no legal swap is possible. The only option is to tell the player that he or she is attempting an illegal move (lines 16–17).

The final job of the doClick() function is to check to see if that click has caused the table to be completely put in order. Line 18 calls the checkWinner() function (which we will create below) to see if this move has created a winner.

The function named swap(), used to exchange cell values, is short and sweet. It takes two arguments, as stated above, that contain the locations of the cells whose values will be exchanged. The function is as follows:

```
function swap (firstCell, secondCell)
{
    swapped = true;
    secondCell.innerHTML = firstCell.innerHTML;
    firstCell.innerHTML = "";
}
```

The Code to Check for a Winner   The game is won when the cells of the table hold the values 1, 2, 3, and 4 in the first row, 5, 6, 7, and 8 in the second row, 9, 10, 11, and 12 in the third row, and 13, 14, and 15 plus an empty space in the fourth row. So, to check for a win, we need to verify that the values in those cells match what we want. We also can easily add an option to play again. The code for this function is given, and the explanation follows:

```
1.   function checkWinner()
2.   {
3.       var win = true;
4.       for (var i = 0; i < 4; i++)
5.       {
6.           for (var j = 0; j < 4; j++)
7.           {
8.               if (!(cells[i][j].innerHTML == i*4 + j + 1))
9.               if (!(i == 3 && j == 3))
10.              win = false;
11.          }
12.      }
13.      if (win)
14.      {
15.          alert("Congratulations! You won!");
16.          if (window.prompt("Play again?", "yes"))
17.              placeNumbers();
18.      }
19.  }
```

Here's how this function works:

The variable, **win**, is initially set to true on line 3. It works as a flag. At any time during the check on lines 4–12, if some cell is found to be out of order, **win** is set back to false to indicate that this arrangement of cells is not a winner.

The outer for loop has four iterations—one for each row. The variable i represents the rows. The inner for loop also has four iterations for the four columns. The variable j represents the columns. The if clause checks the values of each cell using the algorithm (i * 4 + j + 1). Figure 8.3 shows that this algorithm works for all the cells. However, when both i = 3 and j = 3, no check is made. This takes care of the 16th cell which is supposed to be empty. If any of the results is not true, **win** is set to false and no winner is detected.

If **win** is true, the if clause that begins on line 13 does two things. It sends a congratulatory alert to the player and it prompts the player to see if he or she wants to play again. If the player does want to play again, the placeNumbers() function is called, the board is reset, and play begins again. If not, the program ends.

1 = i * 4 + j + 1	2 = i * 4 + j + 1	3 = i * 4 + j + 1	4 = i * 4 + j + 1
1 = 0 * 4 + 0 + 1	2 = 0 * 4 + 1 + 1	3 = 0 * 4 + 2 + 1	4 = 0 * 4 + 3 + 1
= 1 ✓	= 2 ✓	= 3 ✓	✓
5 = i * 4 + j + 1	6 = i * 4 + j + 1	7 = i * 4 + j + 1	8 = i * 4 + j + 1
5 = 1 * 4 + 0 + 1	6 = 1 * 4 + 1 + 1	7 = 1 * 4 + 2 + 1	8 = 1 * 4 + 3 + 1
= 5 ✓	= 6 ✓	= 7 ✓	= 8 ✓
9 = i * 4 + j + 1	10 = i * 4 + j + 1	11 = i * 4 + j + 1	12 = i * 4 + j + 1
9 = 2 * 4 + 0 + 1	10 = 2 * 4 + 1 + 1	11 = 2 * 4 + 2 + 1	12 = 2 * 4 + 3 + 1
= 9 ✓	= 10 ✓	= 11 ✓	= 12 ✓
13 = i * 4 + j + 1	14 = i * 4 + j + 1	15 = i * 4 + j + 1	no math when i = 3
13 = 3 * 4 + 0 + 1	14 = 3 * 4 + 1 + 1	15 = 3 * 4 + 2 + 1	and j = 3 ✓
= 13 ✓	= 14 ✓	= 15 ✓	

Figure 8.3 Algorithm to check cell values for a winning display

Putting It All Together

We now put all the code together. Try it!

```
1.    <html>
2.    <head>
3.    <title>Greg's Gambits | Greg's 15</title>
4.    <link href="greg.css" rel="stylesheet" type="text/css" />
5.    <script type = "text/javascript">
6.        var cells;
7.        var swapped;
8.        function setup()
9.        {
10.           cells = new Array([document.getElementById("cell00"), ↵
                      document.getElementById("cell01"), ↵
                      document.getElementById("cell02"), ↵
                      document.getElementById("cell03")], ↵
                      [document.getElementById("cell10"), ↵
                      document.getElementById("cell11"), ↵
                      document.getElementById("cell12"), ↵
                      document.getElementById("cell13")], ↵
                      [document.getElementById("cell20"), ↵
                      document.getElementById("cell21"), ↵
                      document.getElementById("cell22"), ↵
                      document.getElementById("cell23")], ↵
                      [document.getElementById("cell30"), ↵
                      document.getElementById("cell31"), ↵
                      document.getElementById("cell32"), ↵
                      document.getElementById("cell33")]);
11.           placeNumbers();
12.       }
13.       function placeNumbers()
14.       {
15.           var numbers = new Array();
16.           for (var i=0; i<16; i++)
17.               numbers[i] = i;
18.           var randomLoc;
19.           var temp;
20.           for (i= 0; i < 16 ; i++)
```

```
21.                 {
22.                         randomLoc = Math.floor(Math.random()* 15 + 1);
23.                         temp = numbers[i];
24.                         numbers[i] = numbers[randomLoc];
25.                         numbers[randomLoc] = temp;
26.                 }
27.                 i = 0;
28.                 for (var rows = 0; rows < 4; rows++)
29.                 {
30.                         for (var cols = 0; cols< 4; cols++)
31.                         {
32.                                 if (numbers[i] != 0)
33.                                     cells[rows][cols].innerHTML = numbers[i];
34.                                 else
35.                                     cells[rows][cols].innerHTML = "";
36.                                 ++i;
37.                         }
38.                 }
39.         }
40.     function doClick(row, col)
41.     {
42.             var top = row - 1;
43.             var bottom = row + 1;
44.             var left = col - 1;
45.             var right = col + 1;
46.             swapped = false;
47.             if(top != -1 && cells[top][col].innerHTML == "")
48.                     swap(cells[row][col], cells[top][col]);
49.             else if(right != 4 && cells[row][right].innerHTML == "")
50.                     swap(cells[row][col], cells[row][right]);
51.             else if(bottom != 4 && cells[bottom][col].innerHTML == "")
52.                     swap(cells[row][col], cells[bottom][col]);
53.             else if (left != -1 && cells[row][left].innerHTML == "")
54.                     swap(cells[row][col], cells[row][left]);
55.             else
56.                     alert("Illegal move.");
57.             checkWinner();
58.     }
59.     function swap(firstCell, secondCell)
60.     {
61.             swapped = true;
62.             secondCell.innerHTML = firstCell.innerHTML;
63.             firstCell.innerHTML = "";
64.     }
65.     function checkWinner()
66.     {
67.             var win = true;
68.             for (var i = 0; i < 4; i++)
69.             {
70.                     for (var j = 0; j < 4; j++)
71.                     {
72.                             if (!(cells[i][j].innerHTML == i*4 + j + 1))
73.                                     if (!(i == 3 && j == 3))
74.                                             win = false;
75.                     }
76.             }
77.             if (win)
78.             {
```

```
79.                    alert("Congratulations! You won!");
80.                    if (window.prompt("Play again?", "yes"))
81.                        placeNumbers();
82.                }
83.            }
84.    </script>
85.    </head>
86.    <body onload ="setup()">
87.    <div id="container">
88.            <img src="images/superhero.jpg" class="floatleft" />
89.            <h1 id="logo"><em>Greg's 15</em></h1>
90.            <div id="nav">
91.                <p><a href="index.html">Home</a>
92.                <a href="greg.html">About Greg</a>
93.                <a href="play_games.html">Play a Game</a>
94.                <a href="sign.html">Sign In</a>
95.                <a href="contact.html">Contact Us</a></p>
96.            </div>
97.            <div id="content">
98.            <p>You can move any number into an empty spot by moving up, down, ↵
                    right, or left. Diagonal moves are not allowed. The object ↵
                    is to get all the numbers into correct order, from 1 through ↵
                    15 with the empty space at the end. </p>
99.            <table width = "60%" align = "center">
100.           <tr><td height = "60"><span onclick = "doClick(0,0)" id = ↵
                    "cell00" /> </td>
101.            <td><span onclick = "doClick(0,1)" id = "cell01" /> </td>
102.            <td><span onclick = "doClick(0,2)" id = "cell02" /> </td>
103.            <td><span onclick = "doClick(0,3)" id = "cell03" /> </td>
104.            </tr> <tr>
105.            <td height = "60"><span onclick = "doClick(1,0)" id = ↵
                    "cell10" /> </td>
106.            <td><span onclick = "doClick(1,1)" id = "cell11" /> </td>
107.            <td><span onclick = "doClick(1,2)" id = "cell12" /> </td>
108.            <td><span onclick = "doClick(1,3)" id = "cell13" /> </td>
109.            </tr> <tr>
110.            <td height = "60"><span onclick = "doClick(2,0)" id = ↵
                    "cell20" /> </td>
111.            <td><span onclick = "doClick(2,1)" id = "cell21" /> </td>
112.            <td><span onclick = "doClick(2,2)" id = "cell22" /> </td>
113.            <td><span onclick = "doClick(2,3)" id = "cell23" /> </td>
114.            </tr> <tr>
115.            <td height = "60"><span onclick = "doClick(3,0)" id = ↵
                    "cell30" /> </td>
116.            <td><span onclick = "doClick(3,1)" id = "cell31" /> </td>
117.            <td><span onclick = "doClick(3,2)" id = "cell32" /> </td>
118.            <td><span onclick = "doClick(3,3)" id = "cell33" /> </td>
119.            </tr></table>
120.           </div>
121.           <div id="footer">Copyright &copy; 2013 Greg's Gambits<br />
122.           <a href="mailto:yourfirstname@yourlastname.com"> ↵
                    yourfirstname@yourlastname.com</a></div>
123.    </div>
124.    </body></html>
```

If you use a file from the Student Data Files as a template and create this code, saving the file as greg_15.html, your page will initially look like this, with the numbers in your table generated randomly:

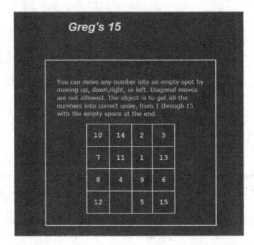

You should be able to play the game yourself. When all the numbers are put in order, you will first see the following alert:

After pressing OK, the following prompt will appear:

Carla's Classroom: Images and Imagination

Carla want her students to learn the "three Rs", but also she encourages creativity. Children love hearing stories and they love telling stories. In this section, we will help Carla develop a site that uses images, form elements, and arrays to create a slide show of photos and allows students to write stories to accompany each picture. We'll call this lesson Images and Imagination.

Setting Things Up

Create a link to a Writing page on Carla's home page. You can use the reading.html page created earlier in the text as a template to create a new writing.html page. The code for this page is shown, including a link to the new page we will create. The new page will be named carla_slideshow.html.

```
1.   <html>
2.   <head>
3.   <title>Carla's Classroom | Writing Lessons</title>
4.   <link href="carla.css" rel="stylesheet" type="text/css" />
5.   </head>
6.   <body>
7.   <div id="container">
8.       <img src="images/writing_big.jpg" class="floatleft" />
9.       <h1 id="logo"><em>Carla's Classroom</em></h1>
10.      <div align="left">
11.      <blockquote><p>
12.         <a href="index.html"><img src="images/owl_button.jpg" />Home</a>
13.         <a href="carla.html"><img src="images/carla_button.jpg" ↵
                    />Meet Carla </a>
14.         <a href="reading.html"><img src="images/read_button.jpg" ↵
                    />Reading</a>
15.         <a href="writing.html"><img src="images/write_button.jpg" ↵
                    />Writing</a>
16.         <a href="math.html"><img src="images/arith_button.jpg" ↵
                    />Arithmetic</a>
17.         <br /></p></blockquote>
18.      </div>
19.      <div id="content">
20.         <p><img src="images/carla_pic.jpg" class="floatleft" /> ↵
                    Writing Lessons: </p>
21.         <p><a href = "carla_slideshow.html">What Happened? Create ↵
                    Your Own Story</a></p>
22.      </div>
23.      <div id="footer">
24.         <h3>* Carla's Motto: Never miss a chance to teach -- and ↵
                    to learn!</h3>
25.      </div>
26.   </div></body></html>
```

The page will look like this:

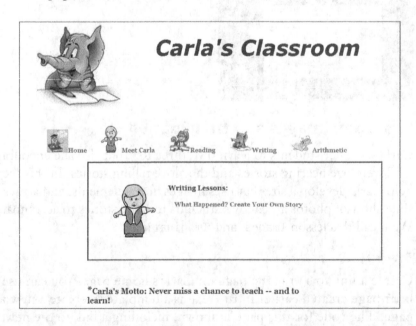

Developing the Program

Now we will create the `carla_slideshow.html` page. The page will include a slide show of images. Under each image will be a text box where the student can enter his or her story about that image. The student should also be able to click a button to advance through the slide show or go back to review previous images.

First we must select some images. Images are included in the Student Data Files but you can, of course, substitute other images.

Next, we need to create a web page with a form and then add the slide show. Before we create the slide show, we will discuss image swapping since this is the basis of how a slide show works.

Setting the Stage   Let's begin by creating the web page. The HTML script is shown below. The page needs to have an area for the images and an area for the student to enter the text. It also should include buttons that will allow the player to scroll through the show. Because the page uses the same template as for the `writing.html` page, the HTML script is only shown for the `"content"` `<div>`.

```
1.   <div id = "content">
2.   <form name="slides">
3.   <table width="95%" align="center" border="0">
4.   <tr>
```

```
5.          <td><p> Use your imagination to tell the story behind each ↵
                       picture</p> </td>
6.   </tr> <tr>
7.          <td>an image will go here </td>
8.          <p><textarea name ="story" rows ="20" cols ="65"> Enter your ↵
                       story here.</textarea><br />
9.          <input type="button" value ="Previous picture" />
10.         <input type ="button" value ="Next picture" />
11.         Picture Number: <input type ="text" value ="1" name = ↵
                       "theslide" size ="5" /></p> </td>
12.   </tr></table>
13.   </form>
14.   <div>
```

We have created a form which allows us to easily access content areas when we start to include the JavaScript code. We have named our form slides and named the textarea box where the student will enter the story with the appropriate name, story. As of now, the page looks empty:

The Image Swap   An image inserted in your page is an object and, therefore, has properties and values. Because an image in a web page is an object, it can be manipulated with JavaScript. A mouse may be rolled over it or off it. It can be clicked on. By using the **onmouseover** and **onmouseout** JavaScript events, simple image swaps can be created.

To create a simple **image swap,** first you must insert the image you want displayed when the page loads. This example will use two images of a horse. The first is the stationary horse and the other is the horse in motion:

```
<img src="horse1.jpg" alt="standing horse" name="horse" />
```

Note that a new property has been added to the image object. The image object now has a name and the name is "horse". When this image is called or referred to by JavaScript, it can be identified by its name.

We are now ready to swap images. The following code should be opened directly before the img tag and should be closed at the end of the img tag:

```
<a href= "#" onmouseover="document.horse.src='horse1.jpg';" ↵
    onmouseout="document.horse.src='horse2.jpg';"> ↵
        <img src="horse1.jpg" alt="standing horse" name="horse" /></a>
```

The onmouseover event alerts the browser that, as a user passes a mouse over some object, something will happen. In this case, the object is the image which has been given the name "horse". The next bit of code, src, tells the browser where the object named horse is located. In this case, the image file (either horse1.jpg or horse2.jpg) is located in the same folder as the web page. If the image had been located in a subfolder named images, that subfolder would, of course, have to be included in the path to the image.

The onmouseout event is similarly coded. Since the entire code is inside an anchor tag, the href = "#" is included because an anchor tag needs an href. In this case, there is no actual address to go to so the # indicates that the link is a dummy link.

Practice the Image Swap Create a folder named image_swap and pick any two images from the Student Data Files to move to this folder. Create a simple web page with the page title JavaScript Image Swap and save the page with the filename swap.html. If you choose the two horse images, your page will look similar to this:

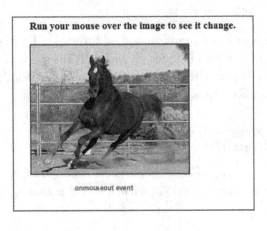

The Slide Show   It seems logical that, if you can swap one image for another, that process can be repeated many times. This is the basis of the slide show which we will use to display a series of photos for which students will view and write stories in corresponding textarea boxes.

When you create this slide show, you will preload a set of images into an array and allow the student to use forward and back buttons to navigate to a new picture. Preloading images requires using an array. Getting the slide show to run requires using functions.

We will use the eight images shown earlier for our page. The images have been sized to ensure that they are the same size and are assumed to be stored in an images folder. For an array of images, we must not only create an array but also tell the browser that each element will contain an image. The code to create the array and load it with the images, as follows, goes in the <head> section, under the <script> tag:

```
var pictures = new Array();
pictures[0] = new Image();
pictures[1] = new Image();
pictures[2] = new Image();
pictures[3] = new Image();
pictures[4] = new Image();
pictures[5] = new Image();
pictures[6] = new Image();
pictures[7] = new Image();
pictures[0].src ="images/tower.jpg";
pictures[1].src ="images/kitten.jpg";
pictures[2].src ="images/gator.jpg";
pictures[3].src ="images/sunset.jpg";
pictures[4].src ="images/horse1.jpg";
pictures[5].src ="images/tree_roots.jpg";
pictures[6].src ="images/pelican_kits.jpg";
pictures[7].src ="images/dog.jpg";
```

Next, we will use another array to hold the stories that the students will create. We will initialize the elements of the array with the simple text, "Enter your story here."

```
var theStories = new Array();
for (var i = 0; i < 8; i++)
    theStories[i] = "Enter your story here.";
```

Now, we will create the JavaScript function and add to the HTML script code that will allow the show to run. This code loads an image as the student clicks the Next or Previous slide button. It tracks the number of the picture, from 1 to 8. This code is placed in the <head> section, under the array declarations:

```
1.  var picNum = 0;
2.  var totalSlides = pictures.length-1;
3.  function showPic(direction)
4.  {
5.      if (direction == "next")
6.          (picNum == totalSlides) ? picNum = 0 : picNum++;
```

```
 7.        else
 8.             (picNum  == 0) ? picNum  = totalSlides : picNum--;
 9.        document.slides.picture.src = pictures[picNum].src;
10.        document.slides.story.value = theStories[picNum];
11.        document.slides.theslide.value = picNum+1;
12.  }
```

The calls to the function must be added to the buttons in the HTML script:

```
<input type="button" value ="Previous picture" onclick ="showPic('previous');" />
<input type ="button" value ="Next picture" onclick ="showPic('next');" />
```

Let's discuss this code in detail.

Line 1 declares a variable named **picNum** and initializes it to 0. Line 2 sets the value of a variable named **totalSlides** initially to the size of the array that holds the pictures. The length method is used to return the number of elements in the **pictures** array. In this case, **pictures**.length has the value of 8. However, the images are identified by the subscripts 0 through 7 so **totalSlides** initially equals **pictures**.length - 1.

The function showPic() begins on line 3. It takes one argument, called **direction**. When showPic() is called, it will receive either the value 'next' or 'previous', depending on which button has been clicked.

Line 5 begins an if...else clause. If **direction** holds the value of 'next' the user wants to see the next slide and line 6 is executed. If not, then the Previous Slide button is chosen and the program skips to line 7.

Line 6 uses the conditional operator. The condition that is checked is the value of **picNum**. If **picNum** is the same as **totalSlides**, we know the user is looking at the last picture in the array. If so, **picNum** is set to 0 which sends the array back to the first picture. If **picNum** is not the last picture, then we want to move to the next picture in the array so **picNum** is incremented by one.

Line 7 starts the else part of the if...else structure. Line 8 tells the computer what to do if the student has pressed the Previous Picture button. In this case, the value of **picNum** has to be re-set if the present picture is the first picture in the array. If the picture on the screen is the first one, the previous picture is actually picture 8 (**pictures[7]**). Therefore, this line says, "If the present picture is the first, reset **picNum** to the value 7. If the present picture is any other number, then decrease the value of **picNum** by 1."

Lines 9–11 simply display the next picture on the web page with the corresponding area for a story and corresponding picture number. To begin the slide show, we add an img tag to link to the first image in the spot that previously held the text "an image will go here" and give this img tag a name so it will be swapped when the Previous Picture or Next Picture button is pressed. The name is "picture" and it is referenced on line 9 of the showPic() function. This code is as follows:

```
<img src="images/tower.jpg" name="picture" alt="slide show" />
```

Putting It All Together

The entire code for the finished website is given:

```
1.   <html>
2.   <head>
3.   <title>Carla's Classroom | Slideshow</title>
4.   <link href = "carla.css" rel = "stylesheet" type = "text/css" />
5.   <script>
6.       var pictures = new Array();
7.       pictures[0] = new Image(); pictures[1] = new Image();
8.       pictures[2] = new Image(); pictures[3] = new Image();
9.       pictures[4] = new Image(); pictures[5] = new Image();
10.      pictures[6] = new Image(); pictures[7] = new Image();
11.      pictures[0].src ="images/tower.jpg";
12.      pictures[1].src ="images/kitten.jpg";
13.      pictures[2].src ="images/gator.jpg";
14.      pictures[3].src ="images/sunset.jpg";
15.      pictures[4].src ="images/horse1.jpg";
16.      pictures[5].src ="images/tree_roots.jpg";
17.      pictures[6].src ="images/pelican_kits.jpg";
18.      pictures[7].src ="images/dog.jpg";
19.      var theStories = new Array();
20.      for (var i = 0; i < 8; i++)
21.          theStories[i] = "Enter your story here.";
22.      var picNum = 0;
23.      var totalSlides = pictures.length-1;
24.      function showPic(direction)
25.      {
26.          if (direction == "next")
27.              (picNum == totalSlides) ? picNum = 0 : picNum++;
28.          else
29.              (picNum  == 0) ? picNum  = totalSlides : picNum--;
30.          document.slides.picture.src = pictures[picNum].src;
31.          document.slides.story.value = theStories[picNum];
32.          document.slides.theslide.value = picNum + 1;
33.      }
34.  </script>
35.  </head>
36.  <body>
37.  <div id="container">
38.      <img src="images/writing_big.jpg" class="floatleft" />
39.      <h2>Images and Imagination </h2>
40.      <div align = "left"><blockquote>
41.          <p><a href = "index.html"><img src = ⏎
                     "images/owl_button.jpg" />Home</a>
42.          <a href = "carla.html"><img src = ⏎
                     "images/carla_button.jpg" />Meet Carla </a>
43.          <a href = "reading.html"><img src = ⏎
                     "images/read_button.jpg" />Reading</a>
44.          <a href = "writing.html"><img src = ⏎
                     "images/write_button.jpg" />Writing</a>
45.          <a href = "math.html"><img src = ⏎
                     "images/arith_button.jpg" />Arithmetic</a>
46.          <br /> </p> </blockquote> </div>
```

```
47.        <div style ="clear:both;"></div>
48.        <div id = "content">
49.        <form name="slides">
50.        <table width="95%" align="center" border="0">
51.        <tr><td>
52.            <p>Use your imagination to tell the story behind each ↵
                        picture</p>
53.        </td></tr> <tr><td>
54.            <img src = "images/tower.jpg" name = "picture" alt = ↵
                        "slide show" />
55.        </td></tr><tr><td>
56.            <p><textarea name ="story" rows = "5" cols = "65"> Enter ↵
                        your story here.</textarea><br />
57.            <input type = "button" value = "Previous picture" ↵
                        onclick ="showPic('previous');" />
58.            <input type = "button" value = "Next picture" onclick ↵
                        = "showPic('next');" />
59.            Picture Number: <input type = "text" value = "1" ↵
                        name = "theslide" size = "5" /></p>
60.        </td></tr></table>
61.    </form>
62.    <div id="footer">
63.        <h3>*Carla's Motto: Never miss a chance to teach -- and ↵
                        to learn!</h3>
64.    </div>
65.    </body></html>
```

Here is what the page will look like when opened:

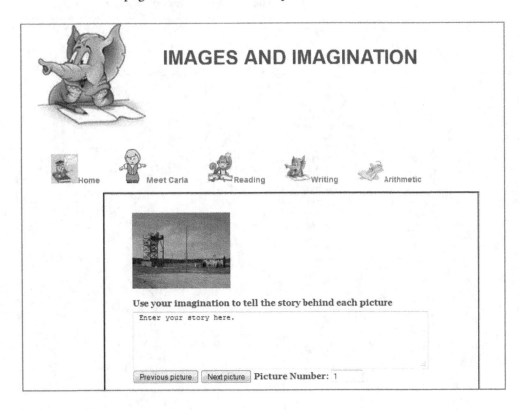

Here is what the page will look like if a student selects Picture 3 and writes a story about the alligator:

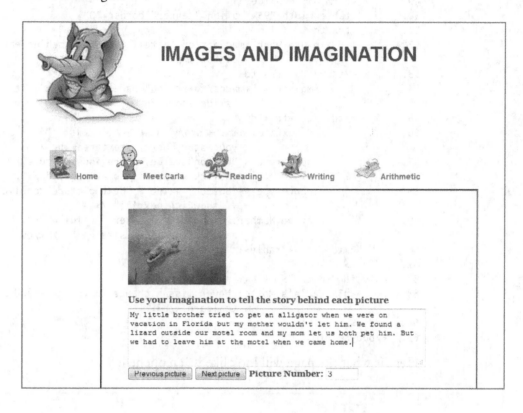

Chapter Review and Exercises

Key Terms

Array object	onmouseover event
image swap	parallel arrays
index number	push() method
length property (of an array)	splice() method
multi-dimensional arrays	subscript
new array ()	square root
new keyword	two-dimensional arrays
one-dimensional array	unshift() method
onmouseout event	var keyword

Review Exercises

Fill in the Blank

1. A list of related data of the same type, referred to by a single variable name and an index number to identify each item is a _____ array.

2. The _____ property of the Array object checks the size of an array at any time.

3. Each element of an array is identified by its _____ value.

4. The _____ method allows you to add several items to the end of an array.

5. The push() and unshift() methods add elements to arrays and return the _____ of the altered array.

True or False

6. T/F   Since arrays are not the same as variables, you do not use the var keyword when you declare an array.

7. T/F   The values to be stored in an array can only be entered by the user at the time the array is created.

8. T/F   Parallel arrays must be of the same size.

9. T/F   The code to add an element to the beginning of an array named **myArray[]** is as follows:

    ```
    myArray.push(0, 1, "new");
    ```

10. T/F   Another word for "index" when referring to a specific element of an array is "subscript."

11. T/F   The push() method allows the user to add one item to the beginning of an array.

12. T/F   The `splice()` method is used to add or remove items from an array.

13. T/F   The `unshift()` method inserts element values at the beginning of an array.

14. T/F   A two-dimensional array has two subscripts.

15. T/F   A two-dimensional array in JavaScript is actually an array of arrays.

Short Answer

16. Given the following array, what is the value of `colors[3]`?

```
var colors = new Array("black", "white", "teal", "mauve");
```

17. Given the following JavaScript code, what is displayed by the `document.write()` statement?

```
var chips = new Array("onion", "barbecue", "salt", "cheese");
document.write("There are " + chips.length + 1 + " types of chips");
```

18. Given the following code, write statements that will assign the values requested:

```
var numbers = new Array(2, 3, 5, 7, 11);
```

   a) Create a variable named **adding** that uses elements in the numbers array such that **adding** = 19.

   b) Create a variable named **divide** that uses elements in the numbers array such that **divide** = 9.

19. Write JavaScript code to create an array named **threes[]** that has five elements. Use a loop to populate the array with the following sequence of numbers: `3, 6, 9, 12, 15`.

20. Write JavaScript code to create an array named **usernames[]** that has 100 elements. Each element contains usernames for a school that assigns usernames to students. Each username concatenates the string `"college"` with a number. The numbers should start at 300 and end at 399.

21. Write JavaScript code to allow a business owner to enter the names of his employees and the number of hours each employee worked in a week. Use parallel arrays named **employees[]** and **hours[]** and a sentinel value so that the boss can enter as many employees as desired.

22. Given an array named **items[]** that holds the names of various items sold in a jewelry business. List three arrays that, as parallel arrays, will hold appropriate data to correspond with each item in **items[]**.

23. Given an array named **snow[]** that contains yearly snowfall amounts in inches in a certain area over a period of 10 years from 2000 to 2009. Use a loop to display these amounts. The output should be on 10 lines, each line of the following form:

```
Snowfall for the year XXXX is YY inches
```

   where XXXX is the year and YY is the amount in inches.

Given: var **snow** = new Array(6, 8, 8, 12, 21, 15, 7, 8, 10, 15);

24. Add code to Exercise 23 to find and display the years with the highest and lowest snowfall amounts.

25. Add code to Exercise 24 to find the average snowfall over the 10 years.

26. Add code to Exercise 25 to find the number of years that snowfall was above the average.

27. Add code to Exercise 26 to find the number of years that snowfall was within two inches (above or below) the average.

28. Add code to the addRings() function of Example 8.14 in the chapter to check if a value Jackie wants to add to her inventory is already part of the inventory.

29. Add code to Example 8.14 in the chapter that will allow Jackie to enter her inventory of pendants and to add or subtract from that inventory.

30. Given the following JavaScript code, what are the values of the eight elements in the **numbers[]** array?

```
var numbers = new Array;
for (var i = 0; i < 8; i++)
      numbers[i] = (i * i) + 1;
```

Programming Challenges

On Your Own

1. Create a web page that will display statistics and calculate the standard deviation on a list of numbers input by the user. The display on the web page should include the following:

   - the entire array of numbers, as entered by the user
   - the mean (average) of the numbers
   - the standard deviation

   Helpful information: Assuming you name your variables as shown, the formulas you need are listed below the variables:

array of numbers: **nums**	two sums: **sum1** and **sum2**
standard deviation: **stdDev**	mean: **mean**
number of elements in the array: **N**	counters as needed: **count, i, j, k**, etc.

   ### Formulas:

   The formula for the standard deviation of a list of **N** numbers in an array named **nums** with a mean of **mean** is the **square root** of

   $$((nums[0] - mean)^2 + (nums[1] - mean)^2 + ... + (nums[N-1] - mean)^2)/(N-2)$$

- to sum the numbers to calculate the mean: **sum1 = sum1 + nums[count]**
- to calculate the average: **mean = sum1/(N)**
- to calculate the first part of the standard deviation, find the differences between each number, **nums[count]** and the **mean** and then square the result of each of these differences. First, find the square of each difference, using a loop:

(nums[count] - mean)^2

then sum all the differences so, in a loop, use

sum2 = sum2 + (nums[count] - mean)^2

and finally, the standard deviation is calculated using the Math.sqrt() method:

stdDev = Math.sqrt(sum2/(N - 1))

Save the page with the filename std_dev.html and submit your work as instructed by your teacher.

2. Add code to Example 8.14 to allow Jackie to create an inventory of pendants and to add or subtract from that inventory using Example 8.14 as a model. Save the page with the filename pendant.html and submit your work as instructed by your teacher.

3. Create a web page that will allow the user to customize the page. The user should be prompted to enter the following information which will be displayed on a new page, along with the customizations the user has chosen.

   User information: name, nickname, email address, favorite movie, favorite book, favorite type of music

   User-selected customizations: page background color, text color, text size

   You can add any features you wish and allow the user to customize each item differently if you want. Save the page with the filename customize.html and submit your work as instructed by your teacher.

4. Create a web page for a business. The page should include parallel arrays which hold names of the items sold and the corresponding price for each item. The user should be prompted to select an item and a quantity and the page will then display the total cost for that quantity of the item chosen. You can create your own inventory or use the following suggestions. Save the page with the filename supplies.html and submit your work as instructed by your teacher.

Item	Price	Item	Price
notebook	$ 5.95	laptop case	$ 29.99
pen	4.95	cell phone case	18.99
mechanical pencil	2.95	3-ring binder	6.95
lead refill pack	.98	3-hole paper refill	2.00

5. Create a web page that will allow a teacher to enter his or her students' names and test scores into parallel arrays. The page should prompt the teacher for the number of students in the class and the number of tests administered. Use this information to create the appropriate number of parallel arrays. Then create the

arrays and prompt the teacher for data to populate the arrays. Display the data on the web page in a table. Also display the high and low score for each test as well as the average for each test. Save the page with the filename class_parallel.html and submit your work as instructed by your teacher.

6. Redo Programming Challenge 5 but use a two-dimensional array instead of parallel arrays for the data. Save the page with the filename class_two_d.html and submit your work as instructed by your teacher.

7. A magic square is a two-dimensional array of positive integers in which the following is true:

- The number of rows equals the number of columns.
- Every row, column, and the two diagonals add up to the same number.

Create a web page with a table that has four rows and four columns. Allow the user to enter values for each cell. Store these values in a two-dimensional array named **magic** and determine if it is a magic square.

Note: if we call the array **magic** then the sums of the two diagonals are as follows:

```
diagonal1 = magic[0][0] + magic[1][1] + magic[2][2] + magic[3][3];
diagonal2 = magic[0][3] + magic[1][2] + magic[2][1] + magic[3][0];
```

Save the page with the filename magic.html and submit your work as instructed by your teacher.

Case Studies

Greg's Gambits

Now you will add a new game to the Greg's Gambits site. The game will be a maze that a player must navigate, while avoiding pitfalls, to save a victim. It will be helpful if you work through the Game of 15 as discussed in this chapter as well as the section on image swapping.

Create a web page using the Greg's Gambits template. Put a table into the "content" area. This table will hold the maze and each cell will be a step that the player can take. You will fill each cell with an image file; you can use the images provided in the Student Data Files or find your own. We will continue the instructions for this game assuming that you are using the files provided: myHero.jpg, saved.jpg, and blue.jpg.

First, create a small 4 × 4 table. After the program is coded and works properly, you can add more rows and columns to make a more challenging game. Next, write the JavaScript code.

Create a two-dimensional array of images and, initially, store the myHero.jpg image in element [0][0] and the saved.jpg image in element [3][3]. All other cells should contain the blue.jpg image.

Next, create the pitfalls. Use a random number generator to identify several cells. At first, start with three pitfalls; you can add more later. You should generate a random value for a row and a column to identify a pitfall cell. You will also need to check to be sure you have not identified the first cell, where the player begins, or the last cell, where the victim awaits, and that the cells you identify do not create an impasse (for example, the three identified pitfalls cannot block the player from moving).

Allow the player to move to any cell above, below, to the left, or to the right. Diagonal moves are not allowed unless you want to get fancy.

Each time the player clicks on a cell (attempts to make a move) you need to check the following:

- Is the desired cell a pitfall? If it is, an alert should tell the player about the pitfall and tell him to make a different move. You may, if you want, create "killer" pitfalls which can end the game.
- Is the desired cell the last cell in the table? If it contains the saved.jpg image, the player has won and should be informed and the game ends.
- If the selected cell is not a pitfall and not a winner, swap the cells and the game continues.

Be sure to give your player the option to replay the game.

Note: You can "hard code" the pitfalls and put them in whatever cells you choose. Using randomly generated pitfalls makes the game more interesting and also makes it easier to enhance the game by increasing the size of the maze.

Save your page as greg_maze.html. Open the index.html page for Greg's Gambits and add a link, under the Play A Game link, that links to this page named Greg's Maze. Submit your work as instructed by your teacher.

Carla's Classroom

In this exercise, you will polish the Images and Imagination page created in the chapter. Therefore, you will need to create the slide show page as instructed in the text. Now add code to this page to extract the story a student has written about one of the images in the slide show. A new page should be created so the student can save a copy of the image selected and his or her story. Allow the student to select a background color for the new page and a text color. Prompt the student for his or her name and for color choices. Use arrays for the color choices and be sure to include a check to ensure that a student does not pick the same color for the page background and text. The page should have the same filename as in the chapter, carla_slideshow.html. Submit your work as instructed by your teacher.

Lee's Landscape

Add a page to the Lee's Landscape website that will allow the customer to select a service and see the options available for that service. Use a two-dimensional array with six rows and five columns to store the information given in the table below. The page should display a list of services. When the customer selects a service, the options should be displayed on the web page.

Services		Options		
lawn mowing	weekly	twice a month	monthly	by call
hedge trimming	weekly	twice a month	monthly	by call
mulch	buy per square yard	delivery	spreading	full yard discounts
pest control	monthly	twice a year	yearly	by call
weed control	weekly	twice a month	monthly	by call
extra services	sod installation	irrigation systems	yard cleanup	ponds, pools, & streams

Be sure to give this web page an appropriate page title such as Lee's Landscape || Services. Save this file with the filename lee_services.html. Add a link to the Lee's Landscape home page to this new page. Submit your work as instructed by your teacher.

Jackie's Jewelry

Add a slide show page to the Jackie's Jewelry website. The page should highlight Jackie's creations. Each image should have a caption that describes the piece. You can use the images in the Student Data Files or you can find your own images online. Remember that if you use an image from a website, you must credit the owner of the image on your web page. Be sure that you size all the images before creating the slide show. If the images are not the same size, your slide show will not display properly.

You may find it helpful to review the Images and Imagination page discussed in this chapter before you begin to create the slideshow.

Be sure to give this web page an appropriate page title such as Jackie's Jewelry || Gallery. Save this file with the filename jackie_gallery.html. Add a link to the Jackie's Jewelry home page to this new page. Submit your work as instructed by your teacher.

Searching and Sorting

Chapter Objectives

Considering the programs we have written in this book, you will remember that many times we wanted to offer a computer user one option out of many. For example, in Chapter 3, we wrote a program for Madame Vadoma and created a list of fortunes. We associated each fortune with a number and a generated random number was matched to a particular fortune through a long `switch` statement. The number of fortunes was limited mainly by the tedium involved in writing the options in the `switch` statement. But if we stored the fortunes in an array, we could have as many as we wanted. Using what we now know about arrays and loops, and what we are about to learn about searching through an array, we could find a fortune that matched a random number using very little code. In Chapter 8, we learned how to create parallel arrays. If, for example, a teacher wanted to store each student's name, homework average, and test average in parallel arrays, being able to sort these arrays could allow the teacher to alphabetize the information, see the scores arranged from highest to lowest, and more. Searching through and sorting information in arrays are programming tools that have a myriad of uses. This chapter discusses two important ways to search through data and two methods used to sort data.

After reading this chapter, you will be able to do the following:

- Use the `sort()` and `reverse()` methods to sort arrays

- Understand how to use the bubble sort algorithm to sort arrays

- Understand how to use the serial search algorithm to find a value in an array

- Understand how to use the binary search algorithm to find a value in an array

- Understand how to use parallel arrays in conjunction with searching and sorting algorithms

- Use more methods of the `Array` object including `indexOf()`, `lastIndexOf()`, and `splice()`

- Create a timer with the `setInterval()` and `clearInterval()` methods

9.1 Sorting Arrays

Often, when we write programs, we find that we must search a one-dimensional array to locate a given item or to sort it in a specific order. Consequently, there are many **algorithms** available to perform each of these tasks. Sometimes we call these **routines**. In this section, we will present several simple techniques to sort an array. In the next section, we will discuss how to search an array for a given value. The JavaScript Array object supports several functions that make it easy to sort arrays. These functions will be discussed first and then we will demonstrate two other sorting methods.

The sort() Method

The **sort()method** will sort an array of strings or numbers. By default, the sort() method sorts strings alphabetically, ascending from A to Z. Recall, however, that each character in a string is stored in the computer as its ASCII value. Therefore, the sort() method will put Apple before aardvark because the uppercase A is stored as its ASCII value (65) and the lowercase a is stored as its ASCII value (97). If, for example, you have an array of names, you can use the toUpperCase() method to ensure that all names begin with uppercase letters and then the sort() method makes the task of alphabetizing the names simple.

The sort() method is called by using dot notation to append it to an array name, as follows: **array_name**.sort(). Example 9.1 demonstrates how to use the sort() method with an array of students' names.

EXAMPLE 9.1

Using the sort() Method to Alphabetize

Assume there is an array named **names** that contains the values shown:

a) This is the simplest way to use the sort() method:

```
1. <script>
2. var names = ["Joe", "Lola", "Anatole", "Zoey", "Ted", "Boris"];
3. document.write(names.sort());
4. </script>
```

The output is as follows:

```
Anatole,Boris,Joe,Lola,Ted,Zoey
```

b) Now we will put the output in a loop so the names are entered by the user and are displayed as they have been entered and sorted, separating each name by a space:

```
1.  <script>
2.  var names = new Array();
3.  var count = 0;
4.  for (count = 0; count < 6; count++)
5.      {
```

```
6.          names[count]= prompt("Enter a name: ");
7.          document.write(names[count] + "  ");
8.          }
9.  names.sort();
10. document.write("<br />");
11. for (count = 0; count < 6; count++)
12. {
13.          document.write(names[count] + "  ");
14. }
15. </script>
```

The output is as follows:

```
Joe Lola Anatole Zoey Ted Boris
Anatole Boris Joe Lola Ted Zoey
```

Sorting Numbers with the sort() Method

The sort() method can be used to sort numbers but needs further discussion. The method compares the ASCII values of the numbers rather than their numeric values. For simple integers that range from 0 through 9, the sort() method would work because the ASCII values for 0 is less than 1, the ASCII value for 1 is less than 2 and so on. But to sort any other numbers, the sort() method, used alone, will not work.

If you wanted to sort the numbers 23, 5, and 17, the sort() method would result in 17, 23, 5. This is because the ASCII value of 1 (49) precedes the ASCII value of 2 (50) and the ASCII value of 5 (53) is the largest. We still can use the sort() method to sort an array of numbers; however, we need to add a function that will compare numbers, not ASCII values. The following function is used to compare numbers:

```
function sortNumber(x,y)
{
     return x - y;
}
```

We use this function to sort an array of numbers by calling it when we call the sort() function as follows:

```
array_name.sort(sortNumber);
```

How does this work? When the sort() method is called, it cycles through the elements in the array and compares all the values in the array. We will learn how this done in Section 9.2 on the bubble sort and Section 9.3 on the selection sort. For now, it is sufficient to understand that elements are compared and the lowest element becomes the first, the next-lowest becomes the second, and so on. But, as mentioned, the comparisons are based on the ASCII values of the elements in the array. When the sortNumber() function is called within the sort() method, for each comparison the sort() method sends two array elements to the sortNumber() function. The first element is passed to x and the second to y. The result of subtracting y from x is returned to the sort(). If it is a positive number, then x must be greater than y. If it is a negative number, then y is greater than x. The sort() method acts upon this result to put the first two values in ascending order. As shown in Example 9.2, the next values are sent and it continues until all the numbers have been sorted.

Note: This little `sortNumber()` function is an excellent addition to a JavaScript source file!

EXAMPLE 9.2

Up and Down: Sorting Numbers

Assume there is an array named **numbers** that contains the values shown:

a) In this example, the numbers are sorted from lowest to highest:

```
1.   <script>
2.   function sortNumber(x,y)
3.   {
4.        return x - y;
5.   }
6.   var numbers = [23, 15, 18, 27, 10, 20];
7.   document.write(numbers.sort(sortNumber));
8.   </script>
```

The output is as follows:

```
10,15,18,20,23,27
```

b) It is easy to change this sort to descending order, sorting from highest to lowest by simply changing the variables in the `sortNumber` function's return statement, as shown on line 4. Now, if the result of calculating **y** - **x** is positive, then **y** is the larger number and **x** is smaller.

```
1.   <script>
2.   function sortNumber(x,y)
3.   {
4.        return y - x;
5.   }
6.   var numbers = [23, 15, 18, 27, 10, 20];
7.   document.write(numbers.sort(sortNumber));
8.   </script>
```

The output is as follows:

```
27,23,20,18,15,10
```

In Example 9.3, we will put two functions in the JavaScript source file we have been building. One will allow us to sort in ascending order, from lowest to highest, and the other in descending order, from highest to lowest. Then we can simplify the code in the page.

EXAMPLE 9.3

Refining the Code by Using the Source File

Code added to the mySource.js file:

```
1.   function sortNumberUp(x,y)
2.   {
3.        return x - y;
4.   }
```

```
5.   function sortNumberDown(x,y)
6.   {
7.        return y - x;
8.   }
```

The new code to sort an array of numbers, ascending first, then descending:

```
1.   <script>
2.   var numbers = [23, 15, 18, 27, 10, 20];
3.   document.write("Part a): " + numbers.sort(sortNumberUp));
4.   document.write("<br />");
5.   var numbers = [23, 15, 18, 27, 10, 20];
6.   document.write("Part b): " + numbers.sort(sortNumberDown));
7.   </script>
```

The output is as follows:

```
Part a): 10,15,18,20,23,27
Part b): 27,23,20,18,15,10
```

The reverse() Method

The **reverse()method** reverses the order of elements in a given array. The first element becomes last, the second element becomes second-to-last, and so on until the last original element becomes first. The syntax is as follows:

```
array_name.reverse()
```

Example 9.4 demonstrates what happens when the reverse() method is used. In this example, the user will enter the names of four players in a game and the program will display the names, as entered, and in reverse order. Assume the user enters "John", "Mary", "Bill", and "Sammy" at the prompts.

EXAMPLE 9.4

Reversing an Array with the reverse() Method

```
1.   <script>
2.   var players = new Array();
3.   var count = 0;
4.   for (count = 0; count < 4; count++)
5.   {
6.        players[count]= prompt("Enter the name of a player: ");
7.        document.write(players[count] + "  ");
8.   }
9.   players.reverse();
10.  document.write("<br />");
11.  for (count = 0; count < 4; count++)
12.  {
13.        document.write(players[count] + "  ");
14.  }
15.  </script>
```

The output is as follows:

```
John Mary Bill Sammy
Sammy Bill Mary John
```

TABLE 9.1	(a) Pre-Sorted Parallel Arrays and (b) Post-Sorted after Sorting One Array				

Pre-Sorted Parallel Arrays   **Post-Sorted, after Purchase Array Is Sorted**

names	emails	purchases	names	emails	purchases
Jane Jones	jane@mymail.com	62.89	Jane Jones	jane@mymail.com	283.45
Harry Hopper	harryh@mymail.com	22.95	Harry Hopper	harryh@mymail.com	125.53
Kim Kesler	kimmie@mymail.com	125.53	Kim Kesler	kimmie@mymail.com	62.89
Mike May	mmay@mymail.com	283.45	Mike May	mmay@mymail.com	22.95
Sally Snoop	snoop@mymail.com	15.26	Sally Snoop	snoop@mymail.com	15.26

The sort() method, along with the accompanying reverse() method are valuable tools. But consider a situation involving parallel arrays. Imagine that Jackie, the jewelry designer, wants to record her customers' information. She stores the information in parallel arrays. One array has the customers' names, another contains their email addresses, and a third contains each customer's last purchase amount. Jackie wants to send all customers who made a purchase greater than $99.99 a special coupon. If she uses the sort() method to sort the purchase array from highest to lowest, she now doesn't know which customer made the highest purchase. If the first five entries of the parallel arrays looked like those shown in Table 9.1(a), after sorting the purchase array, they will look like those shown in Table 9.1(b).

If we only used the sort() method on the purchases array, Jane Jones and Harry Hopper will get the special coupon meant for Kim Kesler and Mike May. We need to find a way to pull along all the elements of all the parallel arrays as we sort one of them.

The sort() method makes sorting an array very easy. As a programmer, not only must you know how to use built-in methods and functions, but also you must understand how and when they can be used, depending on the situation. Many programming algorithms are used to sort data and different situations require different solutions. If you know how a sort routine (method) works, you can use it in any situation. By using one of the sort routines we will discuss now, the index value of the element being moved is available. We use that index value to move all corresponding elements in parallel arrays along with the one we are sorting. This way, when we are finished sorting one array, all the elements in all the parallel arrays correspond.

CHECKPOINT FOR SECTION 9.1 ✓

9.1 Methods used for a specific purpose, such as to sort an array or search for a particular item in an array are known as _____ or algorithms.

9.2 Given the following array, what would be the result of the document.write() statement?

```
numArray = [23, 42, 18, 8];
document.write(numArray.sort());
```

9.3 Given the following function, will this allow the user to sort ascending or descending?

```
function  sortNum(x, y)
{
        return (x - y);
}
```

9.4 Rewrite the function from Checkpoint 9.3, if necessary, so it will sort descending. If it already sorts descending, say so.

9.5 Given the array shown, what is displayed after the document.write() statement is executed?

```
numArray = ["high","jumps","boy","The"];
document.write(numArray.sort());
```

9.6 Write code using the sort() method to sort the following names:

```
Alex, Niral, Howard, Luis, Annie, Marcel
```

9.2 The Bubble Sort

In this chapter, we will discuss two specific sorting routines: the bubble sort and the selection sort. We will discuss the bubble sort first. As long as the number of items to be sorted is relatively small (say, fewer than 100), the **bubble sort** algorithm provides a reasonably quick and simple way to sort. To apply this technique, we make several sweeps (or passes) through the data, and on each pass we compare all adjacent pairs of data items and interchange the data in an adjacent pair if they are not already in the proper order. We continue making passes until no interchanges are necessary in an entire pass, which indicates that the data is sorted.

If you bought a coffee at a coffee shop, you could hand the barista your money with one hand and take the coffee with the other. In one motion you and the barista would have traded items. You start with money and end with coffee; the barista starts with coffee and ends with money. However, for even a fraction of a second, one of you holds both items and the other holds none. A computer cannot make this kind of exchange. In a computer each value is stored in its own location in memory. If you put a coffee in the location that previously held money, the money will be replaced by the coffee and the money would disappear into cyberspace. So before we discuss the bubble sort algorithm, first we must understand how the computer swaps the values of two items.

Swapping Values

How would you change the contents of two boxes if each box can only contain one item at a time? We start with Blue in Box1 and White in Box2 and we want to end with White in Box1 and Blue in Box2. But if we put Blue into Box2, we have lost the value of White. That's the problem a programmer faces. So we create an empty temporary storage space to save the contents of Box1 while we change its value to White, as shown in Figure 9.1.

Example 9.5 shows the **swap routine** in JavaScript.

EXAMPLE
9.5

Swapping Values

```
1.   <html>
2.   <head>
3.   <title>Example 9.5</title>
4.   <script>
5.   var white = "white";
6.   var blue = "blue";
7.   var temp = "hello!";
8.   document.write("contents of white is: " + white + <br />");
9.   document.write("contents of blue is: " + blue + <br />");
10.  document.write("contents of temp is: " + temp + <br />");
11.  temp = white;
12.  white = blue;
13.  blue = temp;
14.  document.write("after the swap: <br />");
15.  document.write("contents of white is: " + white + <br />");
16.  document.write("contents of blue is: " + blue + <br />");
17.  document.write("contents of temp is: " + temp + <br />");
18.  </script>
19.  </head>
20.  <body></body>
21.  </html>
```

The output looks like this:

```
contents of white is: white
contents of blue is: blue
contents of temp is: hello!
after the swap:
contents of white is: blue
contents of blue is: white
contents of temp is: white
```

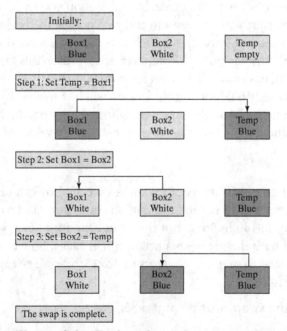

Figure 9.1 Trading places: the swap routine

Using the Bubble Sort Algorithm

To illustrate the bubble sort, we will first walk through an example. We want to sort the following numbers which are stored in an array named **ages**, as shown, from smallest to largest:

```
var ages = new Array(9, 13, 5, 8, 6);
```

A computer can only do one thing at a time, so first it must compare two numbers and decide if they need to switch places. After it decides, it can move on to the next pair. This is why, in this example, there are three passes and each pass has four steps. Figure 9.2 shows, for each pass, the data at the start of the pass on the left and the results of the four comparisons in the next four columns. If an interchange takes place, the arrows cross, indicating which items have been swapped.

In the first pass (the top row of Figure 9.2) the first number (9) is compared with the next number (13) to see if the first is larger than the second. Since 9 is less than 13, no swap is made. Then the second number (13) is compared to the third number (5). In this case, because 5 is less than 13, the numbers are switched. Remember—the computer can only do one thing at a time. Each time you see a switch in Figure 9.2, a swap routine, using a temporary variable as a holding place, has been used.

Further, a computer can't think, as you might, "Well, 5 is also smaller than 9 so I should switch the 5 and 9." It will do that on the next pass, but it can't do it yet. After the 5 and 13 are swapped, the number in the third place (which is now 13) is

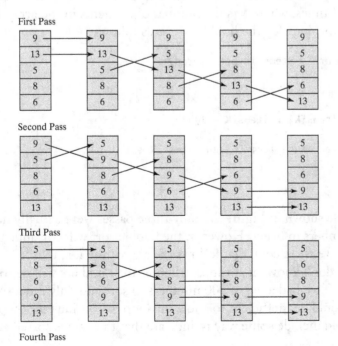

Fourth Pass

No interchanges take place; the numbers are sorted.

Figure 9.2 Using the bubble sort to put five numbers in ascending order

compared to the number in the fourth place (8). Again, because 8 is less than 13, they are swapped. Now 13 is in the fourth place and 13 is compared to the number in the last place (6). Because 13 is larger than 6, they are swapped. One pass is complete. If you review Figure 9.2 carefully and think about what is happening, you will see that, at the end of one pass, the largest number is in the last place. (The opposite will happen if the sort is descending instead of ascending.)

On the second pass, we return to the first number. It is still a 9. But now the second number is a 5, so when these two are compared, the 5 moves to first place. Now the pass continues as before. By the end of the second pass, the second-largest number has moved down to fourth place.

The bubble sort gets its name from the fact that the larger numbers "sink" to the bottom (the end) of the list and the smaller ones "bubble" to the top. In this example, only three passes are needed to sort the numbers. This is simply a result of the way the original list was given. If the list had been written differently, we might have needed up to four passes to sort. In general, to sort N items, it will take at most N – 1 passes through the list to sort them (and, as we will see, one additional pass to determine that they are sorted).

The bubble sort used to sort an array named **items** of N numbers in ascending order is described in the following general pseudocode. Note that the bubble sort requires nested loops. The inner loop compares each element in the array to each of the other elements. By the end of all the iterations in the inner loop on the first time the outer loop executes, the largest number has sunk to the bottom. By the time the inner loop has ended after the outer loop executes a second time, the second-largest number has sunk to the next-to-last space. Therefore, the bubble sort actually fills the array with correct elements from last to first. That's why the outer loop must execute N – 1 times, where N is the number of elements in the array. In general pseudocode, the code for the bubble sort is as follows:

```
while (the array items is not sorted)
{
    for (K = 0; K < N; K++)
    {
        if (items[K] > items[K + 1])
        {
            interchange items[K] and items[K + 1]
        }
    }
}
```

In the example shown in Figure 9.2 only three passes were actually needed to put these five numbers in order. However, the bubble sort will continue to make a fourth pass if we write code that follows the algorithm; i.e., that N – 1 passes should be made. We don't know, in advance, whether the numbers will be sorted in 2, 3, or N – 1 passes. If we had a list of 100 numbers to sort and only 2 numbers were out of order, it would be inefficient to allow the loop to continue for 99 passes. Therefore, we should include some way to indicate that the data is sorted and that the loop can end.

To determine when the list is sorted, we will use a flag. A **flag** is a Boolean variable that takes on one of two values, typically 0 and 1. We will set our flag initially to 0 and continue to reenter the outer loop as long as its value remains 0. Once inside the loop, we set the flag equal to 1 and restore it to 0 if an interchange takes place. If no interchange takes place (meaning the data is sorted), the flag remains 1 and the loop is exited.

Carla, the teacher who runs Carla's Classroom, has administered a new test to her students. She wants to enter the grades into an array and wants to see the results sorted, from highest to lowest. This program in Example 9.6 allows Carla to input as many scores as she wants, stores the scores in an array, sorts them in descending order, and then displays the results. Carla can use these results to decide whether she wants to give a curve to the students or use cut-off values for letter grades.

This program is a little complicated; therefore, try to enter it into a web page and run it. As you work through the program, you will begin to understand better what each line does.

EXAMPLE 9.6

Using the Bubble Sort

```
1.   <html>
2.   <head>
3.   <title>Example 9.6</title>
4.   <script>
5.   function examScores()
6.   {
7.       var scores = new Array();
8.       var count = 0; var flag = 0; var k = 0;
9.       var temp = 0; var oneScore = 0;
10.  //loop to populate the array and find number of elements
11.      while (oneScore != 999)
12.      {
13.          oneScore = prompt("Enter a test score or enter 999 ↵
                            when you are done: ");
14.          if (oneScore == 999)
15.              break;
16.          scores[count] = parseFloat(oneScore);
17.          count++;
18.      }
19.  //begin the bubble sort
20.      while (flag == 0)
21.      {
22.          flag = 1;
23.          for (k = 0; k <= (count - 2); k++)
24.          {
25.              if (scores[k] < scores[k + 1])
26.              {
27.                  temp = scores[k];
28.                  scores[k] = scores[k + 1];
29.                  scores[k + 1] = temp;
30.                  flag = 0;
```

```
31.                        }
32.                   }
33.              }
34.   //Display sorted scores
35.        document.write("Scores sorted from highest to ⏎
                          lowest: <br />");
36.        for (k = 0; k <= (count - 1); k++)
37.              document.write(scores[k] + "<br />");
38.   }
39.   </script>
40.   </head>
41.   <body>
42.   <div id="container" style="width: 700px; margin-left: ⏎
                          auto; margin-right: auto;">
43.        <h2>Enter Test Scores</h2>
44.        <p><input type="button" value = "Start" onclick = ⏎
                          "examScores();" /></p>
45.   </div>
46.   </body></html>
```

Lines 11–18 simply load the array with test scores. A sentinel value (999) is used to indicate when all the scores have been entered. The if clause on lines 14 and 15 ensures that the loop is exited before the counter, **count**, can be incremented. However, because **count** is incremented after the score has been entered, upon exiting this loop, **count** holds the value of the number of elements. By using a break statement in the if clause, we ensure that 999 is not included in the array.

The bubble sort begins on line 19 and ends on line 33. At the end of the previous loop, the value of **count** is the same as the number of scores entered into the array. However, later in the program we want **count** to keep track of the index values of the elements in the array. For example, if there are 45 elements in the array, the subscripts (indexes) of these elements are 0 through 44. We must remember this as we continue with the program.

The variable **flag** has been initialized to 0 and the test condition for the outer while loop is to continue while **flag** remains 0. However, as soon as we enter the while loop, we change the value of **flag** to 1. The inner for loop on lines 23–32 does the sorting. If, at any point in this loop, one value of the **scores** array is swapped with another value, the **flag** is reset to 0. Therefore, the program knows that, on that particular pass, the elements had not been completely sorted. The only way the **flag** will remain at 1 is when, throughout an entire pass of all the elements, no swap is made. And if no swap occurs, then all elements are in their proper order.

Notice that the for loop begins to sort from the first element, when **k** = 0 and **scores[k]** is the first element. It compares the first element to each of the subsequent elements with the test condition **k** <= (**count** - 2). Recall that **count** holds the value of the number of elements in the array. Therefore, the highest array subscript is (**count** - 1). But if **k** represents the index of one element, then (**k** + 1) represents the index of the next element in line for comparison. If there are, for example, four elements in the array, then **count** = 4. But the highest index value is 3 (i.e., (**count** - 1)). We need to compare index 0 to index 1, index 1 to index 2, and index 2 to index 3. We cannot go any higher than index 3 or we will get an error. So when **k** = 2, the loop must stop; this is the last comparison (index 2 compared with index 3). Thus, the loop must end when **k** is 1 less than the highest index value which is ((**count** - 1) - 1) or, as stated on line 23, (**count** - 2).

Finally, lines 35–37 display the values of the sorted array.

If you enter the following test scores, your display should look like this:

Input	Output
98	Scores sorted from highest to lowest:
75	98
67	92
84	84
92	75
999	67

The part of this code that does the actual sorting, the bubble sort, is a valuable addition to your external source file. We'll add the following function to our mySource.js file in Example 9.7, by editing the code from Example 9.6 so it is generic and can be used in a variety of situations. Another piece of code from Example 9.6 is the code to populate the array. Again, we will reuse this code in many different programs. We will create a function that will populate an array and store it in the mySource.js file as well. Then we will update the code from Example 9.6, demonstrating how code can be made extremely succinct and, in programming jargon, more elegant.

Passing Arrays

We have discussed the difference between **passing by value** and **passing by reference**. When passing a variable by value, a copy of the original item passed is created so changes to the new copy do not affect the value of the original. However, when passing by reference, the memory location of the variable is actually passed to a function. Thus, changes to the variable in the function affect the original because the changes are made in the memory location. When arrays are passed to a function, since they are JavaScript objects, they are always passed by reference. This is almost always a good thing. For our purposes, we can pass the array of **scores** to a function that will populate the array, return to the main program, pass the array to another function that will sort it, and not worry at all about returning values.

EXAMPLE
9.7

Adding Useful Functions to the Source File

Add the following two functions to your `mySource.js` file. Remember, it makes no difference where the functions are added; they are accessed as easily from the top of the source file or the bottom.

```
1.   function populateArray(arrayName)
2.   {
3.        var count = 0; var oneElement = 0;
4.        while (oneElement != -9000)
5.        {
6.             oneElement = (prompt("Enter value number " + ↵
                         (count + 1) + " or enter -9000 when ↵
                         you are done: "));
7.             if (oneElement == -9000)
8.                  break;
9.             arrayName[count] = parseFloat(oneElement);
10.            count++;
11.       }
12.  }
13.  function bubbleIt(lgth, arrayName)
14.  {
15.       var flag = 0; var temp = 0;
16.       while (flag == 0)
17.       {
18.            flag = 1;
19.            for (k = 0; k <= (lgth - 2); k++)
20.            {
21.                 if (arrayName[k] < arrayName[k + 1])
22.                 {
23.                      temp = arrayName[k];
24.                      arrayName[k] = arrayName[k + 1];
25.                      arrayName[k + 1] = temp;
26.                      flag = 0;
27.                 }
28.            }
29.       }
30.  }
```

We have changed some variable names in these functions so they can be used in more than one situation. By using functions in an external source file, we have reduced our `main` program to the following:

```
1.   function examScores()
2.   {
3.        var scores = new Array();
4.        var count = 0; var flag = 0; var k = 0;
5.        populateArray(scores);
6.        count = scores.length;
7.        bubbleIt(count, scores);
8.        document.write("Scores sorted from highest to lowest: ↵
                         <br />");
9.        for (k = 0; k <= (count - 1); k++)
10.            document.write(scores[k] + "<br />");
11.  }
```

Example 9.7 sorts exam grades from highest to lowest—in descending order. It is very simple to change the order to ascending. Only one line in the bubble sort code needs to be changed:

Change the following: `if (arrayName[k] < arrayName[k + 1])`

To this: `if (arrayName[k] > arrayName[k + 1])`

We can add value to our source file by including the option to sort either way. One way to do this is to copy the bubble sort function, renaming one function `bubble-ItUp()` (to sort ascending) and the other `bubbleItDown()` (to sort descending). Then we can add a prompt to determine which way the user wants to sort the data. The changes are shown in Example 9.8.

EXAMPLE 9.8

Function to Sort Up or Down

The `bubbleIt()` function has been changed slightly and copied so that the user has the option to sort either from highest to lowest or lowest to highest. The two functions are shown:

```
1.    function bubbleItUp(lgth, arrayName)
2.    {
3.        var flag = 0; var temp = 0;
4.        while (flag == 0)
5.        {
6.            flag = 1;
7.            for (k = 0; k <= (lgth - 2); k++)
8.            {
9.                if (arrayName[k] > arrayName[k + 1])
10.               {
11.                   temp = arrayName[k];
12.                   arrayName[k] = arrayName[k + 1];
13.                   arrayName[k + 1] = temp;
14.                   flag = 0;
15.               }
16.           }
17.       }
18.   }
19.   function bubbleItDown(lgth, arrayName)
20.   {
21.       var flag = 0; var temp = 0;
22.       while (flag == 0)
23.       {
24.           flag = 1;
25.           for (k = 0; k <= (lgth - 2); k++)
26.           {
27.               if (arrayName[k] < arrayName[k + 1])
28.               {
29.                   temp = arrayName[k];
30.                   arrayName[k] = arrayName[k + 1];
31.                   arrayName[k + 1] = temp;
32.                   flag = 0;
33.               }
```

```
34.                }
35.            }
36.  }
```

Then we can add a prompt in the main program, right before calling the sort routine function which will decide whether we call bubbleItUp() or bubbleItDown().

```
1.   function examScores()
2.   {
3.        var scores = new Array();
4.        var count = 0; var flag = 0; var k = 0;
5.        populateArray(scores);
6.        count = scores.length;
7.        option = prompt("Sort highest to lowest? (y/n)");
8.        if(option == "y")
9.            bubbleItDown(count, scores);
10.       else
11.           bubbleItUp(count, scores);
12.       document.write("Scores sorted from highest to lowest:↵
                              <br />");
13.       for (k = 0; k <= (count - 1); k++)
14.           document.write(scores[k] + "<br />");
15.  }
```

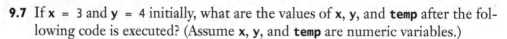

CHECKPOINT FOR SECTION 9.2

9.7 If **x** = 3 and **y** = 4 initially, what are the values of **x**, **y**, and **temp** after the following code is executed? (Assume **x**, **y**, and **temp** are numeric variables.)

```
temp = x;
y = temp;
x = y;
```

9.8 If **x** = 3 and **y** = 4 initially, what are the values of **x**, **y**, and **temp** after the following code is executed? (Assume **x**, **y**, and **temp** are numeric variables.)

```
temp = x;
y = x;
x = temp;
```

9.9 Rewrite the code of Checkpoint 9.8 so that, at the end **x** = 4 and **y** = 3.

9.10 To sort an array of 15 elements, what is the maximum number of passes that
must be completed to ensure that the array is completely sorted?

9.11 What is the purpose of a flag in a bubble sort?

9.3 The Selection Sort

The **selection sort** is a more efficient way to sort data stored in an array than the
bubble sort. The basic idea behind the selection sort is fairly simple. Here is how
we would use it to sort an array in ascending order—from smallest to largest. We
make several passes through the array as follows:

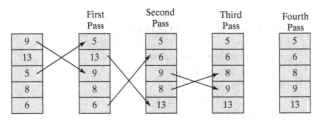

(On the fourth pass, no interchanges take place;
the numbers are sorted.)

Figure 9.3   Selection sort of 9, 13, 5, 8, 6

- On the first pass, we locate the smallest array element and swap it with the first array element.
- On the second pass, we locate the second smallest element and swap it with the second element of the array.
- On the third pass, we locate the next smallest element and swap it with the third element of the array.
- And so forth . . . If the array contains **N** elements, it will be completely sorted after at most **N** – 1 passes.

To illustrate the selection sort, first we will do a simple example by hand. Figure 9.3 demonstrates the process for a data set consisting of the numbers 9, 13, 5, 8, 6. It displays the given data in the first (leftmost) column and the results of the four passes through this data in the next four columns, using arrows to indicate which data values have been swapped.

Example 9.9 repeats the program developed in Example 9.6 but uses the selection sort instead of the bubble sort. This program also allows Carla to enter test scores for her class into an array but uses the selection sort instead of the bubble sort to sort and display the scores. This time we'll sort in ascending order (smallest to largest).

EXAMPLE 9.9

Using the Selection Sort

```
1.    <html>
2.    <head>
3.    <title>Example 9.9</title>
4.    <script type="text/javascript" src="mySource.js"></script>
5.    <script>
6.    function examScores()
7.    {
8.         var scores = new Array();
9.         var littlest = 0; var index = 0; var k = 0; var j = 0;
10.        var count = 0; var temp = 0;
11.        populateArray(scores);
12.        count = scores.length;
13.   //begin the selection sort
14.        for(k = 0; k < (count - 1); k++)
15.        {
16.             littlest = scores[k];
17.             index = k;
18.             for (j = (k + 1); j <= (count - 1); j++)
```

```
19.                {
20.                     if (scores[j] < littlest)
21.                     {
22.                          littlest = scores[j];
23.                          index = j;
24.                     }
25.                }
26.                if (k != index)
27.                {
28.                     temp = scores[k];
29.                     scores[k] = scores[index];
30.                     scores[index] = temp;
31.                }
32.           }
33.      document.write("Scores sorted from lowest to highest: ⏎
                          <br />");
34,      for (k = 0; k <= (count - 1); k++)
35.           document.write(scores[k] + "<br />");
36. }
37. </script>
38. </head>
39. <body>
40. <div id="container" style="width: 700px; margin-left:⏎
                          auto; margin-right: auto;">
41.      <h2>Enter Test Scores</h2>
42.      <p><input type="button" value = "Start" onclick = ⏎
                          "examScores();" /></p>
43. </div>
44. </body></html>
```

Let's take a closer look at this program. Line 11 calls the function populateArray() to load the array with test scores, as in the previous example.

The selection sort begins on line 14 and ends on line 32. The variable **count** holds the number of scores entered into the array. The outer for loop uses **k** as the subscript for each element in the array and it will go around for **N** - 1 passes, given **N** elements in the array. In this case, we could write the test condition as either **k** < (**count** - 1) or **k** <= (**count** - 2).

At the first pass, **index** is initially set equal to **k**. This variable, **index**, will hold the subscript of whatever element is discovered to be the smallest at any time throughout the execution of the program. We also set **littlest** to the value of the first element of the array. This is just a starting value. At the end of the first pass through the outer loop, the smallest value will be in **scores[0]**. It would be a coincidence if **scores[0]** initially happened to be the smallest value.

The inner loop (lines 18–25) compares each element to **littlest**. If the element is smaller than **littlest**, that value becomes the new value of **littlest** (line 22) and the subscript of that element (**j**) becomes the new value of **index**. In this way, we remember which element of the array holds the smallest value.

During the first pass through the outer loop, at the end of the inner for loop we have identified the smallest value in the array. Now line 26 checks to see if that smallest value is in the same place as subscript **k**. On the first pass, **k** = 0 so line 26 asks, "is the smallest value in **scores[0]**?" If it is not, then we want to move the smallest value into the first place in the array. Lines 28–30 swap the smallest value (wherever it happens to be in the array) with the first element. Thus, after the outer loop has completed one pass, the smallest element is now the first element in the loop.

The second pass focuses, initially, on the second element in the loop. Now **k** = 1 and the process begins again. This time we compare the value in the second element of the array (**scores[1]** which is the new value of **littlest**) with every other element. At the end of this pass, the second-smallest element is now in the second place in the array.

This process continues for all elements of the array up to the next-to-last. Clearly, by the time we have filled all elements except the last with the values in ascending order, the last one left must be the largest.

If you enter the following test scores, your display should look like this:

Input	Output
98	Scores sorted from lowest to highest:
75	67
67	75
84	84
92	92
999	98

We do not know how many scores will be entered at first so the array contains **N** + 1 elements. The highest index value is **N** so we need to make (**N** - 1) passes through the loop to complete the selection sort.

Here is another situation where a function can be reused many times in various situations. We should rewrite the selection sort function so that it is generic and put it into our library of functions in the mySource.js file. Then we will call it from this program and streamline the code considerably. Example 9.10 does this.

EXAMPLE 9.10

Adding the Selection Sort Function to the Source File

Add the following function to your mySource.js file. Remember, it makes no difference where the functions are added; they are accessed as easily from the top of the source file or the bottom.

```
1.  function sortItUp(arrayName, num)
2.  {
3.      var littlest = 0; var index = 0; var temp = 0;
4.      for(var k = 0; k < (num - 1); k++)
5.      {
6.          littlest = arrayName[k];
```

```
 7.              index = k;
 8.              for (var j = (k + 1); j <= (num - 1); j++)
 9.              {
10.                  if (arrayName[j] < littlest)
11.                  {
12.                      littlest = arrayName[j];
13.                      index = j;
14.                  }
15.              }
16.              if (k != index)
17.              {
18.                  temp = arrayName[k];
19.                  arrayName[k] = arrayName[index];
20.                  arrayName[index] = temp;
21.              }
22.          }
23.  }
```

It is very easy to sort descending by changing just a few lines. Instead of a variable named **littlest**, we can have a variable named **largest**. The only line of code that needs to be changed is line 10. The variable **largest** will replace **littlest** in the code and line 10 will read as follows:

```
    if (arrayName[j] > largest)
```

We can also add an option to the main program to allow the user to choose whether to sort ascending or descending and the main program is now shorter and more efficient, as follows:

```
 1.  <script>
 2.  function examScores()
 3.  {
 4.      var scores = new Array();
 5.      var choice = ""; var count = 0; var k = 0;
 6.      populateArray(scores);
 7.      count = scores.length;
 8.      choice = prompt("Sort highest to lowest? Enter 'd'. ↵
                        Sort lowest to highest? Enter 'a'.");
 9.      if (choice == 'a')
10.      {
11.          sortItUp(scores, count);
12.          document.write("Scores sorted from lowest ↵
                    to highest:<br />");
13.      }
14.      if (choice == 'd')
15.      {
16.          sortItDown(scores, count);
17.          document.write("Scores sorted from lowest ↵
                    to highest:<br />");
18.      }
19.      for (k = 0; k <= (count - 1); k++)
20.          document.write(scores[k] + "<br />");
21.  }
22.  </script>
```

You probably noticed that both the bubble sort and the selection sort need to swap values. In Chapter 8, Greg's Game of 15 also used a swap function. At this point it would be a good idea to not only add a swap function to our source file but to edit the bubble sort and selection sort functions so these functions call the swap function instead of including the same code in each function. Example 9.11 streamlines our source file further by doing this.

EXAMPLE 9.11

Adding a Swap Function to the Source File

Add the following function which will swap two values:

```
1.  function swapIt(a, b)
2.  {
3.      var temp = a;
4.      a = b;
5.      b = temp;
6.  }
```

Now we can edit the selection sort routines in the source file and make them shorter and cleaner. They will now look like this:

```
1.  function sortItUp(arrayName, num)
2.  {
3.      var littlest = 0; var index = 0;
4.      for(var k = 0; k < (num - 1); k++)
5.      {
6.          littlest = arrayName[k]; index = k;
7.          for (var j = (k + 1); j <= (num - 1); j++)
8.          {
9.              if (arrayName[j] < littlest)
10.             {
11.                 littlest = arrayName[j];
12.                 index = j;
13.             }
14.         }
15.         if (k != index)
16.             swapIt(arrayName[k], arrayName[index]);
17.     }
18. }
19. function sortItDown(arrayName, num)
20. {
21.     var largest = 0; var index = 0;
22.     for(var k = 0; k < (num - 1); k++)
23.     {
24.         largest = arrayName[k]; index = k;
25.         for (var j = (k + 1); j <= (num - 1); j++)
26.         {
27.             if (arrayName[j] > largest)
28.             {
29.                 largest = arrayName[j];
30.                 index = j;
31.             }
32.         }
```

```
33.              if (k != index)
34.                  swapIt(arrayName[k], arrayName[index]);
35.          }
36.  }
```

The main program is now both shorter and offers more options. The JavaScript code now looks like this:

```
1.   function examScores()
2.   {
3.        var scores = new Array();
4.        var choice = ""; var count = 0; var k = 0;
5.        populateArray(scores);
6.        count = scores.length;
7.        choice = prompt("Sort highest to lowest? Enter 'd'. ↵
                           Sort lowest to highest? Enter 'a'.");
8.        if (choice == 'a')
9.        {
10.            sortItUp(scores, count);
11.            document.write("Scores sorted from lowest to highest:<br />");
12.        }
13.        if (choice == 'd')
14.        {
15.            sortItDown(scores, count);
16.            document.write("Scores sorted from lowest to highest:<br />");
17.        }
18.        for (k = 0; k <= (count - 1); k++)
19.            document.write(scores[k] + "<br />");
20.  }
21.  </script>
```

If you enter the following test scores and choose ascending, your display should look like this:

Input	Output
98	Scores sorted from lowest to highest:
75	67
67	75
84	84
92	92
-9000	98

If you enter the following test scores and choose descending, your display should look like this:

Input	Output
98	Scores sorted from highest to lowest:
75	98
67	92
84	84
92	75
-9000	67

CHECKPOINT FOR SECTION 9.3 ✓

9.12 How many passes through an array must be made using the selection sort method to ensure the array is completely sorted? Assume the array has **N** elements.

9.13 Write code using the selection sort method to sort the following numbers in descending order:

```
53, 82, 93, 75, 86, 97
```

9.14 In the selection sort method, if you sort an array in descending order, which element of the array will be the first element after the first pass?

9.15 In a selection sort that sorts in ascending order, what value is held by the variable **littlest**, as used in Example 9.11, at the end of the second pass?

9.4 Searching Arrays: The Serial Search

Suppose you are participating in a multi-user online game that stores information about each player in a table such as the one shown here. For each user, the table displays the username, point score, last game played, and date the game was last accessed. You want to know how your archenemy is doing. You know his username but not his score so you consult the table.

Username	Points	Last Game Played	Last Access
EvilEddy	385	Greg's Tales	4/25/2015, 04:15
DorianDragon	268	Greg's Maze	4/23/2015, 16:12
puppypal	516	Tic-tac-toe	4/20/2015, 23:10
crusher	372	Greg's Hangman	4/20/2015, 02:35
. . .	. . .	. . .	. . .
. . .	. . .	. . .	. . .

To find your foe's point score, you scan the first column for his username and then you move across that row to read the point score, last game played, and last access date.

In computer lingo you have performed a **table lookup**. In data processing terminology the item you were seeking (your foe's point score) is called the **search key**. The search key is a particular item in the list of all such items (all the point scores); we call this list the table keys. In general, the data in the table are called the table values. The way in which you looked for a desired username, checking the numbers in the order listed, makes this a **serial search**.

There are many algorithms available to programmers to search for specific values. We will discuss two of them in this chapter: the serial search and the binary search. We'll start with the serial search.

The Serial Search

The concept of the serial search is pretty simple: The elements in a given array are compared, one by one, to the search key (the value that is searched for). There are only two possible results after a search is complete; either the value is found in the array or it is not. However, if the array being searched is large enough, it may be inefficient to check each element when the search might end (the value may be found) at the beginning of the array. Therefore, we use a flag to identify when the search has been successful and to allow us to exit the search at that time. A simple search of an array is shown in Example 9.12.

In this program, we assume a business that sells tee-shirts wants to determine which color a customer wants. The available colors are stored in an array. The customer can enter the desired color when prompted and the program will search the array to see if that color is available. Depending on the search results, one of two responses will be shown.

EXAMPLE 9.12

Using the Serial Search

```
1.   <html>
2.   <head>
3.   <title>Example 9.12</title>
4.   <script>
5.   function searchColor()
6.   {
7.       var colors = new Array("blue","green","yellow","red", ↵
                       "orange", "purple", "black", "white", "*");
8.       var index = 0; var found = 0;
9.       var searchKey = prompt("What color shirt do you want?");
10.      while ((found == 0) && (colors[index] != "*"))
11.      {
12.          if (colors[index] == searchKey)
13.              found = 1;
14.          index = index +1;
15.      }
16.      if (found == 1)
17.          document.getElementById('result').innerHTML = ↵
                   (colors[index - 1] + " has been found! ↵
                   <br /> Your shirt will be ordered in " ↵
                   + colors[index - 1]);
18.      else
19.          document.getElementById('result').innerHTML = ("The shirt ↵
                   is not available in " + searchKey + ".<br />");
20.  }
21.  </script>
22.  </head>
23.  <body>
```

```
24.   <div id="container" style="width: 700px; margin-left: auto; ⤶
                          margin-right: auto;">
25.        <h2>You want to order a tee-shirt... What color do you want?</h2>
26.        <p><input type="button" value = "Start" onclick = "searchColor();" /></p>
27.        <h3 id = "result">  </h3>
28.   </div>
29.   </body></html>
```

Note that when the searched value is displayed, the index of that element in the array is one less than the value of **index** after the while loop is exited. This is because of the way the program has been written. As an exercise, you can rewrite the program so that the value of **index** at the end of the while loop will match the index value of the item that was identified.

The last element of the array has been denoted "*". It is customary to use an entry that would not, under ordinary circumstances, be an element in the array, as an **end-of-array marker** (similar to a sentinel value) that tells the program when to end.

If the customer wants a red shirt and enters "red" at the prompt, the display will be as follows:

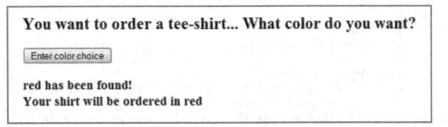

But if the customer wants a mauve shirt and enters "mauve" at the prompt, the display will be as follows:

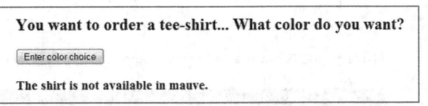

In Example 9.13, we assume that Greg who runs Greg's Gambits has recorded the usernames of his game players in an array called **usernames()**. One of the players notifies Greg to report that although he has been using DorianDragon as a username, his information doesn't appear when he tries to log in. Greg wants to confirm that this username exists in his list of players. He suspects that the player is mistyping the username. For this example, we will use a list of 10 players, but in reality, Greg's list of usernames would probably be much longer. Greg identifies the last element in **usernames()** by "*". Here, we will create and load the array in the function but in "real life" this array would be stored separately.

Using the Serial Search to Find a Name

```
1.   function checkName()
2.   {
3.         var usernames = new Array("EvilEddy", "puppypal", "crusher", ⏎
                          "DorienDragon", "lizard", "SmartCAR", "granny", ⏎
                          "arachnid54",
4.         var index = 0; var found = 0;
5.         var searchKey = prompt("Enter the name to check");
6.         while ((found == 0) && (usernames[index] != "*"))
7.         {
8.              if (usernames[index] == searchKey)
9.                   found = 1;
10.             index = index +1;
11.        }
12.        if (found == 1)
13.             document.getElementById('result').innerHTML = ⏎
                          (usernames[index - 1] + " has been ⏎
                          found!");
14.        else
15.             document.getElementById('result').innerHTML = ⏎
                          (searchKey + " is not on the list.");
16.   }
17.   </script>
18.   </head>
19.   <body>
20.   <div id="container">
21.        <img src="images/superhero.jpg" class="floatleft" />
22.        <h1>Check Usernames</h1>
23.        <div id="content" style="width: 600px; margin-left: ⏎
                          auto; margin-right: auto;">
24.             <p><input type="button" value = "check a username" ⏎
                          onclick="checkName();" /></p>
25.             <div id = "result"><p> </p></div>
26.        </div>
27.   </div></body></html>
```

If Greg enters "DorianDragon" at the prompt, the display will be as follows:

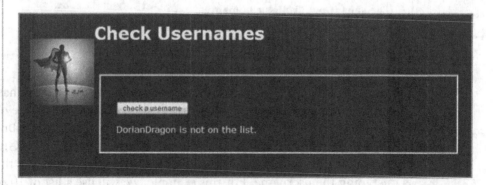

But if Greg enters another user, such as "arachnid54", the display will be as follows:

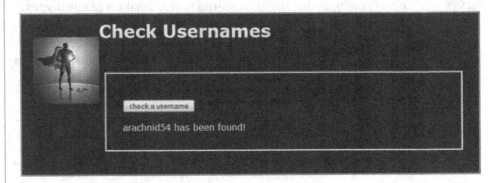

At this point, Greg can tell the player to check his spelling of his username carefully or he can create more programming to try to find a close match to DorianDragon. Greg has confirmed though, that a player with DorianDragon as a username is not on his list.

Using the Serial Search with Parallel Arrays

It's nice to search an array for a particular item, as demonstrated in Example 9.13, but the result is not particularly valuable. All we learned in Example 9.13 was that someone whose username can be found in the list of usernames had, at some time, played one of Greg's games. More often than not, though, we want more information. If different types of information is stored in parallel arrays, we can use a serial search to find one piece of information and use the index of that element to find more.

In Example 9.14, we add a few lines of code to the program in Example 9.13. This allows us to display all the information about one player at the Greg's Gambits site. We will assume that Greg has stored information about players on his site in parallel arrays named **usernames()**, **points()**, **games()**, and **playDates()**. Normally, the arrays would be preloaded before the program is run but, for demonstration purposes, we will load them here.

We'll use a source file for a new purpose. Instead of storing a library of functions that we may want to call on, we will create a new page that stores the arrays we want. Since a source file is a text file, Greg can update it easily and, as we become more proficient, we can update it interactively. We'll call the new file gregPlayers.js and, by using the .js extension, it can be accessed easily from the main program. For demonstration purposes, we will populate the four arrays with 10 values (and an end-of-file marker) by hand. Then we will write code to use our search skills to find the information we want about a specific player.

EXAMPLE
9.14

Parallel Arrays Make Accessing Lots of Information Easy

The following code should be stored in the separate `gregPlayers.js` file:

```
1.   function userArray()
2.   {
3.       var usernames = new Array("EvilEddy","puppypal","crusher", ⏎
             "DorienDragon","lizard","SmartCAR","granny", ⏎
             "arachnid54","joneOfArk","lightfoot","*");
4.       return usernames;
5.   }
6.   function pointsArray()
7.   {
8.       var points = new Array(234,345,567,678,890,1456,2387, ⏎
             6743,221,584,-99);
9.       return points;
10.  }
11.  function gamesArray()
12.  {
13.      var games = new Array("Hangman","Fortunes","Madlibs", ⏎
             "Tictactoe","Hangman","15","Fortunes","15","Hangman", ⏎
             "Battle","*");
14.      return games;
15.  }
16.  function datesArray()
17.  {
18.      var playDates = new Array("Mar 01","Jan 24","Jun 16", ⏎
             "Feb 28","Feb 12","Apr 04","Sep 11","Sep 19", ⏎
             "Dec 02","Jan 15","*");
19.      return playDates;
20.  }
```

Now we can write code that will allow Greg to enter one player's username and get all the information he wants about that player. That page will look like this:

```
1.   <html>
2.   <head>
3.   <title>Example 9.14</title>
4.   <link href="greg.css" rel="stylesheet" type="text/css" />
5.   <script type="text/javascript" src="gregPlayers.js"></script>
6.   <script>
7.   function getInfo()
8.   {
9.       document.getElementById("name").innerHTML = " ";
10.      document.getElementById("pts").innerHTML = " ";
11.      document.getElementById("game").innerHTML = " ";
12.      document.getElementById("date").innerHTML = " ";
13.      document.getElementById("error").innerHTML = " ";
14.      usernames = userArray(); games = gamesArray();
15.      points = pointsArray(); dates = datesArray();
16.      var index = 0; var found = 0;
17.      var searchKey = prompt("Enter the name of the player to check:");
```

```
18.           var message = "Cannot find this player";
19.           while ((found == 0) && (usernames[index] != "*"))
20.           {
21.               if (usernames[index] == searchKey)
22.                   found = 1;
23.               index = index +1;
24.           }
25.           if (found == 1)
26.           {
27.               document.getElementById("name").innerHTML = ("Player's ↵
                          username: " + usernames[index-1]);
28.               document.getElementById("pts").innerHTML = ("Player's ↵
                          points to date: " + points[index-1]);
29.               document.getElementById("game").innerHTML = ("Last ↵
                          game played: " + games[index-1]);
30.               document.getElementById("date").innerHTML = ("Last ↵
                          login: " + dates[index-1]);
31.           }
32.           else
33.               document.getElementById("error").innerHTML = message;
34.  }
35.  </script>
36.  </head>
37.  <body>
38.  <div id="container">
39.      <img src="images/superhero.jpg" class="floatleft" />
40.      <h1>Check On a Player</h1>
41.      <div id="content" style="width: 600px; margin-left: ↵
                      auto; margin-right: auto;">
42.          <p><input type="button" value = "Get player's ↵
                      information" onclick="getInfo();" /></p>
43.          <div id = "name"><p> </div></p>
44.          <div id = "pts"><p> </div></p>
45.          <div id = "game"><p> </div></p>
46.          <div id = "date"><p> </div></p>
47.          <p><div id = "error"> </div></p>
48.      </div>
49.  </div>
50.  </body></html>
```

Lines 9–13 clear out any values from a previous search. Then the arrays are loaded on lines 14 and 15 by calling the corresponding functions in the source file. The code on lines 17–33 is almost the same as in the previous example but, by adding lines 28–30, we not only find one player's username but also the player's points, last game played, and last date the player logged in. This program illustrates the value of storing information in parallel arrays. As soon as we know the index of the item of interest in one array, we know how to access the information stored in all the parallel arrays.

If Greg searches for the player with the username crusher, the result will look like this:

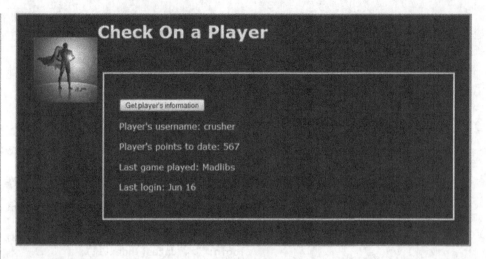

But if Greg searches for the player with the username `kittyCat`, the result will look like this:

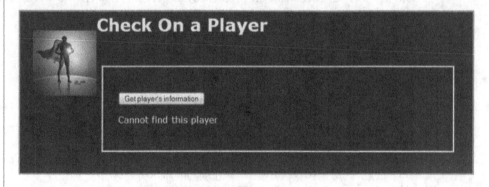

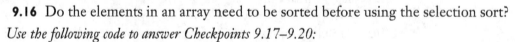

CHECKPOINT FOR SECTION 9.4

9.16 Do the elements in an array need to be sorted before using the selection sort?

Use the following code to answer Checkpoints 9.17–9.20:

```
function userArray()
{
    var cars = new Array("van","convertible","hatchback", ↵
            "sedan","bus","matchbox","XYZ","*");
    var found = 0; var index = 0;
    var key = "sedan";
    while((found == 0) && (cars[index] != "XYZ"))
    {
        if(cars[index] == key)
            found = 1;
        index++;
        if(found == 1)
            document.write("You can buy a " + cars[index - 1]);
        else
```

```
                    document.write("We do not have a " + cars[index - 1] ⏎
                                    + " to sell now.");
          }
     }
```

9.17 What is the end-of-file marker in the array?

9.18 What variable represents a flag in the program?

9.19 How many iterations will the `while` loop in this program make?

9.20 What is the value of **index** in the following line (from the program)?

```
     document.write("You can buy a " + cars[index - 1]);
```

9.5 Searching Arrays: The Binary Search

The **binary search** method is a good way to search a large amount of data for a particular item, which is called the search key. It is considerably more efficient than the serial search technique but requires that the array of data to be searched is in numerical or alphabetical order.

To illustrate how the binary search method works, let's suppose you want to look up a certain word (the target word) in a dictionary. If you used a serial search to find it, starting with the first page and going through the dictionary word by word, it might take hours or even months. A more reasonable approach would be to open the dictionary in the middle and check the target word against an entry on that page to determine if you have gone too far or not far enough. If you've gone too far, check the middle of the front half of the dictionary against your target word; if you did not go far enough, check the middle of the back half of the dictionary. Then repeat these steps until you have located the target word. This example demonstrates the basic idea underlying the binary search procedure.

The Binary Search

To carry out a binary search, first we compare the search key (the **target**) to the element midway through the given array. Because the array data is ordered, we can determine in which *half* of the array the search key lies. We now compare the search key to the element in the middle of this half, and in so doing are able to determine in which *quarter* of the array the search key is located. Then we look at the middle entry in this quarter, and so forth, continuing this process until we find the search key.

In Example 9.15, the variables **low** and **high** represent the smallest and largest array indexes in the part of the array currently under consideration. Recall that the highest index number is actually one less than the number of elements in the array. If the highest index in this array is **N**, then the number of elements in the array is **N + 1**.

Initially, we are searching the entire array, so **low = 0** and **high = N**. However, after the first attempt at locating the value we are searching for, which we call **key**, we are either searching the first half or the last half of the array. Now we want to either zoom in on the first half (from index value 0 to index value N/2) or the second half (from index value N/2 to index value N). But if N is an odd number, N/2 will not be an integer. Therefore, we need to force it to be an integer and here we will use the Math.round() function to round the number to its nearest integer value. Thus, since N/2 will always result in the decimal part being 0.5, Math.round(N/2) will round up. The variable **index** represents the middle element of the part of the array under consideration. Thus, **index** is initially Math.round(N/2), and in general, it is the average of **low** and **high**: **index** = Math.round((**low** + **high**)/2). When N is odd, then **index** will not be the exact middle, of course, but will be 0.5 above the mathematical middle. However, the search is not affected by this. After we have checked the middle of the whole array, we check the half we identify by either setting **low** to 0 and **high** to Math.round(N/2) or **low** to Math.round(N/2) and **high** to N.

EXAMPLE 9.15

The Binary Search for Student Data

Most schools keep records of students that go back many years and these records can become very large. In this program, we demonstrate how to search a large array of student names, stored in alphabetical order to find one name. Then, since data about students is stored in parallel arrays, we can easily access the student's whole record. We assume, for the purposes of this example, that the only data stored is each student's name (in an array **names()**), Grade Point Average (in an array **GPAs()**), and email contact (in an array **emails()**) and we will assume these arrays exist and include data. We will also assume there are 20 students so N will equal 20.

```
1.   <html>
2.   <head>
3.   <title>Example 9.15</title>
4.   <script>
5.   var low = 0; var N = 20; var high = N;
6.   var index = Math.round((N+1)/2);
7.   var found = 0;
8.   var key = prompt("Who are you looking for?");
9.   while (found == 0 && low <= high)
10.  {
11.      if (key == names[index])
12.          found = 1;
13.      if (key > names[index])
14.      {
15.          low = index + 1;
16.          index = Math.round((high + low)/2);
17.      }
18.      if (key < names[index])
19.      {
20.          high = index - 1;
21.          index = Math.round((high + low)/2);
22.      }
23.  }
24   if (key != names[index])
25.      document.write("Student record not found. <br />");
```

```
26.  else
27.  {
28.      document.write("Student: " + names[index] + "<br />");
29.      document.write("Email: " + emails[index] + "<br />");
30.      document.write("GPA: " + GPAs[index] + "<br />");
31.  }
32.  </script>
33.  </head>
34.  <body>
35.  </body>
36.  </html>
```

You can try this program by adding a few lines in the beginning to create and fill three arrays with names, GPAs, and email addresses of fictional students. Doing this and adding more features to the student records (through more parallel arrays) is a Checkpoint exercise.

While students sometimes feel that their teachers know too much information about them, more often, the teacher, who has many students every year, has a hard time recalling specifics about any given student. Carla is a caring, concerned teacher who believes that a good relationship with parents is as important as a good relationship with her students. Therefore, whenever she has a parent-teacher conference she tries to prepare herself with as much information as she can about that particular child. She has kept copious records of her students going back many years. When she prepares for a conference, she checks her records to see how the student is doing but also checks to see if any older siblings have been in her classes over the past years. She keeps records on students from past years in parallel arrays which include each student's name, the parents' names, and an array that stores notes she has made about special circumstances or noteworthy specifics about that family. She also keeps separate records about each of her present students and his or her academic progress.

But, since Carla has been teaching for a good many years, her records have become quite lengthy. A program that will most efficiently get her the information she needs, in this case, utilizes a binary search.

Example 9.16 will allow Carla to find all relevant information about a student quickly. For this example, we will use an external source file which has four functions. Each loads a parallel array with the last name of the student (**pastNames()**), the previous student names (**pastStuNames()**), the names of the parent(s) (**pastParentNames()**), and notes on these students (**pastStuNotes()**). Our example will have 20 records but if Carla was a real teacher and these arrays reflected real records, there would probably be hundreds of records. Our external file is named carlaRecords.js.

Carla will be able to input the last name of one present student and find all information from the past that is relevant to this student. Since we are only using 20 records, N, in this example, will be 20. We will use a binary search to search through the array of last names to find the name Carla is interested in. Since the binary search requires that an array be sorted before the search begins, the external file will also include a bubble sort function that will be called in the main program, after the arrays have been loaded, to sort the arrays before calling on the search. The external file is shown in the example.

EXAMPLE
9.16

Using the Binary Search to Help Carla

```
1.  function pastNames()
2.  {
3.        var pastNames = new Array("Morris" , "Kim" , "Arora" , ↵
            "Anderson" , "Jones" , "Thompson" , "Smith" , ↵
            "Bennett" , "Peterson" , "Rodriguez" , "Lopez" , ↵
            "Vargas" , "McKay" , "Norris" , "Clausen" , "Smolen" , ↵
            "Goldman" , "Stein" , "Franks" , "Chen","*");
4.        return pastNames;
5.  }
6.  function pastStudents()
7.  {
8.        var pastStuNames = new Array("Janey" , "Jo" , "Sonia" , ↵
            "Tommy" , "Gene Junior" , "Anne and Joey" , "Howie, ↵
            Sammy, Margie" , "Summer" , "Cheyenne and Connor" , ↵
            "Eva, Gladys, and Mario" , "Carlos" , "Marisol" , "James" , ↵
            "Charlie" , "Andrew" , "Nick" , "Barbara" , "Rebecca and ↵
            Ruth" , "Morgan" , "Milton, Patricia, and Edward" , "*");
9.        return pastStuNames;
10. }
11. function pastParents()
12. {
13.       var pastParentNames = new Array("Joan and Jim Morris","Kate ↵
            and Chul Kim" , "Achir Arora" , "Janet Anderson" , ↵
            "Eugene and Deborah Jones" , "Trevor Thompson" , "Sue ↵
            and Jim Smith" , "Peter and Rona Bennett" , "Wendy ↵
            Peterson" , "Mike and Misty Rodriguez" , "Rosa Lopez" , ↵
            "Juan Vargas" , "David and Rachel McKay" , "Charles ↵
            Norris" , "Andy and Anna Clausen" , "Dmitri and Masha ↵
            Smolen" , "Herschel Goldman" , "Laura Stein" , "Karen ↵
            and Tom Franks" , "Lilly and Harold Chen" , "*");
14.       return pastParentNames;
15. }
16. function oldNotes()
17. {
18.       var pastStuNotes = new Array("concerned, caring", ↵
            "overanxious but sweet" , "single dad, super bright ↵
            daughter" , "single working mom, tired but helpful" , ↵
            "sensed tension between parents" , "stay-at-home ↵
            dad, disabled, good relationship with children" , ↵
            "very hard to contact, didn't seem to care about ↵
            school" , "artistic family" , "expectations for her ↵
            children too high" , "great people! no wonder kids are ↵
            so great" , "working single mom trying very hard" , ↵
            "language barrier -- no English" , "said grandparents ↵
            do most of the parenting" , "brought in live-in ↵
            girlfriend, seems unaware of son's schoolwork" , ↵
            "blamed each other for everything!" , "recently ↵
            arrived in US, little English but very concerned ↵
            couple" , "single dad, good support from grandparents" , ↵
```

```
                "overachieving mom wants same for daughters - may ↵
                not be possible with older child" , "high-powered ↵
                executives, childcare goes to nannies and household ↵
                help" , "can't they all be like the Chens?" , "*");
19.        return pastStuNotes;
20.    }
21.    function bubbleIt(lgth, arrayName1, arrayName2, arrayName3, arrayName4)
22.    {
23.        var flag = 0; var temp1 = 0; var temp2 = 0;
24.        var temp3 = 0; var temp4 = 0;
25.        while (flag == 0)
26.        {
27.            flag = 1;
28.            for (var k = 0; k <= (lgth - 2); k++)
29.            {
30.                if (arrayName1[k] > arrayName1[k + 1])
31.                {
32.                    temp1 = arrayName1[k];
33.                    arrayName1[k] = arrayName1[k + 1];
34.                    arrayName1[k + 1] = temp1;
35.                    temp2 = arrayName2[k];
36.                    arrayName2[k] = arrayName2[k + 1];
37.                    arrayName2[k + 1] = temp2;
38.                    temp3 = arrayName3[k];
39.                    arrayName3[k] = arrayName3[k + 1];
40.                    arrayName3[k + 1] = temp3;
41.                    temp4 = arrayName4[k];
42.                    arrayName4[k] = arrayName4[k + 1];
43.                    arrayName4[k + 1] = temp4;
44.                    flag = 0;
45.                }
46.            }
47.        }
48.    }
```

Notice that the bubble sort function (on lines 21–48) sorts the four arrays at once. As soon as an element in the first array is identified as the element to be switched, the same swap is made for all four arrays. If we did not sort all the arrays at the same time, Janey might end up with Peter and Rona Bennett for her parents instead of Joan and Jim Morris.

The main code for this program follows with an explanation after the code:

```
1.   <html>
2.   <head>
3.   <title>Example 9.16</title>
4.   <link href="carla.css" rel="stylesheet" type="text/css" />
5.   <script type="text/javascript" src="carlaRecords.js"></script>
6.   <script>
7.   function getInfo()
8.   {
9.        document.getElementById("name").innerHTML = " ";
10.       document.getElementById("sibling").innerHTML = " ";
11.       document.getElementById("parents").innerHTML = " ";
12.       document.getElementById("notes").innerHTML = " ";
13.       document.getElementById("error").innerHTML = " ";
```

```
14.           var sibs = new Array(); var last = new Array();
15.           var parents = new Array(); var myNotes = new Array();
16.           var key = prompt("Enter the last name of the student to check:");
17.           last = pastNames(); sibs = pastStudents();
18.           parents = pastParents(); myNotes = oldNotes();
19.           var N = (last.length - 1);
20.           var low = 0; var high = N; var found = 0;
21.           bubbleIt(N, last, sibs, parents, myNotes);
22.           var index = Math.round((N+1)/2);
23.           var message = "<h3>No past information on " + key + "</h3>";
24.           while (found == 0 && low <= high)
25.           {
26.                if (key == last[index])
27.                     found = 1;
28.                if (key > last[index])
29.                {
30.                    low = index + 1;
31.                    index = Math.round((high + low)/2);
32.                }
33.                if (key < last[index])
34.                {
35.                  high = index - 1;
36.                  index = Math.round((high + low)/2);
37.                }
38.           }
39.       if (key != last[index])
40.             document.getElementById("error").innerHTML = message;
41.       else
42.       {
43.             document.getElementById("name").innerHTML = ⏎
                       ("<h3>Student: "+last[index]+"</h3>");
44.             document.getElementById("sibling").innerHTML = ⏎
                       ("<h3>Sibling(s): "+sibs[index]+"</h3>");
45.             document.getElementById("parents").innerHTML = ⏎
                       ("<h3>Parents: "+parents[index]+"</h3>");
46.             document.getElementById("notes").innerHTML = ⏎
                       ("<h3>Notes: "+myNotes[index]+"</h3>");
47.       }
48.  }
49.  </script>
50.  </head>
51.  <body>
52.  <div id="container">
53.       <h2>Prepare for Parent Conference</h2>
54.       <div id = "content" style="width: 700px; margin-left: ⏎
                       auto; margin-right: auto;">
55.            <p><input type="button" value = "Get student's ⏎
                       information" onclick="getInfo();" /></p>
56.          <div id = "name"><h3>  </h3></div>
57.          <div id = "sibling"><h3>  </h3></div>
58.          <div id = "parents"><h3>  </h3></div>
59.          <div id = "notes"><h3>  </h3></div>
60.          <div id = "error"><h3>  </h3></div>
61.       </div>
```

```
62.        <div style="clear:both;"></div>
63.    </div>
64.    </body></html>
```

The first five lines of the function (lines 9–13) simply clear the <div>s where the information will be displayed on the web page. Lines 14 and 15 create four new Array objects, named **last()**, **sibs()**, **parents()**, and **myNotes()**. These arrays are populated on lines 17 and 18 when each one calls a function on the external page.

Line 16 prompts Carla to enter the last name of the student she is interested in and lines 19 and 20 create and initialize the variables needed for this program. Line 19 sets **N** equal to the number of elements in the array minus one. This is because the length of each array is, right now, 20 elements plus the end-of-file marker. But we do not want to include the end-of-file marker in our search. Now, each time Carla adds information to the arrays, this code will still work.

Line 21 calls the sorting routine, bubbleIt(), in the external file. After this line is executed, all four arrays have been sorted. The first array, **last**, is in alphabetical order and the other three arrays are ordered so that each element corresponds with the correct last name. Line 22 begins the search for the information about the student Carla has entered.

The binary search begins by dividing the array to be searched in half. The lower half starts at element 0 and goes up to the middle of the array. As we have mentioned, we use the Math.round() method to deal with arrays that have an even number of elements. The flag, **found**, is initially set to 0 and will only be changed to 1 when a match has been found between the **key** (the value being searched for) and one of the elements of the array. At that time the index value of this element is the value of the variable, **index**. Since the arrays are parallel, we can identify the correct elements of all the other arrays by using the value of **index**. The search starts with the **low** value = 0, the **high** value equal to the index of the highest element in the array, and the middle equal to Math.round((N+1)/2).

The binary search first compares the **key** to the array element in the middle. If **key** matches (tested on line 26), **found** is set to 1 (line 27) and the search ends. If **key** is greater than the middle value (**last[index]**), we know that the **key** will be found somewhere in the upper half of the array. Thus, we change the boundaries. The **low** value now becomes one higher than the old middle value (line 30) and **high** remains unchanged. The new middle is the average of **low** and **high**, again rounded to an integer (line 31). The next time through the while loop we will compare **key** to the middle value of the upper half of the array.

However, if, initially, **key** is less than the middle value, we know that the value we are looking for is in the lower half of the array. Now we want our **high** to be one less than what was, at first, the middle (line 35) and **low** remains the same. The new middle value is the average of the boundaries (**high** and **low**), rounded to an integer (line 36). The next time through the while loop, we will compare the **key** to the middle of the lower half of the array.

The while loop ends when one of the two possible conditions becomes false. Either **found** no longer equals 0 (which happens when a match is found) or **low** equals **high**. This second condition will only occur when all elements in the array have been checked and none are a match. So, when we leave the while loop we know several things: if **found** = 1, we know there has been a match and the value of **index** tells us which element of the array is the match. If **found** = 0, we know that there is no match and the element in question does not exist in this array.

Thus, we can either display the message that no match has been found (lines 39–40) or display all the requested information (lines 43–46).

If Carla requests information on a student named Stein, the display will first look like this:

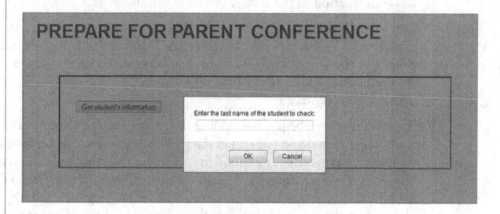

After clicking OK, the information will appear:

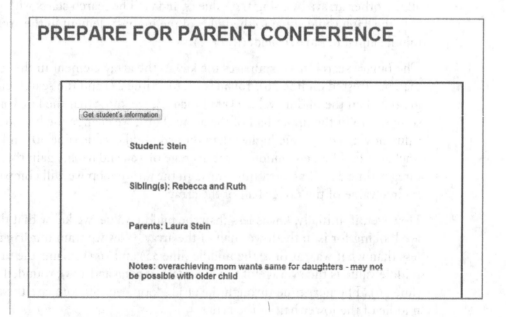

But if Carla requests information on a student named Kruger, the display will look like this:

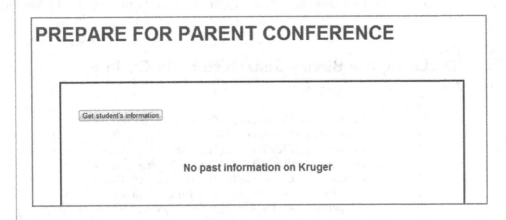

Making Life Easier: The indexOf() Method

Today, it seems that people believe there is a shortcut for everything. Too often, this is true. We learned how to sort an array by coding with two types of sorting routines—the selection sort and the bubble sort. Then we learned that there are methods already written that allow us to sort an array in a single statement. The sort() method will do this. Unfortunately, this is not particularly helpful when we want to use parallel arrays so it is important that we know how to write our own sort code.

We also learned to write code to search arrays using either the serial search or the binary search. But JavaScript has two methods that allow us to find a single value with a single statement. If our parallel arrays are sorted, as shown in Example 9.16, we can use either the indexOf() method or the lastIndexOf() method to search one array for the requested element and access all corresponding elements in parallel arrays from the returned index value.

The indexOf() Method

The **indexOf()method** will search an array for a specified item and return the item's position in the array. The position is the index value of that element in the array. The syntax to use this method is as follows:

```
var veggies = new Array("lettuce", "carrots", "celery", "peppers");
var bestVeggie = veggies.indexOf("celery");
```

The result will be that **bestVeggie** will equal 2 because "celery" is **veggies[2]**.

If the search item is not found, the return value will be -1. The indexOf() method will also allow you to search an array from any place you want to start. The default starting position is 0, the first element. The general syntax for this method, therefore, is as follows:

```
arrayName.indexOf(search_item, start_position)
```

In Example 9.17, we can now shorten the code from the previous example. The new code does not include a binary search but, instead, replaces it with a single statement that uses the indexOf() method. Only the getInfo() function is shown.

EXAMPLE 9.17

Using the Binary Search to Help Carla

```
1.  function getInfo()
2.  {
3.      document.getElementById("name").innerHTML = " ";
4.      document.getElementById("sibling").innerHTML = " ";
5.      document.getElementById("parents").innerHTML = " ";
6.      document.getElementById("notes").innerHTML = " ";
7.      document.getElementById("error").innerHTML = " ";
8.      var sibs = new Array(); var last = new Array();
9.      var parents = new Array(); var myNotes = new Array();
10.     var key = prompt("Enter the last name of the student to check:");
11.     last = pastNames(); sibs = pastStudents();
12.     parents = pastParents(); myNotes = oldNotes();
13.     var N = (last.length - 1);
14.     var low = 0;  var high = N; var found = 0; var index = 0;
15.     bubbleIt(N, last, sibs, parents, myNotes);
16.     index = last.indexOf(key);
17.     var message = "<h3>No past information on " + key + "</h3>";
18.     if (index == -1)
19.         document.getElementById("error").innerHTML = message;
20.     else
21.     {
22.         document.getElementById("name").innerHTML = ⏎
                ("<h3>Student: " + last[index] + "</h3>");
23.         document.getElementById("sibling").innerHTML = ⏎
                ("<h3>Sibling(s): " + sibs[index] + "</h3>");
24.         document.getElementById("parents").innerHTML = ⏎
                ("<h3>Parents: " + parents[index] + "</h3>");
25.         document.getElementById("notes").innerHTML = ⏎
                ("<h3>Notes: " + myNotes[index] + "</h3>");
26.     }
27. }
```

The lastIndexOf() Method

The **lastIndexOf()method** will search an array for a specified item, like indexOf(), but if no starting position is specified, it will begin at the end and search until the beginning value. The return value, if the item is not found, is −1, just the same as the indexOf() method. If the item is found, this method will return the item's position in the array. The syntax to use this method is as follows:

```
var colors = new Array("blue", "red", "yellow", "green", "orange");
var bestColor = color.lastIndexOf("green");
```

The result will be that **bestColor** will be 3 because "green" is **colors[3]**.

The lastIndexOf() method will also allow you to search an array from any place you want to start. The default starting position is the end of the array. The general syntax for this method, therefore, is as follows:

```
arrayName.lastIndexOf(search_item, start_position)
```

Time Out! Using the setInterval() and clearInterval() Methods

The **setInterval()method** will execute a function once for every given time interval. The syntax of this function is as follows:

```
setInterval(function_name, milliseconds);
```

You can stop executions of the function specified in the setInterval() function by using the **clearInterval()method**. This function takes one argument, a variable, which is returned from setInterval(). A general example using these methods follows. The code in Example 9.18 will update the time every two seconds when the user clicks the Start It button and will stop when the user clicks the Stop it! button.

EXAMPLE 9.18

Using a Timer

```
1.   <html>
2.   <head>
3.   <title>Example 9.18</title>
4.   </head>
5.   <body>
6.   <p>Start the timer or stop the timer:</p>
7.   <button onclick="doSomething()">Start it</button>
8.   <button onclick="stopIt()">Stop it!</button>
9.   <script>
10.       var begin;
11.       function doSomething()
12.       {
13.           begin = setInterval(function(){timeIt()},2000);
14.       }
15.       function timeIt()
16.       {
17.           var day = new Date();
18.           var time = day.toLocaleTimeString();
19.           document.getElementById("result").innerHTML = time;
20.       }
21.       function stopIt()
22.       {
23.           clearInterval(begin);
24.       }
25.   </script>
26.   <p><div id = "result"> </div></p>
27.   </body></html>
```

Notice that, in this example, the JavaScript code for the timer was placed within the HTML body. A timer can be used, if you wish, to enhance some of the games we have created or some of the tests we have made for the Greg's Gambits and Carla's Classroom sites.

CHECKPOINT FOR SECTION 9.5 ✓

9.21 Do the elements in an array have to be sorted before using a binary search?

9.22 If an array has 250 elements, what are the initial values of **low**, **high**, and **index** (if **index** represents the middle of the array) in a binary search?

9.23 Why must we use the Math.round() method when determining the middle value when using a binary search?

Use the following array for Checkpoints 9.24 and 9.25:

```
var nums = new Array(12, 14, 20, 22, 29, 32, 35, 35, 43);
```

9.24 How many iterations are necessary in a binary search to locate the index value of 20?

9.25 What is the value of **index** after the following statements are executed?

```
var key = 20;
index = nums.indexOf(key);
```

9.6 Putting It to Work

In this section we will develop a game to add to Greg's Gambits and a math lesson for Carla's Classroom.

Greg's Gambits: Greg's Boggle

This program will be a simplified version of the game of Boggle. In the real game of Boggle, players must form as many words as possible from a square of nine randomly selected letters. The game can be simulated on a computer by generating random letters and using an online dictionary to check if the words a player builds are, in fact, real words. For our example, we will not do this since not everyone has access to an online dictionary. Instead, we will use a short sample of five scrambled sets of letters and develop a program that will display one set of letters and allow the player to enter as many words as he or she can make from those letters. Since the possible words have been created for you, all we need to do is check to make sure the words the player creates are in the array of possible words.

Developing the Program

The arrays that hold the five sets of scrambled letters and possible words are in a file named gregBoggle.js. By using a source file, the main program is kept shorter and easier to manage. Also, at any time, you can add more scrambled sets to this file to enhance the game. The file, gregBoggle.js, in in the Student Data Files. You may find more words than the ones this author found in each set of scrambled letters. If you find a word that is not in the array, simply add it to the list; it will improve the program without necessitating any other changes.

Setting the Stage

Let's begin by creating the web page that will hold this game and putting a link on the `play_games.html` page. We will name the Boggle page `greg_boggle.html` so place a link on the `play_games.html` page to `greg_boggle.html`. The `play_games.html` page will now look like this:

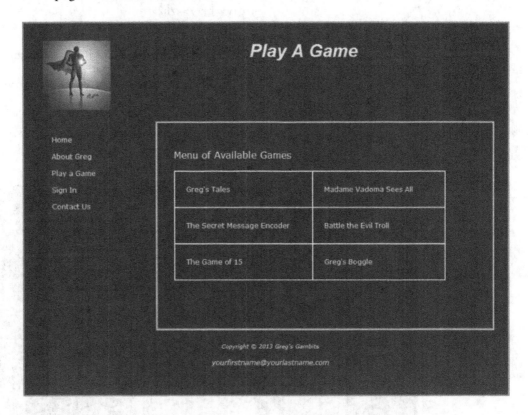

We'll use the template for the `Greg Gambits` site to create the game of `Greg's Boggle`. On this page, we need an area for the scrambled letters to appear, an area for the words the player creates, and an area to display the results, including a score and other relevant information. The code for the HTML part of this page will be as follows:

```
1.  <body>
2.  <div id="container">
3.      <img src="images/superhero.jpg" class="floatleft" />
4.      <h1><em>Greg's Game of Boggle</em></h1>
5.      <div id="nav">
6.          <p><a href="index.html">Home</a>
7.          <a href="greg.html">About Greg</a>
8.          <a href="play_games.html">Play a Game</a>
9.          <a href="sign.html">Sign In</a>
10.         <a href="contact.html">Contact Us</a></p>
11.     </div>
12.     <div id="content">
13.         <p>The object of the game is to create as many words as ↵
                you can, in a given time limit, from the ↵
```

```
                              letters shown below. When you are ready to ⏎
                              begin, click the button.</p>
14.            <p><input type="button" value = "begin the game" onclick = ⏎
                  "boggle();" /></p>
15.            <h2><br /><br />Letters you can use:<br /><div id = ⏎
                  "letters"> </div><br /></h2>
16.            <h2>Your words so far: <br /><div id = "entries">   ⏎
                  </div><br /></h2>
17.            <h2>Results:<br /><div id = "result"> </div></h2>
18.        </div>
19.        <div id="footer">Copyright &copy; 2013 Greg's Gambits<br />
               <a href = "mailto:yourfirstname@yourlastname.com"> ⏎
                              yourfirstname@yourlastname.com</a> </div>
20.   </div>
21.   </body></html>
```

If you enter the HTML code for the "content" <div> into one of the Greg's site pages, your new web page should look like this:

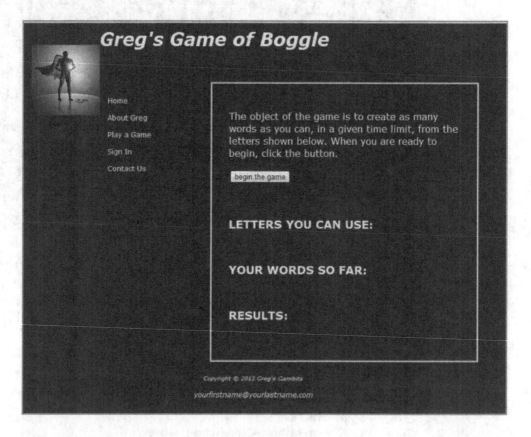

Creating the boggle() Function   Now we'll focus on the JavaScript code to make the game. First, we will add the external file to the head section:

```
<script type="text/javascript" src="gregBoggle.js"></script>
```

This file contains, presently, five arrays of strings. Each array has a certain number of letters which are in no particular order as the first entry. The rest of the entries are real words that can be created from these letters. The main program has to select one of these arrays each time a player plays the game. We will generate a random number from 1 to 5 and send this number, as an argument when it calls the function in the external file. This function will use a `switch` statement to select which array to use, based on the number it receives. The code in the external file looks like the following but, to save space, only the first array is given in its entirety:

```
1.   function words(x)
2.   {
3.        switch (x)
4.        {
5.            case 1:
6.                var word = new Array("balte", "table", "hat", "tab",↵
                          "belt", "lab", "eat", "tea", "ate", ↵
                          "tale", "bale", "let", "bet", "teal", ↵
                          "late", "beat");
7.                break;
8.            case 2:
9.                var word = new Array("atwre", "water", "wet", ↵
                          "wear", "tear", "war", "rat", etc. etc...);
10.               break;
11.           case 3:
12.               var word = new Array("dclaen", "can", etc. etc...);
13.               break;
14.           case 4:
15.               var word = new Array("aepinlar", "air", etc. etc...);
16.               break;
17.           case 5:
18.               var word = new Array("redykboa", "keyboard", "key", ↵
                          "board", "bored", "bore", etc. etc...);
19.               break;
20.       }
21.       return word;
22.   }
```

Now we will develop the game. After declaring some of the necessary variables, we need to generate a random number from 1 to 5 which will be the argument sent to the `words()` function. We will also create several new `Array` objects. One will hold all the words the player creates as the game progresses. Another will hold the array sent back from the `words()` function. A third will hold an array of entries the player makes which are not valid words.

Play will begin when the scrambled letters are displayed on the screen. The player will be prompted for a word and will continue to be prompted until he cannot find any more words in the scrambled letters. Each time the player enters a word, it will be added, using the `push()` method, to the player's array of words. It will also be displayed on the screen so the player can keep track of what he has entered so far.

Once the player has finished entering words, we need to check his score. For this game, the score will simply be the number of valid words the player has found. Therefore, we need to find entries that are not valid words and remove them from the count. We will also keep track of them by adding them to the array of invalid entries.

To display the list of invalid words we will use another method of the Array object—the toString() method.

The toString() Method   The **toString() method** is used to convert a number to a string but is also a method of the Array object. When used with a number or a variable that has a numeric value, it will convert that value to a string. When used with an array it converts all elements in the array to a single string, with each element separated by commas, and returns the result. The original array, of course, remains unchanged. The results of using the toString() method are shown in Example 9.19. The example shows how different applications of the toString() method will yield various results.

A **radix** is a number taken as the base of a system of numbers. Our number system is base 10 so the radix for our number system is 10. By including a radix as a parameter, the toString() method will convert a decimal number to a number in any base from 2 to 36. Of course, we rarely are interested in numbers in base 13 or 25 but we often are interested in the binary or hexadecimal representation of a number. The syntax to convert a number to a different base, assuming **x** is a numeric variable, is as follows:

var **newBase** = **x**.toString(**y**); where **y** represents the radix

The toString() method also has more relevant uses, especially in the game we are developing now. It will convert all elements of an array to a string. Example 9.19 demonstrates how the toString() method will convert a decimal number to both binary and hexadecimal and will also convert an array to a string.

EXAMPLE 9.19

Using the toString() Method

```
1.   <html>
2.   <head>
3.   <title>Example 9.19</title>
4.   <script>
5.   function use_toString()
6.   {
7.       var names = new Array(" Janey", " Joey", " Joanie", " Jimmy", ↵
                     " Jessie", " Johnnie", " Jackie", " Jamie", ↵
                     " Jake", " Jocelyn");
8.       var num = 12345678;
9.       var namesString = names.toString();
10.      var numBase2 = num.toString(2);
11.      var numBase16 = num.toString(16);
12.      document.getElementById("number").innerHTML = num;
13.      document.getElementById("base2").innerHTML = numBase2;
14.      document.getElementById("base16").innerHTML = numBase16;
15.      document.getElementById("array_result").innerHTML = namesString;
16.  }
17.  </script>
18.  </head>
19.  <body>
20.  <div id = "content" style="width: 700px; margin-left: auto; ↵
                     margin-right: auto;">
```

```
21.        <h2>Using the toString() Method</h2>
22.        <p><input type="button" value = "the toString() method" ↵
                        onclick="use_toString();" /></p>
23.        <h3>The original number is: <div id = "number">   ↵
                        </div></h3>
24.        <h3>The number in binary (base 2) is:<div id = "base2"> ↵
                          </div></h3>
25.        <h3>The number in hexadecimal (base 16) is:<div id = ↵
                        "base16">  </div></h3>
26.        <h3>The array consists of the following names:<div id = ↵
                        "array_result"> </div></h3>
27.    </div>
28.    </body></html>
```

If this program is run, the output would be as follows:

Using the toString() Method

[the toString() method]

The original number is:
12345678

The number in binary (base 2) is:
101111000110000101001110

The number in hexadecimal (base 16) is:
bc614e

The array consists of the following names:
Janey, Joey, Joanie, Jimmy, Jessie, Johnnie, Jackie, Jamie, Jake, Jocelyn

Now we are ready to write the function that will run Greg's version of Boggle.

The boggle() Function The code for the boggle() function is as follows:

```
1.  function boggle()
2.  {
3.      var play = "";
4.      var score = 0; var flag = 0;
5.      var num = Math.floor(Math.random()*5) + 1;
6.      compWords = new Array(); notAword = new Array();
7.      playWords = new Array();
8.      compWords = words(num);
9.      yourWord = compWords[0];
10.     document.getElementById("letters").innerHTML = yourWord;
11.     //get player entries
12.     while (play != "Q")
13.     {
14.         play = prompt("enter a word or enter Q when done");
15.         playWords.push(play);
16.         if(play != "Q")
17.             document.getElementById("entries").innerHTML = ↵
                    playWords.toString();
18.     }
19.     //check winning score and list bad words
20.     var complgth = compWords.length;
```

```
21.        var playlgth = (playWords.length - 1);
22.        for (var i = 0; i < playlgth; i++)
23.        {
24.            flag = 0;
25.            for (var k = 0; k < complgth; k++)
26.            {
27.                if(playWords[i] == compWords[k])
28.                {
29.                    score++;
30.                    flag = 1;
31.                }
32.            }
33.            if (flag == 0)
34.                notAword.push(playWords[i]);
35.        }
36.        document.getElementById("result").innerHTML = ("Your score ⏎
                              is " + score + ". The following entries ⏎
                              are not valid words: <br />" + ⏎
                              notAword.toString());
37. }
```

In this code, lines 3 and 4 declare and initialize variables. Line 5 generates a random number that could be 1, 2, 3, 4, or 5. Lines 6 and 7 create the three new Array objects that are needed. Line 8 loads the array of the selected letters by sending the generated random number (**num**) to the function in the external file and stores the result in the **compWords()** array. The external file uses the value of **num** to pick one of the five arrays, using the switch statement. It then returns that array to **compWords()** in the main program.

Line 9 stores the first element of the **compWords()** array in a variable, **yourWord**. These are the scrambled letters that are displayed on the web page (line 10). Then play begins.

The player can continue to enter words until he or she decides to quit, by entering "Q". Each time the player enters a word, it is added to a new array, **playWords()**, using the push() method (line 15). The if statement on lines 16 and 17 checks to see if the user has entered "Q". If not, a string is generated containing all the words so far in the **playWords()** array and displayed. However, if the player has entered a "Q", this clause will not be executed. This ensures that, at the end, a Q will not be displayed as part of the player's entries. Throughout the play, each time the player enters a new word, the web page will continue to display the words entered so far.

Once the player is finished entering words, the program gets the player's score which is simply a count of the number of valid words created. It also separates out the invalid words and displays them on the web page. To do this, the program must compare each word entered with the valid words in the **compWords()** array. The two arrays will rarely (only by coincidence) be the same length so lines 20 and 21 get the lengths of each array. A nested loop is necessary to find which words are valid and which are not.

The outer for loop begins on line 22. It will have as many iterations as there are words in the player's **playWords()** array. In this situation, the **flag** is given a value of 0 on line 24. It is used to identify when a word is valid. If a player's word is compared to each element in the **compWords()** array and no match is found, the **flag** will remain at 0 and we will know that this particular entry is not a valid word.

The inner loop begins on line 25. It takes one word from the **playWords()** array and compares it with each element in the **compWords()** array. Therefore, it will execute for as many times as there are elements in the **compWords()** array. If a match is found the if clause on lines 27–31 is executed. The player's score is incremented by 1 and the **flag** is set to 1. If no match is found, the if clause on lines 33 and 34 are executed. The invalid entry is added to the third array, **notAword()**, using the push() method.

At the end of one pass through the outer loop, the inner loop has compared one of the player's words to each of the computer's words and determined whether there is a match and accompanying increase in score or, if there is no match, the word is added to the list of invalid words.

At the end of all the passes through the outer loop, this process has been completed for each of the player's words so a final score is ready as is a final list of all invalid words. The nested loop ends. Line 36 displays these results on the web page.

Putting It All Together

We now put all the code together. Try it!

```
1.   <html>
2.   <head>
3.   <title>Greg's Gambits | Greg's Boggle</title>
4.   <link href="greg.css" rel="stylesheet" type="text/css" />
5.   <script type="text/javascript" src="gregBoggle.js"></script>
6.   <script>
7.   function boggle()
8.   {
9.       var play = "";
10.      var score = 0; var flag = 0;
11.      var num = Math.floor(Math.random()*5) + 1;
12.      compWords = new Array; notAword = new Array;
13.      playWords = new Array();
14.      compWords = words(num);
15.      yourWord = compWords[0];
16.      document.getElementById("letters").innerHTML = yourWord;
17.      //get player entries
18.      while (play != "Q")
19.      {
20.          play = prompt("enter a word or enter Q when done");
21.          playWords.push(play);
22.          if(play != "Q")
23.              document.getElementById("entries").innerHTML = ⏎
                     playWords.toString();
```

```
24.        }
25.        //check winning score and list bad words
26.        var complgth = compWords.length;
27.        var playlgth = (playWords.length - 1);
28.        for (var i = 0; i < playlgth; i++)
29.        {
30.            flag = 0;
31.            for (var k = 0; k < complgth; k++)
32.            {
33.                if(playWords[i] == compWords[k])
34.                {
35.                    score++;
36.                    flag = 1;
37.                }
38.            }
39.            if (flag == 0)
40.                notAword.push(playWords[i]);
41.        }
42.        document.getElementById("result").innerHTML = ("Your score ↵
                        is " + score + ". The following entries↵
                        are not valid words: <br />" +↵
                        notAword.toString());
43.    }
44.    </script>
45.    </head>
46.    <body>
47.    <div id="container">
48.        <img src="images/superhero.jpg" class="floatleft" />
49.        <h1><em>Greg's Game of Boggle</em></h1>
50.        <div id="nav">
51.            <p><a href="index.html">Home</a>
52.            <a href="greg.html">About Greg</a>
53.            <a href="play_games.html">Play a Game</a>
54.            <a href="sign.html">Sign In</a>
55.            <a href="contact.html">Contact Us</a></p>
56.        </div>
57.        <div id="content">
58.            <p>The object of the game is to create as many words↵
                        as you can, in a given time limit, from the↵
                        letters shown below. When you are ready to ↵
                        begin, click the button.</p>
59.            <p><input type="button" value = "begin the game" ↵
                        onclick = "boggle();" /></p>
60.            <h2><br /><br />Letters you can use:<br /><div id = ↵
                        "letters"> </div><br /></h2>
61.            <h2>Your words so far: <br /><div id = "entries"> ↵
                          </div><br /></h2>
62.            <h2>Results:<br /><div id = "result"> </div></h2>
63.        </div>
64.        <div id="footer">Copyright &copy; 2013 Greg's Gambits<br />
65.            <a href="mailto:yourfirstname@yourlastname.com"> ↵
                        yourfirstname@yourlastname.com</a></div>
66.    </div>
67.    </body></html>
```

If you code and run this program, here are some possible outputs. First the scrambled word is generated:

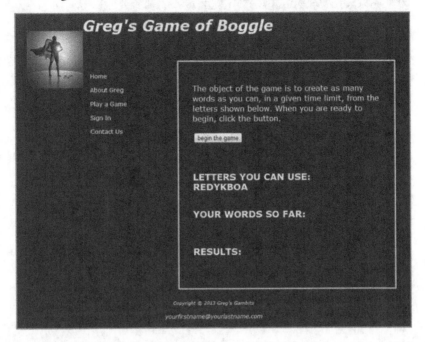

The prompt appears as follows:

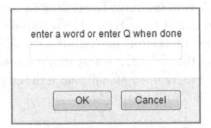

After entering seven words, two of them invalid, the display looks like this:

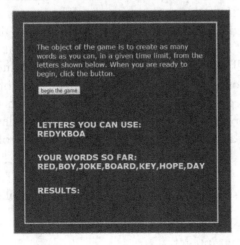

If, at this point, the player enters Q, the results will be as follows:

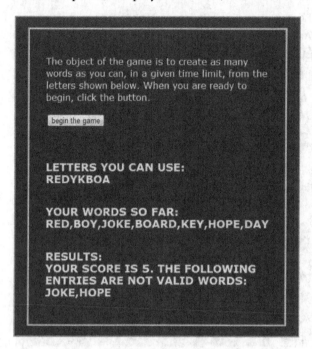

The object of the game is to create as many words as you can, in a given time limit, from the letters shown below. When you are ready to begin, click the button.

[begin the game]

LETTERS YOU CAN USE:
REDYKBOA

YOUR WORDS SO FAR:
RED,BOY,JOKE,BOARD,KEY,HOPE,DAY

RESULTS:
YOUR SCORE IS 5. THE FOLLOWING ENTRIES ARE NOT VALID WORDS:
JOKE,HOPE

Carla's Classroom: A Factoring Lesson

For this lesson, we will add to Carla's math inventory by creating an exercise that she can also use as a test. Students will be presented a number and be required to enter all the factors of that number. Since the program is rather complicated, we will only present the first level of difficulty. However, once this is done, it is easy to add one or more levels of difficulty. This will be your task in a Programming Challenge at the end of the chapter.

Factoring Integers

You have probably learned to factor polynomials in an algebra class, but Carla's students are not ready for algebra. This program will present a student with an integer and the student must find all the factors of that integer. The factors of an integer are all the numbers that, when the number is divided by the factor, the result is another integer. Therefore, 3 is a factor of 12 because $12 \div 3 = 4$ but 5 is not a factor of 12 because $12 \div 5 = 2.4$. All integers have at least two factors: 1 and the number itself. Thus, the only factors of 13 are 1 and 13 because there is no other integer that can result in another integer when 13 is divided by it. Numbers that only have these two factors are called prime numbers. Adding the ability to identify prime numbers will be an option in a Programming Challenge at the end of the chapter.

Developing the Program

This program requires some serious thought. We need to do the following:

- Identify the possible integers to be factored.
- Identify all the factors of that integer.
- Present the student with that integer.
- Prompt for a factor of the integer.

- Test to see if the student's entry is a correct factor.
  - ☐ If correct:
    - The factor must be displayed.
    - The factor should be stored in a new array to avoid allowing the student to enter duplicates.
    - A check should be made to see if the student has found all factors of the number.
  - ☐ If incorrect:
    - The incorrect entry must be displayed.
    - The incorrect entry should be stored in another array.
    - A total of the number of incorrect entries should be updated.
- If a set number of incorrect responses have been made, the student should be presented a new number.
- Once all factors have been identified:
  - ☐ A count of how many times the student has correctly factored a number should be updated.
  - ☐ The student should be presented a new number or given the choice to end.
  - ☐ If the student has correctly factored a set number of integers, the student should move to the next difficulty level or the program will end.

We will write the code in small, manageable pieces. Once complete, this is a robust program that includes most of the concepts we have learned so far but, as you go through the steps, you will see how the most complex programs are built from relatively simple concepts.

Setting the Stage

Let's begin by creating the web page. We will use `carla_factoring.html` for the filename and the page title will be `Carla's Classroom | Fun With Factors` so first add a link to the `Fun With Factors` page on Carla's `math.html` page. The `math.html` page should now look like this:

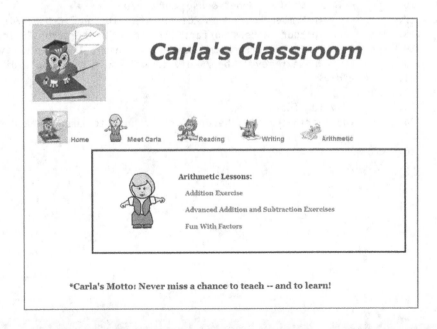

Now we will set up a new web page. The HTML script for the <body></body> of this new page, with the filename carla_factoring.html, is shown below. The page needs to have areas for the number to factor, a running display of the correct factors entered by the student, feedback on whether a given number is incorrect or if the student has discovered all the factors, and an area for the student to enter the response.

```
1.    <body>
2.    <div id="container">
3.        <img src="images/owl_reading.JPG" class="floatleft" />
4.        <h1><em>Carla's Classroom</em></h1>
5.        <div align="left"><blockquote>
6.            <a href="index.html"><img src="images/owl_button.jpg" />Home</a>
7.            <a href="carla.html"><img src="images/carla_button.jpg" ⏎
                      />Meet Carla </a>
8.            <a href="reading.html"><img src="images/read_button.jpg" ⏎
                      />Reading</a>
9.            <a href="writing.html"><img src="images/write_button.jpg" ⏎
                      />Writing</a>
10.           <a href="math.html"><img src="images/arith_button.jpg" ⏎
                      />Arithmetic</a><br />
11.       </blockquote></div>
12.       <div id="content">
13.           <p>This test will increase in difficulty as you prove you are ready ⏎
                      for harder problems. As soon as you get 3 problems ⏎
                      correct in Level One, you will progress to the ⏎
                      next level.</p>
14.           <p>When you begin Level One, you will be given a number ⏎
                      between 1 and 20. You will be prompted for⏎
                      all the factors of that number. When you ⏎
                      find all the factors, you will be given a ⏎
                      new number. If you make 5 incorrect ⏎
                      entries, you will be given a new number.</p>
15.           <p><input type = "button" onclick = "factorIt()" value = ⏎
                      "begin the test" />
16.           <div id = "done"> </div></p>
17.           <p>Number to factor: <div id = "factor_num"> </div></p>
18.           <p>Your factors so far: <div id = "user_factors">  </div></p>
19.           <p>Instant feedback: <div id = "result_1"> </div></p>
20.           <p>Next level:<br /><div id = "result_2"> </div></p>
21.       </div>
22.   </div>
23.       <div id="footer">
24.       <h3>*Carla's Motto: Never miss a chance to teach -- and to learn!</h3>
25.       </div>
26.   </div>
27.   </body>
```

The content of your page will look like this:

> **This test will increase in difficulty as you prove you are ready for harder problems. As soon as you get 3 problems correct in Level One, you will progress to the next level.**
>
> **When you begin Level One, you will be given a number between 1 and 20. You will be prompted for all the factors of that number. When you find all the factors, you will be given a new number. If you make 5 incorrect entries, you will be given a new number.**
>
> `begin the test`
>
> **Number to factor:**
>
> **Your factors so far:**
>
> **Instant feedback:**
>
> **Next level:**

The Code in Pieces

Since this program is complex, we will write the code in pieces and put it all together at the end.

The External File   It's best to put several things we need for this program in an external file. We need an array of integers to give the student to factor. For Level One, the array will include elements of numbers 1 through 20. Once we pick a number, we must find its factors and store them in a new array. This will be used to compare with the student's response when we check to see if the response is a correct factor and when we check to see if the student has identified all the factors.

By putting the numbers for Level One in an external file, it is simple to add new levels or change the range of options for this level. We give this file the filename `carlaFactors.js`.

Loading an array with integers in order from 1 to 20 is easy. But how do we find all the factors of any integer? We know that, if a number is a factor of another number, the result, when dividing one by the other will be an integer. We can use the parseInt() method to check all numbers from 1 up to the integer in question and, if dividing the integer in question by a number results in an integer, it is a factor of that number. In other words, if **x/y** == parseInt(**x/y**) then **y** is a factor of **x**.

The external file, therefore, contains the following functions:

```
1.   function One()
2.   {
3.       var levelOne = new Array()
4.       for (var i = 0; i < 20; i++)
5.           levelOne[i] = i+1;
6.       return levelOne;
7.   }
8.   function Two()
9.   {
10.      //can be added later
11.      return levelTwo;
12.  }
13.  function Three()
14.  {
15.      //can be added later
16.      return levelThree;
17.  }
18.  function getFactors(index)
19.  {
20.      var factors = new Array();
21.      for (i = 1; i <= index; i++)
22.      {
23.          if (index/i == parseInt(index/i))
24.              factors.push(i);
25.      }
26.      return factors;
27.  }
```

Note that the push() method is used on line 24 to create an array of all the factors of a given number. Since the for loop goes from 1 to the number being factored, at the end the array, **factors()**, is sorted from highest to lowest. For our program, it does not matter but the array could be resorted from lowest to highest with one line of code, using either the sort() method or the reverse() method.

The Beginning   The factoring test will begin with a number presented to the student and will end when one of two things happen—either the student factors three numbers correctly or the student opts to end the exercise. The following code is the beginning of the function, factorIt():

```
1.   <html>
2.   <head>
3.   <title>Carla's Classroom | Fun With Factors</title>
4.   <link href="carla.css" rel="stylesheet" type="text/css" />
5.   <script type="text/javascript" src="carlaFactors.js"></script>
```

```
6.   <script>
7.   function factorIt()
8.   {
9.        var yourNum = 0; var total = 0; var test = 0;
10.       var choice = "y"; var factor = 0; var ranOne = 0;
11.       var complgth = 0; var studlgth = 0; var score = 0;
12.       var usedNums = new Array; var myFactors = new Array;
13.       var notAfactor = new Array; var easyNums = new Array;
14.       var allFactors = new Array;
15.       easyNums = One();
16.       easylgth = easyNums.length;
17.  //outer loop goes until student gets 3 right or quits
18.       while (choice == "y")
19.       {
20.            stuff in here
21.       }
22.       function intermediate()
23.       {
24.            alert("nothing here so far");
25.       }
26.  }
27.  </script>
28.  </head>
```

Let's talk about what the variables and arrays will represent:

- **yourNum** holds the integer to be factored.
- **total** holds the number of incorrect responses.
- **test** is used to check to see if a student's entry is a correct factor.
- **choice** holds the student's choice about whether to continue.
- **factor** holds each response the student makes.
- **ranOne** holds the index of the number in the integer array of numbers between 1 and 20 that the student will be asked to factor.
- **complgth** holds the length of the array of factors after the number to be factored is identified and all its factors have been determined by the function getFactors().
- **studlgth** holds the length of the array of factors the student has guessed at any given time. It will be used to compare to **complgth** to see if all factors have been correctly identified.
- **score** holds the value of how many times the student has correctly identified all factors of a number (program moves to next level when **score** = 3).
- **usedNums()** is an array that holds all the numbers given to the student to avoid duplication.
- **myFactors()** is an array that holds all the numbers the student has identified as correct factors at any time.
- **notAfactor()** is an array that holds all the student's incorrect responses at any time.
- **easyNums()** is an array that holds the values from the function One() in the external file.
- **allFactors()** is an array that holds the values from the function getFactors() in the external file.

After the external file is linked to the page (line 5) and the variables and arrays have been declared and initialized, the array of numbers to be used in the program are fetched from the external file and stored in a new array called easyNums() on line 15. Line 16 gets the length of this array and stores that value in **complgth**.

Selecting the Number and Some Housekeeping Tasks   The large outer while loop will continue until the value of **choice** is anything other than "y". This means that, later in the program, when we want to force it to end before giving the student a choice, we can assign any other value to **choice**. We also need to clean out old entries from the web page and identify a number to present to the student. Once we identify the number by randomly picking it from the numbers available, we need to check to make sure it has not been used in this test previously.

After a number that has not been used before has been identified, we want to add it to the array that holds the used numbers and we need to get all the factors of this number. We also want to clean out all old values from the **myFactors()** array which may hold responses from the previous round.

The code for this part of the while loop—which is done each time the student will be offered a new number—is as follows:

```
1.   while (choice == "y")
2.   {
3.        total = 0;
4.        document.getElementById("factor_num").innerHTML = (" ");
5.        document.getElementById("user_factors").innerHTML = (" ");
6.        document.getElementById("result_1").innerHTML = (" ");
7.        ranOne = Math.floor(Math.random()*20);
8.        yourNum = easyNums[ranOne];
9.        usedlgth = usedNums.length;
10.       easylgth = easyNums.length;
11.       incorrectlgth = notAfactor.length;
12.       notAfactor.splice(0, incorrectlgth);
13.       //check if number selected has been used
14.       var check = true;
15.       if (easylgth == usedlgth)
16.              intermediate();
17.       while (check == true)
18.       {
19.            check = false;
20.            for (var i = 0; i <= usedlgth; i++)
21.            {
22.                 if (usedNums[i] == yourNum)
23.                 {
24.                      ranOne = Math.floor(Math.random()*20);
25.                      yourNum = easyNums[ranOne];
26.                      check = true;
27.                 }
28.            }
29.       }
30.       usedNums.push(yourNum);
31.       allFactors = getFactors(yourNum);
32.       myFactors.splice(0, studlgth);
33.  //more code to follow
34.  }
```

The first thing that happens (line 3) is that **total** is set back to 0. After one pass through this loop, the student may have made some incorrect responses but those responses related to a different integer. We want the student to start fresh with each new number. Lines 4, 5, and 6 just clear out old displays on the web page.

Line 7 makes the first attempt at picking a new number to be factored. We want to select one of the elements in the array that holds the possible numbers for this first level. Since the possibilities go from 1 to 20, there are 20 elements in that array. The value picked is stored in **ranOne** and represents the index of the element in the array **easyNums()**. The number the student will see, **yourNum**, is then set equal to the value in **easyNums[ranOne]** (line 8). Line 9 gets the length of the array that holds all the numbers that have already been used. Line 10 gets the length of the array of the factorize-able numbers. Lines 11 and 12 get the length of the array that holds incorrect responses and uses that length to clear out old values in that array (**notAfactor()**) from a prior iteration. We use the **splice()** method which is discussed below.

Now we need to check whether or not the number selected to be given to the student has already been used. Lines 14–29 perform this task. A flag, **check**, is set to **true** (line 14). The **if** statement on lines 15 and 16 check to see if the length of the array of used numbers is the same as the length of the array of options, **easyNums()**. If they are the same length, then the student has already seen all the numbers possible at this level and the next level is called. We do not have any code written for the next level yet so the function **intermediate()** will just display an alert telling us nothing is ready yet.

However, if all the numbers have not been given to the student yet, we need to check if the particular number identified on line 8 has been used. The **while** loop on lines 17–29 will continue until the flag is **false**. First we set the flag to **false** (line 19). If we never find a match for **yourNum** as we test it against every possible number that has been used, **check** will never be set to **true**, the **while** loop will end, and we know that the initial value of **yourNum** is a valid number. The **for** loop on lines 20–28 checks **yourNum** against each number in the **usedNums()** array. If a match is found on lines 22–27, a new random number is selected as the new index value in the **easyNums()** array, a new number is selected and assigned to **yourNum**, and **check** is reset to **true**. This continues until a valid, unused number has been identified.

Once the number to be factored has been picked, line 30 adds this number to the **usedNums()** array. Line 31 calls the **getFactors()** function, sending in the value of the number to be factored (**yourNum**). Line 32 uses a method of the **Array** object that we have not used so far, the **splice()** method. A brief explanation of this method follows.

The *splice()* Method   The **splice()method** will either add elements to an array or remove elements from an array. It returns the new array. The general syntax is as follows:

```
arrayName.splice(index, num_to_remove,add_item1,.....,add_itemX)
```

The **index** parameter is required. This identifies where the **splice()** method should begin. The **num_to_remove** parameter is also required. If, however, you want to use this method to add items to an array, this value should be 0. Then no items will be removed. The third parameter, the items to be added, is optional. If it is left out, no items will be added.

In our program, we use the `splice()` method to clear the array that holds the student's responses as he or she begins to factor a number. After one pass through the program, this array, **myFactors()**, will hold all the student's responses to the first number he or she factored. Line 32 uses the `splice()` method to remove all items from the past trial before beginning the new factorization.

Line 32 says **myFactors.splice(0, studlgth)**;. This means, starting at index = 0, the method will remove all items through the length of the array. Since the numbers given to factor do not have the same number of factors, after each pass, **myFactors()** will have a new length. Therefore, **studlgth** works for any number of factors.

Getting Student Responses   Now we reach the part of the program that gets the student's responses and deals with them. We need to display the number to be factored, prompt the student for a factor, and check several things before getting a second factor. First, we want to know if the response is a factor or an incorrect entry. If it is incorrect, we need to increment the variable that holds the number of incorrect responses. We want to inform the student of this and add this to the array that holds the incorrect responses as well as adding it to the display of incorrect responses so far.

If the response is correct, this value needs to be added to the display of factors so far and it needs to be added to the array of the student's factors for this particular number.

Then we need to see if this response has completed the factorization of this number. If so, the student earns a point since success at this level is determined by the variable **score**. If this response has given the student a score of 3, we must reset choice to something other than "y", congratulate the student on completing this level and move to the next level.

But if the student has not completed the level, we need to give him or her the choice to continue or end. If the student wants to continue, the outer `while` loop begins anew. But if this is an incorrect response that results in five incorrect responses for this number, we need to break out of the loop and start over, at the beginning of the outer `while` loop with a new number.

The code for all of this is as follows:

```
1.  while (score < 3)
2.  {
3.      document.getElementById("factor_num").innerHTML = yourNum;
4.      factor = prompt("enter a factor of " + yourNum);
5.      test = yourNum/factor;
6.      if (test != parseInt(yourNum / factor))
7.      {
8.          notAfactor.push(factor);
9.          document.getElementById("result_1").innerHTML = (factor +↵
                    " is not a factor of " + yourNum + ". Your ↵
                incorrect entries so far are " + ↵
                notAfactor.toString());
```

```
10.              total++;
11.              alert("total incorrect responses: " + total);
12.          }
13.      if (test == parseInt(yourNum / factor))
14.          {
15.              myFactors.push(factor);
16.              document.getElementById("user_factors").innerHTML = ⏎
                        myFactors.toString();
17.          }
18.      complgth = allFactors.length;
19.      studlgth = myFactors.length;
20.      if(complgth == studlgth)
21.          {
22.              score++;
23.              alert("score =" +score);
24.              document.getElementById("result_1").innerHTML = ("All ⏎
                        factors of " + yourNum + " have been identified");
25.              if (score < 3)
26.                  {
27.                      choice = prompt("Ready for another number? Type y ⏎
                            for yes, n for no:");
28.                  }
29.              break;
30.          }
31.      if (total == 5)
32.          {
33.              document.getElementById("result_1").innerHTML = ("You ⏎
                        have had too many errors.");
34.              break;
35.          }
36. }
37. if (score == 3)
38. {
39.      document.getElementById("done").innerHTML = ("Congratulations! ⏎
                You can move to the next level.");
40.      choice = "n";
41.      intermediate();
42. }
```

The while loop on lines 1–36 continues to get factors of the number either until the student has identified all the factors or until the student has had too many errors. After the prompt for a factor (line 4), the input is tested to see if it is a correct factor (line 5). If it is not a factor, the if clause on lines 6–12 is executed. The response is pushed into the array of incorrect responses (line 8), the student is told that the response is incorrect, this response is added to the displayed list of incorrect factors (line 9), the total number of incorrect responses is incremented (line 10), and the number of incorrect responses so far are shown through an alert (line 11). Notice that the toString() method (line 9) converts all the elements of the **notAfactor()** array to a string, with the values separated by commas.

However, if the student's response is a valid factor, the if clause on lines 13–17 is executed. The response is added to the array that holds the student's correct responses so far (line 15) and all the correct responses so far are displayed, again using the toString() method (line 16).

Once the program has dealt with the response, the code checks to see if this response completes the factorization of this number. It compares the length of the array that holds all the number's factors, **allFactors()** with the length of the array that holds all the student's correct responses, **myFactors()**. If the lengths are the same, we know the number has been factored completely. The if clause on lines 20–30 deals with this situation. First, the student's **score** is incremented (line 22) and an alert tells the student his or her present score (line 23). Line 24 informs the student that the number has been completely factored. Then the next options are checked.

If the student's **score** is less than 3, he or she must do another factorization before moving to the next level. This option is checked on lines 25–28. The student is given the **choice** to continue or end the test. If the **total**, which holds the number of errors, is equal to 5, the student is informed of this and the program jumps to the beginning where a new number is generated. This occurs on lines 31–35. But if this iteration has resulted in a **score** of 3, the student is informed that he or she has completed the first level and progresses to the next level (lines 37–42).

Putting It All Together

The code, with all the pieces put together is as follows. The code for the external file, carlaFactors.js, is not repeated here. This code includes some extra comments because it is so long.

```
1.   <html>
2.   <head>
3.   <title>Carla's Classroom | Fun With Factors</title>
4.   <link href="carla.css" rel="stylesheet" type="text/css" />
5.   <script type="text/javascript" src="carlaFactors.js"></script>
6.   <script>
7.   function factorIt()
8.   {
9.        var yourNum = 0; var total = 0; var test = 0;
10.       var choice = "y"; var factor = 0; var ranOne = 0;
11.       var complgth = 0; var studlgth = 0; var score = 0;
12.       var usedNums = new Array; var myFactors = new Array;
13.       var notAfactor = new Array; var easyNums = new Array;
14.       var allFactors = new Array;
15.       var easyNums = One();
16.       var easylgth = easyNums.length;
17.       var incorrectlgth = notAfactor.length;
18.       notAfactor.splice(0, incorrectlgth);
19.  //outer loop goes until student score = 3 or quits
20.       while (choice == "y")
21.       {
22.            total = 0;
23.            document.getElementById("factor_num").innerHTML = ↵
                    (" ");
24.            document.getElementById("user_factors").innerHTML = ↵
                    (" ");
25.            document.getElementById("result_1").innerHTML = (" ");
26.            ranOne = Math.floor(Math.random()*20); //pick num to factor
27.            yourNum = easyNums[ranOne];
28.            usedlgth = usedNums.length;
```

```
29.    //check if number selected has been used
30.            var check = true;
31.        if (easylgth == usedlgth)
32.               intermediate();
33.               while (check == true)
34.               {
35.                     check = false;
36.                     for (var i = 0; i <= usedlgth; i++)
37.                     {
38.                            if (usedNums[i] == yourNum)
39.                            {
40.                                   ranOne = Math.floor(Math.random()*20);
41.                                   yourNum = easyNums[ranOne];
42.                                   check = true;
43.                            }
44.                     }
45.               }
46.        usedNums.push(yourNum); //add number picked to used array
47.        allFactors = getFactors(yourNum); //get all factors of number
48.        myFactors.splice(0, studlgth); //clear out array
49.    //loop until 3 numbers have been correctly factored
50.            while (score < 3)
51.            {
52.                   document.getElementById("factor_num").innerHTML = yourNum;
53.                   factor = prompt("enter a factor of " + yourNum);
54.    //check to see if student response is a real factor
55.                   test = yourNum/factor;
56.                   if (test != parseInt(yourNum / factor))
57.                   {
58.                         notAfactor.push(factor);
59.                         document.getElementById("result_1").innerHTML ↵
                                   = (factor + " is not a factor of " ↵
                                   + yourNum + ". Your incorrect entries↵
                                   so far are " + notAfactor.toString());
60.                         total++;
61.                         alert("total incorrect responses: " + total);
62.                   }
63.                   if (test == parseInt(yourNum / factor))
64.                   {
65.                         myFactors.push(factor);
                           document.getElementById("user_factors"). ↵
                                   innerHTML= myFactors.toString();
66.                   }
67.    //check if number has been completely factored
68.                   complgth = allFactors.length;
69.                   studlgth = myFactors.length;
70.                   if(complgth == studlgth)
71.                   {
72.                         score++;
73.                         alert("score =" + score);
74.                         document.getElementById("result_1").innerHTML ↵
                                   = ("All factors of " + yourNum + ↵
                                   " have been identified");
75.    //check if ready for next level or too many errors
76.                         if (score < 3)
77.                         {
```

```
78.                        choice = prompt("Ready for another number?↵
                              Type y for yes, n for no:");
79.                     }
80.                  break;
81.               }
82.               if (total == 5)
83.               {
84.                  document.getElementById("result_1").innerHTML ↵
                           = ("You have had too many errors.");
85.                  break;
86.               }
87.         }
88.   //if ready for next level
89.            if (score == 3)
90.            {
91.               document.getElementById("done").innerHTML = ↵
                        ("Congratulations! You can move to ↵
                         the next level.");
92.            choice = "n";
93.            intermediate();
94.         }
95.      }
96.      function intermediate()
97.      {
98.         alert("nothing here so far");
99.      }
100.   }
101.   </script>
102.   </head>
103.   <body>
104.   <div id="container">
105.      <img src="images/owl_reading.JPG" class="floatleft" />
106.      <h1><em>Carla's Classroom</em></h1>
107.      <div align="left"><blockquote>
108.         <a href="index.html"><img src="images/owl_button.jpg" />Home</a>
109.         <a href="carla.html"><img src="images/carla_button.jpg"↵
                         />Meet Carla </a>
110.         <a href="reading.html"><img src="images/read_button.jpg"↵
                         />Reading</a>
111.         <a href="writing.html"><img src="images/write_button.jpg"↵
                         />Writing</a>
112.         <a href="math.html"><img src="images/arith_button.jpg"↵
                         />Arithmetic</a><br />
113.      </blockquote></div>
114.      <div id="content">
115.         <p>This test will increase in difficulty as you prove you↵
                         are ready for harder problems. As↵
                         soon as you get 3 problems correct↵
                         in Level One, you will progress↵
                         to the next level.</p>
116.         <p>When you begin Level One, you will be given a number ↵
                         between 1 and 20. You will be ↵
                         prompted for all the factors of ↵
```

```
                                        that number. When you find all the ↵
                                        factors, you will be given a new ↵
                                        number. If you make 5 incorrect ↵
                                        entries, you will be given a new ↵
                                        number. </p>
117.            <p><input type = "button" onclick = "factorIt()" ↵
                                        value = "begin the test" />
118.            <div id = "done"> </div></p>
119.            <p>Number to factor: <div id = "factor_num">  </div></p>
120.            <p>Your factors so far: <div id = "user_factors">   </div></p>
121.            <p>Instant feedback: <div id = "result_1"> </div></p>
122.            <p>Next level:<br /><div id = "result_2"> </div></p>
123.        </div>
124.    </div>
125.        <div id="footer">
126.            <h3>*Carla's Motto: Never miss a chance to teach -- and ↵
                                        to learn!</h3>
127.        </div>
128.    </div>
129.    </body></html>
```

If this code is entered and run, after clicking the begin the test button, the display should look like this:

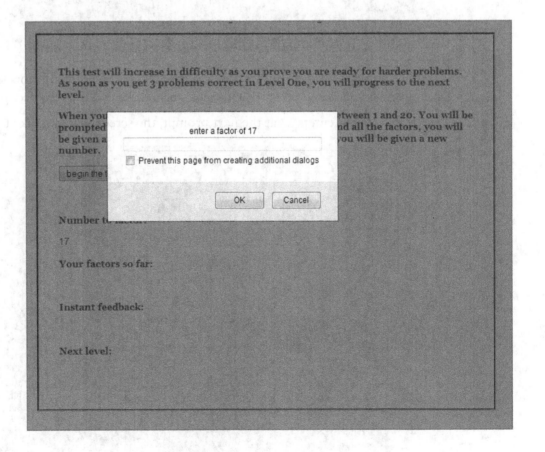

The number to factor is 17. If the student enters 1, 3, and 6, the display will look like this:

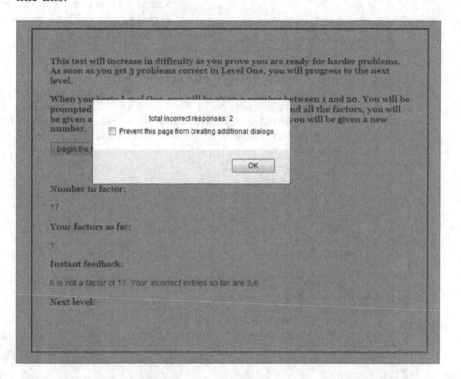

The display shows the number to be factored (17), the correct factors so far (1) and the incorrect factors so far (3 and 6) as well as a total of the incorrect responses so far.

If the student enters 17 at the next prompt, the screen will look like this:

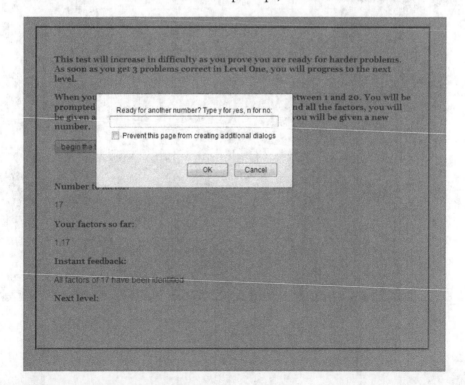

Now the instant feedback tells the student that all factors have been identified and lists those factors. Since the student so far has not completed three factorizations, he is prompted to try another number.

If, at the next number to be factored, the student enters three correct and five incorrect responses, the screen will look like this:

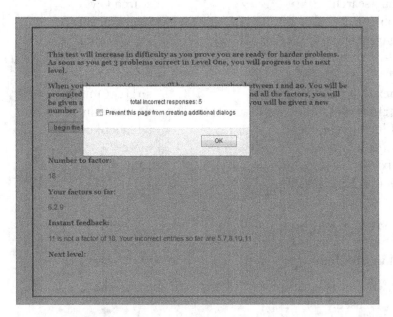

And finally, if the student correctly factors three numbers, the screen will look like this:

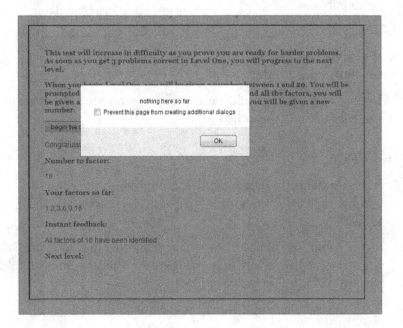

Note that a congratulatory message should appear. The alert is temporary and will be replaced by the second level, when it is written. You will have an opportunity to do that in the Carla's Classroom Case Study at the end of the chapter.

Chapter Review and Exercises

Key Terms

algorithms	routines
binary search	search key
bubble sort	selection sort
clearInterval() method	serial search
end-of-array marker	setInterval() method
flag	sort() method
indexOf() method	splice() method
lastIndexOf() method	swap routine
passing by reference	table lookup
passing by value	target
radix	toString() method
reverse() method	

Review Exercises

Fill in the Blank

1. To reverse the order of elements in an array, the _____ method can be used.

2. To interchange the values of two elements in an array or two variables, you must use a _____ variable to hold the value of one element or variable temporarily.

3. The sort() method sorts an array based on the _____ values of the elements.

4. If a bubble sort is used to sort an array in ascending order, the _____ (largest/smallest) value is in the last place after the first pass.

5. In the _____ search, elements in an array are compared, one by one, to the value that is being searched for.

True or False

6. T/F   At the end of the first pass through the outer loop of a bubble sort that is sorting numbers from highest to lowest, the first number in the array will be the lowest.

7. T/F   At the end of the first pass through the outer loop of a selection sort that is sorting numbers from highest to lowest, the first number in the array will be the lowest.

8. T/F   A selection sort can only be used with numeric data.

9. T/F   Because the sort() method uses ASCII values to sort an array, it can only sort strings in alphabetical order from A to Z.

10. T/F   A Boolean variable is often used as a flag to indicate whether a sort routine has finished sorting the values.

11. T/F   The selection sort is more efficient than the bubble sort.

12. T/F   One problem with the serial search is that it cannot be used with parallel arrays.

13. T/F   The binary search is more efficient than the serial search but requires that the array to be searched must be in alphabetical or numerical order.

14. T/F   The reason the binary search is slow is because it must compare the search key to every element in the array.

15. T/F   When the index value of an element being searched for is identified in a binary search, this index value can be used to identify corresponding data in parallel arrays.

Short Answer

16. Write code using the sort() method to sort the following numbers in descending order:

    53, 82, 93, 75, 86, 97

17. Write code to allow a user to enter the names of five students into an array named students(). Use the reverse() method to display the names in reverse order.

18. Which type of search would be best to use to find the name of student at a large university with a population of 60,000 students if all student names are stored in an array? Justify your answer.

Use the following code for Review Exercises 19 and 20:

Assume there is an array named **customers()** which consists of 150 names and an array called **purchases()** which is a parallel array holding the amount that each customer has spent in this business over the past year. The code sorts the arrays by smallest purchase amount to largest.

```
var littlest = 0; var index = 0; var k = 0; var j = 0;
var count = 0; var temp = 0;
count = purchases.length;
for (k = 0; k < (count - 1); k++)
{
     littlest = purchases[k];
     index = k;
     for (j = (k + 1); j <= (count - 1); j++)
     {
          if(purchases[j] < littlest)
          {
               littlest = purchases[j];
               index = j;
          }
     }
     if (k != index)
     {
          temp = purchases[k];
```

```
            purchases[k] = purchases[index];
            purchases[index] = temp;
        }
    }
```

19. What do the following variables represent?
    a) `littlest`
    b) `index`
    c) `count`

20. Rewrite the swap routine so the parallel **customers()** array will match the **purchases()** array after the sort is complete.

Use the following code for Review Exercises 21–23:

The following code is for a binary search of an array named **names()** which holds 100 names.

```
1.   var low = 0; var N = 100; var high = N;
2.   var index = ???? (middle of the array)
3.   var found = 0; var key = "Joe";
4.   while (found == 0 && low <= high)
5.   {
6.      if(key == names[index])
7.           found = 1;
8.      if(key > names[index])
9.      {
10.          low = ????;
11.          index = ???
12.     }
13.     if(key < names[index])
14.     {
15.          high = ????;
16.          index = ???
17.     }
18. }
```

21. What do the following variables represent?
    a) `low`
    b) `high`
    c) `N`
    d) `index`
    e) `found`

22. Write the expression that creates the appropriate value for **index** on line 2.

23. Fill in the expressions for **low** (line 10), **high** (line 15) and **index** (lines 11 and 16).

24. What are the values of array elements **ages[k]** and **ages[k + 1]** after the following JavaScript code is executed?

```
ages[k] = 12;
ages[k + 1] = 20;
ages[k] = ages[k + 1];
ages[k + 1] = ages[k];
```

25. What are the values of array elements **ages[k]**, **ages[k + 1]**, and the variable **temp** after the following JavaScript code is executed?

```
ages[k] = 12;
ages[k + 1] = 20;
var temp = 15;
temp = ages[k];
ages[k] = ages[k + 1];
ages[k + 1] = temp;
```

26. Use the sort() method to write JavaScript code to sort an array of numbers in ascending order. Recall that, to use this method with numbers in an array, you must include a function to compare numerical values (not ASCII values). The array is as follows:

```
var mynumbers = new Array(16, 8, 5, 25, 13, 7, 9, 3,15, 2);
```

27. Repeat Exercise 26 but sort the numbers in descending order.

Exercises 28–30 refer to the following program that sorts the given array of names in alphabetical order:

```
var names = new Array("Marie", "Jose", "Zack", "Patty", ↵
                      "Ivan", "Tasha");
var N = 5;
for (var k = 0; k <= N; k++)
{
  var min = names[k];
  var index = k;
  for (var j = (k + 1); j < N; j++)
  {
      if (names[j] < min)
      {
          min = names[j];
          index = j;
      }
  }
      if (k != index)
      {
          var temp = names[k];
          names[k] = names[index];
          names[index] = temp;
      }
}
```

28. How many passes are made through the outer for loop?

29. After the first pass through the outer loop, what name is stored in names[0]?

30. After the first pass through the inner for loop, what is the value of **index**?

Programming Challenges

On Your Own

VideoNote
Sorting and Searching
Arrays
On_Your_Own_1_Lottery

1. Create a web page that simulates a lottery. The JavaScript program will create an array of six numbers between 1 and 40 (inclusive). The numbers will be generated randomly. Be sure to check that the array does not contain duplicates. Sort

the array in ascending order. Next, have the user enter the six numbers from an imaginary lottery ticket the user purchased. Sort, if necessary. Check to see how much, if anything, the user has won, using the following table of possible winnings:

Number of Matches	Amount of Winnings
3	$ 5.00
4	$ 50.00
5	$ 100.00
6	$ 100,000.00

The page should display the winning number, the user's number, the number of matches (if any) and the winnings (if any). Save the page with the filename lottery.html. Submit your work as instructed by your teacher.

2. Create a web page that allows a small business owner to enter employee names and salaries in parallel arrays named **employees** and **salaries**. The program will sort the names alphabetically and display the sorted information on the web page. Be sure both arrays are sorted together so each employee receives his/her correct salary! Save your page with the filename employees2.html. Submit your work as instructed by your teacher.

3. Add options to the page created in Programming Challenge 2 to allow the business owner to select how the information will be displayed. The following options should be allowed:
   - select information sorted by employees in alphabetical order
   - select information sorted by salary from highest to lowest
   - select information sorted by salary from lowest to highest
   Save your page with the filename employees3.html. Submit your work as instructed by your teacher.

4. Add to the page you created for Programming Challenge 3. Include parallel arrays called **rate** and **hours** to store each employee's hourly pay rate and the number of hours worked in a given week. Then calculate the salary (**salaries[k] = rate[k] * hours[k]**) and store the result in the corresponding **salaries** array. The web page should display a table with columns for the following information:

Employee name	Hourly rate	Hours worked	Salary
Amanda Jones	10.00	34	$340.00
.	.	.	.
.	.	.	.
.	.	.	.
Bobby Williams	8.50	10	$85.00

Save your page with the filename employees4.html. Submit your work as instructed by your teacher.

5. Create a web page that displays a simulation of rolling two dice. The JavaScript code should use Math.random() to roll the first die (a random number between 1 and 6, inclusive) and the second die (also 1 - 6). Then add the two values. The sums will be between 2 and 12 and there are 11 possible sums. Your program should simulate 10,000 rolls of two dice and sum each roll. Then you will display how often each sum was obtained and check to see if that number is reasonable. The following chart shows the 36 possible outcomes from rolling two dice and summing the two values. Notice that some sums can be obtained by more combinations than others. A second chart shows the probabilities of each sum appearing. Since there are six ways to get a sum of 7 and only one way to get a sum of 2, it is reasonable to assume that there is a much greater possibility of getting a 7. After your program simulates the 10,000 rolls, check your results to see if they agree with the chart shown below. Use an array to keep a tally of how many times each sum appears.

			Die I				Sum and Probability of Rolling That Sum	
	1	2	3	4	5	6	2 = 1/36 = 2.8%	8 = 5/36 = 13.9%
1	2	3	4	5	6	7	3 = 2/36 = 5.6%	9 = 4/36 = 11.1%
2	3	4	5	6	7	8	4 = 3/36 = 8.3%	10 = 3/36 = 8.3%
3	4	5	6	7	8	9	5 = 4/36 = 11.1%	11 = 2/36 = 5.6%
4	5	6	7	8	9	10	6 = 5/36 = 13.9%	12 = 1/36 = 2.8%
5	6	7	8	9	10	11	7 = 6/36 = 16.7%	
6	7	8	9	10	11	12		

(Die 2 labels the leftmost column: 1, 2, 3, 4, 5, 6)

Save the page with the filename dice.html. Submit your work as instructed by your teacher.

6. Create a web page for a real estate agent. The agent should be able to enter the prices of a number of homes in her area which will be stored in an array named **homes**. Then determine the median price of those homes. The median of a list of N numbers is as follows:

- The middle number of the sorted list if N is odd.
- The average of the two middle numbers if N is even.

Save the web page with the filename homes.html. Submit your work as instructed by your teacher.

7. Create a web page that compares the efficiency of two search algorithms: the serial search and the binary search. Create an array of at least 50 elements. One of the arrays in the gregBoggle.js file has 42 elements (it is Case 4) which you can use, adding just a few elements or you can create your own array. The gregBoggle.js file is in the Student Data Files. You can copy just the array to your new page. Your program should call a function that searches for a value, input by the user, using a

serial search. Keep track of how many comparisons are made to locate the item or return the result that the item is not found. Display this information. Then call a function to search for the same value using a binary search and keep track of the number of comparisons made. Be sure to sort the array before doing the binary search. Display that information. Try this out with several values, including items that are in the beginning of the array, toward the end of the array, and not in the array at all. Think about your results. Then, on your web page, comment on what you have seen. Save the web page with the filename `compare.html`. Submit your work as instructed by your teacher.

Case Studies

Greg's Gambits

Add some features to the `Greg's Boggle` game we created in the Putting It to Work section of this chapter. You can do one, all, or as many of these features as you want, depending on your initiative, creativity, or your instructor's requirements:

- Add a timer to each round of play. You can preset the timer to a specific time limit for each word or you can have the player set it.
- Allow for two players and compare the scores of each at the end of each round of play.
- Add more words to the game using the same method as in the chapter.
- Use an online dictionary to get words. You will have to use words that have a specific range of letters and scramble the letters. Then you can use the dictionary to check if words entered by the user are valid words.

Save your page as `greg_boggle2.html`. Be sure to give it an appropriate page title. Open the `index.html` page for `Greg's Gambits` and add a link, under the `Play A Game` link, that links to this page named `Greg's Advanced Boggle`. Submit your work as instructed by your teacher.

Carla's Classroom

Select one of the following (or both if you are motivated or if assigned) exercises:

1. Add two levels to the factoring lesson that we created in the Putting It to Work section. Level Two should have students factor numbers between 101 and 1000. Level Three should ask give students a number between 1 and 1000 and, for that number, find all prime factors. Note: a prime number is a number that only has two factors: itself and 1. Save your page as `carla_factoring2.html`. Open the `math.html` page for `Carla's Classroom` and add a link to this page named `Carla's Classroom | Advanced Factoring`. Submit your work as instructed by your teacher.

2. Create a page that allows Carla to put her students into three groups, based on some test scores. Carla wants to name the groups `Blues`, `Reds`, and `Greens` to avoid emphasizing any "higher" or "lower" stigmas. The page will be linked from Carla's home page. It should do the following:
   - Allow Carla to enter the names of the students alphabetically and store the names in an array called **students**.

- Allow Carla to enter the test scores of the students in a parallel array named **scores**. For this project, restrict the entries to integers.
- The **scores** array should be sorted, keeping the parallel array **students** sorted to correspond to **scores**. Sort from lowest to highest test score.
- Then divide the results into three groups. To do this, you need to find the range of test scores. This is simply the lowest score subtracted from the highest.
- Next, divide the range by 3. If the result is not an integer, round to the nearest integer. Name the variable that holds this value **result**.
- The first group—the Blues—will consist of students who scored from the lowest score up to the lowest plus the number identified in the previous step (which we called **result**).
- The second group—the Reds—will consist of students who scored one point above the highest Blue up to that number plus the value of **result**.
- The third group—the Greens—will consist of students who scored one point above the highest Red up to the highest scoring student.
- The web page should display the three groups with only the names of the students in each group. Don't display the test scores.

Save your page as carla_groups.html. Test your page in a browser. Open the index.html page for Carla's Classroom and add a link, under the Meet Carla link, that links to this page named Carla's Classroom | Carla's Groups. Submit your work as instructed by your teacher.

Lee's Landscape

Lee keeps records of his customers in parallel arrays. Many customers contract him for lawn service, tree trimming, pest control, and so on. He invoices his customers monthly. Lee wants to be able to access a "customer overview." In some situations, he may want an alphabetical list of customers along with the information in the other arrays. Or he may want to see an accounts receivable report. Or he may want to see which customer accounts are past due and by how much.

While Lee keeps other information about each client, for this project we will focus on four arrays only: one that holds the customers' names, one that holds the recurring charges for each customer, and one that holds past due amounts. This information is provided for you in a file called leeCustomers.js and is included in the Student Data Files. Use this file to create a page that allows Lee to sort the arrays by any of the following:

- by customer name, in alphabetical order (by last name)
- by amount of recurring monthly charges allowing Lee to select ascending or descending
- by past due amounts allowing Lee to select ascending or descending
- by number of days past due allowing Lee to select ascending or descending

The results of any sort should be displayed in tabular form (i.e., in columns).

Be sure to give this web page an appropriate page title such as Lee's Landscape || Customer Records. Save this file with the filename lee_billing.html. Add a link to the Lee's Landscape home page to this new page. Submit your work as instructed by your teacher.

Jackie's Jewelry

Jackie records her inventory in parallel arrays. Sometimes she wants to view the inventory and sometimes she needs to add or delete items from the inventory. For this project, we will focus on three arrays: one that holds the names assigned to each jewelry item, one that holds the price charged for each item, and one that contains the number of each item presently in inventory. This information is provided in a file called jackieInventory.js and is included in the Student Data Files. Use this file to create a page that allows Jackie to sort the arrays by any of the following:

- By type: Jackie sells five types of jewelry. She gives each item a name that identifies its appearance and appends an identifier to the end of the name. Rings are identified with an R, bracelets with a B, necklaces with an N, earrings with an E, and ankle bracelets with an A. For example, a silver ring has the name "silver_R" and a silver bracelet is named "silver_B".
- By selling price: This allows Jackie to sort by price in either ascending or descending order.
- By inventory item number: This allows Jackie to sort by quantity on hand in either ascending or descending order.

The results of any sort should be displayed in tabular form (i.e., in columns).

Give this web page an appropriate page title such as Jackie's Jewelry || Inventory. Save this file with the filename jackie_inventory.html. Add a link to the Jackie's Jewelry home page to this new page. Submit your work as instructed by your teacher.

The Document Object Model and XML

Chapter Objectives

We have learned that a web page is actually an object—the document object—which contains other objects. When your browser opens a web page, it actually creates these objects from instructions the web developer has given within the <html></html> tags. The document object is the top level object. Objects that can be contained within the document object are specified in the Document Object Model (DOM). The DOM is organized in a hierarchy of objects. We have been using JavaScript to access, create, and modify these objects throughout this text. Now we will dig deeper into how the DOM works using nodes and hierarchy trees. Then we can create new tags that represent new objects (also called elements or nodes) using an extension of the way HTML works. This is called XML (Extensible Markup Language). By understanding how the model works and how to use XML, we can create customized websites and, eventually, communicate between web pages and databases that reside on a server. By combining these new concepts with our JavaScript skills we can make new pages ever more dynamic and interactive.

After reading this chapter, you will be able to do the following:

- Identify DOM nodes and trees
- Create, add, replace, insert, and remove nodes from a web page
- Use DOM methods to edit a page dynamically with JavaScript
- Use DOM methods to change styles dynamically
- Create an XML (.xml) file
- Understand how to use the parent-child model to create XML elements

- Understand how the XML parser works
- Create and use a DTD and use external DTDs with DOCTYPEs
- Use XSL documents to transform XML documents to HTML pages
- Understand how to use namespaces
- Understand how to create schemas

10.1 The Document Object Model: DOM

The **Document Object Model (DOM)** interface allows programs and scripts to access and modify the content, style, and structure of a document. It is platform-neutral which means it can be used on any computer. It is language-neutral which means it can exchange information between a client and a server, regardless of what language either side is using.

The DOM is an **application programming interface** (an **API**) which defines the logical structure of a document and how the document is accessed and manipulated. The DOM is used for both HTML (and HTML5) and XML documents. Anything found in an HTML or XML document can be accessed, changed, deleted, or added using the DOM, with a few exceptions.

A Brief History of DOM

When JavaScript was first released in 1996 the ability to detect user-generated events was quite limited. These abilities were known as Legacy DOM and allowed for form validation and several other minor capabilities. An updated version, known as Intermediate DOM, was developed in the late 1990s to allow more changes to be made in real time by a user. Unfortunately, many of these capabilities were browser-specific and required separate handling for different browsers. While many browser-specific issues have been addressed since then, browser variance continues to be a problem for web developers.

After the advent of Intermediate DOM, the **World Wide Web Consortium (W3C)** began to work on a standardized DOM. The first DOM standard, known as DOM Level 1, was recommended by W3C in 1998. It provided a complete model to allow changes to any portion of an HTML or XML document.

DOM Level 2 was published at the end of 2000 and included many important additions, without which we would not have been able to do most of the things we have done so far in this text. DOM Level 2 introduced the getElementById() method, included an event model, and support for XML namespaces. In 2004, the current version of DOM—DOM Level 3—was published. Added support for many tasks is included in this version. By 2005, most popular browsers, such as Internet Explorer, Opera, Safari, and Firefox, supported DOM level 3. Chrome, which was not released to the public until 2008, also supports DOM Level 3.

The W3C objective is to provide a standard programming interface through the DOM which can be used in a many different environments and with many different applications.

DOM Nodes and Trees

The DOM sees an HTML (or XML) document as a **tree** or as a group of trees. We don't mean the document can be compared to an elm or an oak tree but its structure, with a top level and branches that form sublevels that have branches and more sublevels is similar. The top level is the document. The document's **root element** is the <html> element. In this case, root does not refer to the underground portion of the tree but rather refers to the primary source. A document that uses the DOM is structured logically where elements are considered nodes. It is possible to see these nodes by using the browser. Most browsers allow you to inspect your document but, since each browser accesses this capability differently, you should use the browser's Help feature to find out how to do this in your browser. Example 10.1 shows a short HTML page and the **tree-node structure** as portrayed when inspected in Firebug through the Firefox browser.

EXAMPLE 10.1

The Node-Tree Structure of a Simple HTML Page

```
<html>
<head>
1.   <title>Example 10.1</title>
2.   <link href="carla.css" rel="stylesheet" type="text/css" />
3.   <script>
4.   function doSomething()
5.   {
6.       var x = 0; var y = 0; var sum = 0;
7.       x = parseFloat(document.getElementById("one_num").innerHTML);
8.       y = parseFloat(document.getElementById("two_num").innerHTML);
9.       sum = x + y;
10.      document.getElementById("result").innerHTML = sum;
11.  }
12.  </script>
13.  </head>
14.  <body>
15.  <div id="container">
16.      <h3>Add the two numbers shown.</h3>
17.      <p><input type="button" value = "add it" onclick = ↵
                               "doSomething();" /></p>
18.      <p><div id = "one_num">81.45</div><br /></p>
19.      <p><div id = "two_num">63.92</div><br /></p>
20.      <p>Sum is:<div id = "result"> </div></p>
21.  </div>
22.  </body>
23.  </html>
```

When run, this page looks like the one shown below in (a) and, after clicking the button, it looks like the one shown in (b).

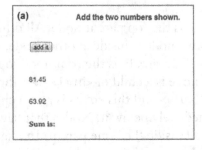

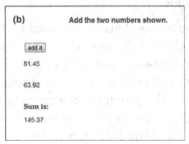

When this document is inspected, the DOM node-tree shown is as follows:

```
 ⚒ ⛏ ‹ › ☰ ▾   Console   HTML ▾   CSS   Script   DOM   Net   Cookies
 ⧉  Edit | body ‹ html
⊟ <html>
   ⊟ <head>
        <title>Example 10.1</title>
      ⊞ <link type="text/css" rel="stylesheet" href="carla.css">
      ⊞ <script>
     </head>
   ⊟ <body>
      ⊟ <div id="container">
           <h3>Add the two numbers shown.</h3>
         ⊟ <p>
              <input type="button" onclick="doSomething();" value="add it">
           </p>
           <p></p>
           <div id="one_num">81.45</div>
           <br>
           <p></p>
           <p></p>
           <div id="two_num">63.92</div>
           <br>
           <p></p>
           <p>Sum is:</p>
           <div id="result">145.37</div>
           <p></p>
        </div>
     </body>
  </html>
```

Each element that has a small rectangle with either a plus (+) or minus (-) sign next to it represents a node. In this document, the top-level node is <html>. The next node is the <head> section which has three sublevels: <title>, <link>, and <script>. The <body> node is the same level as the <head> node. There is only one sublevel under the <body> node; this is the "container" <div>. This node has its own subnodes, including an <h3> node and several <p> and <div> nodes. We will now discuss what this means in more detail.

The Family: The Parent-Child Model

When you first learned to write HTML script, you learned a little about the parent-child model. There are some tags that cannot be nested within other tags because the DOM identifies some nodes as **parent nodes** and others as **child nodes**. A child node can be nested inside a parent node but not the other way around.

The top level node—the root node—is the top parent node. All other nodes are children of the root. However, when a node is inside another node, the outer node also becomes a parent. In Example 10.1, <html> is the root node so it is the parent of all others. Thus, the <body> node is a child of <html>. But the <body> node is also the parent of the container <div> and this <div> is also a child of <body> and a parent of the <h3> node immediately below it. Nodes that have the same level are considered **siblings** if they are all inside the same parent. In Example 10.1 the <head> and <body> nodes are siblings because they are both children of the root and have the same level. Example 10.2 is a simple HTML page that might make the parent-child model a little clearer:

EXAMPLE 10.2

Parents, Children, and Siblings

```
1.   <html> <!-- the root element -->
2.   <head> <!-- child of <html> and parent to <title> -->
3.       <title>Example 10.2</title> <!-child of <head> -->
4.   </head>
5.   <body> <!-- child of <html>, sibling of <head>, and a parent -->
6.       <h2>Hello!</h2> <!-- child of <body>, sibling of <p> and <ul> -->
7.       <p>hello</p> <!-- child of <body>, sibling of <h2> and <ul> -->
8.       <ul> <!-- child of <body>, sibling of <p> and <h2>, parent -->
9.           <li>item 1</li><!-- child of <ul>, sibling of other <li>s -->
10.          <li>item 2</li><!-- child of <ul>, sibling of other <li>s -->
11.          <li>item 3</li><!-- child of <ul>, sibling of other <li>s -->
12.      </ul>
13.  </body>
14.  </html>
```

You can think of the DOM as an internal map of the web page where not all roads are possible. Some nodes cannot be nested within other nodes. For example, if you put your <body> tag after other HTML script, your page will not display as you want. The DOM allows you to access a document's elements when you write programs, as we have been doing with JavaScript. In this section, we will learn to manipulate nodes dynamically—in other words, we will learn to create, insert, add, or remove nodes as the user interacts with a web page.

Table 10.1 lists DOM properties and methods. Table 10.2 shows methods that can be used with HTML elements as well as with node objects. We are familiar with some and others are new. All will be valuable as we continue to develop complex websites.

TABLE 10.1 Some DOM Node Object Properties and Methods

Property	Description
childNodes	returns a list of the child nodes for a node
firstChild	returns the first child of a node
lastChild	returns the last child of a node
nextSibling	returns the next node at the same level as this node
nodeName	returns the name of a node, depending on its type
nodeType	returns the type of a node
nodeValue	sets or returns the value of a node
ownerDocument	returns the root element for a node
parentNode	returns the parent of a node
previousSibling	returns the previous node at the same level as this node
textContent	sets or returns the textual content of a node and its children

TABLE 10.2	**Some Node Object Methods That Can Be Used with Element Objects**
Method	**Description**
appendChild()	adds a new child node to the one specified, as the last child
cloneNode()	creates a clone of a node
compareDocumentPosition()	compares the position in the document of two nodes
createElement()	creates an element of the type specified
hasAttributes()	returns true if node has any attributes, else returns false
hasChildNodes()	returns true if the node has child nodes, else returns false
insertBefore()	inserts a new child node before an existing (specified) node
isEqualNode()	checks if two nodes are equal
isSameNode()	checks if two nodes are the same node
isSupported()	returns true if specified feature is supported, else returns false
lookupNamespaceURI()	returns the namespace URI that matches a specified prefix
lookupPrefix()	returns the prefix that matches a specified namespace URI
normalize()	joins text nodes that are adjacent and removes empty text nodes
removeChild()	removes a child node
replaceChild()	replaces a child node

Creating and Inserting Elements

We will begin manipulating nodes by using a web page that has a simple list. We will then create an element to add to the list and, finally, insert a new element into the list. Example 10.3 shows how this is done.

The createTextNode() Method

The **createTextNode() method** will insert a string of text into a text node. We use this to insert the text into a node that is created by one of the other methods which appends or inserts nodes. The syntax for the createTextNode() method is as follows:

```
var theText = document.createTextNode("text goes here");
```

Now, for example, if we want to insert a paragraph node which has the content "This is a new paragraph", we first create the paragraph element and store it

in a variable. Then we create a text node with the paragraph text. We also identify
the id of this paragraph node with the **setAttribute() method** and then use the
appendChild() method to add it to the page. The syntax is as follows:

```
var newElement = document.createElement("p");
var elementId = "new_text";
newElement.setAttribute("id", elementId);
var theText = "This is a new paragraph";
newElement.appendChild(document.createTextNode(theText));
```

Example 10.3 creates a new node to be inserted into a list and demonstrates
the use of the appendChild() method, the createTextNode() method, and
the createElement() method. We start with a list that has two list items. The
JavaScript code creates a new node and inserts it into the list.

EXAMPLE 10.3

Creating and Inserting Nodes

```
1.   <html>
2.   <head>
3.   <title>Example 10.3</title>
4.   <link href="carla.css" rel="stylesheet" type="text/css" />
5.   <script>
6.   function insertNode()
7.   {
8.      var newItem = document.createElement("LI");
9.      var nodeText = document.createTextNode("Labrador Retrievers");
10.     newItem.appendChild(nodeText);
11.     var list = document.getElementById("puppies");
12.     list.insertBefore(newItem,list.childNodes[0]);
13.  }
14.  </script>
15.  </head>
16.  <body>
17.  <div id="container">
18.     <h3>Love those puppies!</h3>
19.     <p id="demo">Click the button to insert a puppy into the list</p>
20.     <button onclick="insertNode()">Try it!</button>
21.     <ul id="puppies">
22.         <li>Poodles</li>
23.         <li>Jack Russell Terriers</li>
24.     </ul>
25.  </div>
26.  </body>
27.  </html>
```

Initially, the page looks like this:

Love those puppies!

Click the button to insert a puppy into the list

[Try it!]

- Poodles
- Jack Russell Terriers

The HTML <body> is familiar. When the button is clicked, the function insertNode() is executed. Line 8 creates a new variable, **newItem**, that uses the **createElement() method**. In this case, the element we wish to create a list item. List items are identified as "LI" (note the uppercase). We then create a text node on line 9 which uses the createTextNode() method and stores the result in a variable named **nodeText**. Line 10 appends the value of **nodeText** (now a child node) to **newItem** which is a new list element. Line 11 sets a variable, **list**, equal to the value of the element with id = "puppies". In this case, it is the <ul> element. Finally, line 12 uses dot notation and the **insertBefore() method** to insert our new value of "Labrador Retrievers" into the list as the first item. The **list** variable identifies the list as the place to insert something. The insertBefore() method takes two arguments: what to insert (**newItem**) and where to insert it. In this case, we want our new item to be inserted into the list in the first place—i.e., in childNodes[0].

After clicking the button, the page will look like this:

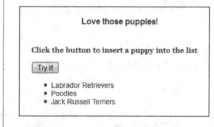

Love those puppies!

Click the button to insert a puppy into the list

Try it!

- Labrador Retrievers
- Poodles
- Jack Russell Terriers

Replacing and Removing Elements

The replaceChild() method replaces one child node with another. The removeChild() method removes a child node.

The removeChild() Method

The **removeChild() method** requires that the parent node is specified. The name of the node to be removed is the required parameter of this method. The syntax is as follows:

```
elementNode.removeChild(node_to_remove)
```

The method will either return the removed node or, if it is not possible, it will return NULL.

The replaceChild() Method

The **replaceChild() method** will replace one child node with another so it has two required parameters—the new node and the node to be replaced. The syntax is as follows:

```
elementNode.replaceChild(new_node, node_to_be_replaced)
```

The method will either return the replaced node or, if it is not possible, it will return NULL.

Example 10.4 demonstrates the use of both of these methods.

The **childNodes property** returns a **NodeList** which contains the child nodes of a selected node. If the node selected does not have any child nodes, the NodeList contains no values. The syntax to use this property is as follows:

```
elementNode.childNodes[]
```

The brackets contain the index value of the node you wish to identify. In Example 10.4, the node we wish to replace or remove has no child nodes so we put 0 in the brackets. In this example, we start two lists. The first list has three types of vehicles and we replace the first vehicle with another. The second list shows a list of four colors and we remove one.

EXAMPLE 10.4

Removing and Replacing Nodes

```
1.   <html>
2.   <head>
3.   <title>Example 10.4</title>
4.   <link href="carla.css" rel="stylesheet" type="text/css" />
5.   <script>
6.   function replaceIt()
7.   {
8.        var newCar = document.createTextNode("red sports car");
9.        var oldCar = document.getElementById("sedan");
10.       oldCar.replaceChild(newCar,oldCar.childNodes[0]);
11.  }
12.  function removeIt()
13.  {
14.       var oldColor = document.getElementById("purple");
15.       oldColor.removeChild(oldColor.childNodes[0]);
16.  }
17.  </script>
18.  </head>
19.  <body>
20.  <div id="container">
21.       <h3>Remove and Replace</h3>
22.       <hr />
23.       <p id="replace">Click the button to replace the sedan with ⏎
                         another car</p>
24.       <button onclick="replaceIt()">Try it!</button>
25.       <p id = "sedan">4-door Sedan</p>
26.       <p id = "truck">Truck</p>
27.       <p id = "cycle">Motorcycle</p>
28.       <hr />
29.       <p id="remove">Click the button to remove the third color ⏎
                        from the list</p>
30.       <button onclick="removeIt()">Try it!</button>
31.       <p id="red">red</p>
32.       <p id = "blue">blue</p>
33.       <p id = "purple">purple</p>
34.       <p id = "orange">orange</p>
35.       <p id = "green">green</p>
```

```
36.        <p id = "brown">brown</p>
37.        <hr />
38.    </div>
39.    </body>
40.    </html>
```

The HTML <body> is familiar. When the first button is clicked, the function replaceIt() is executed. Line 8 creates a new variable, **newCar**, that uses the createTextNode() method to define the new content for the node we are replacing. The variable **oldCar** gets the node we are replacing, using the getElementById() method (line 9). Then, on line 10, the replacement is made. The replaceChild() method replaces the first node of the list of child nodes using the childNodes property.

The page initially looks like this:

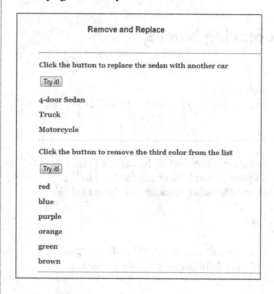

After clicking both buttons, the 4-door sedan is replaced by a red sports car and the color purple has been removed from the list of colors:

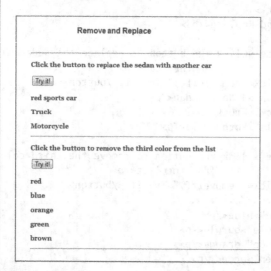

We already know enough JavaScript to be able to do all these things with just JavaScript code so you may be wondering why we are adding the DOM methods and properties. The uses for these new skills will become apparent as we learn more about DOM and add XML to our pages.

CHECKPOINT FOR SECTION 10.1 ✔

10.1 What is the root element of an HTML document object?

10.2 Given the following HTML script, identify the root, parent, child, and sibling nodes:

```
<html>
    <head>
        <title>Checkpoint 10.2</title>
    </head>
    <body>
        <div id = "chk">
            <h1>Checkpoint 10.2</h1>
            <p id = "1">This is a web page</p>
            <p id = "2">There is nothing on this page yet</p>
        </div>
    </body>
</html>
```

10.3 Is getElementById() a property or a method?

10.4 To add content to a node you are creating, you use the _____ method.

For Checkpoints 10.5 and 10.6, use the following:

```
<html>
    <head>
        <title>Checkpoints 10.5 and 10.6</title>
    <script>
        function replaceIt()
        {
            var newStuff = document.createTextNode("new stuff added!");
            var oldStuff = document.getElementById("node_stuff");
            add your code here for Checkpoint 10.5
        }
        function removeIt()
        {
            var oldStuff = document.getElementById("node_stuff");
            add your code here for Checkpoint 10.6
        }
    </script>
    </head>
    <body>
        <div id="container">
            <h3>Remove and Replace</h3>
            <p id="replace">Click the button to remove or replace</p>
            <button onclick="replaceIt()">Replace it!</button>
            <button onclick="removeIt()">Remove it!</button>
            <p id="node_stuff">this is the interesting stuff!</p>
            <p id = "node_2">some other stuff</p>
```

```
                    <p id = "node_3">more other stuff</p>
                </div>
            </body>
        </html>
```

10.5 Write a statement that will replace the node with id = "node_stuff" with the text "new stuff added!".

10.6 Write a statement that will remove the node with id = "node_stuff".

10.2 Using DOM Methods with Timers and Styles

We can use DOM methods and properties to create many more exciting effects on our pages. A timer can be used to create simple animations and styles can be changed dynamically. For example, recall the Boggle game we created in Chapter 9. We can use DOM methods to have an image of a clock ticking away the seconds and growing larger and larger as a time limit is reached. Or, on a business site, we can ask a customer questions and have different options appear, depending on the customer's responses. These and other exciting features can be added to web pages once you understand how to use DOM methods and properties.

The setAttribute()and getAttribute() Methods

The **setAttribute() method** will set the type attribute of an input element. It adds a specific attribute to a value input by a user and gives it the specified value. The syntax for this method is as follows:

```
element.setAttribute(name_of_attribute, value_for_attribute)
```

The **getAttribute() method** will return the value of the attribute you specify. It takes only one argument, the specified attribute. The syntax for this method is as follows:

```
element.getAttribute(name_of_attribute)
```

Example 10.5 demonstrates how to use these methods.

EXAMPLE 10.5

Changing Attributes

```
1.   <html>
2.     <head>
3.        <title>Example 10.5</title>
4.        <link href="carla.css" rel="stylesheet" type="text/css" />
5.     <script>
6.        function buttonIt()
7.        {
8.            document.getElementsByTagName("INPUT")[0].setAttribute ↵
                        ("type", "button");
9.            document.getElementsByTagName("INPUT")[0].setAttribute ↵
                        ("id","who's_a_button?");
10.        }
```

```
11.        function getIt(idName)
12.        {
13.            document.getElementById(idName).innerHTML = ↵
                       document.getElementsByTagName("INPUT")[0]. ↵
                       getAttribute("id");
14.        }
15.    </script>
16.    </head>
17.    <body>
18.        <div id="container">
19.            <h3>Get and Set Attributes</h3>
20.            <hr />
21.            <p id="get_it">See the button's id attribute</p>
22.            <p><button onclick="getIt('old')">Check the button's ↵
                        id</button></p>
23.            <p>Button id attributes <span id = "old"> </span></p>
24.            <hr />
25.            <p id="set_it">Change your input into a button and change ↵
                        the button's id</p>
26.            <p><button onclick="buttonIt()">Make it a button, change ↵
                        its id</button></p>
27.            <p><input id = "a_button" value="type something here"></p>
28.            <hr />
29.            <p id="get_it">See the button's new id</p>
30.            <p><button onclick="getIt('new')">Check button attributes ↵
                        </button></p>
31.            <p>Button's new id attribute: <span id = "new">  ↵
                        </span></p>
32.            <hr />
33.        </div>
34.    </body>
35.    </html>
```

Initially, the page looks like this:

If the top button (that says "Check the button's id") is clicked, the getIt() function will be called, sending in the value of the <span> area where we want the result to be displayed, i.e., the <span> with id = "old". The function getIt(), on lines

11–14, accepts one argument into the parameter **idName**. So, at this point **idName** = "old". Line 13 does the following: it gets the id of the button identified by getElementsByTagName("INPUT")[0] and puts the id of that button into <span id = "old">. At this point the id attribute of our "Make it a button, change its id button" is "a_button". After clicking the top button, the display is as follows:

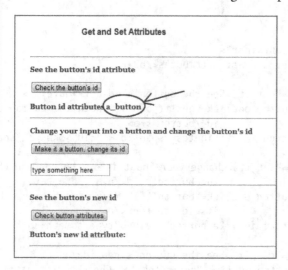

If the user types "Help! Click me!" in the box and clicks the "Make it a button, change its id", the buttonIt() function is called. This function, on lines 6–10, will first set the attribute of the input box to a button (line 8) and then set a new attribute for the id of this button to the text "who's_a_button?". The next display looks like this:

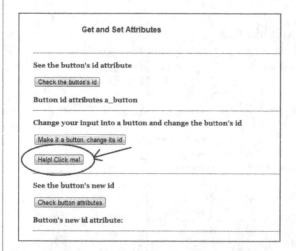

And finally, when the last button, "Check button attributes", is clicked, the new id attribute of the "Make it a button, change its id", are displayed. This happens because the getIt() function is called again, this time sending in a new value of the <span> area where we want the new result to be displayed, i.e., the <span> with id = "new".

The `setInterval()` and `clearInterval()` Methods

Timers can add a lot of interest to our games and can be used for many other interesting effects. The **`setInterval()` method** will begin a timer which will execute until the **`clearInterval()` method** is evoked—either by a condition that is reached or by the user clicking a Stop button. These are methods of the window object and, as such, must be used with the window object.

The `setInterval()` method calls a function or an expression which will be executed at intervals specified by the programmer. It will continue to do this until either the `clearInterval()` method is called or until the window is closed. The intervals between the call `setInterval()` made to the function or JavaScript expression must be given in milliseconds (or thousandths of a second). Thus, to have a function called every two seconds, the time interval should be 2,000. The syntax for the `setInterval()` method is as follows:

```
setInterval(function_or_expression_called, milliseconds)
```

The `clearInterval()` method clears a timer that has been set with the `setInterval()` method. It has one parameter—the identifier used to identify the `setInterval()` method. Its syntax is as follows:

```
clearInterval(id_of_setInterval_method)
```

In order to use a timer, we need to create a variable that will become the identifier for the `setInterval()` method. If this identifier does not have a value—i.e., has a NULL value—the `setInterval()` method will not continue.

We will illustrate the `setInterval()` and `clearInterval()` methods in Example 10.6 with a nonalcoholic rendition of the "99 Bottles of Beer On the Wall" song that many of you may already know.

EXAMPLE
10.6

Using `setInterval()` and `clearInterval()` to Count Bottles of Ginger Ale

This code will count down from 99 bottles of ginger ale on the wall to 1 bottle at 1-second intervals. The button that starts the countdown calls the `timeIt()` function. This function starts the `setInterval()` method which calls the `gingerAle()` function repeatedly at 1-second intervals until the number of bottles of ginger ale has counted down from 99 to 1. Then the `clearInterval()` method stops the countdown and a final message is displayed.

```
1.    <html>
2.      <head>
3.        <title>Example 10.6</title>
4.            <link href="carla.css" rel="stylesheet" type="text/css" />
5.        <script>
6.            var count = 100;
7.            var interval = null;
8.            function gingerAle()
9.            {
10.               count = count - 1;
11.               if( count == 1)
12.               {
13.                   window.clearInterval(interval);
14.                   interval = null;
15.                   document.getElementById("end").innerHTML = ⏎
                              ("That's it, folks!");
16.               }
17.               document.getElementById("bottles").innerHTML = count;
18.            }
19.            function timeIt()
20.            {
21.               interval = window.setInterval("gingerAle()", 1000);
22.            }
23.        </script>
24.      </head>
25.      <body>
26.        <div id="container">
27.            <h3>Ginger Ale Countdown</h3>
28.            <p><button onclick="timeIt()">Start the countdown ⏎
                              </button></p>
29.            <p><span id = "bottles">100</span> bottles of ginger ⏎
                              ale on the wall shelf...</p>
30.            <p><span id = "end"> </span></p>
31.        </div>
32.      </body>
33.    </html>
```

This program demonstrates one of the rare times when we use global variables. Since the variables **count** and **interval** are declared and initialized outside of the two functions, their starting values are available to both functions. We do this because we want these values available at the beginning of both functions and we *do* want changes made locally (inside the functions) to affect what the other function is doing with that same variable. At the beginning we set **interval** to null which means it does not yet have a value.

When the user clicks the button to begin, the timeIt() function is accessed. This function begins on line 19, which is where **interval** is given a value. It sets the interval to 1-second intervals (1,000 milliseconds) and tells the program what to do every second—call the gingerAle() function.

The gingerAle() function decrements the counter and checks to see if the countdown has ended. Since we are counting down from 99 to 1, if **count** is 1, the timer must stop. The check begins with the if statement (line 11). The clearInterval() method is called on line 13 using **interval** as the identifier to identify what setInterval() method is to be stopped. Line 14 sets **interval** back to null and line 15 displays the ending message to the web page. However, if **count** is greater than 1, the new value of **count** is displayed on the web page (line 17).

When this page is first loaded, it looks like this:

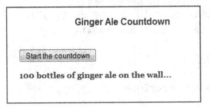

And, after clicking the Start the countdown button and letting 100 seconds pass, the page looks like this:

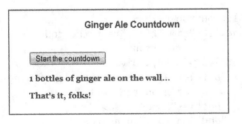

The code for Example 10.6 replaces each line of the display with the next line. Example 10.7 combines the setInterval() and clearInterval() methods with the appendChild() method to allow us to see each line as it displays.

EXAMPLE
10.7

Combining DOM Methods

This code will count down from a given number of bottles of ginger ale on the wall to one bottle at 1-second intervals but each line will be displayed because we will continue to create new elements and append each new element to the web page. For demonstration purposes, we will start the countdown at 10 instead of 100.

```
1.   <html>
2.     <head>
3.        <title>Example 10.7</title>
4.        <link href="carla.css" rel="stylesheet" type="text/css" />
5.        <script>
6.             var count = 10;
7.             var interval = null;
8.             function gingerAle()
9.             {
10.                 count = count - 1;
11.                 if( count == 1)
12.                 {
13.                     window.clearInterval(interval);
14.                     interval = null;
15.                     document.getElementById("end").innerHTML = ⏎
                                    ("That's it, folks!");
16.                 }
17.                 var newBottle = document.createElement("P");
18.                 var oneBottle = document.createTextNode(count + " ⏎
                                bottles of ginger ale on the wall...");
19.                 newBottle.appendChild(oneBottle);
20.                 document.getElementById("count_bottles"). ⏎
                                appendChild(newBottle);
21.             }
22.             function timeIt()
23.             {
24.                 interval = window.setInterval("gingerAle()", 1000);
25.             }
26.        </script>
27.     </head>
28.     <body>
29.        <div id="container">
30.            <h3>Ginger Ale Countdown</h3>
31.            <p><button onclick="timeIt()">Start the countdown ⏎
                                </button></p>
32.            <div id = "bottles"> </div>
33.            <p><span id = "bottles">10</span> bottles of ginger ⏎
                                ale on the wall...</p>
34.            <p id = "count_bottles"> </p>
35.            <p><span id = "end"> </span></p>
36.        </div>
37.     </body>
38.   </html>
```

We have changed several things in this program from the one in Example 10.6. The HTML page now has a <p> tag with id = "count_bottles". Each time a new bottle is counted, a paragraph element will be created and appended to the list of paragraph elements.

The gingerAle() function now creates a new element each time it is called from timeIt(). This happens on lines 17–20. Line 17 uses the createElement() method to create a new paragraph element. The type is "P" (note uppercase!) which identifies a paragraph element. Line 18 uses the createTextNode() method to create the content for the new paragraph. The content concatenates the bottle number (count) with the text " bottles of ginger ale on the wall...". Line 19 puts the content (stored in **oneBottle**) into the new paragraph element. Each time this function is called, the value of **count** will decrement so the content will continue to change. Finally, on line 20 the new element is appended to the area on the web page with id = "count_bottles".

When this page is first loaded, it looks like this:

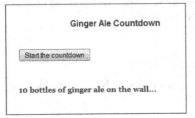

After clicking the "Start the countdown" button and letting four seconds pass, the page looks like this:

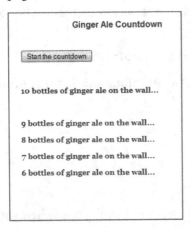

After letting the program finish, the display will look like this:

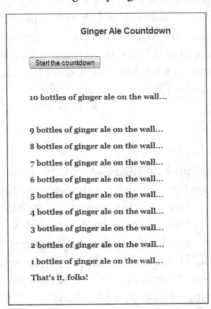

CHECKPOINT FOR SECTION 10.2 ✓

10.7 How many parameters does the setAttribute() method have? How many does the getAttribute() method have?

Use the following statement to answer Checkpoints 10.8 and 10.9:

```
document.getElementsByTagName("INPUT")[0].setAttribute("id", ⏎
                          "love_the_button");
```

10.8 What attribute will be set?

10.9 What will be the value of the attribute?

10.10 What two parameters must be included when using the setInterval() method?

10.11 Given the following statement:

```
window.clearInterval(greenies);
```

What is the identifier of the setInterval() method to be stopped?

10.12 Given the following statement:

```
interval = window.setInterval("jumpIt()", 5000);
```

How long are the intervals between calling the jumpIt() function?

10.3 XML Basics

After learning HTML script and using it for a while, combined with CSS, many of us become complacent. We know that, by combining styles with HTML tags we can pretty much create web pages that look the way we want them to look. But XML allows us to go further. We can now create our own tags and assign them default values for appearance and status as we want. Newer versions of HTML and a trend toward browser standardization allows us even more freedom to create web pages that will appear, to everyone, as we want. But this is only a small part of what the web page script needs to do and only the tip of the iceberg in terms of what XML can do.

What Is XML?

XML stands for **eXtensible Markup Language** and the beauty of XML is that it is **extensible**. You create your own tags and, by combining this with what we now know about the Document Object Model, you can manipulate elements in many ways. XML is not only readable by humans but also by machines. Thus, XML provides capabilities to be used in conjunction with databases and many other application programming interfaces. XML was designed specifically to transport and store data, focusing on what data is, whereas HTML was designed mainly to display data, focusing on how the data appears. Thus, XML doesn't actually do anything except store the data that is transported to and from it. However, it is now as important to the web as HTML was to the foundation of the web. In order to use XML, you need a firm knowledge of both HTML and JavaScript.

Why Do We Need XML?

XML is suited to developing programs to run on the Internet because it comprises a set of tools that allows us to define and create new languages. It allows data to be self-describing. Where HTML tags predefine the default values for content and also have predefined status in the DOM, XML allows us to define our own nodes and tags for elements.

You, as the developer, can create **XML elements** that limit the type of data an element can contain. Consider, for example, an element that is designed to include zip codes. By limiting the type of data to only integers (and, if you wanted an extended zip code, a dash), you would not need to validate every user's zip code entry. The parser (to be discussed later in this section) would not permit any other type of entry in that element.

You can create custom data structures, based on your needs or the needs of your employer. XML has a rich set of tools that can be used for linking and can be used to interchange data between databases and other data structures. It includes robust data-searching capabilities which makes it ideal for any web page that needs to search through large amounts of data.

Recall that we have created JavaScript programs to search arrays for information on players in a game, students in a class, or customers in a business. We used parallel arrays to pull corresponding data onto a web page. But in real life, data quickly becomes unwieldy in parallel arrays and is, normally, stored in databases. Imagine that you work for a large drug store chain. Records of patients are kept in databases that need to include a name, address, contact information, prescribing physicians, prescription refill criteria, dates dispensed, and so on. When a prescription is refilled, information should be updated in several fields, including a field for medication inventory. A pharmacist may need to check two, three, or more fields before filling a prescription. The store may need to check fields before reordering supplies or to create statistical reports. XML, in conjunction with other programs, provides the capabilities to handle these requests.

While we will not deal with data as large as that in a big (or even small) business, we will use the sites we have built in this text to demonstrate how to create and use XML. More functionality will be added in Chapters 11 and 12 where we learn PHP.

XML Components

XML documents are created using tags that may seem very similar to HTML tags. XML documents create a tree-like structure, as we discussed in the sections on the DOM, with leaves and branches. However, since you are defining the elements, you must specify, using the tree structure, which elements are parent and which are child. The components of various parts of an XML document are discussed here.

The XML Declaration

XML documents form a tree structure that starts, as an HTML document, at the root. The root element of an HTML document is the <html> tag. For XML documents, the first line must always be the **XML declaration**. The next line is the XML root element. An XML declaration looks like this:

```
<?xml version = "1.0" encoding = "UTF-8"?>
```

The version is required. XML 1.0 was recommended by W3C first in 1998, and again in 2000, with a second edition that fixed many of the initial bugs. A third edition was created which fixed more bugs. We will use version 1.0.

The **encoding attribute** is not required. It describes the character set that the document uses. If nothing is defined, the default character set is UTF-8. Some other possible character sets are "UTF-16", "ISO-10646-UCS-2", or "ISO-8559-1".

XML Elements

XML elements are the core of an XML document. At the beginning, there aren't any because you must create your own elements. Each XML element consists of three parts and may include a fourth:

- a **start tag**: the name of the element enclosed in < and > symbols, as with an HTML tag
- **content**: data or other elements, as with an HTML tag
- an **end tag**: created like the end tag of an HTML element with a < character, a / (slash), the element name, and a > character
- **attributes**: optional—contains additional information about the element, just as HTML elements can have attributes

While you create your own elements, XML element names must follow certain rules, as follows:

- Names can contain letters, numbers, and other characters.
- Names cannot start with a number or a punctuation character.
- Names cannot start with the letters x, m, l in any form (uppercase, lowercase, or any combination).
- Names cannot contain spaces.
- Tag names are case-sensitive.

As with variables in any programming languages, there are "best practices" that should be followed as well as some **naming conventions** that you may choose to follow. It is also a good idea to be consistent in your naming practices. For example, in this text we have consistently started all variable names with lowercase letters and used camel back notation for variable names that contain two words. This means that if a variable name consists of the words "player" and "score", we use **playerScore** as the variable name. Another developer might choose to use an underscore to separate words in variable names, as in **player_score**. Either of these names are fine variable names but it's best to stick with one convention or another. The same is true for names you give XML elements. In fact, we will use the underscore convention in this book for XML element names as a good way to quickly distinguish them from variable names.

The following are some **best practices** (i.e., practices accepted by the web development community):

- Names should be descriptive. Elements could be named <element_1>, <element_2>, <element_3>, and so on, but it's preferable to name your elements something descriptive like <f_name>, <mid_initial>, <l_name>, and so on.
- Keep names as short as possible. The name <street_address> is much better than <your_street_number_and_name>.
- Avoid the "-" character (the dash or minus sign). Some software might interpret a name like <zip-code> to mean that you want to subtract code from zip.
- Avoid the "." character (the dot or period). Some software might interpret a name like <area.phone> to mean that phone is a property of the object area.
- If you know the naming rules of the database that your XML document will use it is a good idea to use those rules when naming your XML elements.

The second line in an XML document contains the **root element**. This element defines the type of object the XML document represents. All the other elements will describe more things about the root element. For example, if your document is used to hold information about players at the Greg's Gambits website, the root might be <player> and other elements would describe features pertaining to a player, such as <username>, <points>, <game_played>, <avatar>, and so on.

Comments and File Names

An XML document is a text file that usually ends with the **.xml extension**. The syntax for writing **XML comments** is similar to that of HTML. The comment begins with <! -- and ends with -->. For example, a comment which, in XML, is ignored, would be as follows:

```
<!--This is a comment -->
```

In Example 10.8, we will build a simple XML document and add to it in later examples.

EXAMPLE 10.8

A First XML Document

Our first XML document will contain a root element and the elements a business owner might use when sending a memo to employees. We save the file with the filename memo.xml:

```
1.  <?xml version = "1.0" encoding = "UTF-8" ?>
2.  <!- Example 10.8 -->
3.  <memo>
```

```
 4.        <send_to>employee's name</send_to>
 5.        <date>today's date</date>
 6.        <from>boss's name</from>
 7.        <subject>subject in question</subject>
 8.        <memo_body>content of memo</memo_body>
 9.        <shout_out>simple good-bye or good luck or whatever</shout_out>
10.    </memo>
```

This memo is as simple as it gets. Later, we will create styles to use with each element so the different elements have different appearances. Right now, if you viewed this document in a web browser, it would look something like this:

This XML file does not appear to have any style information associated with it. The document tree is shown below.

```
<!-- Example 10.8 -->
- <memo>
    <send_to>employee's name</send_to>
    <date>today's date</date>
    <from>boss's name</from>
    <subject>subject in question</subject>
    <memo_body>content of memo</memo_body>
    <shout_out>simple good-bye or good luck or whatever</shout_out>
  </memo>
```

Because we have not included any information about how to render these tags, the browser displays the **document tree** and informs us of this at the top of the display. Therefore, aside from not displaying the information on line 1 of the code (the XML declaration), the display is virtually identical to the code.

Before we learn how to add style to our elements, we will discuss a few more important facets of XML elements and pages.

XML Attributes

XML element **attributes** are used in a manner similar to the use of attributes in HTML elements. They describe or identify XML elements. Attributes are always contained in the start tag of an element, are case-sensitive, and require a value. They are referred to as **name-value pairs** because each must have a name and a value. As with an HTML attribute, the name of the attribute is on the left of the equals sign and its value, to the right of the equals sign, is enclosed in single or double quotes. The general syntax for two attributes of an element named <my_element> is as follows:

```
<my_element attribute1 = "value one" attribute2 = "value two">
```

Notice that it is unnecessary to separate attributes with anything other than a space. You can define as many attributes as you want (within reason) for an element. XML attributes describe the data in an element in greater detail. However, it may be preferable to use child elements to describe your data. Example 10.9 expands on the previous example and adds some specific content to the elements that were created. Part (a) uses attributes to add detail to some elements and Part (b) uses child elements.

EXAMPLE 10.9

Attributes or More Elements? You Decide

The following code shows two ways to write the XML file named `memo.xml`. Rather than listing the code, these images are from a browser:

```
<!-- Example 10.9 Part a -->
-<memo>
    <send_to title="Princess" first="Leia"> Smith</send_to>
    <date weekday="Monday" month="July"> 23</date>
    <from>Big Bob</from>
    <subject>Performance review</subject>
    <memo_body>You're good at the job but slow</memo_body>
    <shout_out>Speed it up, Princess!</shout_out>
  </memo>
```

```
<!-- Example 10.9 Part b -->
-<memo>
    <send_title>Princess</send_title>
    <send_first>Leia'</send_first>
    <send_last>Smith</send_last>
    <weekday>Monday</weekday>
    <month>July</month>
    <day>23</day>
    <from>Big Bob</from>
    <subject>Performance Review</subject>
    <memo_body>You're good at the job but slow</memo_body>
    <shout_out>Speed it up, Princess!</shout_out>
  </memo>
```

While attributes can be used to add information about the recipient of this memo and about the date, it is probably better to use child elements for this data.

XML Entities

Some characters have special meanings in XML. Thus, if you use these characters inside an element, you will get an error. For example, since the ">" character indicates the end of an element tag, if it is used within the element name or in an attribute name or value, the parser will interpret it to mean a closing character. However, if you need to use the ">" you can replace the character with its **entity** reference, similar to the way you do it in HTML. There are five predefined **entity references** in XML, as shown in Table 10.3.

TABLE 10.3	XML Entity References
Entity Reference	**Character**
&lt;	< (less than sign)
&gt;	> (greater than sign)
&smp;	& (ampersand)
&apos;	' (apostrophe)
&quot;	" (double quotation mark)

Whitespace

We know that, when a page scripted in HTML is displayed, **whitespace** is ignored. However, in XML, whitespace is not ignored.

Well-Formed XML Documents

HTML documents should be well-formed and so should XML documents. A **well-formed XML document** adheres to the following syntax rules:

- XML documents must have one and only one root element.
- XML elements must have closing tags.
- XML tags are case-sensitive.
- XML elements must be properly nested using the parent-child model.
- Every XML attribute must have a value and the value must be in quotes.

XML Parsers and DTDs

An XML **parser** checks your XML document to ensure that the document is well-formed and follows the rules. Parsers are often built into browsers and it was the parser that gave us the message that our first XML document did not have any style information (see Example 10.8).

There are two types of parsers: validating and nonvalidating. To understand the difference, we must first understand what a DTD is. **DTD** stands for **Document Type Definition**. It is the **schema** that defines a document's structure. A schema is an XML document itself and has certain advantages over DTDs when using XML. We will discuss schemas later in the chapter. For now, it is sufficient to know that you can include your own DTD with your XML file and it will define the structure of your XML elements. This is a **validating parser**. For example, using the elements in Example 10.9b, if you defined elements such that each recipient of the memo must have a title identified in Example 10.9b as `<send_title>`, a first name (`<send_first>`), and a last name (`<send-last>`), but did not include a last name for one recipient, the DTD would invalidate the XML document.

However, a **nonvalidating parser** will simply check that the XML document is well-formed but will not check that the structure (i.e., all child elements are included) is sound.

XML Internal DTDs

The purpose of a Document Type Definition—a DTD—is to define the structure of an XML document. However, an alternative to the DTD is a schema which will be covered in greater depth later in the chapter. You can include your DTD at the beginning of your XML file. This is known as an **internal DTD**.

An internal DTD must include all the elements used in the document. It defines the root element and all elements contained in the root. It defines those elements in the order in which they must appear. Each element must be listed with its type (the type of data it contains) and it must have an ending. The syntax for an internal DTD is as follows:

```
<!DOCTYPE root_element_name [
<!ELEMENT element_name        (child_element_A)>
<!ELEMENT child_element_A     (child_a, child_b,...child_x)>
<!ELEMENT child_a             (#TYPE_OF_DATA)>
<!ELEMENT child_b             (#TYPE_OF_DATA)>
...
]>
```

The data types we will use are PCDATA for character data (text), EMPTY (for an empty element), and ANY. Example 10.10 adds an internal DTD to an XML file.

EXAMPLE 10.10

An XML File with an Internal DTD

The following code is similar to the previous examples but adds an internal DTD and creates two parent elements (<recipient> and <body>), each with several child elements. This demonstrates how the DTD is written when some elements are parents of other elements.

```
1.   <?xml version = "1.0" standalone = "yes"?>
2.   <!-- Example 10.10a -->
3.   <!DOCTYPE memo [
4.        <!ELEMENT   memo        (recipient, date, from, subject, body)>
5.        <!ELEMENT   recipient   (title, first, last)>
6.        <!ELEMENT   title       (#PCDATA)>
7.        <!ELEMENT   first       (#PCDATA)>
8.        <!ELEMENT   last        (#PCDATA)>
9.        <!ELEMENT   date        EMPTY>
10.       <!ELEMENT   from        (#PCDATA)>
11.       <!ELEMENT   subject     ANY>
12.       <!ELEMENT   body        (greeting, grade, shout)>
13.       <!ELEMENT   greeting    (#PCDATA)>
14.       <!ELEMENT   grade       (#PCDATA)>
15.       <!ELEMENT   shout       (#PCDATA)>
16.   ]>
17.   <memo>
18.        <recipient>
19.             <title>Princess</title>
20.             <first>Leia"</first>
21.             <last>Smith</last>
22.        </recipient>
23.        <date>Monday</date>
24.        <from>Big Bob</from>
25.        <subject>Performance Review</subject>
26.        <body>
27.             <greeting>Hi there!</greeting>
28.             <grade>You're good at the job but slow: grade = B</grade>
29.             <shout>Speed it up, Princess!</shout>
30.        </body>
31.   </memo>
```

The XML declaration has added a property—the **standalone property** is set to "yes" which means the browser will use the DTD included with this document. This property is optional.

The DTD identifies the parent elements and the child elements. If this file is displayed in a browser, it will look like this but the DTD is not displayed:

```
<!-- Example 10.10a -->
- <memo>
  - <recipient>
      <title>Princess</title>
      <first>Leia</first>
      <last>Smith</last>
  </recipient>
  <date>Monday</date>
  <from>Big Bob</from>
  <subject>Performance Review</subject>
  - <body>
      <greeting>Hi there!</greeting>
      <grade>You're good at the job but slow: grade = B</grade>
      <shout>Speed it up, Princess!</shout>
  </body>
</memo>
```

However, if we change the code slightly and move the closing </recipient> tag to a place before the last child element, as shown below, the parser will display an error. The new code follows:

```
1.   <?xml version = "1.0" standalone = "yes"?>
2.   <!-- Example 10.10b -->
3.   <!DOCTYPE        memo        [
4.        <!ELEMENT  memo        (recipient, date, from, subject, body) >
5.        <!ELEMENT  recipient   (title, first, last) >
6.        <!ELEMENT  title       (#PCDATA) >
7.        <!ELEMENT  first       (#PCDATA) >
8.        <!ELEMENT  last        (#PCDATA) >
9.        <!ELEMENT  date        EMPTY >
10.       <!ELEMENT  from        (#PCDATA) >
11.       <!ELEMENT  subject         ANY >
12.       <!ELEMENT  body        (greeting, grade, shout) >
13.       <!ELEMENT  greeting    (#PCDATA) >
14.       <!ELEMENT  grade       (#PCDATA) >
15.       <!ELEMENT  shout       (#PCDATA) >
16.   ]>
17.   <memo>
18.       <recipient>
19.           <title>Princess</title>
20.           <first>Leia"</first>
21.       </recipient>
22.       <last>Smith</last>
23.       <date>Monday</date>
24.       <from>Big Bob</from>
25.       <subject>Performance Review</subject>
26.       <body>
27.           <greeting>Hi there!</greeting>
28.           <grade>You're good at the job but slow: grade = B</grade>
```

```
29.              <shout>Speed it up, Princess!</shout>
30.         </body>
31.    </memo>
```

The DTD states that the `<recipient>` element requires three child elements, including `<last>` and a parent element named `<last>` is not in the DTD. Now the browser will display an error.

XML Parsing Error: mismatched tag. Expected: </recipient>.
Location: file:///C:/Users/Duck/Desktop/ex_10_10b_memo.xml
Line Number 32, Column 3:

```
</memo>
--^
```

XML External and Public DTDs

You can, if you prefer, create a DTD that is saved in a separate file, just as you can create external CSS files or external JavaScript files. If you do it this way, you must tell the computer where to find the external file and include that line just below the XML declaration. **External DTD** files normally have the extension **.dtd**. The syntax for including an external DTD file is as follows:

```
<!DOCTYPE element_name SYSTEM "path_to_dtd_filename.dtd" >
```

The keyword **SYSTEM** indicates that this is a private DTD. As with style sheets, you can include both internal and external DTDs. If both DTDs reference the same element, the one closest to the element (i.e., the internal DTD) overrides the other, just as an embedded style overrides a style declared in an external style sheet.

CHECKPOINT FOR SECTION 10.3 ✓

10.13 What, exactly, does an XML document do?

10.14 List at least two reasons why XML is needed.

10.15 What is the first line of every XML document?

10.16 What is wrong with the following XML element names?
   a) `<XmL_body>`
   b) `<sender name>`

10.17 What is wrong with the attribute in the following?

   `<sender name = Joey>`

10.18 Identify the error in the following line of code in an XML document and fix it.

   `<num_range>Number must be < 20.</num_range>`

10.19 What is the purpose of a DTD?

10.4   Adding Style and XSL Transformations

By now you're probably wondering what possible use a page that looks like the display shown in Example 10.10a or any of the previous examples could have. You would never want a customer to see the markup when visiting your website. So, before we continue to learn about schemas and namespaces which add to the usability of XML documents, we will discuss how to associate style information with XML elements, as the parsers have noted (see previous examples) is missing. For us, this will be relatively easy since we already understand the concept of styles and style sheets. Now we apply the same concepts used to create styles for HTML to XML.

We have choices. We can use a CSS page to mark up the styles of the XML elements we create. Or we can use a more advanced tool, an XSL (Extensible Style Sheet Language) or XSLT (Extensible Style Sheet Language for Transformations) style sheet. Most often we use both. First we'll just change the presentational aspects of an XML document with CSS.

Using Cascading Style Sheets with XML Documents

When using CSS with XHTML pages, the CSS is used to change the presentational aspects of HTML tags from the default values to whatever we want. For example, without adding a style to the <p> tag, we know that in all browsers it will display smaller than, for example, a <h2> or <h1> tag, will have a common font, and the text will be black. Of course, different browsers may render tags with slightly different fonts or sizes, but, in general, there is a default value that most browsers follow. If we want all our paragraph text to be green, we must add a style to the <p> tag. If we want only some paragraph text to be green, we can add a class and identify the text to be changed by that class. An XML document consists of elements, just as an HTML document consists of elements. The difference is that HTML elements are predefined and we cannot create new ones. In an XML document, no elements are predefined; we create all of them. So we have to create the default values for our new elements.

That, initially, is what we will do with our CSS pages; we will create the way we want each element to be displayed. The syntax to change the style of all <p> elements in an HTML page to blue, bold text is as follows:

```
p {
      font-weight: bold;
      color: #0000FF;
}
```

The syntax to create a style for an XML element named <subject> that will make all text in this element blue and bold is similar:

```
subject {
        font-weight: bold;
        color: #0000FF;
}
```

You can use all the style attributes that are available for HTML style sheets but you must define styles for all elements in your XML page. You can then link the style sheet to the XML document. The syntax to create this link is as follows:

```
<?xml-stylesheet type = "text/css" href = "stylesheet_name.css" ?>
```

In Example 10.11, we will create an XML document that Jackie, our jewelry store owner, wants to use to send information about her latest jewelry making classes. This example shows a new XML document, a corresponding style sheet, and how the two work together to create a display in the browser. The XML file creates a page that advertises a new beading class that Jackie is offering. The CSS file formats the display.

EXAMPLE 10.11

Adding Style to the XML Document

```
1.  <?xml version = "1.0" ?>
2.  <?xml-stylesheet type = "text/css" href = "jackie.css" ?>
3.  <!-- Example 10.11 XML document -->
4.  <courses>
5.      <salutation>Great news!</salutation>
6.      <subject>A new Beading Class!</subject>
7.      <course_info>
8.          <when>Monday evenings, 7 - 9 pm</when>
9.          <where>At Jackie's house: 123 Duckpond Lane</where>
10.         <cost>Only $8.00 per class or $25 for all 4 classes</cost>
11.     </course_info>
12.     <contact>Sign up now: send an email to jackie@jewels.net
                </contact>
13. </courses>
```

This file would be saved with a filename like **new_course.xml**. The style sheet that is referenced on line 2 looks like this:

```
1.  courses         {
2.                  margin: 5%;
3.                  padding: 5%;
4.                  display: block;
5.                  }
6.  salutation      {
7.                  font-family: Georgia,"Times New Roman",Times, serif;
8.                  font-weight: bold;
9.                  color: #333399;
10.                 font-size: 36px;
11.                 display: block;
12.                 }
13. subject         {
14                  font-family: Georgia, "Times New Roman", Times, serif;
15.                 font-size: 24px;
16.                 color: #333399;
17.                 display: block;
18.                 }
19. when, where, cost{
20.                 font-family: Geneva, Arial, Helvetica, sans-serif;
21.                 color: #333399;
22.                 font-weight: bold;
```

```
23.                  display: block;
24.                  }
25.     contact      {
26.                  font-family: Geneva, Arial, Helvetica, sans-serif;
27.                  font-size: 16px;
28.                  font-weight: bold;
29.                  color: #FFFFFF;
30.                  background-color: #333399;
31.                  display: block;
32.                  }
```

Notice that you can use the same styles for several elements (line 19). The style `display: block` results in a carriage return before and after the element to create line breaks. Now the display for this XML page is more pleasing:

> ### Great news!
> A new Beading Class!
> Monday evenings, 7 - 9 pm
> At Jackie's house: 123 Duckpond Lane
> Only $8.00 per class or $25 for all 4 classes
> Sign up now: send an email to jackie@jewels.net

The hierarchy of elements is applied to a style sheet that is used with XML. In other words, if you assign certain styles to a parent element, those styles are inherited by the child elements unless a specific style in the child element overrides them. In the previous example, we could have written one style for `<course_info>` instead of listing all its child elements (`<when>`, `<where>`, and `<cost>`).

In summary, CSS can do the following:

- modify the font size, color, family, and style of text in markup
- define the location and size of an element
- change the background image and color of elements
- create a new look and feel for markup pages to display on the Web

But CSS cannot do the following:

- change the order of elements in a document
- make computations based on the content of the document
- add content to the document
- combine multiple documents into one

If you are looking to transform one document into another, XSL is a powerful tool. It was created to give developers the ability to create data and then transform it to various formats.

The Extensible Style Sheet Language (XSL)

An **XSL document,** like a CSS document, specifies how to render the data in an XML document. But it can do much more. XSL stands for **eXtensible Stylesheet Language** and is actually a group of three technologies.

- **XSL-FO (XSL Formatting Object)** is a vocabulary used to specify formatting.
- **XPath (XML Path Language)** is a language of expressions used to locate structures and data in XML documents.
- **XSLT (XSL Transformation)** is the technology used to transform XML documents into other documents.

Some of the things XSLT can do:

- convert data in a standard XML format to SQL statements, tab-delimited text files, or other database formats for data sharing
- transform XSLT style sheets into new style sheets
- turn Web pages (written in HTML) to a format for handheld devices
- add CSS style sheets to XML documents for viewing in a browser

An in-depth discussion of all these technologies is beyond the scope of this book but we will explain the concepts behind how XSLT works.

To transform an XML document using XSLT two tree structures are required. The **source tree** is the XML document that will be transformed and the **result tree** is the XML document that is created. Example 10.12 demonstrates how the data in an XML file can be transformed into an HTML page.

EXAMPLE
10.12

Using XSL to Transform an XML Document

For this example, we actually need three files. The XML document consists of the data to be displayed. It is considered the source tree. The XSL file will do the transformation—transforming XML data into the specified format. Our specified format is to be an HTML page. This new page is our result tree. The third file is a CSS file that describes how we want the new file displayed.

We begin with the CSS page. Since our XML page will be transformed to an HTML page, the styles needed now are not styles for XML nodes but rather styles that will be used later, by the XSL file. The CSS is given here in case you wish to duplicate this example on your computer.

```
1.  /* Example 10.12: stylesheet for Jackie's Jewelry Classes page */
2.  th        {
3.            color: #FFFFFF;
4.            font-weight: bold;
5.            background-color: #006A9D;
6.            }
7.  td, p     {
8.            color: #006A9D
9.            }
10. h2        {
11.           color: #006A9D;
12.           text-align: center;
13.           }
```

This page will have the filename jackie.css.

Next, we will give the XML code. This code is similar to the ones in previous examples but it has been simplified. Rather than get bogged down in a lot of parent and child nodes, the information has been compressed to include only a root element, one parent element, and two child elements to allow you to focus on the main concepts.

```
1.   <?xml version="1.0" encoding="ISO-8859-1"?>
2.   <?xml-stylesheet type = "text/xsl" href = "ex_10_12.xsl"?>
3.   <!-- Example 10.12: the XML file -->
4.   <jackie_classes>
5.       <course_info id = "Beading">
6.           <when>Mondays, 7 - 9 pm</when>
7.           <where>Room 2</where>
8.       </course_info>
9.       <course_info id = "Silver bracelets">
10.          <when>Tuesdays, 7 - 9 pm</when>
11.          <where>Room 4</where>
12.      </course_info>
13.      <course_info id ="Feathered earrings">
14.          <when>Wednesdays, 7 - 9 pm</when>
15.          <where>Room 2</where>
16.      </course_info>
17.      <course_info id = "Ceramic Beads">
18.          <when>Thursdays, 6 - 10 pm</when>
19.          <where>Room 2</where>
20.      </course_info>
21.      <course_info id = "Pendants">
22.          <when>Saturdays, 10am - noon</when>
23.          <where>Room 3</where>
24.      </course_info>
25.  </jackie_classes>
```

The first eight lines of this code are most important. Line 1 tells the computer that this is an XML document and specifies the version and encoding scheme. Line 2 is similar to Example 10.11 in that it references a style sheet. Note, however, that it does not link to a CSS style sheet. The link is to an XSL style sheet. When this XML file is opened in a browser, the browser will automatically access ex_10_12.xsl and complete the process of displaying the page, using instructions from the XSL file. At this point, our XML file is the source tree.

Line 4 defines the element <jackie_classes> as the root element. Line 5 defines <course_info> as the first (and, in this case, the only) parent element. We have added an id to this element. We could have created a child element called something like <course_name> and included the information in each id in that child node instead. But this is another way to do the same thing and offers us the opportunity to explore certain XSL features.

Lines 6 and 7 define two child elements of <course_info>, <where> and <when>. The parent element is closed on line 8 and the process begins again, on lines 9–12, 13–16, 17–20, and 21–24. Line 25 closes the root and the document is ended.

Finally, the code for the XSL file is written. This is where are the good stuff happens. That code is as follows:

```
1.   <?xml version="1.0"?>
2.   <!--Example 10.12 xsl file -->
3.       <xsl:stylesheet version="2.0" xmlns:xsl = ↲
                          "http://www.w3.org/1999/XSL/Transform">
4.       <xsl:output method = "html" doctype-system = "about:legacy- ↲
                      compat"/>
5.       <xsl:template match="/">
6.       <html>
7.       <head>
8.           <meta charset = "utf-8"/>
9.           <link rel = "stylesheet" type = "text/css" href = ↲
                      "jackie.css"/>
10.          <title>Jackie's Jewelry | Jewelry Making Classes</title>
11.      </head>
12.      <body>
13.          <h2>Jackie's Jewelry Making Classes</h2>
14.          <table border = "1" align = "center" width = "50%">
15.              <tr bgcolor="blue">
                     <th>Course Name</th>
16.                  <th>Location</th>
17.                  <th>Days and Times</th>
18.              </tr>
19. <!-- insert each course information into a table row -->
20.              <xsl:for-each select = "/jackie_classes/course_info">
21.                  <tr>
22.                      <td><xsl:value-of select = "@id"/></td>
23.                      <td><xsl:value-of select = "where"/></td>
24.                      <td><xsl:value-of select = "when"/></td>
25.                  </tr>
26.              </xsl:for-each>
27.                  <tr>
28.                      <td colspan = "3">Each class runs for 4 weeks.
                         The cost is $8.00 per class or $25.00 for each ↲
                             4-week session, payable in advance. </td>
29.                  </tr>
30.              </table>
31.      </body>
32.  </html>
33.  </xsl:template>
34.  </xsl:stylesheet>
```

This code requires some detailed explanation:

- Line 1 defines the XML version that will be used.

- Line 3 begins the XSL style sheet with the style sheet start tag. The version is an attribute and here we specify that this document will conform to XSLT version 2.0. The URI http://www.w3.org/1999/Transform is an instruction to use the W3C's XSLT.

- Line 4 uses the **xsl:output element** to specify that the output (the result tree) will be an HTML page. doctype-system is an attribute and, while HTML5 is still not completely supported, by using the value "about:legacy-compat" we are ensured that the page to be produced will be HTML5 compatible.

- Line 5 has two things to be explained. First, XSLT uses templates to describe how to transform the source tree to the result tree. It means that a template will be applied to the nodes specified in the `match` attribute. The `match` attribute is required. The forward slash ("/") is an XPath character that indicates the root element. Therefore, the **match attribute** now says to select the root element of the source tree and all its included elements and add these to the result tree.

■ Line 6 begins an HTML document. Lines 6–18 should be familiar to you. The `<head>` section gives the page a title (line 10), includes the encoding scheme (line 8), and links to a CSS style sheet (line 9). The `<body>` adds a heading (line 13) and begins a table (line 14). The first row of the table will include column headings so we use the `<th></th>` tags and the style for `<th>` tags will be applied (see the CSS style sheet). All this script will be displayed on the result tree in the ordinary manner.

■ We return to XSL-specific code on line 20. This line begins a loop. We are actually creating an XSL element, **<xsl:for-each...>** and telling it what to search for. The **select attribute** is another XPath expression that specifies the node set that will be searched for. A **node set** is the set of nodes used with the `search` attribute. In this example we set `search = "/jackie_classes/course_info"`. The / between `jackie_classes` and `course_info` means that `course_info` is a child node of `jackie_classes`. This means that the search will look for `course_info` nodes that are child nodes of `jackie_classes`. In this example, we only have one `jackie_classes` node which happens to also be the root node but this may not be the case in all source trees. After finding all `course_info` nodes, they will be processed according to the code that follows.

■ Lines 22, 23, and 24 process the attributes and child nodes of all `course_info` nodes. Line 22 uses the XPath symbol @ to mean that `id` is an attribute node of `course_info`. The **value-of attribute** retrieves the value of a specific child node and places it in a `<td>`. For line 22, this means the value of the `id` in each `course_info` node will be placed in the first column of the table (the first `<td>`). For lines 23 and 24, the values of the `where` and `when` child nodes will be placed in the second and third columns (each in a `<td>` cell). Since the `for-each` attribute puts this sequence of lines (lines 22–24) in a loop, this will be done for each `course_info` element in the XML document.

■ Line 26 closes the loop by closing the `</xsl:for-each>` element.

■ Line 27 adds some more HTML to the page.

■ All HTML tags that are open are then closed on lines 29–32. Finally the open XSL element tags are also closed on lines 33 and 34.

If you create these three files and open the XML file, your result should look like this:

Course Name	Location	Days and Times
Beading	Room 2	Mondays, 7 - 9 pm
Silver bracelets	Room 4	Tuesdays, 7 - 9 pm
Feathered earrings	Room 2	Wednesdays, 7 - 9 pm
Ceramic Beads	Room 2	Thursdays, 6 - 10 pm
Pendants	Room 3	Saturdays, 10am - noon

Jackie's Jewelry Making Classes

Each class runs for 4 weeks.
The cost is $8.00 per class or $25.00 for each 4-week session, payable in advance.

An Important Note

Some web browsers will not perform transformations unless they are accessed on a web server. If you wish to try this example or some of the Review Exercises and do not have a server to post your pages, you may have to try several different browsers to see the final result. This transformation was created in Firefox and worked, regardless of whether the files were accessed from the author's hard drive or the author's server space.

CHECKPOINT FOR SECTION 10.4 ✓

10.20 To display an XML page without doing a transformation, you must include a _____ file.

10.21 Which style is used in an XML document's style sheet to create line breaks?

10.22 An XSL document is which of the following?
   a) a style sheet
   b) an XML document
   c) both

10.23 Which document contains the source tree when creating a transformation using an XSL document to transform an XML document to a web page?

10.24 If you have the following files on your server, what file do you include in the URL in order to view the new page?
   a) `landscape.xml`
   b) `landscape.xsl`
   c) `landscape.css`

10.25 Which attribute is used in an XSL element to specify the nodes to be used in an HTML page?
   a) `match`
   b) `for-each`
   c) `id`
   d) `@`

10.26 Which attribute retrieves the value of a specific node?
   a) `match`
   b) `select`
   c) `value-of`
   d) `for-each`

10.5   XML Namespaces and Schemas

We have seen how an XML document can be transformed into a web page and can imagine many uses for this ability. For example, a bookstore might want to create various pages describing its offerings. Each book has some things in common—a title, an author, and a publisher, for example. But the bookstore might want to create different tables to distinguish books by genre—mysteries, science fiction, romance, biographies, and so on. The elements for each book genre might be the same and it makes sense to name the elements that hold each book's title, author, and publisher by element names `<title>`, `<author>` and `<publisher>`. However, using the `<title>` element in the same document for three different types of books can cause confusion. To distinguish titles of mysteries from titles of books of other genres, we can use namespaces. An XML namespace is a collection of elements and attribute names. It is used so that the person creating the document can refer to elements with the same name and be assured that the `<title>` element of a mystery book will not be confused with the `<title>` element of a romance novel. How to implement namespaces is discussed in the first part of this section.

Earlier in the chapter we learned how to use a DTD to describe the structure of an XML document. However, DTDs have certain limitations. Some of these limitations can be overcome by using an XML schema instead. An **XML schema** consists of two parts. The first part, like a DTD, is used to describe the structure of the XML document. The schema specifies which elements and attributes are valid for a given document, which elements and attributes are required, and which are optional. The second part specifies what data types can be used in an element. We will discuss XML schemas in the second part of this section.

XML Namespaces

Namespaces are used to avoid confusion or naming "collisions" which might occur when two elements have the same name but refer to different things. It is particularly helpful if one XML document is merged with another.

Namespaces must be declared before they are used. A namespace declaration is placed in the start tag of an element and applies to that element and its **descendants** (its child elements). All XML namespaces use the reserved keyword, **xmlns**. This keyword is actually an attribute of the element. Each namespace prefix binds to a series of characters called a **Uniform Resource Identifier (URI),** which uniquely identifies the namespace. The web developer—you—create the URI and the namespace prefix.

The Uniform Resource Identifier (URI)

An XML namespace URI references a server (your server) but it is not an address that can be visited. Its purpose is to provide a unique identity for the namespace. If Jackie, of Jackie's Jewelry business, has `jackie.com` as her domain name, a sample URI for one of her namespaces might be `"http://jackie.com/Namespace_name"`. The syntax for creating a namespace with the name `"beads"` might be as follows:

```
xmlns:beads="http://jackie.com/beads"
```

This is rather confusing. It looks like a URL but, if you were to enter this into a browser, it would go nowhere. The purpose behind using one's own domain name to define a namespace is that it is guaranteed to be a unique string.

Namespace Declarations

A **namespace declaration** has the following syntax:

```
xmlns:prefix = "URI"
```

Here are a few examples of namespace declarations for Jackie's Jewelry pages:

- `xmlns:beads="http://jackie.com/beads"`
- `xmlns:bracelets="http://jackie.com/bracelets"`
- `xmlns:earrings="http://jackie.com/earrings"`

It may be easier to understand namespaces through an example. Imagine you are adding information to the page we created in a previous example that listed Jackie's course offerings. The page already contains five courses: learning to make beaded jewelry, learning to make feathered earrings, learning to make silver bracelets, learning to make ceramic beads, and learning to make pendants. Jackie doesn't charge much for her classes so she cannot afford to supply the students with materials. And she would like to give students the option of bringing their own supplies, using more or less expensive materials, and so on. So she would like to add a table that lists the supplies needed for each course and the prices of supplies she sells. We will create that XML document in Example 10.13 but will only use two courses so we can focus on the new material. The example shows an XML document that has elements to create two courses that Jackie is offering (a beading class and a silver bracelet class) and two options for purchasing supplies for each course. However, we want to distinguish between beading information and bracelet information even though the elements for each have the same names. By specifying a namespace for each <course> element, we avoid naming collisions.

EXAMPLE 10.13

Avoiding Chaos with Namespaces

```
1.   <?xml version="1.0" encoding="ISO-8859-1"?>
2.   <jackie_classes>
3.       <course xmlns:bead = "http://jackie.com/bead">
4.           <description>Beading classes</description>
5.           <when>Monday eve, 7-9</when>
6.           <where>Room 2</where>
7.           <package>Packet of multicolored beads</package>
8.           <pack_cost>$5.00</pack_cost>
9.           <singles>African trade beads</singles>
10.          <single_cost>$2.00 per bead</single_cost>
11.      </course>
12.      <course xmlns:bracelet = "http://jackie.com/bracelet">
13.          <description>Creating necklaces and pendants</description>
14.          <when>Tuesday eve, 7-9</when>
15.          <where>Room 4</where>
16.          <package>silver chain and choice of pendant</package>
17.          <pack_cost>$10.00</pack_cost>
18.          <singles>silver charms - hearts, animals, shapes</singles>
19.          <single_cost>$8.00 per charm</single_cost>
20.      </course>
21.  </jackie_classes>
```

In this code we assigned one namespace to the `<course>` element for beading classes and a different namespace to the `<course>` element for the necklace and pendant classes. Each will now apply to its child elements as well.

We can use the namespace in an XSL transformation, as shown in Example 10.14. This example shows how the XSL file uses the namespaces defined in the XML document of the previous example. We will add two more courses to Jackie's offerings, each with a new namespace, and show how namespaces not only avoid collisions but also allow us to minimize the code in the transformation.

EXAMPLE 10.14

Using Namespaces with an XSL Transformation

```
1.    <?xml version="1.0" encoding="ISO-8859-1"?>
2.    <?xml-stylesheet type = "text/xsl" href = "ex_10_14.xsl"?>
3.    <!-- Example 10.14a: the XML file -->
4.    <jackie_classes>
5.        <course xmlns:bead = "http://jackie.com/bead">
6.            <description>Beading classes</description>
7.            <when>Monday eve, 7-9</when>
8.            <where>Room 2</where>
9.            <package>Packet of multicolored beads</package>
10.           <pack_cost>$5.00</pack_cost>
11.           <singles>African trade beads</singles>
12.           <single_cost>$2.00 per bead</single_cost>
13.       </course>
14.       <course xmlns:bracelet = "http://jackie.com/bracelet">
15.           <description>Creating necklaces and pendants</description>
16.           <when>Tuesday eve, 7-9</when>
17.           <where>Room 4</where>
18.           <package>silver chain and choice of pendant</package>
19.           <pack_cost>$10.00</pack_cost>
20.           <singles>silver charms - hearts, animals, shapes</singles>
21.           <single_cost>$8.00 per charm</single_cost>
22.       </course>
23.       <course xmlns:earrings = "http://jackie.com/earrings">
24.           <description>Creating earrings</description>
25.           <when>Thursday eve, 7-9</when>
26.           <where>Room 3</where>
27.           <package>feathers, beads, hoops, assorted</package>
28.           <pack_cost>$12.00</pack_cost>
29.           <singles>hoops or charms</singles>
30.           <single_cost>$10.00 per hoop or charm</single_cost>
31.       </course>
32.       <course xmlns:mixed = "http://jackie.com/mixed">
33.           <description>Create Your Own: all jewelry types</description>
34.           <when>Saturdays 9am-2pm</when>
35.           <where>Room 3</where>
36.           <package>select any package, one price</package>
37.           <pack_cost>$15.00</pack_cost>
38.           <singles>choose your own items</singles>
39.           <single_cost>prices will vary</single_cost>
```

```
40.        </course>
41.    </jackie_classes>
```

Note that we have added a link to the XSL document on line 2. Each <course> element now has a separate namespace. The XSL document looks almost exactly like the one we created for a previous example but, with the addition of namespaces, it will create a table with four rows, one for each different course (differentiated by the namespaces). The code is as follows:

```
1.   <?xml version="1.0"?>
2.   <!--Example 10.14 xsl file -->
3.       <xsl:stylesheet version="2.0" xmlns:xsl = ↵
                             "http://www.w3.org/1999/XSL/Transform">
4.       <xsl:output method = "html" doctype-system = "about:legacy- ↵
                             compat"/>
5.       <xsl:template match="/">
6.       <html>
7.       <head>
8.           <meta charset = "utf-8"/>
9.           <link rel = "stylesheet" type = "text/css" href = ↵
                             "jackie.css"/>
10.          <title>Jackie's Jewelry | Jewelry Making Classes</title>
11.      </head>
12.      <body>
13.          <h2>Jackie's Jewelry Making Classes</h2>
14.          <table border = "1" align = "center" width = "80%" ↵
                             cellpadding = "5">
15.              <tr bgcolor="blue">
16.                  <th>Course Name</th>
17.                  <th>Location</th>
18.                  <th>Days and Times</th>
19.                  <th>Supply Package</th>
20.                  <th>Package Cost</th>
21.                  <th>Single Items</th>
22.                  <th>Single Item Cost</th>
23.              </tr>
24.      <!-- insert each course information into a table row -->
25.          <xsl:for-each select = "/jackie_classes/course" ↵
                       xmlns:bead='http://jackie.com/bead' ↵
                       xmlns:bracelet='http//jackie.com/bracelet' ↵
                       xmlns:earrings='http//jackie.com/earrings' ↵
                       xmlns:mixed = 'http://jackie.com/mixed' >
26.              <tr>
27.                  <td><xsl:value-of select = "description" /></td>
28.                  <td><xsl:value-of select = "where" /></td>
29.                  <td><xsl:value-of select = "when" /></td>
30.                  <td><xsl:value-of select = "package" /></td>
31.                  <td><xsl:value-of select = "pack_cost" /></td>
32.                  <td><xsl:value-of select = "singles" /></td>
33.                  <td><xsl:value-of select = "single_cost" /></td>
34.              </tr>
35.          </xsl:for-each>
36.              <tr>
37.                  <td colspan = "7">Each class runs for 4 weeks. ↵
                             <br />The cost is $8.00 per class or ↵
```

```
                                    $25.00 for each 4-week session, ↵
                                    payable in advance. </td>
38.                  </tr>
39.                </table>
40.            </body>
41.    </html>
42.    </xsl:template>
43.    </xsl:stylesheet>
```

Most of this code is familiar from Example 10.12. However, by adding the namespace attributes on line 25, the for-each loop will be processed four times, each time creating a new row in the table and each row will be populated with the contents of the elements that correspond to that namespace. If you create these two files and open the XML file in a browser, you will get the following output:

Jackie's Jewelry Making Classes

Course Name	Location	Days and Times	Supply Package	Package Cost	Single Items	Single Item Cost
Beading classes	Room 2	Monday eve, 7-9	Packet of multicolored beads	$5.00	African trade beads	$2.00 per bead
Creating necklaces and pendants	Room 4	Tuesday eve, 7-9	silver chain and choice of pendant	$10.00	silver charms - hearts, animals, shapes	$8.00 per charm
Creating earrings	Room 3	Thursday eve, 7-9	feathers, beads, hoops, assorted	$12.00	hoops or charms	$10.00 per hoop or charm
Create Your Own: all jewelry types	Room 3	Saturdays 9am-2pm	select any package, one price	$15.00	choose your own items	prices will vary

Each class runs for 4 weeks.
The cost is $8.00 per class or $25.00 for each 4-week session, payable in advance.

XML Schemas

Previously we used a DTD to define how we wanted our XML documents structured. An **XML schema** will do the same thing but adds the ability to define and constrain the contents of elements. For this reason, developers often prefer schemas over DTDs. When you use an XML schema, you must declare namespaces in both the XML document and the XML schema document. The namespace for the XML schema document is declared by using the <schema> element as the root of every XML schema, as follows:

```
<xs:schema xmlns:xs = "http://www.w3.org/2001/XMLSchema"
targetNamespace = "http://www.w3schools.com" xmlns =
"http://www.w3schools.com" elementFormDefault = "qualified">
```

We will explain each part of this declaration.

```
xmlns:xs="http://www.w3.org/2001/XMLSchema"
```

This tells us that the elements and data types used in the schema come from the "http://www.w3.org/2001/XMLSchema" namespace and that the elements and data types that come from the "http://www.w3.org/2001/XMLSchema" namespace should be prefixed with xs.

```
targetNamespace="http://www.w3schools.com"
```

This indicates that the elements defined by this schema will come from the "http://w3schools.com" namespace.

```
xmlns="http://www.w3schools.com"
```

This indicates the default namespace which is "http://w3schools.com".

```
elementFormDefault="qualified"
```

This ensures that any elements used by the XML document declared in this schema must be namespace qualified. This means that elements from a target namespace must be qualified with the namespace prefix. The default is "unqualified". The elementFormDefault attribute is optional.

Creating a Reference to a Schema in an XML Document

To reference a schema in an XML document, we might use something like this:

```
<jackie_classes xmlns = "http://www.w3schools.com"
xmlns:xsi = "http://www.w3.org/2001/XMLSchema-instance"
xsi:schemaLocation = "http://jackie.com course_schema.xsd">
```

jackie_classes and **xmlns="http://www.w3schools.com"**

The first item, jackie_classes, is simply the root element of the XML document. The next part (xmlns="http://www.w3schools.com") specifies the default namespace declaration which tells the schema-validator that all elements in this document are declared in the w3schools.com namespace.

```
xmlns:xsi="http://www.w3.org/2001/XMLSchema-instance"
```

This is a namespace that is used for instance documents of XML schemas. When an XML file uses an XML schema to define its valid format, it is said to be an **instance document** of that schema. Thus, this part makes the XML schema instance namespace available.

```
xsi:schemaLocation="http://jackie.com course_schema.xsd"
```

This indicates where the schema document resides (i.e., schemaLocation). The location has two parts. The first part (http://jackie.com) is the namespace to use. The second part, separated from the first by a space, is the name of the schema document.

TABLE 10.4	XML Schema Built-In Data Types	
Data Type	**Syntax**	**Description**
integer	`<xs:element name ="the_int" type = "xs:integer"/>`	integer values
decimal	`<xs:element name ="a_num" type = "xs:decimal"/>`	numeric values
string	`<xs:element name ="my_str" type = "xs:string"/>`	character strings
date	`<xs:element name ="the_date" type = "xs:date"/>`	specifies a date
time	`<xs:element name ="the_time" type = "xs:time"/>`	time in hh:mm:ss
boolean	`<xs:element name ="t_or_f" type = "xs:boolean"/>`	true or false value

In this case, we assume the schema document is named `course_schema.xsd`, where `xsd` is the normal extension for a schema document.

There's More ...

Note that XML schema specifications can contain a great deal more components than we will cover in this book. This is merely an introductory overview.

XML Schema Data Types

There are a number of built-in data types that come with the XML schema specification. Web developers can also create their own data types. For example, you might want to create a data type for a student identification number that consists of eight integers based on the simple `integer` data type or an identification number for business customers that consists of a two-character prefix and a six-digit number based on the `string` data type. Table 10.4 lists some of the more common built-in data types.

Creating an XML Schema

An XML schema document is written as an XML document, using all the same syntax rules of XML. The normal file extension is **.xsd**. Schema definitions for elements are either simple types or complex types. A **simple type element** is an element that has no child elements. They are written as empty elements in the schema. **Complex elements** can contain child elements and attributes. Example 10.15 demonstrates an XML schema consisting of all simple types. Example 10.16 uses complex elements.

An XML Schema Using Simple Type Elements

This first example is as simple as it can be. We have an XML document with one element. Following the XML document is the **XSD document,** the schema for this document.

XML document:

```
1.   <?xml version="1.0" encoding="ISO-8859-1"?>
2.   <!-- Example 10.15: XML document -->
3.   <jackie_classes
4.        xmlns:xsi="http://www.w3.org/2001/XMLSchema-instance"
5.        xsi:schemaLocation="course_schema.xsd">
6.        Jackie offers several jewelry making courses at affordable rates.
7.   </jackie_classes>
```

The schema for this document is saved in a file named `course_schema.xsd` and, in this case, resides in the same folder on a server as the `.xml` file.

XSD document:

```
1.   <?xml version="1.0" encoding="ISO-8859-1"?>
2.   <!-- Example 10.15: the schema document -->
3.   <xsd:schema xmlns:xsd="http://www.w3.org/2001/XMLSchema">
4.        <xsd:element name = "jackie_classes" type="xsd:string" />
5.   </xsd:schema>
```

Line 3 of this document is the namespace declaration for the root element of this document, <xsd:schema>. Line 4 defines the format for the root element of the XML document. Our root element in the XML document is <jackie_classes> so the attribute name references "jackie_classes". This element is an empty element. The type attribute is string because the contents of <jackie_classes> is string content. Line 5 ends the <xsd:schema> element.

An XML Schema Using Complex Type Elements

EXAMPLE 10.16

In this case, our XML file will have both parent and child elements so we need to include complex type elements in the schema document. We have added an element for the date which uses the date data type and included two new attributes: **minOccurs** and **maxOccurs**. Following the XML document is the XSD document, the schema for this document.

XML document:

```
1.   <?xml version="1.0" encoding="ISO-8859-1"?>
2.   <!-- Example 10.16: XML document -->
3.   <jackie_classes
4.       xmlns:xsi="http://www.w3.org/2001/XMLSchema-instance"
5.       xsi:schemaLocation="jackie2_schema.xsd">
6.       <recipient>To: Pat Donnelly</recipient>
7.       <subject>A new Beading Class!</subject>
8.       <date_sent />
9.       <when>Monday evenings, 7 - 9 pm</when>
10.      <where>At Jackie's house: 123 Duckpond Lane</where>
11.  </jackie_classes>
```

The schema for this document is saved in a file named jackie2_schema.xsd and, in this case, resides in the same folder on a server as the .xml file.

XSD document:

```
1.   <?xml version="1.0" encoding="ISO-8859-1"?>
2.   <!-- Example 10.16: the schema document -->
3.   <xsd:schema xmlns:xsd="http://www.w3.org/2001/XMLSchema">
4.       <xsd:element name = "jackie_classes">
5.           <xsd:complexType>
6.               <xsd:sequence>
7.                   <xsd:element: name = "recipient" type = ⏎
                                "xsd:string" minOccurs = "1" ⏎
                                maxOccurs = "unbounded"/>
8.                   <xsd:element: name = "subject" type = ⏎
                                "xsd:string" minOccurs = "1"/>
9.                   <xsd:element: name = "date_sent" type = ⏎
                                "xsd:date"/>
10.                  <xsd:element: name = "when" type = "xsd:string"/>
11.                  <xsd:element: name = "where" type = "xsd:string"/>
12.              </xsd:sequence>
13.          </xsd:complexType>
14.      </xsd:element>
15.  </xsd:schema>
```

A line-by-line explanation of this code is as follows:

- Lines 1 and 3 perform the same tasks as the previous example. The first line is the XML declaration and line 3 is the namespace declaration for the root element of this document, `<xsd:schema>`.

- Line 4 defines the root element of the XML document, `<jackie_classes>`. This time this element is not defined as an empty element because it has child elements. Therefore, it must be closed on line 14.

- Line 5 defines the element as a `complexType` element.

- The `<xsd:sequence>` declaration on line 6 allows the developer to control the order in which the elements appear in the XML document.

- Lines 7, 8, 9, and 10 define the child elements, `<recipient>`, `<subject>`, `<date_sent>`, `<when>`, and `<where>`. All are empty elements (i.e., are closed in the same tag as they are opened) and all contain the `name` attribute which identifies them in the XML document. Some of the attributes are worth explaining.

- The `<recipient>` element on line 7 has two attributes we have not used yet. The `minOccurs` attribute is set to `"1"`, meaning there must be at least one occurrence of this element. The `maxOccurs` attribute is set to `"unbounded"` which means this attribute can occur as many times as desired. That way this document can be used to send this message to as many people as Jackie wants.

- The `<subject>` element on line 8 sets `minOccurs` to `"1"` but does not include the `maxOccurs` attribute. Since the default value for both this attribute and `maxOccurs` is already `"1"`, this attribute was not necessary but is used here to show that it can be used alone, in conjunction with `maxOccurs`, or not at all.

- The `<date_sent>` element on line 9 uses the `date` data type which allows today's date to be included here.

- Lines 10 and 11 include the `name` attributes for the `<when>` and `<where>` elements as well as setting their data types to `string`.

- Finally, all elements that were opened on lines 3, 4, 5, and 6 are closed in correct order on lines 12, 13, 14, and 15.

If we add some styles (through a CSS page) and open this page in a browser, using the information given in the example, the output will be as follows:

> **To: Pat Donnelly**
> A new Beading Class!
> Monday evenings, 7 - 9 pm
> At Jackie's house: 123 Duckpond Lane

CHECKPOINT FOR SECTION 10.5 ✓

10.27 An XML namespace is used to avoid confusion when two or more _____ have the same _____.

10.28 Name one advantage of an XML schema over a DTD.

10.29 What is the purpose of a URI in a namespace declaration?

10.30 What is the attribute in the following namespace declaration?

```
xmlns:start = "http://leeland.com"
```

10.31 What is the root element of every XML schema?

10.32 What type of element should be used in an XML schema for the following XML document?

```
<?xml version="1.0" encoding="ISO-8859-1"?>
    <lees_email
        xmlns:xsi="http://www.w3.org/2001/XMLSchema-instance"
        xsi:schemaLocation="lee_schema.xsd">
        <to>To: Bob Roberts</to>
        <subject>Lawn Maintenance</subject>
        <date_sent>August 3 </date_sent>
        <body>We will be out to mow your lawn this week</body>
        <closing>See you then! Warm regards, Lee</closing>
    </lees_email>
```

10.6 Putting It to Work

We will develop a page for players to use when signing into the Greg's Gambits site and a spelling lesson for Carla's Classroom. Both sites will make use of the DOM, XML, and XSL concepts we have learned in this chapter.

Greg's Gambits: Greg's Avatars

This program will use what we have learned about XML and XSL to create a page that allows players to see the various avatar options available. The player will then be able to view more details about any avatar, using DOM methods to add elements to the page. The information on the initial page will include the following:

Greg's Gambits: The Avatars

Avatar	Special Powers	Home Base	Accessories	Partner
Bunny	hops up to 100 feet	rabbit warren	Easter basket	fox
Princess	mesmerizes anyone	castle	make-up case	knight
Ghost	invisibility	haunted house	sunglasses	vampire
Wizard	fire-maker	cave	magic wand	black cat
Elf	super hearing	inside an oak tree	bow and arrow	dragon

The player will also be able to view detailed information about each avatar. This information will appear only when a specific avatar is chosen.

Developing the Program

The final web page will actually be a compilation of four documents—an XML page to hold information about the five avatars for the initial display, a CSS page for presentational styles, an XSL page to transform the XML page to an HTML web page, and an external JavaScript page which holds the code to display detailed information about each avatar, using DOM methods to create and append nodes. This information is in an external file, gregAvatars.js, in the Student Data Files. You can change the descriptions if you wish, of course. The images used are also in the Student Data Files as well as the CSS style sheet used with this example.

Setting the Stage

Let's begin by creating the XML page that will hold the beginning information about each avatar. We'll call the root element of the page <greg>. When we look at the table above, we see that there are five columns. This means each avatar will be a parent element with five child elements. We will call the parent element <avatar> and the five child elements <name>, <powers>, <home>, <carry>, and <partner>. We will also assign namespaces to each <avatar> element, using the imaginary domain for greg: greg.com. We'll name this file greg_avatars.xml and place a link to this on Greg's index.html page since this page will be used when a new player signs up and selects an avatar. In Chapter 1, we created a sign-in page but that page assumed the player had previously created a username. It allowed players to select an avatar but it was a rather simple process and only showed avatar images. Our new page will allow players to view more information about the avatars before making a selection. We want this page to be used by newcomers to the site so we'll add a link to Greg's home page. It's been a while since we used that page so the code is shown below with a new link to a sign-up page:

```
1.   <html>
2.   <head>
3.       <title>Greg's Gambits</title>
4.       <link href="greg.css" rel="stylesheet" type="text/css" />
5.   </head>
6.   <body>
7.   <div id="container">
8.       <img src="images/superhero.jpg" class="floatleft" />
9.       <h1><em>Greg's Gambits </em></h1>
10.      <h2 align="center"><em> Games for Everyone!</em></h2>
11.      <div style="clear:both;"></div>
12.      <div id="nav">
13.          <p><a href="index.html">Home</a>
14.          <a href="greg.html">About Greg</a>
15.          <a href="play_games.html">Play a Game</a>
16.          <a href="sign.html">Sign In</a>
17.          <a href="contact.html">Contact Us</a>
18.          <a href="aboutyou.html">Tell Greg About You</a>
19.          <a href="sign_up.html">Sign up Now!</a></p>
20.      </div>
21.      <div id="content">
22.          <p>Greg's Gambits offers a variety of games for all ages ⏎
                 and more are added all the time. You can play ⏎
                 our games any time you want for free.</p>
23.          <p>Meet the real-life Greg in the About Greg page. Sign ⏎
                 up to keep your account active or sign in every ⏎
                 time you return through our sign Up link. Choose ⏎
                 your game from the play a Game menu and contact ⏎
                 always looking for new games and new ideas!</p>
24.      </div>
```

```
25.        <div id="footer">
26.            Copyright &copy; 2013 Greg's Gambits<br /> ↵
                    <a href = "mailto:gregory@gambits.net"> ↵
                    gregory@gambits.net</a>
27.        </div>
28.    </div>
29.    </body>
30.    </html>
```

The new link is on line 19. The home page for Greg's Gambits now looks like this:

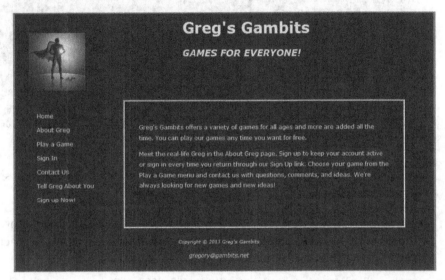

Let's create the simple sign_up.html page for new players to use when they want to sign up. Right now it will only have a link to the XML file we are creating in this section but more pages can be added later as we learn to use PHP. The page uses the same template as all the other pages. The code is as follows:

```
1.    <html>
2.    <head>
3.        <title>Greg's Gambits | Sign Up Now!</title>
4.        <link href="greg.css" rel="stylesheet" type="text/css" />
5.    </head>
6.    <body>
7.    <div id="container">
8.        <img src="images/superhero.jpg" class="floatleft" />
9.        <h1 id="logo">Greg's Gambits </h1>
10.       <h2 align="center"><em> Games for Everyone!</em></h2>
11.       <div style="clear:both;"></div>
12.       <div id="nav">
13.           <p> ... navigation links go here... </p>
14.       </div>
15.       <div id="content">
16.           <p>Sign up now!</p>
17.           <p><a href="greg_avatars.xml">View information ↵
                    about avatars</a></p>
18.       </div>
19.       <div id="footer"> ... footer here ... </div>
20.    </div>
21.    </body>
22.    </html>
```

Notice that the link on line 17 goes to an XML page, not an HTML page. This page looks like this:

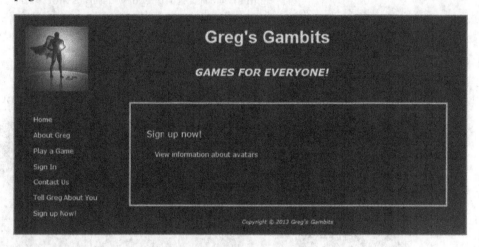

Creating the XML, XSL, and JavaScript Pages

We need four pages for the Avatars page to work. The CSS style sheet is the same as the one we have been using throughout the text.

Creating the XML Page   Now we will create the XML document. It has a root element, a parent element, and five child elements—one set for each avatar. The filename will be greg_avatars.xml. The code is as follows:

```
1.   <?xml version="1.0" encoding="ISO-8859-1"?>
2.   <?xml-stylesheet type = "text/xsl" href = "greg_avatars.xsl"?>
3.   <!-- Greg's Gambits Avatars: the XML file -->
4.   <greg>
5.       <avatar xmlns:bunny = "http://greg.com/bunny">
6.           <name>Bunny</name>
7.           <powers>hops up to 100 feet</powers>
8.           <home>rabbit warren</home>
9.           <carry>Easter basket</carry>
10.          <partner>fox</partner>
11.      </avatar>
12.      <avatar xmlns:princess = "http://greg.com/princess">
13.          <name>Princess</name>
14.          <powers>mesmerizes anyone</powers>
15.          <home>castle</home>
16.          <carry>make-up case</carry>
17.          <partner>knight</partner>
18.      </avatar>
19.      <avatar xmlns:ghost = "http://greg.com/ghost">
20.          <name>Ghost</name>
21.          <powers>invisibility</powers>
22.          <home>haunted house</home>
23.          <carry>sunglasses</carry>
24.          <partner>vampire</partner>
25.      </avatar>
26.      <avatar xmlns:wizard = "http://greg.com/wizard">
27.          <name>Wizard</name>
28.          <powers>fire-maker</powers>
```

```
29.              <home>a cave</home>
30.              <carry>magic wand</carry>
31.              <partner>black cat</partner>
32.          </avatar>
33.          <avatar xmlns:elf = "http://greg.com/elf">
34.              <name>Elf</name>
35.              <powers>super hearing</powers>
36.              <home>inside an oak tree</home>
37.              <carry>bow and arrow</carry>
38.              <partner>dragon</partner>
39.          </avatar>
40.      </greg>
```

Notice that this page links to the XSL page we will create next (line 2). At this point, the XML page is our source tree in the transformation that will happen when it accesses the XSL page.

Each <avatar> element has five child elements, filled with the information shown on the table at the beginning of this section. Each parent element also contains a namespace. We have used the imaginary greg.com domain to ensure that these namespaces are unique. Lines 5, 12, 19, 26, and 33 contain the xmlns attribute, each value assigns a namespace to that <avatar> element and, by inheritance, to the child element descendants. Since no XML styles have been added, if you open this page in a browser at this point, the output will be as follows:

```
<!-- Greg's Gambits Avatars: the XML file -->
<greg>
    <avatar xmlns:bunny = "http://greg.com/bunny">
        <name>Bunny</name>
        <powers>hops up to 100 feet</powers>
        <home>rabbit warren</home>
        <carry>Easter basket</carry>
        <partner>fox</partner>
    </avatar>
    <avatar xmlns:princess = "http://greg.com/princess">
        <name>Princess</name>
        <powers>mesmerizes anyone</powers>
        <home>castle</home>
        <carry>make-up case</carry>
        <partner>knight</partner>
    </avatar>
    <avatar xmlns:ghost = "http://greg.com/ghost">
        <name>Ghost</name>
        <powers>invisibility</powers>
        <home>haunted house</home>
        <carry>sunglasses</carry>
        <partner>vampire</partner>
    </avatar>
    <avatar xmlns:wizard = "http://greg.com/wizard">
        <name>Wizard</name>
        <powers>fire-maker</powers>
        <home>a cave</home>
        <carry>magic wand</carry>
        <partner>black cat</partner>
    </avatar>
    <avatar xmlns:elf = "http://greg.com/elf">
        <name>Elf</name>
        <powers>super hearing</powers>
        <home>inside an oak tree</home>
        <carry>bow and arrow</carry>
        <partner>dragon</partner>
    </avatar>
</greg>
```

Creating the XSL Page   Now we will create the XSL page that will transform the information in the XML page to a new web page. We want to put this information into a Greg's Gambits template in a table within the "content" <div>. Later we will want to add some JavaScript code that will allow the new player to click a button and see more detailed information about any of the avatars. So we will include some HTML script in the beginning of the page and some at the end. In the middle we will use XSL code to populate the table with XML information. The file name for this page will be greg_avatars.xsl and it needs to be stored in the same folder as greg_avatars.xml. The code for this page is as follows:

```
1.   <?xml version="1.0"?>
2.   <!--Example Greg Gambits Avatars: xsl file -->
3.   <xsl:stylesheet version="2.0" xmlns:xsl = ⏎
                        "http://www.w3.org/1999/XSL/Transform">
4.   <xsl:output method = "html" doctype-system = "about:legacy-compat"/>
5.   <xsl:template match="/">
6.   <html>
7.   <head>
8.       <meta charset = "utf-8"/>
9.       <link rel = "stylesheet" type = "text/css" href = "greg.css"/>
10.      <script type="text/javascript" src="gregAvatars.js"></script>
11.      <title>Greg's Gambits | The Avatars</title>
12.  </head>
13.  <body>
14.      <div id="container" style="width: 900px;">
15.          <img src="images/superhero.jpg" class="floatleft" />
16.          <h1 align="center">Avatar Options</h1>
17.          <div style ="clear:both;"></div>
18.          <div id="nav">
19.              <p><a href="index.html">Home</a>
20.              <a href="greg.html">About Greg</a>
21.              <a href="play_games.html">Play a Game</a>
22.              <a href="sign.html">Sign In</a>
23.              <a href="contact.html">Contact Us</a>
24.              <a href="sign_up.html">Sign up Now!</a></p>
25.          </div>
26.          <div id="content">
27.              <table border = "1" align = "center" width = "100%" ⏎
                                cellpadding = "5">
28.                  <tr>
29.                      <th>Avatar</th>
30.                      <th>Special Powers</th>
31.                      <th>Home Base</th>
32.                      <th>Accessories</th>
33.                      <th>Partner</th>
34.                  </tr>
35.  <!-- insert each avatar's information into a table row -->
36.              <xsl:for-each select = "/greg/avatar"
37.              xmlns:bunny = 'http://greg.com/bunny'
38.              xmlns:princess = 'http://greg.com/princess'
39.              xmlns:ghost = 'http://greg.com/ghost'
40.              xmlns:wizard = 'http://greg.com/wizard'
41.              xmlns:elf = 'http://greg.com/elf'>
42.                  <tr>
```

```
43.                          <td><xsl:value-of select = "name" /></td>
44.                          <td><xsl:value-of select = "powers" /></td>
45.                          <td><xsl:value-of select = "home" /></td>
46.                          <td><xsl:value-of select = "carry" /></td>
47.                          <td><xsl:value-of select = "partner" /></td>
48.                  </tr>
49.              </xsl:for-each>
50.              <tr>
51.                  <td colspan = "5">Select an avatar to view more ⏎
                         details.</td>
52.              </tr>
53.              <tr>
54.                  <td align = "center"><img src = "bunny.jpg" /> ⏎
                         <br /><input type = "button" id = ⏎
                         "bunny" value = "Bunny Details" ⏎
                         onclick = "getMore('bunny')" /></td>
55.                  <td align = "center"><img src = "princess.jpg" /> ⏎
                         <br /><input type = "button" id = ⏎
                         "princess" value = "Princess Details" ⏎
                         onclick = "getMore('princess')" /></td>
56.                  <td align = "center"><img src = "ghost.jpg" /> ⏎
                         <br /><input type = "button" id = ⏎
                         "ghost" value = "Ghost Details" ⏎
                         onclick = "getMore('ghost')" /></td>
57.                  <td align = "center"><img src = "wizard.jpg" /> ⏎
                         <br /><input type = "button" id = ⏎
                         "wizard" value = "Wizard Details" ⏎
                         onclick = "getMore('wizard')" /></td>
58.                  <td align = "center"><img src = "elf.jpg" /> ⏎
                         <br /><input type = "button" id = ⏎
                         "elf" value = "Elf Details" ⏎
                         "getMore('elf')" /></td>
59.              </tr>
60.              <tr>
61.                  <td id = "details" colspan = "5">Details</td>
62.              </tr>
63.          </table>
64.      </div>
65.  </div>
66.  </body>
67.  </html>
68.  </xsl:template>
69.  </xsl:stylesheet>
```

The first eight lines of this code were described in detail in Section 10.5. Line
9 links the page to the styles defined in Greg's CSS. Line 10 links to an external
JavaScript file that we will create next. Lines 11–34 are HTML code to set up the
page. The "content" <div> now contains a new table with headings for each avatar's name, special powers, home, accessories, and partner.

The XSL begins on line 36. It begins the loop to populate the table, one row at a
time, with the contents of the elements that correspond to each parent (<avatar>)
element. Lines 37–41 refer to the namespaces for each <avatar> element. Lines
43–47 insert the values in each child element (<name>, <powers>, <home>, <carry>,

and <partner>) into the cells of a row. Line 49 indicates the end of this loop and, for this page, this is the end of the transformation.

Line 50 begins a new row that provides instructions to the user about how to view more details about any of the avatars. The next row contains five cells. Each cell has a picture of one avatar and a button that, when clicked, will access a function on the `gregAvatars.js` page. We will create that page and explain how the function uses DOM methods to display more information about each avatar.

This page cannot do anything by itself. It is used to transform another XML page. Thus, if you opened this page in a browser, you would just see the document tree.

Creating the JavaScript Page and the DOM Code At this point, if we open the XML page, it will be transformed to an HTML page and look like the one shown below but clicking the buttons will do nothing:

Avatar	Special Powers	Home Base	Accessories	Partner
Bunny	hops up to 100 feet	rabbit warren	Easter basket	fox
Princess	mesmerizes anyone	castle	make-up case	knight
Ghost	invisibility	haunted house	sunglasses	vampire
Wizard	fire-maker	a cave	magic wand	black cat
Elf	super hearing	inside an oak tree	bow and arrow	dragon

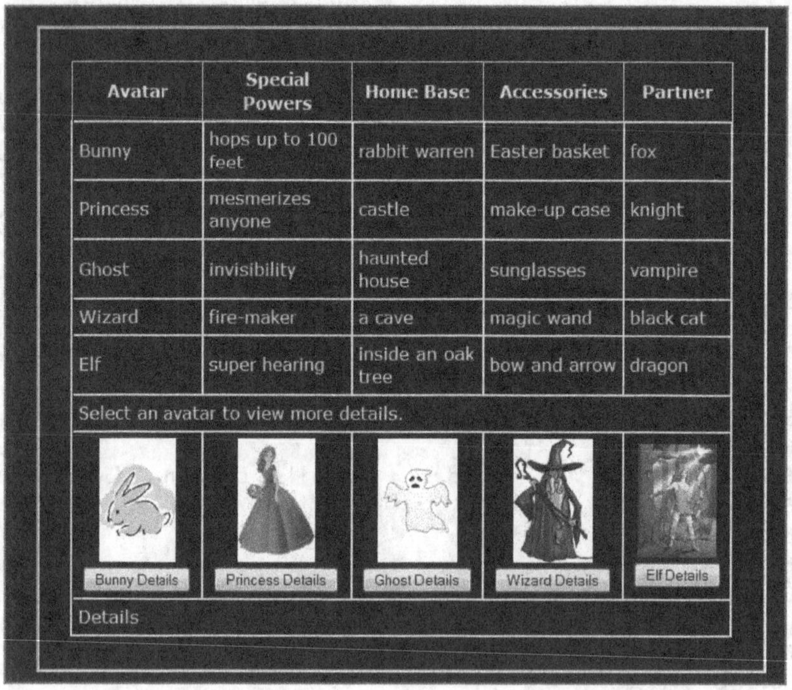

The JavaScript code will display details about the avatar selected by the user. We will use the DOM `createElement()`, `createTextNode()`, and `appendChild()` methods to create and display information in the `"details"` cell. The code uses a `switch` statement and looks like this:

```
function getMore(x)
{
 switch (x)
 {
      case "bunny":
           var bunnyDetails = document.createElement("p");
```

```
7.           var bunnyInfo = document.createTextNode("The bunny can hop ↵
                 to a height of 100 feet and span 100 feet at a time. ↵
                 The Easter Basket is magical and holds anything put ↵
                 into it, even a house (if you can lift it and move ↵
                 it!). The basket comes pre-loaded with supplies like ↵
                 chocolate eggs and a bag of life-sustaining jelly ↵
                 beans. The bunny's partner is a clever fox who is sly ↵
                 and quick-witted. Together with the bunny their ↵
                 intelligence is unmatched. ");
8.           bunnyDetails.appendChild(bunnyInfo);
9.           document.getElementById("details").appendChild(bunnyDetails);
10.          break;
11.     case "princess":
12.          var prinDetails = document.createElement("p");
13.          var prinInfo = document.createTextNode("The princess is so ↵
                 lovely that she mesmerizes anyone who looks at her, ↵
                 man and woman alike. Her makeup case holds her own ↵
                 makeup (although she rarely needs any, as lovely as ↵
                 she already is) but also allows her to transform her ↵
                 appearance to any human or animal form. The princess ↵
                 can call her knight whenever she needs him. He will ↵
                 always appear, garbed in his shining armor.");
14.          prinDetails.appendChild(prinInfo);
15.          document.getElementById("details").appendChild(prinDetails);
16.          break;
17.     case "ghost":
18.          var ghostDetails = document.createElement("p");
19.          var ghostInfo = document.createTextNode("The ghost can appear ↵
                 n ghostly form or become invisible at will. His ↵
                 sunglasses allow him to see through any barrier and ↵
                 increase his sight to a range of 20 miles. The ghost ↵
                 has no need for food, water, or sleep. While the ghost ↵
                 cannot speak, the sunglasses can amplify any sound. To ↵
                 alert a companion to danger, the ghost can tap the ↵
                 sunglasses on any surface. The ghost's best friend is ↵
                 a vampire who can walk among humans (at night, of ↵
                 course) when necessary to aid the ghost.");
20.          ghostDetails.appendChild(ghostInfo);
21.          document.getElementById("details").appendChild(ghostDetails);
22.          break;
23.     case "wizard":
24.          var wizardDetails = document.createElement("p");
25.          var wizardInfo = document.createTextNode("The wizard is a ↵
                 first-class magician. With his magic wand he can ↵
                 weave spells that confound even the hardiest souls. ↵
                 His magic is rivaled by no person or creature, save ↵
                 the evil warlock, Dartmouth Dreadful. The wizard wears ↵
                 a cloak that has bottomless pockets, pre-loaded with a ↵
                 week's supply of food and water. The wizard's cat is ↵
                 very cuddly and provides the wizard with the love and ↵
                 companionship the solitary wizard often craves.");
26.          wizardDetails.appendChild(wizardInfo);
27.          document.getElementById("details").appendChild(wizardDetails);
28.          break;
29.     case "elf":
```

```
30.              var elfDetails = document.createElement("p");
31.              var elfInfo = document.createTextNode("The elf is the ⏎
                 mischief-maker. With the ability to hear sounds as ⏎
                 far as 20 miles off, the elf always knows what or ⏎
                 who is approaching. The elf's bow and arrows shoot ⏎
                 true, rarely missing their mark. The elf also climbs ⏎
                 trees with the agility of a squirrel, climbs mountains ⏎
                 like a mountain goat, and is as comfortable in water ⏎
                 as an otter. The elf's quiver holds a dozen arrows ⏎
                 which are automatically replenished after 11 are ⏎
                 used.  The elf and dragon are rarely parted. The elf ⏎
                 babysits the dragon's one young dragon-ette in a ⏎
                 nursery deep within the elf's giant oak tree and the ⏎
                 dragon provides transportation by air whenever the ⏎
                 elf must travel long distances quickly.");
32.          elfDetails.appendChild(elfInfo);
33.          document.getElementById("details").appendChild(elfDetails);
34.          break;
35.      }
36.  }
```

When the player clicks a button, the id that matches the requested avatar is sent to the getMore() function (see lines 54–58 of the XSL page). The id will be either "bunny", "princess", "ghost", "wizard", or "elf". The switch statement matches that id with one of the cases. For each case, the following happens: On lines 6, 12, 18, 24, and 30 a variable is declared (**bunnyDetails**, **prinDetails**, **ghostDetails**, **wizardDetails**, or **elfDetails**) and set to the value of a new paragraph element, using the createElement() DOM method.

Lines 7, 13, 19, 25, and 31 then create a new variable that stores the value of a text node. These variables are, depending on the avatar selected, **bunnyInfo**, **prinInfo**, **ghostInfo**, **wizardInfo**, or **elfInfo**. The node is created using the DOM createTextNode() method. The text for each avatar is a paragraph that gives details about that avatar.

Lines 8, 14, 20, 26, and 32 use the appendChild() method to add the value of the text to the paragraph element.

Finally, on lines 9, 15, 21, 27, and 33 the element that has been created and filled with text is displayed on the web page. The getElementById() method identifies where the new element should go—into the place with id = "details". The appendChild() method, using the new element's name as its argument (**bunnyDetails**, **prinDetails**, **ghostDetails**, **wizardDetails**, or **elfDetails**) indicates what element will be appended to the "details" area.

Putting It All Together

Each page except the CSS page has been given in its entirety in this section so there is no need to repeat those pages here. Sample displays follow.

If the player wanted to see more detail about the ghost:

Avatar	Special Powers	Home Base	Accessories	Partner
Bunny	hops up to 100 feet	rabbit warren	Easter basket	fox
Princess	mesmerizes anyone	castle	make-up case	knight
Ghost	invisibility	haunted house	sunglasses	vampire
Wizard	fire-maker	a cave	magic wand	black cat
Elf	super hearing	inside an oak tree	bow and arrow	dragon

Select an avatar to view more details.

[Bunny Details] [Princess Details] [Ghost Details] [Wizard Details] [Elf Details]

Details

The ghost can appear in ghostly form or become invisible at will. His sunglasses allow him to see through any barrier and increase his sight to a range of 20 miles. The ghost has no need for food, water, or sleep. While the ghost cannot speak, the sunglasses can amplify any sound. To alert a companion to danger, the ghost can tap the sunglasses on any surface. The ghost's best friend is a vampire who can walk among humans (at night, of course) when necessary to aid the ghost.

But if the player is interested in the wizard:

If the player wanted to see details about several avatars, he or she can click more than one button. If the player selects the bunny, the princess, and the elf, the result will be as follows:

Carla's Classroom: A Spelling Lesson

For this lesson, we will add to Carla's reading inventory by creating a spelling exercise for students. Carla has selected some difficult spelling words. We will use our programming skills to present students with images and students will select the correctly spelled word that matches the picture. We will use what we have learned in this chapter about the DOM to add elements to the page as needed. You can add more words to this page or increase the functionality of the spelling exercise in the Programming Challenges at the end of the chapter.

Developing the Program

Before we start to develop the program we will add a link on Carla's `reading.html` page to this new page. We'll name this file `carla_spell_exercise.html` so, after you add this link, the `reading.html` page will look like this:

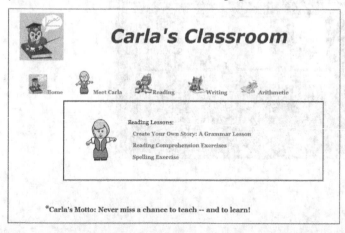

We will, as usual, use one of Carla's pages as a template and the page title for this page will be Carla's Classroom | Spelling Test. We will first create a table with 12 images and below it another table with words describing the images, but in a mixed up order. Since the purpose of this exercise is to learn to use DOM, we will not generate a random order for the images or words; we'll create the order ourselves. The images can be found in the Student Data Files or you can substitute your own images. If you use your own images, be sure they are sized equally so the table looks neat. For each image we need a button for the student to click when he or she selects an image and another button for the student to click when he or she decides on the correct spelling of this image word.

Setting the Stage

The JavaScript program will compare the value of the image name to the value of the word the student selects. When a student clicks a button, the value of the cell's id is sent to a JavaScript function. Therefore, it makes sense to have comparable id values for the cell that holds an image and its corresponding cell with the correct spelling. The code for the <body> of the page looks like this:

```
1.   <body>
2.   <div id="container">
3.       <img src="images/owl_reading.JPG" class="floatleft" />
4.       <h1><em>Carla's Classroom</em></h1>
5.       <div align="left">
6.       <blockquote>
7.           <a href = "index.html"><img src = "images/owl_button.jpg" ↵
                    />Home</a>
8.           <a href = "carla.html"><img src = "images/carla_button.jpg" ↵
                    />Meet Carla </a>
9.           <a href = "reading.html"><img src = "images/read_button.jpg" ↵
                    />Reading</a>
10.          <a href = "writing.html"><img src = ↵
                    "images/write_button.jpg" />Writing</a>
11.          <a href = "math.html"><img src = "images/arith_button.jpg" ↵
                    />Arithmetic</a><br />
12.      </blockquote>
13.      </div>
14.      <div id="content">
15.          <h3>Match the picture with the correct spelling of its ↵
                    name.</h3>
16.          <div id ="pictures">
17.          <table align = "center" border = "1">
18.          <tr>
19.              <td colspan = "6">Click on the little button below ↵
                    a picture</td>
20.          </tr>
21.          <tr>
22.              <td id = "ibananas"><img src = "images/bananas.jpg"/> ↵
                    <button onclick = "getImage('ibananas')"/></td>
23.              <td id = "iwizard"><img src = "images/wizard.jpg"/> ↵
                    <button onclick = "getImage('iwizard')"/> </td>
24.              <td id = "isword"><img src = "images/sword.jpg" /> ↵
                    <button onclick = "getImage('isword')" /> </td>
25.              <td id = "ibracelet"><img src = "images/bracelet.jpg" /> ↵
                    <button onclick = "getImage('ibracelet')" /></td>
```

```
26.                    <td id = "irocket"><img src = "images/rocket.jpg" /> ↵
                          <button onclick = "getImage('irocket')" /> </td>
27.                 <td id = "ilawnmower"><img src = ↵
                       "images/lawnmower.jpg" /> <button onclick = ↵
                       "getImage('ilawnmower')" /></td>
28.            </tr>
29.            <tr>
30.              <td id = "ighost"><img src = "images/ghost.jpg" /> ↵
                    <button onclick = "getImage('ighost')" /> </td>
31.              <td id = "icastle"><img src = "images/castle.jpg" /> ↵
                    <button onclick = "getImage('icastle')" /> </td>
32.              <td id = "irabbit"><img src = "images/rabbit.jpg" /> ↵
                    <button onclick = "getImage('irabbit')" /> </td>
33.              <td id = "inecklace"><img src = "images/necklace.jpg" ↵
                    /><button onclick = "getImage('inecklace')" /></td>
34.              <td id = "icelery"><img src = "images/celery.jpg" /> ↵
                    <button onclick = "getImage('icelery')" /> </td>
35.              <td id = "iflowers"><img src = "images/flowers.jpg" /> ↵
                    <button onclick = "getImage('iflowers')" /> </td>
36.            </tr>
37.          </table>
38.       </div>
39.       <div id = "spellings">
40.       <table align = "center" cellpadding = "10" border = "1">
41.       <tr>
42.              <td colspan = "6">Now click on the spelling that matches ↵
                    the picture</td>
43.       </tr>
44.       <tr>
45.              <td id = "scelery">celery<button onclick = ↵
                    "getSpell('scelery')" /></td>
46.              <td id = "slawnmower">lawnmower<button onclick = ↵
                    "getSpell('slawnmower')" /></td>
47.              <td id = "scastle">castle<button onclick = ↵
                    "getSpell('scastle')" /></td>
48.              <td id = "srocket">rocket<button onclick = ↵
                    "getSpell('srocket')" /></td>
49.              <td id = "sbananas">bananas<button onclick = ↵
                    "getSpell('sbananas')" /></td>
50.              <td id = "sflowers">flowers<button onclick = ↵
                    "getSpell('sflowers')" /></td>
51.       </tr>
52.       <tr>
53.              <td id = "swizard">wizard<button onclick = ↵
                    "getSpell('swizard')" /></td>
54.              <td id = "snecklace">necklace<button onclick = ↵
                    "getSpell('snecklace')" /></td>
55.              <td id = "sbracelet">bracelet<button onclick = ↵
                    "getSpell('sbracelet')" /></td>
56.              <td id = "sghost">ghost<button onclick = ↵
                    "getSpell('sghost')" /></td>
57.              <td id = "srabbit">rabbit<button onclick = ↵
                    "getSpell('srabbit')" /></td>
```

```
58.              <td id = "ssword">sword<button onclick = ↵
                            "getSpell('ssword')" /></td>
59.       </tr>
60.       </table>
61.   </div>
62.       <div id = "the_end"> </div>
63.   </div>
64.   </div>
65.       <div id="footer">  <h3>*Carla's Motto: Never miss a chance ↵
                            to teach -- and to learn!</h3>
66.       </div>
67.   </body>
```

Notice that all cell ids in the `<div id = "pictures">` begin with the character "i" and then include the spelled word that describes the image. Comparably, all the cell ids in the `<div id = "spellings">` begin with the character "s" and then the spelled word is appended. We can use this information in the functions that identify the cells selected and compare their values.

After creating this page, it should look like this:

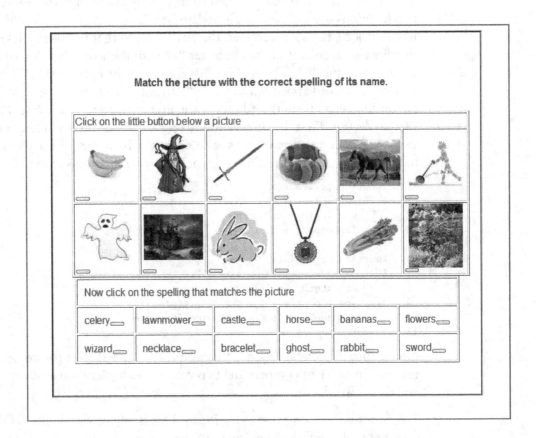

By using buttons without values, the buttons appear as small rectangles.

The Code in Pieces

The code for this program is not complex. Here we will use several global variables. One will hold the value of the spelling of the word that corresponds to the image the student selects. Another will hold the value of the spelling of the word that corresponds to the spelling the student selects. A third variable is a counter that keeps track of how many correct matches have been found. It is used to verify if the student has correctly matched all the images with their spellings.

We have one function to extract this spelling from the image cell's id and another function to extract the spelling from the word cell's id. Then we use a third function to compare the two and this is why we want these variables to be global. After comparing the two values, if they match we will use the DOM capability to append a new element into a cell. If they don't match, the student will receive an alert informing him or her of this. After any match is found, another function will be called to check if this match is the final match and all images have been paired with their correct spellings. When this happens, we'll use DOM again to create a congratulatory message.

The Functions to Extract Values from the Selected Image and Spelling   These two functions use the same logic and are similar so we give both of them here. Each function accepts, as a parameter, the id of the cell that has been clicked. Recall that image ids consist of the character "i" with the word that describes the image appended to the "i". The spelling ids consist of the character "s" with the correct spelling of a word appended to the "s". To compare the words, we need to extract all the characters from the id except the first character. The substr() method is used to do this. First, the function finds the length of the id. Then it creates a new variable (either **imgCompare** or **spellCompare**) which gets all the characters in the id minus the first character. The code for these two functions is as follows:

```
1.   function getImage(x)
2.   {
3.        var iLgth = x.length;
4.        imgCompare = x.substr(1, iLgth -1);
5.   }
6.   function getSpell(x)
7.   {
8.        var sLgth = x.length;
9.        spellCompare = x.substr(1, sLgth -1);
10.       compareThem(imgCompare, spellCompare);
11.  }
```

Notice that the compareThem() function is only called after the getSpell() function because, in order to compare the two values, the student must select an image first and then a word.

The Function to Compare the Values   This is where we use the DOM methods to create new elements and add them to the web page. The code is shown below and an explanation follows:

```
1.   function compareThem()
2.   {
3.        if (imgCompare == spellCompare)
```

```
4.        {
5.              var newStuff = document.createElement("P");
6.              var newMessage = document.createTextNode("CORRECT!");
7.              newStuff.appendChild(newMessage);
8.              document.getElementById("s" + ↵
                                spellCompare).appendChild(newStuff);
9.              count++;
10.             checkEnd();
11.       }
12.       else
13.             alert ("wrong... Try again");
14.  }
```

The compareThem() function does not accept any arguments even though it needs to compare the values of variables from other functions because we have declared those variables as global. At this time, the variables **imgCompare** and **spellCompare** hold the values of the word that describe the image and the word the student has selected as that image's spelling. If the two do not match, the alert on line 13 tells the student the selection is incorrect and prompts the student to try again.

However, if the two variables are a match we want to create a new element and insert it in the cell with the selected word.

Line 5 creates a new paragraph element which is stored in a variable named **newStuff**. Line 6 creates a new text node with the text value "CORRECT!" and stores that in the variable named **newMessage**. Line 7 uses the DOM appendChild() method to append the text node to the new paragraph element. Then line 8 puts the new element in its correct place. We use the getElementById() method to locate the cell where the message should go and use the appendChild() method a second time to add the new element to what is already in that cell.

Next, the counter is incremented (line 9). We have 12 images and words so, when this if clause has been executed 12 times, this means the student has made 12 correct matches and the exercise has been completed successfully. Line 10 calls the next function which will use the value of **count**, a global variable, to check whether the exercise is finished or not.

The Function to Check for Success   The last function checks to see if all images have been correctly matched with the spellings and if so, a new element is created and added to the document. The code for this function is as follows:

```
1.   function checkEnd()
2.   {
3.       if (count == 12)
4.       {
5.           var endIt = document.createElement("H3");
6.           var endMessage = document.createTextNode("Congratulations! ↵
                            You are a great speller!");
7.           endIt.appendChild(endMessage);
8.           document.getElementById("the_end").appendChild(endIt);
9.       }
10.  }
```

This time the new element created is a level 3 header ("H3") and contains the text in the **endMessage** text node.

Putting It All Together

The entire JavaScript code, with all the pieces put together follows. The <body> code is not repeated because it is long and is exactly the same as originally shown.

```
1.  <script>
2.  var imgCompare = ""; var spellCompare = ""; var count = 0;
3.  function getImage(x)
4.  {
5.      var iLgth = x.length;
6.      imgCompare = x.substr(1, iLgth - 1);
7.  }
8.  function getSpell(x)
9.  {
10.      var sLgth = x.length;
11.      spellCompare = x.substr(1, sLgth - 1);
12.      compareThem(imgCompare, spellCompare);
13.  }
14.  function compareThem()
15.  {
16.      if (imgCompare == spellCompare)
17.      {
18.          var newStuff = document.createElement("P");
19.          var newMessage = document.createTextNode("CORRECT!");
20.          newStuff.appendChild(newMessage);
21.          document.getElementById("s" + ↵
                          spellCompare).appendChild(newStuff);
22.          count++;
23.          checkEnd();
24.      }
25.      else
26.          alert ("wrong... Try again");
27.  }
28.  function checkEnd()
29.  {
30.      if (count == 12)
31.      {
32.          var endIt = document.createElement("H3");
33.          var endMessage = document.createTextNode("Congratulations! ↵
                          You are a great speller!");
34.          endIt.appendChild(endMessage);
35.          document.getElementById("the_end").appendChild(endIt);
36.      }
37.  }
38.  </script>
```

The page will originally look exactly like the one shown earlier. After clicking the first image (the bananas) and clicking an incorrect spelling, the page will look like this:

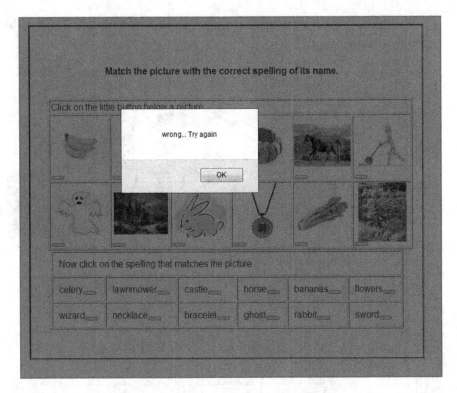

After correctly identifying the spelling of the lawnmover, the wizard, the rocket, and the rabbit, the page will look like this:

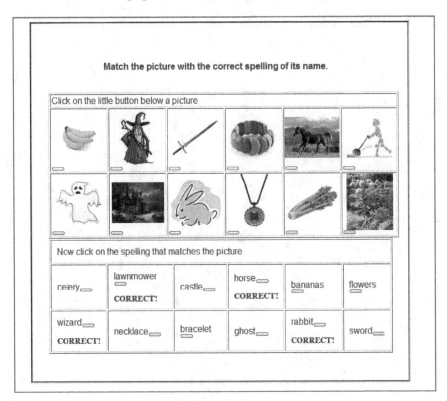

And finally, when all images and words have been matched correctly, the display will look like this:

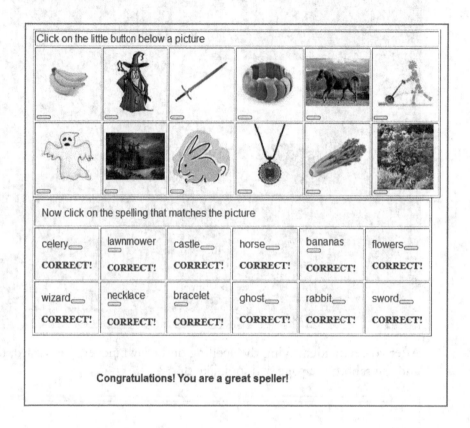

Chapter Review and Exercises

Key Terms

.dtd extension
.xml extension
.xsd extension
appendChild() method
application programming interface (API)
best practices
child nodes/elements
childNodes property
clearInterval() method
complex element
createElement() method
createTextNode() method
CSS page
descendants
Document Object Model (DOM)
document tree
Document Type Definition (DTD)
DOM
DTD
encoding attribute
entity
entity references
eXtensible Markup Language (XML)
eXtensible Stylesheet Language (XSL)
external DTDs
getAttribute() method
insertBefore() method
instance document
internal DTD
match attribute
maxOccurs attribute
minOccurs attribute
namespace declaration
name-value pairs
naming conventions
node set
NodeList

nonvalidating parser
parent nodes
parser
removeChild() method
replaceChild() method
result tree
root element
schema
select attribute
setAttribute() method
setInterval() method
sibling nodes
simple type element
source tree
standalone property
SYSTEM keyword
tree
tree-node structure
Uniform Resource Identifier (URI)
validating parser
value-of attribute
World Wide Web Consortium (W3C)
well-formed document
whitespace
World Wide Web Consortium
XML comments
XML declaration
XML document
XML elements
XML schema
xmlns keyword
XPath (XML Path Language)
XSD document
xsl:for-each attribute
xsl:output element
XSL document
XSL-FO (XSL Formatting Object)
XSLT (XSL Transformation)

Review Exercises

Fill in the Blank

1. The DOM sees an XML or HTML document as a _____ or group of _____.

2. The parent of all nodes in an HTML or XML document is the _____ node.

3. The _____ method is used to define new content for a new element that was created using the DOM createElement() method.

4. The first line of an XML document is always the _____.

5. A _____ parser just checks an XML document to make sure it is well-formed.

True or False

6. T/F   The DOM can be used to access a document's elements.

7. T/F   The setAttribute() method sets the value attribute of an input element.

8. T/F   The setInterval() and clearInterval() methods can only be used with the window object.

9. T/F   All XML documents must include <html> as the root.

10. T/F   An XML declaration must include both the version and the encoding attributes.

11. The following name for an XML element is valid: <x_m_1_3>.

12. T/F   The following name for an XML element is not valid: <player score>.

13. T/F   Attributes, if used, in an XML document must be included in the start tag.

14. T/F   The purpose of a DTD is to define the structure of an XML document.

15. T/F   CSS styles cannot be used with XML.

Short Answer

Use the following statement for Review Exercises 16 and 17:

```
document.getElementsByTagName("INPUT")[0].setAttribute("id",
"this.id");
```

16. What attribute will be set?
    a) INPUT   b) id   c) this   d) this.id

17. What is the value of the attribute?
    a) INPUT   b) id   c) this   d) this.id

Use the following statement for Review Exercises 18 and 19:

```
myInterval = window.setInterval("timeIt()", 100);
```

18. What happens each time this statement is executed?
    a) nothing
    b) the `timeIt()` function is called
    c) there is a 1-second wait
    d) an error is generated

19. How long is the interval set to in this statement?
    a) 1 minute   b) 100 seconds   c) 1/10 of a second   d) 1/100 of a second

20. What, if anything is wrong with the following element name used in an XML document?

    ```
    <my_xmlElement>
    ```

    a) the letters "xml" cannot be included
    b) uppercase letters are not allowed
    c) cannot combine underscores with camel back notation
    d) nothing is wrong

Use the following HTML code for Review Exercises 21–24:

```
<h3>Music Styles</h3>
<button onclick = "insertIt()">Click to insert an element</button>
<button onclick = "removeIt()">Click to remove an element</button>
<button onclick = "replaceIt()">Click to replace an element</button>
<ul id = "music">
    <li>rap</li>
    <li>country</li>
    <li>reggae</li>
    <li>jazz</li>
</ul>
```

21. Write code to create a new element for the list shown above. The new element should contain the text `"classical"`.

22. Write code to insert the element created in Question 21 into the list, at the top of the list. Use a DOM method.

23. Write code to replace the `"jazz"` list item with `"blues"` in the list above. Use a DOM method.

24. Write code to remove any list item from the list above, using a DOM method.

25. Write a function named `jump()` that will call a function named `bunnyHop()` every three seconds.

26. Create an XML document that contains a root element, one parent, and two child elements. The document should be able to be used by a restaurant to list a main course and two side dishes. Fill in any content you want.

27. Find what is wrong with the following XML code and fix it:

```
<? version "1.0" ?>
<my_root>
    <email>
        <to>Some person</to>
        <subject>Some subject</subject>
        <date>July 4, 1889</date>
```

```
        </email>
        <from>Your boss</from>
        <email>
            <to>Another person</to>
            <subject>New subject</subject>
        </email>
        <date>July 5 1889</date>
        <from>The boss's assistant</from>
</my_root>
```

28. Question 27 uses <email> as a parent element. Assuming the code has been fixed and is now well-formed, create two namespaces for the example. One namespace should be "faculty" and the other should be "students". Use the imaginary domain http://administration.edu.

29. What does URI stand for?
    a) Uniform Resource Indent   b) Uniform Result Identity
    c) Uniform Resource Identifier   d) Uniform Resource Identity

30. What is the advantage of using an XML schema over a DTD?

Programming Challenges

On Your Own

VideoNote
Using XML with CSS for a
Web Page
On_Your_Own_1_Menu

1. Create an XML document that a restaurant owner could use to display a luncheon menu. The menu should look similar to the following when the XML page is opened in a browser:

> **XYZ Lunch Menu**
>
> **Soup of the Day**
>
>   Potato Leek Soup
>
> **Sandwiches**
>
>   Ham and Cheese
>
>   Tuna Salad
>
>   Veggie Special
>
> **Sides**
>
>   French Fries
>
>   Cole Slaw
>
>   Fruit Cup

Save the page with the file name menu.xml and the corresponding style sheet menu.css. Submit your work as instructed by your teacher.

2. Create a web page that prompts a user to answer the question "Are you a new user?" If the answer is "no", elements should appear (using DOM methods) that instruct the user to enter his or her username and password. If the answer is "yes", create and display elements to allow the user to create a new username and password or choose the option to enter the site as a guest. Save your page with the file name users.html. Submit your work as instructed by your teacher.

Use the following sample display for Programming Challenges 3, 4, and 5:

Dee's Deli Luncheon Menu

Value Meals: Choose one from each column

Sandwich	Side Dish	Beverage
Roast Beef	French Fries	Soda
Tuna Salad	Coleslaw	Iced Tea
Cheese and Tomato	Onion Rings	Lemonade
Italian Sub	Applesauce	Diet Soda

3. Create an XML document that will display the table shown using a CSS page. Save your pages with the file names dee_menu.xml and dee.css. Submit your work as instructed by your teacher.

4. Use an XSL transformation to create the web page for the XML document you created in Programming Challenge 3 instead of using a CSS page. Save your pages with the file names dee_menu.xml, dee.css and dee.xsl. Submit your work as instructed by your teacher.

5. Use the Dee's Deli Luncheon Menu to create an XML page with styles that will display the following lunches as ordered by a nearby business for take-out.

```
Jane's lunch: tuna sandwich, onion rings, iced tea
Joe's lunch: Italian sub, french fries, soda
Jill's lunch: roast beef sandwich, coleslaw, lemonade
Jack's lunch: tuna salad sandwich, onion rings, soda
```

Save your pages with the file names lunches.xml and lunches.css. Submit your work as instructed by your teacher.

6. Create an XML page with an XSL transformation to display a web page for an employer to list his three employees with the following information for each: hours worked in a week, hourly rate of pay, regular pay amount, and overtime pay amount (calculated at 1.5 time hourly pay rate). Save your pages with the file names emplyees.xml, employees.css and employees.xsl. Submit your work as instructed by your teacher.

Case Studies

Greg's Gambits

Use the Carla's Classroom example in the Putting It to Work section of this chapter and create a game of Concentration for the Greg's Gambits site. In the game, a deck of cards containing image pairs is laid face down. The player must, using memory, turn over one card and try to find its match. It is a game designed to test and enhance memory skills but you can create your own way to win. You might include a timer and establish a deadline; this will increase the difficulty of the project and is optional. Or you could limit the number of incorrect tries; if a player gets all matches before reaching that number, the player wins. This also increases the difficulty of the project and is optional.

For your game, you can use images or simple text for your "cards" and use a table with a cell for each card. Any image that is in one cell should have a match in another cell. Initially, all cells will appear blank (or whatever you use to simulate the back of a card). This can be done by using a blank image, filling the cell with white text, or by creating your own blank cell technique. However, each cell should have some content (image or text) associated with it and another cell should match this content. Thus, if you have a 4 × 4 table with 16 cells, you would have eight different images and each would be associated with two cells. The player should be able to click one cell and attempt to find its match by clicking a second cell. If the two cells match, display the content. If not, have both cells return to the blank content.

Save your page as greg_concentration.html. Be sure to give it an appropriate page title. Open the index.html page for Greg's Gambits and add a link, under the Play A Game link, that links to this page with the page title Greg's Gambits | Greg's Concentration. Submit your work as instructed by your teacher.

Carla's Classroom

Select one of the following (or both if you are motivated or if assigned) exercises:

1. Create a second page to add a second level of difficulty to the Spelling Exercise that was created in the Putting It to Work section. Level two should be similar to the first level. When students have successfully completed Level One, they should be automatically taken to Level Two. Save your page as carla_spell_exercise2a.html. Open the reading.html page for Carla's Classroom and add a link to this page with the page title Carla's Classroom | Advanced Spelling, Part A. Submit your work as instructed by your teacher.

2. Change the page created in the Putting It to Work section so that each image has three possible spellings associated with it. The student must select the correct spelling. You can do this in one table if you want or use the two

tables from the exercise. If you use a single table, the first cell might look like this:

Save your page as `carla_spell_execise2b.html`. Test your page in a browser. Open the `reading.html` page for `Carla's Classroom` and add a link to this page with the page title `Carla's Classroom | Advanced Spelling, Part B`. Submit your work as instructed by your teacher.

Lee's Landscape

Create a web page using an XML document, a CSS style sheet, and an XSL transformation to display Lee's services and costs. The XML document should have three namespaces, using Lee's imaginary domain: `"http://landscape.com"`. The namespaces should be `"lawn"`, `"trees"`, and `"pests"`. The information for the page is shown:

Lee's Services		
Service	**Frequency**	**Cost**
lawn maintenance	monthly	$80
	weekly	$20 for 4 weeks
	as called	$30 per service
tree pruning	yearly	$150
	twice a year	$200 for 2 visits
	as called	$200 per service
pest control	monthly	$50.00
	twice a year	$200 per service
	as called	$250 per service

Be sure to give this web page an appropriate page title such as `Lee's Landscape || Services Offered`. Add a link to the `Lee's Landscape` home page to this new page. Save your pages with the file names `lee_services.xml`, `lee_services.css` and `lee_services.xsl`. Submit your work as instructed by your teacher.

Jackie's Jewelry

Jackie offers several jewelry making classes, as discussed in the examples in this chapter. She wants to keep a record of the people who register for each class. Create an XML document that Jackie can update as new people sign up for her classes. Then create a CSS page for the presentational aspects of the page and an XSL document that will transform the XML document to a web page. The XML document should include the information shown below. Use a namespace for each course ("beads", "any", "necklace", and "earrings"). Use Jackie's imaginary domain: "http://jackie.com". Sample data is given below.

- Costs are as follows. Each class costs $25.00 for 4 sessions.
  - Beading: package of supplies is $5.00, single fancy beads are $2.00 each
  - Necklace-making: package of supplies is $10.00, single charms are $8.00 each
  - Earrings: package of supplies is $12.00, hoops (set of 2) or single charms are $10.00 each
  - Varied jewelry: package of supplies is $15.00, single charms are $8.00, beads $2.00, hoops are $10.00 per set

Be sure to give this web page an appropriate page title such as `Jackie's Jewelry || Students`. Add a link to the `Jackie's Jewelry` home page to this new page. Save your pages with the file names `jackie_students.xml`, `jackie_students.css` and `jackie_students.xsl`. Submit your work as instructed by your teacher.

	Name	Supplies Ordered	Total Cost	Amount Paid	Amount Due
	Ann Axelby	package	30.00	30.00	0
Beading class	Bob Bixby	none	25.00	25.00	0
	Zoey Zacks	package, 3 beads	46.00	20.00	26.00
	Will Warren	package	30.00	10.00	20.00
	Harriet Hart	2 charms	41.00	20.00	21.00
Necklace making	Ira Ingram	package	35.00	15.00	20.00
	Pam Petrova	4 charms	57.00	25.00	27.00
	Oscar Osaka	package	35.00	35.00	0
	Jim Jones	package	37.00	10.00	27.00
Earrings	Katya Kendrick	2 hoops, 1 charm	55.00	55.00	0
	Ned Nichols	package	37.00	30.00	7.00
	Maria Montas	none	25.00	0	25.00
	Tim Thompson	package	40.00	12.00	28.00
Varied jewelry making	Suzie Santos	none	25.00	25.00	0
	Ed Ellis	1 charm, 2 beads	37.00	25.00	12.00
	Felicia Franks	package	40.00	20.00	20.00

PHP: An Overview

Chapter Objectives

You have probably not gotten this far in web development without hearing about PHP. You see it listed in job postings, you hear about it from everyone in the field. And if you do an Internet search and ask, "what is PHP?" the first words of the answer will almost inevitably be "PHP is a server-side scripting language used to create dynamic web pages." But what does that mean? After all, we've been using JavaScript to create dynamic web pages. What makes PHP different? What does "server-side" really mean? That's what this chapter is about. We will learn what PHP is, how to implement it on your computer without an external server, and how to use it. PHP is free, which makes it a widely used, efficient alternative to competitors like Microsoft's ASP. While this book cannot begin to cover the topic of databases, we will learn to use the free MySQL database software in conjunction with PHP.

After reading this chapter, you will be able to do the following:

- Understand the relationship between client and server

- Download and install a free Apache server with MySQL and PHP software

- Understand the concepts of records and fields in a database

- Understand how to create PHP programs

- Use the settype() and gettype() methods and type casting to retrieve and/or change a variable's data type

- Use PHP selection and repetition structures

- Work with PHP arrays, strings, and string comparisons

- Use the preg_match() and preg_replace() methods to search for patterns

- Create an Ajax pipe to communicate from client to server and server to client

- Use several server objects, methods, and properties

11.1   A Brief History of PHP

PHP (Personal Home Page Tools) was created by **Rasmus Lerdorf**. He developed the language to track visitors to his website. He released this package in 1995. By 1997, after a significant rewrite, PHP3 was released and included built-in database support and the ability to handle forms. PHP became very popular. Originally PHP stood for Personal Home Page; today it is said to stand for PHP: Hypertext Preprocessor.

In this text, we have created games and applications that use data. We have stored the data in variables and, as we learned more, we stored more data in arrays. But businesses and large websites need much more functionality to store data than is possible with arrays. Imagine you are a business owner and want to keep customer records. Storing customer information in parallel arrays works nicely when you know beforehand (because you are a student creating an imaginary site) the names of the customers. But in real life, new customers come, old customers go or leave and return after several years of inactivity. A business has more customers than will comfortably fit into an array. Businesses use databases to store information—including information on customers, inventory, employees, and much more. PHP can be used to communicate between a web page that a user will see on his or her computer (i.e., the client) and the database which resides elsewhere (i.e., on the server). This is the power of PHP.

New information can be entered into a database from a form on the user's computer; this is why the capability to handle forms is noteworthy. When you create an account on a website, you enter information into a form. The form processes that information and adds it to the appropriate databases. In other words, it sends information from the client to the server. This may be one of the most important things PHP does.

PHP allows information to flow the other way too—from the server to the client. When you return to a site where you have an account, your information is retrieved from the databases on that site's server and returned to you, the client. That's how websites can greet you by name, display your ordering history, and much more.

Presently, the current version of PHP is 5.4.X (the X indicates that small changes may occur between the time of this writing and the time you read this book). PHP is open-source code, free to everyone. This is one of the advantages of PHP; the large PHP community is willing to share. If you're looking for a particular script, chances are someone else within the PHP community has already created something similar and it probably is available. Check out `http://php.net/` for assistance and great ideas.

What Does a Server Do?

When a user clicks a link, a request is sent to a server. Then the **server,** as we know, sends the requested page back to the **client,** i.e., the user's computer. That's all the normal user knows and expects. But there's more to it. The URL tells the browser what page or other resource (a video, a song, etc.) the user wants to retrieve. The server makes that resource available to the browser. We already know what the parts of a URL mean. In the sample URL,

```
http://www.jackie.com/courses/beading.html
```

we know the following: `http://` indicates that the protocol HyperText Transfer Protocol will be used; the web page requested resides on the web server `www.jackie.com`; there is folder named `courses` which contains a file named `beading.html`; and this file is the resource requested. A protocol, in general, includes the customs and regulations, normally relating to some diplomatic formality or etiquette. A **communications protocol** is a system of digital message formats and rules for exchanging messages between computing systems. While `http` is the most common communications protocol, others include `ftp`, `IP`, and `TCP`. The hostname, `www.jackie.com`, is actually an IP address which is a series of numbers. These numbers have been converted into text to make it easier for us to type. An Internet Domain Name System (DNS) maintains a database of hostnames and their corresponding IP addresses. It automatically translates the text hostname to its IP address.

HTTP get and post Request Types

Normally, when a user performs a website search, the user wants to get some information that resides on the site's server. And often the user wants to send information to a server, such as when logging into a site or, as a business owner, to update information that resides, most likely in a database, on the business's server. Therefore, the `get` and `post` **request types** are the two most common HTTP request types.

A **get request** appends data to the URL to specify what it should get. The information requested is sent as form data and the server's ability to process form data is used. A **post request** is similar. In this chapter, we will learn to use these requests to communicate from the client to the server.

The Apache HTTP Server, MySQL, and PHP

To complete the examples, exercises, and projects in this chapter and the next, you need to have access to a web server, a database, and PHP software. We will use the Apache HTTP server, the MySQL database, and PHP.

The Apache HTTP Server

An **Apache Web Server** (most commonly called **Apache**) is a free open-source web server. It was originally created for Unix, but there are now versions that run under other platforms such as Linux and Windows. To continue to learn to communicate between client and server, you must have server software on your computer or you must have access to a server.

The MySQL Database

To use PHP in a way that makes it valuable to website development we need to use a database. Learning to use databases is far beyond the scope of this book but it is assumed that you know what a database is. In general terms, a **database** is an organized collection of data. The databases we refer to in this chapter are **relational databases**. The information in the database is stored in **tables**. Tables contain groups of related data called **records**.

For example, a business might store varied information about its customers such as name, contact information, dates of purchases, types of purchases, special interests, and more. One table might hold the demographic information about a customer (name, address, contact information, age, gender, marital status, and the like). All of the information relating to one customer comprises a single record. Each data item in a record is called a **field**. In this case, the fields would include the customer's name, contact information, age, and so on. A second table in this sample database might hold a customer's purchasing history (date of last purchase, dates of previous purchases, items purchased, and more). A single record would be the data referring to one customer and the fields in this table would be the specific information (purchase date, items purchased, etc.). A third table might hold the business's inventory. In this table, each record might be an item that is sold and the fields could include information like number on hand, warehouse location, production costs, and retail price.

A relational database is so called because the user can pull information from several tables to find relationships between data. For example, the business owner, using database queries, can find out how many customers from Georgia purchased a widget, or how many women shoppers bought gadgets over a particular period of time, pulling and combining data from the table with demographic information and the table with purchase histories. The ability to store massive amounts of data and use it in multiple and various ways makes relational databases invaluable to businesses, government organizations, and the academic community.

Databases can hold many different types of information. The same business owner might have another database that stores each employee as a record. In this case, the fields would be different from the customer database, including such items as hours worked, pay rate, tax deductions, and so forth. A third database the business owner might maintain would include information about inventory. A record might be the name of a particular item for sale. If the business owner sold men's clothing, one record could be wool sweaters. The fields, in this case, might be size, color, number in stock, wholesale price, retail price, and so on. To summarize: Databases are made up of records and records are made up of fields.

The beauty of a database is that it can retrieve and put together information in numerous ways. The business owner can ask the database to find out how many customers purchased green wool sweaters in July or how many employees who earn more than $15 an hour have requested more than 10 hours of overtime in a given period. In this text, we will create several of our own databases, using simple tools. To do this, we need the database software. **MySQL** is a free open-source relational database system, especially popular for web applications.

PHP and XAMPP

Finally, we need PHP. PHP is a general-purpose scripting language that is especially suited for web development and can be embedded into HTML. In order to get everything we need—Apache, MySQL, and PHP—we can install free software called **XAMPP:**

- **X:** for "cross", because it is cross-platform (can be used on many different platforms)
- **A**pache HTTP Server
- **M**ySQL
- **P**HP and **P**erl (although we do not need Perl in this text)

The software can easily be installed on most machines, regardless of the operating system platform. It includes, in one package, the Apache HTTP Server, the MySQL database program, and PHP software. The next section gives instructions about how to complete this installation. If you already have access to a server which uses Apache, a database, and PHP you do not need to install XAMPP but the information in this chapter and Chapter 12 will assume you are using XAMPP.

CHECKPOINT FOR SECTION 11.1 ✓

11.1 Who is Rasmus Lerdorf?

11.2 Given the following URL, what part represents the IP address?

```
http://www.leesland.com/services/mowing.html
```

11.3 If Lee of the Lee's Landscape business maintains a database that contains a table with data relating to the services he offers and each service is considered a record, such as lawn maintenance, landscaping, and pest control, list three possible fields for each record.

11.4 What does the "X" in XAMPP stand for and what does it mean?

11.2 XAMPP

Installation of XAMPP is easy. You only need to download it and let the installer do the work. If, after you finish the programs in this book or decide you don't want XAMPP installed on your computer, simply delete the XAMPP directory (wherever you put it on your computer) and it will be completely removed from your system. However, if you use the Windows installer version of XAMPP it is recommended that you use the Windows Uninstall feature because, as every installer does, it will make registry entries that you may want to remove.

Installing XAMPP

There are a few things you may want to note before installing XAMPP. While there are many places on the web where you can get XAMPP, in this book we will use the Apache Friends website.

Security

The Apache Friends website built an easy to install XAMPP distribution for developers so they can enter the world of Apache. Thus, XAMPP is configured with all features turned on. This default configuration is not secure enough for a production environment; do not use it for such. It can be used by web developers in a **development environment** which means nothing from this server will go "live."

The License

XAMPP is a compilation of free software and can be copied and used under the terms of the GNU General Public License (check it out at `http://www.gnu.org/licenses/`). If you plan to use XAMPP for reasons other than the examples and projects in this text, please check the licenses of the contained products to see what is and what is not allowed.

The Install

Go to

```
http://www.apachefriends.org/en/xampp.html
```

Scroll down and select your platform. Be sure to read the pertinent information provided for your platform. Then begin the download.

Note: This is a pretty large file. Don't expect it to take a minute or two to download. Depending on your Internet connection speed, the download could take up to an hour. However, once you have downloaded the program, installing it takes only a few minutes.

It is recommended that, when prompted, you accept the default installation. This is what will be assumed throughout this chapter and the next.

Note for Windows Vista users: Because of missing or insufficient write permissions in `"C:\Program Files"`, it is recommended that you use an alternate folder for XAMPP. You can accept the folder suggested by the installer (`"C:\xampp"`) or create your own.

Try It

If you select the option to show the XAMPP control panel, your Control Panel will look like this:

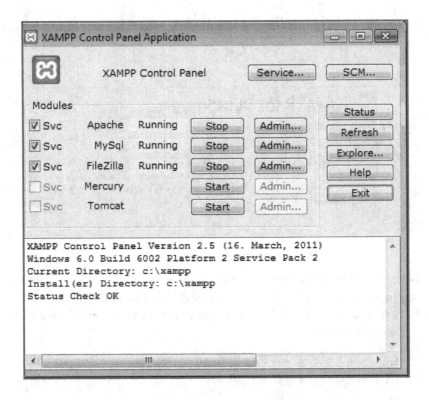

If you do not have the Control Panel, go to the folder where you stored XAMPP and click the xampp-control.exe file.

Linux users: To start XAMPP open a shell and enter the following command:

```
/opt/lamp/lamp start
```

To stop, enter the following command:

```
/opt/lamp/lamp stop
```

All Users: To test that your program is properly installed, go to any browser and enter the following:

```
http://localhost/
```

If everything is working correctly, you should see a display similar to the following:

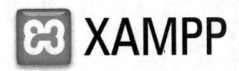

If you have a Windows machine and click **English,** you should see a screen similar to the following:

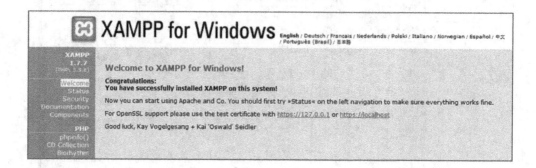

Note for Windows Vista users: You must run the XAMPP Control Panel as an **administrator**. To do this, you can click the **Admin** button on the Control Panel. However, to have XAMPP run as **administrator** automatically each time you use it, do the following:

- Right-click the XAMPP icon to view your options (shown below)
- Click **Properties** (shown below)
- Check the **Run this program as an administrator** box (shown below)
- Click **Apply**

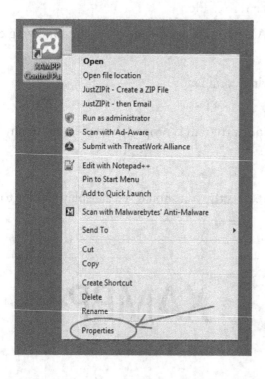

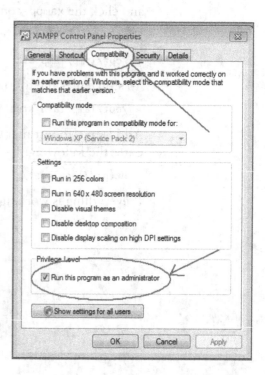

Let's Get Started

In the Control Panel, click **Start** for Apache and MySQL. You're now running a server. Next, we will enable PHP. Click the **Admin** button next to MySQL in the Control Panel and the phpMyAdmin screen will open in your browser, as shown:

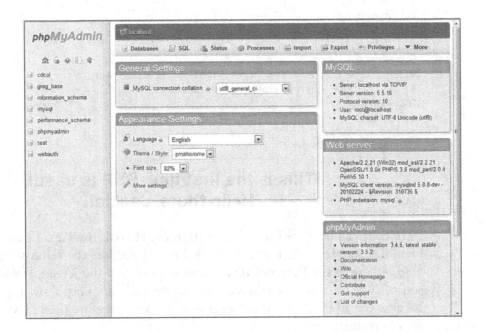

You can leave the default settings. Be aware that by leaving the defaults, including no password, you are running the server with no security. This text assumes you are only using the programs you create for learning and demonstration purposes.

Your First PHP Program

PHP code is commonly embedded into text documents. For now, we will embed some PHP into an HTML document so you can see how it works. A simple HTML document is interpreted and rendered on your screen by your browser. The browser resides on your computer so this means the HTML is rendered on the client side. PHP, however, even though it may be embedded into an HTML document, is interpreted by the server before it is delivered to you (the client).

PHP script is inserted between **<?php and?> tags**. All PHP variables begin with the **$**. Example 11.1 will display a welcome message on a web page, using PHP. You can create this code but, before saving it and running it, you should read Section 11.3.

Creating a Welcome to PHP! Using PHP

```
1.   <!DOCTYPE html>
2.   <html>
3.   <?php
4.       $name = "Jackie";
5.   ?>
6.   <head>
7.   <title>Example 11.1</title>
8.   </head>
9.   <body>
10.      <h2>This is the first time PHP is used! <br />
11.      Hello there, <?php print("$name"); ?>!</h2>
12.  </body>
13.  </html>
```

The display will be as follows:

This is the first time PHP is used!
Hello there, Jackie!

PHP code can be placed anywhere within the HTML markup. The variable **$name** identifies Jackie as the name in line 4. Line 11 accesses the value of that variable and, using the PHP **print() function,** puts it on the screen. If you view the source code for this page you will see that the code does not show any PHP. This is because the all PHP operations occur on the server, before the HTML document is sent to your computer.

The last sentence in the discussion following the Example 11.1 code is important and bears repeating. All PHP operations occur on the server, before the HTML document is sent to your computer. This happens behind the scenes when you are on the web. But as you learn to use PHP, this distinction becomes important.

CHECKPOINT FOR SECTION 11.2 ✓

11.5 What is meant by a development environment?

11.6 How do you test that your installation of XAMPP is working properly?

11.7 What type of document can use PHP?

11.8 Where can PHP be placed in an HTML document?

11.9 When a .php document is accessed from a browser, where and when is the PHP code processed?

11.10 What is the first character in all PHP variable names?

11.3 PHP Basics

In this chapter, we will discuss some familiar concepts and learn how PHP uses them. In Chapter 12, we'll put it all together and create some complete projects that utilize the features of HTML, CSS, JavaScript, XML, XSL, PHP, and MySQL.

PHP File Names, the htdocs Folder, and Viewing Your PHP Pages

We have said that PHP can be placed anywhere in a page with HTML markup. This means you can put it in the <head> section or anywhere in the <body>, just as with JavaScript or CSS. The difference is that if a page has any PHP included at all—even one line—the page normally must have the .php extension.

If you tried Example 11.1 and named the file hello.html, and opened it as you normally do in a browser the display would simply be as follows:

This is the first time PHP is used!
Hello there, !

The browser would ignore code that it considers unintelligible (the PHP statements). However, if you view the page's source code, you will see the unprocessed PHP statements. You need to name this page something like hello.php.

If you then opened the hello.php page on your computer in the ordinary way—by putting in the path to that file in a browser—your display would still be as follows:

This is the first time PHP is used!
Hello there, !

Why is this? We have said that PHP operations occur on the server, before the page is rendered by your browser. If you are using XAMPP or any version of a local (on your computer) server, the pages you test must go through that server. If you put the hello.php file on your computer in, for example, a folder named javascript_course and then attempted to open it from that folder, the browser would simply try to display whatever script it understands. And that would be the HTML markup. The PHP code would, once again, be ignored. While we learn how to use PHP on a local server, all the PHP documents we create must be stored in the **htdocs folder**. This folder was created for you when you installed XAMPP, as shown in the following listing of folders in the xampp folder:

Name	Date mo
anonymous	7/13/201
apache	7/13/201
bProtectorForWindows	7/13/201
cgi-bin	7/13/201
contrib	7/13/201
FileZillaFTP	7/13/201
htdocs	7/14/201
install	7/13/201
licenses	7/13/201
locale	7/13/201
mailoutput	7/13/201
mailtodisk	7/13/201
MercuryMail	7/13/201
mysql	7/13/201
perl	7/13/201
php	7/13/201
phpMyAdmin	7/13/201
searchplugins	7/13/201
security	7/13/201
sendmail	7/13/201

We're almost ready to view our page, but there is one more thing. To open this page on your computer and allow the server to process the PHP before the browser takes over, we do not create a path directly to this file. Instead, we tell the browser to use the **local host**—the Apache server that was installed with XAMPP. The path thus is as follows:

```
localhost/hello.php
```

By using **localhost** in the path, the computer knows the server is on the local machine and knows to look in the htdocs folder. Now the display for Example 11.1 will appear as desired:

This is the first time PHP is used!
Hello there, Jackie!

Variables and Methods

PHP variable names begin with **$**, as we have seen in Example 11.1. PHP variables, like JavaScript variables, are **loosely typed**. Recall that this means a variable can contain different types of data at different times. Often we may need to convert a variable from one data type to another and this can be accomplished with certain PHP functions. Table 11.1 presents a list of PHP's data types.

Here are a few examples of variable name declarations and assignments:

```
$username = 'puppypal'; // declares a string variable with the value
       puppypal
$points = 234; // declares an integer variable with the value 234
$cost = 45.87; // declares a float variable with the value 45.87
$response = true; // declares a Boolean variable with the value true
```

TABLE 11.1	PHP Data Types
PHP Data Type	**Description**
int, integer	a whole number, positive, negative, or zero
float, double, real	all real numbers; i.e., numbers that can be expressed as $\frac{a}{b}$. Floats must include a decimal part, even if that decimal part is 0, such as 34.0
string	text enclosed in single or double quotes
bool, boolean	used for values that are either true or false
array	a group of elements
resource	used for variables that hold data or reference to an external source
NULL	means the variable has not been assigned any value
object	a group of associated data and methods

Note the double slashes (//) make the text following into a single-line comment.

Converting Data Types with the settype() and gettype() Methods

As with JavaScript, a variable's data type is determined by the value assigned to it. In JavaScript, you can use the parseInt() method to truncate a float to an integer. In PHP, you can use the settype() method to set the data type of a variable. The gettype() method will return the data type of its argument.

The **settype() method** takes two arguments. The first argument is the variable whose type will be changed and the second argument is the variable's new type. The syntax for settype() is as follows:

```
settype($variableName, "new_datatype");
```

The **gettype() method** takes only one argument—the name of the variable whose type will be returned. The syntax for gettype() is as follows:

```
gettype($variableName);
```

Converting Data Types by Type Casting

The settype() method actually changes the type of a variable. If the variable starts out as a float and settype() is used to change its type to integer, the variable is then an integer. Sometimes this is undesirable. You may want an integer to display on a web page but want to use the entire value of the variable later. Another option to convert a variable's type is **casting** (also called **type casting**). Rather than changing the value of the variable, when casting is used, a temporary copy of the variable's value is created in memory. The syntax to cast one variable to another type is as follows:

```
(datatype_desired) $variableName;
```

Example 11.2 will demonstrate how variables are declared and will use these methods to set, alter, and retrieve the variables' data types.

EXAMPLE

11.2

Declaring Variables and Displaying Values

```
1.    <!DOCTYPE html>
2.    <html>
3.    <?php
4.        $name = "Jackie";
5.        $numStudents = 47;
6.        $costNecklaceA = 23.95;
7.        $studentID = "0001";
8.    ?>
9.    <head>
10.       <title>Example 11.2</title>
11.   </head>
12.   <body>
13.       <h2>This website is run by
14.       <?php print("$name"); ?>.</h2>
15.       <p>She has
16.       <?php print("$numStudents"); ?>
17.       students in her jewelry-making classes.</p>
18.       <p>Jackie will assign ID numbers to students beginning with
19.       <?php print("$studentID"); ?> .</p>
20.       <p>The cost of a silver necklace with a dove pendant is $
21.       <?php print("$costNecklaceA"); ?>.</p>
22.       <h3>Original variables and their values:</h3>
23.       <p>The value of the variable $name is
24.       <?php print("$name"); ?> .</p>
25.       <p>The value of the variable $studentID is
26.       <?php print("$studentID"); ?>.</p>
27.       <p>The value of the variable $numStudents is
28.       <?php print("$numStudents"); ?>.</p>
29.       <p>The value of the variable $costNecklaceA is
30.       <?php print("$costNecklaceA"); ?>.</p>
31.   </body>
32.   </html>
```

Line numbers are included here each time PHP code has started but this is done only for explanatory purposes. Lines 3 and 8 open and close the PHP code that is included before the <head> section of the document. Lines 4–7 declare four variables and their data types are assigned through their values. Therefore, originally, **$name** and **$studentID** are strings since their values have been enclosed in quotes. **$costNecklaceA** is a float (also called a double) because its original value is a floating point number. The last variable, **$numStudents**, is an integer because it is assigned an integer value.

Lines 13–21 use the values of these variables with HTML script to display some information. We can look more closely at any pair of these lines and the rest are comparable. Lines 15, 16, and 17 create the display: "She has 47 students in her jewelry-making classes."

Line 15 starts the HTML by opening a paragraph tag and including the text "She has ". Line 16 starts more PHP. It uses the PHP print() method to display the value of the variable **$numStudents** next. The variable is the argument in the print() method but, as we shall see, we can include HTML script as an argument, similar to the write() method in JavaScript. The semicolon ends this PHP statement and the PHP code is closed with the ?> closing tag. Line 17 finishes the HTML text for this <p></p> element.

If this page were saved with a file name such as example_2.php, stored in the htdocs folder, and the following path typed into a browser, the display would be as shown below:

```
localhost/example_2.php
```

This website is run by Jackie.

She has 47 students in her jewelry-making classes.

Jackie will assign ID numbers to students beginning with 0001.

The cost of a silver necklace with a dove pendant is $ 23.95.

Original variables and their values:

The value of the variable $name is Jackie.

The value of the variable $studentID is 0001.

The value of the variable $numStudents is 47.

The value of the variable $costNecklaceA is 23.95.

We can include the HTML inside the print() method instead of breaking up each statement into three parts (a beginning HTML tag and text, the PHP code, and an ending HTML tag) as shown in the alternate code for lines 13–21:

```
lines 13-14   <h2><?php print("This website is run by $name."); ?></h2>
lines 15-17   <p><?php print("She has $numStudents students in her ⏎
                             jewelry-making classes."); ?></p>
lines 18-19   <p><?php print("Jackie will assign ID numbers to students ⏎
                             beginning with $studentID."); ?></p>
lines 20-21   <p><?php print ("The cost of a silver necklace with a
                             dove pendant is $ $costNecklaceA."); ?></p>
```

Example 11.3 will build on this page. We'll use the settype() and gettype() methods to change the data types of these variables and to retrieve their data types.

EXAMPLE 11.3

Using the settype() and gettype() Methods

The following code uses the gettype() method to get the data type of a variable, uses settype() to change that variable's type, and then displays its new value. The gettype() method is used again to show the new data type of that variable.

```
1.   <!DOCTYPE html>
2.   <html>
3.   <?php
4.        $name = "Jackie";
5.        $numStudents = 47;
6.        $costNecklaceA = 23.95;
7.        $studentID = "0001";
8.   ?>
9.   <head>
10.       <title>Example 11.3</title>
11.  </head>
12.  <body>
13.       <h3>Original variables and their values:</h3>
14.       <p>The value of the variable $name is <?php print("$name"); ?>.</p>
15.       <p>The value of the variable $studentID is
16.       <?php print("$studentID"); ?>.</p>
17.       <p>The value of the variable $numStudents is
18.       <?php print("$numStudents"); ?>.</p>
19.       <p>The value of the variable $costNecklaceA is
20.       <?php print("$costNecklaceA"); ?>.</p>
21.       <h3>We can find out the data type of a variable:</h3>
22.       <p>The data type of the variable, $costNecklaceA is
23.       <?php print gettype($costNecklaceA); ?></p>
24.       <h3>But we can convert the values to other data types:</h3>
25.       <p>The value of the variable, $costNecklaceA, converted to an integer is
26.       <?php settype($costNecklaceA, "integer"); print($costNecklaceA); ?> </p>
27.       <p>So the data type of the variable, $costNecklaceA is now
28.       <?php print gettype($costNecklaceA); ?></p>
29.  </body>
30.  </html>
```

The original values of the variables are displayed on lines 13–20. Line 23 uses the gettype() method to get the data type of **$costNecklaceA**. At this point, since the variable was originally assigned a floating point value, its data type is double and this is what will be displayed.

Line 26 both changes the data type of **$costNecklaceA** and displays its new value. The statement settype(**$costNecklaceA**, "integer"); identifies the variable whose data type will be changed (**$costNecklaceA**) and its new type ("integer"). Notice that the new data type is in quotes.

The second PHP statement on line 26 is print(**$costNecklaceA**); and it displays the new value of the variable.

Line 28 uses the gettype() method again to display the new data type of **$costNecklaceA**.

If this file was saved in the htdocs folder as example_3.php and localhost/example_3.php is entered into a browser's address bar, the output will be as follows:

> **Original variables and their values:**
>
> The value of the variable $name is Jackie.
>
> The value of the variable $studentID is 0001.
>
> The value of the variable $numStudents is 47.
>
> The value of the variable $costNecklaceA is 23.95.
>
> **We can find out the datatype of a variable:**
>
> The datatype of the variable, $costNecklaceA is double
>
> **But we can convert the values to other datatypes:**
>
> The value of the variable, $costNecklaceA, converted to an integer is 23
>
> So the datatype of the variable, $costNecklaceA is now integer

Notice that **$costNecklaceA** originally has the value 23.95 and is of the double data type. After changing its type to an integer, it has the value 23 and its data type is integer. If Jackie decided to change the price of this necklace from a double to an integer, she would have lost almost $1.00. This may be a problem when using the settype() method to change a data type in some cases. We can use another option—type casting—to change data types without this loss of data, as shown in Example 11.4.

EXAMPLE 11.4

Using Type Casting to Change a Variable's Data Type

The following code is similar to the previous examples but adds the type casting option which can be used instead of settype() and maintains the original value of a variable.

```
1.   <!DOCTYPE html>
2.   <html>
3.   <?php
4.       $name = "Jackie";
5.       $numStudents = 47;
6.       $costNecklaceA = 23.95;
7.       $studentID = "0001";
8.   ?>
9.   <head>
10.      <title>Example 11.4</title>
11.  </head>
12.  <body>
13.      <h3>Original variables and their values:</h3>
14.      <p>The value of the variable $name is <?php print("$name"); ?>.</p>
15.      <p>The value of the variable $studentID is
16.      <?php print("$studentID"); ?>.</p>
17.      <p>The value of the variable $numStudents is
18.      <?php print("$numStudents"); ?>.</p>
19.      <p>The value of the variable $costNecklaceA is
20.      <?php print("$costNecklaceA"); ?>.</p>
21.      <h3>We can find out the data type of a variable:</h3>
```

```
22.        <p>The data type of the variable, $costNecklaceA is
23.        <?php print gettype($costNecklaceA); ?></p>
24.        <h3>But we can convert the values to other data types:</h3>
25.        <p>The value of the variable, $costNecklaceA, converted to an integer is
26.        <?php settype($costNecklaceA, "integer"); print($costNecklaceA); ?> </p>
27.        <p>So the data type of the variable, $costNecklaceA is now
28.        <?php print gettype($costNecklaceA); ?></p>
29.        <h3>Using type casting instead of settype():</h3>
30.        <p>The value of the variable $studentID when cast as an integer is
31.        <?php print(integer) $studentID; ?></p>
32.        <p>The value of the variable, $studentID, still remains
33.        <?php print($studentID); ?></p>
34.        <p>The data type of the variable, $studentID is still
35.        <?php print gettype($studentID); ?></p>
36.  </body>
37.  </html>
```

The new lines of code in this example are lines 29–35. Line 31 casts **$studentID** as an integer. The print() method takes the new data type, "integer", as its argument and then displays the value of requested variable, **$studentID**, with its new value, as an integer. Originally, **$studentID** was a string so its value was 0001. As an integer, however, only the integer numeric value counts so it is simply 1. But line 33 displays the actual value of **$studentID** which remains 0001 and, as demonstrated by line 35, it also remains a string. You could, if you wished, use the type cast value in a numeric operation while retaining the string value for other purposes.

If this file was saved in the htdocs folder as example_4.php and localhost/example_4.php is entered into a browser's address bar, the output will be as follows:

Original variables and their values:

The value of the variable $name is Jackie.

The value of the variable $studentID is 0001.

The value of the variable $numStudents is 47.

The value of the variable $costNecklaceA is 23.95.

We can find out the datatype of a variable:

The datatype of the variable, $costNecklaceA is double

But we can convert the values to other datatypes:

The value of the variable, $costNecklaceA, converted to an integer is 23

So the datatype of the variable, $costNecklaceA is now integer

Using type casting instead of settype():

The value of the variable $studentID when cast as an integer is 1

The value of the variable, $studentID, still remains 0001

The datatype of the variable, $studentID is still string

PHP Keywords

The scope of this book will not allow us to experiment with all that PHP can do. However, as with other programming and scripting languages, each language's keywords are reserved by the language. **Keywords** (or **reserved words**) are words that have special meaning in the language. These words cannot be used as a name of a function, method, class, or namespace. It is sometimes possible but always inadvisable to use any of these words as variable names. Therefore, we list the **PHP keywords** in Table 11.2.

Operators

An **operator** is something that takes one or more values or expressions and, after processing, yields a new value. There are many types of operators; in JavaScript we discussed arithmetic operators, relational operators, and logical operators. We will discuss how these work in PHP. One way to group operators is by how many values they take. PHP operators can take one, two, or three values.

Unary Operators

An operator that acts on a single value is known as a **unary operator** (see Example 11.5). For example, the NOT operator takes a boolean value (true or false) and returns the opposite. If **$idea** is a boolean variable that has the value true, when the NOT operator (which is the exclamation point in PHP, as in JavaScript: !) acts on **$idea**, the result is false. Some other unary operators are the increment (++) and decrement (--) operators.

TABLE 11.2	PHP Keywords			
		PHP Keywords		
abstract	declare	endswitch	include	require
and	default	endwhile	include_once	require_once
array()	die()	eval()	instanceof	return
as	do	exit()	interface	static
break	echo	extends	isset()	throw
callable	else	final	list()	trait
case	elseif	for	new	try
catch	empty()	foreach	or	unset()
class	enddeclare	function	print	use
clone	endfor	global	private	var
const	endforeach	if	protected	while
continue	endif	implements	public	xor

The Unary Operator

EXAMPLE 11.5

Given the following variables and their initial values:

```
if $choice = true;  then ! $choice = false;
```

PHP follows the same rules as JavaScript regarding pre-increment/decrement and post-increment/decrement. Thus, if **$number** = 14;

- ■ **++$number** results in 15 because the variable is incremented before it is used
- ■ **$number++** results in 14 and then **$number** is incremented to 15
- ■ **--$number** results in 13 because the variable is decremented first
- ■ **$number--** results in 14 and then **$number** is decremented

Binary Operators

The majority of operators are **binary operators**. We know that all the arithmetic operators take two values. Comparison (or relational) operators, such as greater than (>), less than (<), and so on are all binary operators. The logical operators AND (&&) and OR (||) are also binary operators. PHP uses common symbols for many operators but adds a few that are new to us. Table 11.3 includes the arithmetic operators, relational operators, and binary logical operators. Other operators listed are not covered in this text, but you may use them, as needed, in the future.

The operators in Table 11.3 include two we have not seen in JavaScript—the identical (===) and the not identical (!==) operators. These are rarely used. The situation involving && and and or || or or is similar. The two pairs of operators differ only in precedence and the && and || operators are almost always preferred.

TABLE 11.3 **PHP Binary Operators**

Operator	Description
Arithmetic Operators	
+	addition
–	subtraction
*	multiplication
/	division
%	modulus
Comparison Operators	
<	less than
>	greater than
<=	less than or equal to

TABLE 11.3	**Continued**
Operator	**Description**
>=	greater than or equal to
==	equal to
!=	not equal to
===	identical: true if the two values are the same and have the same type
!==	not identical: true if the two values are not the same or they are the same but have different types
Logical Operators	
&&	AND
||	OR
and	does same thing as && but has lower precedence
or	does same thing as || but has lower precedence
Concatenation Operators	
.	concatenates two strings
.=	appends the argument on right side to argument on left

Operator Precedence   In general, operators in PHP follow the same **order of precedence** as we have used in JavaScript. Arithmetic operators follow the usual order: parentheses → multiplication/division/modulus in order from left to right → addition/subtraction in order from left to right. Comparison operators do not have an order of precedence. Logical operators take their order from left to right. The PHP code in Example 11.6 demonstrates some results of using various binary operators.

EXAMPLE 11.6

The Binary Operators in Action

```
1.   <!DOCTYPE html>
2.   <html>
3.   <?php
4.        $numX = 2; $numY = 9; $numZ = 6; $numW = 3;
5.   ?>
6.   <head>
7.        <title>Example 11.6</title>
8.   </head>
9.   <body>
10.       <h3>Original variables and their values:</h3>
11.       <p>$numW: <?php print("$numW"); ?><br />
12.       $numX: <?php print("$numX"); ?><br />
13.       $numY: <?php print("$numY"); ?><br />
14.       $numZ: <?php print("$numZ"); ?></p>
15.       <p>The value of $numX + $numY * $numW is <?php $result = ↵
```

```
                        $numX + $numY * $numW; print($result); ?> ↵
                        <br />because multiplication is done ↵
                        before addition.</p>
16.          <p>The value of $numY / $numW * 3 + $numZ * $numX is <?php ↵
                        $result2 = $numY / $numW *3 + $numZ * $numX; ↵
                        print($result2); ?> <br />because multiplication ↵
                        and division are done in order from left<br />to ↵
                        right and addition and subtraction are done ↵
                        last.</p>
17.     </body>
18.     </html>
```

The output will look like this:

Original variables and their values:

$numW: 3
$numX: 2
$numY: 9
$numZ: 6

The value of $numX + $numY * $numW is 29
because multiplication is done before addition.

The value of $numY / $numW * 3 + $numZ * $numX is 21
because multiplication and division are done in order from left
to right and addition and subtraction are done last.

In order to demonstrate the comparison and logical operators we need to use PHP conditional statements, which are covered in the next section.

Ternary Operators

The one **ternary operator** in PHP that takes three values will be familiar to you from JavaScript. It is not truly an operator in the sense that unary and binary operators are; that is, it does not evaluate to a variable. It is, rather, a conditional statement. It evaluates to the result of whichever condition is true. The operator is written ?: but normally uses the following syntax where an expression is inserted between the ? and :, as follows:

```
(expression_1) ? (expression_2) : (expression_3);
```

This expression will evaluate to the result of expression_2 if expression_1 is true. If expression_1 is false, it will evaluate to the result of expression_3. It is also possible to leave out the middle expression. This syntax is as follows:

```
(expression_1) ?: (expression_3);
```

In this case, it will return the value of expression_1 if expression_1 is true. If expression_1 is false, it will evaluate to the result of expression_3. The PHP code in Example 11.7 demonstrates some results of using the ternary conditional operator.

EXAMPLE
11.7

Using the Ternary Operator

```
1.   <!DOCTYPE html>
2.   <html>
3.   <?php
4.       $numX = 2; $numY = 9; $numZ = 6; $numW = 3;
5.       $result_true = "This is true!"; $result_false = "Nope, not true!";
6.       $result = " ";
7.   ?>
8.   <head>
9.       <title>Example 11.7</title>
10.  </head>
11.  <body>
12.      <h3>Original variables and their values:</h3>
13.      <p>$numW: <?php print("$numW"); ?><br />
14.      $numX: <?php print("$numX"); ?><br />
15.      $numY: <?php print("$numY"); ?><br />
16.      $numZ: <?php print("$numZ"); ?><br />
17.      $result_true: <?php print("$result_true"); ?><br />
18.      $result_false: <?php print("$result_false"); ?></p>
19.      <hr />
20.      <h3>Using the conditional operator:</h3>
21.      <p>Check to see if $numX and $numY are the same.<br /> If they ⏎
                 are, the output will be $result_true.<br /> If ⏎
                 not, the output will be $result_false. <br /> ⏎
                 (This tests to see if 2 = 9) And this is:
22.      <?php $result = ($numX == $numY) ? ($result_true) : ⏎
                 ($result_false); print($result); ?> </p>
23.      <p>Check to see if $numZ is the same as ($numX * $numW). <br /> ⏎
                 If they are, the output will be $result_true. ⏎
                 <br /> If not, the output will be ⏎
                 $result_false. <br />(This tests to see if ⏎
                 6 = 2 * 3) And this is:
24.      <?php $result = ($numZ == ($numX * $numW)) ? ($result_true) : ⏎
                 ($result_false); print($result); ?> </p>
25.  </body>
26.  </html>
```

The output will look like this:

Original variables and their values:

$numW: 3
$numX: 2
$numY: 9
$numZ: 6
$result_true: This is true!
$result_false: Nope, not true!

Using the conditional operator:

Check to see if $numX and $numY are the same.
If they are, the output will be $result_true.
If not, the output will be $result_false.
(This tests to see if 2 = 9) And this is: Nope, not true!

Check to see if $numZ is the same as ($numX * $numW).
If they are, the output will be $result_true.
If not, the output will be $result_false.
(This tests to see if 6 = 2 * 3) And this is: This is true!

The Concatenation Operators

There are two **string operators:** the concatenation operator which concatenates two strings and the concatenating assignment operator which appends the argument on the right side to the argument on the left side.

The **concatenation operator** is a dot (' . '). The syntax for the concatenation operator is as follows:

```
argument1 . argument2;
```

The **concatenating assignment operator** is a dot and an equals sign (' .= '). The syntax for the concatenating assignment operator is as follows:

```
argument1 .= argument2;
```

Spaces before and after these operators is optional and is a matter of preference. Example 11.8 demonstrates the use of these two concatenation operators.

EXAMPLE 11.8

The String Concatenation Operators

Given: **$fName** = "Jessie "; **$lName** = "Jumper";

a) **$fullName** = **$fName** . **$lName**;
   will result in **$fullName** = "Jessie Jumper"

   The concatenation operator concatenates the values of **$fName** and **$lName** into the single new variable, **$fullName**.

b) But **$fName** .= "Leaper";
   will result in **$fName** = "Jessie Leaper"

   The concatenating assignment operator concatenates the original value of **$fName** with the new text, "Leaper" into the single variable, **$fName**.

CHECKPOINT FOR SECTION 11.3 ✓

11.11 Why must all pages that contain PHP have the `.php` extension?

11.12 Why must all PHP pages that you want to run from your computer using XAMPP be put in the `htdocs` folder?

11.13 What are the differences between the following variables?
   $myVarA = "678";   **$myVarB** = 678;   **$myVarC** = 678.0;

Use the following statement for Checkpoints 11.14–11.16:
   $oneNum = "765";

11.14 Write a PHP statement to change the data type of the variable to `integer`.

11.15 Write a PHP statement to determine the data type of the variable.

11.16 Write a statement to cast the variable as an integer.

11.17 Give one example of each of the following types of operators: unary, binary, and ternary.

11.18 Given the following:

```
$numA = 3;        $numB = 5;        $numC = 8;
$yes = "yes";     $no = "no";
```

Write a statement, using the variables given, that will check if 3 is the result of subtracting 5 from 8. If it is true, output "yes" and if not, output "no".

11.4 Using Conditionals and Loops

The logic of a PHP program is the same as the logic of any programming or scripting language. You can create decision statements (conditionals), write repetition statements (loops), use arrays, search and sort, and more. In this section, we will cover the basics of how these structures are handled in PHP.

Making Decisions: The `if` Structure

PHP uses the same logic when making decisions as JavaScript. The `if` structure evaluates an expression and, if it is true, one thing happens. If it is not true, either something else happens or nothing happens. There is also an `else` construct and an `elseif` (or `else if`) construct. These work in the same manner as we are accustomed to with JavaScript. As mentioned in the previous section, the conditional operator, `?:`, is another way to execute a selection statement but it should probably not be used when there are nested conditions. In other words, the conditional operator is useful for a single decision but if you have multiple `elseif` conditions, stick to the `if...elseif...else...` construction.

The syntax for an `if` structure is as follows:

```
if(condition):
    result if condition is true;
endif;
```

The syntax for an `if...elseif` structure is as follows:

```
if(condition):
    result if condition is true;
    elseif (condition):
        result if condition is true;
endif;
```

And the syntax for an `if...elseif...else` structure is as follows:

```
if(condition):
    result if condition is true;
    elseif (condition):
        result if condition is true;
        else:
            result;
endif;
```

The echo Construct

Before we continue to create more examples, we will mention the **echo construct**. So far in this chapter, we have used the print() method to pass information from PHP code to a web page, in a manner similar to the JavaScript document.write() statement. The echo construct does the same thing but is shorter and easier to use if you simply want to see the results of some code on your web page. The syntax is simple:

```php
<?php echo "Hi there!"; ?>
```

This will output the text "Hi there!". There are times when print() is more appropriate than echo because print() behaves like a function. From now on, in our examples, we will use either print() or echo, depending on the context, to output data to the web page. Example 11.9 shows how to use an if structure, an if... elseif structure, and an if...elseif...else... structure.

EXAMPLE 11.9

Making Decisions: if, if...else, if...elseif...

```
1.    <!DOCTYPE html>
2.    <html>
3.    <?php
4.        $X = 2;      $Y = 9;  $Z = 9;
5.    ?>
6.    <head>
7.        <title>Example 11.9</title>
8.    </head>
9.    <body>
10.       <p>The value of $X is <?php print("$X"); ?>.<br />
11.       The value of $Y is <?php print("$Y"); ?>.<br />
12.       The value of $Z is <?php print("$Z"); ?>.</p>
13.       <hr />
14.       <p>This PHP code uses the if structure to compare two variables. ↵
                      <br /> If the result is true, it will display ↵
                      that result. If the result <br /> is not true, ↵
                      nothing will appear:</p>
15.       <h3><?php
16.           if($X > $Y):
17.               echo $X." is greater than ".$Y;
18.           endif;
19.       ?></h3>
20.       <hr />
21.       <p>This PHP code uses the if...elseif structure to compare two ↵
                      variables. <br /> If the result is true, it will ↵
                      display that result. If the result <br /> is not ↵
                      true, a new message will appear:</p>
22.       <h3><?php
23.           if($X > $Y):
24.               echo $X." is greater than ".$Y;
25.               else:
26.                   echo $X." is not greater than ".$Y;
27.           endif;
28.       ?></h3>
29.       <hr />
```

```
30.        <p>This PHP code uses the if...elseif...else structure to ⏎
                    compare variables. <br/> If the first condition ⏎
                    is true, that message will display.<br /> If ⏎
                    that is not true, another test will be made. If ⏎
                    that <br /> is not true, a different message ⏎
                    will display:</p>
31.        <h3><?php
32.            if($Z > $Y):
33.                echo $Z." is greater than ".$Y;
34.                elseif($Z < $Y):
35.                    echo $Z." is less than ".$Y;
36.                    else:
37.                        echo $Y." and ".$Z." are equal";
38.            endif;
39.        ?></h3>
40.    </body>
41.    </html>
```

The syntax is similar to JavaScript except you must include colons after the condition in the if, elseif, and else statements. If you created and ran this program, the output would be as shown below. Notice that nothing displays in the if statement because the comparison is not true.

The value of $X is 2.
The value of $Y is 9.
The value of $Z is 9.

This PHP code uses the if structure to compare two variables.
If the result is true, it will display that result. If the result
is not true, nothing will appear.

This PHP code uses the if...elseif structure to compare two variables.
If the result is true, it will display that result. If the result
is not true, a new message will appear.

2 is not greater than 9

This PHP code uses the if...elseif...else structure to compare variables.
If the first condition is true, that message will display.
If that is not true, another test will be made. If that
is not true, a different message will display:

9 and 9 are equal

The switch Statement

The syntax of the switch statement is similar to JavaScript. The case expression in a PHP switch statement may be any expression that evaluates to a simple type. This includes integers, floats, and strings. The syntax for a PHP statement follows. The break; statement is required each time you want to exit the switch.

```
switch ($variable)
{
    case (option_1):
        statements;
        break;
    case(option_2):
        statements;
        break;

        .

        .

        .

    case(option_N):
        statements;
        break;
    default:
        statements;
}
```

Example 11.10 shows how the switch statement looks in PHP. Just as with JavaScript, without the break; statements at the end of each case, the next case will be executed.

EXAMPLE
11.10

Using the PHP switch Statement

```
1.   <!DOCTYPE html>
2.   <html>
3.   <?php
4.       $grade = 4;
5.   ?>
6.   <head>
7.       <title>Example 11.10</title>
8.   </head>
9.   <body>
10.  <h3>Given that the value of $grade = 4, the student's grade is:
11.  <?php
12.      switch ($grade)
13.      {
14.          case 5:
15.              print "A";
16.              break;
17.          case 4:
18.              print "B";
19.              break;
20.          case 3:
21.              print "C";
22.              break;
23.          default:
24.              print "No credit";
25.      }
26.  ?></h3>
27.  </body>
28.  </html>
```

The output of this code will be as follows:

Given that the value of $grade = 4, the student's grade is: B

Cycling Through: Repetitions and Loops

PHP has loop structures that are the same as the ones we have been using in JavaScript. Therefore, we will touch only briefly on each so you can see how they are used in PHP. PHP has while, do...while, and for loops.

The syntax for a while loop is as follows:

```
while (expression)
{
    statements to be executed
}
```

or:

```
while (expression):
    statements to be executed
endwhile;
```

Notice that you can either group the statements to be executed in the loop between curly braces or you can use the endwhile; statement so long as you include the : after the while().

A similar situation exists with for loops; alternate syntaxes are available. The syntax for the for loop that is most familiar to us in this book is as follows:

```
for ($variable = start_value; test_condition; increment)
{
    statements to be executed
}
```

And there is the alternate syntax:

```
for ($variable = start_value; test_condition; increment):
    statements to be executed
endfor;
```

Notice that, if you choose the second syntax, as with the while loop, you must end the loop with the endfor; (or endwhile;) statement that includes a semicolon.

There is only one syntax for the do...while loop, as follows:

```
do
{
    statements to be executed
} while (condition);
```

Examples 11.11 through 11.13 demonstrate each of these loop structures in PHP.

The PHP while Loop Structure

This example uses the while loop syntax to count by twos. The code is as follows:

```
1.  <!DOCTYPE html>
2.  <html>
3.  <?php
4.      $numX = 2; $num = 1;
```

```
5.    ?>
6.    <head>
7.        <title>Example 11.11</title>
8.    </head>
9.    <body>
10.   <div id="content" style="width: 600px;">
11.       <h3>Original variables and their values:</h3>
12.       <p>$num: <?php print("$num"); ?><br />
13.       $numX: <?php print("$numX"); ?><br />
14.       <hr />
15.       <h3>Using the while loop:</h3>
16.       <p>This loop will display the result of multiplying the ⤶
                        numbers 1 through 5<br /> by the value of ⤶
                        $numX using a while loop.<br />
17.       <?php
18.           while ($num < 6):
19.               print($num * $numX)."<br/>";
20.               $num++;
21.           endwhile;
22.       ?> </p>
23.       <hr />
24.   </div>
25.   </body>
27.   </html>
```

The output should look like this:

Original variables and their values:

$num: 1
$numX: 2
$numY: 5

Using the while loop:

This loop will display the result of multiplying the numbers 1 through 5
by the value of $numX using a while loop.
2
4
6
8
10

The PHP do...while Loop Structure

EXAMPLE 11.12

This example uses the do...while loop syntax to count by fives. The code is as follows:

```
1.    <!DOCTYPE html>
2.    <html>
3.    <?php
4.        $num = 1; $numY = 5;
```

```
5.    ?>
6.    <head>
7.       <title>Example 11.12</title>
8.    </head>
9.    <body>
10.   <div id="content" style="width: 600px;">
11.      <h3>Original variables and their values:</h3>
12.      <p>$num: <?php print("$num"); ?><br />
13.      $numY: <?php print("$numY"); ?></p>
14.      <hr />
15.      <h3>Using the do...while loop:</h3>
16.      <p>This loop will display the result of multiplying the numbers ⏎
                      1 through 5 by the value of $numY using a ⏎
                      do...while loop.<br />
17.      <?php
18.          do
19.          {
20.                  print($num * $numY)."<br/>";
21.                  $num++;
22.          }
23.          while($num < 6);
24.      ?> </p>
25.      <hr />
26.   </div>
27.   </body>
28.   </html>
```

The output should look like this:

Original variables and their values:

$num: 1
$numY: 5

Using the do...while loop:

This loop will display the result of multiplying the numbers 1 through 5
by the value of $numY using a do...while loop.
5
10
15
20
25

EXAMPLE
11.13

The PHP for Loop Structure

This example uses the for loop syntax to count down from 10 to 1. The code is as follows:

```
1.   <!DOCTYPE html>
2.   <html>
```

```
3.    <?php
4.        $num = 10; $message = "BLAST OFF!";
5.    ?>
6.    <head>
7.        <title>Example 11.13</title>
8.    </head>
9.    <body>
10.   <div id="content" style="width: 600px;">
11.       <h3>Original variables and their values:</h3>
12.       <p>$num: <?php print("$num"); ?><br />
13.       $message: <?php print("$message"); ?></p>
14.       <hr />
15.       <h3>Using the for loop:</h3>
16.       <p>This loop will count down from 10 to 1 and display a message ⏎
                             at the end. The for loop is used.</p>
17.       <h2><?php
18.           for ($num = 10; $num > 0; $num--)
19.           {
20.               print($num )."   ...<br/>";
21.           }
22.           print ($message);
23.       ?> </h2>
24.       <hr />
25.   </div>
26.   </body>
27.   </html>
```

The output should look like this:

Original variables and their values:

$num: 10
$message: BLAST OFF!

Using the for loop:

This loop will count down from 10 to 1 and display a message at the end.
The for loop is used.

10 ...
9 ...
8 ...
7 ...
6 ...
5 ...
4 ...
3 ...
2 ...
1 ...
BLAST OFF!

11.19 Which of the following is not a selection structure?

a) `if...endif` b) `if...elseif...endif`

c) `switch` d) all are selection structures

11.20 The body of which of the following repetition structures will always execute at least once?

a) `while` b) `do...while`

c) `for` d) all will execute at least once

11.21 Rewrite the following PHP statement using echo instead of `print()`:

```php
print("$X is older than $Y");
```

11.22 Rewrite the following using `else` statements instead of three `if` statements:

```php
<?php
    $age = 22;
    if ($age < 12)
    {    print ("Child tickets cost $8.00");      }
    if ($age >= 12 && $age < 65)
    {    print ("Adult tickets cost $15.00");      }
    if ($age >= 65)
    {    print ("Senior citizen tickets cost $9.00");      }
?>
```

11.23 Rewrite the following using a for loop:

```php
<?php
    $count = 0;
    while ($count < 5)
    {
        print ($count * 10);
        $count++;
    }
?>
```

11.5 Arrays and Strings

Arrays

Just as PHP allows you to store data in variables, PHP allows you to store data in arrays. The elements of an array behave as variables, and arrays are used in the same manner as JavaScript and other programming languages—to store many related elements. Array names in PHP begin with the **$**. Individual array elements are accessed by using the array's name and the element's index number, enclosed in square brackets ([ ]).

In PHP, if a value is assigned to an element in an array but the array does not exist, PHP creates that array. If an array does exist but a value is assigned to an element without indicating an index, the new element will be appended to the end of the array.

There are several ways to initialize an array. The **array function** can be used or you can simply start declaring array elements. Examples 11.14 and 11.15 demonstrate how to initialize arrays and fill them with values. A loop is used to display the values after the array has been created and filled.

EXAMPLE 11.14

Creating an Array in PHP "On the Fly"

This example creates an array with five elements and loads each element as it is created. Then a for loop displays the names. The code is as follows:

```
1.  <!DOCTYPE html>
2.  <html>
3.  <head>
4.       <title>Example 11.14</title>
5.  </head>
6.  <body>
7.  <div id="content" style="width: 600px;">
8.       <h3>Creating and loading an array</h3>
9.       <p>This PHP code will create an array named $names and load ⌐
                   it with 5 names. The loop will then display ⌐
                   these names.</p>
10.      <h3><?php
11.          $names[0] = "Mary";
12.          $names[1] = "Howard";
13.          $names[2] = "Annabelle";
14.          $names[3] = "Marvin";
15.          $names[4] = "Pat";
16.          for ($num = 0; $num < 5; $num++)
17.          {
18.                  print($names[$num]." <br />");
19.          }
20.      ?> </h3>
21.  </div>
22.  </body>
23.  </html>
```

Notice that the array **$names** was not declared before its first element was initialized. By doing this on line 11, PHP automatically created the **$names** array. Array subscripts in PHP begin with 0 and we can use PHP variables to represent index values, as on line 18. If coded and opened, the page will look like this:

Creating and loading an array

This PHP code will create an array named $names and load it with 5 names.
The loop will then display these names.

Mary
Howard
Annabelle
Marvin
Pat

EXAMPLE 11.15

Creating Arrays with the array Function and with a Loop

This example creates two arrays, each with five elements. The first array is an array of strings and is loaded using the PHP array function with the values loaded by the programmer as the array is created. The second array uses a loop to load an array of integers. Loops display the results. The code is as follows:

```
1.   <!DOCTYPE html>
2.   <html>
3.   <head>
4.         <title>Example 11.15</title>
5.   </head>
6.   <body>
7.   <div id="content" style="width: 600px;">
8.         <h3>Creating and loading an array</h3>
9.         <p>This PHP code will create an array named $names and load ⏎
                    it with 5 names. This code uses the array ⏎
                    function. The loop will then display ⏎
                    these names.</p>
10.        <h3><?php
11.          $names = array ("Mary", "Howard", "Annabelle", "Marvin", "Pat");
12.          for ($num = 0; $num < 5; $num++)
13.          {
14.                  print($names[$num]." <br />");
15.          }
16.        ?> </h3>
17.        <hr />
18.        <p>This PHP code will create an array named $byFours and load ⏎
                    it with 5 elements. A loop will be used to load ⏎
                    the array with numbers, beginning at 0 and ⏎
                    counting by fours up to 16. A second loop will ⏎
                    then display the array contents.</p>
19.        <h3><?php
20.          $byFours = array();
21.          for ($i = 0; $i < 5; $i++)
22.          {
23.                  $byFours[$i] = ($i * 4);
24.          }
25.          for ($num = 0; $num < 5; $num++)
26.          {
27.                  print($byFours[$num]." <br />");
28.          }
29.        ?> </h3>
30.  </div>
31.  </body>
32.  </html>
```

You can see that the behavior of the array elements, once created, is the same as in JavaScript. In this program, line 11 creates and fills an array. Line 20 creates a second array which, at this time, is empty. But the loop on lines 21–24 fills the array with the numbers 0, 4, 8, 12, and 16. If coded and opened, the page will look like this:

Creating and loading an array

This PHP code will create an array named $names and load it with 5 names.
This code uses the array function. The loop will then display these names.

Mary
Howard
Annabelle
Marvin
Pat

This PHP code will create an array named $byFours and load it with 5 elements.
A loop will be used to load the array with numbers, beginning at 0 and counting by fours up to 16.
A second loop will then display the array contents.

0
4
8
12
16

The reset() Method

The **reset() method** will reset the computer's internal pointer to the first element of an array. The syntax is simply reset(**$array_name**). This can be valuable when you are stepping through an array for one purpose and want to begin to step through the array at the beginning for another purpose.

The foreach Construct, the as keyword, and the ==> Operator

The **foreach construct** provides an easy way to iterate over arrays. It works on arrays and objects only. It automatically resets the computer's internal pointer to the first element of an array so, when using foreach, you do not need to use the reset() method. The syntax for the foreach construct is as follows:

```
foreach($array_name as $element ==> $value)
{
        statements to be executed
}
```

The foreach construct uses the **as keyword** and the **==> operator**. The value to the left of the ==> operator is the index of the array element to begin with and the value to the right of the ==> operator is the value of that element.

The key() Method

The **key() method** returns the element key from the current internal pointer position. The syntax is simply key(**$array_name**).

Example 11.16 creates the array of names as in Example 11.15 but uses the foreach construct to display the names, rather than a while, do...while, or for loop. Remember, though, that the foreach construct can only be used with arrays or objects so it cannot substitute for other types of loops in every situation.

Using the foreach Construct

```
1.   <!DOCTYPE html>
2.   <html>
3.   <head>
4.        <title>Example 11.16</title>
5.   </head>
6.   <body>
7.   <div id="content" style="width: 600px;">
8.        <h3>Using the foreach construct</h3>
9.        <p>This PHP code will create an array named $names which ⏎
                        contains 5 names. It will display the ⏎
                        names using the foreach construct instead ⏎
                        of a loop.</p>
10.       <h3><?php
11.           $names = array ("Mary", "Howard", "Annabelle", "Marvin", ⏎
                        "Pat");
12.           foreach ($names as $element)
13.           {
14.               echo $element." <br />";
15.           }
16.       ?></h3>
17.  </div>
18.  </body>
19.  </html>
```

If coded and opened, the page will look like this:

Using the foreach construct

This PHP code will create an array named $names which contains 5 names. It will display the names using the foreach construct instead of a loop.

Mary
Howard
Annabelle
Marvin
Pat

Why Are We Learning All This?

So far, we have not discussed the purpose of using PHP and we have seen that there is a lot of syntax in PHP that is similar to JavaScript and other programming languages. But we do not need to learn PHP as a programming language; the programming part is assumed. In this chapter, we focus mainly on the basics of PHP code so you can use it for its true purpose. In Chapter 12, we will put it all together, pulling from everything we have learned throughout the text and creating websites that truly work in the real world.

You can think about a working website as a house with various rooms. In the living room, you turn on the lights, TV, or radio. The electricity comes from outside the room. In the kitchen, you turn on the water in the sink. The water is pumped in from elsewhere. In the bedroom, you turn on your computer or you listen to music through your smart phone. The Internet connection comes from someplace else. Your home is heated or air conditioned from units that are housed outside the rooms themselves. A website can be thought of similarly. One web page may ask you to register for the site's benefits or log in. The information you provide is stored in one place on the site's server. An "About Us" page may highlight information about the company that runs the site. This information may be directly provided from the HTML script on that page. Another page might present items the site is selling; these items are probably stored in a database, elsewhere on the server. When you add items to a shopping cart, the information about your purchase, before you actually buy anything, most likely comes from JavaScript code, either directly in the web page or from an external JavaScript file. Once you make a purchase, you receive a confirmation email, generated from other server-side code.

Just as heat, cool air, or water is piped in through vents or pipes in your house, information that goes from your browser to the site's server and back is piped in through various scripts. PHP is one of the most important of these scripts. With PHP, you can access enormous amounts of data stored on a server, save customer or user information, use it whenever an individual returns to the site, and much much more.

Since PHP is often used to access and process data—and since that data is often presented as text (as opposed to numbers), it is appropriate that PHP has specific ways to handle string data which make it easier for a programmer to work with such data.

Working with Strings

One way to process string data is to use the **equality** and **comparison operators**. These operators can check to see if two strings are the same or if one comes before or after another in the alphabet. Also, PHP often needs to do more than simply compare strings. We may need to substitute one string for another or one part of a string for another. We may need to extract parts of a string, search through many strings, or sort string data. Most often, this type of processing is done using regular expressions. A **regular expression** provides a way to match strings of text which can be specific characters, words, or patterns of characters. We will discuss the various types of string data manipulation here.

Comparing Strings

The relational operators can be used to compare strings. We have done this before in JavaScript. We can use this code in a sort routine to sort values alphabetically. However, PHP has many sort functions which make it redundant for us to write our own. Example 11.17 uses comparison operators in conjunction with a PHP sort routine to determine if a given item is the same as the first element in an array, sorted alphabetically, or if it should go before or after the first element.

EXAMPLE
11.17

Comparing String Data

```
1.   <!DOCTYPE html>
2.   <html>
3.   <head>
4.       <title>Example 11.17</title>
5.   </head>
6.   <body>
7.   <div id="content" style="width: 600px;">
8.       <h3>The original array of usernames is:</h3>
9.       <h3><?php
10.          $usernames = array ("Puppypal", "EvilEd", "DorienDragon", ↵
                                "PammyPrincess", "PeterRabbit");
11.          foreach ($usernames as $element)
12.          {
13.              echo $element." <br />";
14.          }
15.          sort($usernames);
16.          echo "<p>Here are the names sorted: </p>";
17.          foreach ($usernames as $element)
18.          {
19.              echo $element." <br />";
20.          }
21.          $newName = "CoolCat";
22.          if ($newName < $usernames[0])
23.          {
24.              echo "<p>$newName belongs before $usernames[0]</p>";
25.          }
26.              else if ($newName == $usernames[0])
27.              {
28.                  echo "<p>$newName is the same as $usernames[0] ↵
                            </p>";
29.              }
30.                  else
31.                  {
32.                      echo "<p>$newName should not be the first ↵
                              item in the list of names</p>";
33.                  }
34.      ?></h3>
35.   </div>
36.   </body>
37.   </html>
```

Line 10 initializes the array, **$usernames**, and the foreach construct on lines 11–14 print out the unsorted array. Line15 uses the **sort()** method to sort the names alphabetically and they are displayed again (lines 17–20). Line 21 declares and initializes a new variable, **$newName**. Lines 22 and 26 use comparison operators to see if **$newName** should go before the first name in the alphabetized list, is the same as that first name, or should be sorted somewhere else in the list. If coded and opened, the page should look like the first one shown. By changing the value of **$newName** to DorienDragon, the output should look like the second one shown.

```
The original array of usernames is:          The original array of usernames is:

Puppypal                                     Puppypal
EvilEd                                       EvilEd
DorienDragon                                 DorienDragon
PammyPrincess                                PammyPrincess
PeterRabbit                                  PeterRabbit

Here are the names sorted:                   Here are the names sorted:

DorienDragon                                 DorienDragon
EvilEd                                       EvilEd
PammyPrincess                                PammyPrincess
PeterRabbit                                  PeterRabbit
Puppypal                                     Puppypal

CoolCat belongs before DorienDragon          DorienDragon is the same as DorienDragon


          Part 1                                        Part 2
```

Searching for Expressions: The `preg_match()` and `preg_replace()` methods

Using comparison operators is a simple way to search for string expressions. But it is often not enough for what we need to accomplish. PHP provides more ways to identify strings.

A regular expression is a pattern of characters. We often need to match specific characters to items in an array or database. For example, our schoolteacher, Carla, might want to find all the students in her database whose names are John, Johnny, Johnathan, and Johnnie but not Johanna or Johwann. A program that allows her to enter the characters "John" would do the trick. Or Greg of our Greg's Gambits site might want to assign all users an identification name that uses the username part of their email addresses without anything that follows the @ sign. A program that allows everything up to the @ sign of an email address to be added to another pattern of characters would be helpful. The PHP `preg_match()` function is used in these situations.

The first parameter in this method is the regular expression to search for. In Carla's case, this would be "John". Regular expressions can also contain special characters and some special characters identify specific patterns. The caret (∧) matches the beginning of a string, the dollar sign ($) matches the end of a string, and the dot (.) matches any single character. For example:

- `preg_match("/∧cat/", $string)` searches for the pattern "cat" in the beginning of the string while
- `preg_match("/cat$/", $string)` searches for the pattern "cat" at the end of the string

You can add a **bracket expression** which contains a list of characters enclosed in square brackets ([ ]). A single character can be included, or a list of characters, or a range of characters. The \b before and after the parentheses indicates the beginning or end of a word; i.e., it means we are searching for a match to a whole word. The

/i indicates that the match can be case-insensitive (either uppercase or lowercase). For example:

- `preg_match("/\b(cat[a-z]+\b/", $string)` searches for any word beginning with the pattern "cat" while

- `preg_match("/\b([a-z]*cat\b/i", $string)` searches for any word ending with the pattern "cat"

The third parameter in the **preg_match() method, $match,** is optional. It is an array that stores matches to the regular expression. The first element in the array stores the text that matches the full pattern. The second element will have the text that matched the first captured subpattern and so on. A loop can be used to display the results of this array. For example:

```
preg_match("/\b(cat[a-z]+\b/", $string, $match);
print ("Word found that begins with c-a-t is: ".$match[1]);
```

This will display the first whole word that begins with the pattern "cat".

Another optional parameter is the offset. Normally, the search starts at the beginning of a string. However, the **offset parameter** can be used to specify an alternate place from which to start the search.

Example 11.18 shows how to use the preg_match() method with various parameter specifications.

EXAMPLE 11.18

Using the preg_match() and preg_replace() Methods

This example uses the preg_match() and **preg_replace()** methods. First, it searches through a short story to see if the first word in the story is a specific word or if the last word in the story is that word. Then, it looks for words that either begin or end with a specific character. Some of this code has been explained previously and some will be explained after the code shown below:[1]

```
1.   <!DOCTYPE html>
2.   <html>
3.   <head>
4.      <title>Example 11.18</title>
5.   </head>
6.   <body>
7.      <div id="content" style="width: 600px;">
8.      <h3>Using preg_match() to find words in a paragraph</h3>
9.      <?php
10.         $myStory = "Once when a Lion was asleep a little Mouse ↵
                       began running up and down upon him. This soon ↵
                       wakened the Lion, who placed his huge paw upon ↵
                       the mouse and opened his big jaws to swallow ↵
                       him. 'Pardon, O King,' cried the little Mouse, ↵
                       'forgive me this time and I shall never forget ↵
```

---

[1] This fable is one of Aesop's Fables. It can be accessed at Page By Page Books (http://www.pagebypagebooks.com/Aesop/Aesops_Fables/The_Lion_and_the_Mouse_p1.html)

```
                              it. Who knows but what I may be able to do you ↵
                              a turn some of these days?' The Lion was so ↵
                              tickled at the idea of the Mouse being able to ↵
                              help him that he lifted up his paw and let him ↵
                              go. Sometime after the Lion was caught in a ↵
                              trap. The hunters who desired to carry him alive ↵
                              to the King tied him to a tree while they went ↵
                              in search of a waggon to carry him on. Just then ↵
                              the little Mouse happened to pass by and, seeing ↵
                              the sad plight in which the Lion was, went up to ↵
                              him and soon gnawed away the ropes that bound ↵
                              the  King of the Beasts. 'Was I not right?' said ↵
                              the little Mouse.";
11.       print ("<h3>Little Friends May Prove to Be Great Friends
                              </h3><p>".$myStory."</p>");
12.       print ("<h3>Is the first word 'Mouse'?</h3>");
13.       if (preg_match("/^Mouse/", $myStory))
14,           print ("<p>'Mouse' is the first word in this story</p>");
15.       else print ("<p>'Mouse' is not the first word in this story</p>");
16.       print ("<h3>Is the last word 'Mouse'?</h3>");
17.       if (preg_match("/Mouse.$/", $myStory))
18.           print ("<p>'Mouse' is the last word in this story</p>");
19.       else print ("<p>'Mouse' is not the last word in this story</p>");
20.       print ("<h3>What words in this story begin with the letter ↵
                              'p', either upper or lower case?</h3>");
21.       while (preg_match("/\b(p[[:alpha:]]+)\b/", $myStory, $match))
22.       {
23.           print ($match[1]." ");
24.           $myStory = preg_replace("/".$match[1]."/", "", $myStory);
25.       }
26.       $myStory = "Once when a Lion was asleep a little Mouse ↵
                              began running up and down upon him. This soon ↵
                              wakened the Lion, who placed his huge paw upon ↵
                              the mouse and opened his big jaws to swallow ↵
                              him. 'Pardon, O King,' cried the little Mouse, ↵
                              'forgive me this time and I shall never forget ↵
                              it. Who knows but what I may be able to do you ↵
                              a turn some of these days?' The Lion was so ↵
                              tickled at the idea of the Mouse being able to ↵
                              help him that he lifted up his paw and let him ↵
                              go. Sometime after the Lion was caught in a ↵
                              trap. The hunters who desired to carry him alive ↵
                              to the King tied him to a tree while they went ↵
                              in search of a waggon to carry him on. Just then ↵
                              the little Mouse happened to pass by and, seeing ↵
                              the sad plight in which the Lion was, went up to ↵
                              him and soon gnawed away the ropes that bound ↵
                              the  King of the Beasts. 'Was I not right?' said ↵
                              the little Mouse.";
27.       print ("<h3>What words in this story end with the letter 'p'?</h3>");
28.       while (preg_match("/\b([[:alpha:]]*p)\b/", $myStory, $match))
29.       {
30.           print ($match[1]." ");
31.           $myStory = preg_replace("/".$match[1]."/", " ", $myStory);
```

```
32.           }
33.       ?></h3>
34.     </div>
35.   </body>
36. </html>
```

We'll discuss what happens in specific lines of this code. The string variable, **$myStory**, holds a whole short story which, in this case, is one of Aesop's Fables. Line 13 checks to see if the first word in the story is "Mouse". An ordinary if...else structure prints out one message if the first word is "Mouse" and another if it is not. The preg_match() function takes the character string to be matched (in this case it is "Mouse") as the first argument. The characters are enclosed in slashes, / /. The ^ before Mouse indicates that we are looking for the character pattern at the beginning of the string. The second argument, **$myStory**, is the string to be searched.

Line 17 does almost exactly the same thing as line 13 but, in this case, it uses the $ after the pattern "Mouse" inside the / / to indicate that we want to know if the pattern is at the end of the string, **$myStory**.

Things get a bit more complicated on line 21. Here we want to identify all words that begin with a specific character. However, the preg_match() function just identifies the first instance of the item being looked for. We'll discuss the part of line 21 that is the while loop condition:

```
preg_match("/\b(p[[:alpha:]]+)\b/", $myStory, $match))
```

The beginning and ending / / mark off the pattern we are looking for. The \b at the beginning and end of this area indicates that we are looking at whole words. In the nested parentheses, the 'p' means we are looking for words that begin with 'p'. PHP has **character classes** and alpha is one of those classes. A character class is delimited by [: and :]. Thus, [:alpha:] means that we are looking at the alphanumeric character class. This is placed inside another set of square brackets. The + sign is a **quantifier** and means we are looking for one or more times. The possible quantifiers are shown in Table 11.4 and the possible character classes are shown in Table 11.5.

Since preg_match() looks for the first instance of the character ('p' in this case) but we want to find all words that start with 'p', we must put this expression in a loop and replace the first instance found with something that does not start with 'p'. Line 23 displays the first word found and line 24 replaces that word with an empty space. The expression

```
$myStory = preg_replace("/".$match[1]."/", " ", myStory);
```

will replace the first word found which has been stored in **$match[1]** with an empty space. The new value of **$myStory** is the same story as the original but now the first few sentences:

```
"Once when a Lion was asleep a little Mouse began running up and down upon
him. This soon wakened the Lion, who placed his huge paw upon the mouse
and opened his big jaws to swallow him. 'Pardon, O King,' cried the little
Mouse..."
```

will be as follows:

> "Once when a Lion was asleep a little Mouse began running up and down upon him. This soon wakened the Lion, who his huge paw upon the mouse and opened his big jaws to swallow him..."

The second time the loop executes, this sentence will read as follows:

> "Once when a Lion was asleep a little Mouse began running up and down upon him. This soon wakened the Lion, who his huge upon the mouse and opened his big jaws to swallow him..."

and so on. Lines 27–31 do almost the same thing except, in this case, we are searching for words that end with the letter 'p'. In this case, line 27 is almost identical to line 21 but we place the character we are searching for after the character class with a * to indicate we are looking for words that end in 'p'.

If this example were entered in a program and run, the output would be as follows:

Using preg_match() to find words in a paragraph

Little Friends May Prove to Be Great Friends

Once when a Lion was asleep a little Mouse began running up and down upon him. This soon wakened the Lion, who placed his huge paw upon the mouse and opened his big jaws to swallow him. 'Pardon, O King,' cried the little Mouse, 'forgive me this time and I shall never forget it. Who knows but what I may be able to do you a turn some of these days?' The Lion was so tickled at the idea of the Mouse being able to help him that he lifted up his paw and let him go. Some time after the Lion was caught in a trap. The hunters who desired to carry him alive to the King tied him to a tree while they went in search of a waggon to carry him on. Just then the little Mouse happened to pass by and, seeing the sad plight in which the Lion was, went up to him and soon gnawed away the ropes that bound the King of the Beasts. 'Was I not right?' said the little Mouse.

Is the first word 'Mouse'?

'Mouse' is not the first word in this story

Is the last word 'Mouse'?

'Mouse' is the last word in this story

What words in this story begin with the letter 'p', either upper or lower case?

placed paw pass plight

What words in this story end with the letter 'p'?

asleep up help trap

TABLE 11.4	PHP Quantifiers	
Quantifier	**Number of Matches**
{n}	exactly n times
{m, n}	between m and n times, inclusive
{n, }	n or more times
+	one or more times
*	zero or more times
?	zero or one time

TABLE 11.5 | **Some PHP Regular Expression Character Classes**

Character Class	Description
alnum	alphanumeric characters (i.e., letters [a-zA-Z] or digits [0-9])
alpha	letters (i.e., [a-zA-Z])
digit	digits
space	white space
lower	lowercase letters
upper	uppercase letters

CHECKPOINT FOR SECTION 11.5 ✓

11.25 Create an array with 10 elements where each element has the value of six times its index. Call the array **$bySixes**.

11.25 Given the following array, use the foreach() method to display the square of each array element:

$squares = array (0, 1, 2, 3, 4);

11.26 True or False? PHP can use logical and relational operators to compare string data.

11.27 Use the sort() method to sort and display the following array (after sorting). Use the foreach() method for the display.

$cars = array ("Ford", "Chevrolet", "Kia", "Rolls Royce", ↵
"Porsche", "Dodge", "Toyota", "Cadillac");

Use the following statement for Checkpoints 28–31:

preg_match("/\b(sedan[a-z]+)\b/", **$carStyles**, **$match**);

11.28 What pattern is being searched for?

11.29 What string will be searched?

11.30 Where is the first match stored?

11.31 What would need to be changed if the search pattern was '4door' and what should it be changed to?

11.6   Putting It to Work

The output here will be surprisingly dull. However, the back end (the part we will create) is complex and, by working through this project, you will learn a tremendous amount about how PHP communicates with JavaScript and HTML and even a little about Ajax. We will develop a sign-in page for the Greg's Gambits site that uses PHP to respond to the player, and for Carla's Classroom, we will develop a page Carla can use to find all her students, past and present. We have done similar things using JavaScript and HTML. Now, we will now use our own servers to perform these tasks using PHP and server-side technologies.

Greg's Gambits: PHP Welcome Messages

We will create a web page that allows a player to enter his or her name and the program will respond with another page that uses the name in a message. We will, at the same time, learn how websites are created by putting together various files. Some of these files may be used with every page on a site while others may be used for specific purposes on various pages. Once we create the new (and improved) template for Greg's Gambits, we are ready to add more server-side capabilities. We'll use PHP to communicate with the user in this section and build on this in Chapter 12. This material is learned more easily through doing than through reading about doing, so let's get started.

Developing a New Format for Greg's Pages: Organizing a Site

By now, most likely you have realized that every page on this site contains the same information at the top and the bottom as most of the other pages. The middle, what we have previously identified as the container <div>, is where the new content is placed each time we create a new page. We can put the information that will always be displayed at the top and bottom of each page into two files—a header file and a footer file—and, just as we include a CSS style sheet, we can include these two files in each page. This saves rewriting the code each time and ensures that the information on each page is always the same. Furthermore, if we ever need to change any information, by changing it on the header or footer file, we are assured that it will be changed everywhere.

The code from our previous Greg Gambits pages that should be included in the header file is as follows:

```
<img src="images/superhero.jpg" class="floatleft" />
<h1><em>Greg's Gambits</em></h1>
<h2 align="center"><em>Games for Everyone!</em></h2>
<p> </p>
<div id="nav">
    <p><a href="index.php">Home</a>
    <a href="greg.html">About Greg</a>
    <a href="play_games.html">Play a Game</a>
    <a href="sign.html">Sign In</a>
    <a href="contact.html">Contact Us</a>
    <a href="aboutyou.html">Tell Greg About You</a></p>
</div>
```

The code for the footer file is as follows:

```
<div id="footer">Copyright &copy; 2013 Greg's Gambits<br />
    <a href="mailto:gregory@gambits.net">gregory@gambits.net</a>
</div>
```

There's a little more to it than this, but generally this is what will be included in the two new files we are creating. Once they are created, each web page will include a PHP statement that instructs the browser to include these pages before displaying the requested page on the player's computer.

We also need to link to a CSS page and, as we have seen in the past, we often link to an external JavaScript page too. One web page is often the compilation of many pages—the instructions on the web page are moving from page to page, from client to server—all invisible to the user.

It makes sense, then, for us to add to the organizational scheme used to store a website. Until now, you have probably had a folder for Gregs_Games and an images folder inside that one. Let's add a few more folders. We have used a single CSS page for the whole site but large websites often have several different CSS pages and, depending on a web page's content, one or another or several may be applied to that page. So we will have a css folder.

We also decided that we will develop pages that include the material that always goes at the top of each web page (the header) and the material that always goes at the bottom (the footer). Since these are included in every page, we'll put them in a separate folder. Other PHP files may need to be included in a page (depending, of course, on the page's content). We'll now add an include folder to our website to hold these pages.

Other things may enhance our pages. In this project, we will develop a page that uses Ajax to take player-entered information and use it to respond to the player. We'll put that in another folder which we will call assets. Other "assets" we might have are JavaScript pages, XML pages, or, as we become proficient in more scripting languages, other scripts. We'll create a subfolder of assets which we will call scripts.

Before you go further with this section, create the following folder structure in the htdocs folder of XAMPP:

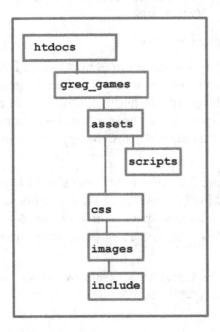

Since much of the code in these new files will be unfamiliar, extensive comments will be included with the code as well as explanations in the text following the code.

The Header and Footer Files

Our header file initially will contain just the top of every page on the Greg's Gambits site. This means it should include the beginning <html> tag, whatever we want in the <head> section, the navigation links, and both the page title and the title that appears on the page. We will add to this file as we develop the PHP code. Create (or copy and paste from a previous page) the following script and name the file header.php. Store it in the include folder in htdocs.

```
1.   <!DOCTYPE HTML PUBLIC "-//W3C//DTD HTML 4.01 ⏎
                Transitional//EN""http://www.w3.org/TR/html4/loose.dtd">
2.   <html>
3.     <head>
4.         <title>Greg's PHP Demo</title>
5.         <link href="css/greg.css" rel="stylesheet" type="text/css" />
6.         <script language="JavaScript" type="text/javascript">
7.     </head>
8.     <body>
9.     <!-- html to be inserted into calling page -->
10.        <div id = "header">
11.            <img src="images/superhero.jpg" class="floatleft" />
12.            <h1><em>Greg's Gambits</em></h1>
13.            <h2 align="center"><em>Games for Everyone!</em></h2>
14.            <div id="nav">
15.                <p><a href="index.php">Home</a>
16.                <a href="greg.html">About Greg</a>
17.                <a href="play_games.html">Play a Game</a>
18.                <a href="sign.html">Sign In</a>
19.                <a href="contact.html">Contact Us</a>
20.                <a href="aboutyou.html">Tell Greg About
                            You</a></p>
21.            </div>
22.        </div> <-- closes container div -->
```

Notice that this page opens the <body> tag but does not close it. It will be closed in the footer file. You can open a tag in any page that is included with a web page so long as it is appropriately closed later in another page. You will see that we wrap all the HTML script inside a <div> with id = "header". As we continue to develop this project we will add PHP to this page. Be sure to copy your greg.css page into the new css folder in htdocs.

Repeat this process with the footer file. Your new footer should have the file name footer.php and should be saved into the include folder in htdocs. This is the only code that is necessary; you do not have to specify <html> or <body> or anything else because this text is simply called as soon as the rest of the script on the main page has finished loading.

```
1.   <div id="footer">Copyright &copy; 2013 Greg's Gambits<br />
2.       <a href="mailto:gregory@gambits.net"> gregory@gambits.net</a>
3.   </div>
4.   </body>
5.   </html>
```

Setting the Stage

From now on, all pages will include, at least, the header.php and footer.php and a page that will contain the content. If you wish, you can revisit the games and other pages created throughout this text and edit them to mirror what we are doing here. For now, we will create the content for this new page. It will be included in a separate PHP file and will begin with a <div> with id = "content". This first PHP demonstration will allow the player to enter his or her name and PHP code will use that name, stored on the server, to respond to the player. The file name for this page should be phpDemo.php and it should be stored outside of the subfolders but inside the gregs_games folder inside htdocs. The code is as follows:

```
1.   <!-- The first statement, an include() statement, places the ⏎
     contents of the header.php file, located in the include folder, ⏎
     into this page -->
2.   <?php include ('include/header.php'); ?>
3.       <div id = "content">
4.           <p class="phpH2">PHP DEMO</p>
5.           <table>
6.   <!-- Re: the input elements: the id attributes identify user inputs ⏎
     which will be submitted to a JavaScript function (in this case ⏎
     ajax_post()) via the onclick() event of the input element. Follow ⏎
     the data (via the id names) in the ajax_post() which is located in ⏎
     the header.php file -->
7.               <tr>
8.               <td style="border: none;">First Name: </td>
9.               <td style="border: none;"><input id="firstName" ⏎
                         name = "firstName" type = "text" /></td>
10.              </tr>
11.              <tr>
12.              <td style="border: none;">Last Name: </td>
13.              <td style="border: none;"><input id="lastName" ⏎
                         name = "lastName" type = "text" /></td>
14.              </tr>
15.              <tr>
16.              <td style="border: none;"> </td>
17.              <td style="border: none;"><input name = "btnSubmit" ⏎
                         type = "submit" value = "Submit" ⏎
                         onclick = "javascript:ajax_post();" /></td>
18.              </tr>
19.          </table>
20.          <br />
21.          <div id = "status"></div>
22.      </div>
23.      <br /><br style = "clear: both;" />
24.  <?php include ('include/footer.php'); ?>
```

The one thing that you have not seen so far (line 17) is the syntax of the onclick event that occurs when the player clicks the Submit button. We will discuss the JavaScript function ajax_post() in the next section.

Notice that line 2 calls the `header.php` file so the header script is displayed. Then this content is displayed and line 24 calls on the `footer.php` file so that file's content is displayed.

At this point, if you enter the code for the three files listed so far, save them in your `htdocs` folder as explained, and enter the following link in a browser, the display should be as shown. If you type your name, however, nothing will happen.

```
localhost/gregs_games/phpDemo.php
```

The `ajax_post()` Function

After the player clicks the `Submit` button, what happens? Here's where all the action is. The next process is complex. By including extensive comments in the pages and an explanation in the text, you should begin to understand how the client-server model works with PHP.

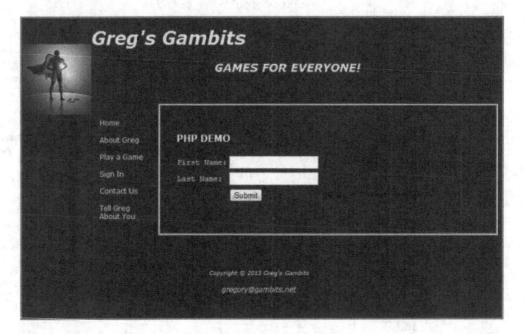

What Is Ajax?   We've mentioned Ajax several times in this example. What is it? **Ajax,** which stands for **Asynchronous JavaScript and XML,** is a technique used to create dynamic web pages. It's fast and it allows web pages to be updated asynchronously by exchanging small amounts of data behind the scenes. In programming, **asynchronous events** are events that occur independently of the `main` program. This means that they can occur while the `main` program (or web page in our case) can continue to flow. By using Ajax, we can update parts of a web page without reloading the whole page. In pages that do not use Ajax, each time the contents of a page changes, the entire page must be reloaded. For this example, a little Ajax is the perfect venue.

The `onclick = "javascript:ajax_post();"` *event*   We are used to seeing functions in the <head> section of a web page or in external files. But the page created by the previous code now has the code from the `header.php` file available. And that file has the JavaScript we need to execute the `ajax_post()` function. The following code is the expanded `header.php` file with the JavaScript functions that we need. It includes detailed comments to explain each section of the `ajax_post()` function:

```
1.    <!DOCTYPE HTML PUBLIC "-//W3C//DTD HTML 4.01 ⏎
            Transitional//EN""http://www.w3.org/TR/html4/loose.dtd">
2.    <html>
3.    <head>
4.       <title>Greg's PHP Demo</title>
5.       <link href="css/greg.css" rel="stylesheet" type="text/css" />
6.       <script language="JavaScript" type="text/javascript">
7.         function ajax_post()
8.         {
9.    // create HttpRequest object to allow communication with ⏎
      server. This object is an Application Programming Interface ⏎
      (api) that is used to transfer and manipulate XML data to and ⏎
      from a web server using HTTP. This object establishes an ⏎
      independent connection channel between our client-side web ⏎
      page and the server-side php script.
10.             var objHttpRequest = new XMLHttpRequest();
11.   // location of our server-side Common Gateway Interface ⏎
      (cgi) script (our php script)
12.             var url = "assets/ajaxDataPipe.php";
13.   // variable to hold data from user (the value associated ⏎
      with the element that is referenced with the id attribute)
14.             var fName = document.getElementById("firstName").value;
15.   // variable to hold data from user (the value associated with ⏎
      the element that is referenced with the id attribute)
16.             var lName = document.getElementById("lastName").value;
17.   // variable to hold field-value pairs that will be sent to ⏎
      server side script for processing. Note '&' is used to indicate ⏎
      a new field-value pair.
18.             var vars = "postFirstName = " + fName + ⏎
                  "&postLastName = " + lName;
19.   // open(method,url,async) : method = POST: the method ⏎
      or way the request is being sent (this means that our ⏎
      field-value pair, currently held in our client-side javascript ⏎
      variable vars, will be stored in the server-side accessible ⏎
      Super Global Variable $_POST), url is the location of the ⏎
      server-side cgi script where processing will take place, ⏎
      asynch set to TRUE means that server-side script processing ⏎
      continues after the send() method, without waiting for ⏎
      a response.
20.             objHttpRequest.open("POST", url, true);
21.   // Set content type header information for sending url encoded ⏎
      variables in the request. By defining 'Content-type' as ⏎
      "application/x-www-form-urlencoded" we are stating that the ⏎
```

```
          kind of data contained in the body of the request will be ⏎
          form data.
22.                objHttpRequest.setRequestHeader("Content-type", ⏎
                        "application/x-www-form-urlencoded");
23.       // Access the onreadystatechange event for the XMLHttpRequest ⏎
          object. The onreadystatechange event is triggered every time ⏎
          the readyState changes.
24.                objHttpRequest.onreadystatechange = function()
25.                {
26.       //checks if readyState is 4 (means request is finished and ⏎
          response is ready) and status is 200 (the page is found). ⏎
          If TRUE then response is ready.
27.                   if(objHttpRequest.readyState == 4 && ⏎
                            objHttpRequest.status == 200)
28.                   {
29.       // since request is finished and response is ready we can ⏎
          access the server's response to the request. The ⏎
          'responseText' property is used to retrieve the server's ⏎
          response as a string (as opposed to XML)
30.                      var returnData = ⏎
                                   objHttpRequest.responseText;
31.       // Set the html element's (whose id = status) value to the ⏎
          server's string response
32.                      document.getElementById("status")⏎
                                   .innerHTML = returnData;
33.                   } // end if
34.                } // close function()
35.       // Send the data to PHP now. Wait for response to update ⏎
          the status <div>
36.       // The next line executes the request
37.                objHttpRequest.send(vars);
38.       // The following displays while server side php is processing vars
39.                document.getElementById("status").innerHTML = ⏎
                                   "doing work ...";
40.          } // end function ajax_post()
41.       </script>
42.       </head>
43.       <body>
44.          <div id = "header">
45.   <!-- html to be inserted into calling page -->
46.             <img src="images/superhero.jpg" class="floatleft" />
47.             <h1><em>Greg's Gambits</em></h1>
48.             <h2 align="center"><em>Games for Everyone!</em></h2>
49.             <p> </p>
50.             <div id="nav">
51.                <p><a href="index.php">Home</a>
52.                <a href="greg.html">About Greg</a>
53.                <a href="play_games.html">Play a Game</a>
54.                <a href="sign.html">Sign In</a>
55.                <a href="contact.html">Contact Us</a>
56.                <a href="aboutyou.html">Tell Greg About ⏎
                            You</a></p>
57.             </div>
58.   <!-- close header div -->
59.          </div>
```

What is happening, in plain English? We'll discuss it one bit at a time.

First, on line 10 an object is created which is of the type HttpRequest() and is used to transfer and manipulate XML data—and yes, the data we send in is actually XML data—to and from a server using HTTP. You don't need to know any more about the **HttpRequest() object** now except that it is used to get the data your user enters to the server and back to the page the user is looking at. So we create one of those objects on line 10 and give it the name **objHttpRequest**.

We also have to create a script to tell the server what to send back to the page after the incoming data has been processed. We will create that script next, but for now, we will assume it has been created. It will be stored in a page with the file name ajaxDataPipe.php and we'll put it in our assets folder. Thus, line 12 creates a variable named **url** which holds the path to this file.

Lines 14 and 16 should be familiar. Here, we create two JavaScript variables (**fName** and **lName**) that hold the values the player enters for his or her first and last names.

Field-Value Pairs   Line 18 creates a new variable that holds the player's whole name. However, instead of simply concatenating **fName** and **lName** as we have done in the past, this variable is identified as a **field-value pair**. A field-value pair consists of the field (a term we will use extensively with databases) and the value of that field. The line

```
var vars = "postFirstName = " + fName + "&postLastName = " + lName;
```

contains two field-value pairs. The first pair is the field which is the server statement "postFirstName = " and its value which is the value of **fName**. The second pair is the server statement "postLastName = " but when the "&" is appended to it in front, this indicates that it is a new field-value pair. The value of the second field is the value of **lName**. When the server receives the variable **vars**, it will know there are two field-value pairs and know which fields to place the values of **fName** and **lName**. The "postFirstName =" and "postLastName =" statements are server-side instructions.

Now we use some methods of the server. The **open()method** on line 20 says that our field-value pairs, **vars**, will be stored in the server as a **Super Global Variable** (also called a **superglobal**) named **$_POST**. Note that the $ indicates that it is a PHP variable. Super Global Variables are built-in to PHP and are available to all scripts. A list of Super Global Variables is given in Table 11.6. The general form of the open() method contains three arguments: open(method, url, async). A breakdown of the arguments in the statement on line 20 follows:

- method: The method is POST.
- url: The location of the server-side cgi script, where our information will be processed, is stored in our variable, **url**.

- asynch: If set to `true`, the server-side script processing will continue after the `send()` method without waiting for a response.

Line 22 sets the type of content we are sending in the request. Our data comes from a form, albeit a very small form (just two text boxes). The **setRequestHeader()method** takes two arguments. The first is, for our purposes, "Content-type" and the second is the type of content. Since our content is from a form, we use "application/x-www-form-urlencoded".

TABLE 11.6	PHP Super Global Variables
Pre-Defined PHP Super Global Variables (Superglobals)	
$GLOBALS	
$_SERVER	
$_GET	
$_POST	
$_FILES	
$_COOKIE	
$_SESSION	
$_REQUEST	
$_ENV	

To describe the next expression (line 24) in depth is beyond the scope of this text. Basically, the server needs to know the "state" it is in. Is it ready to move on or not? The **onreadystatechange event** is triggered every time the `readyState` changes. The **readyState property** holds the status of the `XMLHttpRequest()`. In this program, we set this property to call a `function()`. That function does several things:

- if `readyState` is ready to move on (line 27) then line 30 is executed.
- Line 30 says that the request has been made and we need to get the server to respond to the request. The **responseTextproperty** is used to get the server's response as a string. The value of this string (which we will create later) is now stored in a variable, **returnData**.
- The value of **returnData** is displayed on the web page on line 32 using familiar JavaScript code.
- The `if` statement is closed on line 33 and the function is closed on line 34.

Line 37 uses the **send()method** to send the data and line 38 uses JavaScript to display a message if there is any delay while the server processes the player's entry and responds. If you code this page and look closely you will see the "doing work..." message flash briefly on your screen.

Finally, line 40 ends the `ajax_post()` function, the JavaScript script closes, and the HTML script begins again.

The ajaxDataPipe.php Page   This file is short and sweet. It creates a string using the values the player enters and our own text. This will be the result when the player enters his or her name and clicks the Submit button. The file should have the file name ajaxDataPipe.php and should be stored in the assets folder in htdocs. The code is as follows:

```
1.   ?php
2.   // creates a string (using the values stored in the Super Global ↵
     Variable $_POST, i.e., the value of the data that originated from ↵
     the user in the HTML input elements). This will be sent back to the ↵
     XMLHttpRequest object
3.       echo 'Thank you '. $_POST['postFirstName'] . ' ' . ↵
             $_POST['postLastName'] . ', says the PHP file. ↵
             You have sent your name to the server and for that, ↵
             Greg thanks you. Hope you enjoy this site and keep ↵
             playing our games. ';
4.   ?>
```

Line 2 explains what this file does. Line 3, the PHP statement, describes what to display on the web page.

Putting It All Together

In this section, we do not need to revisit the code for each page but we will review what we need for this web page to work, including the files, the file names, and the location where the code should be stored. The files are as follows:

- All files must be inside the htdocs folder of the XAMPP program on your computer.
- It is recommended that you have a subfolder in htdocs called gregs_games and put all the files for this section in that folder. You can add files when we create a more advanced project in Chapter 12.
- Inside greg_games, have the following subfolders with their contents:
  □ assets should contain ajaxDataPipe.php.
  □ css should contain greg.css.
  □ images should contain superhero.jpg.
  □ include should contain header.php and footer.php.
- In the gregs_games folder but not in any other subfolder, include phpDemo.php.

If you set everything up like this and use the following URL:

```
localhost/gregs_games/phpDemo.php
```

the display will look like this:

If the player enters the name Michael Murphy and clicks the Submit button, the display will look like this:

Carla's Classroom: Using PHP for Hints

In this section, we will use PHP to help Carla when she searches for a student. This project uses only a PHP file and an HTML file which calls the PHP code. Carla has saved information about all her students, past and present. We will assume the students' names, along with other valuable information, is kept in a database. However, because there are many students and many of their siblings have been in her classes, Carla cannot remember each student's full name and that student's brothers and sisters. Thus, we will create a program that will allow Carla to type a last name, part of a last name, or even a first letter in the last name and have the program display all entries that match what she typed. Eventually, Carla will be able to use that information to get the full data on a particular student from her database, but that requires that we know database commands, queries, and more. When a database is queried, the necessary information is extracted from the database and temporarily stored in an array. Since we are not yet using a database, we will simply create and use an array with the information sought.

Developing the Program

This page does not have to be connected to the Carla's Classroom site because only Carla will use it. However, for consistency, we will use the same style sheet as for all of Carla's pages. A file called names.txt is in the Student Data Files. You can copy the contents of this file into the PHP page we will create or make up your own names. This text file contains more than 100 names so you can see how the program works. Of course, it would work with only a few names but it is far more interesting with a lot of names.

First, let's create the appropriate folder structure to put in htdocs and separate out the header and footer as we did for the Greg's Gambits site.

The Folders   Create the following folders, as you did for Greg's Gambits and be sure they are in the htdocs folder of XAMPP.

- carlas_class is the top folder.
- Subfolders are: assets, css, images, and include.
- Put the style sheet, carla.css into the css folder.
- Put the following images into the images folder: arith_button.jpg, carla_button.jpg, carla_pic.jpg, owl_button.jpg, owl_reading.jpg, read_button.jpg, and write_button.jpg.

The header.php File   The header file needs to contain all the information that should be in the <head> section, any JavaScript or PHP code that we want in the <head> section, and the part of the web page that will remain the same for all of Carla's page. For now, however, we will not include the JavaScript; we will develop it later. This part of the code for Carla's header.php file follows. The file should be stored in the include folder.

```
1.   <!DOCTYPE HTML PUBLIC "-//W3C//DTD HTML 4.01 ⏎
          Transitional//EN""http://www.w3.org/TR/html4/loose.dtd">
2.   <html>
3.   <head>
4.       <title>Carla's Classroom | Find Students With PHP Hints</title>
5.       <link href="css/carla.css" rel="stylesheet" type="text/css" />
6.   </head>
7.   <body>
8.       <div id = "header">
9.           <img src="images/owl_reading.jpg" class="floatleft" />
10.          <h1><em>Carla's Classroom</em></h1>
11.          <h2 align="center">Making Learning Fun!</h2>
12.          <div align="left">
13.              <blockquote>
14.                  <p><a href = "index.html"><img src = ⏎
                         "images/owl_button.jpg" />Home</a>
15.                  <a href = "carla.html"><img src = ⏎
                         "images/carla_button.jpg" />Meet Carla</a>
16.                  <a href = "reading.html"><img src = ⏎
```

```
                                "images/read_button.jpg" />Reading</a>
17.                 <a href = "writing.html"><img src = ⌐
                                "images/write_button.jpg" />Writing</a>
18.                 <a href = "math.html"><img src = ⌐
                                "images/arith_button.jpg" />Arithmetic</a>
19.                 <br /></p>
20.             </blockquote>
21.         </div>
22.     </div>
```

The *footer.php* File   The footer file simply contains the Motto that Carla includes on all of her pages and closes the <body> and <html> tags. This file must be named footer.php and saved in the carlas_class folder inside the include folder in htdocs. The code is as follows:

```
1.      <div id="footer">
2.          <h3>*Carla's Motto: Never miss a chance to teach -- and ⌐
                        to learn!</h3>
3.      </div>
4.      </div>
5.  </body>
6.  </html>
```

The *carla_phpDemo.php* File   This file should be saved inside the carlas_class folder in htdocs but not inside any other subfolder. It will contain the content of the page. If you were developing Carla's Classroom into a live site, you might want to edit all previous pages to use the header.php file and the footer.php file, and use a separate "middle" file for each page. This ensures consistency throughout the site and makes updating content easy.

This file will contain an input box for Carla to enter a student's name and a space for the names our PHP code finds. Notice that this file includes two PHP statements—one at the top to tell the browser to include the header.php file first and one at the bottom to tell the browser to finish the page by including the footer.php file. The code is as follows:

```
1.  <?php include ('include/header.php'); ?>
2.  <div id="content">
3.      <p><img src="images/carla_pic.jpg" class="floatleft" /></p>
4.      <h3>Forgot your student's full name? <br />
5.      Want to see other family members?<br />
6.      Start typing a name in the input box below:</h3>
7.      <form>
8.          <h3>First name: <input type = "text" onkeyup = ⌐
                        "showHint(this.value)" size = "20" /></h3>
9.      </form>
10.     <h3>Suggestions: <span id="txtHint"></span></h3>
11. </div>
12. <?php include ('include/footer.php'); ?>
```

The only thing that is new in this code is the onkeyup event. The **onkeyup event** executes a JavaScript function when a key on the keyboard is released. Therefore, each time a letter is typed, the showHint() function is executed. This is a JavaScript function that we will now create and put in the header.php file. This function will create a request to the server to get all the names of students that match what Carla types. However, the function showHint() must work with the server to look through all the names in the array. We will give the code for both the JavaScript showHint() function that will reside in the header.php file and the code that resides on the server which contains all the names in Carla's array. First, we will write the JavaScript showhint() function and then create the getHint.php page that processes the data on the server side.

The showHint() Function   The following code should be placed in the <head> section of the header.php file. It could also be placed in an external JavaScript file so long as you are sure to include the proper path to that page and include a link to the file where necessary in the code. An explanation of the code is given by the comments and also following the code.

```
1.   <script language="JavaScript" type="text/javascript">
2.   //str is passed to the function by the onkeyup event
3.        function showHint(str)
4.        {
5.   //if nothing is typed, nothing is returned
6.            if (str.length==0)
7.            {
8.                document.getElementById("txtHint").innerHTML="";
9.                return;
10.           }
11.  //the if-else construct checks to see if the browser is older. Most ↵
     modern browsers can create an XMLHttpRequest() object but older ↵
     browsers use an ActiveXObject(). Either object establishes an ↵
     independent connection channel between our client-side web page ↵
     and the server-side php script.
12.           if (window.XMLHttpRequest) //for most modern browsers
13.           {
14.               var xmlhttp = new XMLHttpRequest();
15.           }
16.           else // code for older browsers
17.           {
18.               var xmlhttp = new ActiveXObject("Microsoft.XMLHTTP");
19.           }
20.  //The onreadystatechange event is triggered every time the ↵
     readyState changes.
21.           xmlhttp.onreadystatechange = function()
22.           {
23.  // checks if readyState is 4 (request is finished and response is ↵
     ready) and status is 200 (page is found). If TRUE then response is ↵
     ready.
24.               if (xmlhttp.readyState==4 && xmlhttp.status==200)
25.               {
26.  // The 'responseText' property is used to retrieve the server's ↵
     response as a string
27.  document.getElementById("txtHint").innerHTML = ↵
                                      xmlhttp.responseText;
28.               }
```

```
29.                }
30.    // open(method,url,async) has 3 arguments. Here the ⏎
       method = GET. The second argument is the location of ⏎
       server-side processing - gethint.php with an appended ⏎
       parameter, q, equal to str which holds whatever was ⏎
       typed into the input box. The asynch argument is set ⏎
       to TRUE so that server-side script processing continues ⏎
       after the send() method, without waiting for a response.
31.                xmlhttp.open("GET","gethint.php?q = "+str,true);
32.    //the send() method executes the request
33.                xmlhttp.send();
34.        }
35.    </script>
```

As soon as a key in the input box is released, the content of the box is passed to this function (line 3). Lines 6–10 check to see if nothing is in the box. If this is the case, nothing is returned. The next if...else structure, on lines 12–19, checks which browser is in use. This is necessary because, for older browsers, an ActiveXObject must be used instead of an XMLHttpRequest() object. We have now opened up a channel to the server where processing will be done.

Line 21 checks the state of the XMLRequestObject() (which is now identified by the variable **xmlhttp**). Line 31 uses the open() method which was discussed win the Greg's Gambits project. Here, we use the GET method instead of POST. These two methods are very similar. The main difference is that, with GET, the URL of the page used is displayed in the browser's address bar. Sometimes, for security, this is not preferable. For our purposes, it doesn't matter so GET was used in this example to show that both GET and POST can be used almost interchangeably.

The open() method then uses gethint.php as the location argument. This means the code on this page (which we have not created yet) will be executed. A parameter, identified as "q" is sent with the location and, appended to it, is the value that was typed in. This value is stored in the variable, **str**. Finally, the asynch property is set to true. In virtually all cases, asynch is set to true. Finally, line 33 sends the request.

At this point, if you save the header.php page with the JavaScript code in your carlas_class folder in htdocs and type in the following URL, your page will look as shown below. However, if you type something into the input box, nothing will happen:

```
localhost/carlas_class/Carla_phpDemo.php
```

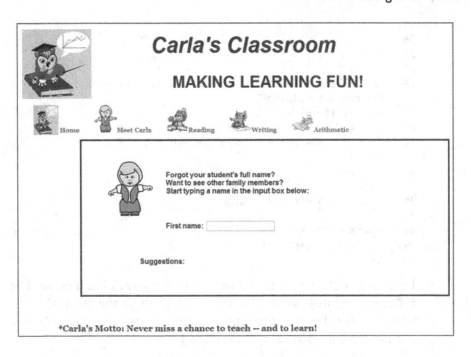

The gethint.php File   The code for the gethint.php page is short but includes an array of the names of Carla's students. You will need to create this array. You can use the names.txt file from the Student Data Files to avoid typing in the names yourself. The code for this file is as follows. To save space, not all the names in the array are shown.

```php
1.  <?php
2.  // Fill array with names (sample names are shown)
3.      $a[]="Adams, Anna"; $a[]="Adams, Sam"; $a[]= "Adams, Brittany";
4.      $a[]="Blue, Chester"; $a[]="Blue, Charity";
5.      ... all the rest of the array entries go here...
6.      $a[]="Chen, Karen"; $a[]="Lee, Michelle"; $a[]="Lee, Cooper";
7.      $a[]="Weare, James"; $a[]="Krantz, Otto"; $a[]="Schultz, Cheryl";
8.  //identify the $q parameter
9.      $q = $_GET["q"];
10. //lookup all hints from array if length of $q > 0
11.     if (strlen($q) > 0)
12.     {
13.         $hint = "";
14.         for($i = 0; $i < count($a); $i++)
15.         {
16.             if (strtolower($q) == strtolower(substr($a[$i], ↵
                                     0, strlen($q))))
17.             {
18.                 if ($hint == "")
19.                 {
20.                     $hint = $a[$i];
21.                 }
22.                 else
23.                 {
24.                     $hint = $hint." ; ".$a[$i];
```

```
25.                              }
26.                       }
27.                  }
28.          }
29.   // Set output to "no suggestion" if no hint were found or to ⌐
      the correct values
30.       if ($hint == "")
31.       {
32.             $response = "no names match";
33.       }
34.       else
35.       {
36.             $response = $hint;
37.       }
38.   //output the response
39.       echo $response;
40.   ?>
```

Lines 3–7 contain a truncated version of the array of names, **$a**. Line 9 uses the **$_GET** superglobal variable. It will search through the array using the parameter **$q** which is what the user is typing. If anything is typed (strlen($q) > 0), first **$hint** is set to nothing (**$hint** = ""; on line 13).

The $_GET superglobal Variable   The **$_GET** superglobal variable is an array of variables passed to the current script via the URL parameters. In this case, **$_GET** gets the value of the key that has been pressed by the user and it is now stored in **$q**.

The count() Method   The **count()method** is a PHP method that counts all the elements in an array. Thus, it is used as the test condition for the loop in this program.

The strtolower() Method   The **strtolower()method** returns whatever string is inside the parentheses with all the alphabetic characters converted to lowercase.

Therefore, as soon as the user presses and releases a key, the following happens:

- The **$hint** variable is reset to nothing.
- The keypress(es) is/are stored in **$q**.
- The loop checks each element in the array against the key (or keys) that have been pressed.

The last item in the bulleted list happens on line 16. This line says the following:

```
if (strtolower($q))== strtolower(substr($a[$i], 0, strlen($q))))
```

If, for example, the user has pressed "Abc", then strtolower($q) is now "abc". This string is compared to the first three characters in array element **$i**. Notice that it uses the substr() method where the string to be used is **$a[$i]**, the character to begin at is character 0, and the number of characters to compare is the length of **$q**, i.e. strlen($q).

The loop that begins on line 14 searches through the array. If there is a match and if **$hint** is still equal to "", lines 18–21 are executed and **$hint** now takes on the value of **$a[$i]**. Thus, if someone has typed "Ada", **$hint** will, on the first pass through the loop, be "Adams, Anna". On the second pass through the loop, "Ada" will match "Adams, Sam". Now **$hint** is not empty so line 24 is executed. This concatenates the previous value of **$hint** with a semicolon to separate the names and the new name. If there are no more names in the array that begin with "ada", when the loop ends, **$hint** will be "Adams, Anna ; Adams, Sam".

Lines 30–39 output the results. If no matches are found (lines 30–33), an appropriate message is displayed. But if matches have been found (lines 34–37), the value of **$hint** is stored in **$response** and this is displayed with the echo statement on line 39.

Putting It All Together

We will not repeat all the code for each page but we will review what we need for this web page to work, including the files, each file name, and where it should be stored. These files are as follows:

- All files must be inside the htdocs folder of the XAMPP program on your computer.
- It is recommended that you have a subfolder in htdocs called carlas_class and put all the files for this section in that folder. You can add files when we create a more advanced project in Chapter 12.
- Inside carlas_class, have the following subfolders with their contents:
  - assets should contain ajaxDataPipe.php.
  - css should contain carla.css.
  - images should contain all the images that go with Carla's pages.
  - include should contain header.php and footer.php.
- In carlas_class, but not in any other subfolder, include carla_phpDemo.php and gethint.php.

If you set everything up like this, use the following URL,

```
localhost/carlas_class/carla_phpDemo.php
```

and begin typing "s", the display will be as follows:

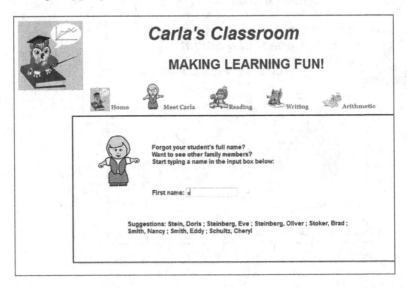

But if you continue typing a "t", the display will be as follows:

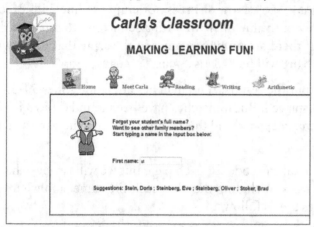

But if you narrow the field even more by typing an "o" your display will narrow to this:

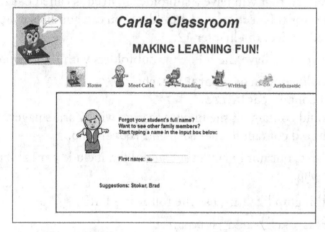

And finally, if you type "m" you will see the following since there are no names in the array that begin with stom:

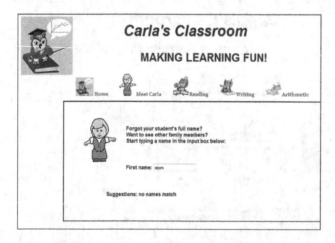

Chapter Review and Exercises

Key Terms

$match() array
<?php and ?> tags
==> operator
Ajax
Apache Web Server (Apache)
array function
as keyword
asynchronous events
Asynchronous JavaScript and XML
binary operators
bracket expression
casting
character classes
client
communications protocol
comparison operator
concatenation assignment operator
concatenation operator
count() method
database
development environment
echo construct
equality operator
fields
field-value pairs
foreach construct
get request
gettype() method
htdocs folder
HttpRequest() object
key() method
local host
localhost
loosely typed variables
MySQL
offset parameter

onkeyup event
onreadystatechange event
open() method
operators
order of precedence
PHP
PHP code
PHP keywords
post request
preg_match() method
preg_replace() method
print() function
quantifier
Rasmus Lerdorf
readyState property
records
regular expressions
relational databases
request types
reserved words
reset() method
responseText property
send() method
server
setRequestHeader() method
settype() method
sort() method
string operators
strtolower() method
Super Global variable
superglobals
tables
ternary conditional operator
type casting
unary operators
XAMPP

Review Exercises

Fill in the Blank

1. Two types of communications _____ are ftp and IP.

2. The two most common HTTP request types are _____ and _____.

3. The ending PHP tag is _____.

4. PHP operations all occur on the _____. (server/client).

5. The _____ method will tell you what the data type of a variable is.

True or False

6. T/F   In a database, a field consists of one or more records.

7. T/F   In the following URL, `http://` represents the IP address:

   `http://www.jackiesjewels.com/junk/oldstuff.xml`

8. T/F   Any file that contains even one line of PHP must have the `.php` extension.

9. T/F   All PHP variable names begin with **$**.

10. T/F   All PHP code must be placed in the `<head>` section of an HTML document.

11. T/F   PHP variables can contain different types of data at different times within a PHP program.

12. T/F   The `settype()` method actually changes the data type of a variable while type casting does not.

13. T/F   The statement **$myNum** = "4"; creates a PHP string variable.

14. T/F   To display text on a web page with PHP, either the `print()` function or the `echo` construct can be used.

15. T/F   PHP does not use any unary operators.

Short Answer

16. A professor wants to store information about his students in a database. For each student, list at least four appropriate fields that will help the professor keep track of student progress.

17. What URL would you enter into your browser to open a file named `my_file.php` which is stored in the `htdocs` folder of the Apache server that resides on your computer?

18. What is the difference between the `settype()` method and type casting when you need to change the data type of a variable?

19. Using the following variables, create a PHP statement that will output the sentence "My dog is named Spike.":

   $pet = "dog";   **$name** = "Spike";

Use the following variables for Exercises 20–22:

   $A = 3;   **$B** = 5;   **$C** = 6;   **$D** = 30;
   $yup = "true"; **$nope** = "false";

20. What will display after the following code is executed:

```
if ($D == $A * $B * 2)
{     echo $yup;      }
else
     {     echo $nope;      }
```

21. What will display after the following code is executed:

```
if ($C * $A < $D)
{     echo $yup;     }
else
    {     echo $nope;     }
```

22. What will display after the following code is executed:

```
echo ($C == ($A * $A)) ? $yup: $nope);
```

Use the followin'g variable for Exercises 23–24:

```
$G = "43.65";
```

23. Write PHP statements to do the following:
    a) check the data type of **$G**
    b) change the data type of **$G** to double using the settype() method
    c) check the data type of **$G** again

24. Write PHP statements to do the following:
    a) check the data type of **$G**
    b) cast **$G** as a double
    c) check the data type of **$G** again

25. What will be the output of the following PHP program?

```
<?php
    $num = 2;  $age = 24;
    echo "<p>You are now " . $age . " years old.</p>"
    while ($num < 12)
    {
        echo "<p>In " . $num . " years you will be " . ($age ↵
                + $num). " years old.</p>";
        $num = $num + 2;
    }
?>
```

26. Rewrite the code of Exercise 25 using a for loop.

27. Create an array named **$myNums** and load it with 20 elements. The contents of each element should be the index of the element squared. For example:

```
$myNums[0] = 0, $myNums[1] = 1, $myNums[2] = 4
$myNums[3] = 9, $myNums[4] = 16 and so on
```

28. Create PHP code to display the results of the array created in Exercise 27 using the following example line of output. Your output should have 20 lines, displaying the squares of the numbers 0 through 19 inclusive:

```
The square of x is x²
```

where x is the index of the array element and x^2 is the value of that element.

Use the following statement for Exercises 29–30:

```
preg_match("/\b(mauve[a-z]+\b/", $colors, $match);
```

29. a) What pattern is being searched for?
    b) What string will be searched?

30. Change the statement to search for the pattern "lavender".

Programming Challenges

On Your Own

1. Create a PHP program that displays the possible rating scale for a company's Quality Control page. The display should be as shown:

```
5 = Excellent
4 = Good
3 = Fair
2 = Poor
1 = Unsalvageable
```

Save the page with the file name `ratings.php`. Submit your work as instructed by your teacher.

Use the following tale from Aesop's Fables for Programming Challenges 2 and 3. (Note: This story is also a text file, available in the Student Data Files, named `two_mice.txt`*, which you can use instead of typing in the whole thing.)*

The Town Mouse and the Country Mouse

Now you must know that a Town Mouse once upon a time went on a visit to his cousin in the country. He was rough and ready, this cousin, but he loved his town friend and made him heartily welcome. Beans and bacon, cheese and bread, were all he had to offer, but he offered them freely. The Town Mouse rather turned up his long nose at this country fare, and said: "I cannot understand, Cousin, how you can put up with such poor food as this, but of course you cannot expect anything better in the country; come you with me and I will show you how to live. When you have been in town a week you will wonder how you could ever have stood a country life." No sooner said than done: the two mice set off for the town and arrived at the Town Mouse's residence late at night. "You will want some refreshment after our long journey," said the polite Town Mouse, and took his friend into the grand dining-room. There they found the remains of a fine feast, and soon the two mice were eating up jellies and cakes and all that was nice. Suddenly they heard growling and barking. "What is that?" said the Country Mouse. "It is only the dogs of the house," answered the other. "Only!" said the Country Mouse. "I do not like that music at my dinner." Just at that moment the door flew open, in came two huge mastiffs, and the two mice had to scamper down and run off. "Good-bye, Cousin," said the Country Mouse, "What! going so soon?" said the other. "Yes," he replied; "Better beans and bacon in peace than cakes and ale in fear."[2]

VideoNote
Using the preg_match()
and prereg_replace()
PHP Methods
On_Your_Own_2_AesopFable

2. Create a program using the `preg_match()` and/or `preg_replace()` methods to display the following information about the Aesop's fable, The Town Mouse and the Country Mouse (given above):
   - A list of words that begin with "A" or "a"
   - A list of words that end with "g"

Save your page with the file name `fable_q2.php`. Submit your work as instructed by your teacher.

---

[2]This fable is one of Aesop's Fables. It can be accessed at Page By Page Books (http://www.pagebypage books.com/Aesop/Aesops_Fables/)

3. Create a program using the Aesop's fable, `The Town Mouse and the Country Mouse` (given above) that replaces all instances of the word "`Mouse`" with "`Lion`" and all instances of the word "`town`" with "`metropolis`". Save your page with the file name `fable_q3.php`. Submit your work as instructed by your teacher.

4. Create a page using PHP for a business website that will ask the user to enter his or her name into text boxes and will display a welcome message that uses the user's name. Save your page with the file name `welcome.php` and be sure to include any necessary accompanying files. Submit your work as instructed by your teacher.

5. Add to the page you created in Programming Challenge 4. Create a new page or add to the existing page but use PHP code that will ask the user to enter the color and size of a jacket he or she wants to purchase. The program should return the following statement:

   "`Your order of a size X jacket in Y will be shipped to you today.`"

   where `X` is the size entered by the user and `Y` is the color. Save your page with the file name `order.php` and be sure to include the necessary accompanying files. Submit your work as instructed by your teacher.

6. Create a page that contains an array of at least 20 movie titles or book titles (your choice). The page should have an input box for the user to enter the title and, as the user continues typing, the page should display all possible matches (i.e., hints). Use the `Carla's Classroom` project from the Putting It to Work section as a guide. Save your page with the file name `title_hints.php` and be sure to include any necessary accompanying files. Submit your work as instructed by your teacher.

7. Create a page that incorporates the code from Programming Challenges 4 and 6 that uses PHP to allow the user to enter a username and find a favorite movie or book. After the user enters a username, the page should display a welcome message. The page should look something like this:

```
On Your Own
Program 7


enter username    [            ]

        Hello, username!


What is your favorite    [          ]
movie/book?

Did you mean ...  Hints display here
```

Save your page with the file name `welcome_and_hints.php` and be sure to include any necessary accompanying files. Submit your work as instructed by your teacher.

Case Studies

Greg's Gambits

Using the `Carla's Classroom` project in the Putting It to Work section of this chapter as a guide, create a page that will help a player who has registered on the `Greg's Gambits` site to retrieve his or her username if the player has forgotten the spelling of it. The player should be able to start typing the first letter or letters of his or her username and the program will display all possible usernames that begin with that letter or letters. A file named `greg_usernames.txt` is provided in the Student Data Files with an array of usernames or you can make up your own. If you want to use the names provided, simply copy and paste the usernames from the text file into your program.

Save your page as `greg_hints.php`. If you have been creating the `Greg's Gambits` website throughout the text or have completed the `Greg's Gambits` project from the Putting It to Work section, use a `header.php` file, a `footer.php`, and a `greg_hints.php` file. Be sure to include the necessary accompanying files to communicate with the server. You can add a link, under the `Sign In` link on Greg's home page to this page with the page title `Greg's Gambits | Find Your Username`. Submit your work as instructed by your teacher.

Carla's Classroom

Eventually Carla plans to create a website that parents can use to track a child's progress. Create the initial login page for this proposed site. The parents should be able to enter a child's first and last name and received the following message:

```
"Welcome to Carla's Classroom! Let's talk about FirstName LastName now."
```

Later you will be able to add increased functionality to this page. For now, just the welcome message will suffice.

Save your page as `carlas_parents.php`. If you have been creating the `Carla's Classroom` website throughout the text or have completed the Carla's project from the Putting It to Work section, use a `header.php` file, a `footer.php`, and a `carlas_parents.php` file. Be sure to include the necessary accompanying files to communicate with the server. You can add a link from the `Meet Carla` page to this page with the page title `Carla's Classroom | Parents Page`. Submit your work as instructed by your teacher.

Lee's Landscape

Create a web page that uses PHP to allow a customer to enter his or her name, a required service, and the day of the week that is convenient for service. The page should display a table with services offered, the days Lee performs those services, and the time frame choices. When the customer enters the information into text boxes, the PHP will generate a message confirming the entry, as shown below. Later you can build on this to generate an email from Lee to the customer to confirm the contract. The information for the page is shown below, followed by a sample output:

Lee's Services

Service	Days Available	Times Available
lawn maintenance	Monday	morning
	Monday	afternoon
	Thursday	morning
	Thursday	afternoon
tree pruning	Tuesday	morning
	Tuesday	afternoon
pest control	Wednesday	morning
	Wednesday	afternoon
	Friday	morning
	Friday	afternoon

Note: Morning services begin at 8 AM and Lee's Crew will be done before noon Afternoon services start at 1:30 PM and Lee's Crew will be done before 5:30 PM

A sample output, if Lucy Lebowskaya requests pest control on Wednesday afternoon would be as follows:

Be sure to give this web page an appropriate page title such as Lee's Landscape || Sign Up for Service. Add a link to the Lee's Landscape home page to this new page. Be sure to include the necessary accompanying files to communicate with the server. Save your page with the file name lee_signup.php. Submit your work as instructed by your teacher.

Jackie's Jewelry

Jackie sells jewelry and also teaches jewelry making classes. We will use the program created in the `Carla's Classroom` site for a different purpose now; we'll use it to allow a customer to view various options. Create a PHP file that contains Jackie's products and services in an array, and when the customer enters something, displays all the options.

A text file has been created for you with approximately 100 elements in an array, `$j`. The file is named `jackies_jewelry.txt` and is in the Student Data Files. Each element of the array begins with a letter and an underscore. Elements that begin with t_ are classes that Jackie teaches, r_ indicate rings she sells, b_ indicates bracelets, p_ indicates pendants, e_ indicates earrings, and c_ indicates charms that can be used with other jewelry. Here is a sample of what this page might look like:

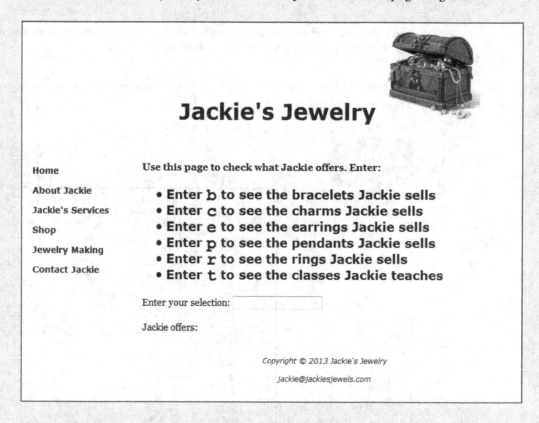

Your page should have an input box for the customer to begin typing as well as instructions that explain what to type. Be sure to give this web page an appropriate page title such as `Jackie's Jewelry || Inventory for Customers`. Add a link to the `Jackie's Jewelry` home page to this new page. Be sure to include the necessary accompanying files to communicate with the server. Save this page with the file names `jackie_inventory.php`. Submit your work as instructed by your teacher.

Using PHP With Cookies and MySQL

Chapter Objectives

When students first begin to learn programming, often they look for a button to click to complete a task and are surprised to learn that they actually need to write out all the statements. It is hard, in the twenty-first century, to remember a time when there were no buttons to click and all commands were created, line by line, by the user. For example, to average a bunch of numbers using Microsoft's Excel spreadsheet program, you can enter the numbers and the AVERAGE function does the work. Someone has programmed Excel to add the numbers, count the numbers, and divide the sum of the numbers by the count. We—people who study programming and scripting—write those programs! You've seen how JavaScript has built-in methods to sort an array or search for a value in an array. And you have also seen that there are situations when these methods aren't sufficient and you need to create your own.

Now, using a server and PHP, you will be pleasantly surprised at how many methods are already provided and will do just what you need them to do. This is because many of these methods complete website tasks that, while producing a wide range of results, use the same logic to perform what is needed. Of course, you can still create your own PHP functions (and in this chapter we will) but often built-in functions get the job done.

There are many more things that can be accomplished by a web server running MySQL (or any database), PHP, and Perl than we can cover in one chapter. Therefore, we will concentrate on using what we know and what we will learn here to complete some important website tasks. We will learn to create cookies on a user's computer and retrieve them when the user revisits the site; we will learn about form processing to access information on a database, and we will learn to use database data from a website to generate customized emails to be sent to users.

After reading this chapter, you will be able to do the following:

- Create and read cookies

- Use cookies to customize a user's website

- Use $_COOKIE as $key => $value with the foreach construct

- Use MySQL to create a database and manage database users

- Create tables with appropriate fields and attributes in a database

- Use PHP methods to create and close a connection to a MySQL database

- Use PHP and SQL statements to create new records in a MySQL database

- Use PHP methods to query a MySQL database

- Use PHP to retrieve database information to generate emails

- Use PHP and SQL to validate records in a MySQL database

- Understand what a session is and how to use the $_SESSION superglobal

12.1   Cookies

Just about everyone has heard of cookies. Even those who don't use computers know what cookies are. Of course, those cookies—the ones you eat—have no relation to the cookies we are talking about. On the Internet, a **cookie** is a little text file that resides on the user's computer. It is placed there by the browser when the browser receives some information from the website's server.

Cookies have no evil intent; their main purpose is to identify users and possibly prepare some customizations on a web page when the user revisits the site. Cookies cannot carry viruses and cannot install malware on a user's computer. Some cookies may be used to track records of a user's long-term browsing history, but generally this is not a major concern.

Although security is always important, cookies are normally quite safe. The information in a cookie on a client computer can only be retrieved by the server that originally set the cookie. Cookies perform valuable work. In fact, some of the functions performed by cookies are essential. For example, **authentication cookies** allow a web server to know whether a user is logged in and which account the user is logged in under. Without such information, the site would not know whether or not to send sensitive information. Imagine if someone who used your computer could access your bank information!

Types of Cookies

Cookies were designed to be a reliable method for a website to remember information about a user's activity and preferences on that site. There are various types of cookies and we will list some of them here.

One important distinction between cookie types is whether the cookie is a session cookie or a persistent cookie. A **session cookie** exists only while a user is on a particular website. It is normally deleted by the browser when the user exits the browser. A **persistent cookie** remains on the user's computer for a specified length of time, even after the user has left the site, exited the browser, and turned off the computer.

Other types of cookies include the following:

- A **secure cookie** has the secure attribute enabled and is only used via HTTPS. This ensures that the cookie will be encrypted when transmitting from client to server.

- A **httponly cookie** is supported by most modern browsers and is used when transmitting HTTP or HTTPS requests. This feature only applies to session cookies.

- A **third-party cookie** is set with a different domain from the one that shows in the address bar of the browser. These cookies are often set by advertisers to gain information about what website a user has visited. Third-party cookies differ from normal (first-party) cookies that are set with the same domain as the website being accessed.

Writing Cookies

The **setcookie() function** is used to define a cookie. The cookie must be set before any output from your script. This is a restriction of the protocol. It means that the setcookie() function must be called before any output, including the <html> and <head> tags. Once a cookie has been set, it can be accessed the next time the page loads using the **$_COOKIE** superglobal or **$_REQUEST**.

The setcookie() function accepts up to six arguments and all except the **$name** argument are optional. The general syntax for this function is shown here with an explanation of all the arguments following.

```
bool setcookie(string $name [, string $value [, int ↵
    $expire = 0 [, string $path [, string $domain [, bool ↵
    $secure = false [, bool $httponly = false ]]]]]] )
```

An explanation of the parameters in this function follows:

- **$name:** This is the name of the cookie.
- **$value:** This the value stored on the client's computer. It will be retrieved by the server.
- **$expire:** This sets the expiration date of the cookie. The time is expressed in number of seconds since a specific date/hour/minute/seconds. Therefore, it is easier to use the time() function, adding to the time the number of seconds until

you want it to expire. If no expiration is specified or if it is set to 0, the cookie will expire when the browser closes.

- **$path:** This is the path on the server in which the cookie will be available. If this is set to '/' the cookie will be available to the entire domain.
- **$domain:** This is the domain (and subdomain) to which the cookie is available. For example, a cookie that sets www.drake.jackiejewels.com is not available to www.drake.leesland.com.
- **$secure:** As a boolean, this can be set to either true or false. When set to true, the cookie will only be transmitted if a secure HTTPS connection exists.
- **$httponly:** This boolean will be made accessible only through the HTTP protocol when set to true. This means that the cookie will not be accessible to other scripting languages like JavaScript.

If you wish to skip any of these parameters, you can replace the parameter with an empty string ("") or do nothing. Because **$expire** is an integer, you must either skip it or enter '0'.

If output exists before calling this function, the setcookie() function will fail and return false. If the setcookie() function runs successfully, it will return true. This return value simply says whether or not the function ran; it does not indicate whether or not the cookie was accepted by the client.

The time() Function

The **time() function** returns the current time measured as the number of seconds since the Unix epoch. Unix time is the number of seconds since January 1, 1970 00:00:00 GMT. For our purposes, it really doesn't matter what that number actually is. At the time of this writing, the value of time() was approximately

$$\frac{142 \; years}{since \; 1970} * \frac{365 \; days}{year} * \frac{24 \; hours}{day} * \frac{60 \; minutes}{hour} * \frac{60 \; seconds}{minute} = 4{,}478{,}112{,}000 \text{ seconds.}$$

There are $\dfrac{24 \; hours}{day} * \dfrac{60 \; minutes}{hour} * \dfrac{60 \; seconds}{minute} = 86{,}400$ seconds in one day.

Therefore, at the time of this writing, tomorrow will be 4,478,112,000 seconds + 86,400 seconds

And next week will be 4,478,112,000 seconds + 86,400 seconds * 7

The time() function sets a base time and then we can add or subtract a specific number of seconds to that base time. Thus, if you want your cookie to expire in 14 days, set **$expire** to time() + (14 * 86,400).

Writing Your First Cookie

To create a cookie, we need the setcookie() function, as described above, but we also need some information to put into it. First, we need to get that information. Then, we need to put that information into a cookie. And finally, we must check that the information has been stored correctly. This requires three files so we will do them, one at a time, in Examples 12.1 and 12.2.

EXAMPLE
12.1

Writing Your First Cookie

This example will show you how to set a cookie. Since it uses PHP code to send information to a server, remember that, to try this, all the files must be stored in the htdocs folder of your xampp folder on your computer. To access the files, you must use the URL localhost and then the path to your files.

a) Getting the information: We'll use a form to allow a user to enter three pieces of personal information. Then the user will click a button that will call the setcookie() function. The submit button at the end tells the form to submit the information. This is an HTML page so the file name should have the .htm or .html extension. We will name this page ex_12_1_data.html. The output of this first page is displayed below the code.

```
1.   <html>
2.   <head>
3.       <title>Example 12.1: Get Cookie Data</title>
4.       <style type="text/css">
5.       <!--
6.           .style3    {
7.               color: #4f81bd;        font-weight: bold;
8.               font-family: Geneva, Arial, Helvetica, sans-serif;
9.               font-size: larger; text-indent: 20px;
10.                  }
11.      -->
12.      </style>
13.  </head>
14.  <body>
15.      <form method = "post" action = "ex_12_1_set_cookie.php">
16.      <div style="width: 75%;" ><br />
17.          <h2>Welcome to the <span class="style3">Your Favorite ↵
                        Things!</span> Website</h2>
18.          <h2>Tell us a bit about yourself:</h2>
19.          <p><strong>Your name:    
20.          <input type="text" name="name" size = "30" value ↵
                        = ""/></p>
21.          <p>What month were you born?    
22.          <input type="text" name="month" size="20" value = ↵
                        ""/></p>
23.          <p>What do you most like to do in your free time? ↵
                           
24.          <input type="text" name="free_time" size="30" value = ↵
                        ""/></p>
25.          <p><input type = "submit" value = "send in my ↵
                        information"/></p>
26.      </div>
27.      </form>
28.  </body></html>
```

This page looks like this:

Welcome to the Your Favorite Things! Website

Tell us a bit about yourself:

Your name: _____

What month were you born? _____

What do you most like to do in your free time? _____

send in my information

b) Setting the cookie: Now that data has been collected, we can write the page that creates the cookie. For demonstration purposes, we will also write HTML script to display the user the information that was sent to the hard drive in the cookies. As you remember from Chapter 11, since this page includes some PHP code, the file name must have the .php extension. We will name this page ex_12_1_set_cookie.php. The code for this page is as shown with an explanation following:

```
1.   <?php
2.       define("NEW_TIME", 60*60*24*7);
3.       $username = $_POST['name'];
4.       $usermonth = $_POST['month'];
5.       $userfreetime = $_POST['free_time'];
6.       setcookie("name", $username, time() + NEW_TIME);
7.       setcookie("month", $usermonth, time() + NEW_TIME);
8.       setcookie("free_time", $userfreetime, time() + NEW_TIME);
9.   ?>
10.  <html>
11.  <head>
12.      <title>Example 12.1: Set the Cookie</title>
13.      <style type="text/css">
14.      <!--
15.          .style3    {
16.              color: #4f81bd;   font-weight: bold;
17.              font-family: Geneva, Arial, Helvetica, sans-serif;
18.              font-size: larger;   text-indent: 20px;
19.                  }
20.      -->
21.      </style>
22.  </head>
23.  <body>
24.      <div style="width: 75%;" ><br />
25.          <h2>We set up a cookie on your hard drive!</h2>
26.          <h2>It contains:</h2>
27.          <p><strong>Who you are:
28.          <?php echo ($username) ?></p>
29.          <p>The month you were born:
30.          <?php echo ($usermonth) ?></p>
31.          <p>What you like to do in your free time:
```

```
32.            <?php echo($userfreetime) ?></p>
33.            <p>Want to read your cookie?
34.            <a href = "ex_12_2_read_cookie.php">Check it out.</a>
35.            </strong></p>
36.        </div>
37.    </body>
38.    </html>
```

Let's talk about some of the lines of code. First, as previously noted, the code to set the cookies must be included before anything else, including the <html> tag, is read by the browser. So, our PHP code to set the cookies begins at the top of the page.

The *define()* Method The **define()method** defines a named constant and it takes two or three parameters. Its syntax, in general, is as follows:

```
bool define(string $name, mixed $value[, bool $case_insensitive])
```

The first parameter is the name of the named constant. It must be a string. The second parameter is the value of that constant and can be of the following types: integer, float, string, or boolean. The third parameter, $case_insensitive, is optional. If it is not included, the default is false which means the named constant's value will be case sensitive.

Line 2 uses the define() method to define a named constant that will be used for the expiration date of our cookies. The cookie must be set for a time based on the time() method plus or minus some number of seconds. In this case, the cookies will be set for a week. A week, converted to seconds, is

$$\frac{24\ hours}{day} * \frac{60\ minutes}{hour} * \frac{60\ seconds}{minute} * \frac{7\ days}{week}.$$

To avoid repeating this calculation, we set NEW_TIME, the named constant, equal to 24 * 60 * 60 * 7 or 604,800 seconds.

The second parameter in the setcookie() function is the value to be set. It will be retrieved from the form by the superglobal $_POST. Lines 3, 4, and 5 create three PHP variables, each equal to the value of an HTML element (in this case, the input boxes from the previous page). The line:

```
$username = $_POST['name'];
```

sets **$username** equal to the value typed into the input box with id = 'name'. The same is true for **$usermonth** and **$userfreetime**.

Lines 6, 7, and 8 set three cookies. The first parameter in each is the name of the cookie, the next parameter is the value of the cookie, and the third is the expiration date. The body of the web page (lines 23–37) use PHP to display the values of these three cookies.

If a user named Stephen Sandoval, born in July, who loves to explore caves enters that information on the first page, then clicks the "send my information" button, the output will be as follows:

We set up a cookie on your hard drive!

It contains:

Who you are: Stephen Sandoval

The month you were born: July

What you like to do in your free time: explore caves

Want to read your cookie? Check it out.

The last thing we need to do before we are satisfied with our first cookies is to check that the information has been stored correctly. We have included a link on this page to the file that will read the cookies (line 34). Example 12.2 shows how to do this.

<table>
<tr><td>**EXAMPLE**
12.2</td><td></td></tr>
</table>

Reading Your First Cookie

The code to read a cookie is pretty simple. Remember that only the server that set the cookie can read the cookie. This is a comforting thought. It means that no site can access your computer and read the cookies that have been placed there by other sites. Here is the code for a file named ex_12_2_read_cookie.php:

```
1.   <html>
2.   <head>
3.        <title>Example 12.2: Read the Cookie</title>
4.        <style type="text/css">
5.        <!--
6.          .style3    {
7.                 color: #4f81bd;  font-weight: bold;
8.                 font-family: Geneva, Arial, Helvetica, sans-serif;
9.                 font-size: larger;  text-indent: 20px;
10.                   }
11.       -->
12.       </style>
13.  </head>
14.  <body>
15.      <div style="width: 75%;" ><br />
16.          <h2>This data was saved as a cookie on your ⏎
                        computer:</h2>
17.          <?php
18.              foreach ($_COOKIE as $key => $value)
19.                  print("<p>$key; $value</p>");
20.          ?>
21.      </div>
22.  </body>
23.  </html>
```

Lines 18 and 19 are the lines that read the cookie.

- The PHP foreach construct iterates through each value of the **$_COOKIE** superglobal.

- **$_COOKIE** is actually an array of variables. Each element in the array contains one of the values previously set as a cookie.

- The expression **$_COOKIE** as **$key** => **$value** will assign the current element's key to the **$key** variable on each iteration. The value of that key (what the user entered) is stored in **$value**. Thus, for each iteration, a new <p> tag opens, the value of **$key** (in this case it is "name", "month", or "free_time") is displayed, then the actual value of that key's contents (what the user entered) is displayed, and the <p> tag is closed. Since we set three cookies, this foreach construct will have three iterations.

If Morris Catts uses this page, enters the month he was born as November, and says his favorite thing to do is play soccer, the output will be as shown. Remember, to access the page to set the cookies and the page to read the cookies, the URL must be as follows: localhost/path_to_ex_12_1_data.htm.

This data was saved as a cookie on your computer:

name: Morris Catts

month: November

free_time: play soccer

Now let's do something a little more interesting. In Example 12.3, we will allow the user to customize a web page by selecting a background color, a text color, and a username.

The isset() Method

The **isset()method** is a convenient way to check if a value has been given to a variable. We will use it often in this chapter, and now in Example 12.3. The method is a boolean which means, of course, that it has only two possible outcomes—true or false. If the argument in the parentheses has been set and is not NULL, isset() will return true. Otherwise, it will return false. The syntax is simply as follows:

```
bool isset($var);
```

If **$var** has a value, this statement returns true but if **$var** has not been assigned a value, the statement returns false.

EXAMPLE
12.3

Customizing a Web Page with Cookies

When trying this example, be sure to save the file as a PHP file in your htdocs folder in xampp. Here is the code to allow the user to set the way he or she wants a page to look when it's revisited.

```
1.  <?php
2.      if (isset($_POST['submitted']))
```

```
3.          {
4.              $newBgColor = $_POST['bgColor'];
5.              $newColor = $_POST['txtColor'];
6.              $newUsername = $_POST['username'];
7.              define("NEW_TIME", 60*60*24*7);
8.              setcookie("bgColor", $newBgColor, time() + NEW_TIME);
9.              setcookie("txtColor", $newColor, time() + NEW_TIME);
10.             setcookie("username", $newUsername, time() + NEW_TIME);
11.         }
12.     // for first-time users
13.     if ((!isset($_COOKIE['bgColor']) ) && ↵
                        (!isset($_COOKIE['txtColor'])) ↵
                        &&(!isset($_COOKIE['username']) ))
14.         {
15.             $bgColor = "White";
16.             $txtColor = "Black";
17.             $username = "Guest";
18.         }
19.     //if cookies are set then use them
20.     else
21.         {
22.             $bgColor = $_COOKIE['bgColor'];
23.             $txtColor = $_COOKIE['txtColor'];
24.             $username = $_COOKIE['username'];
25.         }
26. ?>
27. <html>
28. <head>
29.     <title>Example 12.3</title>
30. </head>
31.     <body bgcolor = "<?php echo $bgColor ?>" text = "<?php ↵
                                echo $txtColor ?>">
32.     <form action = "<?php echo $_SERVER['PHP_SELF']; ?>" method ↵
                                = "POST">
33.     <div style="width: 80%; margin: 10%;">
34.         <h3>Hello, <?php echo ($username) ?></h3>
35.         <h2>Customize your page! Simply select the options you ↵
                                prefer and the next time you visit ↵
                                this page, it will look the way you ↵
                                want it to look.</h2>
36.         <h3>What name do you want displayed on the page? ↵
                                   
37.         <input type = "text" name = "username" size = "30" ↵
                                value = "guest"/></h3>
38.         <h3>Select a background color for the page:</h3>
39.         <select name = "bgColor">
40.             <option value ="Red">Red</option>
41.             <option value ="Green">Green</option>
42.             <option value ="Blue">Blue</option>
43.             <option value ="Yellow">Yellow</option>
44.             <option value ="Black" selected>Black</option>
45.             <option value ="Brown">Brown</option>
46.             <option value ="White">White</option>
47.         </select>
48.         <h3>Select a color for the text:</h3>
49.         <select name = "txtColor">
```

```
50.                    <option value ="Green">Green</option>
51.                    <option value ="Red">Red</option>
52.                    <option value ="Blue">Blue</option>
53.                    <option value ="Yellow">Yellow</option>
54.                    <option value ="Black">Black</option>
55.                    <option value ="Brown">Brown</option>
56.                    <option value = "White" selected>White</option>
57.                </select>
58.                <p><input type = "hidden" name = "submitted" value ↵
                           = "true"></br>
59.                <input type = "submit" value = "click here twice to ↵
                               check your settings"></p>
60.         </div>
61.         </form>
62.  </body>
63.  </html>
```

We'll start the discussion by following the sequence of events, rather than following the lines of code (although at times they may be the same).

A web page displays as shown:

> **Hello, guest**
>
> **Customize your page! Simply select the options you prefer and the next time you visit this page, it will look the way you want it to look.**
>
> **What name do you want displayed on the page?** guest
>
> **Select a background color for the page:**
>
> Black ▾
>
> **Select a color for the text:**
>
> White ▾
>
> click here twice to check your settings

The PHP code on lines 1–26 checks to see if the value of the hidden button on line 58 is "true". This will occur after the user has clicked the submit button (line 59) to select his or her customized setting. If the hidden button (name = "submitted") is true, the cookies are set. This occurs on lines 4–10 and we will discuss them later.

For a first time user, lines 13–18 display the default settings where the background color, **$bgColor**, is "white", the text color, **$txtColor**, is "black", and the username, **$username**, is "guest". That's what initially displays. The PHP code on lines 31, 32, and 34 use the values of the PHP variables which are set on lines 15, 16, and 17 for this initial display.

Next, the user selects a username from the input box (lines 36–37), a background color from the first drop-down menu (lines 39–47), and a text color from the second drop-down menu (lines 49–57). After clicking the submit button (line 59), the form action on line 32 executes. This method uses the **$_SERVER('PHP_SELF)** method.

The $_SERVER() Method and PHP_SELF   **$_SERVER** is a superglobal. It's an array which contains different types of information such as headers, paths, and script locations. **PHP_SELF** is one of the possible indices of **$_SERVER**. It is the file name of the script that is currently executing, relative to the document root. In this case, if we assume our file has the file name ex_12_3.php and is in a folder named ch12 in htdocs, **$_SERVER('PHP_SELF')** is /ch12/ex_12_3.php.

In this case, the form action points to the page itself. Therefore, when the submit button is clicked, the PHP code at the top of the page begins. Now line 2 is true and the cookies will be set.

Lines 4, 5, and 6 get the new values for the variables **$newBgColor**, **$newColor**, and **$newUsername** by using the **$_POST** superglobal as in Example 12.1 to retrieve the user-selected options from the boxes with id = "bgColor", id = "txtColor", and id = "username". In this example, we set the expiration date of these cookies to a week (line 7) and set the cookies on lines 8, 9, and 10. If a user with username Tweety has selected "Blue" for the background color and "White" for the text color, the page will now look like this:

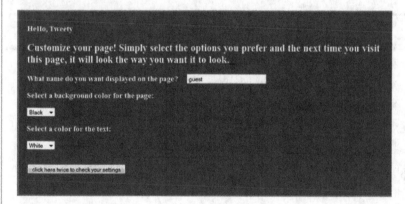

The next time Tweety returns to this site within a week, the else clause of the if...else structure on lines 13–25 will be executed. Since cookies were previously set, they will be reused. Line 22 says that **$bgColor** should be the value of **$_COOKIE('bgColor')**. The same is true for **$txtColor** and **$username** on lines 23 and 24. Therefore, for a week, each time Tweety returns, the values he initially set as cookies will be displayed first. Remember, to access this page to set the cookies, the URL must be as follows:

```
localhost/path_to_ex_12_3.php
```

CHECKPOINT FOR SECTION 12.1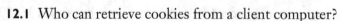

12.1 Who can retrieve cookies from a client computer?

12.2 What is the difference between a session cookie and a persistent cookie?

12.3 When must the setcookie() function be called?

12.4 What parameters can the setcookie() function take?

12.5 How would you create an expiration time for a cookie to last one day?

Use the following for Checkpoints 12.6–12.8:

```
$choice = "free";
setcookie('choice', $choice, time() + 60 * 5);
```

12.6 What is the name of the cookie?

12.7 What is the value of the cookie?

12.8 How long will this cookie last?

12.2 A Database Server: MySQL

As you are aware, today's Internet relies heavily on databases. Without them, businesses, organizations, game sites, and so forth would be unable to provide the varied services offered to millions of people. To learn how databases work and manipulate them with ease is beyond the scope of this book. However, we will provide an overview of databases, show how they can be used, and give you a chance to perform some simple manipulations. Luckily, we have installed MySQL, a database server, when we installed XAMPP.

An Overview of MySQL

MySQL, an open source **relational database management system (RDBMS),** may be the most popular RDBMS in the world. It runs as a server and provides multiuser access to a number of databases. It was founded by **Michael Widenius,** who was working for TcX, a Swedish consulting firm in 1994. Widenius was the principal author of the original version of MySQL. We pronounce MySQL as "my sequel" and the **SQL** part stands for **Structured Query Language**. MySQL is now owned by the Oracle Corporation.

What's Good about MySQL?

MySQL has several important benefits, including the following:

- There are implementations of MySQL for many operating system platforms, including Windows, Mac, Linux, and Unix.
- It can handle large databases that may include tens of thousands of tables with millions of rows.
- It is scalable and can be embedded in an application or used in an enormous data warehouse environment.
- It supports many programming languages, which means it can be accessed regardless of the programming language that wants to use it. It offers comprehensive support for application development needs.
- It offers many security features that ensure data protection. While it is doubtful that security is a concern while completing the examples in this chapter, it is of great concern to anyone dealing with real-life web development and programming.
- It includes many self-management features, which not only assist database administrators on the job but also allow us to use MySQL without having to learn about database management first.

The License

For our purposes, MySQL is completely open source. However, for some commercial situations, a commercial license may be required. If you plan to use MySQL for purposes other than those outlined in this chapter, please check www.mysql.com/about/legal.

Setting Up a MySQL User Account

In order to use MySQL in the examples in this chapter, you will need to create and modify databases. To do this, you have to set up a **user account**. We will administer MySQL through the **phpMyAdmin** software that comes with XAMPP. To access phpMyAdmin, click the **Admin** button from the MySQL option in the XAMPP Control Panel:

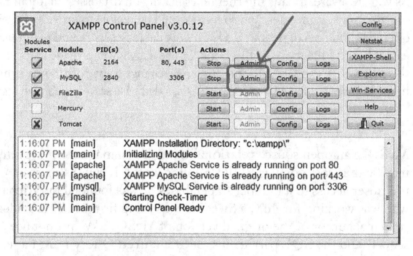

You will see the following. We use the Users tab to create a new user:

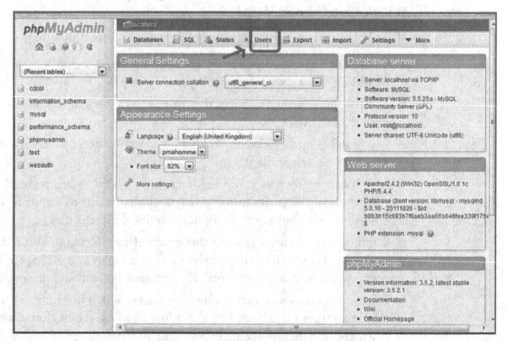

Create a New User

When you first installed XAMPP, a general user was set up. This general user has full access to anyone who can call on the host. You may, in the future, want to set up other users with restricted privileges—for example, a user who can create queries but not otherwise alter the database. For now, you will create a user (yourself) with a specific password who will have unlimited access to your databases. First, click the **Users** tab as shown above. Then, click the **Add user** link in the middle of the screen. Enter the username you want to use and the password (enter and retype) you want to use but select Local for the Host. Your screen should look similar to the following:

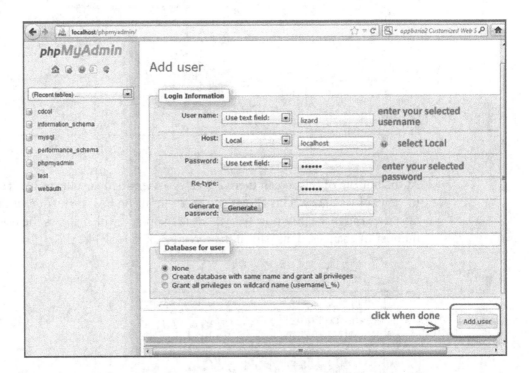

When you are satisfied with the new user's information, click the **Add user** button at the bottom of the screen. You should see a confirmation alert and then a screen with an overview of all users created so far. At the next screen, called Users Overview, you can add or delete users as you wish.

Assigning Privileges

Now you need to assign privileges to your new user. Select (by clicking in the checkbox) your newly created user and click the **Edit Privileges** link.[1] We will give our new user Global privileges so you can select **Check All** at the next screen which should look like this:

---

[1]Tip: If this screen is partially hidden, put your cursor in the top-left corner of the Edit Privileges window and, when the four-way arrow appears, move the mouse quickly to the *left*. You may need to play with this a few times before this window is centered.

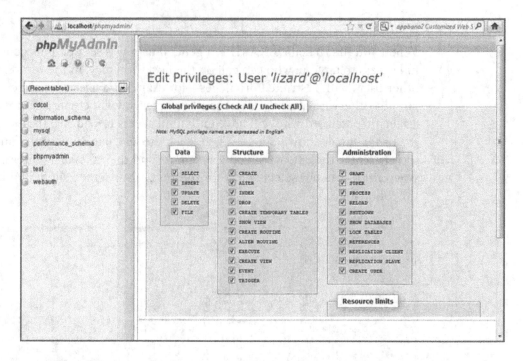

At the bottom of this screen there is a category entitled Resource limits. Scroll down to view this category. This allows you to set limits on how many queries, updates, and so on a user can make. For now we will leave them at 0 which allows the user an unlimited number of changes. This part of the screen should look like this:

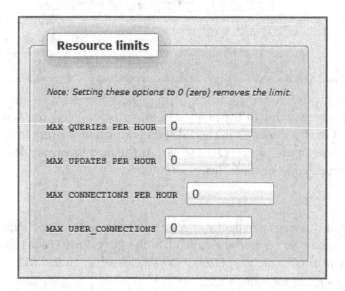

Congratulations! You have created a new user. From now on we will call the user by the username created here, lizard.

To return to the home screen with all the options at any time, click the **Home** button on the navigation bar at the left:

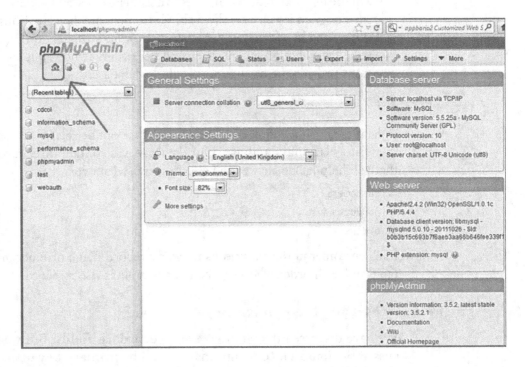

The Database Structure

It's simple to create a database using phpMyAdmin. But before we do, we must consider what the database may need to do and create its structure. The general purpose of a database is to allow you to manipulate large amounts of data in many different ways. For example, a pharmacy has customers who buy medications which are prescribed by various doctors. One doctor may prescribe the same medication for many people. Some of those people may take a second medication; others may take a different second medication. Another doctor may prescribe the same medications to other patients. Or some patients may get different prescriptions from several doctors. The pharmacy may need to know when to order more of a particular drug or the generic version of another. Most likely it needs to record which combinations of medications are taken by a specific customer to avoid dangerous drug interactions. A database allows a pharmacist to find the answers to many queries. For example, the pharmacist might need to know which customers are prescribed a certain medication from a specific physician. Or which medications have been prescribed by a certain physician over a given time. Or which customers in a given age range take a specific medication. The questions that can be answered by a properly constructed database are many and varied.

Thus, before we create a database, we will think about what we want that database to do. In this example, we will not be overly ambitious. We'll create a database that we can build on later in the chapter, by using more PHP, JavaScript, and HTML skills.

Building a Small Business Database

We will create a database for the `Jackie's Jewelry` site. Jackie sells her custom-designed jewelry on the web. Customers buy her creations. Therefore, Jackie needs to keep track of her customers (who buys her stuff?), her stock (does she have enough inventory?), and her orders (who is buying what?). These questions provide the basis for our sample database.

Jackie's Tables

A database is a collection of tables of data that can be related to each other; thus, the term **relational database**. Our database will contain three tables, each with data that will help Jackie answer the questions posed above:

- `customers`
- `products`
- `orders`

Each customer in the `customers` table is a record. Each product in the `products` table and each order placed in the `orders` table is also a record.

The Primary Key and the Foreign Key

We have discussed the fact that every **record** has **fields**. But we have not discussed the importance of a primary key. The **primary key** of each table in a relational database is the **unique identifier** for each record. The primary key should always be something that no other record will have. For example, two customers may have the same name or two people may place an identical order. Therefore, neither the customer's name nor the order description is an appropriate primary key. On the other hand, if each customer is assigned a unique ID number, there is no chance that two customers will have that same number. If each order has an invoice number, there is, again, no chance that two orders will have the same invoice number. Most colleges issue student ID numbers to avoid the possibility that information about one student will get mixed up with another student. Every database table must have one column designated as the primary key.

A **foreign key** is a field in a relational database that matches the primary key column of another table. For example, if we wanted to know if customer Janet Johansen ordered a jade necklace, we would match the ID number assigned to customer Janet Johansen with the product key for jade necklaces.

Table Fields

Let's consider the three tables included in Jackie's database and see what information is required for each table. This helps determine the fields we need to assign to each table. Keep in mind that we are drastically simplifying things for this sample database. A real database for a large business would have many more tables and each record would consist of more fields.

customer table fields:

- `customerID`—This is the primary key because it is unique to each customer.
- `customerName`—This is the full name of a customer.
- `customerEmail`—This is how an order confirmation will be sent or other promotional ads can be distributed.

There are other fields one might include, such as a customer's shipping address, preferences, and preferred payment method. But for our sample database, three `customer` table fields are sufficient.

orders table fields:

- `orderInvoice`—This is the primary key because it is unique to each order.
- `orderCustomer`—This is the name of the customer who placed the order.
- `orderProduct`—This is the product that was ordered.
- `orderQuantity`—This is how many items were ordered by the customer.

products table fields:

- `productID`—This is the primary key because it is unique to each product.
- `productName`—This is the description of each item Jackie sells.
- `productQuantity`—This is the number of each item Jackie has in stock.

Field Attributes

There is something else to consider. Each field can have certain attributes that, by using phpMyAdmin, we can set as we want, leave a default value, or not set at all. We will see these attributes as we begin to create the database but we will list them here. Some of them are only used in special situations and don't concern us here so we can ignore them:

- Name: The name given to a field. For example, we will name the ID of the customers in the customer table `customerID` and the email address field `customerEmail`. It's a good idea to keep naming conventions the same throughout. Since, in this database, the fields are named using the table name and appending a descriptive word, beginning with an uppercase letter, it would make sense to name the ID of the product in the products table `productID` and the quantity of products in stock `productQuantity`. The name you assign each table and each field is up to you but you should be consistent.
- Type: This is the data type of the information in a field. A quantity would be an INT but a name would be TEXT. While phpMyAdmin offers both TEXT and VARCHAR options for text fields, we will use VARCHAR because it saves space when the database is stored.
- Length/Values: This allocates the number of spaces needed for a field. For example, you may want to allocate 25 spaces for a name but only 5 or 6 for an

integer. Most integer values in a database count the number of something and five spaces allows for an integer of, maximum, 99,999.

- `Default`: We will leave this attribute set to `None`. It will give us the current timestamp; i.e., when that record was created or changed.

- `Collation`: Ignore this one.

- `Attributes`: This allows us to set the type of numeric value in a numeric field. When the numbers we are dealing with are integers we will set this to `UNSIGNED` or `UNSIGNED ZEROFILL`.

- `Null`: Leave blank.

- `A_I`: This attribute stands for `auto_increment` and is used for fields like IDs. Each time a new record is added to the customer table, we want to assign that customer a new and unique ID. By using this feature, each new customer's ID will be the next number following the ID of the last customer. We will check this box for our three primary keys (`customerID`, `productID`, and `orderInvoice`).

- `Comments`: Leave blank.

- `MIME type`: Aids in sending emails with database information but we will leave it blank.

- `Browser Transformation`: Leave blank.

- `Transformation Options`: Leave blank.

Creating the Database with phpMyAdmin

Now we can create the database using phpMyAdmin. As you work through phpMyAdmin, notice that each time you execute a command by checking a box or clicking a button, the corresponding SQL command will display under a green or pink banner at the top of the screen. This can help you learn SQL commands while you use the phpMyAdmin GUI software. For example, a sample database named `'lizardtest'` was created and then deleted. The command to delete a database in SQL is `DROP DATABASE 'databaseName';`. The screen display follows:

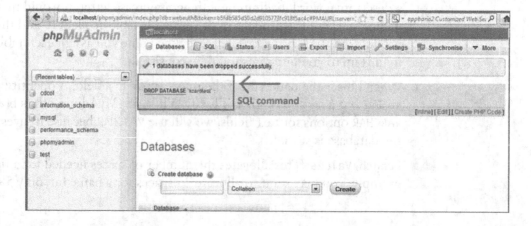

Create the `jackiejewelry` Database

From the Home screen in phpMyAdmin, click the **Databases** tab. Type the database name into the box under `Create database`. We will name our database `jackiejewelry`. Then click the **Create** button.

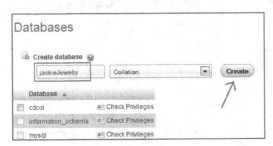

You should get a confirmation alert saying that this database has been created and it should be added to the list of databases on the `Databases` screen. Now we will begin creating the tables discussed previously. We'll talk through creating the first table with screenshots and you can create the second and third table on your own.

When you click the **jackiejewelry** database you will see a screen that says no tables are found. We will create three tables. The first table, `customer`, will have three fields so we will enter the table name, `customer`, and a 3 in the `Number of columns` box. Then click the **Go** button.

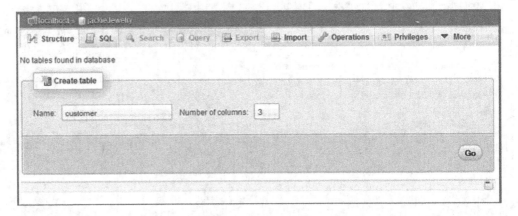

The next screen will provide three rows—one for each of our fields. You can always add or delete fields later. Now enter the following values (shown in Table 12.1) for each field. Table 12.1 shows two lines for the list of field structure attributes, but in phpMyAdmin they are on one line.

When you finish entering the `Structure` attributes for the three fields, press the **Save** button. You will receive an alert confirming that the table has been created. This table will now use `customerID` as the primary key. Each time a new customer is entered into the database, an ID number will be created, starting at number 000001 and incrementing automatically by one. Thus, the second customer will have `customerID = 000002` and the 435th customer will have `customerID = 000435`. The next screen you see will look like this:

TABLE 12.1 Table Field Structure for the customers Table of the jackiejewelry Database

Structure for customers Table

Name	Type	Length/ Values	Default	Collation	Attributes
customerID	INT	6	NONE		unsigned
customerName	VARCHAR	20	NONE		
customerEmail	VARCHAR	40	NONE		

(Structure continued)

Null	Index	A_I	MIME type	Browser Transformation	Browser Options
	PRIMARY	✓			

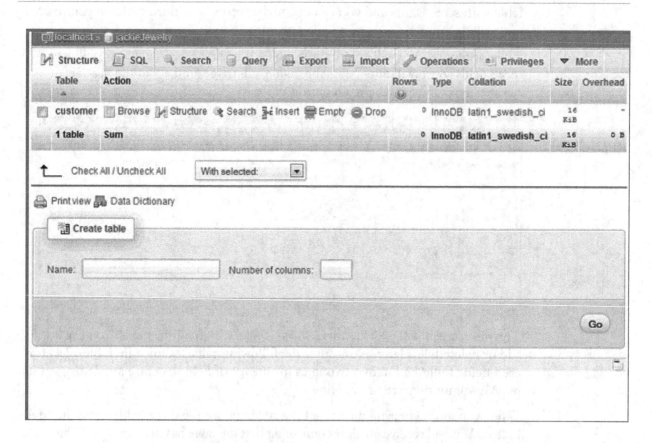

Now create two more tables, orders and products. The structure of each are shown in Tables 12.2 and 12.3.

TABLE 12.2	Table Field Structure for the orders Table of the jackiejewelry Database

Structure for orders Table

Name	Type	Length/Values	Default	Collation	Attributes
orderInvoice	INT	6	NONE		unsigned
orderCustomer	VARCHAR	20	NONE		
orderProduct	VARCHAR	30	NONE		
orderQuantity	INT	4	NONE		unsigned

(Structure continued)

Null	Index	A_I	MIME type	Browser Transformation	Browser Options
	PRIMARY	✓			

TABLE 12.3	Table Field Structure for the products Table of the jackiejewelry Database

Structure for products Table

Name	Type	Length/Values	Default	Collation	Attributes
productID	INT	6	NONE		unsigned
productName	VARCHAR	30	NONE		
productQuantity	INT	3	NONE		unsigned

(Structure continued)

Null	Index	A_I	MIME type	Browser Transformation	Browser Options
	PRIMARY	✓			

When you are finished creating the three tables, you should see a screen like this:

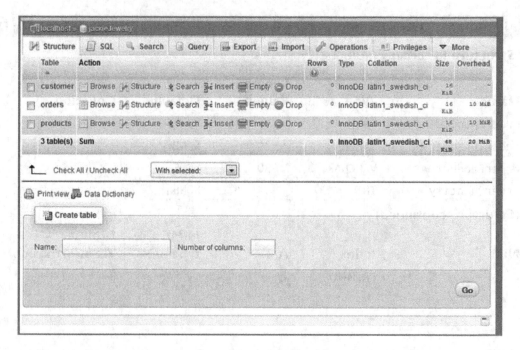

In the next section, we will learn to populate this database with information from a form on a web page.

12.9   Who is Michael Widenius?

12.10 List at least three reasons why a business might choose MySQL over different database software?

12.11 What is phpMyAdmin used for?

12.12 If you were a database administrator, why might you need several users?

12.13 In a table in a database that includes all the users of a particular website, is each user a record or a field?

12.14 In a database table that contains the following fields, which field should be designated as the primary key? Why?

fields: userName, userPhone, userSSN, userAge

12.3   Populating a Database from the Web

In this section, we will learn how to add records to the jackiejewelry database we just created. There are many ways to populate a database but, since we are programming for the web, the most appropriate format is to create a web form where information entered by a user will become a record in the proper table in the database. This requires several PHP files and a folder structure similar to the ones we created in Chapter 11 for the Greg's Gambits and Carla's Classroom sites. To follow along with this example, create the following folders inside your htdocs folder in the xampp folder where you have installed XAMPP. The two images (jackie_logo.jpg and jackie_logo2.jpg) and the style sheet (jackie.css) files are available in the Student Data Files.

```
jackie
    assets
    css (put jackie.css in this folder)
    images (put jackie_logo.jpg and jackie_logo2.jpg in this folder)
    include
```

The Web Page Form

We need three more files in order to create a form that can be used to add customers to the database. One file will be the form to enter the customer's information, a second file will connect to the database, and a third file will insert the information into the customer table of the database. When SQL commands are used, we will explain what they do but, unless you have already completed a course on the SQL language, you will not be expected to create the SQL code.

The main page is named index.php and should be stored in the jackie folder but not in any subfolders. The code for this page is shown in Example 12.4. The other two pages are essential but very short.

EXAMPLE 12.4

The index.php File

```
1.   <?php include ('assets/insert.php'); ?>
2.   <html>
3.   <head>
4.       <title>Jackie's Jewelry | Add Customers</title>
5.       <link href = "css/jackie.css" rel = "stylesheet" ↵
                                        type = "text/css" />
6.   </head>
7.   <body>
8.       <div id="container">
9.           <div align="center">
10.              <img src="images/jackie_logo.jpg" />
11.              <img src="images/jackie_logo2.jpg" /> </div>
12.              <div id="nav">
13.                  <a href="index.html">Home</a>
14.                  <a href="jackie.html">About Jackie</a>
15.                  <a href="services.html">Jackie's Services</a>
16.                  <a href="products.html">Shop</a>
17.                  <a href="tips.html">Jewelry Making</a>
18.                  <a href="contact.html">Contact Jackie</a>
19.              </div>
20.              <div id="content">
21.              <div style="width: 600px; float: right;">
22.              <div style="float: right; width: 500px; ↵
                                    padding: 1px; margin-right: ↵
```

```
                                      10px; margin-left: 10px;">
23.                <p>Add a new customer to Jackie's Jewelry ⏎
                               database:</p>
24.                <form action = "<?php echo ⏎
                               $_SERVER['PHP_SELF'];?>" ⏎
                               method = "post">
25.                    <table>
26.                    <tr>
27.                        <td><hr />
28.                            Enter customer's full name:<br />
29.                            Last name, First name, Middle or ⏎
                               other <br />
30.                            Examples:
31.                            <ul>
32.                                <li>Smith, John</li>
33.                                <li>Morrisey, Edward III</li>
34.                                <li>Chen, Kimmie X.</li>
35.                            </ul>
36.                        </td>
37.                        <td><input type = "text" name = ⏎
                               "customerName" size = "35"/>
38.                        </td>
39.                    </tr>
40.                    <tr>
41.                        <td><hr />
42.                            Enter customer's email address:
43.                            <br />Include full address <br />
44.                            Examples:
45.                            <ul>
46.                                <li>john.smith@yahoo.com</li>
47.                                <li>EddieD@gbdmail.net</li>
48.                                <li>chen.kim@myschool.edu</li>
49.                            </ul>
50.                        </td>
51.                        <td><input type = "text" name = ⏎
                               "customerEmail" size = "35" />
52.                        </td>
53.                    </tr>
54.                    <tr>
55.                        <td colspan = "2" style = ⏎
                               "text-align:center;">
56.                        <input type="submit" name = ⏎
                               "frmAddCustomer" />
57.                        </td>
58.                    </tr>
59.                    </table>
60.                </form>
61.            </div>
62.            </div>
63.        </div>
64.    </div>
65.    </body>
66.    </html>
```

Some lines need explanation. Line 1 uses PHP to include the file that will receive the information from this page, contain instructions about how to connect to the database (through another included file), and add the new customer's information into the `customer` table.

Line 24 tells the computer that the information from this form will be posted (`method = "post"`), and the PHP code uses the **$_SERVER['PHP_SELF']** superglobal with the `PHP_SELF` indices to indicate that the information will be posted on a database located on a server on this computer.

Two items of information are collected—the new customer's name and email address. We have used only one field for the customer's name to simplify things; in a real database, the name could be stored in three or four fields including, most likely, a first name, last name, middle initial, and honorifics (such as Mr., Ms, Dr. and so on). The information collected is entered in the two input boxes (lines 37 and 51). The `names` of these input boxes (`customerName` and `customerEmail`) have been chosen to correspond with the fields in the database table.

If you enter this code, the page will look as shown but will not be functional.

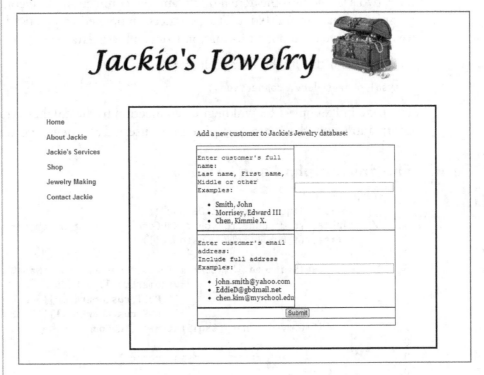

Example 12.5 will create the `insert.php` page. Before we show the example we will explain several methods that will be used.

The die() Method

While a method called `die()` looks pretty dramatic, the **die() function** is simply a PHP function that can be used as an alternate to the `exit()` function. It is normally used when trying to connect to a database or website and includes a message that will be displayed if the connection is unable to be made. The syntax is as follows:

```
die(message);
```

The mysql_error() Method

The **mysql_error() method** will return the error description of a MySQL operation that cannot be completed. If there is no error, then the empty string ("") is returned. Otherwise, the error message will correspond to whatever error has occurred. For example, if the user does not have access to the required database, the error could be "Access denied for user 'whoever'@'whatever_host'" or, if a specified database does not exist, the mysql_error() method would return a message to that effect. This method is often used in conjunction with the die() method. Thus, if a connection is not possible, the program will stop and the appropriate error will be generated. The syntax for this sequence of events is as follows:

```
die(mysql_error());
```

The mysql_query() Method

The **mysql_query() method** executes a query on a MySQL database. The method takes two arguments—the actual query and the connection. The connection argument is optional. If omitted, the last connection opened will be used. A **query** is the way we retrieve or import information from and to a database.

The syntax for this method is as follows:

```
mysql_query(query, connection);
```

The page in Example 12.5 will begin a connection to the database and send in the information from the index.php page to be inserted as a new record in the database.

EXAMPLE
12.5

The insert.php Page

```
1.   <?php
2.       include("include/connectDB.php");
3.   // variables from connectDB.php: $dbConn - connection object
4.       if(isset($_POST['frmAddCustomer']))
5.       {
6.           $sqlStatement="INSERT INTO customer (customerName, ↵
                           customerEmail) VALUES ↵
                           ('$_POST[customerName]', ↵
                           '$_POST[customerEmail]')"; ↵
7.           if (!mysql_query($sqlStatement,$dbConn))
8.           {
9.               die('Error: '. mysql_error());
10.          }
11.          echo "<h2>RECORD ADDED</h2>";
12.          include("include/closeDB.php");
13.      }
14.  ?>
```

We will discuss this code in detail. Line 2 says to include another file, connectDB.php, which does not yet exist. This file, given in the next example, will connect to the database. For now, we will assume the connection is made. The comment on line 3 tells us that a variable, **$dbConn**, has been declared and given a value in the connectDB.php page. It's there so that, if a new programmer edits this code, he or she will know that the variable (used later, on line 7) is not an un-instantiated variable.

Line 4 uses the `isset()` method to check that the information has arrived from the `index.php` page. If this is `true`, the statements on lines 6–12 are executed.

Line 6 contains a SQL statement on the right side of the `'='` sign. Since we are not learning SQL in this text, you can accept the syntax of this statement to mean that the values of the customer's name and email will be inserted into the `customerName` and `customerEmail` fields of the `customer` table of the `jackiejewelry` database. The values come from `$_POST(customerName)` and `$_POST(customerEmail)` input boxes in `index.php`. The entire right side of the statement is now stored in the PHP variable, `$sqlStatement`.

Line 7 checks to see if the query is valid. If the connection and the SQL statement on line 6 are valid, the expression will be `true` and the `NOT` operator will give this condition a value of `false`. In this case, the `if` clause will be skipped. On the other hand, if there is a problem with the query or the connection, the expression `mysql_query($sqlStatement,$dbConn)` will be `false`. The `NOT` operator will change the value of the `if` condition to `true`, the user will receive an appropriate message, and the code will end. The `mysql_error()` method will display whatever error caused this statement to execute.

If lines 7–10 are not executed, then a connection to the database has been made and the field values have been appropriately entered in the customer table. Line 11 displays a message on the web page that a record has been added.

Line 12 includes a fourth file, `closeDB.php`, which we will create in a following example and which will close the connection to the database.

Before we do a screen shot of the display we will create the `connectDB.php` and `closeDB.php` files because, until these are created, nothing can happen to change the display shown in the previous example.

The `mysql_connect()` Method

The **`mysql_connect()`** PHP method opens a connection to a MySQL database. If successful, it returns the connection but if unsuccessful, it returns `false`. The function takes up to five (all optional) parameters, as follows:

- `server`: This parameter can specify a server or a port. The default value, if this is not included, is `localhost:3306`.
- `user`: This parameter can specify a username or, by default, it is the name of the user who owns the server process.
- `pwd`: If left blank, the default is `""`.
- `newlink`: This is a way to return the identifier of an already-opened connection.
- `clientflag`: This can be used to specify certain constants which are not necessary for our purposes.

The syntax for this method is as follows:

```
mysql_connect(server, user, pwd, newlink, clientflag);
```

The `mysql_select_db()` Method

This PHP method picks the database to use. It sets the MySQL database that will be active for the connection. The **mysql_select_db() method** takes two parameters:

- `database`: This is required and specifies the database to select.
- `connection`: This is optional and, if not specified, will use the last connection opened by `mysql_connect()`.

The syntax for this method is as follows:

```
mysql_select_db(database, connection);
```

Example 12.6 creates and closes a connection to the `jackiejewelry` database.

EXAMPLE 12.6

Creating and Closing a Connection to the Database

The connectDB.php file: The following code creates the connection:

```
1.  <?php
2.      $dbConn = mysql_connect('localhost', 'lizard2', 'lizard');
3.      if (!$dbConn)
4.      {
5.          die('Could not connect: ' . mysql_error());
6.      }
7.  //jackieJewelry is the name of the db
8.      $dbObj = mysql_select_db('jackiejewelry', $dbConn);
9.  ?>
```

Line 2 creates a new variable, **$dbConn** that will take the value of the `mysql_connect()` function. In this case, we specified a server (`localhost`), a username (`lizard2`), and a password (`lizard`) but these parameters are optional if you want to use the defaults.

Line 3 checks to see if **$dbConn** is valid. If it is not, the `die()` method is used to display the message "`Could not connect:`" concatenated with the appropriate reason from the `mysql_error()` function.

If a connection is made, line 8 creates a variable, **$dbObj**, that takes the value of the expression `mysql_select_db('jackiejewelry', $dbConn)`. In this case, the jackiejewelry database is selected from the connection made previously. This information is now available to the `insert.php` page.

The closeDB.php file: The following code closes the connection database:

```
1.  <?php
2.      mysql_close($dbConn);
3.  ?>
```

Both of these files should be stored in the `include` folder in `htdocs`.

Now, if you open the `index.php` file you are ready to add records to the `jackiejewelry` database. Be sure you have stored all the files in the correct places in your `jackie` folder of `htdocs` in `xampp` on your computer. Then use the following URL:

```
localhost/jackie/index.php
```

If you enter a user named `Victor Vanderhoff Jr.` whose email address is vv2@myschool.edu, you should see the following:

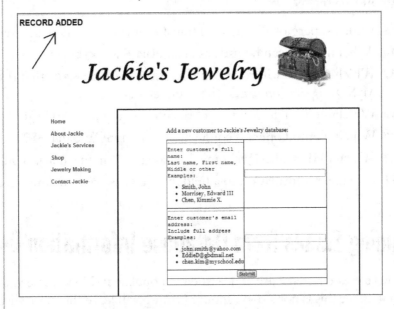

Now you can use this page each time you want to add a record to the customer table of the jackiejewelry database. As an end-of-chapter exercise, you will be asked to create forms to populate the orders and products tables.

To view the records you have added, click the **jackiejewelry** database in phpMy-Admin, then click the **customer** table and you will see the added customer records. The following screenshot shows a list of four customers. Their customerIDs are not sequential because previously customers with customerIDs 1, 2, 4, 5, 6, 7, and 8 have been deleted.

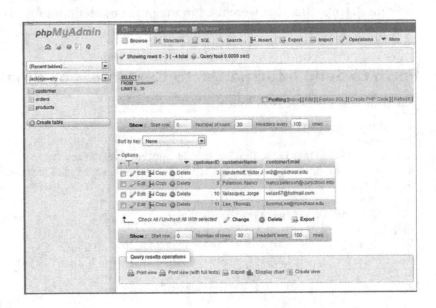

CHECKPOINT FOR SECTION 12.3 ✓

12.15 Which superglobal is used to transmit form data to the server?

12.16 What method can be used as an alternate to exit()?

12.17 Which method will return the description of the error that results when a MySQL operation cannot be completed?

12.18 Which method do you use to execute a query on a MySQL database?

12.19 Which method opens a connection to a MySQL database?

12.20 Which PHP method picks the database that is used when sending in form data?

12.21 Is sending information to a field in a database record considered a query?

12.4 Sending Emails from Database Information Using PHP

We have created a database and learned to populate it. Now we need to do things with it. Since this is not a book about SQL, we will leave the more advanced queries and data mining alone. In this section, we will learn to use information that exists in a database to send emails to people in that database. We will use the database we created in the previous section and, in the Carla's Classroom site in the Putting It to Work section, we will create a more detailed database and send a more complex email.

The Form

The form that we will use to allow Jackie to select a customer to send an email to is straightforward. Since we are building on the previous example, we will use the same look and feel for Example 12.7. This file will be named sale_email.php and should be saved in the jackie folder inside htdocs. It will use the connectDB.php and closeDB.php files that were used in the previous section. However, we will need to create a new page to get the customer's record, format the email, and send it.

EXAMPLE 12.7

Form to Send Information to Customers by Email

The code for this page is as follows:

```
1.   <html>
2.   <head>
3.       <title>Jackie's Jewelry | Add Customers</title>
4.       <link href="css/jackie.css" rel="stylesheet" type="text/css" />
5.   </head>
6.   <body>
7.       <div id = "container">
8.           <div align = "center">
9.               <img src = "images/jackie_logo.jpg" />
10.              <img src = "images/jackie_logo2.jpg" /> </div>
11.          <div id = "nav">
12.              <a href = "index.html">Home</a>
```

```
13.                          <a href = "jackie.html">About Jackie</a>
14.                          <a href = "services.html">Jackie's Services</a>
15.                          <a href = "products.html">Shop</a>
16.                          <a href = "tips.html">Jewelry Making</a>
17.                          <a href = "contact.html">Contact Jackie</a>
18.                  </div>
19.                  <div id = "content">
20.                      <div style = "width: 600px; float: right;">
21.                      <div style = "float: right; width: 500px; padding: ↵
                                    1px; margin-right: 10px; ↵
                                    margin-left: 10px;">
22.                          <p>Send an email to a customer</p>
23.                          <form action = "assets/getCustomer.php" ↵
                                    method = "post">
24.                          <table>
25.                          <tr>
26.                              <td>Customer's Name: </td>
27.                              <td><input type = "text" name = ↵
                                        "get_customername" /></td>
28.                          </tr>
29.                          <tr>
30.                              <td colspan = "2" style = "text-align: ↵
                                        center;">
31.                              <input type="submit" /></td>
32.                          </tr>
33.                          </table>
34.                          </form>
35.                      </div>
36.                      </div>
37.                  </div>
38.              </div>
39.      </body>
40.  </html>
```

In this script, the input box on line 27 allows Jackie to enter the name of the customer that she wants to send the email to. The name of this box is "get_customername" and this identifier will be used later.

When the submit button is clicked, the form's action takes place. The action on line 23 says to go to the assets folder and retrieve the file named getCustomer.php. We will create that file in the next example. For now, the page looks like this but if you enter a name and click the submit button, nothing will happen:

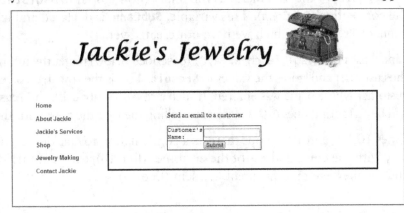

In Example 12.8, we will write the file that will create and send an email. We will store this file in the assets folder and give it the file name getCustomer.php.

EXAMPLE

12.8

Using PHP to Create and Send an Email

```php
1.  <?php
2.      include('../include/connectDB.php');
3.      $sqlStatement = "SELECT * FROM customer WHERE (customername = ↵
                            '$_POST[get_customername]')";
4.      $result = mysql_query($sqlStatement, $dbConn);
5.      $customerRecord = mysql_fetch_array($result);
6.      if (!$customerRecord)
7.      {
8.          die('Error: ' . mysql_error());
9.      }
10.     echo "<p>Email = " . $customerRecord['customerEmail'] . "</p>";
11.     echo "<p>customer = " . $customerRecord['customerName']."</p>";
12. // Send the email to the customer
13.     $to = $customerRecord['customerEmail'];
14.     $subject = "Jackie's Jewelry Holiday Sale!";
15.     $message = "<--Great Holiday Sale! --> \n Check out our ↵
                            great deals!\n Up to 50% off and ↵
                            free shipping now through the end ↵
                            of the month.";
16.     $from = "jackie@jackiesjewels.com";
17.     $headers = "From:" . $from;
18.     mail($to,$subject,$message,$headers);
19.     echo "Email sent.";
20.     include('../include/closeDB.php');
21. ?>
```

Line 2 is an instruction to include the file connectDB.php. Notice that, in this example, since this file is included in a file that is inside one of the folders in the jackie folder, to access it, we must back out of assets and then go into include (../).

Line 3 assigns the result of a SQL statement to the variable **$sqlStatement**. This SQL statement retrieves the customername from the customer table.

Line 4 assigns the result of a SQL query to the variable **$result**. Recall that the mysql_query() method includes the query (now stored in **$sqlStatement**) and the connection (**$dbConn**). This variable, **$dbConn**, is declared and initialized in the connectDB.php file which we have not created yet.

Line 5 uses the mysql_fetch_array() (described below) to get the information about the customer and stores the values in **$result**. This is the row that corresponds with the customer whose name was entered. If such a row does not exist, the **$customerRecord** will be false and lines 6–9 will execute, telling the user the reason for the query's failure.

Lines 10, 11, and 19 are put there as a confirmation for Jackie. A new page will display with the email address of the customer (line 10), the customer's name (line 11) and the message that the email was sent (line 19).

Line 13 begins the code to send the email. The **$to** variable sets the value of the email address that will be used. Line 14 assigns a value to the subject line of the email, stored in **$subject**. The email we are creating will be the same for every customer. We want to announce a sale that Jackie is having. Therefore, the text of the message will be the same for all. Later, we will learn to use other data from the database to customize each email for each customer. For this example, however, the email message body will consist of the text stored in **$message** on line 15. Notice that we use the "\n" escape character to format text on a new line because our email will be sent in plain text.

Other information that will go into the email are the values of Jackie's email address (stored in **$from** on line 16) and the header of the email (stored in **$headers** on line 17). Line 18 uses the mail() function (described below) to send the message to the email address pulled from the customerEmail field in the customer table of the jackiejewelry database.

The mysql_fetch_array() Method

The **mysql_fetch_array() method** returns an array of strings that corresponds to the fetched row. If there are no more rows, the return will be false. It takes one argument: the result which is the resource that is being evaluated. A **resource** is a special variable that holds a reference to an external source, such as, in our case, the result of a SQL query. The syntax for this method is as follows:

```
mysql_fetch_array(resource $result[, $result_type_if_desired]);
```

The mail() Method

The **mail()method** is used to send email with PHP. It contains at least three parameters. Others can be added if desired.

- **$to:** includes the email address(es) of the receiver or receivers of the email. More than one recipient can be included, with each email address separated by commas.
- **$subject:** includes the text to be included in the subject line of the outgoing email.
- **$message:** contains the body of the email. Each line in the body should be separated by a linefeed (LF) which is written "\n". No line can be greater than 70 characters.
- **$headers:** includes the sender of the email. It is a string that will be inserted at the end of the email header.
- Additional headers and additional parameters are available and optional.

The syntax for this method is as follows:

```
mail mail($to,$subject,$message,$headers);
```

Before we can actually use this page we need to create the two files that will connect with the database and close the connection. We will do this in Example 12.9.

Opening and Closing the Connection to the Database

The connectDB.php and the closeDB.php files are the same files that were used in the previous section. We copy them here for your convenience but no explanation is necessary.

connectDB.php:

```php
1.  <?php
2.      $dbConn = mysql_connect('localhost', 'lizard2', 'lizard');
3.      if (!$dbConn)
4.      {
5.          die('Could not connect: ' . mysql_error());
6.      }
7.      $dbObj = mysql_select_db('jackiejewelry', $dbConn);
8.  ?>
```

closeDB.php:

```php
1.  <?php
2.      mysql_close($dbConn);
3.  ?>
```

Both of these files should be stored in the include folder in htdocs. Now, if you open the sale_email.php file and enter a user named Nancy Peterson whose email address is nancy.peterson@ourschool.edu, you should see the following confirmation:

```
Email = nancy.peterson@ourschool.edu
customer = Peterson, Nancy
Email sent.
```

If nancy.peterson@ourschool.edu was a real email address, Nancy should receive an email message with the subject line and body as shown:

CHECKPOINT FOR SECTION 12.4 ✔

12.22 The method used to send an email using PHP is _____.

12.23 Which parameters should always be included with the mail() method?

12.24 What action should be placed in a <form> tag from a page in the root directory to retrieve a file named getUserData.php that is in a folder named data inside an assets folder?

12.25 What will be returned by the mysql_fetch_array() method if the desired row of data does not exist?

12.5 Putting It to Work

We will now pull together everything we have learned so far. We'll create a database for Greg's Gambits that will allow a player to do several things, including creating an account, logging into an account already created, and playing a game. In this section, we will only create the code to create and log in to an account. Using a database with PHP and JavaScript for more features is beyond the scope of this book.

We will also create a way for Carla of Carla's Classroom to enter student progress into a database and then create and generate customized student reports to parents by pulling the information from the database. An email will be sent to the parent with the information about the student.

Greg's Gambits: Create or Validate an Account and Log In

We will use the same format for the site as we used in Chapter 11. We'll have a header.php page, a footer.php, and several other pages. However, before we begin to develop the PHP, we need a database to work with.

Creating the Database

We will name our database gregs_gambits. We'll use phpMyAdmin to create this database with tables and fields. For this project, we need only one table for users but to keep it real, we will also create a table for one game. We'll use the game of Boggle as the example but you can add tables for each game if you wish. Use the process described earlier in the chapter to create a database named gregs_gambits. The two tables and their fields are listed below. If a field from XAMPP is not listed, leave the default value:

- Table: users
  - Fields:
    - user_ID: type: INT, size: 6, AUTO_INCREMENT
    - first_Name: type: VARCHAR, size: 20
    - last_Name: type: VARCHAR, size: 20
    - userName: type: VARCHAR, size: 30
    - password: type: VARCHAR, size: 8
- Table: game_boggle
  - Fields:
    - user_ID: type: INT, size: 6, AUTO_INCREMENT
    - userName: type: VARCHAR, size: 30
    - points_Earned: type: INT, size: 5
    - played: type: TINYINT, size: 3 (how many times player has played this game)

Notice that this structure allows for up to 999,999 players (the user_ID size maximum is six digits). Each player can have a userName of up to 30 characters and a password of eight characters. You can change these field sizes if you wish. For now, we will not put any other restrictions on what can be used as a password so any characters or combinations within the eight-character limit are valid. We have also put a limit of 999 on how many times a player can play this game; the played field is restricted to three digits for a maximum of 999.

Creating User Accounts and Login Pages

We will be creating several PHP pages that tie together. First, we need a page that allows a new player to create an account. This information will then become part of the users table. Since we have explained much of this code previously, only new PHP and SQL statements will be explained. This file will be named newUser.php. There will be a second similar page created for existing users to log in. We will continue to use the technique described earlier where each new page will include the header.php and footer.php files.

Before you begin, create a folder structure in the htdocs folder on XAMPP and remember to store all your pages for this site in that folder. You can use the folder names given here but can change the names if you wish. Some of the names shown in the structure that follows are normally used, by convention:

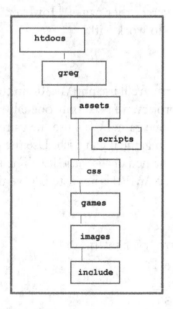

The first page we will create is the page to create a new user. The file name for this page is newUser.php and it should be stored in top-level greg folder in htdocs.

The newUser.php File: The code for the page to create a new user is as follows:

```
1.   <?php include ('include/header.php'); ?>
2.   <?php include("assets/addUser.php"); ?>
3.       <div id = "content">
4.           <p>Create User </p>
5.           <hr />
6.           <form action = "<?php echo $_SERVER['PHP_SELF']; ?>" ↵
                          method = "post">
7.           <table>
```

```
8.              <tr>
9.                  <td style = "border: none;">First Name: </td>
10.                 <td style = "border: none;"><input id="idFirstName" ⏎
                        type = "text" name = "firstName" /></td>
11.             </tr>
12.             <tr>
13.                 <td colspan = "2" style="border: none;"></td>
14.             </tr>
15.             <tr>
16.                 <td style = "border: none;">Last Name: </td>
17.                 <td style = "border: none;"><input type = "text" ⏎
                        name = "lastName" /></td>
18.             </tr>
19.             <tr>
20.                 <td colspan = "2" style = "border: none;"></td>
21.             </tr>
22.             <tr>
23.                 <td style = "border: none;">User Name: </td>
24.                 <td style = "border: none;"><input type = "text" ⏎
                        name = "userName" /></td>
25.             </tr>
26.             <tr>
27.                 <td colspan = "2" style = "border: none;"></td>
28.             </tr>
29.             <tr>
30.                 <td style = "border: none;">Password:</td>
31.                 <td style = "border: none;"><input type="password" ⏎
                        name = "passWord" /></td>
32.             </tr>
33.             <tr>
34.                 <td colspan = "2" style = "border: none;"></td>
35.             </tr>
36.             <tr>
37.                 <td style = "border: none;"> </td>
38.                 <td style = "border: none;"><input style = "margin: ⏎
                        5px 0px 5px 0px;" type = "submit" ⏎
                        name = "frmAddUser" value = "Create ⏎
                        User Account" /></td>
39.             </tr>
40.             </table>
41.             </form> <!-- close insert form -->
42.         </div>
43.    <?php include ('include/footer.php'); ?>
```

This page creates a form with four input boxes for a new player to enter his or her full name and login information. It includes the header.php file (line 1) and a second file, addUser.php (line 2) which will be created later. Once the form has been completed by the new player and the submit button is clicked, the form's action sends the information to the server (line 6). The footer.php file is also included (line 43).

For your convenience, before creating the login page and the page that will add the new player to the database, we will repeat the code for the header.php and footer.php files here. Both of these files should reside in the include folder.

The header.php File:

```
1.   <html>
2.       <head>
3.           <title>Greg's Games</title>
4.           <link href = "css/greg.css" rel = "stylesheet" ↵
                     type = "text/css" />
5.           <script language = "JavaScript" type = "text/javascript" ↵
                     src = "assets/scripts/scripts.js"></script>
6.       </head>
7.       <body>
8.       <div id = "header">
9.           <div id = "nav">
10.              <img src = "images/superhero.jpg" />
11.              <p><a href = "index.php">Greg's Game Home</a></p>
12.              <p><a href = "index.php">Sign In</a></p>
13.              <p><a href = "addUser.php">Create User ↵
                        Account</a></p>
14.              <p><a href = "games.php">Play a Game</a></p>
15.              <p><a href = "index.php">About Greg</a></p>
16.              <p><a href = "contact.php">Contact Us</a></p>
17.          </div>
18.          <div id = "banner" class = "banner">
19.              <h1 align = "center"><em>Greg's Gambits</em></h1>
20.              <h2 align = "center"><em>Games for ↵
                        Everyone!</em></h2>
21.          </div>
22.      </div>
```

Notice that this header file includes a link to a JavaScript page, scripts.js, which is in a folder named scripts in the assets folder. This page will include various snippets of JavaScript code that will be required in different pages on the site. Here is another good reason to separate out a header file that will be included in all pages. By including the link once in the header.php file, we can add JavaScript wherever needed and know that all pages have access to it. Also, if we need to add a JavaScript function, we can add it to the scripts.js file and know that it will be included wherever needed.

The footer.php File:

```
1.   <div style = "clear: both;" id = "banner" class = "banner">
2.       <p>Copyright &copy; 2013 Greg's Gambits<br />
3.       <a href = "mailto:gregory@gambits.net"> ↵
                        gregory@gambits.net</a></p>
4.   </div>
5.   </body>
```

Connecting to the Database Using the connectDB.php File: This page will be called from the next page where we will actually add the new user. This code will check that a connection to the server can be made. It creates a variable, **$dbConn** that includes the values of the host (for us, this is localhost), the user who has rights to add to the database (in this case our user uses lizard2 as a username) and that user's password (which, here, is lizard). If you recreate this page, you will want to put in your own username and password and be sure that, in phpMyAdmin, this user has been given privileges to add to the database.

If a connection is made, a new variable, **$dbObj**, now takes the value of the requested database. In our case, this is the gregs_gambits database. This code is identical to the code for the connectDB.php file created in an earlier example.

```php
1.  <?php
2.      $dbConn = mysql_connect('localhost', 'lizard2', 'lizard');
3.      if (!$dbConn)
4.      {
5.          die('Could not connect: ' . mysql_error());
6.      }
7.      $dbObj = mysql_select_db(' gregs_gambits', $dbConn);
8.  ?>
```

If a connection cannot be made, the die() method will display the message to the user that a connection was not possible and will display whatever error caused the problem, using the mysql_error() method. If a connection is made, the **$dbObj** and **$dbConn** variables are now available for use in the addUser.php page which we create following the closeDB.php file.

Closing the Connection Using the closeDB.php File   This page will be called whenever the work extracting information from a database or sending information to a database is completed. The code is repeated here. Both the opening and closing files—connectDB.php and closeDB.php—should be stored in the include folder. This file is only three lines:

```php
1.  <?php
2.      mysql_close($dbConn);
3.  ?>
```

The addUser.php File: This page contains most of the PHP code that is used to take the information a new player enters and add it to the database if necessary. The file name of this page is addUser.php and it belongs in the assets folder of the greg folder. The code is as follows, with comments added within the page and additional explanations after the code.

```php
1.  <?php
2.      include("include/connectDB.php");
3.      // variables from connectDB.php: $dbConn, the connection object
4.      if(isset($_POST['frmAddUser']))
5.      {
6.          $returnToLogin = false;
7.          $dbObj = mysql_select_db('gregs_gambits', $dbConn);
8.          $sqlStatement = "SELECT * FROM users";
9.      /*the next line loads a variable, $users, with the ↵
        result of a SQL query that selects values from the ↵
        users table */
10.         $users = mysql_query($sqlStatement, $dbConn);
11.         while($row = mysql_fetch_array($users))
12.         {
13.             if($row['user_Name'] == $_POST['userName'] ↵
                    && $returnToLogin == false)
```

```
14.                   {
15.                         echo "<script>alert('Username already ⏎
                                  exists. Try a new one.'); ⏎
                                  location.href = '../greg/newUser.php'; ⏎
                                  </script>";
16.                         $returnToLogin = true;
17.                   } // end if to check if userName already exits
18.                   elseif($returnToLogin==false && $row['first_Name'] ⏎
                                  = $_POST['firstName'] && ⏎
                                  $row['last_Name'] == ⏎
                                  $_POST['lastName'])
19.                   {
20.                         echo "<script>alert('You are already a ⏎
                                  member. Please log in.'); ⏎
                                  location.href = ../greg/index.php'; ⏎
                                  </script>";
21.                         $returnToLogin = true;
22.                   } // end if to check name already exists
23.             } // end while to sift through all records
24.             if($returnToLogin == false)
25.             {
26.                   $sqlStatement = "INSERT INTO users (first_Name, ⏎
                                  last_Name, user_Name, password) ⏎
                                  VALUES ('$_POST[firstName]', ⏎
                                  '$_POST[lastName]','$_POST ⏎
                                  [userName]','$_POST[passWord]')";
27.                   if (!mysql_query($sqlStatement,$dbConn))
28.                   {
29.                         die('Error could not add: ' . mysql_error());
30.                   }
31.                   echo "<script>alert('User has been added. ⏎
                                          Please log in.') ⏎
                                          location.href = ⏎
                                          '../greg/index.php';</script>";
32.             } // end if returnToLogin == false
33.       } // end if isset
34.       include("include/closeDB.php");
35.  ?>
```

After the connection is made (line 2), line 4 checks to see if the form action has been initiated. If this is true (i.e., isset($_POST['frmAddUser'])) then a new variable, $returnToLogin is declared and set, initially, to false. This will serve as a flag.

There are three possible outcomes when comparing the rows in the users table of the database with the player's entries: either a player with the same username but different first and last names already exists, or a player with the same username and same first and last names already exists (i.e., this person has already set up an account), or there are no matches (i.e., this is a new player with a username that has not been taken). This is what we are checking on lines 11–23.

Line 11 begins a while loop that checks all the rows in the users table. Line 13 begins an if clause that checks a row to see if the username given ($_POST['userName']) matches one entry in the table ($row['userName']) and the flag, $returnToLogin, is still false. This means that this username has already been used. If this is all true, line 15 uses JavaScript to send an alert to the player that

he or she needs to pick a different username. It also sends the player back to the
newUser.php page and ends the JavaScript. Line 16 sets the flag to true. Now the
while loop will end without going through the rest of the table.

If this clause is not executed, the elseif clause on line 18 checks the following
conditions:

- is the flag still false? AND
- is the first name in the row being inspected ($row['first_Name']) the same as
  the first name of this player ($_POST['firstName'])? AND
- is the last name in the row under inspection ($row['last_Name']) the same as
  the last name of this player ($_POST['lastName'])?

If all these things are true, we know that this player has already created an account.
An alert informs the player (line 20) and sends him or her back to the login page,
index.php. The flag is now set to true. This ensures that the while loop will end.

However, if neither the if or elseif clauses have been executed, we know that
the person entering the information is truly a new user and should be added to the
database. The if clause on line 24 checks to ensure the $returnToLogin flag is still
false. If so, line 26 uses a SQL statement to insert the new values into the appropriate fields in the users table. The last possibility, that, for some reason, this player
cannot be added to the database, line 29 sends that message to the player along with
the MySQL reason for the error.

Finally, if all goes well and this is really a new user, the information will be added to
a new row in the users table and line 31 sends a JavaScript alert to the player that
he or she has been added to the Greg's Gambits database. The player is then sent
to the index.php page to log in and begin using the site. Line 34 includes the page,
closeDB.php, to close the connection to the database.

Testing It

At this point the index.php page looks like this:

If our new player, Pat Pennyweather, does not have an account, he can click the Not a member? Create an account now. link and will be taken to the following page, addUser.php. Initially, the page looks like this:

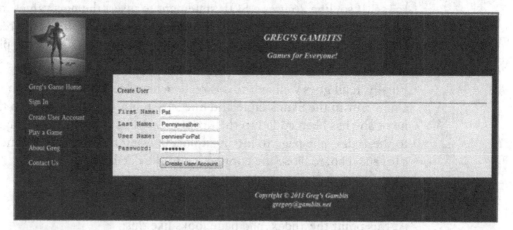

If Pat Pennyweather enters his first and last names and wants penniesForPat as a username and pat^345 as a password, the display will be as follows:

Assuming Pat has not previously created an account, when the CreateUser Account button is clicked, the new account will be created, Pat will receive a confirmation alert, and the display will be as follows:

When `Pat` clicks the `OK` button, he will be redirected to the original login page, `index.php`. Then, when `Pat` logs in with his username and password, he will receive the following `alert`:

We will create a page with a player's information and give `Pat` the choice of several games or the option to log off. This new page, `userPage.php` will look as shown, with `Pat Pennyweather's` information. The `password`, for obvious reasons, is masked. But before we create this page we will try a few more login options to check that our `addUser.php` page works correctly.

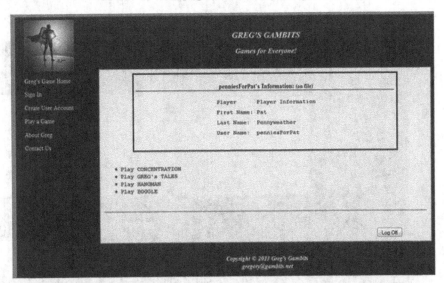

Let's assume that `Priscilla Patterson` wants to sign up at `Greg's Gambits`. She always uses `penniesForPat` as her username so that's what she enters on the `addUser.php` page, along with her name and her chosen password, `PrisCat1`.

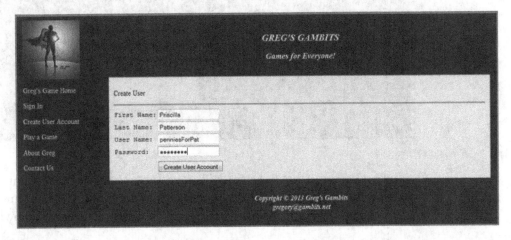

After clicking the Create User Account button, she gets the following alert and then is redirected to the previous page to retry:

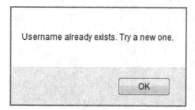

After clicking the OK button, she is returned to the newUser.php page. At this time, if she enters Priscilla Patterson, a new username, dollarsForPat, her original password, PrisCat1, and then clicks Create User Account, her account will be successfully created and she will be prompted to log in:

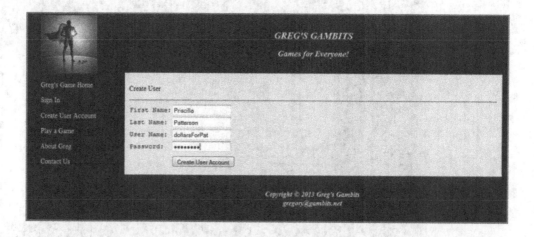

Now let's assume that Pat's sister, Patty, wants to set up an account. All her friends call her Pat and she has been signing her name as Pat for a long time. She wants to use babyPat as a username and password. She will receive the following alert after entering `Pat` for a first name, `Pennyweather` for a last name, `babyPat` as a username, and `babyPat` as a password:

. . . but when she tries to log in on the `index.php` page, using `babyPat` as both username and password, she will get the following:

Clicking `OK` will take her back to the login page. There are other things we can do to make this site more realistic but they are beyond the scope of this text. With your current knowledge, you could create pages to check if a player remembered a correct username but forgot his or her password or if a user forgot both but already has an account. Then, after using the features we will discuss in the `Carla's Classroom` section, you could send an email to the user with a username and/or password reminder.

The New Beginning: The `index.php` Page

Our new `index.php` page contains some significant new PHP concepts. It also links to another page which is necessary to start a session for a player, validate that player, and allow the rest of the session to continue. So we will begin with a discussion about sessions.

The Session   Each time a player logs into a site, a session begins. A PHP **session** begins when the player logs in and ends when he or she logs off. The session variable, `$_SESSION`, is used to store information about the user or to change settings for that user during the session. This variable (which is, as all superglobals, actually an array) holds information about one user and the information is available to all pages in one application. When a session is started, in this case, certain information will be retrieved from the `users` table in the database and stored in `$_SESSION` to make that information available to all the pages throughout the session. For each of our sessions, the `$_SESSION` values should include the player's first and last names, username, and user ID. Later, after the player has played a game, the user ID can be used to identify which score should be updated in the `game_boggle` table of the database.

The `index.php` Page   This page is stored in the `gregs_games` folder in `htdocs` but not in any subfolder. The code for the `index.php` page is as follows:

```php
1.  <?php include ('assets/logIn.php'); ?>
2.  <?php include ('include/header.php'); ?>
```

```
3.          <div id = "content">
4.          <p>Log In </p>
5.          <hr />
6.          <form action = "<?php echo $_SERVER['PHP_SELF']; ?>" method = ↵
                             "post" onsubmit = "return ↵
                             validate_loginForm(this);">
7.              <table>
8.              <tr>
9.                  <td style = "border: none;">User Name: </td>
10.                 <td style = "border: none;"><input id="idUserName" ↵
                             type = "text" name = "userName" /></td>
11.             </tr>
12.             <tr>
13.                 <td style = "border: none;">Password:</td>
14.                 <td style = "border: none;"><input id="idPassWord" ↵
                             type = "password" name = "passWord" /></td>
15.             </tr>
16.             <tr>
17.                 <td style = "border: none;"> </td>
18.                 <td style = "border: none;"><input type = "submit" ↵
                             name = "frmLogin" /></td>
19.             </tr>
20.             <tr>
21.                 <td colspan="2" style="border: none;"><br /><hr /> ↵
                             <a class="contentAnchor" style="margin- ↵
                             top: 15px;" href = "addUser.php"> Not a ↵
                             member? Create an account now.</a> ↵
                             <br /></td>
22.             </tr>
23.             </table>
24.         </form>
25.         <br /><hr />
26.     </div>
27.     <?php include ('include/footer.php'); ?>
```

Most of this code is clear. Lines 1, 2, and 27 include the necessary files. Line 6 needs some explanation. The form action is "<?php echo $_SERVER['PHP_SELF']; ?>". This statement sends the computer to the logIn.php page where the session variables are defined. We will create that page next. The form method is "post". The onsubmit action is "return validate_loginForm(this);". This JavaScript function is included in the scripts.js page and we will create it below.

The *logIn.php* Page

```
1.  <?php
2.  session_start();  // BEGIN session for User
3.  include("include/connectDB.php");
4.  if(isset($_POST['frmLogin']))
5.  {
6.      $sqlStatement = "SELECT * FROM users";
7.      $users = mysql_query($sqlStatement, $dbConn);
8.      if (!$users)
9.      {
10.         die('Error: ' . mysql_error());
```

```
11.        }
12.        while($row = mysql_fetch_array($users))
13.        {
14.            if($row['user_Name'] == $_POST['userName'] && ⏎
                                $row['password'] == ⏎
                                $_POST['passWord'])
15.            {
16.                $_SESSION['userID'] = $row['user_ID'];
17.                $_SESSION['user'] = $row['user_Name'];
18.                $_SESSION['userFirstName'] = $row['first_Name'];
19.                $_SESSION['userLastName'] = $row['last_Name'];
20.                echo "<script>alert('Login successful!'); ⏎
                                location.href = 'userPage.php'; ⏎
                                </script>";
21.            } //end if to check if username & password match DB entry
22.        } // end while to sift through all records
23.        echo '<script>alert("Login failed."); location.href = ⏎
                                "index.php";</script>';
24.    } // end if isset
25.    include("include/closeDB.php");
26.    ?>
```

Line 2 starts a session using the session_start() PHP method.

The *session_start()* Method and the *$_SESSION* Superglobal   Each time a player logs into the site, a session must begin. The PHP function, **session_start()** will begin a session the first time it is encountered. From now on, any page that relates to this session will begin with session_start() and it will resume the session that has been started. The session variable, **$_SESSION**, stores information about this player and can be used to change settings for that player (such as updating a game score) during the session.

Lines 6 and 7 create a SQL statement to go to the users table of the gregs_gambits database. The while loop on lines 12–22 checks the values entered which are all elements of the **$_SESSION** array ('userID', 'user', 'userFirstName', and 'userLastName') against the value of all the rows in that table. If a match is found, the "Login successful!" alert is displayed (line 20) and the user is redirected to the userPage.php. If no match is found, line 23 displays a failed login alert and the player is redirected back to the index.php page where he or she can try again.

The *validate_loginForm(thisform)*, *validate_userName()*, and *validate_passWord()* JavaScript Functions   The following JavaScript code will validate the username and password for a player who attempts to log in. Alerts will display when either field is invalid.

```
1.    var gatherInvalids = new Array(); //alerts for invalid entries
2.    function validate_loginForm(thisform)
3.    {
4.        with (thisform)
5.        {
6.            validate_userName(userName);
7.            validate_passWord(passWord);
8.        }
```

```
9.          if (gatherInvalids.length)
10.         {
11.             var displayInvalids = '';
12.             var count;
13.             for (count = 0; count < gatherInvalids.length; ↵
                                         count++)
14.             {
15.                 displayInvalids += gatherInvalids[count] + "\n";
16.             }
17.             alert(displayInvalids);
18.             document.getElementById("idUserName").innerHTML="";
19.             document.getElementById("idPassword").innerHTML="";
20.             displayInvalids = '';
21.             gatherInvalids = [];
22.             return false;
23.         }
24.     } // close validate form
25.     function validate_userName(field)
26.     {
27.         with(field)
28.         {
29.             if(value.length > 29)
30.             {
31.                 gatherInvalids.push("username length cannot ↵
                                    exceed 30 characters");
32.             }
33.             if(value.length < 1)
34.             {
35.                 gatherInvalids.push("Please enter a username.");
36.             }
37.         }
38.     } // end function to check username entered and length
39.     function validate_passWord(field)
40.     {
41.         with(field)
42.         {
43.             if(value.length > 7)
44.             {
45.                 gatherInvalids.push("Password length cannot ↵
                                    exceed 8 characters");
46.             }
47.             if(value.length < 1)
48.             {
49.                 gatherInvalids.push("Please enter a password.");
50.             }
51.         }
52.     }// end function to check password
```

This code becomes part of the scripts.js page that is included with all pages on the site. There are three functions here. The validate_loginForm() function receives the form name from the index.php page. It calls on two other functions—validate_userName() and validate_passWord(). The with keyword is a new JavaScript reserved word and it is described here.

The with() Reserved Word (Keyword)   The **with() reserved word** (or keyword) allows you to leave the object name off the front of all property and method references within a block of code. All the references within the block are assumed to be properties or methods of the object specified in the with() statement. When the with() reserved word is used, it knows to apply statements to the argument that it is working with. Therefore, given the following code (lines 27–32):

```
27.  with(field)
28.  {
29.      if(value.length > 29)
30.      {
31.          gatherInvalids.push("User name length cannot ...");
32.      }
```

The **field** argument refers to the argument passed into the function on line 25. In this case, the **field** is username. Thus, because of how the with() statement works, **value** on line 29 means the value of username. Using the with() statement can be a convenient way to shorten your code so you do not have to add the object name to all of the references.

The three functions, validate_loginForm(thisform), validate_userName(), and validate_passWord() complete the following tasks:

- Line 6 calls validate_username()
  - □ If the username entered exceeds the 30-character limit (line 29), the first element of the **gatherInvalids** array will be the message that a username must be no more than 30 characters.
  - □ If nothing has been entered (**value**.length < 1) (line 33) the message will be to enter a username.
- When this function ends, line 7 will call validate_passWord().
  - □ This function is similar to validate_userName() but checks to make sure the password does not exceed eight characters and that a password has been entered (lines 43 and 44).
- After the username and password validation has been completed, line 9 checks to see if there are any messages to display—that is, if **gatherInvalids**.length exists.
  - □ If so, the messages are displayed (lines 11–19), the **gatherInvalids** array is emptied (line 21) and the function ends.

Creating the User Information Page

Once a player has reached the userPage.php page, he or she can click a game to play. Since we are not developing any further functionality, we will simply create the userPage.php. Creating pages to allow the player to play games and have the database keep track of scores, number of games played, and more, is left for a more advanced course. This is the code for the page that displays the player's information and sets up the player to play games.

```
1.  <?php include ('assets/userPage.php'); ?>
2.  <?php include ('include/header.php'); ?>
3.  <div id = "content">
4.      <div style="width: 80%; border:3px solid black; padding: 5px; ↵
                     background-color: #C3F9FF;">
5.          <h3 class = "phpH3">
6.              <?php echo $_SESSION['user']; ?>'s Information: (on ↵
```

```
                                                      file)</h3>
7.              <table style = "margin: 0px auto 0px auto;">
8.              <tr>
9.                  <td>Player</td>
10.                 <td>Player Information</td>
11.             </tr>
12.             <tr>
13.                 <td>First Name: </td>
14.                 <td><?php echo $_SESSION['userFirstName']; ?></td>
15.             </tr>
16.             <tr>
17.                 <td>Last Name: </td>
18.                 <td><?php echo $_SESSION['userLastName']; ?></td>
19.             </tr>
20.             <tr>
21.                 <td>User Name: </td>
22.                 <td><?php echo $_SESSION['user']; ?></td>
23.             </tr>
24.             <tr>
25.                 <td colspan="2" style="border: none;"> </td>
26.             </tr>
27.             </table>
28.         </div>
29.         <br />
30.         <ul>
31.             <li><a class = "contentAnchor" href = ↵
                            "game_Concentration.php"> Play ↵
                            CONCENTRATION</a></li>
32.             <li><a class = "contentAnchor" href = "game_Tales.php"> ↵
                            Play GREG's TALES</a></li>
33.             <li><a class="contentAnchor" href="game_Hangman.php"> ↵
                            Play HANGMAN</a></li>
34.             <li><a class = "contentAnchor" href = "game_Boggle.php"> ↵
                            Play BOGGLE</a></li>
35.         </ul>
36.         <br /><hr /><br />
37.         <p>
38.             <input style="float: right; margin-right: 60px;" name = ↵
                            "btnSubmit" type="submit" value="Log ↵
                            Off" onclick="logOff(); return false;" />
39.         </p>
40.     </div>
41.     <?php include ('include/footer.php'); ?>
```

Most of this code is straightforward. The first PHP page that is included is a second page also named `userPage.php` but is stored in `assets`. This page simply keeps the session going. The page code looks like this:

```
1.  <?php
2.      // Resume session
3.      session_start();
4.  ?>
```

While it may seem strange to name two pages with the same file name, this can be helpful in the future. You probably already see how confusing the structure of the site can become. By having pages that relate to each other but are in different folders with the same file names, you will be able to see the relationships between pages more easily. The header.php and footer.php pages are also included and these will be included in virtually all the site pages.

Lines 7–27 create a table with four rows and two columns to display the information about the player who has logged in. Lines 30–35 create a list of the games that the Greg's Gambits site offers and each item on the list links to one of the games. We've only listed four games here but more can easily be added. The **$_SESSION** superglobal retrieves the player's information from the database and displays it on the screen.

Let's Play a Game!

If you store the games you have created throughout the text in the games folder in your greg folder, you will be able to create an account, log in to the site, and play a game. However, you will need to set up each game to be part of this site in htdocs. Here is a sample, using Boggle, of how to edit your game files and store them.

We'll start by repeating the Boggle game here, with PHP code added. When a valid user has logged in and clicks Play Boggle from the userPage.php, a redesigned page will appear. First, we need some PHP to acknowledge that the player is a registered user. This page is named game_Boggle.php and is stored in the greg folder but not in any subfolder.

```
1.   <?php
2.        include ('assets/userPage.php');
3.        include ('include/header.php');
4.   ?>
5.      <div id = "content">
6.          <h2>BOGGLE</h2>
7.          <h3><?php echo $_SESSION['user']; ?>'s Session</h3>
8.          <hr />
9.          <p>The object of the game is to create as many words as ↵
                    you can, in a given time limit, from the ↵
                    letters shown below. When you are ready to ↵
                    begin, click the button.</p>
10.         <p><input type = "button" value = "begin the game" ↵
                    onclick = "boggle();" /></p>
11.         <h2><br />Letters you can use:<br />
12.             <div id = "letters"> </div><br />
13.         </h2>
14.         <h2>Your words so far: <br />
15.             <div id = "entries"> </div><br />
16.         </h2>
17.         <h2>Results:<br />
18.             <div id = "result"> </div>
19.         </h2>
20.         <hr />
21.         <p style = "float: right; margin-right: 60px;"> <input ↵
                    name = "btnSubmit" type = "submit" value ↵
                    = "Log Off" onclick = "logOff(); return ↵
                    false;" /></p>
22.      </div>
23.   <?php include ('include/footer.php'); ?>
```

Lines 2, 3, and 23 include the necessary PHP files. Line 7 uses the session variable to personalize this session for the player. If our player, Pat Pennyweather, logs in and clicks Play BOGGLE, the screen will display as follows:

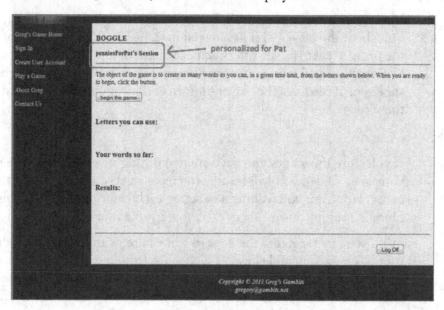

Once Pat begins to play, the Boggle game works with JavaScript, as created in Chapter 9. We have put the JavaScript code for this game inside the scripts.js page and, since we include the header.php file which contains a link to scripts.js, the Boggle game code is available to this page.

Later, you can add code to store Pat's results and send them to the boggle table in the database. Two nonfunctional buttons are included—Submit Boggle Score and Log Off—which can be used when you become proficient with PHP and SQL. If Pat plays the game once, the display will now look like this:

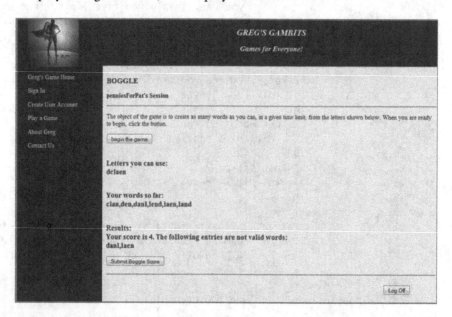

Putting It All together

In this section, we will review the files needed for this project, include a brief summary of their functions, and describe where they should be saved in the folder structure. If you are following along and creating this database and these files, be sure your structure matches this one:

- All files must be inside the htdocs folder of the XAMPP program on your computer.
- All files for this project will be stored in a subfolder in htdocs called greg.
- The following files are needed:
    - □ index.php is the opening page. It is in the top-level greg folder and it calls the logIn.php page.
    - □ greg.css is the style sheet and is in the css folder.
    - □ superhero.jpg is in the images folder.
    - □ All the images that go with each game should also be in the images folder.
    - □ newUser.php creates a new user and is in the top-level greg folder. It creates a new user.
    - □ header.php is in the include folder and links to the the style sheet (greg.css) and the JavaScript scripts (scripts.js).
    - □ footer.php is in the include folder.
    - □ connectDB.php is in the include folder and creates a connection to the database.
    - □ closeDB.php is in the include folder and closes the connection with the database.
    - □ userPage.php is in the top-level greg folder. It includes the userPage.php which is stored in assets to keep the session going. This page displays the information for a valid user who has logged in and allows the user to select a game to play.
    - □ userPage.php is the second page with this file name but is stored in the assets folder. It keeps a session open.
    - □ addUser.php is in the assets folder. It makes a connection to the database and adds information from newUser.php to the database. Then it closes the connection.
    - □ logIn.php is in the assets folder. It connects to the database, checks that the login information is valid, and closes the connection.
    - □ game_Boggle.php is the page that allows the user to play Boggle and it is in the top-level greg folder. It calls the scripts.js page to play the game and it displays game information as the game is being played.
    - □ scripts.js contains all the JavaScript functions needed throughout the site. It is stored in the scripts subfolder of assets.

Carla's Classroom: Using PHP to Send Student Reports by Email

In this section, we will create a database for Carla where she can store information about her students and, eventually, tap into the information she requires. For now, we will allow her to enter a student's name, three grades (Math, Reading, and

Writing), and some comments. Then, she will use PHP to call up that information from the database and send it, by email, to the student's parents, as a report card.

Creating the Database

We will name our database `carlas_class`. Using phpMyAdmin, create a database with one table and eight fields. The table and the fields are listed below. If a field from XAMPP is not listed, leave the default value:

- Table: `students`
  - □ Fields:
    - student_ID: type: INT, size: 4, attributes: unsigned, index: primary, AUTO_INCREMENT
    - last_Name: type: VARCHAR, size: 20
    - first_Name: type: VARCHAR, size: 20
    - contact_Email: type: VARCHAR, size: 40
    - grade_Math: type: FLOAT, size: 5
    - grade_Read type: FLOAT, size: 5
    - grade_Write: type: FLOAT, size: 5
    - comment: type: VARCHAR, size: 300

The Folders   Create the following folders, as you did for `Greg's Gambits` and be sure they are in the `htdocs` folder of XAMPP.

- The top folder is `carlas_class`.
- Subfolders are `assets`, `css`, `images`, and `include`.
- Put the style sheet, `carla.css`, into the `css` folder.
- Put the following images into the `images` folder: `carla_pic.jpg` and `owl_reading.jpg`.

Adding a Student to the Database

To add a record to Carla's database we need a form to allow her to enter the information, a connection to the database, and a file to insert the new record.

The `index.php` File   This page allows Carla to enter information about a specific student, which will then be added to the database. Since this page will not be seen by students, it is a stand-alone page. Therefore, we don't need all the links to other places on Carla's site so we will not use the header or footer files. We have included an image of Carla and her favorite owl, and we have used her style sheet for aesthetics, but there is no real need for special styles or images. The file will be a form where Carla can enter a student's name, grades, and comments she wants to send to the parent. The file name for this file is `index.php` and it is stored in the `carla` folder but not in any subfolder. The code is as follows:

```
1.   <?php include ('assets/insert.php'); ?>
2.   <html>
3.   <head>
4.        <title>Carla's Classroom | Add Students</title>
5.        <link href = "css/carla.css" rel = "stylesheet" type = ⏎
                                "text/css" />
```

```
6.    </head>
7.    <body>
8.        <div id = "container">
9.            <img src = "images/owl_reading.jpg" class="floatleft" />
10.           <h1 id = "logo"><em>Carla's Students</em></h1>
11.             <div id = "content">
12.                 <img src = "images/carla_pic.jpg" class = ↵
                                "floatleft" />
13.                 <div style = "width: 400px; float: right;">
14.                 <div style = "float: right; width: 400px; border: ↵
                                1px solid black; background- ↵
                                color: #FFEAA3; padding: 5px; ↵
                                margin-right: 50px;">
15.                 <p>Add Students Form </p><hr />
16.                 <form action="<?php echo $_SERVER['PHP_SELF']; ?>" ↵
                                method = "post">
17.                 <table>
18.                 <tr>
19.                     <td><p>Last name: </td>
20.                     <td><input type = "text" size = "30" name = ↵
                                "lastName" /></p></td>
21.                 </tr>
22.                 <tr>
23.                     <td><p>First name: </td>
24.                     <td><input type = "text" size = "30" name = ↵
                                "firstName" /></p></td>
25.                 </tr>
26.                 <tr>
27.                     <td><p>Email: </td>
28.                     <td><input type = "text" size = "30" name = ↵
                                "contactEmail" /></p></td>
29.                 </tr>
30.                 <tr>
31.                     <td><p>grade_Math: </td>
32.                     <td><input type = "text" size = "30" name = ↵
                                "gradeMath" /></p></td>
33.                 </tr>
34.                 <tr>
35.                     <td><p>grade_Read: </td>
36.                     <td><input type = "text" size = "30" name = ↵
                                "gradeRead" /></p></td>
37.                 </tr>
38.                 <tr>
39.                     <td><p>grade_Write: </td>
40.                     <td><input type = "text" size = "30" name = ↵
                                "gradeWrite" /></p></td>
41.                 </tr>
42.                 <tr>
43.                     <td><p>Comments: </td>
44.                     <td><textarea rows = "6" cols = "23" name = ↵
                                "comment"> </textarea></p></td>
45.                 </tr>
46.                 <tr>
47.                     <td colspan = "2" style = "text-align: ↵
                                center;"><input type = "submit" ↵
                                name = "frmAddStudent" /></td>
48.                 </tr>
```

```
49.                     </table>
50.                     </form>
51.                     <hr />
52.                     <p><a href = "sendEmail.php">Send a report by ↵
                            email</a></p>
53.                     </div>
54.                     </div>
55.                 </div>
56.             </div>
57.     </body>
58.     </html>
```

This script creates a form with input boxes for Carla to enter the student's name, grades, and her own comments. Line 47 creates a submit button that, when clicked, will send the information to the database. Line 16 is the form action and method. The method is the familiar "post" method. The form action says (echo $_SERVER['PHP_SELF'];) to send the information from the form to the same server that this page is on. Line 52 links to the next page we will create which will allow Carla to send an email to a parent.

The insert.php file has been included with this file (line 1). This is how the information will be added to the database. We will create this file next. At this point, even though it is not yet functional, if you enter this code and run it from localhost, your page will look like this:

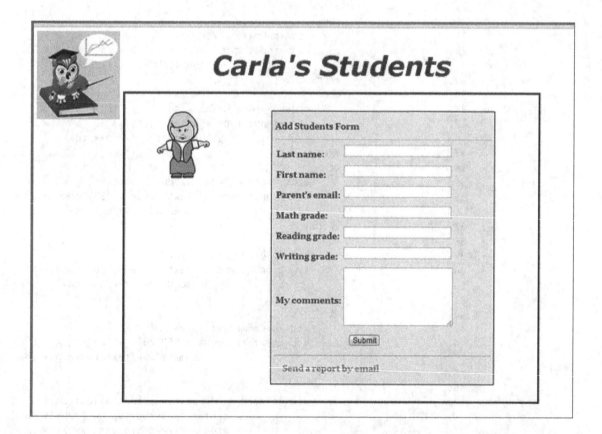

Inserting a New Record: Making the Connection   The insert.php file takes the information entered on the form and sends it to the database. If the connection can be made, if the database exists, and the fields are valid, Carla will get a message that the new record has been created and added to the database. If there is a problem, a message to that effect will be displayed. To achieve this we need to connect to the database and, after updating the database, close the connection. These two files, connectDB.php and closeDB.php, are similar to those we created for Greg's Gambits but we will show the code here:

connectDB.php:

```
1.   <?php
2.       $dbConn = mysql_connect('localhost', 'lizard2', 'lizard');
3.       if (!$dbConn)
4.       {
5.           die('Could not connect: ' . mysql_error());
6.       }
7.   ?>
```

Recall that the user who has rights to add to this database must be included (line 2) as well as the location of the database ('localhost') and the user's password. In our case, the designated user's username is 'lizard2' and this user's password is 'lizard'. The file, connectDB.php, should be stored in the include folder.

closeDB.php:

```
1.   <?php
2.       mysql_close($dbConn);
3.   ?>
```

This file should also be stored in the include folder.

The insert.php *File*   This file inserts information into the appropriate fields in the carlas_class database. Comments have been included as well as explanation following the code.

```
1.   ?php
2.       include("include/connectDB.php");
3.   // variables from connectDB.php: $dbConn
4.       if(isset($_POST['frmAddStudent']))
5.       {
6.           // the $dbObj sets the active MySQL database, ↵
                carlas_class
7.           $dbObj = mysql_select_db('carlas_class', $dbConn);
8.           // Sets the variable, $sqlStatement, equal to the MySQL ↵
                       query that is built on the right side ↵
                       of the '=' sign.
9.           $sqlStatement = "INSERT INTO students (last_Name, ↵
                       first_Name, contact_Email, grade_Math, ↵
                       grade_Read , grade_Write , comment) ↵
                       VALUES('$_POST[lastName]', ↵
                       '$_POST[firstName]', ↵
                       '$_POST[contactEmail] ↵
```

```
                               ','$_POST[gradeMath]', ↵
                               '$_POST[gradeRead]', ↵
                               '$_POST[gradeWrite]', ↵
                               '$_POST[comment]')"; ↵
10.          if (!mysql_query($sqlStatement,$dbConn))
11.          {
12.               die('Error: ' . mysql_error());
13.          }
14.          echo "<h2>RECORD ADDED</h2>";
15.          include("include/closeDB.php");
16.     }
17.  ?>
```

Line 4 checks to make sure data has been sent from the form. The isset() method will return true if data from frmAddStudent is in the **$_POST** superglobal.

Line 7 creates a variable, **$dbObj**, that uses the mysql_select_db() method to set the database being used. The database that is being used here is carlas_class and the **$dbConn** is the connection.

Line 9 has two parts. The left side of the '=' sign creates a PHP variable, **$sqlStatement**. This variable will hold the value of the MySQL query that is built on the right side of the '=' sign. In this case, we are inserting a record (i.e., a row) into the students table with the fields (i.e., columns) expressed in the first set of parenthesis, i.e. last_Name, first_Name, contact_Email and so on. These are field names in this table; each record in the table has these fields associated with it. The MySQL statement 'VALUES' tells MySQL that the following values will be inserted into their respective fields for this particular record; i.e., the value stored in **$_POST[lastName]** will be stored in the field 'last_name', the value stored in **$_POST[gradeMath]** will be stored in the field 'grade_Math', and so on for all seven fields. The only field that is not mentioned is the student_ID because this one is automatically incremented by MySQL each time a record is added. This is the result of denoting it the PRIMARY KEY and checking the Auto_Increment attribute.

Lines 10–13 check to see if the query was properly executed. If the result of mysql_query(**$sqlStatement,$dbConn**)is true, the query worked. The NOT operator will turn the true into a false and the if clause will be skipped. However, if the query fails it will return false and, because of the NOT operator, it will become true and the die() function will execute.

Line 14 displays a message to Carla that a record has been added and line 15 closes the connection to the database.

Here is what will happen if Carla enters the following for a student named Jean-Paul Lejeune who is a great math student (Math grade = 97.6) but not a particularly avid reader (Reading grade = 80.4) or writer (Writing grade = 73.9). Mr. and Mrs. Lejeune use lejeune@gmail.com for their email. Carla wants to encourage Jean-Paul to read more.

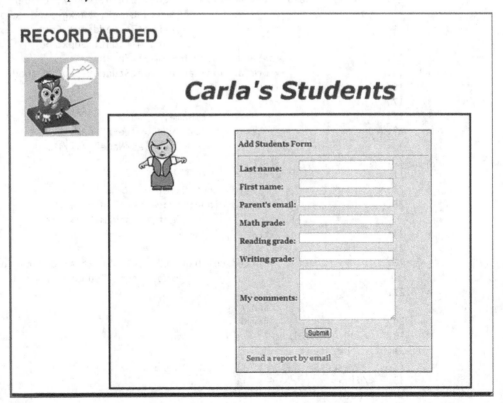

After entering the information, Carla clicks the submit button and the following screen displays:

Creating and Sending the Email

When Carla is ready, she can click the `Send a report by email` link at the bottom of this page and be connected to a page where she can enter a student's name and an email will automatically be generated and sent to that student's parent(s). This will require two pages—one for the form where Carla will enter the name of the student and one to create the email.

The sendEmail.php File   This page creates a short form, similar to the `index.php` page, which simply gets the name of a student and sends it on to be processed. It is stored in the `carla` folder but not in any subfolder. The code is as follows:

```
1.    <?php include('assets/insert.php'); ?>
2.    <html>
3.    <head>
4.        <title>Carla's Classroom | Send Student Reports</title>
5.        <link href = "css/carla.css" rel = "stylesheet" type = ↵
                            "text/css" />
6.    </head>
7.    <body>
8.    <div id = "container">
9.        <img src = "images/owl_reading.jpg" class = "floatleft" />
10.       <h1 id = "logo"><em>Carla's Students</em></h1>
11.       <div id = "content">
12.           <img src = "images/carla_pic.jpg" class = "floatleft" />
13.           <div style = "float: right; width: 400px; border: 1px ↵
                            solid black; background-color: ↵
                            #FFEAA3; padding: 5px; ↵
                            margin-right: 50px;">
14.               <p>Send report by email</p><hr />
15.               <form action="assets/getStudent.php" method="post">
16.               <table>
17.               <tr>
18.                   <td>Last Name: </td>
19.                   <td><input type = "text" name = ↵
                            "get_lastName" /></td>
20.               </tr>
21.               <tr>
22.                   <td>First Name: </td>
23.                   <td><input type="text" name = ↵
                            "get_firstName" /></td>
24.               </tr>
25.               <tr>
26.                   <td colspan="2" style="text-align: center;"> ↵
                            <input type="submit" /></td>
27.               </tr>
28.               </table>
29.               </form>
30.           </div>
31.       </div>
32.       </div>
33.   </div>
34.   </body>
35.   </html>
```

Except for the single PHP statement on line 1, this code is just an HTML table with a form for Carla to enter a chosen student's name. The form action, on line 15, sends the form information into a file named getStudent.php in the assets folder. We will create that file next. If coded, this file would now appear as shown below but will, as yet, do nothing.

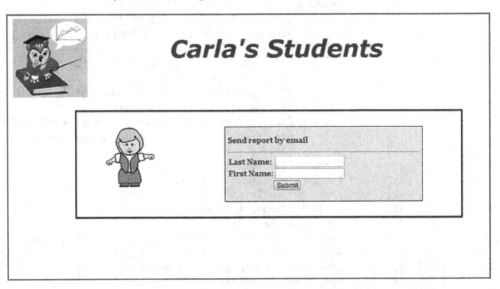

The *getStudent.php* File   This page is where the email is created. The page opens a connection to the host and then uses a SQL query to retrieve the information about the record associated with the name Carla entered. Finally, it creates an email message from the information in the record and sends it. This file is named getStudent.php and is stored in the assets folder. The code is as follows:

```
1.   <?php
2.       include("../include/connectDB.php");
3.       $dbObj = mysql_select_db('carlas_class', $dbConn);
4.       // builds a MySQL statement to get all field values from ↵
                    the record of the selected student.
5.       $sqlStatement = "SELECT * FROM students WHERE (last_Name ↵
                    = '$_POST[get_lastName]') AND (first_Name ↵
                    = '$_POST[get_firstName]')";
6.       //The mysql_query() processes the previous statement and ↵
                    stores the result in the '$result' variable.
7.       $result = mysql_query($sqlStatement, $dbConn);
8.       //The mysql_fetch_array() returns a row from a recordset ↵
                    as an  array.
9.       $studentRecord = mysql_fetch_array($result);
10.      if (!$studentRecord)
11.      {
12.          die('Error: ' . mysql_error());
13.      }
14.      $firstName = $studentRecord['first_Name'];
15.      $lastName = $studentRecord['last_Name'];
16.      $stuEmail = $studentRecord['contact_Email'];
17.      $mathGrade = $studentRecord['grade_Math'];
```

```
18.        $readGrade = $studentRecord['grade_Read'];
19.        $writeGrade = $studentRecord['grade_Write'];
20.        $stuComments = $studentRecord['comment'];
21.        //build the email to send
22.        $to = $studentRecord['contact_Email'];
23.        $subject = "Student's Report";
24.        $message = "<-- Course Grade Report --> \n ↵
               Student First Name: ".$_POST['get_firstName']. "\n ↵
               Student Last Name: " . $_POST['get_lastName'] . "\n ↵
               ------------------------------------------------- \n ↵
               Math Grade:   "  . $mathGrade . "\n ↵
               Reading Grade:  " . $readGrade . "\n ↵
               Writing Grade: " . $writeGrade . "\n ↵
               My comments: " . $stuComments . "\n ↵
               Email = " . $studentRecord['contact_Email'] . "\n ↵
               Feel Free to call me with any questions.\n ↵
               Carla";
25.        $from = "carla@carlasclass.com";
26.        $headers = "From:" . $from;
27.        //the PHP mail function
28.        mail($to,$subject,$message,$headers);
29.        echo "Mail Sent.";
30.        echo "<p>Student: " . $firstName . " " . $lastName . "</p>";
31.        echo "<p>Email: " . $stuEmail . "</p>";
32.        echo "<p>Math grade = " . $mathGrade . "</p>";
33.        echo "<p>Reading grade = " . $readGrade . "</p>";
34.        echo "<p>Writing grade = " . $writeGrade . "</p>";
35.        echo "<p>Carla's comments: " . $stuComments . "</p>";
36.        include("../include/closeDB.php");
37.    ?>
```

The first line of interest is line 5. This builds a MySQL statement that stores the result in the variable, **$sqlStatement**. The statement is a SELECT statement which tells MySQL to select FROM the students table the record where lastName = '$_POST[get_lastName]' and first_Name = '$_POST[get_firstName]'. The WHERE clause in the SQL statement is an instruction to select all the field values. These values come from the previous form in the sendEmail.php file.

Line 7 stores the result of the query in a variable named **$result**.

Line 9 stores an array that contains the values of **$result** in a new variable named **$studentRecord**. It uses the PHP mysql_fetch_array() method which makes the data received in the previous query more accessible.

Lines 10–13 check to make sure everything is working so far. If there are any problems, the process is aborted and a message is sent to Carla.

Lines 14–20 create new variables. Each variable holds the value of a single field in the row. Recall that **$studentRecord** is an array of the values of all the fields in the record under consideration. Therefore, for example, **$studentRecord['first_Name']** holds the value of the first name field in that specific record. Line 14 now assigns that value to **$firstName**. Similarly, **$studentRecord['comment']** holds the value of whatever is in the comment field of that record and this value is now stored in the **$stuComments** variable. We do this so we can build an email that makes sense to the recipient.

As we learned earlier in the chapter, the `mail()` method takes four parameters: **$to**, **$subject**, **$message**, and **$headers**. The values of those parameters are created on lines 22, 23, 24, and 26. Line 24 formats the message body of the email. All the information, including line breaks ('\n') are included in the variable **$message**. Line 25 creates a **$from** parameter which is optional.

The message is sent on line 28. Lines 29–35 are included simply to let Carla know what information was sent and also for us, to check that the correct information for the requested student was sent out.

We cannot see what this page looks like because it is a processing page. However, if Carla requests that an email be sent to the parents of the student we just added, `Jean-Paul Lejeune`, an email will go to his parents that looks like this:

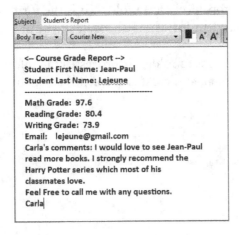

And Carla will see the following:

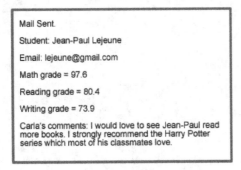

Putting It All Together

In this section, we will review the files needed for this project, include a brief summary of their functions, and describe where they should be saved in the folder structure. If you are following along and creating this database and these files, be sure your structure matches this one:

- All files must be inside the `htdocs` folder of the XAMPP program on your computer.
- A subfolder in `htdocs` called `carla` is where all the files for this project will be stored.

- The following files are needed:
  - ☐ index.php is the opening page. It is in the top-level carla folder and it calls the insert.php page. This is where Carla will enter student information.
  - ☐ carla.css is the style sheet and is in the css folder.
  - ☐ owl_reading.jpg and carla_pic.jpg are the two images used and are in the images folder.
  - ☐ insert.php processes the information entered from the index.php page and creates a new student record. It is in the assets folder.
  - ☐ connectDB.php is in the include folder and creates a connection to the database.
  - ☐ closeDB.php is in the include folder and closes the connection with the database.
  - ☐ sendEmail.php is in the top-level carla folder. It is the form that Carla uses to enter the name of a student for whom she wants to send out an email report.
  - ☐ getStudent.php is in the assets folder. It processes the information requested by sendEmail.php, and creates and sends an email.

Chapter Review and Exercises

Key Terms

$_COOKIE
$_POST
$_REQUEST
$_SERVER() method
$_SESSION
$domain cookie argument
$expire cookie argument
$headers (parameter of mail() method)
$httponly cookie argument
$key
$message (parameter of mail() method)
$name cookie argument
$path cookie argument
$secure cookie argument
$subject (parameter of mail() method)
$to (parameter of mail() method)
$value cookie argument
authentication cookie
cookie
define() method
die() method
field argument
fields
foreign key
httponly cookie
isset() method
mail() method

Michael Widenius
MySQL
mysql_connect() method
mysql_error() method
mysql_fetch_array() method
mysql_query() method
mysql_select_db() method
persistent cookie
PHP_SELF
phpMyAdmin
primary key
query
records
relational database
relational database management system (RDBMS)
resource
secure cookie
session
session cookie
session_start() method
setcookie() function
SQL (Structured Query Language)
third-party cookie
time() function
unique identifier
user account
user privileges
value
with() keyword

Review Exercises

Fill in the Blank

1. A _____ cookie remains on a user's computer for a specified length of time.

2. Superglobal variables, such as **$_COOKIE** or **$_POST** are actually _____ and not variables.

3. The _____ superglobal retrieves values entered by a user into form elements.

4. A unique identifier in a database is known as the _____ _____.

5. To post information from a form to a database located on a server on the same computer as the form file, use the _____ index of the **$_SERVER** superglobal.

True or False

6. T/F   A cookie can only be retrieved by the server that set it.

7. T/F   The only attribute of the setcookie() function that is not optional is the name.

8. T/F   A cookie can be set in any place on an HTML page.

9. T/F   The foreach construct can be used in place of an if...else structure.

10. T/F   The isset() method only returns true or false.

11. T/F   The main drawback to using MySQL is that it can only be implemented through XAMPP.

12. T/F   The field attribute in a MySQL database that is automatically created each time a record is added is the UniqueID attribute.

13. T/F   If a field in a database is an integer and has a length of 3, this means it can range from 100–399.

14. T/F   The mysql_error() method takes two parameters: the name of the database and the name of the file where the error should be recorded.

15. T/F   The mysql_select_db() method takes two parameters: the database to select (required) and the connection (optional).

Short Answer

16. Create a cookie named 'birthday' that will store the user's birthday in the PHP variable **$bday**, and will expire when the browser is closed.

17. Redo Exercise 16 but have the cookie persist for a month (30 days).

18. Redo Exercise 17 but use the define() method to define a named constant, **MY_TIME**, to set the cookie to last 30 days.

Use the following cookie for Exercises 19–22:

```php
$color = "blue";
define ("YEAR", 60 * 60 * 24 * 365);
setcookie("pageColor", $color, time() + YEAR);
```

19. What is the name of this cookie?

20. What is the value of this cookie?

21. How long will this cookie last?

22. What would be displayed after the following statements are executed?

```php
<?php
    foreach($_COOKIE as $key => $value)
        print ("<p>$key; $value </p>");
?>
```

Use the following code for Exercises 23–25:

```
<body>
    <form method = "XXX" action = "XXX.php">
        <p>What do you want to be called?
        <input type = "text" name = "callMe" value = "" /></p>
        <p>What is your best friend's name?
        <input type = "text" name = "bestie" value = "" /></p>
        <p><input type = "submit" value = "submit" /></p>
    </form>
</body>
```

23. Fill in the "XXX"s in the form method and action so that the form will send this information to a PHP page named "meAndBff.php" which will set the cookies that have information about this user's name and best friend's name.

24. Write the code for the meAndBff.php page to set two cookies: one for the user's requested name and one for the name of the best friend. The cookies should expire in a week.

25. Add code to the page created in Exercise 24 to read the cookies that were created.

26. Create a PHP page to open a connection to a database named mybase which is located on the user's localhost. The user's username is dbQueen and the password is royalty. Be sure to include code to display a message if a connection with the database could not be made and display the reason for the connection problem.

27. Assuming you have installed and use XAMPP, describe how you can view the records in a table named scores in a MySQL database named math_tests.

28. If you have a table in a database that stores information about a doctor's patients, which of the following fields should be the primary key?

    patientLastName   patientFirstName   patientMedication
    patientNumber   patientApptDate   patientInsurance

29. Which fields must be included in the mail() method to send an email with PHP?

30. Given the following files for a site that uses a database for a doctor's office, identify which folders should hold which files:

folders:	files:
doctors	connectDB.php
assets	closeDB.php
scripts	index.php
css	doctor.css
images	drWho.jpg
include	drOffice.jpg
	docStuff.js
	headerDoc.php
	footerDoc.php
	addPatient.php
	sendBill.php

Programming Challenges

On Your Own

VideoNote
Creating Cookies with PHP
On_Your_Own_1_Cookies

1. Create a page that will request the following information from a user and will use this information to set cookies that expire in a week: user's name, user's age, and user's gender. Save your page with the file name cookiesOne.php. Submit your work as instructed by your teacher.

2. Add code to the page you created in Programming Challenge 1 that will use the cookies that were set to customize the user's page when the page is revisited within a week:
   - If the user's gender is male, the background color of the page should be orange with brown text.
   - If the user's gender is female, the background color of the page should be yellow with blue text.
   - If the user entered anything else or nothing, the background color of the page should be green with white text.

   Save your page with the file name custom.php. Submit your work as instructed by your teacher.

3. Create a database structure that holds information for a doctor's office. The doctor wants to store demographic information about patients (address, age, gender, marital status), medications dispensed (when, what, quantity), and billing information (amount billed, amount and date paid, insurance information). You do not have to create the database. Sketch out the structure as follows: There should be three tables and each record should have at least four fields. You must include the information given in this problem but you can add other information you feel is significant. Save this file as either an HTML page named doctors. html or a text file named doctors.txt. Submit your work as instructed by your teacher.

4. Create the database from Programming Challenge 3. Name the database doctorWho. Then create a page that allows Doctor Who's assistant to add a new patient record. You will need to give the assistant rights to this database. The assistant's username is 'helper' and the password is 'feelBetter'. For this to work, you will need to create several pages so be sure to include all of them when submitting your work. Name the main page addPatient.php. Submit your work as instructed by your teacher.

5. Add at least five records to the patients table in the doctorWho database you created in Programming Challenge 4. Now create a page that will display three or more fields from each of these records. The display should consist of, at a minimum, the patient's first and last names and a unique identifier. Name the page getPatient.php and be sure to include the necessary accompanying files when you submit your work. Submit your work as instructed by your teacher.

6. Create a page that will display all records from any one table from any database you have created in this chapter. Name this page getRecords.php and be sure to include any necessary accompanying files. Submit your work as instructed by your teacher.

Case Studies

Greg's Gambits

Using the Carla's Classroom project in the Putting It to Work section of this chapter as a guide, add to the Greg's Gambits site. Create pages that allow Greg to enter a player's name and generate an email to that player. First, you will have to add to the gregs_gambits database. Add a table named contact which contains the following fields: player's last name, first name, username, email address, and identification number. Next, create a web page that prompts Greg to enter a player's username. The following email should be generated:

- **$to:**   player's email address
- **$from:**   greg@gregsgambits.com
- **$subject:** Hello from Greg
- **$message:** Thank you for using my games!
                 Game Master, Greg
- **$headers:** From concatenated with **$from**

Save your page as send_mail.php. Be sure to include the necessary accompanying files. Submit your work as instructed by your teacher.

Carla's Classroom

If you have not created the carla_class database, create it now with the tables specified in the Putting It to Work section. Add a new table named projects. This table will have eight fields: the primary key (same as in the students table), a student's first and last name, comments, and four fields named project_1, project_2, project_3, project_4. Carla has her students complete four major projects throughout the year. Create a page that allows Carla to update a student's grade each time a project is completed. The file name of this page is projects.php.

Challenge: Add a new page, like the one in the Putting It to Work section, to allow Carla to email parents with updates on their child's progress. Save this page as project_email.php.

Be sure to include the necessary accompanying files. Submit your work as instructed by your teacher.

Lee's Landscape

Create a database for the Lee's Landscape business called landscape. The database should have at least two tables with, at minimum, the following fields:

Table customers: Fields:	Table billing: Fields:
customer_ID	customer_ID
customer_L_Name	customer_L_Name
customer_F_Name	service
customer_Title (Mr, Ms, Dr. etc,)	customer_bill
street_Address	amt_paid
city_State_Zip	bill_date
customer_Phone	date_paid
customer_Email	

Create a PHP page that will extract a customer's bill amount and the amount paid. Then it will calculate the amount due. If the amount due is greater than 0, an email should be generated and sent to the customer with that amount in the message. If the amount due is zero or there is a credit, generate a thank-you email that thanks the customer for his or her payment and expresses Lee's wishes for continued business with this customer.

Name the main page sendBill.php and be sure to include all the necessary accompanying files when you submit your work as instructed by your teacher.

Jackie's Jewelry

Using the files and the jackiejewelry database you created earlier in this chapter, create forms that will allow Jackie to populate her products table with the jewelry she sells and add to her orders table each time a customer places an order. You can populate these databases with as much data as you wish.

Be sure to create the files you need and store them in appropriate folders. Using everything you have learned so far, see how *few* files you can create by adding to or changing values in the files that are already created. Save the pages with appropriate file names. Submit your work as instructed by your teacher.

ASCII Characters

The ASCII Character Set: Nonprintable and Printable Characters

The ASCII Character Set			
Nonprintable ASCII Characters			
Decimal	Hexadecimal	Character	Description
0	0		null
1	1		start of heading
2	2		start of text
3	3		end of text
4	4		end of transmit
5	5		enquiry
6	6		acknowledge
7	7		audible bell
8	8		backspace
9	9		horizontal tab
10	A		line feed
11	B		vertical tab
12	C		form feed
13	D		carriage return
14	E		shift out
15	F		shift in
16	10		data link escape
17	11		device control 1
18	12		device control 2

The ASCII Character Set

Nonprintable ASCII Characters

Decimal	Hexadecimal	Character	Description
19	13		device control 3
20	14		device control 4
21	15		negative acknowledge
22	16		synchronous idle
23	17		end transmit block
24	18		cancel
25	19		end of medium
26	1A		substitution
27	1B		escape
28	1C		file separator
29	1D		group separator
30	1E		record separator
31	1F		unit separator
127	7F		delete

The ASCII Character Set

Printable ASCII Characters

Decimal	Hexadecimal	Character	Description
32	20		space
33	21	!	exclamation point
34	22	"	double quotes
35	23	#	number sign
36	24	$	dollar sign
37	25	%	percent sign
38	26	&	ampersand
39	27	'	single quote
40	28	(	opening parenthesis
41	29	)	closing parenthesis
42	2A	*	asterisk
43	2B	+	plus sign
44	2C	,	comma
45	2D	–	minus sign—hyphen
46	2E	.	period
47	2F	/	slash

The ASCII Character Set
Printable ASCII Characters

Decimal	Hexadecimal	Character	Description
48	30	0	zero
49	31	1	one
50	32	2	two
51	33	3	three
52	34	4	four
53	35	5	five
54	36	6	six
55	37	7	seven
56	38	8	eight
57	39	9	nine
58	3A	:	colon
59	3B	;	semicolon
60	3C	<	less than sign
61	3D	=	equal sign
62	3E	>	greater than sign
63	3F	?	question mark
64	40	@	at symbol
65	41	A	
66	42	B	
67	43	C	
68	44	D	
69	45	E	
70	46	F	
71	47	G	
72	48	H	
73	49	I	uppercase characters
74	4A	J	
75	4B	K	
76	4C	L	
77	4D	M	
78	4E	N	
79	4F	O	
80	50	P	
81	51	Q	

The ASCII Character Set
Printable ASCII Characters

Decimal	Hexadecimal	Character	Description
82	52	R	
83	53	S	
84	54	T	
85	55	U	
86	56	V	uppercase characters
87	57	W	
88	58	X	
89	59	Y	
90	5A	Z	
91	5B	[	opening bracket
92	5C	\	backslash
93	5D	]	closing bracket
94	5E	^	caret—circumflex
95	5F	_	underscore
96	60	`	grave accent
97	61	a	
98	62	b	
99	63	c	
100	64	d	
101	65	e	
102	66	f	
103	67	g	
104	68	h	
105	69	i	
106	6A	j	lowercase characters
107	6B	k	
108	6C	l	
109	6D	m	
110	6E	n	
111	6F	o	
112	70	p	
113	71	q	
114	72	r	
115	73	s	

The ASCII Character Set
Printable ASCII Characters

Decimal	Hexadecimal	Character	Description
116	74	t	
117	75	u	
118	76	v	
119	77	w	lowercase characters
120	78	x	
121	79	y	
122	7A	z	
123	7B	{	opening brace
124	7C	|	vertical bar
125	7D	}	closing brace
126	7E	~	equivalency sign—tilde
160	A0		nonbreaking space
161	A1	¡	inverted exclamation mark
162	A2	¢	cent sign
163	A3	£	pound sign
164	A4	¤	currency sign
165	A5	¥	yen sign
166	A6	¦	broken vertical bar
167	A7	§	section sign
168	A8	¨	spacing diaeresis—umlaut
169	A9	©	copyright sign
170	AA	ª	feminine ordinal indicator
171	AB	«	left double angle quotes
172	AC	¬	not sign
173	AD		soft hyphen
174	AE	®	registered trade mark sign
175	AF	®	spacing macron—overline
176	B0	°	degree sign
177	B1	±	plus-or-minus sign
178	B2	^{2}	superscript two—squared
179	B3	^{3}	superscript three—cubed
180	B4	´	acute accent—spacing acute

The ASCII Character Set
Printable ASCII Characters

Decimal	Hexadecimal	Character	Description
181	B5	µ	micro sign
182	B6	¶	pilcrow sign—paragraph sign
183	B7	·	middle dot—Georgian comma
184	B8	¸	spacing cedilla
185	B9	¹	superscript one
186	BA	º	masculine ordinal indicator
187	BB	»	right double angle quotes
188	BC	¼	fraction one quarter
189	BD	½	fraction one half
190	BE	¾	fraction three quarters
191	BF	¿	inverted question mark
192	C0	À	Latin uppercase letter A with grave
193	C1	Á	Latin uppercase letter A with acute
194	C2	Â	Latin uppercase letter A with circumflex
195	C3	Ã	Latin uppercase letter A with tilde
196	C4	Ä	Latin uppercase letter A with diaeresis
197	C5	Å	Latin uppercase letter A with ring above
198	C6	Æ	Latin uppercase letter AE
199	C7	Ç	Latin uppercase letter C with cedilla
200	C8	È	Latin uppercase letter E with grave
201	C9	É	Latin uppercase letter E with acute
202	CA	Ê	Latin uppercase letter E with circumflex
203	CB	Ë	Latin uppercase letter E with diaeresis

The ASCII Character Set

Printable ASCII Characters

Decimal	Hexadecimal	Character	Description
204	CC	Ì	Latin uppercase letter I with grave
205	CD	Í	Latin uppercase letter I with acute
206	CE	Î	Latin uppercase letter I with circumflex
207	CF	Ï	Latin uppercase letter I with diaeresis
208	D0	Đ	Latin uppercase letter ETH
209	D1	Ñ	Latin uppercase letter N with tilde
210	D2	Ò	Latin uppercase letter O with grave
211	D3	Ó	Latin uppercase letter O with acute
212	D4	Ô	Latin uppercase letter O with circumflex
213	D5	Õ	Latin uppercase letter O with tilde
214	D6	Ö	Latin uppercase letter O with diaeresis
215	D7	×	multiplication sign
216	D8	Ø	Latin uppercase letter O with slash
217	D9	Ù	Latin uppercase letter U with grave
218	DA	Ú	Latin uppercase letter U with acute
219	DB	Û	Latin uppercase letter U with circumflex
220	DC	Ü	Latin uppercase letter U with diaeresis
221	DD	Ý	Latin uppercase letter Y with acute
222	DE	Þ	Latin uppercase letter THORN

The ASCII Character Set
Printable ASCII Characters

Decimal	Hexadecimal	Character	Description
223	DF	ß	Latin lowercase letter sharp s—ess-zed
224	E0	à	Latin lowercase letter a with grave
225	E1	á	Latin lowercase letter a with acute
226	E2	â	Latin lowercase letter a with circumflex
227	E3	ã	Latin lowercase letter a with tilde
228	E4	ä	Latin lowercase letter a with diaeresis
229	E5	å	Latin lowercase letter a with ring above
230	E6	æ	Latin lowercase letter ae
231	E7	ç	Latin lowercase letter c with cedilla
232	E8	è	Latin lowercase letter e with grave
233	E9	é	Latin lowercase letter e with acute
234	EA	ê	Latin lowercase letter e with circumflex
235	EB	ë	Latin lowercase letter e with diaeresis
236	EC	ì	Latin lowercase letter i with grave
237	ED	í	Latin lowercase letter i with acute
238	EE	î	Latin lowercase letter i with circumflex
239	EF	ï	Latin lowercase letter i with diaeresis
240	F0	ð	Latin lowercase letter eth
241	F1	ñ	Latin lowercase letter n with tilde
242	F2	ò	Latin lowercase letter o with grave

The ASCII Character Set
Printable ASCII Characters

Decimal	Hexadecimal	Character	Description
243	F3	ó	Latin lowercase letter o with acute
244	F4	ô	Latin lowercase letter o with circumflex
245	F5	õ	Latin lowercase letter o with tilde
246	F6	ö	Latin lowercase letter o with diaeresis
247	F7	÷	division sign
248	F8	ø	Latin lowercase letter o with slash
249	F9	ù	Latin lowercase letter u with grave
250	FA	ú	Latin lowercase letter u with acute
251	FB	û	Latin lowercase letter u with circumflex
252	FC	ü	Latin lowercase letter u with diaeresis
253	FD	ý	Latin lowercase letter y with acute
254	FE	þ	Latin lowercase letter thorn
255	FF	ÿ	Latin lowercase letter y with diaeresis

APPENDIX

B

Operator Precedence

Operators and Operator Precedence

Arithmetic Operators

Arithmetic Operator	Computer Symbol	Example
Addition	+	2 + 3 = 5
Subtraction	–	7 – 3 = 4
Multiplication	*	5 * 4 = 20
Division	/	12 / 3 = 4
Exponents	^	2 ^ 3 = 8
Modulus	%	14 % 4 = 2

Relational Operators

Relational Operator	Definition
<	is less than
<=	is less than or equal to
>	is greater than
>=	is greater than or equal to
==	is equal to (is same as)
!=	is not equal to

Logical Operators

Logical Operator	Definition
&&	AND operator: false unless both expressions are true
||	OR operator: true unless both expressions are false
!	NOT operator: true if expression is false and false if expression is true

Truth Table for Logical Operators

X	Y	X || Y	X && Y	! X
true	true	true	true	false
true	false	true	false	false
false	true	true	false	true
false	false	false	false	true

Hierarchy of Operator Precedence

Description	Symbol
Arithmetic Operators Are Evaluated First in the Order Listed	
First: Parentheses	( )
Second: Exponents	^
Third: Multiplication / Division / Modulus	*, /, %
Fourth: Addition / Subtraction	+ −
Relational Operators Are Evaluated Second and All Relational Operators Have the Same Precedence	
Less than	<
Less than or equal to	<=
Greater than	>
Greater than or equal to	>=
The same as, equal to	==
Not the same as	!=
Logical Operators Are Evaluated Last in the Order Listed	
First: NOT	!
Second: AND	&&
Third: OR	||

HTML Characters and Entities

HTML Entities

Reserved Characters in HTML

Some characters are reserved in HTML and XHTML. Characters like the < (less than) and > (greater than) signs indicate the start and end of an HTML tag. Similarly, single and double quotes are also used in HTML markup. Therefore, to use these symbols as part of your web page output, you must use entities to represent them.

Character	Entity Number	Entity Name	Description
"	&#34;	&quot;	quotation mark
'	&#39;	&apos;	apostrophe
&	&#38;	&amp;	ampersand
<	&#60;	&lt;	less than
>	&#62;	&gt;	greater than

ISO 8859-1 Symbols

Character	Entity Number	Entity Name	Description
			nonbreaking space
¡	&#161;	&iexcl;	inverted exclamation mark
¢	&#162;	&cent;	cent
£	&#163;	&pound;	pound
¤	&#164;	&curren;	currency
¥	&#165;	&yen;	yen
¦	&#166;	&brvbar;	broken vertical bar (pipe)
§	&#167;	&sect;	section
¨	&#168;	&uml;	spacing diaeresis

Character	Entity Number	Entity Name	Description
©	&#169;	&copy;	copyright
a	&#170;	&ordf;	feminine ordinal indicator
«	&#171;	&laquo;	angle quotation mark (left)
¬	&#172;	&not;	negation
—	&#173;	&shy;	soft hyphen
®	&#174;	&reg;	registered trademark
®	&#175;	&macr;	spacing macron
°	&#176;	&deg;	degree
±	&#177;	&plusmn;	plus-or-minus
^{2}	&#178;	&sup2;	superscript 2
^{3}	&#179;	&sup3;	superscript 3
´	&#180;	&acute;	spacing acute
µ	&#181;	&micro;	micro
¶	&#182;	&para;	paragraph
·	&#183;	&middot;	middle dot
¸	&#184;	&cedil;	spacing cedilla
^{1}	&#185;	&sup1;	superscript 1
º	&#186;	&ordm;	masculine ordinal indicator
»	&#187;	&raquo;	angle quotation mark (right)
¼	&#188;	&frac14;	fraction 1/4
½	&#189;	&frac12;	fraction 1/2
¾	&#190;	&frac34;	fraction 3/4
¿	&#191;	&iquest;	inverted question mark
×	&#215;	&times;	multiplication
÷	&#247;	&divide;	division

JavaScript Objects

JavaScript Objects and Methods

Array Object

The Array object is used to store multiple values in a single variable.

The Array object is created with: var myArrayName = new Array();

Properties

Property	Description
constructor	returns the function that created the Array object's prototype
length	sets or returns the number of elements in the array

Methods

Method	Description
concat()	joins two or more arrays, returns a copy of the joined arrays
indexOf()	searches the array for an element, returns its position
join()	joins all elements of an array into a string
lastIndexOf()	searches the array for an element, starting at the end, returns its position
pop()	removes the last element of an array, returns that element
push()	adds new elements to the end of an array, returns the new length
reverse()	reverses the order of the elements in an array
shift()	removes the first element of an array, returns that element
slice()	selects a part of an array, returns the new array
sort()	sorts the elements of an array
splice()	adds or removes elements from an array

Method	Description
toString()	converts an array to a string, returns the result
unshift()	adds new elements to the beginning of an array, returns the new length
valueOf()	returns the primitive value of an array

Boolean Object

The Boolean object is used to convert a non-Boolean value to a Boolean value (true or false).

The Boolean object is created with: var myNewBool = new Boolean();

Properties

Property	Description
constructor	returns the function that created the Boolean object's prototype
prototype	allows you to add properties and methods to a Boolean object

Methods

Method	Description
toString()	converts a Boolean value to a string, returns the result
valueOf()	returns the primitive value of a Boolean object

Date Object

The Date object is used to work with dates and times.

The Date object is created with var myNewDate = new Date();

Properties

Property	Description
constructor	returns the function that created the Date object's prototype
prototype	allows you to add properties and methods to an object

Methods

Method	Description
getDate()	returns the day of the month (from 1–31)
getDay()	returns the day of the week (from 0–6)

Method	Description
getFullYear()	returns the year (four digits)
getHours()	returns the hour (from 0–23)
getMilliseconds()	returns the milliseconds (from 0–999)
getMinutes()	returns the minutes (from 0–59)
getMonth()	returns the month (from 0–11)
getSeconds()	returns the seconds (from 0–59)
getTime()	returns the number of milliseconds since midnight Jan 1, 1970
getTimezoneOffset()	returns the time difference between UTC time and local time, in minutes
getUTCDate()	returns the day of the month, according to UTC time (from 1–31)
getUTCDay()	returns the day of the week, according to UTC time (from 0–6)
getUTCFullYear()	returns the year, according to UTC time (four digits)
getUTCHours()	returns the hour, according to UTC time (from 0–23)
getUTCMilliseconds()	returns the milliseconds, according to UTC time (from 0–999)
getUTCMinutes()	returns the minutes, according to UTC time (from 0–59)
getUTCMonth()	returns the month, according to UTC time (from 0–11)
getUTCSeconds()	returns the seconds, according to UTC time (from 0–59)
getYear()	deprecated; use getFullYear()
parse()	parses a date string and returns the number of milliseconds since midnight of January 1, 1970
setDate()	sets the day of the month of a Date object
setFullYear()	sets the year (four digits) of a Date object
setHours()	sets the hour of a Date object
setMilliseconds()	sets the milliseconds of a Date object
setMinutes()	sets the minutes of a Date object
setMonth()	sets the month of a Date object
setSeconds()	sets the seconds of a Date object
setTime()	sets a date and time by adding or subtracting a specified number of milliseconds to/from midnight January 1, 1970
setUTCDate()	sets the day of the month of a Date object, according to UTC time
setUTCFullYear()	sets the year of a Date object, according to UTC time (four digits)
setUTCHours()	sets the hour of a Date object, according to UTC time

Method	Description
setUTCMilliseconds()	sets the milliseconds of a Date object, according to UTC time
setUTCMinutes()	sets the minutes of a Date object, according to UTC time
setUTCMonth()	sets the month of a Date object, according to UTC time
setUTCSeconds()	Sets the seconds of a Date object, according to UTC time
setYear()	deprecated; use setFullYear()
toDateString()	converts the date portion of a Date object into a readable string
toGMTString()	deprecated; use toUTCString()
toISOString()	returns the date as a string, using the ISO standard
toJSON()	returns the date as a string, formatted as a JSON date
toLocaleDateString()	returns the date portion of a Date object as a string, using locale conventions
toLocaleTimeString()	returns the time portion of a Date object as a string, using locale conventions
toLocaleString()	converts a Date object to a string, using locale conventions
toString()	converts a Date object to a string
toTimeString()	converts the time portion of a Date object to a string
toUTCString()	converts a Date object to a string, according to UTC time
UTC()	returns the number of milliseconds in a date string since midnight of January 1, 1970, according to UTC time
valueOf()	returns the primitive value of a Date object

Math Object

The Math object allows you to perform various mathematical tasks.

All properties and methods of the Math object are called by using the Math object without creating it. For example, var answer = Math.sqrt(64); returns the square root of 64.

Properties

Property	Description
E	returns Euler's number (≈ 2.718)
LN2	returns the natural logarithm of 2 (≈ 0.693)
LN10	returns the natural logarithm of 10 (≈ 2.302)
LOG2E	returns the base-2 logarithm of E (≈ 1.442)
LOG10E	returns the base-10 logarithm of E (≈ 0.434)

Property	Description
PI	returns PI (≈ 3.14)
SQRT1_2	returns the square root of 1/2 (≈ 0.707)
SQRT2	returns the square root of 2 (≈ 1.414)

Methods

Method	Description
abs(x)	returns the absolute value of x
acos(x)	returns the arccosine of x, in radians
asin(x)	returns the arcsine of x, in radians
atan(x)	returns the arctangent of x as a numeric value between $-PI/2$ and $PI/2$ radians
atan2(y,x)	returns the arctangent of the quotient of its arguments
ceil(x)	returns x, rounded upward to the nearest integer
cos(x)	returns the cosine of x (x is in radians)
exp(x)	returns the value of E^x
floor(x)	returns x, rounded downward to the nearest integer
log(x)	returns the natural logarithm (base E) of x
max(x,y,z,...,n)	returns the number with the highest value
min(x,y,z,...,n)	returns the number with the lowest value
pow(x,y)	returns the value of x to the power of y
random()	returns a random number between 0 and 1
round(x)	rounds x to the nearest integer
sin(x)	returns the sine of x (x is in radians)
sqrt(x)	returns the square root of x
tan(x)	returns the tangent of an angle

Number Object

The Number object is an object wrapper for primitive numeric values.

The Number object is created with var myNewNum = new Number(x); where x is a numeric value.

Properties

Property	Description
constructor	returns the function that created the Number object's prototype
MAX_VALUE	returns the largest number possible in JavaScript
MIN_VALUE	returns the smallest number possible in JavaScript

Property	Description
NEGATIVE_INFINITY	represents negative infinity
NaN	represents a Not-a-Number
POSITIVE_INFINITY	represents infinity
prototype	allows you to add properties and methods to an object

Methods

Method	Description
toExponential(x)	converts a number into exponential notation
toFixed(x)	formats a number with x numbers of digits after the decimal point
toPrecision(x)	formats a number to x length
toString()	converts a Number object to a string
valueOf()	returns the primitive value of a Number object

String Object

The String object is used to manipulate a stored piece of text.

The String object is created with var myWord = new String();

Properties

Property	Description
constructor	returns the function that created the String object's prototype
length	returns the length of a string
prototype	allows you to add properties and methods to an object

Methods

Method	Description
charAt()	returns the character at the specified index
charCodeAt()	returns the Unicode value of the character at the specified index
concat()	joins two or more strings, returns a copy of the joined strings
fromCharCode()	converts Unicode values to characters
indexOf()	returns the position of the first found occurrence of a specified value in a string

Method	Description
lastIndexOf()	returns the position of the last found occurrence of a specified value in a string
match()	searches for a match between a regular expression and a string, returns the matches
replace()	searches for a match between a substring (or regular expression) and a string, replaces the matched substring with a new substring
search()	searches for a match between a regular expression and a string, returns the position of the match
slice()	extracts a part of a string, returns a new string
split()	splits a string into an array of substrings
substr()	extracts the characters from a string beginning at a specified start position through the specified number of characters
substring()	extracts the characters from a string between two specified indices
toLowerCase()	converts a string to lowercase letters
toUpperCase()	converts a string to uppercase letters
valueOf()	returns the primitive value of a String object

String HTML Wrapper Methods

The HTML wrapper methods return the string wrapped inside the appropriate HTML tag.

Method	Description
anchor()	creates an anchor
big()	displays a string using a big font
blink()	displays a blinking string
bold()	displays a string in bold
fixed()	displays a string using a fixed-pitch font
fontcolor()	displays a string using a specified color
fontsize()	displays a string using a specified size
italics()	displays a string in italic
link()	displays a string as a hyperlink
small()	displays a string using a small font
strike()	displays a string with a strikethrough
sub()	displays a string as subscript text
sup()	displays a string as superscript text

RegExp Object

The RegExp object describes a pattern of characters. It is used to perform pattern matching or "find-and-replace" functions on text.

The RegExp object is created with either of the following:

```
var myPattern = new RegExp(pattern, modifiers);
var myPattern = /pattern/modifiers;
```

Modifiers

Modifiers are used to perform case-insensitive and global searches.

Modifier	Description
i	performs case-insensitive matching
g	performs a global match
m	performs multiline matching

Brackets

Brackets are used to find a range of characters.

Expression	Description
[abc]	finds any character between the brackets
[^abc]	finds any character not between the brackets
[0-9]	finds any digit from 0 to 9
[A-Z]	finds any character from uppercase A to uppercase Z
[a-z]	finds any character from lowercase a to lowercase z
[A-z]	finds any character from uppercase A to lowercase z
[adgk]	finds any character in the given set
[^adgk]	finds any character outside the given set
(red|blue|green)	finds any of the alternatives specified

Metacharacters

Metacharacters are characters with a special meaning.

Metacharacter	Description
.	finds a single character, except newline or line terminator
\w	finds a word character
\W	finds a nonword character
\d	finds a digit
\D	finds a nondigit character
\s	finds a whitespace character

Metacharacter	Description
\S	finds a nonwhitespace character
\b	finds a match at the beginning/end of a word
\B	finds a match not at the beginning/end of a word
\0	finds a NULL character
\n	finds a newline character
\f	finds a form feed character
\r	finds a carriage return character
\t	finds a tab character
\v	finds a vertical tab character
\xxx	finds the character specified by an octal number xxx
\xdd	finds the character specified by a hexadecimal number dd
\uxxxx	finds the Unicode character specified by a hexadecimal number xxxx

Quantifiers

Quantifier	Description
n+	matches any string that contains at least one n
n*	matches any string that contains zero or more occurrences of n
n?	matches any string that contains zero or one occurrence of n
n{X}	matches any string that contains a sequence of X n's
n{X,Y}	matches any string that contains a sequence of X to Y n's
n{X,}	matches any string that contains a sequence of at least X n's
n$	matches any string with n at the end
^n	matches any string with n at the beginning
?=n	matches any string that is followed by a specific string n
?!n	matches any string that is not followed by a specific string n

Properties

Property	Description
global	specifies if the "g" modifier is set
ignoreCase	specifies if the "i" modifier is set
lastIndex	specifies the index at which to start the next match
multiline	specifies if the "m" modifier is set
source	specifies the text of the RegExp pattern

Methods

Method	Description
compile()	compiles a regular expression
exec()	tests for a match in a string, returns the first match
test()	tests for a match in a string, returns true or false

JavaScript Global Properties and Functions

The JavaScript global properties and functions can be used with all JavaScript objects.

Global Properties

Property	Description
Infinity	indicates a numeric value that represents positive or negative infinity
NaN	indicates a Not-A-Number value
undefined	indicates that a variable has not been assigned a value

Global Functions

Function	Description
decodeURI()	decodes a URI
decodeURIComponent()	decodes a URI component
encodeURI()	encodes a URI
encodeURIComponent()	encodes a URI component
escape()	encodes a string
eval()	evaluates a string and executes it as if it was script code
isFinite()	determines whether a value is a finite, legal number
isNaN()	determines whether a value is not a number
Number()	converts an object's value to a number
parseFloat()	parses a string, returns a floating point number
parseInt()	parses a string, returns an integer
String()	converts an object's value to a string
unescape()	decodes an encoded string

jQuery

jQuery

What Is jQuery?

jQuery is a library of JavaScript Functions. It can be added to a web page with a single line of markup. The jQuery library contains the following features:

- HTML elements manipulation
- CSS manipulation
- HTML event functions
- JavaScript effects and animations
- HTML DOM traversal and modification
- AJAX
- Utilities

To use the jQuery library, you download a small file and add the following line to the <head> section of a web page:

```
<script type="text/javascript" src="jquery.js"></script>
```

Downloading jQuery

Two versions of jQuery are available for downloading:

- the production version (minified and gzipped)
- the development version (uncompressed code)

Both versions can be downloaded from jQuery.com. The file is a 91 KB text file and should be saved on your computer as jquery.js.

If you don't want to store the jQuery library on your computer, you can use the hosted jQuery library from Google or Microsoft. Add the following lines to the <head> section of your web page:

```
<script type="text/javascript"
src="http://ajax.googleapis.com/ajax/libs/jquery/1.8.0/⏎
                  jquery.min.js">
</script>
```

Sample jQuery Code

We have repeatedly mentioned that whitespace is ignored by a computer when interpreting code. jQuery is a wonderful example. To make the code as efficient as possible, the entire jQuery library is written without the whitespace and indents that we use to make code easier to read, understand, and debug. Following are examples of the first two functions in the jQuery library:

Directly from the download:

```
{function G(a){var b=F[a]={};return p.each(a.split(s), function(a,c)
{b[c]=!0}),b}function J(a,c,d) {if (d===b&& a.nodeType===1){var e="data-"+c.
replace(I,"-$1").toLowerCase ();d=a.getAttribute(e); if(typeof d=="string")
{try{d=d=== "true"? !0:d==="false"?!1:d==="null"?null:+d+""===d?+d:H.test(d)?
p.parseJSON(d):d}catch(f){}p.data(a,c,d)}else d=b}return d}
```

What these functions look like with whitespace and indents:

```
function G(a)
{
     var b=F[a]={};
     return p.each(a.split(s),function(a,c){b[c]=!0}),b
}
function J(a,c,d)
{
     if(d===b&&a.nodeType===1)
     {
          var e="data-"+c.replace(I,"-$1").toLowerCase();
          d=a.getAttribute(e);
          if(typeof d=="string")
          {
               try{d=d==="true"?!0:d==="false"?!1:d==="null"?↵
               null:+d+""===d?+d:H.test(d)?p.parseJSON(d):d}↵
               catch(f){}p.data(a,c,d)
          }
          else d=b
     }
     return d
}
```

Notice that the variables and parameters are as general as possible; they are simply single lowercase characters. To use a jQuery function, you need to understand what the function does and how to pass in any necessary arguments.

DOM Properties, Methods, and Events

DOM Properties, Methods, and Events

The Document Object Model: DOM

In the DOM, HTML documents consist of a set of node objects. The nodes can be accessed with JavaScript or other programming languages. DOM is defined by standard properties and methods.

Some DOM Properties

Here, x is a node object, i.e., an HTML element:

- x.innerHTML—the text value of x
- x.nodeName—the name of x
- x.nodeValue—the value of x
- x.parentNode—the parent node of x
- x.childNodes—the child nodes of x
- x.attributes—the attributes nodes of x

Some DOM Methods

Here, x is a node object, i.e., an HTML element:

- x.getElementById(id)—gets the element with a specified id
- x.getElementsByTagName(name)—gets all elements with a specified tag name
- x.appendChild(node)—inserts a child node to x
- x.removeChild(node)—removes a child node from x

Some Events

Every element on a web page has certain events that can trigger JavaScript functions. The events are defined in the HTML elements. Events are normally used in combination with functions. The function will not be executed until the event occurs:

- a mouse click
- a web page or an image loading
- running the mouse over, up, down, on, or away from a hot spot on the web page
- selecting an input box in an HTML form
- submitting an HTML form
- using a specific keystroke

Node Properties

Three important node properties are as follows:

- nodeName
- nodeValue
- nodeType

The nodeName Property

The nodeName property specifies the name of a node:

- nodeName is read-only
- nodeName of an element node is the same as the tag name
- nodeName of an attribute node is the attribute name
- nodeName of a text node is always #text
- nodeName of the document node is always #document

Note: nodeName always contains the uppercase tag name of an HTML element.

The nodeValue Property

The nodeValue property specifies the value of a node:

- nodeValue for element nodes is undefined
- nodeValue for text nodes is the text itself
- nodeValue for attribute nodes is the attribute value

The nodeType Property

The nodeType property returns the type of node. nodeType is read only. The following are the most important node types:

- element
- attribute
- text
- comment
- document

PHP Reserved Words

PHP Reserved Words and Predefined Constants

Keywords

This list contains words that have special meaning in PHP. They cannot be used as constants, class names, or function and method names. While it is all right to use them as variable names, doing so could lead to confusion and therefore should be avoided.

_halt_compiler()	abstract	and	array()
as	break	callable	case
catch	class	const	continue
declare	default	die()	do
echo	else	elseif	empty()
enddeclare	endfor	endforeach	endif
endswitch	endwhile	eval()	exit()
extends	final	for	foreach
function	global	goto	if
implements	include	include_once	instanceof
insteadof	interface	isset()	list()
namespace	new	or	print
private	protected	public	require
require_once	return	static	switch
throw	trait	try	unset()
use	var	while	xor

Predefined Constants

These following constants are defined by the PHP core:

Constant	Description
PHP_VERSION	string, current PHP version
PHP_MAJOR_VERSION	integer
PHP_MINOR_VERSION	integer
PHP_RELEASE_VERSION	integer
PHP_VERSION_ID	integer
PHP_EXTRA_VERSION	string
PHP_ZTS	integer
PHP_DEBUG	integer
PHP_MAXPATHLEN	integer
PHP_OS	string
PHP_SAPI	string, the server API for this build of PHP
PHP_EOL	string, returns correct end-of-line symbol
PHP_INT_MAX	integer, largest integer supported
PHP_INT_SIZE	integer
DEFAULT_INCLUDE_PATH	string
PEAR_INSTALL_DIR	string
PEAR_EXTENSION_DIR	string
PHP_EXTENSION_DIR	string
PHP_PREFIX	string
PHP_BINDER	string, specifies where binaries were installed
PHP_BINARY	string, specifies the PHP binary path during script execution
PHP_MANDIR	string, specifies where manual pages were installed
PHP_LIBDIR	string
PHP_DATADIR	string
PHP_SYSCONFDIR	string
PHP_LOCALSTATEDIR	string
PHP_CONFIG_FILE_PATH	string
PHP_CONFIG_FILE_SCAN_DIR	string
PHP_SHLIB_SUFFIX	string, the build-platform's shared library suffix (such as "dll" for Windows or "so" for most Unix systems)
E_ERROR	integer, error reporting constant
E_WARNING	integer

Constant	Description
E_PARSE	integer
E_NOTICE	integer
E_CORE_ERROR	integer
E_CORE_WARNING	integer
E_COMPILE_ERROR	integer
E_COMPILE_WARNING	integer
E_USER_ERROR	integer
E_USER_WARNING	integer
E_USER_NOTICE	integer
E_DEPRECATED	integer
E_USER_DEPRECATED	integer
E_ALL	integer
E_STRICT	integer
_COMPILER_HALT_OFFSET_	integer
TRUE	boolean
FALSE	boolean
NULL	boolean

PHP MySQL Functions

Common PHP MySQL Functions

The following functions have been used in this text or are common functions that you may want to use.

Function	Description
mysql_affected_rows()	gets the number of rows affected by the previous MySQL operation
mysql_close()	closes a connection to a MySQL server
mysql_connect()	opens a connection to a MySQL server
mysql_create_db()	creates a MySQL database
mysql_data_seek()	moves the internal result pointer
mysql_db_query()	selects a MySQL database and executes a query
mysql_drop_db	drops a MySQL database
mysql_error()	returns the text of the error message from the previous MySQL operation
mysql_fetch_array()	fetches a row as an array
mysql_fetch_field()	gets column information from a result and returns it as an object
mysql_fetch_lengths()	gets length of each output in a result
mysql_fetch_object()	fetches a row as an object
mysql_insert_id()	gets the id generated in the last query
mysql_list_dbs()	lists databases available on a MySQL server
mysql_list_fields()	lists MySQL table fields
mysql_list_tables()	lists tables in a MySQL database
mysql_num_fields()	gets the number of fields in the result
mysql_num_rows()	gets the number of rows in the result

Function	Description
mysql_pconnect()	opens a persistent connection to a MySQL server
mysql_query()	sends a MySQL query
mysql_result()	gets result data
mysql_select_db()	selects a MySQL database
mysql_tablename()	gets the table name of a field

Answers to Checkpoint Exercises

Answers to Checkpoint Exercises

Chapter 0

Checkpoint for Section 0.1

0.1 c

0.2 Analytical Engine

0.3 Vacuum tubes were replaced by transistors

0.4 the microchip or microprocessor

Checkpoint for Section 0.2

0.5 TCP/IP

0.6 Answers will vary.

0.7 `http://www.widgets.com/gallery/fidgety_widget.html`
  a) the protocol → `http`
  b) the server → `www`
  c) the domain → `widgets`
  d) the TLD → `.com`
  e) the path → `gallery/fidgety_widget.html`
  f) the name of the file to be displayed → `fidgety_widget.html`

Checkpoint for Section 0.3

0.8 c

0.9 ROM is Read-Only memory and it is permanent (non-volatile). RAM is Random Access Memory and it is temporary (volatile).

0.10 Answers will vary.

0.11 Answers will vary.

Checkpoint for Section 0.4

0.12 printer, mouse, monitor, etc.

0.13 games, database, photo editor, etc.

0.14 helps applications communicate with the computer hardware; provides an interface between user and the computer

0.15 compiled: translated to machine language before execution, interpreted: translated to machine language while executing

Checkpoint for Section 0.5

0.16 A browser is a software application that resides on the user's computer and retrieves, displays, and allows the user to surf for information resources on the World Wide Web.

0.17 When a user types a URL (or clicks a link which also tells the browser the requested URL), the browser sends a request to the web server, requesting that information. This function goes from client to server back to client.

0.18 HTML5 is an attempt to standardize how HTML and XHTML is displayed. It attempts to define a single HTML or XHTML markup language.

0.19 An internet is any connected collection of networks. The Internet is the largest internet on the planet.

0.20 The World Wide Web is just one part of the Internet.

0.21 Answers will vary but making sure everything displays as the creator wants should be part of the answer.

Checkpoint for Section 0.6

0.22 Netscape and Livescript

0.23 XHTML is stricter and cleaner.

0.24 Client-side runs on the user's computer and server-side runs on the website's server.

0.25 Answers will vary.

0.26 It is a server-side scripting language that is embedded in the HTML document.

0.27 nothing, they just store and transport data

Chapter 1

Checkpoint for Section 1.1

1.1 understand the problem, devise a plan of action, carry out the plan, review the results

1.2 Answers will vary.

1.3 analyze the problem, design a program to solve the problem, code the program, test the program

1.4 Answers will vary.

Checkpoint for Section 1.2

1.5 Answers will vary; include from a file, keyboard, mouse, etc.

1.6 Answers will vary; include to a screen, printer, file.

1.7 sequence, selection, repetition

1.8 A selection has a branch point where either a block of statements will be executed or not. A repetition structure will repeat a certain block of statements until a condition no longer is true.

Checkpoint for Section 1.3

1.9 a) True   b) True

1.10 `calculation = myNumber + 3`

1.11 a) `result *= z;`   b) `result += x;`   c) `result /= (y * z);`

1.12 a) `greeting = hello + " " + name + "! Glad you're here."`

b) `greeting = name + " Your shipping cost is $ " + shipping`

c) `total = price + shipping;`
`greeting = "The total cost of your purchase is $ " + total;`

Checkpoint for Section 1.4

1.13 This is a way to break a program into smaller pieces, with each piece accomplishing a task.

1.14 Pseudocode uses English phrases instead of actual code to design a program. It allows the programmer to think through the logic of the program design without worrying about specific syntax.

1.15 the diamond

1.16 Answers will vary.

Checkpoint for Section 1.5

1.17 the type (`type = javascript`)

1.18 It will display alternate content for users who have disabled JavaScript.

1.19 nothing

1.20 An alert will pop up which will say `Boo!`

1.21 An alert will pop up that will say `Ouch! Be gentle, friend!`

1.22 when you want some JavaScript code to occur as soon as the page is finished loading

Checkpoint for Section 1.6

1.23 properties and methods or attributes and functions

1.24 `write()`

1.25 `document.write("<h2>Welcome to my world!</h2>");`

Use the following code for Checkpoints 1.26 and 1.27

```
<html>
<head>
<title>Checkpoints 1.26 and 1.27</title>
<script type = "text/javascript">
```

```
            function getValue()
            {
                  fill in the blank for Checkpoint 1.26
                  document.write("Your car is a <br />");
                  fill in the blank for Checkpoint 1.27
            }
            </script>
            </head>
            <body>
            <h3 id = "cars" onclick = "getValue()">Lamborghini</h3>
            </body>
            </html>
```

1.26 var **auto** = document.getElementById("cars");

1.27 document.write(**auto**.innerHTML);

1.28 document.window.open("","extraInfo", "width = 400, height = 600");

Checkpoint for Section 1.7

1.29 a group of instructions that can be used by other parts of a program

1.30 function warning()
```
       {
             document.write("<h3>Don't go there! You have been
                           warned.</h3>");
       }
```

1.31 values that are passed into a function

1.32 **first** and **last**.

1.33
```
       <html>

       <head>
             <title> JavaScript Events</title>
             <script type = "text/javascript">
             function ouch()
             {
                   document.write("<h2>Don't be so pushy!<br />One click is
                                 enough.</h2>");
             }
             </script>
       </head>
       <body>
             <h2 id = "hello"2>Who are you?</h2>
             <button type = "button" ondblclick = "ouch()">Enter your name</button>
       </body>
       </html>
```

Chapter 2

Checkpoint for Section 2.1

2.1 a memory location in the computer's memory

2.2 you, the programmer

2.3 no spaces; no punctuation; no JavaScript keywords; cannot begin with a number; cannot have a mathematical, relational, or logical operator

2.4 a) **Shipping Cost** contains a space

b) **1_number** begins with a number

c) **JackAndJillWentUpTheHillForWater** nothing but is too long

d) **OneName** nothing

e) **thisName** contains a JavaScript keyword

f) **Bob,Joe,Mike** contains punctuation

Checkpoint for Section 2.2

2.5 In a strongly typed language, a variable retains its type throughout the program. In a loosely typed language, a variable's type can change during the execution of the program. JavaScript is a loosely typed language.

2.6 Answers will vary; sample answers shown here:

a) var **try** = 0;

b) var **tax** = 0.0;

c) var **answer** = 0;

2.7 Answers will vary; sample answers shown here:

a) var **username** = " ";

b) var **choice** = "A";

c) var **welcome** = " ";

2.8 Answers will vary; sample answer shown here: var **DISCOUNT** = 0.20;

Checkpoint for Section 2.3

2.9 a) 2   b) 1   c) 5   d) 9

2.10 a) 4   b) 11   c) 4   d) 12

2.11 a) Correct statement:

```
document.write(name + " is a " + beastie + ".");
```

2.12 It is used to join two strings or it is used as the addition operator.

2.13 parseInt() gives the integer value of a string, if that string begins with a number while parseFloat gives the decimal value of the string, if that string begins with a floating point number. Both functions do not recognize any characters after the last numeric character. If the first character in the string is not a number, both functions return **NaN**.

2.14

```
<html>
<head>
<title>Sale price calculator</title>
<script type = "text/javascript">
    var number = prompt("Enter the percent of the discount:", 0);
    number = parseFloat(number) / 100;
    var price = prompt("Enter the price of an item: " , 0);
    price = parseFloat(price);
    var cost = price * (1 - number);
    document.write("The item originally cost $ " + price + "<br />") ;
    document.write("With a discount, the item costs $ " + cost + "<br />");
</script>
</head>
```

Checkpoint for Section 2.4

2.15 a) 81   b) 113   c) 47   d) 52   e) 38

2.16 a) false   b) true   c) false   d) false

2.17 a) false   b) true   c) false   d) true

2.18 The assignment operator adds two expressions. The comparison operator compares the two expressions and returns a value of `true` or `false`.

2.19 a) false   b) true   c) true   d) true

2.20 a) true   b) false   c) true   d) false

Checkpoint for Section 2.5

2.21 a) relational   b) arithmetic or mathematical   c) logical

2.22 a) true   b) false   c) false   d) false

2.23 **variableName** is where you store the result of the conditional operator (condition) checks if a condition is `true` or `false`.

If the condition is true, `value1` is stored in **variableName**, else `value2` is stored in `variableName`.

2.24 2

2.25 Lizzie

Chapter 3

Checkpoint for Section 3.1

3.1 A selection structure consists of a test condition together with one or more groups of statements. The result of the test determines which of these blocks is executed.

3.2 In a single-alternative, one set of statements executes if the test condition is true; if not, nothing happens. In a dual-alternative structure, one set of statements executes if the test condition is `true`; if it is `false`, another set of statements executes.

3.3 In a dual-alternative structure, one set of statements executes if the test condition is `true`; if it is `false`, another set of statements executes. In a multiple-alternative structure it is possible to have many different outcomes.

3.4 Answers will vary.

3.5 Answers will vary.

3.6 Answers will vary.

Checkpoint for Section 3.2

3.7 a true/false expression

3.8 true or false

3.9 display will be as follows:

```
You are eligible for a learner's permit.
```

3.10

```
if (age > 16)
{
        document.write("<p>You are " + age + " years old.</p>");
        document.write("<p>You are eligible for a learner's permit.</p>");
}
```

3.11 change test condition to if (**age** >= 16)

Checkpoint for Section 3.3

3.12 Curly brackets are used to enclose the statements in either if or else clauses and are used when there is more than one statement in the clause.

3.13

```
else
    document.write("<p>You are too young for a learner's permit.</p>");
```

3.14 and 3.15

```
<head>
  <title>Checkpoint 3.14 and 3.15</title>
<script>
function getNumbers()
  {
        var num1 = parseInt(prompt("Enter one number"," "));
        var num2 = parseInt(prompt("Enter another number"," "));
        var add = prompt("Do you want to add the numbers? (yes or no)? ⏎
                  If not, I will multiply them"," ");
        if (add == "yes")
            var answer = num1 + num2;
        else
            var answer = num1 * num2;
        document.write("<p>The result is " + answer + ".</p>");
        if (add == "yes")
            document.write("<p>I added the numbers " + num1 + " and " ⏎
                + num2 + ".</p>");
        else
            document.write("<p>I multiplied the numbers " + num1 + " and " ⏎
                + num2 + ".</p>");
  }
</script>
</head>
<body>
<h1>Math</h1>
<h3>Click the button! </h3>
<p><input type = "button" id = "numbers" value = "Enter your numbers"
onclick = "getNumbers();" /></p>
</body>
</html>
```

Checkpoint for Section 3.4

3.16 Answers will vary.

3.17

```
function getAge()
{
        var age = prompt("How old are you?"," ");
```

```
                    if (age < 16)
                    {
                        document.write("<p>You are " + age + " years old.</p>");
                        document.write("<p>You are not eligible for a learner's ↵
                                     permit.</p>");
                    }
                    else
                    {
                        if (age == 16)
                        {
                            var birthday = prompt("Is today your birthday? (yes/no)", " ");
                            if (birthday == "yes")
                                document.write("<h2>Happy Birthday!</h2>");
                        }
                        document.write("<p>You are " + age + " years old.</p>");
                        document.write("<p>You are eligible for a learner's permit.</p>");
                    }
                }
```

3.18
```
    function getResult()
    {
        var x = parseInt(prompt("Enter x"," "));
        var y = parseInt(prompt("Enter y"," "));
        var product = prompt("Do you want to multiply the numbers ↵
                         (yes or no)?"," ");
        if (product == "yes")
        {
            var result = x * y;
            document.write("<p>I multiplied the numbers " + x + " and " ↵
                       + y + ".</p>");
            document.write("<p>The result is " + result +".</p>");
        }
        else
        {
            var dividey = prompt("Do you want to divide x by y
                                 (yes or no)?"," ");
            if (dividey == "yes")
            {
                var result = x / y;
                document.write("<p>I divided " + x + " by " + y + ".</p>");
                document.write("<p>The result is " + result + ".</p>");
            }
            else
            {
                result = y / x;
                document.write("<p>I divided " + y + " by " + x + ".</p>");
                document.write("<p>The result is " + result + ".</p>");
            }
        }
    }
```

3.19
```
    var answer = parseInt(prompt("What is 3 plus 5?"," "));
    if (answer == 8)
        document.write("Correct!</p>");
```

```
        else
        {
            if (answer == 12)
                document.write("<p>Looks like you multiplied ⏎
                                instead of added</p>");
                document.write("<p>Your answer is incorrect</p>");
        }
```

Checkpoint for Section 3.5

3.20 Answers will vary.

3.21

```
function changeGrade()
{
        var grade = 0;
        var letterGrade = " ";
        var letterGrade = prompt("What is this student's letter ⏎
                          grade?" , " ")
    if (letterGrade == "A")
      {
      grade = 95;
      document.write("<p>The student's grade is now " + grade + ".</p>");
      }
        else if (letterGrade == "B")
      {
          grade = 85;
          document.write("<p>The student's grade is now " + grade + ".</p>");
      }
        else if (letterGrade == "C")
      {
            grade = 75;
            document.write("<p>The student's grade is now " + grade + ".</p>");
      }
        else if (letterGrade == "D")
      {
            grade = 65;
            document.write("<p>The student's grade is now " + grade + ".</p>");
      }
        else
            document.write("<p>The student's grade is now 50.</p>");
}
```

3.22

```
function changeGrade()
{
        var grade = 0;
        var letterGrade = " ";
        var letterGrade = prompt("What is this student's letter grade?","");
        switch (letterGrade)
        {
        case "A":
            grade = 95;
            document.write("<p>The student's grade is now " + grade + ".</p>");
            break;
```

```
                case "B":
                    grade = 85;
                    document.write("<p>The student's grade is now " + grade + ".</p>");
                    break;
                case "C":
                    grade = 75;
                    document.write("<p>The student's grade is now " + grade + ".</p>");
                    break;
                case "D":
                    grade = 65;
                    document.write("<p>The student's grade is now " + grade + ".</p>");
                        break;
                default:
                    document.write("<p>The student's grade is now 50.</p>");
            }
        }
```

3.23 Add to program, before default:

```
            case "black":
                document.body.bgColor = "black";
                break;
            case "red":
                document.body.bgColor = "red";
                break;
```

Checkpoint for Section 3.6

3.24 switch

3.25

```
        function changeGrade()
        {
            var grade = 0;
            var letterGrade = " ";
            var letterGrade = prompt("What is this student's grade?", " ");
            if (letterGrade == "A")
            {
                grade = 95;
                document.write("<p>The student's grade is now " + grade + ".</p>");
            }
            else if (letterGrade == "B")
            {
                grade = 85;
                document.write("<p>The student's grade is now " + grade +".</p>");
            }
            else if (letterGrade == "C")
            {
                grade = 75;
                document.write("<p>The student's grade is now " + grade + ".</p>");
            }
            else if (letterGrade == "D")
            {
                grade = 65;
                document.write("<p>The student's grade is now " + grade +".</p>");
            }
            else
                document.write("<p>The student's grade is now 50.</p>");
        }
```

3.26

```
function changeGrade()
{
    var grade = 0;
    var letterGrade = " ";
    var letterGrade = prompt("What is this student's grade?", " ");
    switch (letterGrade)
    {
    case "A":
        grade = 95;
        document.write("<p>The student's grade is now " + grade +".</p>");
        break;
    case "B":
        grade = 85;
        document.write("<p>The student's grade is now " + grade + ".</p>");
        break;
    case "C":
        grade = 75;
        document.write("<p>The student's grade is now " + grade + ".</p>");
        break;
    case "D":
        grade = 65;
        document.write("<p>The student's grade is now " + grade + ".</p>");
        break;
    default:
        document.write("<p>The student's grade is now F.</p>");
    }
```

3.27 and 3.28

```
function pageColor()
{
    var color = prompt("enter color ", " ");
    switch (color)
    {
    case "green":
        document.body.bgColor = "green";
        break;
    case "blue":
        document.body.bgColor = "blue";
        break;
    case "yellow":
        document.body.bgColor = "yellow";
        break;
    case "lavender":
        document.body.bgColor = "lavender";
        break;
    case "black":
        document.body.bgColor = "black";
        break;
    case "red":
        document.body.bgColor = "red";
        break;
    default:
        document.write("Invalid entry");
    }
}
```

Chapter 4

Checkpoint for Section 4.1

4.1 the loop

4.2 one pass through a loop

4.3 the thing that is tested and if it's true, the loop performs another iteration

4.4 infinite loop

4.5 There is no way for user to exit loop unless he enters 0 by accident.

4.6 An infinite loop will run forever (unless stopped) but one that traps the user could end if the user enters the right thing.

Checkpoint for Section 4.2

4.7 Add the following code to the `<script>`:

```
document.write('<h1 align = "center">Game Players</h1>');
document.write('<table width = "40%" border = "1" align = "center">');
document.write('<td><h3>Players</h3></td><td><h3>Points</h3></td>');
```

4.8

```
do
{
        item = prompt("What do you choose for item number " + (num + 1) + "?");
        document.write('<tr>');
        document.write('<td>item ' + (num + 1) + ' : ' + item + '</td>');
        document.write('</tr>');
        num = num + 1;
}
while (num < 10)
```

4.9 The new function looks like this:

```
function getPay()
{
        document.write('<table width = "40%" align = "center">');
        var name = " ";
        var hours = 0;
        var rate = 0;
        var grossPay = 0;
        var netPay = 0;
        var overtime = 0;
        document.write('<tr><td>name</td><td>gross pay</td><td>net pay</td> ↵
                        <td>regular pay</td> <td>overtime pay</td></tr>');
name = prompt("Enter the first employee's name:");
do
{
    hours = parseFloat(prompt("How many hours did " + name + " ↵
                                work this week?"));
    rate = parseFloat(prompt("What is " + name + "'s hourly pay rate?"));
        if (hours > 40)
        {
                var regular = 40 * rate;
                overtime = ((hours - 40) * 1.5 * rate);
                grossPay = regular + overtime;
        }
```

```
              else
              {
                    grossPay = hours * rate;
                    overtime = 0;
                    regular = grossPay;
              }
              netPay = grossPay * .85;
              document.write('<tr><td>' + name + '</td><td>$ ' + ↵
                          grossPay.toFixed(2) + '</td><td>$ ' + ↵
                          netPay.toFixed(2) + '</td><td>' + ↵
                          regular.toFixed(2) + '</td><td>$ ' + ↵
                          overtime.toFixed(2) + '</td></tr>');
              name = prompt("Enter another employee's name or enter 'done' ↵
                          when finished:");
          }
      while  (name != "done")
      document.write('</table>');}
  }
```

4.10 Add the following to the list of variables:

```
var dependents = 0;
var taxRate = 0;
```

add the switch after the if...else clause and change the algorithm to calculate net pay:

```
switch (dependents)
{
    case 0:
      taxRate = 0.28;
      break;
    case 1:
    case 2:
    case 3:
      taxRate = 0.22;
      break;
    case 4:
    case 5:
    case 6:
      taxRate = 0.17;
      break;
    default:
      taxRate = 0.12;
      break;
}
netPay = grossPay * (1 - taxRate);
```

4.11 Change **username** expression to **username** = fname.toLowerCase() + "_" + id;.

4.12 a) **myCounter**++; or ++**myCounter**;   b) **countdown** -= 5;
c) **multiply** *= 2;   d) **j** += 3;

Checkpoint for Section 4.3

4.13 Change the line: while (**num** < 10) to for(**num** = 0; num < 10; **num**++).

4.14 a) **age** += 2;   b) **counter**--;   c) **num** *= 3;   d) **id** += 5;

4.15 Using the ++ operator before the variable results in the same value as using it after the variable. But given **counter**++ = **x**, **x** will have the value of counter before the increment. Using ++**counter** = **x**, **x** will have the value of counter after the increment.

4.16 Change the for statement to: for (i = 0; i < 7; i++).

4.17 Change the for statement to: for (i = 0; i <= (**beans** - i); i++).

Checkpoint for Section 4.4

4.18 validate for numeric entry, integer, number >= 1 and <= 20

4.19
```
var tShirts = (prompt("How many tee shirts do you want?"," "));
var check = parseFloat(tShirts) % 1;
while (check != 0)
    {
        tShirts = prompt("Please enter a whole number. How many tee shirts ⌐
                do you want?"," ");
        var check = parseFloat(tShirts) % 1;
    }
document.write("You want " + tShirts + " tee shirts.");
```

4.20 a) _   b) 4   c) empty space   d) ,

4.21 a) **username**.length → 9   b) **address**.length → 21

4.22 Add the following code right before the for loop:
```
if (email.charAt(0) != "@")
{
```
Add the following code right after the last else clause:
```
}
else
{
    document.getElementById("message").innerHTML = "<h3>You entered " ⌐
            + email + ". This is not a valid email address.</h3>";
}
```

Chapter 5

Checkpoint for Section 5.1

5.1
```
function getRange()
{
    var number = 0; var count = 0; var high = 0; var low = 0;
    number = parseInt(prompt("Enter a number:"," "));
    low = number;
    high = number;
    while (count < 9)
    {
        count++;
        number = parseInt(prompt("Enter the next number:"," "));
        if (number > high)
            high = number;
        if (number < low)
            low = number;
    }
```

```
        document.write("<p>The lowest score is: " + low + ".</p>");
        document.write("<p>The highest score is: " + high + ".</p>");
    }
```

5.2

```
function getNum()
{
    var num = 0; var odd = false; var even = false;
    var newInt = 0; var count = 0;
    var result = " ";
    num = parseInt(prompt("Enter any number or enter -999 to quit: "));
    while (num != -999)
    {
      if (num % 2 == 0)
            result = "even";
      else
            if (num % 2 != 0)
                result = "odd";
        document.write("<p>You originally entered " + num + ":</p>");
        document.write("<p>Your number is " + result + "</p>");
        num = parseInt(prompt("Enter any number or enter -999 to quit: "));
    }
    document.write("<p>-999 is an odd number</p>");
}
```

5.3

```
function getStats()
{
    var num = 0; var roundValue = 0; newNum = 0;
    roundValue = parseFloat(prompt("At what decimal value do you ↵
                    want the number to be rounded up? ", " "));
    num = parseFloat(prompt("Enter any number or enter -999 to quit: "));
    while (num != -999)
    {
      newNum = Math.round(num + (.5 - roundValue));
        document.write("<p>You originally entered " + num + ":</p>");
        document.write("<p>This number, rounded your way, is " + ↵
                    newNum + "</p>");
        num = parseInt(prompt("Enter another number or enter -999 ↵
                    to quit: "));
    }
}
```

5.4 After the `while` loop that determines the highest and lowest scores, change the average calculation to:

```
if ((count - 1) == 0)
    {
        document.write("<p>No average can be calculated at this ↵
                    time. </ br>");
        document.write("It would cause a division by zero error ↵
                    to occur. </p>");
    }
    else
    {
      average = Math.round(sum / (count - 1));
        document.write("<p>The average of these scores is: " + ↵
                    average + ".</p>");
    }
```

5.5 Add the following code in the loop, after the prompt for a response to the first question:

```
while ((question != "n") && (question != "y"))
    question = (prompt("Please enter a valid response for
question " + count + ": ", " "));
```

5.6 Add the following code in the loop, after the first prompt for a response:

```
question = question.toLowerCase();
```

Checkpoint for Section 5.2

5.7 Add the following line to the prompt for item:

```
item = item.toUpperCase(item);
```

5.8 Add the following code after the prompt for the item:

```
while (((item < "A") || (item > "I")) && (item != "X"))
{
    item = prompt("Enter a valid choice for the item number " ⌐
            + count + " or enter 'X' when you are finished.");
    item = item.toUpperCase(item);
}
```

5.9 Add the following code after the prompt for choice:

```
while ((choice != "y") && (choice != "n"))
    choice = prompt("Enter either 'y' to continue shopping ÷ ⌐
                    or 'n'to stop now:" , " ");
```

5.10 Here is the new function:

```
function getFives()
{
    var i = 0;
    for (i = 0; i <= 100; i++)
    {
        if ((i / 5) != parseInt(i / 5))
        {    continue;  }
        document.write(i + "   ");
    }
}
```

5.11 Answers will vary.

5.12 Answers will vary.

Checkpoint for Section 5.3

5.13 walking through code, keeping track, with pencil and paper, of all variable values and output; used for debugging logic errors.

5.14 cannot nest loops with same variable as the test condition

5.15 false

5.16 change line 9 to:

```
for(week = 1; week < 53; week++)
```

5.17

```
function flipCoin()
{
    var response = prompt("Flip a coin (y/n)?"," ");
    response = response.toLowerCase();
```

```
            while (response == "y")
            {
                var coin = Math.floor(Math.random() * 2);
                if (coin == 0)
                {   response = prompt("This toss was heads. Flip again ⏎
                                      (y/n)?", " ");
                    response = response.toLowerCase();
                }
                else
                    if(coin == 1)
                    {
                        response = prompt("This toss was tails. Flip again ⏎
                                          (y/n)?", " ");
                        response = response.toLowerCase();
                    }
            }
        }
```

Checkpoint for Section 5.4

5.18
```
    function getShape()
    {
        var star = 1; symbol = "*";
        document.write("    " + symbol + "<br />");
        document.write("   " + symbol + symbol + symbol ⏎
                        + "<br />");
        document.write("  " + symbol + symbol + symbol + ⏎
                                    symbol + symbol + "<br />");
        for(var j = 1; j < 8; j++)
        {
            document.write(symbol);
        }
    }
```

5.19
```
    for (row = base; row >= 1; row--)
    {
        for(col = 1; col <= row; col++)
            document.write(symbol + " ");
        document.write("<br />");
    }
```

5.20
```
    <a href = '#' onmousedown = "document.photo.src = 'troll.jpg';">
    <img src = "wizard.jpg" alt = "the winner" name = "photo" /></a>
```

5.21
```
    <head>
    <title>Checkpoint 5.21</title>
    <script>
    function getSwap()
    {
        var pic = 1;
        while (pic <= 3)
        {
            if (pic == 1)
            {
                document.getElementById('photo').innerHTML = "<img src ⏎
                                = 'troll.jpg' />";
```

```
                        pic = parseInt(prompt("Enter 2 or 3 for a new image ⏎
                                    or 4 to quit", " "));
                }
                if (pic == 2)
                {
                        document.getElementById('photo').innerHTML = "<img src ⏎
                                    = 'wizard.jpg' />";
                        pic = parseInt(prompt("Enter 1 or 3 for a new image ⏎
                                    or 4 to quit", " "));
                }
                if (pic == 3)
                {
                        document.getElementById('photo').innerHTML = "<img src⏎
                                    = 'bunny.jpg' />";
                        pic = parseInt(prompt("Enter 1 or 2 for a new image ⏎
                                    or 4 to quit", " "));
                }
            }
        }
        </script>
        </head>
        <body>
            <table align = "center" width = "70%">
            <tr><td colspan = "2">
                <h1>Swapping Images</h1>
                <p><input type = "button" id = "swap" value = "Push me to change ⏎
                                the image" onclick = "getSwap();" /></p>
                <p>Enter a 1 to see troll, a 2 to see a wizard, a 3 to see ⏎
                                a bunny, or a 4 to quit</p>
            <tr><td id = "photo" name = "photo">
                <img src = "troll.jpg" alt = "troll" name = "myPhoto" />
            </td></tr>
            </table>
        </body></html>
```

Chapter 6

Checkpoint for Section 6.1

6.1 yes, but not nested

6.2 submit and reset

6.3 `<input type = "reset" value = "let me start over">`

6.4 `<input type = "submit" value = "send it off!">`

6.5

```
<html>
<head>
        <title>Checkpoint 6.5</title>
</head>
 <body>
        <form name = "problems" method = "post" action = ⏎
                        "mailto:john.doc@nowhere.com" enctype = ⏎
                        "text/plain">
        </form>
 </body>
</html>
```

6.6 CGI script is a program that tells the computer what to do with form data that is sent to it. It is stored on a web server, in a `cgi-bin` folder.

Checkpoint for Section 6.2

6.7 All the names are different. For a radio button group to work, each button must have the same name as the others.

6.8
```
function checkIt()
{     document.getElementById("agree").checked = true    }
```

6.9 Textboxes can only have widths configured; textarea boxes can be set to however many rows and columns are desired.

6.10
```html
<html><head><title>Checkpoint 6.10</title>
<script>
    function firstName(name)
    {
            var fname = document.getElementById(name).value;
            document.getElementById('f_name').innerHTML = fname;
    }
    function lastName(name)
    {
            var lname = document.getElementById(name).value;
            document.getElementById('l_name').innerHTML = lname;
    }
</script>
</head>
<body>
    <p>Enter your first name:<br />
    <input type = "text" name = "firstname" size = "30" maxlength = "28" ⏎
                        id = "firstname">
    <input type = "button" onclick = "firstName('firstname')" ⏎
                        value = "ok"></button></p>
    <p>Enter your last name:<br />
    <input type = "text" name = "lastname" size = "30" maxlength = "29" ⏎
                        id ="lastname">
    <input type ="button" onclick = "lastName('lastname')" ⏎
                        value = "ok"></button></p>
    <h3>Your first name: <span id = "f_name"> </span> </h3>
    <h3>Your last name: <span id = "l_name"> </span> </h3>
</body></html>
```

6.11
```html
<form name = "myform" method = "post" enctype = "text/plain" action = ⏎
            "mailto:lily.field@flowers.net? Here is the requested ⏎
            information&cc = henry.higgins@flowers.net">
```

6.12 Each control in the email is identified by its name. The user's selection is listed by the form control's `value`.

Checkpoint for Section 6.3

6.13 Answers will vary.

6.14 Add the following to the web page `<body>`:
```html
<input type = "hidden" name = "sides" id = "sides" value = "add lemon wedge
with salmon, ketchup with fries, dressing with salad " />
```

6.15 `middle = username.substr(4,2);`

6.16 `var nameLength = username.length;`
`endChar = username.substr((nameLength - 1), 1);`

6.17

```
<script>
function showWord(pword)
{
        var username = document.getElementById(pword).value;
        var nameLength = username.length;
        var charOne = username.substr(0,1);
        var charEnd = username.substr((nameLength - 1),1);
        var middleLength = nameLength - 2;
        var middle = "";
        for (i = 0; i <= middleLength; i++)
                middle = middle + "*";
        var word = charOne + middle + charEnd;
        alert(word);
}
</script>
</head>
<body>
<h3> Enter a password in the box below. </h3>
        <p><input type = "password" name = "user_pwrd" id ↵
                        "passwrd" size = ""/>
        <input type = "button" onclick = "showWord('passwrd')" ↵
                        value = "ok"></button></p>
</body>
```

6.18

```
<script>
function checkAmp(pword)
{
        var checkSpecial = false;
        var pword = document.getElementById(pword).value;
        var nameLength = pword.length;
for (i = 1; i <= (nameLength - 1); i++)
        {
                if (pword.charCodeAt(i) == 38)
                checkSpecial = true;
        }
        if (checkSpecial == false)
            alert("You don't have an ampersand (&) in ↵
                        your password.");
else
            alert("Ampersand (&) found!");
}
</script>
</head>
<body>
<h3> Enter a password in the box below. </h3>
 <p><input type = "password" name = "user_pwrd" id = "passwrd" size = ""/>
<input type = "button" onclick = "checkAmp('passwrd')" value = "ok"></
button></p>
</body>
```

Checkpoint for Section 6.4

6.19 size

6.20 multiple

6.21 size = "1"

6.22 Answers will vary.

6.23 Answers will vary.

6.24
```
<select multiple = "multiple" name = "cars" size = "2" id = "cars">
      <option>Ford</option>
      <option>Chevrolet</option>
      <option>Kia</option>
      <option>Lexus</option>
      <option>Mercedes Benz</option>
      <option>Honda</option>
</select>
```

Chapter 7

Checkpoint for Section 7.1

7.1 isFinite(), isNaN(), parseInt(), etc.

7.2 a) document.write(parseFloat(6.83);
     b) document.write(parseFloat(**age** - 2.385));
     c) document.write(parseFloat(**score**));

7.3 value

7.4 d

7.5 multiplies two numbers and returns the product

Checkpoint for Section 7.2

7.6 in function yy(), **one** = 1

7.7 in function yy(), **two** = 2

7.8 in function yy(), **three** = 3

7.9 in function xx(), **one** = 1

7.10 in function xx(), **three** = 3

7.11 in function xx(),**four** = 4

7.12 **one** = 1, **three** = 3, **four** = 4

Checkpoint for Section 7.3

7.13 arguments: **age**, parameters: **num**

7.14 The function takes two arguments.

7.15 The function takes two numeric arguments.

7.16 Nothing is wrong.

7.17 one

7.18 When passed by value changes to their values in the function *do not* affect the value of the corresponding (argument) variables in the calling function. When passed by reference changes in their values *do* affect the corresponding arguments in the calling function.

Checkpoint for Section 7.4

7.19 reusable

7.20 allows you to perform mathematical tasks

7.21 by reference?

7.22
```
var newDay = new Date();
newDay = newDay.setFullYear(1852,4,27);
```

7.23
```
var today = new Date(); var timer;
var sec = today.getSeconds();
document.getElementById('clock').innerHTML = sec;
timer = setTimeout('startClock()',500);
```

Checkpoint for Section 7.5

7.24 inline, in the <head> section, and as an external file

7.25 the one in the <head> section

7.26 Source files do not use the <script></script> tags.

7.27 The call has only two arguments but the function has three parameters.

Chapter 8

Checkpoint for Section 8.1

8.1 data type

8.2 var **array_name** = new Array()

8.3 var **byFives** = new Array(5)
```
byFives[0] = 5;
byFives[1] = 10;
byFives[2] = 15;
byFives[3] = 20;
byFives[4] = 25;
```

8.4 ???????????????? → document.write(**mycars**.length);

Checkpoint for Section 8.2

8.5 directly: values are entered by programmer; interactively: values are entered by the user

8.6
```
<script type = "text/javascript">
var music = new Array("jazz","blues","classical","rap","opera");
</script>
```

8.7

```
<script type = "text/javascript">
    var i;
    var twos() = new Array(20);
    for (i = 0; i<20; i++)
    {
        twos[i] = i * 2;
    }
</script>
```

8.8

```
<script type = "text/javascript">
    var rain = new Array(3,4,3,5,6,7,8,2,9,3,4,5);
    var i = 0;
    for (i = 0; i < 12; i++)
    {
    document.write("Month number " + (i + 1) + " is: " + rain[i] + "<br />");
    }
</script>
```

Checkpoint for Section 8.3

8.9 They are arrays of the same size in which elements with the same subscript are related.

8.10 Answers will vary.

8.11 a) not parallel   b) parallel   c) parallel

8.12

```
<html>
<head>
<script type = "text/javascript">
    var scores = new Array();
    var sum = 0;
    var count1 = 0;
    var count2 = 0;
    var count = 0;
    var average = 0;
    var avg_count = 0;
    var count3 = 0;
    while (scores[count1] != 999)
    {
        scores[count1] = prompt("Enter the student's grade ⏎
            or enter 999 when you are done: ");
        scores[count1] = parseFloat(scores[count1]);
        if (scores[count1] == 999)
        {
            break;
        }
        sum = sum + scores[count1];
        count1 = count1 + 1;
    }
    average = sum / count1;
    for (count = 0; count < count1; count++)
    {
        if ((scores[count] > (average - 0.5)) && (scores[count] < ⏎
            (average + 0.5)))
```

```
            { avg_count = avg_count + 1; }
            if (scores[count] > (average + 0.5))
            {  count2 = count2 + 1; }
            if (scores[count] < (average - 0.5))
            {   count3 = count3 + 1;      }
      }
      document.write("The average is: " + average + "<br />");
      document.write("The number above the average is: " + count2 + "<br />");
      document.write("The number below the average is: " + count3 + "<br />");
      document.write("The number at the average is: " + avg_count + "<br />");
```

Checkpoint for Section 8.4

8.13 splice()

8.14 **games**.push("hangman", "hide-and-seek");

8.15 **colors**.splice(3, 0, "magenta", "lime");

8.16 function repeated here with added code highlighted:

```
function deleteRings(rings)
{
      var r = rings.length;
      numSubt = parseInt(prompt("If you want to subtract from the ⏎
                  inventory, enter the number of rings you want ⏎
                  to subtract (or enter 0):"));
      for (i = 0; i <= (numSubt - 1); i++)
      {
          if (numSubt == 0)
              break;
          var oldRing = prompt("Enter a ring to delete:");
          var flag = 0;
          for (j = 0; j <= (r - 1); j++)
          {
              if (rings[j] == oldRing)
              {
                    rings.splice(j,1);
                    flag = 1;
              }
              if (flag == 0)
              {
                    alert(oldRing + " is not part of the inventory.");
                    break;
              }
          }
      }
      displayRings(rings);
}
```

8.17 same as for **rings** with array name changed and variables changed, as appropriate

Checkpoint for Section 8.5

8.18 a) 83   b) 100   c) 65

8.19
```
var mixedArray = new Array(4);
mixedArray[0] = new Array(2);
mixedArray[1] = new Array(5);
```

```
    mixedArray[2] = new Array(1);
    mixedArray[3] = new Array(8);
```

8.20

```
var myArray = new Array(100);
for (i = 0; i < 100; i++)
{
    myarray[i] = new Array(3);
}
for (i = 0; i < 100; i++)
{
    for (j = 0; j < 3; j++)
    {
        myarray[i][j] = (i + 1);
    }
}
```

8.21

```
var myarray = new Array(100);
    for (i = 0; i < 100; i++)
    {
        myarray[i] = new Array(3);
    }
    for (i = 0; i < 100; i++)
    {
        for (j = 0; j < 3; j++)
        {
            if (j == 0)
                { myarray[i][j] = "X";  }
            if (j == 1)
                { myarray[i][j] = "Y";  }
            if (j == 2)
                { myarray[i][j] = "Z";  }
        }
    }
```

8.22

```
var myarray = new Array(100);
for (i = 0; i < 100; i++)
{
    myarray[i] = new Array(3);
}
for (i = 0; i < 100; i++)
{
    for (j = 0; j < 3; j++)
    {
        myarray[i][j] = prompt("Enter a value:");
    }
}
```

Chapter 9

Checkpoint for Section 9.1

9.1 routines

9.2 18   23   42   8

9.3 ascending

9.4
```
function sortNum(x, y)
{
    return (y - x);
}
```

9.5 The,boy,jumps,high

9.6
```
<script type = "text/javascript">
    var names = ["Alex", "Niral", "Howard", "Luis", "Annie", "Marcel"];
    document.write(names.sort());
</script>
```

Checkpoint for Section 9.2

9.7 x = 3, y = 3, temp = 3

9.8 x = 3, y = 3, temp = 3

9.9
```
temp = x;
x = y;
y = temp;
```

9.10 14

9.11 It allows the loop to be exited early if an array is completely sorted before the (N − 1) passes are made.

Checkpoint for Section 9.3

9.12 N − 1

9.13
```
function sortNums()
{
    var nums = new Array(53, 82, 93, 75, 86, 97);
    var count = nums.length; var k = 0;
    count = nums.length;
    document.write("numbers sorted from highest to lowest: <br />");
    var largest = 0; var index = 0;
    for(var k = 0; k < (count - 1); k++)
    {
        largest = nums[k];
        index = k;
        for (var j = (k + 1); j <= (count - 1); j++)
        {
            if (nums[j] > largest)
            {
                largest = nums[j];
                index = j;
            }
        }
        if (k != index)
        {
            var temp = nums[k];
            nums[k] = nums[index];
            nums[index] = temp;
        }
```

```
        }
        for (k = 0; k <= (count - 1); k++)
            document.write(nums[k] + "<br />");
    }
```

9.14 the largest

9.15 the second-smallest

Checkpoint for Section 9.4

9.16 No

9.17 "XYZ"

9.18 found

9.19 four

9.20 4

Checkpoint for Section 9.5

9.21 yes

9.22 low = 0, high = 249, index = 125

9.23 to make the value always into an integer

9.24 two

9.25 2

Chapter 10

Checkpoint for Section 10.1

10.1 <html>

10.2
```
    <html>→ root and parent,
    <head> → parent,
    <title>→child of <head>,
    <body> → parent,
    <div> → parent and also child of <body>,
    <h3> → child of <div>
    <p id = "1"> and <p id = "2"> → child elements of <div> and siblings
```

10.3 method

10.4 creatTextNode()

10.5 oldStuff.replaceChild(newStuff,oldStuff.childNodes[0]);

10.6 oldStuff.removeChild(oldStuff.childNodes[0]);

Checkpoint for Section 10.2

10.7 setAttribute() has 2 parameters, getAttribute() has one

10.8 the id

10.9 "love_the_button"

10.10 a function or expression to be called/executed and a time interval

10.11 greenies

10.12 5 seconds

Checkpoint for Section 10.3

10.13 nothing

10.14 allows us to create our own tags, stores data to be transported elsewhere, is used for searching large databases, other answers possible

10.15 the XML declaration

10.16 a) cannot use the sequence of letters xml to start an element name
b) element names cannot have spaces

10.17 Joey must be in quotes.

10.18 The < character cannot be used—change it to the entity <.

10.19 to define the structure of an XML document

Checkpoint for Section 10.4

10.20 CSS style sheet

10.21 `display:block`

10.22 c

10.23 the XML document

10.24 a

10.25 a

10.26 c

Checkpoint for Section 10.5

10.27 elements, name

10.28 A schema allows you to specify the data type of element contents as well as maximum or minimum number of occurrences of an element.

10.29 to give a unique identification of a namespace because no two people will have the exact same domain name.

10.30 `xmlns`

10.31 `<schema>`

10.32 complex

Chapter 11

Checkpoint for Section 11.1

11.1 the original creator of PHP

11.2 `www.leesland.com`

11.3 Answers will vary; could be price per service, package deals, customers who used the service, supplies needed, etc.

11.4 cross-platform, means it can be used on various operating systems like Windows, Mac, Linux, etc.

Checkpoint for Section 11.2

11.5 a place where web content is developed by web developers before anything is put out live to the public.

11.6 go to http://localhost

11.7 any text document, such as an HTML page

11.8 anywhere in the markup

11.9 It is processed on the server before the document is displayed to the client.

11.10 $

Checkpoint for Section 11.3

11.11 PHP must be processed by the server and the extension indicates this.

11.12 The page must first be processed by the Apache server which resides on the computer.

11.13 $myVarA is a string, $myVarB is an integer, $myVarC is a float

11.14 settype($oneNum, "integer");

11.15 gettype($oneNum);

11.16 (integer)$oneNum;

11.17 Answers will vary.

11.18 (($numC - $numB) == $numA) ? ($yes) : ($no);

Checkpoint for Section 11.4

11.19 d

11.20 b

11.21
```
print("$X is older than $Y");
echo $X." is older than ".$Y;
```

11.22
```php
<?php
    $age = 22;
    if ($age >= 65)
    {
        print ("Senior citizen tickets cost $9.00");
    }
        elseif ($age >= 12)
        {
            print ("Adult tickets cost $15.00");
        }
        else
        {
            print ("Child tickets cost $8.00");
        }
?>
```

11.23

```php
<?php
    for ($count = 0; $count < 5; $count++)
    {
        print ($count * 10);
    }
?>
```

Checkpoint for Section 11.5

11.24

```php
<?php
    $bySixes = array();
    for ($i = 0; $i < 5; $i++)
    {
        $bySixes[$i] = ($i * 6);
    }
    for ($num = 0; $num < 5; $num++)
    {
        print($bySixes[$num]." <br />");
    }
?>
```

11.25

```php
<?php
    $squares = array();
    for ($i = 0; $i < 5; $i++)
    {
        $squares[$i] = $i * $i;
    }
    foreach ($squares as $element)
    {
        echo $element."<br />";
    }
?>
```

11.26 True

11.27

```php
<?php
    $cars = array ("Ford", "Chevrolet", "Kia", "Rolls Royce", ↵
            "Porsche", "Dodge", "Toyota", "Cadillac");
    sort($cars);
    echo "<p>Here are the cars: </p>";
    foreach ($cars as $element)
    {
        echo $element." <br />";
    }
?>
```

11.28 sedan

11.29 $carStyles

11.30 $match[1]

11.31 change [a-z] to [[:alnum:]]

Chapter 12

Checkpoint for Section 12.1

12.1 only the web server that originally set the cookies

12.2 Session cookies last only until the browser is closed; persistent cookies last as long as the time set by the cookie creator.

12.3 before any output occurs

12.4 `$name, $value, $expire, $path, $domain, $secure, $httponly`

12.5 `time() + 60 * 60 * 24`

12.6 choice

12.7 free

12.8 5 minutes

Checkpoint for Section 12.2

12.9 the main author of the original version of MySQL

12.10 It is free, open-source, scalable, supports many programming languages, etc.

12.11 to create and manage MySQL databases

12.12 to give various people different types of access (some may be able to alter the database while others may only be allowed to add records, etc.)

12.13 a record

12.14 The userSSN should be the primary key because it is unique to every user.

Checkpoint for Section 12.3

12.15 `$_SERVER()`

12.16 `die()`

12.17 `mysql_error()`

12.18 `mysql_query()`

12.19 `mysql_connect()`

12.20 `mysql_select_db()`

12.21 yes

Checkpoint for Section 12.4

12.22 `mail()`

12.23 `$to, $subject, $message` and probably `$headers`

12.24 `action = "assets/data/getUserData.php"`

12.25 `false`

Index

Credits

Page 728 Windows® view of XAMPP logo w/right-click menu open and embedded logos-screenshot, XAMPP Properitelialog box in Windows Page 732 htdocs in hierarchical explorer view screenshot

Mozilla Corporation: screenshots—page 33 prompt box, page 35 display on screen in Firefox, pages 52–54 The page looks like thwhen loaded: and The page looks like this after the button has been clicked: and This is what the page looks like after the user clicks the OK button, pag 60, 61, 62 the output looks like this: "Welcome to my first JavaScript Page!", page 64 Page originally looks like this:, After clicking on the word Poodlehe screen now looks like this:, pages 66, 67 When first loaded, the page looks like this: and After clicking on the Open a small window button, the screen lks like this:, page 386 Screenshots: email: manager@mealstogo.com, page 432 Screenshot: email: Carla@carlasschool.net

phpMyAdmin: Screenshots courtesy of phpMyAdmin. Reproduced with permission. Page 729 phpMyAdmin software screenshot, age 806, phpMyAdmin users highlight screenshot, page 807 phpMyAdmin Add user screenshot, page 808 phpMyAdmin Edit Privileges screenshot, phpMAdmin Resource Limits screenshot, phpMyAdmin Databases, page 809 phpMyAdmin arrow towards HOME icon screenshot, page 812 phpMyAdmin SQ command screenshot, page 816 phpMyAdmin select/drom/limit screenshot, page 813 phpMyAdmin create table, page 814 phpMyAdmin create table 2, page 816 phpMyAdmin create table 3

Aesop's Fables; Page 788 FABLES, RETOLD BY JOSEPH JACOBS, by Aesop. Vol XVII, Part 1. The Harvard Classics, published 1909–14 by P. F. Collier & Sons.

Shutterstock: Cover: kayak red isolated on white background/andrea crisante, page 83 elf female archer, a character from mythologyand folklore legend, vector illustration/ensiferum, cartoon wizard with staff isolatd on white/Anton Brand, illustration of ghost flying on white background/vectomart, beautiful princess/tanik, page 215 vector illustration of ecological conservation character mowing the grass/Joan Kerrigan, page 77 vector superhero on top of the world/solarseven